THE SOCIOLOGY OF
ANDREW M. GREELEY

South Florida-Rochester-Saint Louis
Studies on Religion and the Social Order
EDITED BY

Jacob Neusner William Scott Green William M. Shea

THE SOCIOLOGY OF ANDREW M. GREELEY

by
Andrew M. Greeley

THE SOCIOLOGY

OF

ANDREW M. GREELEY

Andrew M. Greeley

Scholars Press
Atlanta, Georgia

The Sociology of Andrew M. Greeley

by
Andrew M. Greeley

Published by Scholars Press
for the University of South Florida, University of Rochester,
and Saint Louis University

Library of Congress Cataloging in Publication Data
Greeley, Andrew M., 1928-
    The sociology of Andrew M. Greeley / Andrew M. Greeley.
        p.   cm. — (South Florida-Rochester-Saint Louis studies on
religion and the social order ; v. 4)
    ISBN 1-55540-910-5 (alk. paper)
    1. Sociology, Christian (Catholic) 2. Catholic Church—Education.
I. Title. II. Series.
BX1753.G66   1993
306.6'3—dc20   93-32119
                                      CIP

Printed in the United States of America
on acid-free paper

PERMISSIONS

"Americans and Their Sexual Partners," with Robert T. Michael and Tom W. Smith, *Society*, Vol. 27, July/August 1990. © 1990 Society/Transaction Publishers. All rights reserved.

"The Demography of American Catholics: 1965-1990" in *Religion and Social Order*, Vol. II, 1991 by JAI Press, Inc. © 1991 by JAI Press, Inc. All rights reserved.

"American Exceptionalism: The Religious Phenomenon" in Byron E. Shafer (ed.) *Is American Different? A New Look at American Exceptionalism*, Clarendon Press Oxford, 1991. © 1991 by Clarendon Press Oxford. All rights reserved.

"Religion and Attitudes Towards AIDS Policy," *Sociology and Social Research*, Vol. 75, No. 3, April 1991. © 1991 *Sociology and Social Research*. All rights reserved.

"The Paranormal is Normal: A Sociologist Looks at Parapsychology," The *Journal of the American Society for Psychical Research*, Vol . 85, October 1991. © 1991 *The Journal of the American Society for Psychical Research*. All rights reserved.

"A Model of Religious Choice Under Uncertainty: On Responding Rationally to the Nonrational" with John T. Durkin, Jr. *Rationality and Society*, Vol. 3, No. 2, April 1992. © 1992 by Sage Publications, Inc. All rights reserved.

CONTENTS

FOREWORD

Michael Hout*
University of California, Berkeley

People ask me what it is like working with Andrew Greeley. Well, Andy is an avid boatsman and water skier, and working with him is a lot like water skiing. Imagine him up ahead there in the boat going full throttle. Imagine yourself back here clasping the bar, white-knuckled, just trying to stay up on the boards. Now when you are about to lose control of your feet, he glances over his shoulder, smiles that Irish smile, and gives you a grand thumbs up sign.

In a career that spans—can it be?—thirty years, a dozen of us have taken our turn on the boards. The throttle is still wide open, too. In the fifty days between Easter and Pentecost of 1992 I received six academic papers from Andy. We are all enjoying an amazing ride.

By going full throttle, Andrew Greeley has done nothing less than single-handedly remake the sociology of religion. He entered a field that equated religion with premodern, traditional thought and mistook religious people as marginal to society. In those days the practitioners of the sociology of religion debated theories about how and why religion would continue to decline in Europe and America. At their peril, they never bothered to establish the parameters of the decline that was "sweeping" Western society. Why waste time establishing the obvious? With their disciplinary blinders firmly in place they were actually ignoring the obvious. They scorned the Catholic Democrats who voted for Eisenhower because Stevenson was divorced without asking how a supposedly dying institution could so profoundly affect American politics. They ignored the role of religion in the 1960 election. They failed to notice that the leaders of the Civil Rights Movement were clergymen. None of them wrote about the Vatican Council. They misread Catholics' reaction to the birth control encyclical Humanae Vitae (at least they paid attention this time). They thought of Catholic schools as impediments to the intellectual development of Catholic youth.

Andrew Greeley up-ended this myopic complacency. From the beginning, he has challenged the theories, practices, and unscientific assumptions of the field as he found it. Andy's work—from his dissertation on why Catholics do not go to graduate school (answer: they do) to his latest work on the parish as a sacrament—is marked by a focus on the practical questions of pastoral workers and politicians and on the academic questions of professional social scientists. His style is to sub-

*Michael Hout is Professor of Sociology and Director of the Survey Research Center at the University of California, Berkeley. He teaches social stratification and quantitative methods. In addition to the research on religion that he and Andrew Greeley have done together, Hout has published research on social mobility, education, politics, and methodology. In 1991 he directed national surveys of Russia and the United States. He is currently analyzing the results of those surveys.

ject the taken-for-granted, "obvious" assumptions of the field to empirical test and to measure the quantities that people need to know if they are to be practitioners or theorists.

A working class metaphor: Three of my brothers-in-law are carpenters. Their big, yellow Stanley tape measures are always on their belts. Their motto is "don't guess; measure it." That could be Andy's motto, too. Micro-computers are still bigger than twenty five-foot Stanley tapes, but Andy's Compaq packed with survey data is always at-the-ready. Of course, my working class metaphor plays right into the hands of the "above data" crowd who have styled themselves as theoreticians who need not concern themselves with measurement. They fancy themselves architects who draw up the blue prints that dictate the carpenters' measurements, but their disregard for the empirical terrain makes their blueprints useless. To be successful at "don't guess; measure it" you have to know what "it" to measure and how to carry out the measurement. Andy does. He has written or selected the key questions that now make up the religion modules in all of those surveys. He is the one who insists on national surveys, high response rates, and replication.

The first precept of Greeley sociology (and all good sociology) is that quality data present an opportunity for learning. Fond as Andy is of rituals, data analysis is not a ritual for him. Some people's ideas are so vague that they can write the text before the data come in. One of Andy's great strengths is the ability to think so clearly that every datum is grist for the theorist's mill.

What has this dialogue between theory and data produced? A new "naturalist" sociology of religion. The old sociology of religion assumed a contradiction between modern reason and religious devotion. Andrew Greeley's research shows that there is no contradiction. He supplants the false contradiction with the assumption that the quest for meaning is an integral part of human nature. Religious institutions give expression to that quest. Religion and society are not in tension. Religion emerges from society; it is how people express to one another the meaning they experience in life. Religions are systems of sacraments (small "s"), i.e., outward signs of the difficult-to-express ideas that are central to the community of believers. Among the radical implications of this theory are the predictions that:

- religious practice be more-or-less constant (neither necessarily waxing or waning) unless it is repressed by the state,

- religious practice bears no necessary relationship to the advance of industrialism, rationality, or higher education,

- religious practice will be positively correlated with social integration (stable employment, higher education, marital stability, political efficacy, and happiness) and negatively correlated with alienation and dysfunction (psychological distress, family problems, nonvoting, and anger),

- religious imagery will have masculine and feminine elements.

The primary documents in the development of this new sociology of religion are contained in this volume. It is a work-in-progress that continues to gain new dimensions all the time. It would be missing the point of what has gone before to expect these ideas to be accepted without further tests. That is not how the new sociology of religion is done. The empirical frontiers will be continually pushed back with new data on different time periods, different religious indicators, and different nations. Particularly exciting is the recent enrichment of the data base for comparative analysis through the International Social Survey Project.

This volume is also the chronicle of how sociology of religion has moved from the margins of sociology (back) into the core of the discipline (Weber and Durkheim were both sociologists of religion). The indicators of the change are on the rise: the leading journals are publishing more articles, university presses are publishing more books, and fewer people refer to religious subcultures. Andy has reinvigorated the field by showing that religion is a matter of great importance to real people, that it is subject to empirical investigation, and that it is a persistent phenomenon to be explained—not a passing relic of a fading era to be explained away.

A contribution of this magnitude would be a career for most of us. But Andy's interests in politics and ethnicity complement his knowledge of religion. He has made major contributions to understanding these well-springs of identity as well. His work on ethnicity and politics follow the "don't guess; measure it" principle. He has interjected empirical correctives into a number of debates that were weak on the facts before he arrived on the scene. Notions about sexist, racist Irish were dispelled by data that consistently show the Irish to be among the country's most progressive groups. Claims about the twilight of ethnic identity were countered by data on persistent identification, differential drinking, family visits, and marriage patterns.

This volume celebrates Andy's successes to date. We his readers eagerly await future installments.

Some aspects
of interaction
between religious groups
in an upper middle class
Roman Catholic parish

Andrew M. Greeley

reprinted from
SOCIAL COMPASS, 1962 IX / 1-2

Andrew M. Greeley

Some aspects of interaction between religious groups in an upper middle class Roman Catholic parish[*]

Quoique habituellement l'Amérique soit considérée comme « the great melting-pot », il est un fait que la religion ne semble pas participer aux systèmes de valeur qui se perdent dans les processus d'acculturation. Une théorie est suggérée distinguant trois niveaux dans les processus d'interpénétration. Même si les Américains se mêlent entre eux sur le plan économique sans tenir compte de la religion, sur les plans matrimonial et des loisirs les vieilles barrières religieuses restent fermes et ne montrent aucun signe d'affaiblissement. Cela apparaît clairement dans une paroisse périphérique à population appartenant aux classes supérieures. L'homogénéité de la population, quant à la plupart des indices sociaux et économiques, donnerait plutôt à croire que l'on y rencontrerait une absence des barrières religieuses. Or les faits montrent que « Westwood » est divisé en deux « ghettos invisibles ». Il y a très peu de mariages entre les deux, on se mêle très peu les uns aux autres d'un groupe à l'autre, il y a très peu d'associations et ce, jusque sur le terrain de golf. Les Catholiques ont tendance à vivre dans certains quartiers résidentiels et les non-Catholiques dans d'autres, cela, apparemment en relation avec l'implantation de l'église catholique. En dépit de ces murs invisibles, il y a très peu de conflits ouverts dans la communauté, chaque groupe écartant avec précaution tout ce qui pourrait donner lieu à des troubles, et allant jusqu'à nier l'existence de quelque barrière que ce soit. En ce sens, les résultats de l'enquête à « Westwood » tendent à confirmer la thèse de l'interpénétration différente selon les plans.

[*] Submitted to the Department of Sociology of the University of Chicago, February 1961.

Some aspects of interaction between religious groups...

Introduction

In one of those intriguing and spacious generalizations which are so characteristic of his work David Riesman[1] once remarked that the future shape of America depended to a considerable extent on the fate of the new Catholic upper middle class which has been emerging since the end of the second world war[2]. Whether one agrees with Riesman or not, it seems clear enough that the transformation going on in the American Catholic population is one of the most interesting sociological phenomena of the post war decades. The Church in the United States is rapidly ceasing to be the Church of the immigrant working class. Other groups (some of them nominally Catholic, but of a vastly different background than earlier immigrant groups) have replaced the European Catholic immigrants at the bottom of the economic and social ladder and Catholics of the third and fourth generation are pushing their way out into the suburbs and up into the professional and managerial élites (and indeed have recently annexed the very top position in the political élite).

It is legitimate to wonder how this new generation of Catholics will differ from its ancestors. On the one hand the hope is expressed that suburban Catholics will become thoroughly « American » and on the other hand the fear is heard that by becoming « American » they will in some sense cease to be Catholic. Both the hope and the fear seem to be based on a historical model that is thoroughly discredited, but nonetheless still very much part of our popular and scientific folklore—the melting pot hypothesis. Warner in his Yankee City[3] and Jonesville[4] studies, for example, seems to imply that the assimilation process involves the shedding of most of the old world values, including the religious ones. The upper class Irish of Yankee City differ from their neighbors on Hill Street only in that they have a few vestigial loyalties to the religion of their ancestors[5].

[1] In an article in the *Chicago Review,* in the late 1950's. I have been unable to locate the exact reference.
[2] For help in the preparation of this paper, I am indebted to Professors Everett C. Hugues, Harrison White and James A. Davis, and to Messrs, Robert Crain and James Casey.
[3] W. Lloyd Warner and Leo Srole, *The Social System of American Ethnic Groups,* New Haven, 1945, p. 67-103.
[4] W. Lloyd Warner et.al., *Democracy in Jonesville,* New York, 1949, p. 163-192.
[5] CF of first chapter of *The Social System of American Ethnic Groups.*

... in an upper middle class Roman Catholic parish

Houtart[6] in his study of national parishes in the Archdiocese of Chicago predicts that the disintegration of the national parish is the sign of the ultimate assimilation of the offspring of the immigrant, the beginning of a defection from the Church similar to that experienced in European industrial centers.

Ruby Jo Reeves Kennedy[7] and Will Herberg[8] dissent from this view. They rather suggest a « triple melting pot » phenomenon in which the old ethnic barriers are indeed weakening, but the religious barriers are remaining as strong as ever. In fact, Herberg suggests that the so called religious revival of the post war era is merely a manifestation of the growing use of religion as a means of « social location ». A person, in this hypothesis, is a Protestant, a Catholic, or a Jew because he must be *something*.

It is the purpose of this article to test the multiple[9] melting pot hypothesis against certain data from an upper middle class Roman Catholic parish[10] on the fringe of a large midwestern metropolis.

In this paper the multiple melting pot (or alternatively the « open ghetto ») hypothesis means essentially that religion is not one of the facets of a person's value system which is likely to be the object of the assimilation processes; on the contrary, it is more likely to be a rallying point around which he finds new « in groups » to help him meet problems of social identity. In this view assimilation is not an uninterupted and progressive phenomenon. On the contrary, after several generations the various assimilation curves tend to level off and to combine on three « separate but equal » plateaus. The old ethnic groups are in the process of dying; but religious distinctions are not, contrary to some popular belief, dying with them. Members of the various American religious

---

6 François Houtart, *The Parishes of Chicago*, mimeographed, 1953.
7 Ruby Jo Reeves Kennedy, « Single or Triple Melting Pot ».
8 Will Herberg, *Protestant-Catholic-Jew*, Doubleday: Garden City, 1955, p. 59 et. seq.
9 In addition to the three groups usually considered there is also the Orthodox Christian melting pot and perhaps the secular humanist melting pot. In the present study only two groups were considered since the Jews, the Orthodox Christians, and the Secular Humanists (if there is really such a group and tradition distinct from American Protestantism) are present in Westwood in very small numbers.
10 This a departure from the normal sociological approach to the parish. Most works in the field have been concerned with religious practice. In the United States at least other questions might also be asked.

Some aspects of interaction between religious groups...

groups may cooperate in the economic and political worlds, but in their recreational and social lives they still keep a certain distance from each other, a distance which does not seem to be appreciably lessening. The concept of « cultural pluralism » has been widely used[12] in recent years to describe the theological-ethical situation in our society. According to the multiple melting pot hypotheses, this concept is capable of a much wider application since it could also be used to describe the social interaction of the members of the three religious groups. According to such a theory, members of the three groups may cooperate in many ways but when it comes to leisure time activities, friendship groups, and marriage, they will stand on separate plateaus staring at each other with a mixture of friendly interest and cautious reserve. Indeed, some of the descendents of the immigrants may have been « assimilated away » from their religious in the way Warner describes, but these were merely the first lonely pioneers who moved out into the main territory of American life. Those who followed after in large groups—especially Catholics involved in the « great leap forward » after the end of the Second World War, would not only maintain the religion of their ancestors, but would even engage in some of its practices with greater fervor than those who had gone before them.

The neighborhood

At first glance Westwood[13] might appear to be the place where the open ghetto would be least likely to appear. Located just inside the city limits of Lakeport, Westwood, unlike most suburban-type regions, has a long history as an exclusive residential neighborhood. The earliest construction within Upper Westwood (which is coterminous with St. Praxides Roman Catholic parish) dates back to the turn of the century. Fully half of the area was built up by 1930 and most of the rest of home construction was completed before 1950. Home values in the 1950 census were over $ 25,000. Only three census tracts of the 1,000 tracts in the Lakeport metropolitan

---

[12] C.F. Gustave Weigel S.J. and Robert McAfee Brown, *An American Dialogue*, Doubleday, 1960; John Courtney Murray S.J. *We hold These Truths*, Sheed and Ward, 1960; and Jarsolav Pelikan, *The Riddle of Roman Catholicism*, Abdington Press, 1958.
[13] All Proper names in this paper are fictitious.

... in an upper middle class Roman Catholic parish

region had a median income higher than Westwood's $ 8,000 and none topped its 12.6 median education level. Its citizens are middle-aged business and professional men who pay the highest taxes in all of Lakeport for the privilege of living on the shady, curving streets of Westwood and enjoying the lovely vista of impeccably landscaped Georgian, Dutch Colonial and contemporary homes. As one might well expect, Westwood is a conservative neighborhood. In the 1952 election it went for Eisenhower 4 to 1 and, despite the large number of Catholics in the community, Kennedy lost to Nixon by a 2 to 1 margin. As one might not expect, however, the neighborhood has been traditionally Democratic in local politics and has consistently sent a Democratic alderman to the city hall. Westwood is also a worried neighborhood since it feels that its peaceful serenity is threatened by the Negro ghetto which is slowly moving towards it on three sides.

The parish

Forty-five percent of the population of Upper Westwood is Catholic.

St. Praxides, the parish church of the community, was founded in 1936 and included not only the handful of well-to-do Catholics then living in the half finished region of Upper Westwood, but also a tiny working class group clustered around the business district of the then insignificant suburb of Redwood Park[14]. Oral tradition has it that Catholics were not welcome in Westwood. A fiery cross is supposed to have been burned on the front lawn of St.Luke's (the parish from which St. Praxides was cut off) in the late 1920's. Catholics were excluded from the Tennis Club and only a handful were admitted to the Country Club. A petition was circulated to prevent the pastor of St. Praxides from building the parish school in 1937[15]. These events are in the distant past now, but they are remembered at least vaguely by the parishoners of St. Praxides—and with resentment.

---

[14] Three parishes now serve the suburban development which has occured in Redwood Park since the end of the war.

[15] It is dubious how serious this petition was meant to be. It was forwarded to Alderman Kelly who was a member of the parish and probably was certain that he never got any of the votes of the signers anyhow.

Some aspects of interaction between religious groups...

Table 1   Parish and School Growth 1936-1960

Year	Parish	School
1936	650	0 (151 in 1937)
1940	1500	307
1945	1800	320
1950	2500	435
1955	3000	550
1960	3500	700

Source : Annual parish report

The parish doubled in size from its founding until 1940, declined somewhat in the early 1940's (after the loss of Redwood Park) spurted up to 1800 by the end of the war and then added about one hundred members a year in the ensuing decade and a half. The increase from 1936 to 1945 dramatically demonstrates how Westwood was part of the tiny construction boom of the late 1930's and early 1940's. Growth since 1950 is due to the increased size of families in the post war baby boom and the replacement of non-Catholic families by Catholic families—especially in the older part of the neighborhood.

St-Praxides fits the image of the vigorous, active modern Catholic parish. Somewhere between 85 and 90 per cent[16] of its admitted members crowd into the striking contemporary style Church each Sunday morning. Over 3,000 Holy Communions are distributed each week, approximately half on Sunday and the rest at week day masses. Four priests, twelve nuns, and thirteen salaried lay people (including five lay teachers) serve the parish « plant ». More than twenty projects and organizations—from a community lecture series with nationally known speakers to a parish blood bank—keep its meeting rooms going each night of the week. Its athletic teams are the terror of the Southwest Catholic Conference, and its laity are almost chauvinistically proud of their « progressive » parish (although, at times they are just a bit afraid that it might be too « progressive »). Its young people especially feel a close loyalty to the parish as a center of much of their activity (even though there is not a parish high school). More than 90 % of its children of

[16] The statistics on religious practice in St. Praxides have been calculated according to a procedure described in A.M. Greeley *Some Aspects of Interaction between Members of an Upper Middle Class Roman Catholic Parish and their Non Catholic Neighbors,* Unpublished Masters Dissertation, University of Chicago, 1961, p. 45-50.

... in an upper middle class Roman Catholic parish

grammar school and high school age are in Catholic schools. Perhaps more than 10 % of its families would fit in Fichter's nuclear category[17]. Forty-two of its young men are students for the priesthood—the diocesan high from one of the smallest parishes in Lakeport.

There is no simple test which would prove or disprove the multiple melting pot hypothesis as an accurate description of the relation between the members of St. Praxides parish and their non Catholic neighbors. Four different kinds of statistical evidence have been compiled each one bearing on a different aspect of the Protestant Catholic relation. The presentation of this « hard » data will be followed by a summary of field work observations which will add some impressionistic « flesh and bones » to the skeleton presented in statistical tables.

Place of residence

Before addressing ourselves to the question of the interaction of Protestants and Catholics it might be wise.to see whether religion has anything to do with choice of residence in Westwood.

Table 2.   Percent of homeowners who are catholic
                              in tiers of blocks at increasing intervals
                              of one block from the Church
                              (East and West Zones Separated)

	WEST					EAST					
Tier	V	IV	III	II	I	I	II	III	IV	V	VI
* blocks	1	14	16	8	6	5	6	12	10	5	5
* Cath.	15	114	164	129	83	51	69	90	74	23	6
* N-C	25	136	188	64	30	51	74	176	150	60	65
% Cath.	37	46	46	68	75	50	47	33	32	28	8
% of all Cath. in tier	1.8	14	20	16	10	6.2	8.4	11	9	3	1
% of all N-C in tier	2.3	13	18	6	3	5	7.14	17.6	15	6	6.5

KEY : * = number of Cath. -   N-C - Non-Catholics.
      Catholics   P is less than .001.
                                   Delta = 21.6

[17] C. F. Joseph Fichter, *Social Relations in the Urban Parish*, Chicago: The University of Chicago Press, Chapter 3.

Some aspects of interaction between religious groups...

Table 2 shows the spacial distribution of the Catholic and non-Catholic families[18] in Upper Westwood arranged in tiers of one block width receding from the parish Church and divided into eastern and western zones (thus, tiers I are the closest to the Church). It is obvious that the Catholic population is concentrated in the area near the Church with 40 % of the Catholics living within two blocks of the Church. As a result, the Catholic population density is greatest in the area nearest the Church. The Catholic population also tends to be concentrated in the western end of the neighborhood where the more recent home construction has occured with 62 % of the Catholics living in this zone. Using the block tiers as divisions a coefficient of dissimilarity is calculated which equals 21,6[15]. It is difficult to say how meaningful such a segregation index without other neighborhoods available for comparison. However, it seems fairly clear that there is a substantial amount of physical segregation between the two groups; for example in the area within two blocks of the Church there can be found 40 % of the Catholic population and only 20 % of the non-Catholic.

No claim is made that this segregation is the result of a conscious choice on one side or the other. According to real estate men, home buyers rarely, if ever, inquire as to the religion of their neighbors. However, Catholics are especially eager to buy homes near a Church, as is evidenced by the real estate ads in the Lakeport press which often give the distance to the nearest Catholic Church. Nor can this be dismissed merely as a desire to be near a school for their children, since the public school is right across the street from St. Praxides, and yet the Catholics easily win the competition for homes in the vicinity[19]. The parish then, is viewed as more of a valued community center by Catholics than the public school is by the non-Catholics. This data, if duplicated in other parishes would tend to throw serious doubt on the oft-heard[20] contention that the modern Catholic parish does not have strong community ties with its people[21].

[18] Cf. Greeley, *op. cit.*, p. 78 for data on each block in the community.
[19] In the square around the public school and its yard there are 25 homes, 21 of them owned by Catholics.
[20] Cf. Fichter, *op. cit.*, p. 9.
[21] The information on distribution of home ownership was compiled from the parish census records, tax lists, and voting lists, Cf. Greeley, *op. cit.*, p. 77.

... in an upper middle class Roman Catholic parish

Intermarriage

Hughes distinguishes three kinds of social interaction between members of different cultural groups: the kind that would lead to marriage, the kind that would not lead to intermarriage, but does involve socializing in each others homes, the kind that is limited to recreational activity. In the remaining pages of this paper, data will be presented on each of these types of interaction.

Table 3   **Religious and ethnic mixed marriages in St. Praxides by five year periods**

Years	* of Marriages	I-I	I-*I*	*I*-I	*I*-*I*	Mixed Religion C-C	C-C	%mixed
1936-40	68	19	12	4	14	10	9	28
1941-45	74	29	9	10	6	13	7	27
1946-50	105	37	9	16	21	20	6	22
1951-55	117	35	16	16	16	17	7	20
1956-60	128	37	34	23	30	3	1	3
TOTALS:	*492*	*157*	*80*	*69*	*87*	*63*	*30*	*100*

KEY: *I* - Irish   C - non-Catholic
     I - other than Irish   In each heading the first is female, the
     C - Catholic   second male.
Source: Parish marriage records   eg. I-*I* = the woman is Irish
                                        the man is not Irish

Table 3 shows the pattern in religious and ethnic mixed marriages during the twenty-five year history of St. Praxides. It is obvious from a quick glance at Table 3 that the multiple melting pot model applies to the marriages in St. Praxices. In approximately half the marriages in which people with Irish names[23] were involved during the last quarter of a century, there was a crossing of ethnic lines in the case of marriages between two Catholics. On the other hand, 81 % of the marriages were between two Catholic parties[24].

[22] Everett C. Hughes, *French Canada in Transition*, Chicago: The University of Chicago Press, 1943, p. 160.
[23] 48 % of the parish was Irish according to the names in the 1960 parish census records, 24 % German, 13 % Italian, 5 % Polish, 10 % other.
[24] About the same percentage as Bogue.has found on the national level. Cf. Donald Bogue, *The Population of the United States*, Glencoe: The Free Press, 1959, p. 695.

Some aspects of interaction between religious groups...

In two-thirds of the mixed religious marriages the bride was the Catholic party; in slightly more than half of the ethnic mixed marriages, the bride was Irish; however, no consistent long term pattern emerged in the brides' nationality.

The fluctuation in the number of marriages between two non-Irish can be explained by the cut off of Redwood Park in the early 1940's. The Redwood Park community was largely non-Irish and accounted for most of the Irish and non-Irish marriages of the late 1930's. This community was also responsible for some two-thirds of the religious mixed marriages in the first five year period. In the years after the war an increasing number of non-Irish joined the Irish pioneers in Upper Westwood and the number of marriages in which they were involved rose steadily.

The most striking fact about the whole table is that although ethnic intermarriages have steadily increased during the twenty-five year history of the parish, religious intermarriages remained rather constant in the 20 % area (with some slow decline) until 1955 when suddenly they dropped drastically. Thus, in the 1955 to 1960 period, when for the first time, the number of Irish involved in ethnic intermarriages exceeded the number marrying other Irish, there were only four religious intermarriages. This decline is so sharp that one might be tempted to dismiss it as a temporary phenomenon. However, most of the twenty-four religious mixed marriages in the preceeding period occured in the first two years. Since 1952 there have been only sixteen religious intermarriages in St. Praxides.

The increase in ethnic intermarriages can readily be explained in terms of long run trends which were recognized by Kennedy in 1940[25]. It would be very difficult to establish a long run national trend for religious intermarriages to decline.

A possible explanation would be the increase in the religious integration of the Catholic community in Upper Westwood. In the 1920's and 1930's the Catholics of Upper Westwood and Redwood Park were in the minority group of a dominantly Protestant community and in the case of the Redwooders, a religiously disorganized minority. The effects of this minority and disorganized status persisted for at least a decade after the founding of St. Praxides since those who were being married in the late 1930's and the first

[25] Kennedy, *op. cit.*, p. 331.

... in an upper middle class Roman Catholic parish

two-thirds of the 1940's were young people whose childhood and adolescent years were spent in a community where the Church was not well organized. According to this hypothesis, there would be a lag of ten or fifteen years between the achievement of some kind of religious parity and parochial integration and the results of these factors being recorded in the marriage register. In other words, religion as a marriage melting pot begins to operate at peak efficiency only when a religious organization becomes fairly well integrated[26].

Social acceptability

These speculations merit further investigation in other communities. Certainly they fit with the idea[27] that religious intermarriage occurs normally where one religious group is a rather weak and disorganized minority. Unfortunately, instances where variables can be controlled and date obtained with the relative simplicity as in St. Praxides are rare[28].

[26] The increase in population of Catholics and in grammar school enrollment was great during the 1940's, but the grammar school graduation classes were small until the 1950's. It was only when those who began to graduate in the relatively large classes of the early 1950's came to marriage age in the last few years, that religious mixed marriages began to vanish almost totally. Another interesting clue into this problem comes from the fact that 37 of the 42 members of the class of 1952 were the oldest members of their family. The would represent, in all probability, families which were formed in 1938 or 1939 and came to Westwood during the 1940's. They represent the first wave of those who spent all their years in Westwood as part of a strongly organized Catholic parish.

[27] Professor Hughes has suggested that the concept of « critical mass » could be applied to this phenomenon.

[28] It might be argued that the decline in religious intermarriages is only apparent, that what is actually happening is that people who are marrying non Catholics are now marrying outside the Church, and, in effect, leaving the Church at the time of marriage. This is certainly a possible explanation and might have considerable validity in many parts of a city and a country. However, it does not seem to fit the facts in St. Praxides. The parish census cards (the census is taken each year), show little evidence of such marriages. It must be remembered that St. Praxides is a small parish and Westwood is a small community. Very few events transpire in the neighborhood that are not public knowledge in a very short order. The classes which are in the marrying years at present are bigger than the early classes in the parish's history, but they are still relatively small. It is possible for the clergy to keep accurate track of where the various young parishioners are and what they are doing. In facts, it is possible to assemble a group of knowledgeable young people and go through the five classes that would be in the twenty to twenty five age bracket and account for all but a handful of those who graduate from St. Praxides grammar school. Only the marriages outside the Church were discovered. There may have been a few more, but certainly not very man.

Some aspects of interaction between religious groups...

The second position on the Hughes scales of interaction is the choice of friends for ones social life. To get some idea of how Catholics in Westwood choose their friends, it was decided to administer a questionaire to a group of high school senior girls. The questionaire consisted of thirty-nine items and was administered to a group of thirty-three girls, practically all the high school seniors in the parish. The girls were told to assume that a new girl had moved into the community and was trying to become part of the most desirable clique of girls (other than the one the respondent was in). They were asked to evaluate the items on the questionaire in terms of whether they would help or hurt the girl in her search for acceptance[29]. The girls were asked to be as realistic as possible in reporting things the way they are and not the way they should be.

Eight types of items were listed on the questionaire — style of life, educational plans, father's occupation, religion, ethnic background, talent, ethical values and personality factors[30].

The respondents seem to think that certain elements of life style would be more important than others. Only 30 % thought that country club membership would be a help, while 57 % thought that having her own car would matter, and 63 % thought that frequency of entertainment would be a decisive factor. 69 % thought that being the « best dressed » girl in Westwood would impress new neighbors, but 84 % insisted that the absence of flashy clothes (« She wears hand-me-downs ») would not make any difference. 60 % would say that lots of spending money would be immaterial, although 18 % thought it would hurt and 21 % thought it would help. 81 % felt that living in a « rundown » home would be a handicap.

The four colleges which a girl's future plans involved would not make much difference in her acceptability, whether the college

---

[29] Three qualifying factors must be kept in mind when evaluating these data: 1) The questionaire was administered by a religious functionary whom the girls had known for 6 of their 17 years. 2) There is no certainty that the norms of social acceptability among teenage females are the same as among their parents and 3) there may be a tendency for the young to be more idealistically egalitarian in their views of class structure than adults. The questionaire was administered in the very relaxed atmosphere of a Westwood living room as the girls were lounging around on a Sunday evening, waiting for a sonority meeting to begin (the organization had no connection with the parish).

[30] In Greeley *op. cit.*, pp. 117 & 118 the data are arranged in Gutman scales. Rep. was over 9.

... in an upper middle class Roman Catholic parish

was an eastern prestige school, a middlewestern prestige school, a commuter college with little prestige (the first three Catholic schools) or a state university. Once again the girls insisted strongly that the father's occupation, whether he be a steel worker or a medical doctor (one of the very high prestige occupations in the community) would make no difference in her acceptability. Such egalitarianism is perhaps something of an exageration in its interpretation of reality. However, there is some information[31] which would indicate that at this age the young people of Westwood will not discriminate against their peers on the grounds of father's occupation alone. One young man summed up his impression this way: « What is important is not so much what your father is, as what it looks like you're going to be. »

The responses on religious items indicate that religion is of considerable, indeed, decisive importance in obtaining acceptance among Westwood Catholics. 63 % felt that daily Mass attendance would be a help in becoming popular. On the other hand, 90 % were of the opinion that not going to Sunday Mass would be an obstacle and 66 % thought that it would be a serious obstacle. Even non practice, by the girl's parents would weigh against her according to 60 % of the respondents. But a non-Catholic parent would be no problem to 84 %[32]. A member of another faith would be a great disadvantage in breaking into the group: 69 % thought that a Protestant girl would have a hard time and 81 % thought it would be difficult for a Jewish girl.

Except for those who were Negroes, girls would not be rejected because of their nationality according to sizeable majorities. Only one girl[33] thought that a Negro would have no problem but 72 % thought that a girl from a Polish parish would encounter no difficulty and 66 % made the same judgement about a girl from an Italian parish. 72 % thought that a mother who spoke broken English would not be an obstacle.

In a mobile upper middle class society, it might be suspected

---

[31] Cf. Greeley, *op. cit.* A study of those elected to positions of responsibility in teenage organizations showed that neither father's occupation nor ethnic background seemed to be very important.

[32] Hence it is better, according to the respondents, to have a non-Catholic parent than a Catholic parent who does not practice the faith.

[33] And she probably misread the question.

Some aspects of interaction between religious groups...

that a person would be judged not merely by where he came from, but also by where he seemed to be going. Talents and « personality » would be of great importance in gaining acceptance, no matter what your nationality or family background. The president of a student council would have no trouble breaking into a clique of her own (81 %). (There is at least one case where such a girl was assimilated into a Westwood clique without having to move into the parish.) Nor would the editor of the school paper (69 %) or a talented musician (72 %) experience any difficulty. Good looks (72 %), popularity with boys (57 %), a sense of humor (78 %), ability to make others feel important (96 %) and helpfulness to others (81 %) — these are the qualities that Westwood girls look for in a newcomer. In a group which has just moved into the expanding upper.middle class because of its ability at self marketing, it would be expected that skills in human relations and marketable personality traits would be considered to be especially desirable characteristics in a newcomer. If these are to be found—*and she is a reasonably good Catholic*—she will have no trouble breaking into most groups, no matter what her ethnic background.

Recreational companionship

For information on the third item in the Hughes scale—recreational companionship—we turn to data gathered at the Westwood Country Club. Westwood Country Club, since its founding in 1908, has been known as one of the most exclusive golf clubs in the Lakeport region. Although its elegant Victorian club house may lack the plush spaciousness of some of the newer clubs and its social life may be less frantic, its cuisine is excellent, its swimming pool is impressive and its eighteen hole golf.course is probably the best in Lakeport.

The religious history of the club since its founding is shrouded in myth and legend. Indeed, there are practically no records of any kind of what happened at the club for anything but the last ten years. It cannot be established with certainty that Catholics were completely excluded from membership—though there were not

[34] The religion of members was rated by several judges. In case of doubt, the vote of the majority of the raters was accepted. Only four or five families were doubtful, religion being a highly visible quality at the Club.

... in an upper middle class Roman Catholic parish

very many Catholics until the 1940's and not an approach to parity until the 1950's. The first Catholic president did not serve until 1945 and the next Catholic was not elected until 1956. Apparently, the present policy (though unwritten) is for Catholics and non-Catholics to alternate in office. At present, the balance between the two groups is almost exactly equal[34]. There are 168 Catholic members and 163 non-Catholic members (with 62 members of St. Praxides belonging and 26 other Upper Westwoodians holding membership)[35]. Two of the four officers and five of the nine board members are Catholic. In the woman's auxilary all four of the officers are non-Catholic, but four of the eight directors are Catholic. Seven of the committee chairmen are Catholic and five are non-Catholic. Four of the seven membership committee members are non-Catholic. Of the fourteen new members admitted in the past two years exactly half have been Catholic.

It should be noted that this balance is maintained without any conscious communication between the two groups on the subject of balance. Apparently, everyone takes it for granted that some kind of rough parity must be maintained. The Club president (a Catholic) denies that there is even a tacit agreement to maintain this parity; but he will admit that two years ago he was the first Catholic ever to nominate a non-Catholic to the board of directors (and only after prior agreement with a non-Catholic to nominate a Catholic).

If one looks at the present situation and tries to piece together some idea of the past history, it is possible to argue that a succession phenomenon has gone on and that the present delicate and complex balance may be an unstable transition state. It seems reasonable to suspect that Catholics were a distinct minority in the club until 1950, that the big surge in Catholic membership came between the end of the Second War and 1955, that the parity situation has existed for the last five years since both groups have found it in their temporary interest to maintain parity. The remaining Protestants do not want to give up « their » club without a battle and the Catholics do not especially want to see them go since their departure will force the club to dip lower down in the Catholic ethnic pool for new members whose money will be necessary to keep

[35] Catholics tend to play moe golf than non Catholics but not significantly more.

Some aspects of interaction between religious groups...

the club running (which, of course, is the very reason why Catholics were admitted in the first place). How long this situation will last is at its best problematic. A highly significant indicator of future trends is the fact that only twenty-six non-Catholic families from Upper Westwood are still members. One would very much like to know how many non-Catholics from Upper Westwood have let their memberships lapse in the last decade, but unfortunately, such information is not available.

In any case, the present situation is one in which the invisible walls of the ghetto cut across the fairways of Westwood Country Club instead of being coterminous with its fences. Depending on whom one is talking to, one can get varied pictures of the amount of fraternizing at the club's social affairs. Everyone agrees, however, that there is no segregation on the golf course. However, the starting sheets from July 1950 indicate a different picture. 2,408 games of golf were played during the month, 1,293 by Catholics and 1,115 by non-Catholics. Catholics from St. Praxides played in 324 golfing groups and in only 86 of these did they mix with non-Catholics. 584 games were played by members of St. Praxides; in the 86 groups in which they encountered non-Catholics, they met 150 non-Catholic golfers of whom almost half (66) were in the twenty-two foursomes where one Catholic played with three non-Catholics. The mathematics of arranging this material are complex since there are three different kinds of golf patterns (twosomes, threesomes, and foursomes)[36]. Table 4 gives ratios of actual to expected (by random distribution) interaction between Catholics and non-Catholics.

Table 4   **Ratios of distribution of golfers from St. Praxides to the distribution which might have occured had mere chance been operating**

Twosomes

Both from parish	With a Catholic not from the neighborhood	With a non-Cath. neighbor	With a non-Cath. not from neighborhood
3.5	.74	.2	.12

[36] Cf. Greeley *op. cit.*, for a fuller discussion, p. 129.

54

... in an upper middle class Roman Catholic parish

	Threesomes		
All from parish	At least one Cath. not from neighborhood	At least one non-Cath. neighbor	At least one non-Cath. not from the neighborhood
7.0	.9	.3	.3

	Foursomes		
7.0	.9	.5	.3

It is clear from the tables that in groups of three and four golfers, members of St. Praxides tend to play with each other about seven times as often as they would in a random model. As a result, their golfing with other Catholics is more or less random and they considerably underchoose non-Catholics as partners. It might be argued that one would expect people to play golf more with their neighbors than with non-neighbors; indeed this is true. It is apparent even that members of St. Praxides slightly overchoose their non-Catholic neighbors in comparison to non-Catholics from outside the neighborhood. However, those non-Catholics from the neighborhood are still substantially underchose[37].

The open ghetto in Westwood

The data presented in the four previous sections establishes that the amount of interaction between the religious groups is very close to the open ghetto model. In the concluding sections of this paper an attempt will be made to report explain the mechanics by which such a ghetto situation operates and at the same time to find some kind of causes.

A visitor to Westwood would think at first glance that he had come upon a remarkable homogeneous neighborhood. Its citizens work at the same kind of jobs, are in frequent business contact with each other or similar people, wear the same kind of clothes, drive the same kind of cars, belong to the same clubs, vote the same way in elections, ride the same commuter trains, frequent the same vaca-

---

[37] There had been some hope of finding patterns of interaction at the Country Club, of uncovering a « type » of person or an occupation which would figure more frequently in religious mixed golf. No such patterns emerged. It is interesting to note that seven men — a doctor, a lawyer, a real estate man, a travel agent, a business executive, and two presidents of small steel companies — accounted for two thirds of the mixing that went on in foursomes.

Some aspects of interaction between religious groups...

tion spots, share the same values and life goals, and die of the same kinds of diseases. But, if the visitor tarried a bit, he would find that there were two distinct groups in the community. The first thing he would notice would be that the children—after kindergarten—went to different schools. Although the two schools were across the street from each other, the playgrounds very close, the two schools had little contact between the children in them. Their starting and finishing times were different and rarely were students from one school walking home at the same time as the students of the other school. If groups from one school should pass groups from another, there might be an occasional polite « hello » but more frequently no exchange of greetings. Indeed, it seemed that one group was unaware of the other's existence. The two playgrounds were but half a block away, but never did the children from one group mingle with the children from the other. Members of the Catholic group would frequently play softball or touch football on the public playground, but never with the « publics ». Two softball games could be going on at opposite diamonds without either group being aware of the other's presence, except occasionally to throw back a stray ball.

If the visitor were to probe into the infancy of these youngsters, he would learn that little children played with next door neighbors no matter which group they belonged to, but that by the latency years, as if by mutual consent, such relations were terminated. He would also learn that the two groups went to separate high schools and colleges and continued to be unaware of each other's existence —except as a part of the scenery— until they had married and left the neighborhood[38]. Should the visitor be brave enough to venture into the chaos of a St. Praxides « High Club » social, he would find that among the four hundred milling, noisy adolescents there was to be found not a single member of the other group. They were not turned away, they simply never came.

If the puzzled investigator was invited to the many cocktail parties which form the main stream of Westwood social life, he would notice that it was a rare party where a member of one group

---

[38] One girl from St. Praxides summed up the attitude perfectly: « Oh, there was a non Catholic girl who lived next door to us, but she rode horses all the time. »

... in an upper middle class Roman Catholic parish

was admitted into the home of someone from the other group (unless there was a case of mixed marriage and there are only about eighty of them in Upper Westwood). He might have taken up bridge and found that it was quite possible to engage in this popular pastime for years and never sit across a table from one who was in the other group.

He could have continued his investigations to the Westwood Tennis Club and learned that while occasionally a young tennis star might take on a member of the other group, he (or she) would never choose the other as a partner in tournament doubles. He could have gone on to the Country Club and noted that the young people from the two groups would be clustered at the opposite ends of the pool, that there was no dancing with members of the other group at teen-age dances, that at adult parties the two groups stayed on opposite sides of the room and that even on the links it was a rare foursome which contained members of both groups.

With all this data gathered, our researcher would have expected to find a considerable amount of social conflict between the two groups; but he would have been disappointed. He would find that in seven years there was only one relatively minor issue on which the members of Upper Westwood (or at least a group of them) publically disagreed on strictly religious lines. (The issue was a swimming pool for the Tennis Club.) At other times the religious issue might be raised by certain individuals on either side who claimed to see a plot on the part of the other group. But the issue would quickly be batted down by leaders of both the factions in the debate, who would quickly point out that there were prominent Catholics and non-Catholics on both sides.

The religious issue was always lurking in the background with the possibility of coming out into the open, but both groups seemed to have a major interest in seeing that the serenity of the community was not disturbed by religious conflict. Indeed even the existence of the religious division is often stoutly denied.

To what extent is parish activity a cause of this division? The American Catholic parish has traditionally been a social and recreational center for its people. The « national » parish which smoothed the transition from the Old World to the New was equipped to meet virtually every need of the immigrant from a credit union to a boxing

Some aspects of interaction between religious groups...

ring. It was argued by the clergy—and with good reason[39]—that without such social and recreational services the Church would « lose » the immigrants. One would have expected that with the disappearance of the immigrants and the decline of the national parish, the need for these social and recreational services would have lessened. The need may no longer be present, but the demand for them still is[40].

It is obvious that the existence of the parish as a recreational center will inhibit the amount of social interaction between Catholics and non-Catholics. On the basis of time alone, Catholics are so busy interacting with fellow parishioners that they will not interact with non-Catholics. It is important to note, however, that the recreational and social activities of the parish are not part of a plot to keep Catholics away from non-Catholics. Such a function is very latent indeed. The clergy promote such activities because they vaguely feel that the activities are good for « parish spirit » and because the laity want the activities and because these are things which parishes have « always done ». The laity in their turn want the activities because these are the things which parishes have always done (and hence « should do ») and because the parish facilities are a convenient social center. No one seriously believes that in the absence of such facilities the people of St. Praxides would cease to be good Catholics.

Thus, when dissatisfaction arose with the Park District and the Catholic Youth athletic leagues, it was « natural » for St. Praxides to join with other suburban parishes to form the Southwest Catholic Conference. No one thought of inviting any of the non-Catholic churches in the area to join the conference; indeed it is doubtful that

[39] Houtart, for example, argues that the flexibility of the national parishes was the main reason why the working class did not leave the church in America as it did in Europe. Cf. François Houtart, *Aspects Sociologiques du Catholicisme Américain*, Les Editions Ouvrières, Paris, 1957.

[40] In fact there is every reason to suspect that all the recreational and social activities in St. Praxides could be suppressed tomorrow and there would be no change in the level of religious practice in the foreseeable future (which is not to imply that the activities *should* be suppressed). Some neighborhing parishes have no such activities and yet the level of religious practice is virtually the same as in St. Praxides. This raises the highly intriguing hypothesis, which must some day be investigated, that in the present state of American society, the level of a religious practice of a parish depends on social and economic factors and is almost totally independent of what the parish clergy may or may not do.

... in an upper middle class Roman Catholic parish

they would have been flattered by an invitation. The Conference continued the separation between the two groups—and by emphasizing the park league—perhaps heightened the separation somewhat. No one planned such a result, but tradition and structure made it practically inevitable.

Conclusion

There are many short term functions which the open ghetto serves for the Churches in Upper Westwood. Religious mixed marriages, which both sides consider to be undesirable, are kept at a minimum. Members of neither religious group are in any danger of being « contaminated » by the other's ideas. The conflicting situations or at least the social embarassment which would probably arise, if there were more communication between the two groups are kept at a minimum. Both sides can feel secure that they have the loyalties of their people, that their congregations are lively, bustling organizations. Both sides can be reasonably confident that they have enough strength to resist the encroachments which the other is likely to be plotting. The clergy on both sides are faced with far less complicating factors than would be encountered if the ghetto walls should vanish.

Nevertheless, many of the long run effects of the open ghetto are almost certain to be dysfunctional—for the churches, for Westwood and for the larger society. No one in their right mind would imagine that the difference between Catholicism and Protestantism would be resolved if there were only more communication between the two groups. On the other hand, neither religion is going to develop, even to a reasonably full extent the potentials of its own tradition as long as it studiously pretends that the other tradition is non-existent in a community. Nor is there a ghost of a chance that Westwood will solve the problems which the oncoming Negro ghetto is going to bring unless the two groups are willing to cooperate intensively with each other.

In the course of this paper we have attempted to report on the situation in Upper Westwood without probing too deeply for causes, much less seeking for someone to « blame ». In such a delicate and controversial problem as the relation between religious groups, the temptation to blame one side or the other is great, even for the

Some aspects of interaction between religious groups...

social scientist. Since the view of Westwood is from the Catholic side, most of the emphasis has been on how Catholics do not interact with their non-Catholic neighbors. Such a perspective might give the impression that the author is blaming his fellow religionists for being « ghetto minded ». Such is not his intention. If Catholics do not interact with non-Catholics, neither do non-Catholics interact with Catholics. If one asks who does not interact first, one finds himself facing the problem of the chicken and the egg.

If one goes beyond the fruitless search for a scapegoat[41] and seeks to find causes, one is inevitably forced to look into the operation of historical trends—an investigation which may well seem speculative by the more rigid standards of contemporary sociology. Nevertheless, it might well be asked on what grounds one could reasonably expect the situation to be any different. Admittedly the Reformation occured some four centuries ago. Yet, there have been very few situations in these four centuries where Catholics and Protestants have faced each other in the same community and with relatively equal power. Some of the European countries have similar percentages of Catholics and non-Catholics, but normally the division of population is territorial, with Catholics dominating in one section and the Protestants in another. A condition of direct confrontation in a framework where there are constitutional limitations on the amount of conflict permitted is comparatively rare. In addition, the United States was for more than a century a Protestant nation. It has been only in very recent years that the Catholic population has been admitted to some kind of equal partnership. It would be surprising if either of the partners were happy with the present situation. Catholics are no longer immigrants, but the immigrant experience is still fresh in their minds. Protestants are no longer the dominant majority, but the majority experience is still fresh in

---

[41] It seems pointless to the present writer to say the open ghetto is a function of the Catholic school system. The ghetto seems to exist in areas where there is not a Catholic school system in New England. There would be more mixing if there were not a Catholic school system, but how much more is open to question. In any case it seems to the present writer that the school system is the dependent variable and that to explain the multiple melting pot as being the result of the school system is to invert the causal relationship. The important question to ask would be why the American Church, alone of all Churches in the Western World, has felt it necessary to build a school system which extends from kindergarten to graduate school. The answer to this question would be the explanation of the multiple melting pot.

... in an upper middle class Roman Catholic parish

their minds.   It is possible to argue that under such circumstances
the *absence* of a multiple melting pot situation would be surprising.

Perhaps Westwood is untypical.   It is Irish; it is middlewestern;
it is a place of numerical parity; it has a history; its Catholic population came more or less « all at once » after the war; it is composed
largely of independent professionals and entrepreneurs[42] not organization men.   Only further research in the multiple melting pot
hypothesis will reveal whether a change in any of these variables
might substantially affect the theory.   However, on the basis of
field work observations, distribution of home ownership, intermarriage, norms of social acceptability and choice of recreational companionship, it seems safe to say that at least some of the data from
Westwood fit the multiple melting pot hypothesis[43].

Andrew M. GREELEY

[42] As one young Westwoodian put it in a rare epigramatic mood, « This place is
the last stronghood of inner directed man. »

[43] As this paper is being readied for mimeographing, I have come across a study
by Goddijn (W. Goddijn, « Catholic Minorities and Social Integration »,
Social Compass, 1960, VII, 2, p. 161-176) in which research carried on in
Friesland (northern Holland) has uncovered a situation not at all unlike that
in Westwood.   A Catholic minority, just coming to be accepted as a junior
partner in the Dutch Polity exhibits many characteristics similar to those in
the United States — high levels of religious practice, large numbers of
Catholic organizations, universal school system, little interaction with members of the outgroup.   The similarity is quite striking.

Anti-Intellectualism in Catholic Colleges

Andrew M. Greeley
University of Chicago

The frequently heard charge of anti-intellectualism against Ameri-can Catholic colleges is examined against data taken in a June 1961 representative sample of college graduates. On most indicators of "intellectualism" the graduates of Catholic colleges scored no lower than the national average. There seemed to be no disinclination on the part of these graduates to enter scholarly careers. Some evi-dence is present that this is the result of a major social change and that the faculties of Catholic colleges are putting pressure on their gifted students to consider academic careers.

It has been generally assumed that the Catholic colleges in the United States are inferior in the production of scholars. The Knapp studies[1] indicated that few scientists or scholars had emerged from Catholic institutions; the productivity of 16 Catholic men's colleges was 1.96 while the index of 23 non-Catholic men's colleges was 10.95.[2] Knapp advances some explanations for his findings: ....

> First Catholic institutions are in good part concen-trated in the eastern sections of the United States, a re-gion not noted for high production of scientists. Second, the Catholic population of America, from which these in-stitutions have largely drawn their students, has come from parent European cultures not conspicuous in recent times for scientific accomplishments. Third Catholicism has permitted comparatively little secularization of out-look among its constituents and has maintained a firm

[1] R. H. Knapp and H. B. Goodrich, *Origins of American Scientists,* Chicago: University of Chicago Press, 1952 and R. H. Knapp and J. J. Green-baum, *The Younger American Scholar,* Chicago: University of Chicago Press, 1953.

[2] Knapp and Greenbaum, *op. cit.,* p. 46. All the Catholic colleges in the sample produced 97 Ph.D.'s. Harvard produced 288.

authoritarian structure. Fourth, Catholicism has been a consistent opponent of physical monism, that philosophic tradition under which science has for the most part advanced.[3]

Gerhard Lenski[4] in his study of the religious groups in the Detroit Metropolitan area found that Catholics were not only low scorers on indices of economic rationality (the "Protestant Ethic") but that Catholics also tended to be much more "anti-intellectual" than non-Catholics:

> *On the basis of the findings of this study is appears that overt conflict between the churches and the modern scientific movement . . . is only one of the factors accounting for the disinclination of Catholics to enter scientific careers. In our opinion, other less visible factors are equally important; perhaps far more important. Especially influential is the basic intellectual orientation which Catholicism develops, an orientation which values obedience above intellectual autonomy. Also influential is the Catholic tendency to value family and kin group above other relationships. In brief at both the conscious and subconscious levels of thought and action, membership in the Catholic group is morel ikely to inhibit the development of scientific careers than is membership in other Protestant or Jewish groups. The implications of this for the future of American society are not difficult to discover.*[5]

Much more vigorous criticisms have come from within the Catholic community, with the works of Weigel,[6] O'Dea,[7] and Ellis[8] being the best known of the self-criticisms.[9] The self-critics blame the inferior condition of the Catholic colleges on clerical domination, lack of concern for the values of this world, fear of science, inse-

---

[3] Knapp and Goodrich, *op. cit.,* p. 24.

[4] Gerhard Lenski, *The Religious Factor,* New York: Doubleday, 1961.

[5] Lenski, *ibid.,* p. 255.

[6] Gustave Weigel, S.J., "American Catholic Intellectualism—A Theologian's Reflections," *The Review of Politics,* XIX (July, 1957).

[7] Thomas F. O'Dea, *American Catholic Dilemma: An Inquiry into the Intellectual Life,* New York: Sheed and Ward, 1958.

[8] Msgr. John Tracey Ellis, "American Catholics and the Intellectual Life," *Thought,* XXX (Autumn, 1955).

[9] The vast literature of self-criticism is excerpted in Frank L. Christ and Gerard E. Sherry, *American Catholicism and the Intellectual Ideal,* New York: Appleton Century Crofts, 1959.

352   THE AMERICAN CATHOLIC SOCIOLOGICAL REVIEW

curity in faith, the defensive mentality of the ghetto spirit, the absence of an intellectual tradition among American Catholics, the materialism of the Catholic laity who are more interested in making money than in the pursuit of truth, and the absence of training in initiative and curiosity in Catholic schools. O'Dea comments, "The fact is that although American Catholics have the largest and most expensive educational system of any Catholic group in the world, a genuine Catholic intellectual life is still dependent upon translation of European works."[10] And the Callahans add, "Surely the Catholic college which says, in effect, 'you are intellectually mediocre, you need our strict control to mature and to keep your faith, and it might be harmful if you were left to your own devices in your newspapers and student groups,' cannot be said to foster a spirit of engagement and responsibility."[11] Weigel sums up the theme of the self-critics when he says, "The general Catholic community in America does not know what scholarship is."[12]

There has been little in the way of recent data to substantiate these theories. Ellis collected materials from a number of studies, most of which were more than a decade old at the time of his writing. Lenski's survey was limited to Detroit and included only a small number of graduates of Catholic colleges. The Knapp data pertain to people who had graduated from college before the Second World War. Most of the self-critics are unencumbered by empirical data, though a few comparisons have been made on the basis of graduate scholarship grants.[13]

A recent survey conducted by the National Opinion Research Center makes possible a reevaluation of the anti-intellectualism theory. Questionnaires were administered to some 35,000[14] June 1961 college graduates in 135 colleges and universities, of which 15 were Catholic. The investigation was concerned primarily with the academic experience, career plans, and occupational values of the graduates.[15] It is therefore possible to make a comparison be-

[10] O'Dea, *op. cit.,* p. 9.

[11] Daniel and Sidney Callahan, "Do Catholic Colleges Develop Initiative?" *The Catholic World,* (December, 1957).

[12] Weigel, *op. cit.,* quoted in Christ and Sherry, *op. cit.,* p. 221.

[13] Christ and Sherry, *op. cit.,* have reprinted several articles on Catholic college failures in Rhodes, Fulbright and National Science Foundation grants.

[14] This analysis is based in great part on computations made with a 10% representative sample of the total sample (N for the 10% sample = 3397 of which 368 were graduates of Catholic colleges).

[15] The preliminary report of this study is contained in James A. Davis and Norman Bradburn, *Great Aspirations: The Career Plans of June 1961 College Graduates,* Chicago: National Opinion Research Center, 1961. Further reports from this survey are in preparation.

tween the contemporary graduates of the Catholic colleges and graduates of other colleges. Although such an investigation is not able to predict the future scholarly accomplishments of these graduates, it at least may give some insight into the processes which are at work in Catholic colleges.

From the various threads of the anti-intellectualism theory, the following hypotheses may be drawn together which are testable against the NORC data:

1. Graduates of Catholic colleges will be less likely to attend graduate school.

2. Graduates of Catholic colleges who do go to graduate school will be less likely to choose the academic fields— the arts and sciences.

3. Graduates of Catholic colleges who do choose the arts and sciences will be less likely to choose the physical sciences (and more likely to choose the humanities).

4. Graduates of Catholic colleges who do go to graduate school in the arts and sciences will be less likely to be religious than those who do not.

5. Graduates of Catholic colleges will be more likely to choose business and the professions.

6. Graduates of Catholic colleges will be less likely to see the purpose of education as intellectual and more likely to see it as career training.

7. Graduates of Catholic colleges will be less likely to be loyal to their schools because of the rigid control to which they were subject.

8. Graduates of Catholic colleges will be more likely to seek the security of a large corporation for their employment, will be more interested in avoiding high pressure on the job, less interested in working in a world of ideas or in opportunities to be original and creative, less interested in freedom from supervision, and less interested in making a lot of money. (Most of the items in this hypothesis flow from Lenski's modernization of the Protestant Ethic Theory.)

Table 1 presents a summary of demographic and socio-economic differences between graduates of Catholic colleges and graduates of all other colleges. Only two of the differences are sig-

TABLE 1
Summary of Demographic and Socio-Economic Differences Between Graduates of Catholic Colleges and Graduates of Other Colleges

	Catholic College	Other College
Percent male	57	60
Hometown over 500,000	48	28*
Married	5	26*
Have children	4	17
Father went to college	40	39
Mother went to college	37	36
Income over $7,000	48	47
Parent professional or manager	54	49
	N = 368	N = 3029

* Significant at .01 level.

nificant and neither surprising.[16] Graduates of Catholic colleges are more likely to be from large cities and less likely to be married.[17] No significant differences emerge on sex ratio, parental income, parental education, or parental occupation. In short, there is nothing in the NORC material which would lead us to believe that there are any notable demographic or socio-economic differences between the graduates of Catholic colleges with the exception of the size of hometown and the possibility of being married.

Table 2 summarizes the available data on the academic experience of the graduates of Catholic colleges as compared with the graduates of other colleges. We note that there is no significant difference between the two groups on academic performance,[18] plans to go to graduate school in the coming fall, disinclination ever to go to graduate school, and inclination to go to graduate school in the academic areas. In short, there is no support for the

[16] Significance standards were obtained by multiplying numbers taken from Davies, *Tables Showing Significant Differences Between Percentages* by a 1.5 correction factor. The correction factor was necessitated by the fact that the survey was based on cluster sampling techniques. Ten per cent was a significant difference at the .01 level and eight per cent at the .05 level.

[17] One would assume that Catholics are less likely to get married at least in part because their Church's doctrine would put them in a position of trying to raise children while still in college.

[18] Academic performance was based on grade point average adjusted by a school quality index which index was in turn based on the performance of students at a given college on the National Merit Scholarship exam (in addition to certain other factors). High performers represented the upper fifth of the total sample.

anti-intellectualism hypotheses in the first four items on the table, and indeed the percentages on fall graduate school and choice of arts and sciences run in a direction opposite to the hypotheses.

The next set of items in Table 2 have to do with the purpose of college education; the respondents were asked what they thought the purpose of college education was and what they thought their classmates considered to be the purpose of college education. In direct contradiction to expectations, the graduates of Catholic colleges were significantly more likely to see the purpose as intellectual and less likely to see it as career training. They were also more likely to regard their fellows' intention as intellectual. It should be noted that just an evaluation of education does not of course make the evaluators intellectuals; neither on the other hand does it confirm the notion that such a group is incapable of understanding the meaning of scholarship.[19]

TABLE 2

SUMMARY OF ACADEMIC EXPERIENCE OF GRADUATES OF CATHOLIC COLLEGES AND GRADUATES OF OTHER COLLEGES

	Catholic College	Other College
High Academic Performance	17	18
Graduate school in fall	36	31
No graduate school plans	25	24
Arts and science grad school in fall	15	13
Purpose of school objective		
Appreciation of ideas	77	65*
Career training	19	33*
Purpose of school subjective		
Appreciation of ideas	50	36*
Career training	35	40
School Loyalty		
Liked school very much	45	30*
Liked it	29	43*
Mixed feelings	20	18
Did not like	4	4
Strongly disliked	—2	3
	N = 368	N = 3029

    * Significant at .01 level.

[19] Perhaps the tradition of Catholic education would place more stress on emphasizing the "liberal" purpose of education and hence would provide its students with a better answer to the question. It is difficult to go through a

The next set of items on Table 2 are concerned with school loyalty. It would appear that, despite the fears of the self-critics that the graduates of Catholic colleges are under a clerical oppression, there is no significant difference between the two groups on general patterns of school loyalty, with about three-fourths of both groups expressing positive feelings towards their school. Indeed, in direct contradiction to the expectations, graduates of Catholic colleges are significantly more inclined to say that they liked their colleges very much.

TABLE 3
SUMMARY OF FUTURE PLANS OF GRADUATES OF CATHOLIC COLLEGES AND GRADUATES OF OTHER COLLEGES

Future Occupation

	Catholic College	Other College
Science	4	7
Social Science or Humanities	10	8
Medicine	3	3
Law	7	7
Engineering	6	8
Education	25	31
Business	24	16*
Other professions	15	13
Other	6	6
	N = 355	N = 2808

Future Career Employer

	Catholic College	Other College
Large company	33	27
Small company	13	10
Family business	4	2
Self-employed	8	7
Research organization	6	7
College	11	12
Elementary or secondary education	23	32*
Other education	1	0.5
Federal government	15	13
State or local government	7	5
Welfare organization	7	8
	N = 368	N = 3029

* Significant at .01 level.

Catholic college and not hear (and perhaps even read) Newman's ideas about the purpose of a university. One who had contact with *The Idea of a University* would hesitate to dismiss education as "career training" no matter what he thought it was really for.

Table 3 compares the two groups of collegians on their future occupational plans. The first group of items shows that there is only one significant difference between the groups: graduates of Catholic colleges overchoose business according to the prediction. Catholics also underchoose education, though the margin falls just short of significance on this item. On the next set of items, however, (future career employer) we see the opposite phenomenon as far as significance is concerned: here the Catholic underchoice of education is significant and the overchoice of the large company (called for by the prediction) is merely suggestive. The net impression we obtain from Table 3 is that Catholics do indeed overchoose business as a career, but as a result of an underchoice of teaching and not of the more scholarly fields such as the sciences or the humanities.

Table 4 presents information on value differences between the two groups. Once again very little in the way of significant differences emerges. Graduates of Catholic schools are significantly less interested in "working in a world of ideas" than others as our predictions would require. On all other items, predictions fail to be confirmed by significant differences although margins are suggestive on "opportunities to be original and creative" and "freedom from supervision." On the other hand, differences run in directions opposite to the hypothesis on "avoiding high pressure" and "slow and sure progress." Table 4 offers somewhat more support to the anti-intellectualism hypotheses than did Table 2 or Table 3, but falls far short of definitive confirmation. No support is to be found for the "Protestant Ethic" hypothesis.

The second section of Table 4 reports the responses on certain self-description items in the questionnaire. Catholic college graduates are significantly more likely to think of themselves as conventional and religious than graduates of other colleges and less well disposed to modern art and political liberalism than other graduates, though the differences are not significant on these last two items. These findings are in keeping with the notion inherent in much of the comment on Catholic schools that they tend to be more conservative than other schools, although the differences are not especially great. It is interesting to note that the Catholic population in all colleges (non-Catholic as well as Catholic) is more likely to consider itself politically liberal than Protestant graduates.[20]

[20] Cf. A. M. Greeley, "Religion and the College Graduate" (Unpublished Ph.D. Dissertation, The University of Chicago, 1962).

TABLE 4

SUMMARY OF VALUE DIFFERENCES BETWEEN GRADUATES OF
CATHOLIC COLLEGES AND OTHER COLLEGES
Occupational Values

	Catholic College	Other College
Making a lot of money	26	24
Opportunities to be original and creative	46	52
Opportunities to be helpful to others	66	65
Avoiding high pressure	14	16
Living and working in a world of ideas	32	40**
Freedom from supervision	12	19
Slow and sure progress rather than chance of extreme success or failure	26	33
Chance to exercise leadership	38	41
Remaining in area where I grew up	9	7
Getting away from area	8	13
Opportunity to work with people instead of things	58	56
	N = 368	N = 3029

Self Description

	Catholic College	Other College
Favorable to modern art	43	48
Politically liberal	41	47
Conventional	59	51**
Religious	92	58*
	N = 368	N = 3029

* Significant at .01 level.
** Significant at .05 level.

Table 5 turns to the potential scholars of the survey, those who were definitely going to attend graduate schools in the arts and sciences in the fall of 1961.[21] We note that the expected Catholic college lead in the humanities is significant, but that this results from a lack of Catholic college inclination to the biological sciences and not, as the prediction would have expected, from a disinclination to go into the physical sciences.

Table 6 shows that potential scholars from Catholic colleges are somewhat less likely to plan a career of research than graduates

[21] In this part of the analysis, it was possible to use cards representing all the Catholic college graduates in the survey, hence the high total. The non-Catholic colleges were represented by the 10% sample. Significant percentage differences in the middle range were seven per cent at the .05 level and nine per cent at the .01 level.

ANTI-INTELLECTUALISM   359

TABLE 5

CAREER FIELDS OF GRADUATES GOING TO ACADEMIC GRADUATE
SCHOOL IN THE COMING FALL FOR CATHOLIC COLLEGES
AND OTHER COLLEGES

	Catholic College	Other College
Physical Sciences	30	31
Biological Sciences	6	13**
Social Sciences	20	21
Humanities	44	35*
Total	100 (482)	100 (3405)

(N = 3887, representing all potential scholars in the survey)

** Significant at .05 level.
 * Significant at .01 level.

from other colleges, although the difference falls just short of significance. This difference is in all probability related to the Catholic overchoice of the humanities where research is not so imperative as in the sciences.

TABLE 6

CAREER INTERESTS OF POTENTIAL SCHOLARS BY SCHOOL TYPE

	Catholic College	Other College
Teaching	72	72
Research	56	63
	N = 482	N = 3405

At this point, it seems reasonably safe to say that there is very little in the way of confirmation for the main themes of the Catholic college anti-intellectualism theory, although there is some suggestive evidence for certain aspects of it. However, on the most important points—the choice of graduate school, the choice of the arts and sciences, and the choice of the physical sciences—there is absolutely no support for the theory.

The findings in this paper may come as a considerable surprise to many—as indeed they did to the author. It may be possible that a major social change is going on within the Catholic educational system as the descendants of the immigrants become more closely integrated into American life (an integration that was ritually symbolized by the Douay Bible on Inauguration Day). One might argue that the lack of scholarship from graduates of Catholic colleges in past years was not due to the ideological and organizational reasons advanced by the self-critics, but rather a result of the stage in the acculturation process at which the Catholic group was operating. In a qualitative report on a study which has

360   THE AMERICAN CATHOLIC SOCIOLOGICAL REVIEW

yet to be published, Donovan makes the same suggestion: "The independent spirit, the open mind, the critical insight and the dedicated and industrious scholar are today more frequent companions in our colleges and universities. . . . Indeed, during the past 15 years, the stature of Catholic intellectual life in the United States has grown dramatically. The evidences of this growth are not yet fully reflected in the records of productive scholarship because it is a transition to maturity which is still in process."[21]

This transitional explanation certainly fits the findings reported in this paper: a general absence of difference between the two kinds of graduates on major items and yet at least suggestive differences on items such as research plans or a desire to work in a world of ideas.

It is possible to put this "transition" hypothesis to one test. The author suspected that a "system" in transition would be eager to acquire the status symbols of the "system" which it was adopting as a reference group and that therefore one might expect the Catholic colleges to put more pressure on their students to attend graduate school in the arts and sciences. Since we had available information on the amount of influence students attributed to their advisor or to other faculty members, we might test such a theory. Little in the way of difference emerged on this test. However, a second thought suggested that perhaps schools involved in the transitional process here hypothesized would not want just any student going into the groves of academia, but only the more impressive ones. Tables 7 and 8 show that there is some confirmation for this hypothesis.

TABLE 7

PERCENTAGE REPORTING INFLUENCE OF FACULTY ADVISER
IN MAKING CAREER DECISIONS FOR CATHOLIC
AND OTHER SCHOOLS BY API SCORE

API	Catholic Schools*		
	Arts and Sciences	Professional	Not going
High	61 (241)	45 (198)	49 (652)
Not high	58 (340)	43 (754)	48 (4580)

Weighted N = 6765 (representing all Catholic school
graduates in survey)

	Other Schools		
High	53 (126)	38 (108)	40 (331)
Not high	65 (105)	43 (172)	49 (2187)

N = 3029 (all graduates of non-Catholic colleges in 10%
representative subsample)

TABLE 8

PER CENT REPORTING INFLUENCE OF OTHER FACULTY MEMBERS
IN MAKING DECISION BY API SCORE AND SCHOOL TYPE

A P I	Catholic Schools		
	Arts and Sciences	Professional	Not going
High	80 (241)	69 (198)	53 (652)
Not high	67 (340)	50 (754)	56 (4580)
	Other Schools**		
High	69 (126)	43 (108)	49 (331)
Not high	75 (105)	55 (172)	54 (2187)

      * Weighted N = 6765.
    ** N = 3029.

We note in Tables 7 and 8 that for Catholics going to graduate school the higher influence percentages are in the first row—the row representing the students who did exceptionally well academically while in the other schools the higher influence percentages tend to be in the second row—for those who were not among the high academic achievers. However, when we look at those not going to graduate school we see that the Catholic non-achievers report either more influence or practically the same as achievers. In some instances, the percentage differences are rather small, although it is quite clear that the low achievers in non-Catholic schools are more likely to report influence than the high achievers, while this is clearly not the case in the Catholic schools. The overall impression seems to be that the influence "weight" among graduate school planners in the Catholic schools is with the higher achievers and in the other schools the "weight" is with the lower achievers.

Professor James A. Davis has suggested to me an ingenious explanation for this phenomenon. In schools unworried by the status problems of the transition process, the faculty is more concerned with giving advice to the less gifted students on the premise that these are the ones who are in most need of assistance and that the gifted students can take care of themselves. On the other hand, in schools in the transition process towards full-fledged acceptance in the American academic system, the desire for prestige will lead the faculty to desire to send its most promising members into the "big leagues" of graduate school training.

Table 9 shows that the phenomenon under consideration is not a private school function. Indeed the pattern displayed in Catholic schools is more likely to be found in public schools than in other private schools—a finding in keeping with the assumptions of the "transition status search" theory.

TABLE 9

Per Cent Reporting Influence of Faculty Adviser and Other Faculty Members in Public and Private Non-Catholic Schools by API

Faculty Adviser

	Public Schools			Private Schools (Non-Catholic)		
	Arts and Sciences	Professional	Not going	Arts and Sciences	Professional	Not going
High	68 (52)	39 (33)	37 (152)	48 (74)	36 (75)	45 (180)
Not high	53 (46)	48 (84)	54 (1274)	64 (59)	47 (88)	52 (912)

Public N = 1641
Private N = 1388

Total N = 3029

	Public Schools			Private Schools (Non-Catholic)		
	Arts and Sciences	Professional	Not going	Arts and Sciences	Professional	Not going
High	80 (52)	66 (33)	37 (152)	66 (74)	51 (75)	50 (180)
Not High	66 (46)	68 (84)	54 (1274)	77 (59)	54 (88)	52 (912)

Public N = 1641
Private N = 1388

Total N = 3029

Table 10 shows that the influence pattern at work in the Catholic colleges is also to be found in non-Catholic religious colleges (a religious college being one with denominational affiliation and more than 80% of its student body reporting that they are "religious"), although the numbers involved are quite small. One might argue, therefore, that the influence pattern is a function of the religious atmosphere of a college, although such an argument does not exclude the "transition status search" explanation, since virtually all the small Protestant denominational colleges in the study might be assumed to be as eager for the status conferred by Ph.D. alumni as the Catholic colleges are.

TABLE 10

INFLUENCE OF ADVISORS AND OTHER FACULTY BY API AS
REPORTED BY STUDENTS IN NON-CATHOLIC DENOMINATIONAL
COLLEGES WITH HIGH (OVER 80) STUDENT RELIGIOSITY SCORE

A P I	Arts and Sciences	Advisor Professional	Not going
High	85 (7)	55 (11)	47 (47)
Not high	75 (60)	56 (81)	50 (367)

Other Faculty			
High	70 (7)	72 (11)	70 (47)
Not high	41 (60)	75 (81)	57 (367)

N = 573

It might well be wondered to what extent this weight of faculty influence has an effect on the "mix" of students a given school system sends on to graduate school in the academic fields. There are actually two roles a college can play in the production of graduate students—it can recruit people who had no orientation towards such a career at the beginning of their college education or it can retain in an academic orientation those students who came to college with such an orientation. Astin[22] and Davis[23] have suggested that colleges act more as a "pipe line" of talent and that those colleges which have high productivity of scholars are the ones which have attracted students who already have an orientation towards a career which will require graduate work or whose

[22] Alexander W. Astin, "A New Approach to Evaluation College 'Productivity'" Mimeographed Manuscript, National Merit Scholarship Corporation, 1962.

[23] Davis and Bradburn, op. cit., p. 24.

364   THE AMERICAN CATHOLIC SOCIOLOGICAL REVIEW

academic abilities would make them likely candidates for graduate school (since there is a high correlation between academic ability and graduate school inclination). Thus instead of measuring productivity by the number of Ph.D.'s a school turns out, we might be better advised to measure productivity by the number of recruits it is able to gain for the academic profession. Some 60% of those who had academic occupations for their career choice at graduation time had come to college with this kind of orientation; so 40% of the future academics were recruited for academia while in college. Table 11 shows that 41% of the high academic performers from Catholic colleges who were going into scholarly occupations were recruits, while only 31% of the low performers with scholarly plans were recruits. Almost the exact opposite percentages are recorded for other colleges. Thus the Catholic college high performers who are going into scholarly pursuits are more likely to be recruits than the low performers, while the non-Catholic college high performers are less likely to be recruits than the low performers. In other words, those high performing Catholic college graduates who are going into scholarly careers have a higher proportion of recruits among their numbers than do non-Catholic college high performers or Catholic college low performers. It would appear that the faculty "weight" which we have described is increasing the proportion of academically gifted Catholic college graduates who are oriented towards the arts and sciences.

TABLE 11

PER CENT OF THOSE CHOOSING ACADEMIC CAREERS WHO WERE RECRUITED TO THOSE CAREERS WHILE THEY WERE IN COLLEGE BY API FOR CATHOLIC AND NON-CATHOLIC COLLEGES

API	Catholic Colleges*	Other Colleges**
High	41 (123)	28 (76)
Not high	31 (305)	40 (179)

* All Catholic college graduates in survey.
** Ten per cent subsample.

In Table 12 we attempt to determine whether faculty influence plays a more important role in recruiting or retaining potential scholars. Even though the numbers are very small in most of the cells, it would appear that there is a tendency for Catholic college recruits to report more faculty influence than Catholic college retainees or other college recruits at both levels of academic performance. Catholic college high level recruits report the highest amount of faculty influence. In other colleges the lower level retainees report more influence than the lower level recruits and there is only a small difference between the influence reported by the high level recruits and the high level retainees. The relatively small numbers in the table make definite interpretation uncertain, but it would appear once again that the weight of influence in Catholic colleges towards an academic career is concentrated on brighter students who have not chosen such a career and is not without its effect in swaying the choice of some students.

TABLE 12
INFLUENCE OF FACULTY MEMBERS ON RECRUITING OR RETAINING STUDENTS FOR ACADEMIC CAREERS BY API FOR CATOLIC AND NON-CATHOLIC COLLEGES
(% REPORTING FACULTY INFLUENCE IN CAREER DECISION)

Catholic Colleges

A P I	Recruited	Retained
High	90 (51)	68 (72)
Not high	60 (94)	55 (211)

N = 428

Other Colleges

High	78 (23)	73 (53)
Not high	51 (70)	69 (109)

N = 259

We can therefore suggest tentatively that faculty pressure at Catholic colleges is not producing more arts and science graduate students, or more recruits for the arts and sciences from those who did not originally plan such a career, or even a greater proportion of high performing graduate students than other colleges. But what the pressure is apparently doing is producing a higher proportion of *recruits* among the high performing Catholic college graduates who are going into the arts and sciences. Thus the "mix" of Catholic college graduates choosing an academic career will have a higher proportion of bright recruits than might be expected and less recruits from the lower four-fifths of academic performers than might be expected. (Another way of saying the same thing would be to observe that the Catholic college "mix" will have a lower proportion of bright retainees and a higher proportion of less gifted retainees.)

Obviously the mechanism we have described is working in a situation created by the acculturation of the Catholic ethnic groups. In Defarri's study three decades ago of 14,000 graduate students, only seven per cent were Catholic.[24] In Davis' 1957 study 26% were Catholic.[25] This change, to which we intend to devote further study, has made it possible for young Catholics to plan academic careers in proportions similar to other Americans, for Catholic colleges to strive to recruit their more promising students for such careers, and for the college faculties to see a positive value in the status which comes from having produced "scholars." It is only against the background of this larger social change that the mechanism reported in this paper can be seen in operation.[26] We would claim for the mechanism that it is an intervening specification of the acculturation process.

We might note in conclusion that the Catholic college graduate planning a scholarly career does not appear to see any conflict between such a career and his religion. Ninety-one per cent of all the Catholic college graduates think of themselves as "religious" while 89% of the potential scholars would so describe themselves.

CONCLUSION

Little evidence was found to support the hypotheses of antiintellectualism among graduates of Catholic colleges. Graduates of these colleges were no less likely to go to graduate school, to choose the arts and sciences, to specialize in the physical sciences, or to have a high academic record. They were more likely to see the purpose of education as intellectual and to think that their fellow students shared this concept; they were also more likely to be very loyal to their schools. They were more inclined to business as a career, but because of an underchoice of education, not because of an underchoice of the sciences and the humanities. They were less interested in working in a world of ideas and there was suggestive evidence that they were less interested in opportunities to be original and creative and less interested in research if they were going to graduate school in the arts and sciences. However, none of these differences was very large. There was also evidence that

[24] Roy J. Deferri, "Catholics and Scholarship," *The Commonweal*, XIV (June 4, 1931) quoted in Christ and Sherry, *op. cit.*, p. 95.

[25] James A. Davis, *Stipends and Spouses*, Chicago: The University of Chicago Press, 1962.

[26] As will be reported in another paper, there were few significant differences between Catholics in Catholic colleges and Catholics in other colleges, although the former were somewhat more likely to choose academic careers, especially if they were in the upper fifth of the academic performers.

they were more religiously inclined[27] and more conventional and perhaps slightly more conservative politically. There was no confirmation for the hypotheses derived from Lenski's adaptation of the Protestant Ethic theory.

It was suggested that the situation described in this paper—so contrary to most expectations from previous theory as well as from Catholic self-criticism—might be the result of a transitional process which is accompanying the later stages of the acculturation processes of the Catholic immigrant groups. As a test of one aspect of this transition theory, it was predicted that there would be a tendency for Catholic faculties to put considerable pressure on their more gifted students to go to academic graduate school, a pressure which would be manifested especially by a higher proportion of recruits among the high level students choosing academic careers. This prediction was substantiated and it was suggested that alumni with Ph.D.'s are status symbols that a school or a school system in transition might seek as it attempts to move into the more prestigious sections of the Academic Groves. One suspects that the competition for future Nobel prize winners will grow more acute.

It is not the intention of this paper to claim that the anti-intellectual hypothesis was false when it was first advanced or that self-criticism has not made a contribution to American Catholicism or that American Catholics have now become part of the intellectual elite in their proper proportion. We do maintain that the lack of confirmation for the hypothesis among the June 1961 graduates of Catholic Colleges would suggest that there has been a drastic social change in the last decade and a half. The change is not complete; the work of self-criticism is by no means finished;

[27] They would be much less likely to leave their religion. Less than one per cent of the graduates from Catholic colleges no longer considered themselves Catholics, while some 12% of the Catholics who had graduated from other colleges no longer considered themselves Catholics. However, the fact that 88% of those who were raised Catholics still considered themselves to be Catholic at the time of their graduation from a non-Catholic college would indicate that there is no massive apostasy among Catholics at non-Catholic colleges. (Another study by the present writer would indicate that about eight per cent of those born Catholic in the general population are no longer Catholic. Cf. A. M. Greeley, "Some Information on the Present Situation of American Catholics," *Social Order* (forthcoming).

368   THE AMERICAN CATHOLIC SOCIOLOGICAL REVIEW

there are no Catholic colleges among the very elite schools as yet;[28] a Catholic intellectual elite is at best just beginning to be formed. But just as it would be a mistake to argue that there is no room for further progress, it would also be a mistake, at least in view of the data reported in this paper, to deny that there has been dramatic progress.

[28] Since this paper was completed a tabulation has become available (through Mr. Richard McKinlay of the National Opinion Research Center) which enables us to compare the graduate school inclinations of Catholic College graduates with graduates of other groups of colleges:

	Ivy	Other Prestige	Middle Western	Big Ten	Catholic	National Average
Arts and Science	21	25	15	9	15	12
All Graduate schools	52	63	32	26	36	31

We note that the Catholic colleges are less likely to produce arts and science graduate students (or any kind of graduate students) than the Ivy League schools or the other high quality schools in the sample but more likely than the Big Ten schools or the national average and about the same as the Middle Western liberal arts colleges. These figures give us a rough idea of where the Catholic college system would be rated in the total American picture—neither at the top nor at the bottom, but a bit above the average.

Areas of Research on Religion And Social Organizations

Andrew M. Greeley

The University of Chicago

Reprinted from
THE AMERICAN CATHOLIC SOCIOLOGICAL REVIEW
Fall, 1962

Areas of Research on Religion
And Social Organizations*

Andrew M. Greeley

The University of Chicago

*Little empirical research exists on the impact of religion on
social organization in the United States, partly because of the
lack of adequate theoretical tools; partly because of the difficulties in separating religious influences from class and ethnic
influences; partly, because of the absence of a clear vocabulary
to delineate the different religious groups. It is suggested that
the "triple melting pot" hypothesis of Herberg, Kennedy and
Lenski might be a useful tool in examining "religious segregation"
in the marriage market, clique formation, recreational activity,
civic interaction, occupational association, political alliance
and spatial integration. The possibility that competition between
the various creeds leads to some kind of functional balance
requires further research, especially since the condition of
religious pluralism presently existing in the United States is
almost unique in the history of human society.*

There has been very little research done on the impact of
religion on social organization in the United States—a fact which
is especially surprising in view of the classic notion of data of the integrative "function" of religion. A considerable amount of data
has been amassed on the differential behavior of the members
of the three major American religious groups,[1] but very little
has been done to determine how (or whether) Protestants, Catholics, and Jews interact with each other and to what extent this
interaction (or non-interaction) affects the social organization
of a given community or a larger society.

* For help in various stages of preparation of this paper I am indebted
to Professors Peter M. Blau, Donald J. Bogue, James A. Davis, Everett C.
Hughes, Peter H. Rossi and Harrison C. White.

[1] We know for example about voting patterns, socialization techniques,
sexual practices, fertility expectations, and scores on "V" and "F" scales.

A fair body of literature exists on religious intermarriage[2]: Hughes has made a cultural study of the English Protestant and French Catholic confrontation in Canada;[3] Underwood has reported a conflct situation in a New England community;[4] Herberg has generalized Kennedy's triple marriage melting pot theory to cover a much larger body of phenomena[5]; Rosenthal has asked whether the acculturation of the Jewish population of Chicago will necessarily lead to assimilation[6]; Solomon has pointed out the connection between the religious hospital system in Chicago and the career of a physician[7]; Meier and Bell have suggested that religion might be considered in the evaluation of a person's social-economic status.[8] Lenski has recently suggested that the triple melting pot hypothesis can be used to explain not only interaction patterns, but value differences which he sees affecting the attitudes of members of the various religions on politics, economics, education, science, and family life.[9] Even though Lenski's work is most suggestive, the relatively small size of his sample and its limitation to Detroit cause one to have some reservations about his conclusions.

Such a small collection of studies bound together by very little in the way of even low level theory is all the more astonish-

[2] For example John L. Thomas, *The American Catholic Weekly*, New York: Prentice Hall, 1956; Ruby Jo Reeves Kennedy, "Single or Triple Melting Pot," *American Journal of Sociology*, XLIX (January, 1944), p. 331; Loren E. Chancellor and Thomas Monahan, "Religious Preference and Interreligious Mixture in Marriages and Divorces in Iowa," *American Journal of Sociology*, LXI (November, 1955), p. 233; Judson T. Landis, "Marriage of Mixed and non-Mixed Religious Faith, *The American Sociological Review*, XIV (June, 1949), p. 401; A. B. Hollingshead, "Cultural Factors in the Selection of Marriage Mates," *The American Sociological Review*, XV (October, 1950), p. 619.

[3] Everett C. Hughes, *French Canada in Transition*, Chicago: The University of Chicago Press, 1943.

[4] Kenneth Underwood, *Protestant-Catholic*, Boston: The Beacon Press, 1957.

[5] Will Herberg, *Protestant Catholic Jew*, Garden City Doubleday, 1955; Kennedy, *op. cit.*, p. 331.

[6] Erich Rosenthal, "Acculturation Without Assimilation, *American Journal of Sociology*, ZLVI.

[7] David Solomon, "Ethnic and Class Differences Among Hospitals as Contingencies in Medical Careers," *American Journal of Sociology*, LXVI (March, 1961), p. 463.

[8] Dorothy L. Meier and Wendell Bell, "Anomia and the Achievement of Life Goals," *The American Sociological Review*, XXIV (April, 1959), p. 189.

[9] Gerhard Lenski, *The Religious Factor: A Sociologist's Inquiry*, New York: Doubleday, 1961.

RELIGION AND SOCIAL ORGANIZATIONS 101

ing when one considers the vast amount of journalistic and philosophical writings on the problems of religious tension in a pluralistic society and the substantial popular interest in the subject. Indeed almost everyone with a rotary press and newsprint became an "expert" on inter-religious relations during and after the 1960 election campaign, even though few of the writers had little in the way of factual data at their disposal.

DIFFICULTIES IN THE STUDY OF RELATION AND SOCIAL ORGANIZATION

Rossi has hinted at one of the reasons for the difficulty in the study of this area when he says (speaking of all research in social organization): "If we view social organization as a system of relationships, we may immediately recognize that the stuff with which we must be concerned is not directly available . . . The discernment of relations becomes a job of abstraction. Hence the development of adequate conceptual schemes for the study of social organization is a task of formidable magnitude for which a first approximation in the form of an adequate common sense vocabularly is largely missing."[10]

The study of religion and social organization has at least the beginnings of such a vocabulary in the triple melting pot theory of Ruby Jo Reeves Kennedy and Will Herberg which, for all its metaphorical aura, can serve as a hypothesis with which to begin. The notion that religious membership operates as a reference in the formation of groups outside of the religious sphere certainly admits of empirical testing. It will be the purpose of this paper to describe some of the difficulties in testing with this hypothesis and to enumerate various areas of human activity to which it might be applied. Some findings from a study of an upper middle class suburban community will be used as illustrations.

The first problem is that granting the multiple melting pot assumption, it is by no means clear how many melting pots there are. Some 97 per cent of the American population claim adherence to one of the three main religious groups, but only 60 per cent of the population are listed as Church members.[11] Are the non-members who still ally themselves with one of the

[10] Peter H. Rossi, "Comment," *American Journal of Sociology*, LXV (September, 1957), p. 149.

[11] Donald J. Bogue, *The Population of the United States*, Glencoe: The Free Press, 1959, p. 695.

102   THE AMERICAN CATHOLIC SOCIOLOGICAL REVIEW

three groups to be assigned, for hypothetical purposes, to the group to which they are vaguely connected or do they represent another melting pot? Probably some could be assigned to one of the three melting pots and others could not, but the establishment of criteria for such a decision would not be easy. One also might postulate a "secular humanist" group which has formed for itself a distinct world view that involves much more than mere non-membership in a Church and yet may coexist with some kind of weak tie with one of the organized religions. As Talcott Parsons has commented, "Religious and secular orientations may, to an important degree, thus be seen as constituting different aspects of the same system of orientation to 'problems of meaning.' "[12]

Zelan has collected some evidence that this "religion of the intellectual" is a functional substitute for traditional faith.[13] The members of this secular humanist melting pot may not constitute a large group in American society, yet since they are concentrated in positions of key importance, it is at least possible that they should be considered as a fourth (or a fifth) religious division. Finally one should weigh whether the presence of an Eastern Christian patriarch on the Presidential Inauguration platform is evidence that this rather small group has become of sufficient importance at least in certain parts of America to be listed as yet another "official" branch of American religion.

A second problem has to do with the relation between religion and ethnicity. Kennedy's use of the triple melting pot notion implies that the old ethnic groups are breaking up and the former members of such groups are realigning themselves within religious reference groups—at least for the purpose of choosing marriage patners. However her data, admittedly twenty years old now, showed that, while the influence of ethnicity in choice of marriage partner was declining, it had by no means vanished. In their analysis of material from the 1930 and 1950 consensus, Duncan and Lieberson found that the segregation of ethnic groups declined as social-economic status increased and

---

[12] Talcott Parsons, "Some Comments on the Pattern of Religious Organization in the United States" in *Structure and Process in Modern Societies*, Glencoe: The Free Press, 1960.

[13] Joseph Zelan, "Correlates of Religious Apostasy," (A paper presented at the Thirty-Seventh Annual Institute of the Society for Social Research, The University of Chicago, 1960). I am grateful to Mr. Zelan for making this information available to me.

RELIGION AND SOCIAL ORGANIZATIONS   103

as length of the groups' time in the United States increased.[14] However, their data covered only the foreign born and the children of the foreign born. In one well-to-do suburb it has only been in the five years that those with Irish names (one half the Catholic population of the community and one quarter of the total population) have chosen marriage partners independent of ethnicity.[15] As a matter of fact, we know very little about what ethnicity means in American society today. We have some notion of its influence upon first and second generation behavior but very little about its effect on the third and the fourth generation. One has the impression in a city like Chicago that there continue to be ethnic concentrations among third and fourth generation families, but whether such concentration is directly related to ethnicity or not remains to be seen. The third and fourth generation may still feel some vague and diffuse loyalty to the land of their birth or rather more precisely to other Americans who are descended from immigrants from such a land.[16] However, we do not have a very clear picture of what this loyalty might mean or what effect it would have on human interaction. Thus it is extremely difficult to say how a given type of segregation might arise from religious or ethnic factors or a mixture of both. It is at least possible that there has been a reversal in the relationship between religion and ethnicity. At one time a person may have been Catholic because he was Irish; it is possible that his son or grandson considers himself Irish because he is a Catholic whose parents happen to be descendents of Irish immigrants.[17]

Another problem in the investigation of religious segregation along the lines of a multiple melting pot hypothesis is that it

[14] Otis Dudley Duncan and Stanley Lieberson, "Ethnic Segregation and Assimilation," *American Journal of Sociology*, LXX, p. 403.

[15] This statement is based on a model assuming that in a random choice of mates the Irish in the community would choose partners in proportion to the percentage of the various groups in the community. The choice of Irish by Irish exceeded chance at the .05 level from 1936 to the early 1950's. In the last seven years the choice of Irish by Irish did not exceed chance. Cf. Andrew M. Greeley, "Religious Segregation in a Suburb," unpublished M.A. thesis, The University of Chicago, 1961. Westwood is a fictitious name of the suburb.

[16] In one Chicago ward, with a heavy population of second and third generation Poles Nixon carried some 70 per cent of the votes but a liberal Democratic congressman with a Polish name won handily.

[17] The Irish in the suburban community surveyed showed practically no identification with the land of their ancestors and seemed to view their Irishness as part of their Catholicity. Cf. Greeley, *op. cit.*, p. 95.

104   THE AMERICAN CATHOLIC SOCIOLOGICAL REVIEW

is extremely difficult to hold class factors constant. Much of
the segregation one might encounter in testing the hypothesis
could be accounted for as a function of social-economic status
rather than religous affiliation. The problem is complicated by
the fact that we lack any clear idea of what class or status are
in American society or of the relation between these factors and
religion. We have been aware for some time that class influences
the nature or at least the style of religious belief (with changes
in religion marking a family's ascent of the status ladder). There
has been far less investigation of whether religion might affect
status. Meier and Bell suggest that one of the reasons Catholics
and Jews scored higher on Srole's amonie scale is that membership in these groups automatically lowers one's position in the
status heirarchy.[18] Thus Catholics and Jews might think of themselves as being at a disadvantage with the members of the
dominant Protestant group even if they had attained educational,
economic, and occupational parity. A given segregated situation
may be the result of a complicated interconnection of religious
and class factors such that one would be able to sort out the
independent variable only with great difficulty. In Westwood
for example there was very little association on any level between Protestants and Catholics even though the community was
remarkably homogenous according to all the standard indicators
of social class. Certainly the religious factor was at work in this
situation, but one had the impression that the two groups felt
themselves separated by a status distinction: The Protestants
viewing the Catholics as *nouveau riche* interlopers in the community and the Catholics viewing the Protestants as prejudiced
aristocrats who would rather like to keep the neighborhood to
themselves. It might be suggested that the Catholic arrival as
a more or less equal partner in American society (as symbolized
ritually by the Douay bible at the Presidential inauguration) is so
recent and unsure as to leave both the junior and senior partner un-
comfortable in each other's presence. The connection between religion and social status deserves far more careful investigation.

Research in these areas is made more complicated by the
fact that the terms "Protestant," "Catholic," and "Jew" (to say
nothing of the term "humanist") can be compared only in the
most general fashion. Each term implies not only religious beliefs, but hundreds of years of history and culture tangled to-

[18] *Op. cit.*, pp. 199-200.

gether in an intricate web. To be Jewish implies far more than merely a connecton with a group which has certain religious dogmas and certain moral practices. To say that a man is "Jewish" is to say something more about him than if one were to say he is a "Protestant," for there are different notions implicit in the concept "Jewish" than are to be found in the concept "Protestant." On the other hand while "Jewish" gives us hints about certain aspects of a man that "Protestant" does not, it is equally true that "Protestant" subsumes certain kinds of information that "Jewish" does not. The same paradigm could be expanded to include the terms "Catholic" and "humanist." Each of the four terms contains certain comparable elements, but each also implies a considerable number of non-comparable factors. One does not intend to argue that these terms should not be used in an attempt to describe the impacts of religion on social organization. However it should be realized that the use of these terms as though they represented comparable qualities is a highly abstract codification fraught with some danger.

A final difficulty which might face the investigator of possible religious segregation is the temptation to search for the group which is "causing" the segregation. If there are indeed several invisible religious ghettos cutting across the social organization of the republic (or of parts of the republic), the first tendency is to argue that where there is segregation there must be a party segregating and a party segregated. Indeed there may well be a division. However in this new and delicate area of research it might be wise not to assume that the ordinary rules of segregation apply, especially since the word segregation may be too strong a description of what is taking place. It would be far better to establish with some clarity exactly what effect religion does have on social organization in this country before endeavouring, except in a very tentative fashion, to discover how the responsibility for such divisions can be parceled out. Rosenthal's article is very suggestive on this point.[19] He suspects that the Jews of Chicago are consciously resisting assimilation (especially as represented by intermarriage) by providing a modicum of Jewish education and living in well-to-do and voluntarily segregated areas (at least relatively voluntarily and relatively segregated). He argues that in part this is a reaction to anti-semitism and thus similar to the "return to the ghetto" de-

[19] Rosenthal, *op. cit.*, p. 36.

scribed by Louis Wirth, but also in part the result of a new sense of pride (or more appropriately of different sense of pride) in being Jewish, a pride which is partly a reaction to anti-semitism and partly an independent factor. In Westwood something of the same reactions were to be found among Catholics.[20] One suspects that Herberg and Hansen may very well be right in maintaining that the grandson tends to return to what the son has rejected. In any event the causality of religious segregation is so involved that a careful study of it would be much more fitting after its nature and extent are more clearly delineated.

RELIGIOUS INTERMARRIAGE

The multiple melting pot hypothesis can be applied to many different areas of human actvity, but there is available no neat typology of areas. At present the investigator is forced to make up a list almost arbitrarily. Hughes describes three levels of interaction: marriage, clique formation, and recreation.[21] To these one might add formal (in the sense of intercredal) cooperation, civic interaction, occupational association, political alliance, and spatial integration.

The area of interaction we know most about is that of religious intermarriage. Bogue quotes census figures to show that some 93 per cent of marriages in the country are within the same religious group.[22] Ninety-one per cent of the Protestants, 92 per cent of the Jews and 78 per cent of the Roman Catholics marry within their own groups. Most of the regional studies tend to confirm these figures, although data from Iowa and Marin County in California seem to indicate a Jewish intermarriage level in the 25 per cent to 35 per cent bracket in these areas.[23] Thomas' analysis of Catholic intermarriages (based on Catholic Chancery Office data) seems to indicate a somewhat higher percentage for Catholics than Bogue's figures.[24] The Iowa study also indicated a slightly higher percentage for Catholics in this state than Kennedy found in New England or Bogue reported for the national level.

[20] Greeley, *op. cit.*, p. 36.

[21] Hughes, *op. cit.*, p. 160.

[22] Bogue, *loc. cit.*

[23] Doren E. Chancellor and Thomas Monahan, "Religious Preferences and Inter-Religious Mixture in Marriages and Divorces in Iowa," *American Journal of Sociology*, LXI (November, 1955), p. 233; Judson T. Landis, "Marriages of Mixed and non-Mixed Religious Faith," *The American Sociological Review*, XIV (June, 1949), p. 401.

[24] Thomas, *op. cit.*, pp. 121-136.

RELIGION AND SOCIAL ORGANIZATIONS 107

It seems safe to say, therefore, that with some obscurites and some regional variations, the triple melting pot hypothesis is a useful way to describe the effect of religion on marriage in the United States. However, there are many interesting questions still to be answered. To what extent, for example, does the intermarriage rate vary with size of place, income, education, degree of religious activity, percentage of local population in the given religion, and past intermarriage history?

Thomas maintains that the degree of mixed marriages for Catholics varies with the percentage of Catholics in a city, the cohesiveness of ethnic groups, the size of the city, and the level of social class.[25] For cities of 100,000 and over the rate is 14.9 per cent, for cities between 5,000 and 100,000, the rate is 24 per cent and for cities under 5,000 it is 19 per cent. (His data are based on the middle west where the rate is lower than in the rest of the country because of the higher percentage of Catholics in the middle west.) He also found that in Chicago the rate increases from 8.5 in low rental areas to 12.2 in middle areas to 19.3 in suburban areas.

The findings in the Westwood survey were at variance with Thomas' data.[26] Although the average had been around 20 per cent for the early history of the Catholic parish in Westwood, the figure has declined to less than five per cent as Westwood becomes more Catholic and the parish communty becomes more integrated. The Westwood data tend to suggest that as a religious group achieves something like numerical parity in a community and its members become more and more intimately connected with church activities the level of intermarriage will decline, no matter what the economic and social factors in the neighborhood might be. Hence the high intermarriage rate for Jews in Iowa and Northern California might not be a sign, as Rosenthal hints, that assimilation is following acculturation but merely that the Jews in these areas are not sufficiently numerous or well enough integrated in a Jewish community to keep the rate down to the national average.

Even though the melting pot theory seems to fit the data on intermarriage, the precise nature of this fit is not clear. Considerably more research is required before the pattern of religious intermarriage can be described with any degree of confidence.

[25] *Ibid.*, p. 160.
[26] Greeley, *op. cit.*, pp. 93-103.

108 THE AMERICAN CATHOLIC SOCIOLOGICAL REVIEW

CLIQUE FORMATION AND RECREATIONAL ACTIVITY

The present writer knows of little recent information on the other two areas Hughes lists—clique formation and recreational activity. The Warner studies represent a situation that is now more than twenty years in the past; and even at the time the studies were made they described highly stratified small communities.[27] In the Westwood survey, the choice of golf partners and the formation of teen age cliques was investigated. At the Westwood Country Club the two religious groups maintained a power balance that was almost as complicated as a Lebanese cabinet balance with precise (but always unspoken) arrangements for equality in membership and official position.[28] On the golf course itself the invisible ghetto was found to be at work, despite the apparently sincere protestations of club members that golf was "the great equalizer." Indeed members of the Catholic parish overchose other Catholics as golf partners at a ratio seven to one (a comparison between actual distribution of partners and that which would be expected by chance if religion was not a factor). Teen age cliques were formed completely on religious lines with no members of a clique being of dfferent religion than that of the other members of the clique.[29] It should be noted that such segregation in Westwood coexisted with a high degree of external tranquility. Indeed the few people in the community who tried to make the religious issue explicit in any of the minor controversies whch erupted in this exclusive suburb were quickly silenced by the leaders within their own group.

It is by no means evident that the Westwood findings can be generalized to other areas. Westwood is in the middle west, the Catholics are at least half Irish, the community has a long history (unlike many suburbs), the Catholic population is almost exactly the same size as the non-Catholic. Nevertheless, the existence of such segregation in a community where one would expect that the traditional barriers of religion and nationality would be weakened by the social and economic homogeneity of members of the third and fourth generation, at least suggests that other communities should be studied to see if the same factors are operating.

---

[27] W. Lloyd Warner and Leo Srole, *The Social System of American Ethnic Groups*, New Haven: Yale University Press, 1945; W. Lloyd Warner, et al., *Democracy in Jonesville*, New York, 1949.

[28] Greeley, *op. cit.*, pp. 121-136.

[29] *Ibid.*, pp. 103-121.

It is the writer's suspicion that a very clever survey interviewer equipped with a very sophisticated questionnaire would have a difficult time unearthing information on the effect of religion on leisure time activities. This is not to imply that a "one shot" visit by a survey research worker would not provide all kinds of useful information; but religion plays such a peculiar and, one might almost say, delicate role in American life, that definitive information may well require the kind of minute observation which Blau used in his study of interaction in bureaucratic agencies.[30] Americans are subject to conflicting notions about members of other religions (one might almost say that there is here another "American dilemma"). On the one hand they are told by their "official ideology" that religion is a good thing, that one religion is pretty much the same as another, and that a man should be judged on his own merit and not on his religious faith. On the other hand, Protestants often hear that the Catholic hierarchy is planning to take over the country or, alternately, planning the subversion of the public school system; and Catholics hear that they are being deprived of their educational rights and the Protestants resent the rising political power of Catholics. Depending on which cross current happens to be salient the average American would have almost two sets of answers to questions about associations with members of other groups. Survey interviews on religious segregation would certainly have great value, but it is possible that they would have to be backed up with "harder" data obtained from watching a particular community in operation.

RESIDENTIAL SEGREGATION

It is at least possible that there might even be a spatial segregation between the members of the various groups within a given metropolitan community. Rosenthal's findings on Jews in Chicago would seem to indicate that there is a segregation of Jews even in the new suburbs. The impressions one has of various nationalities continuing their segregation even to the fourth generation would also confirm such a hypothesis. A detailed study of this aspect of the problem will have to wait for the possible inclusion of a religious question in the 1970 census. In the microanalysis used in Westwood it was discovered that Catholics were concentrated within certain blocks and non-

---

[30] Peter M. Blau, *Dynamics of Bureaucracy,* Chicago: The University of Chicago Press, 1955.

110   THE AMERICAN CATHOLIC SOCIOLOGICAL REVIEW

Catholics in other blocks. The concentration seemed to be a function of the location of the Catholic Church in the community with 40 per cent of the Catholic population living within a two block radius of the church as opposed to 20 per cent of the non-Catholic population in the same radius (551 homes were in this two block radius). This finding was especially surprising since it could not be attributed to school location, the public school being across the street from the Catholic school.[31] Whether such micro-segregation is widespread can only be established by further study. However it is suggestive that real estate ads in newspaper often list the distance of a new real estate development from the nearest Catholic Church.

FORMAL COOPERATION

We have virtually no information on what kind of formal cooperation (official or unofficial) goes on between the various religious groups at the various levels in their respective organizational hierarchies. Nor do we know the extent of civic cooperation between the religious bodies or their members. It would be helpful to know if religion plays a role in the formation of the various civic bodies (hospital boards, welfare agencies, crime commissions, citizens leagues etc.) within a large metropolitan community. Perhaps the "snowball sample" type of survey might be useful in such investigation of the religious factor at work among those groups which hold what remains of rational power in a metropolis. That there is relatively little social interaction at the very top ranks of the elite in a city like Chicago is suggested by the rather clear religious divisions which mark such "socially prominent" functions as debutante balls. Even if one does not subscribe to the Community Power Structure approach of Hunter one would still like to know if those who make whatever decisions are still made in a big city are divided on religious lines or even if they communicate with each other.[32]

Party politics make a bow to the multiple melting pot hypothesis in the form of "balanced" tickets. There seems to be considerable doubt as to how necessary such "balance" is, but party leaders are disinclined to take a chance that the balance is not needed. The suspicion seems to be that if a voter sees a name that he judges to be affiliated with his group he will be more inclined to vote for that name than for another, especially

---

[31] Greeley, *op. cit.*, pp. 77-93.

[32] Floyd Hunter, *Community Power Structure*, Chapel Hill: University of North Carolina Press.

on the lower echelons of the long ballot where the voter is unlikely to know anything more about a candidate than his name. If there is still room for disagreement by the experts on what part the religious factor played in a dramatic presidential election, it is obvious that we know very little about what part it plays in the much less spectacular local elections which are the bread and butter of party politics.

OCCUPATIONAL LIFE

One cannot even presume that religion does not play a role in the organization of occupational life. In a large city there are law firms, medical partnerships, and, more recently, brokerage offices which are known to be Protestant or Catholic or Jewish. We do not know what part if any religion plays in the workings of the large corporation either at the level of friendships in the plant or office or at the level of the politics of the upper echelon of the corporate bureaucracy. It may play no part; but, considering the segregation which exists in the marriage market and which there is some reason to believe exists in other areas as well, one cannot rule out the possibility of such an operation of the multiple melting pot without careful investigation. Solomon's article on medical careers, mentioned above, gives interesting insights in this area.

CONCLUSION

In considering these problems one is faced with the fact that the single melting pot concept is stubbornly entrenched in our national subconscious. Indeed it has become so much a part of the American official mythology that one is tempted to dismiss the questions raised in this paper as being unimportant when they are discussed for the first time. It is indeed curious that, although acculturation and assimilation are among the great facts of the American experience, we know next to nothing about what is going on in the late stages of these processes. Indeed about all we have is a body of tacit assumptions based on concepts like the single melting pot which we know are not especially helpful. Such assumptions crop up, for example, in the frequent reference to homogeneous suburbs. When they use this term skilled researchers mean that the suburbs in question are homogenous *on the variables investigated*, which are normally the variables found in census tract data. But one wonders if the significant information for understanding the social organization of a suburb like Skokie or like Westwood is that the income,

112   THE AMERICAN CATHOLIC SOCIOLOGICAL REVIEW

education, and occupational levels show rather little dispersion around a central measure or that the former is 32 per cent Jewish and the latter is 45 per cent Catholic. There are relatively few criteria by which one could judge whether one set of variables was more important than the other in any attempt to explain the social organization of the community in question.

It has recently been suggested that the conflict or at least competition between the various religious groups serves to bring about a balance and a higher unity in a pluralistic society.[33] Such a notion would not be at variance with the notions of Simmel and Coser about the functions of social conflict.[34] Perhaps competition between the various religious groups is a safety valve mechanism which does contribute to the dynamic unity of a complex society, although one must admit that such an idea is indeed a strange transmutation of the old "functional" theory of religion. However, the validity of such an assumption must be subjected to searching investigation. It is by no means proven that competition between religious groups does contribute to social integration, nor is it proven that it does not. In any case the connection between religion and social organization has nothing to do with the claim of organized religion to play an important part in human affairs. Such a claim is based on other grounds than religion's effect on social organization.

The concept of religious segregation implied in the multiple melting pot theory should not be unduly shocking. In urban America for the first time since Martin Luther tacked his thesis on the door of the monastery church the major religious groups stand in a position of relative social and economic parity, occupying the same physical space, engaged in competition with each other, bound by certain rules of the game, and committed to some kind of consensus about the nature and function of the political society which supervises their competition. Such a situation is quite new in human history and on a priori grounds one would be surprised if something like a multiple melting pot did not exist and promise to continue to exist in the foreseeable future. It would be inexcusable for students of social organization to ignore this highly interesting phenomenon which is going on before their eyes.

[33] Leo Pfeffer, *Creeds in Competition*, New York: Harper, 1958.
[34] Georg Simmel, *Conflict*, trans. Kurt H. Wolff, Glencoe: The Free Press, 1956.

Reprinted for private circulation from the
JOURNAL OF HIGHER EDUCATION, Vol. XXXIV, No. 3, March, 1963

Catholic Colleges: System in Transition

A Report Based on the Findings of a Questionnaire Survey

By ANDREW M. GREELEY

IT HAS been generally assumed that the Catholic colleges in the United States are inferior in the production of scholars. The studies of R. H. Knapp in the early 1950's showed that the number of Ph.D.'s among graduates of Catholic colleges was astonishingly low; all the Catholic colleges in his sample produced only 97 doctorates, whereas Harvard alone produced 288. Knapp suspected that among the reasons for such a dearth of scholars were the Catholic opposition to the philosophy of physical monism and the firm authoritarian structure of the Catholic Church.[1] Similarly, according to his recent book *The Religious Factor*, Gerhard Lenski apparently discovered a disinclination of Catholics to go into scientific careers; he argued that the Catholic tendency to value obedience above intellectual autonomy, and family ties above other relationships, was partially responsible for this disinclination.[2]

These criticisms were relatively mild compared to the attacks leveled at the quality of the Catholic college system by persons within American Catholicism. Gustave Weigel, Thomas O'Dea, John Tracey Ellis, and Theodore Hesburg have been the most outspoken but by no means the only self-critics. The inferior quality of Catholic colleges has been attributed by them to clerical domination, lack of concern for the values of this world, fear of science, insecurity in faith, the defensive mentality of the ghetto spirit, the absence of an intellectual tradition among American Catholics, the materialism of the Catholic laity who are more interested in making money than in the pursuit of truth, and the absence of training in initiative and curiosity in Catholic schools. O'Dea comments, "The fact is that although American Catholics have the largest and most expensive educational system of any Catholic group in the world, a genuine Catholic intellectual life is still dependent upon translation of European works."[3] And Weigel sums up the theme of the self-critics

[1] R. H. Knapp and H. B. Goodrich, *Origins of American Scientists* (Chicago: University of Chicago Press, 1952).

[2] New York: Doubleday and Company, Inc., 1961, pp. 282–83.

[3] *American Catholic Dilemma: An Inquiry into the Intellectual Life* (New York: Sheed and Ward, 1958), p. 22.

ANDREW M. GREELEY *is senior study director at the National Opinion Research Center, University of Chicago.*

159   JOURNAL OF HIGHER EDUCATION

when he says, "The general Catholic community in America does not know what scholarship is."[4]

There has been little in the way of recent data to substantiate these theories, which have become almost axiomatic. Ellis collected materials from a number of studies, most of which are now two or three decades old. Lenski's survey was limited to Detroit and was based on a small number of graduates of Catholic colleges. Knapp's data pertain to Ph.D.'s who received their degrees before 1952 and who therefore graduated from college before, during, or immediately after the Second World War. Most of the self-critics are unencumbered by empirical data.

A recent study made by the National Opinion Research Center of the University of Chicago makes possible a re-evaluation of the anti-intellectualism theories. In the spring of 1961, under a grant from the National Institutes of Health, the National Science Foundation, and the Office of Education, the Center undertook a study of the career plans and aspirations of some of the June, 1961, graduating classes of American universities and colleges. A probability sample of 135 schools granting the B.A. degree was drawn, and questionnaires were obtained from the students within these schools. About 34,000 students returned questionnaires, of whom some 4,000 were graduates of 16 Catholic colleges (approximately 45 per cent of the Catholics who graduated from college in June, 1961, attended Catholic colleges).[5]

On the basis of virtually all available information, one would have expected that the graduates of Catholic colleges would be less likely than others to go to graduate school, that those who went to graduate school would be less likely to choose the traditional academic fields (the arts and sciences), that those who did choose these academic fields would be less likely to choose the physical sciences, that those who entered the academic life would be less tied to the Catholic Church than their peers, and that graduates of Catholic colleges would be less likely to be loyal to their schools (because of the rigid control to which they were subject) and less likely to see the purpose of education as intellectual. Not to keep the results a secret any longer, none of these assumptions was valid.

BEFORE we report in greater detail on these somewhat startling findings, we must note that across a broad range of social, economic, and demographic factors, the profile of the graduate of a Catholic college was little different from the profile of the total sample. Catholic graduates

[4]"American Catholic Intellectualism: A Theologian's Reflections," *The Review of Politics*, XIX (July, 1957), p. 299.

[5]The preliminary report of this survey is contained in *Great Aspirations: The Career Plans of America's June, 1961, College Graduates*, by James A. Davis and Norman Bradburn (Chicago: National Opinion Research Center, 1961). A final report on the first phase of this ongoing study is now in preparation. For information concerning the technical background of the present article as well as for detailed statistical tables, see Andrew M. Greeley, "Anti-Intellectualism in Catholic Colleges," *American Catholic Sociological Review*, XXIII (Winter, 1962), pp. 350–59. The writer wishes to express his gratitude to Peter H. Rossi, James A. Davis, and Richard McKinlay of the NORC staff for assistance in this study.

CATHOLIC COLLEGES   160

were less likely to be married and more likely to come from large cities, but the sex ratio, and the income, occupation, and education of parents, were virtually the same.

Approximately 31 per cent of the June, 1961, graduates planned to go to graduate school in the following autumn; one would have expected the percentage to be considerably lower for Catholic colleges than for the total sample; however, it was actually 5 per cent higher. Nor was the high proportion of the Catholic graduates merely the result of an over-choice of the traditional professions such as law, medicine, and business, since 15 per cent of them were going to the arts and sciences as opposed to 13 per cent for the total sample. Finally, the Catholics who had chosen to do graduate work in the arts and sciences were no less inclined to say that research was a major career interest than the total sample (about 60 per cent of the potential scholars—those who were going to enroll in graduate school in the arts and sciences in the fall—considered research to be a major career interest).

TABLE I
PLANS OF A SAMPLE OF COLLEGE SENIORS
WHO GRADUATED IN JUNE, 1961*

TYPE OF COLLEGE OR UNIVERSITY	PERCENTAGE OF PROSPECTIVE GRADUATE STUDENTS	
	All Fields	Arts and Sciences Only
(1)	(2)	(3)
Ivy League.................	52	21
High-quality private........	63	25
Midwest....................	32	15
Big Ten....................	26	9
Catholic...................	36	15

*Source: Richard McKinlay, *Students at the Midway* (Chicago: National Opinion Research Center, 1962).

It may be wondered where this level of production of potential scholars places the Catholic college system with regard to other schools. Table I offers some indication of the status of the Catholic system. The sample was made up of seven Ivy League schools, eight other high-quality private schools, twelve Middle Western liberal-arts colleges, and eight schools belonging to the Big Ten Conference. In the production of potential scholars, the Catholic schools were behind the high-quality private schools, about even with the Middle Western schools, and ahead of the Big Ten as well as of the sample mean. They were neither the most productive nor the least productive.

Father Weigel may be correct when he says that the American Catholic community does not know what scholarship is, but there seems to be no evidence that the graduates of Catholic colleges are less informed about what scholarship is than anyone else—at least if a tendency to choose a scholarly life signifies a knowledge of what scholarship is.

Neither is there any evidence that graduates of Catholic schools have an aversion to the physical sciences. About one-third of those planning to attend graduate school report that they have chosen the physical sciences as their field of specialization, exactly the same proportion as for the total sample. Perhaps at long last the troubled spirit of Galileo Galilei will be put to rest. Catholics are somewhat underrepresented in the biological sciences—as are Jews (in both cases this is apparently related to their urban origins)—and somewhat overrepresented in the humanities; but there is no indication that the graduate of a Catholic college is running away from science.

To complete the picture of surprises, the graduate of a Catholic college is more likely than the average graduate to see the purposes of college as intellectual (77 per cent as opposed to 65 per cent for the total sample) and to have liked his school very much (45 per cent as opposed to 30 per cent). Finally, the potential scholar from the Catholic college is no less likely to consider himself religious than the non-scholar (89 per cent for the former and 91 per cent for the latter).

IT IS quite obvious that the potential scholar is not yet a scholar and may never be. Enrollment in graduate school does not guarantee that scholarship will result ten years later. Many things may intervene between the first year of graduate school and the Ph.D.; many more may intervene between the doctorate and respectable scholarly work; and many, many more between respectable work and pre-eminence. Nevertheless, it seems unlikely that any group will produce a substantial number of competent workers and a handful of great ones unless it has an even larger group that begins to climb the ladder. Whether graduates of Catholic colleges have begun to climb the ladder of scholarship can only be judged in years to come, when some of them have reached the top (or failed to). All we can say at this stage of the proceedings is that the situation at present is very different from that in the early 1930's, when only 7 per cent of the graduate students in the country were Catholics (as opposed to 25 per cent today).

There is some reason to suspect that the difference between the findings of the NORC study and, let us say, the Knapp volumes represents a notable social change, one associated in some fashion with the acculturation of the Catholic immigrant groups and the movement of the large elements of the Catholic population into the expanding upper middle classes. Indeed one might guess that the GI Bill represented the turning point in this social change. In a report on a study which has yet to be completed, John Donovan of Boston College makes a similar suggestion:

> The independent spirit, the open mind, the critical insight, and the dedicated and industrious scholar are today more frequent companions in our colleges and universities. . . . Indeed during the past fifteen years, the structure of Catholic intellectual life in the United States has grown dramatically. The evidences of this growth are not yet fully reflected in the records of productive scholarship because it is a transition to maturity which is still in process.

CATHOLIC COLLEGES 162

We might ask whether this transition occurring in the American Catholic population is giving rise to any mechanisms within the Catholic colleges which may be accelerating the process. One would expect that these colleges, spurred on by the taunts of the self-critics, would be eager to acquire some of the status symbols which are considered important in the prestigious sections of the academic groves. Hence it might be argued that there would be special efforts within the Catholic colleges to turn out as many Ph.D.'s as possible and that therefore faculties would put considerable pressure on their students to consider the advantages of an academic career. Since there was a question in the survey about the influence of the faculty on the respondent's plans for a career, it is possible to make some tentative probings to learn whether such mechanisms are really at work. Our first probe turned up no evidence: Catholic graduate students reported no more faculty influence than graduate students from other colleges. However, on second thought it occurred to us that the faculties would be interested in sending, not their average students, but their promising ones, to graduate school. The students were therefore divided into the upper fifth academically and the lower four-fifths. When faculty influence was investigated along these lines, a very surprising phenomenon emerged. The gifted students from the Catholic colleges who were going to specialize in arts and sciences in graduate school reported more faculty influence than the less gifted students who had chosen the same career, whereas the exact opposite was true of the students from other colleges. The influence "weight" among prospective graduate students in the Catholic schools is with the higher achievers; in the other schools it is with the lower achievers.

James A. Davis has suggested an ingenious explanation of this phenomenon: In schools unworried by the status problems of the transition process, the faculty is chiefly concerned with giving advice to the less gifted students on the premise that these are the ones who are most in need of assistance and that the gifted students can take care of themselves. Conversely, in the schools in the transition process toward full-fledged acceptance in the American academic system, the desire for prestige will lead the faculty to send its most promising protégés to graduate school.

It should be noted that this is not a private-school phenomenon. Indeed, if the respondents who are not in Catholic colleges are divided into private- and public-college categories, the influence pattern at the public schools is more likely to resemble that of the Catholic colleges than is the pattern of the non-Catholic private schools. Furthermore, the pattern existing at Catholic colleges was also found at the small Protestant denominational colleges covered in the survey. One might argue that the influence pattern is a function of the religious atmosphere of a college, although such an explanation does not exclude the desire for prestige as a motivating factor, since it can be assumed that virtually all the small Protestant denominational colleges in the study are as eager for the status conferred by Ph.D. alumni as the Catholic colleges are.

There is a considerable amount of discussion today as to whether colleges really recruit for graduate school or merely channel students into it who had plans to attend graduate school before they came to college. It is beyond the purpose of the present article to engage in discussion of this general question. However, a series of fairly complex probings into the NORC materials strongly suggests that the influence of the faculty at the Catholic colleges is indeed recruiting gifted students for the academic life who did not come to college with such an orientation, and that this recruiting effort is more successful than in the average college (as determined by the sample mean).

There is apparently a major social change going on within American Catholicism as the immigrant groups become acculturated and more Catholics enter the upper middle class; the change manifests itself partly in faculty pressure on gifted students at Catholic schools to pursue academic careers, a pressure which has not been unsuccessful. Apparently the Catholic schools are permanently in the competition for future Nobel Prize–winners.

Reprinted from the AMERICAN CATHOLIC SOCIOLOGICAL REVIEW, Vol. 24, No. 1
Spring, 1963

An Upper Middle Class Deviant Gang

Andrew Greeley

National Opinion Research Center
The University of Chicago

James Casey

Criminal Division
The Department of Justice

Theoretical explanations of deviant gangs do not appear adequate to explain middle class delinquency. It is the contention of this paper that for some members of the upper middle class, socially sanctioned means of maintaining their social position are difficult to realize and that these young people organize subcultures which fit the definition of a delinquent gang. The theory is illustrated through and ex post facto application to a middle class gang.

Middle-class delinquency has always been a stumbling block for most theoretical explanations of deviant gangs. The Sutherland "white collar crime"[1] scheme would have no trouble in accounting for middle and upper-middle-class gangs; it would see such gangs as merely a manifestation of the differential opportunity structure for dishonesty and crime. However, some middle-class gangs (including the one to be described in this paper) do not seem very different—except possibly in degree—from lower-class gangs. Talcott Parsons' notion of the absence of a father figure in the life of young middle-class males is persuasive,[2] but does not explain the origin of the gangs as such. The Bloch-Niederhoffer[3] explanation

[1] Edwin Sutherland, *Principles of Criminology*, Chicago: J. B. Lippincott, 1955.
[2] Talcott Parsons and Robert F. Bales, *Family Socialization and Interaction Process*, Glencoe: The Free Press, 1955.
[3] H. A. Bloch and Arthur Neiderhoffer, *The Gang—A Study in Adolescent Behavior*, New York: Philosophical Library, 1958.

of gangs as a kind of self-imposed puberty rite which cuts across class lines is interesting and certainly would apply to middle-class gangs, but their arguments for the general validity of their theory are not completely convincing. The social disorganization theory of Shaw and McKay[4] and their followers presumably does not apply to middle-class society. And the various anomie theories of Merton,[5] Cohen,[6] and Ohlin and Cloward[7] by definition would not apply to those who have access to socially sanctioned means—and middle- and upper-middle-class boys are assumed to have such access.

Cohen and Short[8] suggest two possibilities; they argue that middle-class delinquency will "arise in response to problems of adjustment which are characteristic products of middle-class socialization and middle-class life situations." They also suspect that "it seems probable that the qualities of malice, bellicosity, and violence will be underplayed in the middle-class subcultures and that these subcultures will emphasize more the deliberate courting of danger . . . and a sophisticated, irresponsible 'playboy' approach to activities symbolic in our culture of adult roles and centering largely around sex, liquor and automobiles."

England's[9] theory is similar but has a different conclusion. He argues that the emergence of a teen age culture, promoted in part by mass media development since World War II, have created a new sense of ingroup feeling among young people and an increased sense of alienation from adult society. Within this teen subculture, hedonistic values are stressed to compensate for status ambiguity. Thus the teen delinquents are selectively imitating certain adult roles, but enlarging them to fill the whole role repertoire.

Kvaraceus and Miller[10] also think that the media must share

[4] Clifford R. Shaw and Henry D. McKay et al., *Juvenile Delinquency and Urban Areas*, Chicago: The University of Chicago Press, 1942.

[5] Robert K. Merton, *Social Theory and Social Structure*, Glencoe: The Free Press, 1957.

[6] Albert K. Cohen, *Delinquent Boys: The Culture of the Gang*, Glencoe: The Free Press, 1955.

[7] Richard A. Cloward and Lloyd E. Ohlin, *Delinquency and Opportunity*, Glencoe: The Free Press, 1960.

[8] Albert K. Cohen and James F. Short, Jr., "Research in Delinquent Subcultures," *Journal of Social Issues*, 14 (1958), p. 28.

[9] Ralph W. England, Jr., "A Theory of Middle Class Delinquency," *Journal of Criminal Law, Criminology and Police Science*, 50 (March-April, 1960), p. 565.

[10] William C. Kvaraceus and Walter B. Miller, *Delinquent Behavior:*

much of the blame since they view middle-class delinquency as the result of a diffusion of working class behavior among middle class youth, partly by the mass media. Bohlke[11] with perhaps better logic argues that what has happened is not the diffusion of working-class norms among middle-class youth, but of working-class youth among the middle class. He argues that a good part of the middle class are "nouveau bourgeoise," families whose income may be middle class but whose values, attitudes and behavior patterns have yet to become middle class. Another element of the middle class which might be expected to contribute to delinquency are those whose position in the income hierarchy has not remained consistent with their place in the prestige hiearchy. This group is economically downwardly mobile and their delinquency is a revolt against a system which is disenfranchising them. Bohlke suggests that both these groups are victims of what he calls "stratification inconsistency." Finally he raises the problem of middle-class youth whose failure in the reward system—particularly at school—seems to destine them for failure in the struggle for success to attain the middle-class goals they aspire to maintain. We find this last point highly suggestive. It will be our contention that for some members of the upper middle class, socially sanctioned means of maintaining their social position are difficult to utilize and that these young people will, in the absence of countervailing forces, organize their own little subcultures that may not be as violent as gangs in other neighborhoods, but nevertheless fit the definition of a delinquent gang quite well. The main difference between these gangs and lower-class subcultures in the anomie theories is that the lower-class group is unable to rise to the middle-class goals to which they aspire while the middle- and upper-middle-class groups are unable to maintain the standards which their parents have achieved. To illustrate this theory—though hardly to prove it—we will apply the theory to one upper-middle-class gang with which the writers are familiar.

There are several weaknesses inherent in this paper. First of all, it is an ex post facto explanation of a gang which has since been dissolved. Secondly, the field work study of the gang was not carried out in an organized fashion with intentions to record the events in the gang's history. The authors had their own theories to explain the gang and did not perceive how these theories "fit" into the anomie

Culture and the Individual, National Education Association of the United States, 1959.

[11] Robert H. Bohlke, "Social Mobility, Stratification Inconsistency and Middle-Class Delinquency," _Social Problems,_ 8 (Spring, 1961), p. 351.

theory tradition before reading Bohlke's article.[12] Thirdly, since the gang members are scattered and hardly disposed to be friendly to the present writers, it is impossible to administer any standardized tests to validate our hunches about their motivation. Finally, the writers are anything but impartial observers to the rise and fall of the gang. In fact at the bitter end, the writers presided—with some qualms of conscience, over its liquidation. However, despite all these difficulties, it would seem that there is so little material available about upper-middle-class gangs that the halting attempts of this paper are not without some value.

Certain points of information about "Westwood" (the semi-suburban community where the gang operated) should be made clear:

(1) It is, as we have noted in another work,[13] a community where friendship lines are usually drawn on a religious basis. Teen-age cliques are seldom ecumenical.

(2) Friendship groups in Westwood usually follow school grade lines; thus the graduates of the Catholic grammar school will continue to associate with their classmates through the years of high school and college (and graduate school). The group will expand to include young people from the neighboring Catholic parish during the teen years and there will be some dating across grade lines in the later years of high school—with two grades often combining at this point. Westwoodians also have friends from other communities, some of whom will be able to break into the Westwood crowd, but their close friends are pretty much those young people with whom they grew up. Occasional isolates will drift away from the Westwood cliques and seek friends elsewhere but the dominant groups are, to put it mildly, strongly oriented toward their own community and its activities.

(3) The Catholic group in Westwood is for the most part "new rich"—families whose wealth was largely of the post war variety. For some families the change from the lower to the upper class was swift with no apprenticeship in the lower middle class. For others the change was less abrupt,

[12] One of the authors had leaned heavily on the adolescent subculture theory to explain the problems of the non-delinquent teenagers in Andrew M. Greeley, *Strangers in the House,* Sheed and Ward, 1961.

[13] Andrew M. Greeley, "Religious Segregation in an Upper-Middle-Class Suburb," Unpublished M.A. Thesis, The University of Chicago, 1961.

AN UPPER MIDDLE CLASS GANG 37

but for very few is there enough of a background of affluence for anything like an aristocratic tradition to emerge (Westwood has its millionaires, but few debutantes and fewer patrons of the arts).

(4) Delinquent gangs are rare in Westwood. This is not to say that there is no deviant behavior; there is a considerable amount of it, but it is usually of isolated individuals or pairs.[14] Many of the teen age cliques occasionally engage in something which might be considered delinquent, but such behavior is not habitual and is contrary to their normal values. The Westwoodians who usually get into trouble with the police are those who have not been able to break into the dominant cliques and have gone off on their own or associated with groups from other communities. These troubles that young Westwoodians do find themselves involved in are usually such that they can be hushed up before the cases reach court—and sometimes even before they reach the police station.

(5) For the purposes of this paper we are not considering habitual drinking as deviant behavior.

THE PERSONNEL OF THE GANG

The gang had its inner core and its hangers on, but the five members of the inner group are our principal concern in this paper. Four of the five were from well to do families, three of them very well to do. None of the families represented old wealth, however; nor did any of them represent professional or business wealth. The heads of several of the families were labor leaders or construction contractors, often with vague political connections. Two of the families had moved into Westwood in the very recent past. In all instances the transition from the lower class to the upper middle class had been very quick. These families were members of Bohlke's "nouveau bourgeoise," except we might add the adjective "haut."

In every family the father was largely an absent figure, either through sickness or separation or almost total non-involvement in family affairs (to a degree unusual even in Westwood). In each instance there was a long record of trouble with school authorities. Some of the boys were simply not bright enough to do well in school, while others had the mental ability but not habits of study required for the level of academic performance required of a young

---

[14] Significantly enough, kleptomania is a not uncommon problem in Westwood.

Westwood male. Some of the families had reacted to these school problems with repressive disciplinary measures (which were usually applied with considerable inconsistency) while others had reacted by blaming the school and engaging in running battles with the teachers. In neither case was there any improvement in academic performance.

Two of the boys apparently had major ego problems. The leaders of the gang were both on the border of serious mental disturbances. Periodically they experienced moods of extreme hatred for adult society, hatred which led to the violence and vandalism which became the trade-mark of the gang. If these two leaders had not been inclined to vandalism, it seems unlikely that the other three would have begun such activity on their own; for these latter could be characterized as having defective—almost nonexistent—superegos. The absence of parental discipline meant that they were not equipped with the kind of internal controls necessary for high performance in school or for avoiding the constant opportunities for mischief which a well-to-do neighborhood like Westwood offered its young.

The five members of the gang had more than their share of problems. In every case there was a serious defect in the father-son relationship. More importantly, because of home background, lack of ability, lack of study habits, and resistance to discipline, they were constantly at odds with the authorities in their schools. They would certainly not have verbalized their problem in this fashion, but it was clear enough to everyone who watched that none of these lads had too much of a chance of achieving "success" as dictated by the Westwood ideal. Nature or their families or their old neighborhood had not equipped them with the mental and personality traits necessary to be "successful" in school as a prelude to being "successful" in life. The Westwood norm said "do well in school, go to college, and be a professional man." The gang realized only very dimly that they could not follow this norm but they did realize that the community institutions—school, church, adult cliques—were in conflict with them. Even though they were members of the upper middle class, they were still anomic individuals —at war with a society which was oppressing them and which they hated—only now it was not a society of another social class, but of their own social class, a class of which their parents in some fashion or the other were members.

Adolescents like these had existed in Westwood before, but no group had ever been composed of so many that were so disturbed;

AN UPPER MIDDLE CLASS GANG 39

nor was there ever such a complete absence of any other forces within the grade group. In other grade groups there was always an inner nucleus of the typical Westwood teen-age male—intelligent, athletic, socialized and docile (though not without their own emotional problems). These emergent aristocrats looked on violent deviant behavior as being stupid since it would interfere with their careers. Deeply disturbed individuals like the leaders of the gang were either ostracized or neutralized. But in this particular group the countervailing powers had been removed (the grade leaders had gone to the seminary) and there was not one to prevent the emergence of a delinquent gang.

They were delinquent only in some senses of the word. They did not break into any homes; they did not engage in street fights; they did not drink very much until toward the end of their existence as a gang; the Irish mores in Westwood were strong enough to prevent the gang from indulging in any heterosexual irregularities as might be expected in gangs from other cultural levels. (A few of the girls who associated themselves with the group—and to some extent egged them on—engaged in minor vandalism, though they were even more clumsy than their male friends and a gentle warning from the local clergy was enough to frighten them off.) The gang's chief pastimes were vandalism and minor theft, the victims, almost always local churches and schools (public as well as parochial). Perhaps their vandalism exceeded only in degree the occasional vandalism in which their predecessors had engaged. However this degree was considerable: before the gang was disbanded at the end of its sophomore year in high school the amount of damage had run into several thousands of dollars.

It is interesting to note in passing that the Church and the schools were the object of much of the vandalism and that the efforts of the parish to establish contact with the gang were in the end futile—despite persistent and dedicated effort. In a community like Westwood the parish and the schools are very much part of The Establishment; they represent in a powerfully symbolic fashion the adult world against which the teenager is revolting. If a gang strikes at them, then the gang is striking at everything it hates and fears. (Durkheim's notion of religion as a collective representation seems to be applicable to these circumstances.) The Church represents middle-class culture perhaps to a far greater extent than it would in a poorer neighborhood. Thus, even though the gang was flattered by the attention the parish showered on it, it was never able to trust the parish or its workers.

40   THE AMERICAN CATHOLIC SOCIOLOGICAL REVIEW

CONCLUSION

We are suggesting that this gang, an example of a group of disturbed adolescents at odds with the socially sanctioned means created by their own class, turned to vandalism as an expression of their frustration and anomie. We further suggest that the absence of father figures in their lives and the social disorganization of a new rich suburb contributed to the creation of the anomic situation. From these facts we would argue that the subculture which this gang evolved for its year of existence could easily be explained by the Merton-Cohen-Cloward theories of delinquency, especially as refined by Bohlke. There is no reason why certain upper-middle-class young people should not feel as anomic as lower-class young people, although the direction and ferocity of their revolt will be colored by their middle-class background. The particular gang in question reached the power it did because of two accidents—the juxtaposition of a relatively large number of problem people in one group and the absence of any strong countervailing power within the group. Its activities were pretty much the projection of the personalities of its two strongest members. But its career was bound to be short because its subcultural norms were so much at variance with the norms of the larger culture. If the gang had contented itself with drinking, it would probably still exist as some kind of middle-class retreatest subculture. However the mercurial temperament of the two leaders assured it a spectacular but brief career.

We would agree with England[15] and Coleman[16] that the adolescent society is a subculture or rather a collection of subcultures. Middle-class youth groups, we would predict, will tend toward delinquency when it has: (a) a large number of "nouveau bourgeoise" members; (b) a large number of notable "father absent" members; (c) a large number of poor academic performers; and (d) an insufficient number of countervailing personalities" to control deviant tendencies.

A group, because of the foregoing factors, perceives itself not only at odds with adult society (a normal enough stage for teen-age groups), but in revolt against it, since it will not be able to achieve the goals that adult society demands of it.

At the present stage of our knowledge we are not in a position to predict how many of the first four conditions need to be met in

---

[15] Op. cit.
[16] James Coleman, *The Adolescent Society*, Glencoe: The Free Press, 1961.

AN UPPER MIDDLE CLASS GANG 41

order that revolt might become operative. Nor are we certain what size a group must be before the "critical mass" necessary for delinquency has been achieved. We would conclude by observing that the lower classes have no monopoly on anomie in our society.

Reprinted for private circulation from
THE AMERICAN JOURNAL OF SOCIOLOGY
Vol. LXVIII, No. 6, May 1963
Copyright 1963 by the University of Chicago
PRINTED IN U.S.A.

INFLUENCE OF THE "RELIGIOUS FACTOR" ON CAREER PLANS AND OCCUPATIONAL VALUES OF COLLEGE GRADUATES[1]

ANDREW M. GREELEY

ABSTRACT

Previous studies have indicated a strong tendency toward antiscientism among American Catholics; in particular, the recent work of Lenski has suggested that Catholics will score low on indicators of economic rationality (the "Protestant Ethic"). These hypotheses are not substantiated by data gathered in a survey of June, 1961, college graduates. Catholics were as likely to go to graduate school, to choose an academic career, to specialize in the physical sciences, and to plan a life of research as Protestants, even under a battery of socioeconomic and demographic controls. Nor was there any indication that Catholics were any less inclined to economic rationality than Protestants. It is suggested that the differences between these findings and those of Lenski might be connected with the different ethnic compositions of the two samples. A reexamination of an earlier study supports this suggestion.

Considerable interest has been expressed recently in the use of religion as a predictor variable.[2] Gerhard Lenski has maintained that, across a wide range of political, economic, intellectual, and family-value dependent variables, religion is at least as efficient a predictor as social class.[3] He also suggests that Catholics will score lower on items indicating economic rationality (the "Protestant Ethic") and higher on items indicating antiscientism. In attempting to find explanations for the latter phenomenon, he discovers both conscious and subconscious forces at work:

On the basis of the findings of this study it appears that overt conflict between the churches and modern scientific movement . . . is only

one of the factors accounting for the disinclination of Catholics to enter scientific careers. In our opinion, other less visible factors are equally important—perhaps far more important—especially influential is the basic intellectual orientation which Catholicism develops: an orientation which values obedience above intellectual autonomy. Also influential is the Catholic tendency to value family and the kin group above other relationships. In brief, at both the conscious and subconscious levels of thought and action, membership in the Catholic group is more likely to inhibit the development of scientific careers than is membership in either Protestant or Jewish groups. The implications of this for the future of American society are not difficult to discover.[4]

Lenski would find substantial agreement for his analysis from the self-critics within American Catholicism. Writers like O'Dea,[5] Weigel,[6] Ellis,[7] and others[8] attribute the in-

---

[1] The author is grateful for the help of Professors James A. Davis and Peter H. Rossi in the preparation of this paper.

[2] One thinks especially of the voting and fertility studies: on fertility cf. Ronald Freedman, Pascal K. Whelpton, and Arthur A. Campbell, *Family Planning, Sterility and Population Growth* (New York: McGraw-Hill Book Co., 1959) and Charles Westoff, Robert Potter, Philip Sagi, and Elliot Mishler, *Family Growth in Metropolitan America* (Princeton, N.J.: Princeton University Press, 1961). On voting cf. Paul Lazarsfeld, Bernard Berelson, and Hazel Gaudet, *The People's Choice* (New York: Duell, Sloan & Pearce, 1944); Bernard Berelson, Paul Lazarsfeld, and W. N. McPhee, *Voting* (Chicago: University of Chicago Press, 1954); and Philip E. Converse, Angus Campbell, Warren E. Miller, and Donald E. Stokes, "Stability and Change in 1960: A Reinstating Election," *American Political Science Review*, June, 1961.

[3] *The Religious Factor* (Garden City, N.Y.: Doubleday & Co., 1960).

[4] *Ibid.*, p. 255.

[5] Thomas O'Dea, *American Catholic Dilemma* (New York: Sheed & Ward, 1958).

[6] Gustave Weigel, "American Catholic Intellectualism—a Theologian's Reflections," *Review of Politics*, XIX (1957), 275–307.

[7] John Tracey Ellis, "American Catholics and the Intellectual Life," *Thought*, Vol. XXX (Autumn, 1955).

[8] Summarized in Frank L. Christ and Gerard E. Sherry, *American Catholicism and the Intellectual Ideal* (New York: Appleton-Century-Crofts, Inc., 1961).

INFLUENCE OF THE "RELIGIOUS FACTOR" ON CAREER PLANS   659

tellectual deficiencies of American Catholicism to the absence of a scholarly tradition, clerical domination, fear of modern science, lack of concern for temporal values, materialism among the Catholic laity, low valuation on curiosity and initiative in Catholic training, and the tendency to encourage talented youth to enter the religious life. The findings of Knapp and his associates on the poor productivity of scholars by Catholic schools apparently confirm these conclusions.[9]

However the Knapp data refer to graduates in the years before 1950, and the self-critics have materials that are even older. Lenski's study, although recent, was limited to the Detroit metropolitan area. A recent survey by the National Opinion Research Center (NORC) permits us to test the Protestant Ethic and antiscientism hypotheses against contemporary data from a national sample.[10] Some 35,000 questionnaires were administered to June, 1961, graduates from 135 colleges and universities in a study of career plans, academic experiences, and occupational values.[11] Since questions about original and current religion were included in the questionnaire, it is possible to analyze the influence of religion on these dependent variables.[12]

The following hypotheses were constructed from the conclusions of previous studies to be tested against the NORC materials:

1. Catholics will be less likely to go to college.
2. Catholic graduates will be less likely to go to graduate school.
3. Catholics who go to graduate school will be less likely to choose the arts and sciences, that is, the academic fields.

4. Catholics in the academic fields will be less likely to go into the most scientific of sciences, that is, the physical sciences.
5. Catholics who go into the academic fields will be less likely to plan a research career.
6. Catholics who go into the academic fields will be less likely to be religious and more likely to be apostates.
7. Catholics will tend to overchoose large corporations as employers, business as an occupation, and security and the avoidance of high pressure as occupational values.

Previous research findings would also lead us to suspect that, on both the "intellectualism" and economic rationality scales devised in the hypotheses, Protestants would be intermediate between Catholics and Jews.

The use of the word "intellectualism" in this paper needs to be clarified. It is clear that going to graduate school in the physical sciences and planning a career of research in this area, for example, are not necessarily indicators of intellectuality, much less of potential scholarship. It is argued merely that the first six hypotheses proposed above would seem to follow logically from those writings that question the intellectuality or at least the orientation toward science of

---

[9] Robert H. Knapp and H. B. Goodrich, *Origins of American Scientists* (Chicago: University of Chicago Press, 1952), and Robert H. Knapp and Joseph J. Greenbaum, *The Young American Scholar: His Collegiate Origins* (Chicago: University of Chicago Press, 1953).

[10] The survey was carried out under grants from the National Institutes of Health, the National Science Foundation, and the United States Office of Education. The careers of the respondents will be followed for several years to come by a continuing series of surveys.

[11] The sample was of stratified-cluster design. All American colleges and universities were grouped into four strata based on previous productivity of students going on to graduate degrees. Then schools were sampled randomly within each stratum. Twenty-page questionnaires (with sixty-two questions, principally about future career and educational plans) were administered to all graduating seniors within these schools; the response rate was well in excess of 90 per cent for most schools. Schools in the more productive strata were oversampled. In order to compensate for the unequal sampling rates, the observations were then weighted proportionately to the reciprocals of these rates, thus providing unbiased estimates. An indication of the interest of the students in the survey is that the response rate to a second questionnaire sent to the same graduates in June of 1962 was over 85 per cent.

[12] The part of the analysis reported in this paper was done on a 10 per cent representative subsample. The preliminary report on the total project is contained in James A. Davis *et al.*, *Great Aspirations: The Career Plans of America's June 1961 Collegiate Graduates* (Chicago: National Opinion Research Center, 1962).

THE AMERICAN JOURNAL OF SOCIOLOGY

American Catholics. If the hypotheses are not supported by the data, previous researches are not necessarily disproved, but at least must be seriously re-examined. It might well be true that Catholics are entering "intellectual" careers for reasons different, and somehow less "intellectual," than Protestants and Jews, but surely this explanation cannot be presumed.[13]

Table 1 shows the distribution of the 10 per cent subsample by original religion.[14] It will be noted that about one-fourth of the graduates are Catholic,[15] approximately the same proportion of Catholics in the population of the United States.[16] An immediate

TABLE 1

RELIGIOUS DISTRIBUTION OF
1961 COLLEGE GRADUATES*

	Per Cent
Protestant............	61
Catholic.............	25
Jew.................	8
Other...............	3
None................	3

* $N = 3,330$; no answer = 67; total 10 per cent sample = 3,397.

[13] It is embarrassing but probably necessary to enter a word about personal bias. At the present state of American culture it may not be true that, if a Catholic researcher discovers some indications that Catholics are not as antiscientific as previously thought, his findings are immediately subject to grave suspicion. Nevertheless, let it be recorded that the six "intellectualism" hypotheses in this paper were not straw men; the writer is close enough intellectually and personally to the self-critics to have thought "before the data" that this study would provide grist for the self-critics' mill. The findings of the NORC survey were therefore something of a rude surprise.

[14] It was felt that the religion in which one was reared was the most important in shaping one's values, if indeed they were shaped at all by religion.

[15] The vagaries of the sampling process selected sixteen Catholic schools; some 45 per cent of the graduates whose religion was Catholic came from these schools. However, as we hope to point out in another paper, the differences between Catholic graduates of Catholic colleges and Catholic graduates of other colleges were minimal on virtually all items herein reported. The differences that do exist would have the graduates of Catholic colleges scoring *higher* on "intellectual" and "Protestant" items than Catholic graduates of other colleges.

reaction would be to maintain that the first hypothesis (Catholics are disinclined to go to college) is not supported. The matter is not that simple, however, since there are more Protestants who are rural or Negro and these two latter groups are less likely to go to college. The kind of comparison that would be most satisfactory would be between urban white Catholics and Protestants at the specific ages of college graduation.

There are, however, no available national population figures that permit such a comparison to be made. However, if the racial factor is taken into account, it appears that Catholics are still slightly underrepresented in the college population, comprising 28 per cent of the white population[17] of the nation and 26 per cent of the white population of the NORC sample. On the other hand, it seems quite certain that the educational gap between white Protestants and white Catholics is narrowing rapidly; Catholics make up 18 per cent of the total population with college education but 25 per cent of the June, 1961, graduates, despite the fact that the proportion of the Catholic population at college graduation age is about the same as the proportion of the national population at this age.[18] One can, therefore, say of the first hypothesis that there is no strong evidence supporting it, and that whatever differences exist between Catholics and non-Catholics in college education seem to be diminishing rather rapidly.[19]

[16] For a discussion of the Catholic population in the United States see my "Some Information on the Present Situation of the American Catholics," *Social Order*, April, 1963, pp. 9–24.

[17] The percentages in this sentence are based on data reported by Bernard Lazerwitz in "A Comparison of Major United States Religious Groups," *Journal of the American Statistical Association*, LVI (September, 1961), 568–79.

[18] *Ibid.*

[19] Significant demographic differences among the three religious groups were computed from the Davies *Table of Significant Differences* with a correction factor added because of the fact that the sample was taken by a cluster technique. The independent assessment of the significance of Protestant-Catholic,

INFLUENCE OF THE "RELIGIOUS FACTOR" ON CAREER PLANS   661

EDUCATIONAL EXPERIENCE

Table 2 summarizes the different educational experiences of the three religious groups. Jews are more likely to have attended "quality" colleges.[20] They are also more likely to score high (upper 20 per cent) on the Academic Performance Index. (The difference between Catholics and Protestants approaches significance; however,

there is no difference between the two groups when a comparison is made of the upper half academically.) All three groups contain about the same proportion of graduates who would attribute a "liberal" purpose to college, although Catholic graduates are more likely than Protestants and Protestants more likely than Jews to concede to their fellow students a "liberal" orientation. Prot-

TABLE 2

SUMMARY OF DIFFERENCES ON EDUCATIONAL EXPERIENCES
(Percentage Distribution)

EDUCATIONAL EXPERIENCES	PROTESTANT (P)	CATHOLIC (C)	JEW (J)	STATISTICAL SIGNIFICANCE		
				P-C	P-J	C-J
School quality A or B..............	12	12	26	N.S.	.01	.01
High academic performance..........	19	15	26	N.S.	.05	.01
Appreciation of ideas:						
Purpose of college:						
Subjective...................	65	65	65	N.S.	N.S.	N.S.
Projective...................	35	44	27	.01	.01	.01
Positive school loyalty..............	77	71	71	.01	N.S.	N.S.
Course reactions:						
Science interesting................	34	33	37	N.S.	N.S.	N.S.
Mathematics interesting...........	32	34	37	N.S.	N.S.	N.S.
Biology interesting................	44	37	37	.01	.05	N.S.
Social science interesting..........	63	65	65	N.S.	N.S.	N.S.
English interesting................	49	54	37	.01	.01	.01
N...........................	(2,007)	(833)	(272)			

Protestant-Jewish, and Catholic-Jewish differences is not completely legitimate, owing to the intercorrelation among them. However, the complicated nature of the sampling technique left little other choice. It was not feasible to modify the χ^2 test to take into account the cluster sample. The differences between Protestants and Catholics, however, are still relatively minor in almost all instances, and the differences between Jew and gentile are sufficient enough to be of importance, even if the tests are relatively crude. It might be noted that in an analysis of the total weighted sample of some 55,000, to be published shortly by J. A. Davis of the NORC staff, the same conclusions with regard to the religious factor have been reached as are reported in this article.

[20] The quality of the schools was based on an index prepared from the scores of students in the colleges on the National Merit Scholarship examinations. The Academic Performance Index mentioned in the next sentence was based on grade-point average weighted for school quality.

estants have a somewhat higher percentage who feel loyal to their schools than the other two groups. Protestants found the biological sciences more interesting than the other groups, and Catholics found English more interesting than the other groups. Each course was rated separately, so the respondents were not forced to choose one course as their favorite. The former finding might result from the more rural origins of American Protestants and the latter from the supposed tradition of humanistic studies in the Catholic colleges. The Catholic interest in science and mathematics is not what prevous findings would lead us to expect. Generally speaking, there was little in the way of major differences in reactions to courses.

662   THE AMERICAN JOURNAL OF SOCIOLOGY

FUTURE PLANS

Table 3 summarizes information on future plans of the college graduates of the three religious groups. The Jews are most likely to plan to attend graduate school in the coming year and Protestants least likely. There is no significant difference in the proportions of each group going into graduate study in the academic fields. These findings are in direct opposition to the hypotheses derived from previous research. No support

and medicine, Catholics more inclined to business, Protestants more inclined to education and "other professions." No other differences are significant.

OCCUPATIONAL VALUES

Table 4 gives the reaction of the graduates of the three religious groups to the question: "Which of these characteristics would be important in picking a career?" The "Protestant Ethic" hypothesis is not sup-

TABLE 3

SUMMARY OF DIFFERENCES ON FUTURE PLANS

(Percentage Distribution)

FUTURE PLANS	PROTESTANT	CATHOLIC	JEW	STATISTICAL SIGNIFICANCE		
				P-C	P-J	C-J
Graduate school next year..........	28	33	47	.05	.01	.01
Per cent of graduate students in arts and sciences....................	43	46	39	N.S.	N.S.	N.S.
Career employer:						
Large company..................	25	33	26	.01	N.S.	N.S.
Small company..................	7	11	21	N.S.	.01	.01
Self...........................	7	8	14	N.S.	.05	.05
Education......................	36	27	27	.01	.01	N.S.
Career occupation:						
Science........................	7	6	8	N.S.	N.S.	N.S.
Social science and humanities......	10	10	10	N.S.	N.S.	N.S.
Medicine.......................	2	3	6	N.S.	.05	.05
Law...........................	2	3	10	N.S.	.01	.01
Engineering....................	7	8	8	N.S.	N.S.	N.S.
Education......................	34	26	27	.01	.01	N.S.
Business.......................	15	23	17	.01	N.S.	.01
Other professions...............	16	12	6	.05	.01	.01
Other..........................	7	9	8			
N..........................	(2,007)	(833)	(272)			

is found for the notion of Catholic anti-intellectualism.

Catholics overchoose large companies[21] (according to the prediction), Jews overchoose small companies and self-employment (no difference between Protestants and Catholics on this item), and Protestants overchoose elementary education for future career employment.[22] In the choice of future occupations, Jews are more inclined to law

[21] The percentages on career employer do not add to 100 because only those items that showed a difference are included in Table 3.

ported for Catholic-Protestant differences. Catholics are more interested in making money than Protestants, no different in avoiding high pressure, and no different in the quest for security through slow, sure progress. They are also more interested in "leadership," which may or may not be a

[22] It has been suggested that the Protestant lead in education is the result of the fact that Negro Protestants overchoose this field; they do, indeed, but no more than other Protestants, according to the NORC data. It should be noted also that Negro Protestants who graduate from college are just as likely to go to graduate school as white Protestants.

INFLUENCE OF THE "RELIGIOUS FACTOR" ON CAREER PLANS   663

"Protestant Ethic" type of item. Protestants are more interested in being helpful to others, which, however praiseworthy it might be, is hardly in keeping with the economic individualism of the "Protestant Ethic." Jews score higher on monetary ambition but also on the desire for creativity, and on a chance to work in a world of ideas. The basic cleavage on occupational values is between Jew and Gentile, not between Protestant and Catholic.

Catholics were six percentage points ahead of Protestants in plans for graduate school the autumn after graduation. This lead continues (by four points) in the key group of high-SES, large-home-town males and is also unaffected in all female groups (Table 5). Only among small-city, low-SES males do Catholics fall behind Protestants (5 per cent) in graduate-school plans; among large-city, low-SES males there is exact parity. In general, we can say that the sur-

TABLE 4

OCCUPATIONAL VALUES, BY RELIGION

(Percentage Distribution)

OCCUPATIONAL VALUES	PROTESTANT	CATHOLIC	JEW	STATISTICAL SIGNIFICANCE		
				P-C	P-J	C-J
Making a lot of money..............	21	27	38	.01	.01	.01
Chance to be creative..............	50	50	64	N.S.	.01	.01
Helpful to others..................	68	61	60	.01	.01	N.S.
Avoid high pressure................	15	17	15	N.S.	N.S.	N.S.
World of ideas.....................	39	35	50	N.S.	.01	.01
Freedom from supervision...........	18	17	21	N.S.	N.S.	N.S.
Slow and sure progress.............	33	32	25	N.S.	.05	N.S.
Leadership........................	34	40	40	.01	N.S.	N.S.
Same area.........................	4	8	9	.05	.05	N.S.
New area..........................	10	10	11	N.S.	N.S.	N.S.
Work with people, not things........	57	55	56	N.S.	N.S.	N.S.
N...........................	(2,007)	(833)	(272)			

THE EFFECT OF CONTROLS

Only three control variables seem to produce much in the way of a change in the measures described in the preceding paragraphs, so these three were combined into a new index—the Index of Background Characteristics (IBC). Each religious group was subdivided into eight subgroups based on sex, home-town size (over 100,000 or under 100,000), and socioeconomic status (SES) (upper half or lower half). Even though the numbers in some of these subgroups are rather small and comparisons must be made with some care, there are enough respondents in the important groups (e.g., big-city, high-SES males) for each of the three religions to enable us to judge to what extent background characteristics are responsible for the similarities and differences above.

prising showing of Catholics in the matter of graduate-school plans cannot be explained away by background characteristics. In all but one of the eight comparison groups, Catholics are either ahead of Protestants in graduate-school plans or even with them. In the four groups in which there are enough cases to make a comparison, the Jewish lead over the other two groups continues, although it seems that among high-SES males from large home towns, the Jewish lead is substantially reduced (from thirteen to seven points ahead of Catholics).

We saw previously that there was virtually no difference among the three religions in those planning arts and science careers, despite the prediction that Jews would be more likely than gentiles to plan such careers and Protestants more likely than Catholics. Table 6, part A, shows a very interesting phenomenon for Jews. More than twice as large a proportion of low-SES Jewish males choose the academic professions as do high-SES males (although the reverse is true for Jewish girls). Indeed, high-SES Jewish males are much less likely to choose the academic life than either Protestants or Catholics. There is little difference

TABLE 5

Per Cent Going to Graduate School in Fall, 1961, by Religion and Background Characteristics

	Protestant	Catholic	Jewish
	Male		
Large home town:*			
High SES†.....	44 (248)	48 (159)	55 (103)
Low SES.......	39 (161)	39 (161)	55 (48)
Small home town:			
High SES......	35 (304)	38 (94)	36 (14)
Low SES.......	26 (431)	21 (115)	50 (4)
	Female		
Large home town:			
High SES......	29 (260)	28 (96)	44 (60)
Low SES.......	24 (92)	28 (67)	35 (23)
Small home town:			
High SES......	15 (248)	29 (74)	27 (18)
Low SES.......	16 (263)	22 (67)	....

* Large home towns are those with a population over 100,000.

† High socioeconomic status (SES) indicates those whose parents had attended college and had a white-collar job (professional or manager) or who had a white-collar job and made more than $7,500 a year even if they had not attended college or who had a blue-collar job, but made more than $7,500 a year and had attended college.

between Protestants and Catholics in the large home towns, whether they be male or female, in their plans for academic careers, though the small home-town Protestant males are ahead of the Catholics and the small home-town Catholic females are ahead of the Protestants. We note once again no evidence for a disinclination of Catholics to go into the academic life, and a somewhat surprising underchoice of academia by well-to-do Jewish sons.

The reason for the underchoice of academia by this group becomes clear in Table

6, part B; almost two-fifths of the high-SES Jewish males from big cities are choosing the traditional professions of law and medicine, while only one-tenth of the low-SES Jewish males are making the same choice. Thus well-to-do Jewish sons choose the traditional professions and "lower" class sons choose the academic professions. Even though the numbers on which this last statement is based are somewhat small, it should be noted that the differences are statistically significant. The Catholic overchoice of the professions in comparison with Protestants holds up in all male categories.

Table 6, part C, supports the finding that primary and secondary education is the Protestant field. The Protestant lead over Catholics in this career is to be found in all groups with the exception of the low-SES, small home-town females (where there are so few Catholics that the finding is dubious). It is worth noting that Jewish girls are the ones most likely to choose education, while Jewish males are the least likely. It is also worth noting that while Protestant males are ahead of Catholic males in all categories in the choice of education, the lead is especially pronounced among the low-SES groups. Apparently education is the popular means of upward mobility for "poor" Protestant males just as the academic life is for "poor" Jewish males.

Something of the same phenomenon is to be observed among Catholics in the choice of business careers (Table 6, part D). Catholics are ahead of Protestants in choosing business in all categories (except the troublesome low-SES, small home-town females), but the biggest overchoice is among low-SES males. Each religious group apparently has its own favorite path of upward mobility—the Protestants choosing education, the Catholics choosing business, and the Jews choosing academia. For the first two groups the choice is merely an exaggeration of what the upper-SES groups are choosing, but for the Jews the choice is totally different from the upper-SES choice of the traditional professions.

Background characteristics have no ef-

TABLE 6

FUTURE CAREER PLANS, BY RELIGION AND
BY BACKGROUND CHARACTERISTICS

A. PER CENT CHOOSING ACADEMIC PROFESSION (PHYSICAL SCIENCES,
BIOLOGICAL SCIENCES, SOCIAL SCIENCES, HUMANITIES)

	Protestant	Catholic	Jewish
	Male		
Large home town:			
High SES............	22 (248)	18 (159)	12 (103)
Low SES............	18 (161)	20 (161)	28 (47)
Small home town:			
High SES............	19 (304)	12 (94)	7 (14)
Low SES............	17 (431)	11 (115)	25 (4)
	Female		
Large home town:			
High SES............	25 (260)	28 (96)	29 (60)
Low SES............	14 (92)	15 (67)	13 (23)
Small home town:			
High SES............	16 (248)	23 (74)	23 (18)
Low SES............	9 (263)	7 (67)	....

B. PER CENT PLANNING CAREER IN PROFESSIONS (LAW AND MEDICINE)

	Protestant	Catholic	Jewish
	Male		
Large home town:			
High SES............	12 (248)	18 (159)	38 (103)
Low SES............	7 (161)	10 (161)	9 (47)
Small home town:			
High SES............	13 (304)	16 (94)	28 (14)
Low SES............	4 (431)	7 (115)	0 (4)
	Female		
Large home town:			
High SES............	0 (260)	1 (96)	0 (60)
Low SES............	1 (92)	0 (67)	4 (23)
Small home town:			
High SES............	0 (248)	1 (74)	0 (18)
Low SES............	0 (265)	2 (67)	....

C. PER CENT PLANNING CAREER IN PRIMARY OR SECONDARY EDUCATION

	Protestant	Catholic	Jewish
	Male		
Large home town:			
High SES............	11 (248)	7 (159)	4 (103)
Low SES............	25 (161)	15 (161)	13 (47)
Small home town:			
High SES............	15 (304)	12 (94)	0 (14)
Low SES............	27 (431)	22 (115)	0 (4)

666 THE AMERICAN JOURNAL OF SOCIOLOGY

TABLE 6—*Continued*

C—*Continued*

	Female		
Large home town:			
High SES.............	48 (260)	41 (96)	64 (60)
Low SES.............	59 (92)	57 (67)	74 (23)
Small home town:			
High SES.............	58 (248)	53 (74)	56 (18)
Low SES.............	68 (263)	69 (67)	....

D. PER CENT PLANNING CAREER IN BUSINESS

	Protestant	Catholic	Jewish
	Male		
Large home town:			
High SES............	30 (248)	35 (159)	30 (103)
Low SES............	19 (161)	28 (161)	9 (47)
Small home town:			
High SES............	26 (304)	36 (94)	43 (14)
Low SES............	19 (431)	34 (115)	50 (4)
	Female		
Large home town:			
High SES............	10 (260)	15 (96)	7 (60)
Low SES............	5 (92)	10 (67)	4 (23)
Small home town:			
High SES............	3 (248)	4 (74)	11 (18)
Low SES............	6 (263)	3 (67)	....

fect on the ordering of the three religions as to the importance of money as an occupational value (Table 7). It is more important to Jews than to Catholics in all categories and to Catholics than to Protestants. The slight Catholic deficiency in the desire to be "original and creative" seem to result primarily from the performance on this item of low-SES Catholics in large home towns, regardless of sex, and of Catholic girls from large home towns. The Jewish lead in "people, not things" on the other hand is a high-SES phenomenon, probably not unrelated to the interest of this group in the professions of law and medicine. We find no evidence in these values of any anti-intellectualism or anti-economic achievement in Catholics.

To sum up this section, we may say that

Catholics are more likely to choose business, Jews more likely to choose law and medicine, and Protestants more likely to choose education. All three groups are about equally represented in the arts and sciences. There seem to be different paths of upward mobility for the lower-SES members of each religion. One need not look too far for a historical explanation of the differences we have reported: the American public school system, whatever its present orientations, was surely Protestant in its origins and early history; the Jews, traditionally victims of prejudice, would be inclined to look to the professions as the best way to get ahead despite prejudice; and the Catholics as latecomers to the economic battles, would find that the business corporation was best suited to their needs. Whether there is anything in

SELECTED OCCUPATIONAL VALUES, BY RELIGION AND
BY BACKGROUND CHARACTERISTICS

A. "MAKING A LOT OF MONEY"

	Protestant	Catholic	Jewish
	Male		
Large home town:			
High SES............	30 (248)	38 (159)	56 (103)
Low SES.............	25 (161)	28 (161)	46 (48)
Small home town:			
High SES............	29 (304)	35 (94)	36 (14)
Low SES.............	26 (431)	30 (115)	0 (4)
	Female		
Large home town:			
High SES............	12 (260)	16 (96)	18 (60)
Low SES.............	7 (92)	12 (67)	8 (23)
Small home town:			
High SES............	10 (248)	12 (74)	33 (18)
Low SES.............	13 (263)	24 (67)	....

B. "OPPORTUNITIES TO BE ORIGINAL AND CREATIVE"

	Protestant	Catholic	Jewish
	Male		
Large home town:			
High SES............	59 (248)	58 (159)	61 (103)
Low SES.............	55 (161)	49 (161)	62 (48)
Small home town:			
High SES............	47 (304)	41 (94)	43 (14)
Low SES.............	42 (431)	43 (115)	50 (4)
	Female		
Large home town:			
High SES............	59 (260)	53 (96)	68 (60)
Low SES.............	52 (92)	46 (67)	76 (23)
Small home town:			
High SES............	56 (248)	56 (74)	72 (18)
Low SES.............	42 (263)	51 (67)	....

C. "OPPORTUNITY TO WORK WITH PEOPLE INSTEAD OF THINGS"

	Protestant	Catholic	Jewish
	Male		
Large home town:			
High SES............	46 (248)	46 (159)	54 (103)
Low SES.............	45 (161)	50 (161)	35 (48)
Small home town:			
High SES............	46 (304)	45 (94)	64 (14)
Low SES.............	46 (431)	46 (115)	74 (4)
	Female		
Large home town:			
High SES............	71 (260)	68 (96)	72 (60)
Low SES.............	68 (92)	64 (67)	64 (23)
Small home town:			
High SES............	72 (248)	64 (74)	61 (18)
Low SES.............	72 (263)	82 (67)	....

each religion that would predispose its members in these directions remains to be seen. It could be argued that the practical bent of rabbinic scholarship would incline the Jews to the professions, and the large organizational apparatus of the Catholic church would orient its members toward the large corporation. Perhaps even the "service" tradition of much of American Protestantism could be linked with primary and secondary education. But such propositions require much more careful investigation.

note that the only significant difference in field of choice is the Protestant lead over Jews in the biological sciences. We note further that, in the career activities favored by members of the three religious groups, the Jews lead both other groups significantly in choosing research. There is no support for the hypotheses that Catholics will underchoose physical sciences or research. Table 9 compares religiosity rates[24] and apostasy rates[25] for "scholars" and the group mean on these rates for each of the religious groups.

TABLE 8

PLANS OF POTENTIAL SCHOLARS, BY RELIGION

(Percentage Distribution)

	PROTESTANT	CATHOLIC	JEWISH	SIGNIFICANCE		
				P-C	P-J	C-J
Field of study:						
Physical sciences......	30	32	33	N.S.	N.S.	N.S.
Biological sciences....	14	11	9	N.S.	.01	N.S.
Social sciences........	20	18	25	N.S.	N.S.	N.S.
Humanities..........	36	39	32	N.S.	N.S.	N.S.
Total per cent......	100	100	99			
Total N..........	2,159	970	489			
Career activities:						
Teaching............	73	73	76	N.S.	N.S.	N.S.
Research............	62	60	73	N.S.	.05	.01
Administration.......	17	17	16	N.S.	N.S.	N.S.
Service.............	8	9	15	N.S.	.05	N.S.
None of these........	2	2	4	....	....	......

POTENTIAL SCHOLARS

Table 8 begins an investigation of the potential scholars from the three religious groups (those with no religion are added). A potential scholar was defined as someone who was planning to go to graduate school in the arts and sciences the coming fall.[23] We

[23] A different deck of cards was used for the analysis reported in this paragraph. It represented all respondents who planned fall graduate school in the arts and sciences: $N = 3,816$. It will be noted that in this deck the proportion for each religious group is different from that in the deck analyzed in previous paragraphs. The reason for this is that the three groups enter arts and sciences graduate school in different proportions than they exist in the total population.

[24] The "group mean" is the percentage religious or apostasizing in the total college population as measured by the survey; the "scholar mean" is the percentage in the scholar deck.

[25] Two questions were used to measure apostasy: "In what religion were you raised?" and "What is your present religious preference?" An apostate was defined as one who had listed "religion in which he was raised" as Protestant, Catholic or Jew, and listed his present religion as "none." It is to be noted that only among Catholics is there no appreciable increase of apostasy among "scholars." This could mean that Catholics perceive little conflict between orientation to the arts and sciences as a career and religious membership or that Catholics are better able to compartmentalize their lives than members of the other groups. A forthcoming paper will discuss the fact of apostasy and the variation in rates within the three major religious groups.

INFLUENCE OF THE "RELIGIOUS FACTOR" ON CAREER PLANS 669

There is a slight increase in apostasy among Catholic "scholars" (about 2 per cent), and the amount of irregular church attendance increases moderately; however, in neither apostasy nor irregular church attendance is the increase among Catholic "scholars" comparable to the increase among the other religious groups. There is no evidence that the apparently heightened interest in the academic life among American Catholics has led to a large scale movement away from the Church.

As a conclusion to this section, we might note that in a resurvey a year after graduation, 87 per cent of the Jews, 81 per cent of

pected). Why our findings are so different from Lenski's needs to be explored. A possible explanation (suggested by Bernard Rosen[26] and others) is that the ethnic composition of the two Catholic samples might be considerably different. Lenski gives no data on ethnic subdivisions within the Catholic sample and no ethnic question was asked in the NORC survey. However, it is generally assumed that the Catholic population of Detroit has a very large Polish element. An earlier study made of graduate students by NORC[27] did ask an ethnic question and enables us to see whether there are any differences between the various Catholic ethnic

TABLE 9

RELIGIOUS ORIENTATION OF ARTS AND SCIENCES GRADUATE STUDENTS

(Per Cent)

	PROTESTANTS		CATHOLICS		JEWS	
	Graduate Students	All Protestants	Graduate Students	All Catholics	Graduate Students	All Jews
Regular church attendance*......	36	65	73	85	36	68
Irregular church attendance......	33	20	16	6	37	16
Apostate.....................	31	15	11	9	27	16
N	(2,159)†	(2,007)‡	(970)†	(833)‡	(489)†	(272)‡

* For Catholics, weekly or several times a month; for Protestants, at least once a month; for Jews, at least two or three times a year.

† Total sample.

‡ Ten per cent sample.

the Protestants, and 80 per cent of the Catholics who said that they were going to graduate school the autumn after their graduation were in fact taking graduate-school courses; 24 per cent of the Jewish graduates of June, 1961, 22 per cent of the Protestants, and 21 per cent of the Catholics affirmed their eventual intention of getting the Ph.D. (although an approximately equal proportion of each group had not yet begun their academic work for the degree).

THE ETHNIC FACTOR

Only two predictions of our initial hypotheses have been supported. Catholics overchoose large corporations and business as a career (although the general Jew-gentile differences emerge pretty much as ex-

groups. It seemed possible that those ethnic groups who came in the later waves, largely southern and eastern European groups, might be experiencing a somewhat slower acculturation process than the earlier groups and, therefore, would be less likely to go to college, to plan academic careers, and to be strongly oriented toward economic or academic achievement. Two items in the graduate-student study enabled us to measure the college plans and the self-confidence of the various ethnic groups within American

[26] In his review of Lenski's book in *American Sociological Review*, XXVII (February, 1962), 111.

[27] This survey was reported by James A. Davis in *Stipends and Spouses: The Consumer Finances of Graduate Study in America* (Chicago: University of Chicago Press, 1962).

670   THE AMERICAN JOURNAL OF SOCIOLOGY

Catholicism: a question about whether college was taken for granted in high school and a question about evaluation of one's own abilities. In Table 10 we note that the Irish-German-British wave was more likely to have taken college for granted when in high school and to have a higher estimate of its own abilities than the Italian-Slavic group. There seems to be sound reason for suggesting that the differences between Lenski's findings and those reported here might be connected with ethnicity. It would appear that perhaps ethnicity has no ceased to be an important factor for sociological concern.

The question remains as to whether the influence of the ethnic factor that we described in the preceding paragraph is truly

ethnic or is rather the result of the fact that members of one group have simply less in the way of an American background, since their families have been in America for a shorter period of time. Will the ethnic effect vanish under a control for generation or socioeconomic status? In Table 11 we note that a control for father's occupation does not eliminate the two differences that had correlated with ethnicity. First-wave ethnic groups are more likely to have a higher estimate of their native ability than second-wave ethnic groups regardless of father's occupation, even though both increase their estimate of native ability as status improves. Further, ethnic groups of the first wave with white-collar background are more likely to have come from families where college education was taken for granted than such groups of the second wave. The reverse seems to be true of the lower class of both waves, although the case base is very small.

Nor does a control for generation eliminate the differences between the two waves. It is true that the early (first to third) generations of both waves have about the same percentage ranking their native ability high. However the later generations of the first wave have far more self-confidence than the later generations of the second wave. Finally, the later generations of the first wave

TABLE 10

DIFFERENCES AMONG CATHOLIC
ETHNIC GROUPS

(Percentage Distribution)

	Irish-German-British	Italian-Slavic	Significance
College taken for granted........	43	30	.01
High estimate of abilities........	33	23	.05
N..........	(556)	(147)	

TABLE 11

ETHNIC VARIABLES BY FATHER'S OCCUPATIONAL STATUS AND BY GENERATION
(Percentage Distribution)

	HIGH ESTIMATE OF NATIVE ABILITY		COLLEGE TAKEN FOR GRANTED WHEN IN HIGH SCHOOL	
	First Wave*	Second Wave†	First Wave*	Second Wave†
Father's occupational status:				
Upper class‡..............	35 (424)	27 (80)	52 (424)	45 (80)
Lower class..............	32 (132)	18 (67)	15 (132)	19 (67)
Generation:				
1st to 3d generation§.......	26 (140)	23 (107)	31 (140)	36 (107)
4th or after..............	38 (416)	25 (40)	47 (416)	33 (40)

* Irish, German, British.
† Italian, eastern European.
‡ Non-manual occupation.
§ At least one grandparent not born in America.

are substantially more likely to have taken college for granted than the later generations of the second wave (although the reverse seems to be true for the earlier generations). Since the number of respondents involved is rather small and since the interactions under controls are often ambiguous, we can hardly regard this analysis as definitive. However the finding that differences in self-confidence and the taking of college for granted do not disappear even in the fourth generation of the two ethnic categories strongly suggests that the pure ethnic factor deserves much further investigation.

SUMMARY

It was the purpose of this essay to examine certain hypotheses about the influence of the Protestant Ethic and of Catholic anti-intellectualism in light of the data gathered by a national cluster sample of college graduates. Only one item in the Protestant Ethic complex (the overchoice by Catholics of large corporations) and one item in the anti-intellectualism syndrome of the self-critics within the American Catholic church (the overchoice of business as a career) were supported. There was no substantial evidence of anti-intellectualism among Catholic college graduates. (And as we will report elsewhere there were no significant differences between graduates of Catholic colleges and Catholic graduates of other colleges.) The main lines of division on the variables examined were on the Jew-gentile axis rather than on the Protestant-Catholic axis. It was further suggested after a brief examination of materials from another survey that the differences between our findings and those of other investigators might have to do with the different ethnic composition of the samples and that, therefore, the ethnic factor was still an important one in American society.

The abandonment of previously held concepts does not and must not proceed precipitously. Many of the survey findings reported in this paper are at variance with ideas that have been popular both within and outside of the American Catholic community. One survey does not a revolution make. The NORC data provide little support for theories of antiscientism among American Catholics. Considerably more research will be required, however, before one can in fact argue that the values of Catholics with regard to scholarship are not different from their non-Catholic fellow Americans. It will then be necessary to determine whether this similarity represents a major social change and, if it does, what the mechanisms of this change have been.

NATIONAL OPINION RESEARCH CENTER
UNIVERSITY OF CHICAGO

A NOTE ON THE ORIGINS OF RELIGIOUS DIFFERENCES

ANDREW M. GREELEY
National Opionion Research Center
The University of Chicago

AT least three different models could be used to describe the relationship between religion as a sub-cultural system[1] and society. In the Weberian model religion influences the personality variables of its members and the members in their turn, acting under the influence of their religious values, influence the organization of the social system.[2] A second model, which might trace its origin to the positivist followers of Marx or the functionalist disciples of Durkheim, would view the influence flowing in the opposite direction: the social system would create certain "need dispositions" in the personalities of its participants, which need dispositions would in their turn lead to certain kinds of religious activity and belief. In the first model religion is the independent variable, in the second it becomes an "epiphenomenon"—a dependent variable.

A third model would view religion as neither necessarily an independent variable nor necessarily a dependent variable; rather it would see religion as a "correlate," as a "predictor" variable which is perhaps independent and perhaps dependent; but whose precise causal influence must be determined in each correlation and not as a matter of general principle. In this view a person's religion could influence his personality organization which in turn would influence the role he plays in the social system. On the other hand, the role he plays in the social system could shape the value system he espouses (or that his children will espouse) and in turn affect the religious belief he professes. In such a model the relationship between culture, personality, and society are recognized to be so complex—especially when the factor of the past history of the culture or the society is introduced—that the sociologist is extremely hesitant to generalize about the direction of causality. His more immediate concern is prediction.

There is little reason to doubt that religion is a useful predictor variable in a study of American society. Differences in family values,[3] political attitudes,[4] and economic orientations[5] have been reported for the three major religious groups. Lenski found that in his survey religion

---

[1] In a pluralist society a religion would be described as a subculture both because a given religion involves only a certain number of people and because it involves only certain parts of the value system of its members.

[2] Obviously such a model represents considerable simplification of Weber's complex and at times difficult thought on the subject.

[3] Cf., Ronald Freedman, Pascal K. Whelpton, and Arthur A. Campbell, *Family Planning, Sterility, and Population Growth*, (New York: McGraw-Hill, 1959); and Charles Westhoff, Robert Potter, Philip Sagi, and Elliot Mishler, *Family Growth in Metropolitan America* (Princeton: Princeton University Press, 1961).

[4] Cf., Paul Lazarsfeld, Bernard Berelson, and Hazel Gaudet, *The People's Choice* (New York: Duell, Sloan, and Pearce, 1944); and Bernard Berelson, Paul Lazarsfeld, and W. N. McPhee, *Voting* (Chicago: The University of Chicago Press, 1954).

[5] Gerhard Lenski, *The Religious Factor* (New York: Doubleday, 1961).

22   THE ORIGINS OF RELIGIOUS DIFFERENCES

was at least as efficient a predictor as social class. The two recent fertility studies found that religion was by far the most important predictor of family size.

However, not too much thought has been given to the question as to what there is in a religious group which causes differences across a range of dependent variables. Lenski defines a "religion as a system of beliefs about the nature of the force[s] ultimately shaping man's destiny and the practices associated therewith, shared by members of a group."[6] He views the religious group as a "network of informal, primary type relations"[7] which constitute "segregated communications networks limited to the adherents of the same faith [and] facilitate the development and transmission of distinctive political and economic norms." He insists that the norms which are communicated are not merely the result of the socio-economic condition of the religious group but also "reflect the exposure of past generations of believers to the social environments of other eras";[8] religions are "carriers of complex subcultures relevant to almost all phases of human existence" and "products of the social heritage of the group."[9]

Lenski's theory is certainly a useful contribution to the sociology of religion and his proofs that religious variation cannot be dismissed merely as the result of the operation of current economic and social forces are quite convincing. However, at least one question remains to be answered: to what extent are the formal creed, code and cult of a given religion responsible for the variations observed among members of the different groups? Are religious differences the result of the theology and the morality of a religion or are they result of the social

experiences of the group which are, in turn, the result of historical "accidents"? In some instances the answers seem rather obvious: the connection between Catholic family morality and the Catholic birth rate seems obvious enough, especially when we learn that frequency of Church attendance correlates with family size. In other instances the answer is by no means so clear. Is the Jewish inclination to professional careers caused by any article of Jewish belief, or rather by the historical and cultural experiences of the Jewish group which indeed happened to a religious group but in no sense flowed from their religious creed? In other words, to what extent are the religious differences reported in so many studies the result of theology and to what extent are they the result of social history which has no direct connection with theology?

To investigate this question further, we propose to consider thirty-one "religiously-linked" traits discovered in a recent study of the career plans of college graduates.[10] We will first of all present a table listing the distinctive traits of each religious group. Second, we will attempt to discover whether there is a direct relation between the existence of this trait and the degree of religiosity of members of each group. Third, the absence of such a relationship will lead us to suggest that certain traits may be related with membership in a religious group, but not necessarily with the religious ideology of the group; to test such a hypothesis we will offfer suggestive evidence that those who live in areas where the religious group is a minority

---

[6] *Ibid.*, p. 298.

[7] *Ibid.*, p. 301.

[8] *Ibid.*, p. 311.

[9] *Ibid.*

[10] The preliminary report of this study is contained in James A. Davis, *et al.*, *Great Aspirations: The Career Plans of American June 1961 College Graduates.* Some 35,000 students in 135 colleges and universities were chosen by a stratified, cluster sampling technique. The analysis reported in this note was based on a 10% representative subsample.

THE ORIGINS OF RELIGIOUS DIFFERENCES   **23**

will not exhibit the trait to the same degree as those who live where the group is strong. Finally, we will indulge in some speculation about the origins of these religiously connected but non-religiosity related traits and suggest some areas of further research in the problem.

THE RELIGIOUS TRAITS

At least 31 traits are available for analysis—9 Protestant, 7 Catholic, and 15 Jewish. Each trait correlates with religion and maintains the correlation even when social, economic, and personality factors are controlled. In most instances the trait represents one group differing from the other two—for example Jews scoring high on the choice of self-employment as opposed to the other groups. In some cases all three groups differ among themselves—thus, each group has a different score on graduate school plans. Table 1 lists the traits.

TABLE 1

DISTINCTIVE RELIGIOUS TRAITS

Trait	Item
Protestant	
1. High not going to graduate school	Fall Plans
2. Education	Future Career
3. Other Professional	Future Career
4. Elementary Education	Career Employer
5. No Pressure	Occupational Value
6. Slow Sure Progress	Occupational Value
7. High Academic Performance	Academic Performance Index
8. Per cent Conservative	Political Orientations
9. Drive	Drive Scale (from Self-description)
Catholic	
1. High going to graduate school	Fall Plans
2. Intellectual	Intellectual Ideal Scale (Self-description)
3. Business	Future Career
4. Large Corporation	Career Employer
5. Low Academic Performance	Academic Performance Index
6. Per cent Liberal	Political Orientations
7. Per cent Against Modern Art	Artistic Orientation
Jewish	
1. High going to graduate school	Fall Plans
2. Science	Future Career
3. Medicine	Future Career
4. Law	Future Career
5. Small Companies	Career Employer

24   THE ORIGINS OF RELIGIOUS DIFFERENCES

6. Self-Employment   Career Employer
7. Chance to Make Money   Occupational Value
8. Chance to be Creative   Occupational Value
9. Working in World of Ideas   Occupational Value
10. High Academic Performance   Academic Performance Index
11. Per cent Liberal   Political Orientation
12. Per cent Unconventional   Conventionality Orientation
13. High Sophistication   Personality Scales (from Self-description)
14. High Emotionality   Personality Scales
15. High Extroversion   Personality Scales
16. High Intellectual   Personality Scales

The first hypothesis to be tested is that these traits are religious in the strict sense of the word—that is, they result directly from the beliefs and practices of the religion to which the possessors of that trait belong. Unfortunately we do not have the array of tools which Lenski possessed to measure different kinds of religiosity. We are forced to use the one question in which the repondents were asked to rate their own religiosity. We are not sure what standards they used to rank themselves, so we are forced to assume that the religiosity index stands for a combination of three of Lenski's indices—orthodoxy, devotionalism, and associational involvement.[11] In any event, if ideology in some sense is responsible for the traits we would expect a direct correlation between religiosity and the trait. For example, the Catholic choice of a large corporation should be higher among very religious Catholics than in non-religious. The members of the three religious groups were divided into three categories according to their religiosity. Catholics

and Protestants were separated into the very religious, the fairly religious, and the not religious. Since the distribution of the Jews on the scale was different and since the Jewish subsample was much smaller, a different division was necessary: the religious, the non-religious and the "none's." (The last group were those who were raised Jews but no longer consider themselves Jewish in religion.) Such a division is not altogether at variance with theory because, as both Lenski and Glazer point out, the non-practicing Jews are still Jews, although the same could hardly be said of apostate Catholics or Protestants.

THE INFLUENCE OF RELIGIOSITY

Table 2 presents data to test the hypothesis that the religious traits vary with religiosity. For a trait to be accepted as religious it would be necessary for it to vary directly with religiosity for the group which scores high on it and not to vary with religiosity for the other groups (or at least to such a great extent).

Table 2 shows that only in a very few instances is the hypotesis upheld. Only four traits—all of them Protestant—seem to be religiously correlated in the sense of the hypothesis. It can be said that education as a career, elementary education as an expected employer, drive, and the desire to help others are Protestant traits in some sense of the word.[12] A

---

[11] Self rating as "Religious" is not a completely useless tool by any means. We would expect a valid measure of religiosity to show women scoring higher than men, students of denominational colleges scoring higher than other students, and Catholics scoring higher than Protestants or Jews. As a matter of fact, the religiosity tool used in this analysis does vary along the predicted lines.

[12] However, the other two religious groups

THE ORIGINS OF RELIGIOUS DIFFERENCES 25

TABLE 2

Religious Traits by Religiosity

N's		Prot	Cath	Jew
High Religious		346	259	105
Medium Religious		985	417	122
Low Religious		337	141	41

A. *Protestant Traits*		High Rel	Med Rel	Low Rel
1. High Go Grad School	Prot	27	23	30
	Cath	36	30	38
	Jew	47	49	54
2. Education	Prot	45	35	24
	Cath	28	25	20
	Jew	33	25	22
3. Other Professional	Prot	22	15	12
	Cath	28	25	20
	Jew	33	25	22
4. Elementary Education	Prot	43	34	25
	Cath	29	23	25
	Jew	32	26	20
5. Helpful	Prot	82	67	64
	Cath	74	46	54
	Jew	73	56	55
6. Slow sure progress	Prot	27	37	34
	Cath	31	29	30
	Jew	23	34	17
7. High API	Prot	16	16	21
	Cath	15	16	15
	Jew	19	30	31
8. Per cent Conservative	Prot	46	36	42
	Cath	34	31	31
	Jew	22	11	25
9. Drive Scale	Prot	62	53	52
	Cath	52	38	42
	Jew	55	48	44

also vary directly on these items, so we cannot say with confidence that the effect results from Protestantism since the variation may be merely the result of religiosity as such and *as* Protestant religiosity. By the strictest standards, there are no traits that are religious in the sense that they vary directly only for one religious group.

26   THE ORIGINS OF RELIGIOUS DIFFERENCES

B. *Catholic Traits*

1. High Go   (Cf. A-1)

2. Intellectual   Prot   22   13   15
                            Cath   25   16   25
                            Jew   18   30   35

3. Business   Prot   7   16   19
                            Cath   20   28   15
                            Jew   24   14   15

4. Large Corporation   Prot   10   24   32
                            Cath   29   34   29
                            Jew   21   29   20

5. Low API   (Cf. A-7)

6. Per cent Liberal   Prot   30   44   38
                            Cath   47   50   54
                            Jew   67   70   60

7. Per cent Against   Prot   27   25   23
   Modern Art   Cath   18   31   27
                            Jew   23   20   13

C. *Jewish Traits*

1. High Go   (Cf. A-1)

2. Science   Prot   7   7   6
                            Cath   6   6   6
                            Jew   7   7   10

3. Medicine   Prot   2   2   3
                            Cath   2   4   3
                            Jew   5   8   5

4. Law   Prot   1   1   7
                            Cath   3   6   8
                            Jew   7   12   12

5. Small Company   Prot   9   14   21
                            Cath   15   26   22
                            Jew   12   13   12

6. Self-Employment   Prot   1   2   3
                            Cath   2   4   1
                            Jew   4   4   1

7. Chance to Make Money   Prot   14   18   30
                            Cath   18   18   39
                            Jew   36   38   41

8. Chance to be Creative   Prot   48   48   47
                            Cath   49   47   54
                            Jew   64   66   70

THE ORIGINS OF RELIGIOUS DIFFERENCES   27

9. Working in a World of Ideas	Prot	35	35	37
	Cath	33	30	50
	Jew	47	51	57
10. High API	(Cf. A-7)			
11. Per cent Liberal	(Cf. B-6)			
12. Per cent Unconventional	Prot	24	19	33
	Cath	19	21	54
	Jew	43	38	75
13. Sophistication	Prot	13	10	13
	Cath	18	11	13
	Jew	15	19	10
14. Emotionality	Prot	8	18	15
	Cath	8	13	23
	Jew	18	20	27
15. Extroversion	Prot	61	61	65
	Cath	63	63	61
	Jew	58	74	77
16. Intellectual	(Cf. B-2)			

high score on the drive scale would fit the Protestant Ethic theory nicely. Social service and the helping of others is certainly part of the tradition of American Protestantism, though somewhat at variance with the strict *sola fide* doctrine. One might even fit the inclination to education, especially elementary education, into the Protestant tradition of service, all the more so since to a large extent the American public education system grew out of the Protestant "social improvement" impulse.

The complete absence of religious correlation for Jewish and Catholic traits is surprising. Two possible explanations might be offered. First of all, the religiosity index might be worthless for these two groups. Certainly this is a possibility not to be rejected, particularly in view of Lenski's finding that the various component elements which he defined in religiosity do not correlate. However, it is worth noting that in the Lenski study there were few consistent correlation patterns for any of the religiosity indices with the exception of Catholic

family values. While we cannot say with certainty that there is no correlation between religious involvement and the supposedly religious traits, we can say that we have some suggestive evidence for this conclusion, especially since there is at least persuasive data to support an alternative explanation of the differences between members of the various religious groups.

This second explanation is that the traits are the result of the socio-cultural experiences the various groups have had during their history. Stated more specifically, such a hypothesis would maintain that the deviations of Catholics and Jews from the American Protestant mode can be explained by the differential experiences the two groups had of the immigration and assimilation experience —the Jews as members of a highly developed middle class transplanted to a middle class culture, the Catholics as remnants of a peasant "folk" society transplanted into the midst of urban industrialism. These different experiences happened to the members of the religious

28   THE ORIGINS OF RELIGIOUS DIFFERENCES

groups because they were members of the group but not in so far as they were members. In other words, there would be, in this hypothesis, nothing specific in Jewish doctrine or modal practice which would make the Jews more interested in earning money, but much in the two millenia of Jewish cultural experience would make this exceedingly reasonable. Nor would there be anything in the Catholic creed, code or cult which would incline Catholics to work for large corporations more often than Protestants, but there might be much in the history of a group arriving at the threshold of economic and social success at this moment in America's history which would incline the group to regard the large company as an important means of upward mobility.

We would certainly hold with Lenski that religious groups are primary groups which form segregated communication networks limited to the adherents of the same faith and facilitating the development and transmission of distinctive political and economic norms, or, alternatively, distinctive role images. We would merely affirm that these differences do not flow from religious ideology but cultural experience.

THE SOCIAL MARGINALITY HYPOTHESES

How could such an hypothesis be tested? There are no questions in our interview schedule which would perfectly fit our requirements. However, there are certain procedures which might give us "a hint of an explanation." To the extent that one is physically isolated from the members of one's religious "communication network" there is some possibility that the norms the network carries would not come through so clearly. Thus, we might suggest that Protestants, Catholics, and Jews who are socially marginal to their religious groups might score less high on the religious traits than do their brothers. If you simply do not live in an area where there are, for example,

very many Catholics or Jews, it might be much less likely that you will absorb the norms of your socio-religious community. The reason is not that you are a poorer Catholic or Jew religiously, but that you are, physically speaking, living on the margin of the Jewish or Catholic community.[13]

Therefore, we would expect, in this hypothesis, that Catholics from rural or small hometown background and Jews living in medium-sized cities (there were no rural or small city Jews in the subsample) would decline in their respective religious traits while Protestants in the same area would not decline in these traits, or at least would not decline so much. The test was therefore applied to 25% of the Catholics (N = 206) who live on farms or in towns under 50,000 and to the 23% of the Jews (N = 61) who live in cities under 500,000. Table 3 presents the results.

In the first part of the table, dealing with Catholic traits, the first column shows the percentage for the "social marginal" (small town) Catholics and the second column gives the percentage for all the Catholics in the subsample. The third and fourth columns present comparable figures for Protestants. The fifth column is the "difference between the differences." Thus, the Catholic average on the first item is 33% and the marginal Catholic score is 24% for a difference of 9%; the Protestant average is 28% and the small town Protestant average is 24% for a difference of 4%. The

_____

[13] Partial confirmation of this hypothesis comes from the studies on religious mixed marriages which seem to increase according to the social marginality of a member of a religious group with relation to his group. Cf., A. M. Greeley, "Religious Segregation in a Suburb" (Unpublished M. A. Thesis, The University of Chicago, 1961), and Rudolph K. Hairle, "A Survey of the Literature on Religious Intermarriage" (Unpublished M. A. Thesis, The University of Chicago, 1961).

THE ORIGINS OF RELIGIOUS DIFFERENCES   29

TABLE 3

RELIGIOUS TRAITS BY SOCIAL MARGINALITY

A. *Catholic Traits*	Catholics Small Town	Average	Protestants Small Town	Average	Net Dif
1. High Go	24	33	24	28	+5
2. Intellectual	15	22	15	17	+5
3. Business	22	24	15	15	+2
4. Large Corporation	23	33	21	25	+6
5. Modern Art	29	29	24	26	—2
6. Liberal	48	50	44	44	+2
7. High API	90	85	82	80	—8
8. Religiosity	77	80	74	70	+7
N	(206)	(830)	(1060)	(2007)	

B. *Jewish Traits*	Jews Medium	Large	Protestants Medium	Large	Net Dif
1. High Go	36	50	30	37	+7
2. Science	7	9	8	8	+2
3. Medicine	2	7	2	3	+4
4. Law	3	10	3	3	+7
5. Small Company	25	18	9	10	—8
6. Self-Employment	15	15	5	7	—2
7. Make Money	36	40	20	20	+4
8. Creative	53	63	54	59	+5
9. World of Ideas	41	51	38	43	+5
10. High API	21	27	18	27	—5
11. Liberal	64	67	42	44	+1
12. Unconventional	28	40	28	35	+7
13. Sophistication	18	16	13	13	—2
14. Emotionality	14	21	13	13	+7
15. Extroversion	28	31	23	23	+3
16. Intellectual	15	30	20	20	+15
N	(63)	(209)	(460)	(480)	

Protestant score declines 4%, the Catholic score declines 9%, the difference between the two declines is 5% which is the number found in the fifth column.

In the second part of the table, the first column shows the percentage for Jews in medium cities (cities between 100,000 and 500,000)—the presumable social mar-

ginal Jews. The second column reports on the large city Jews. The third and fourth columns give the comparable Protestant data.

To establish the hypothesis the figure in the first column must be lower than that in the second, while the figure in the third must not be lower than that

30   THE ORIGINS OF RELIGIOUS DIFFERENCES

in the fourth or not as much lower as the first is in relation to the second. Thus, in the first item, the first column is lower than the second, but the third is also lower than the fourth. However, the decrease is less sharp in the latter case so that the net difference is plus 5%, and the hypothesis is supported.

In six of the eight Catholic traits and in 13 out of the 16 Jewish traits the predicted result occurs. In 4 of the Catholic traits and 9 of the Jewish traits is the net difference (difference between minority group scores minus difference between majority group scores) five or more percentage points. The other six cases are close, some of them very close indeed. The main burden of our argument, however, rests not so much on specific point differences on individual traits, but the rather overwhelming *direction* of the data in favor of the hypothesis. The proof that these norms have something to do with the socially transmitted histtorical tradition is not absolutely conclusive, but the data are persuasive.

The contrary hypothesis—that the differences are the result of religious ideology and not of a non-religious, but religiously linked cultural tradition— is not disproved by the above data unless one accepts the religiosity test described earlier in the essay. Even in the face of the evidence from the last paragraph it could be argued that the religiosity indicator was not valid and that social marginality to a religious group was the same as religious marginality, but that the religiosity indicator used in this paper does not reveal that religious marginality. Therefore, the argument might run, if control was made for religiosity the differences listed in Table 3 might disappear. Such an argument might indeed be valid, but since the argument rejects the only religiosity indicator we have at our disposal, there is no way of disproving it.

Thus, our social but not religious marginality hypothesis is dependent on two assumptions: (1) that the religiosity indicator we use is a valid measure of religious involvement, and (2) that the convergence of the scores in Table 3 in the direction of the hypothesis indicates that the Catholics and the Jews who live in areas where presumably there are few Catholics or Jews will be less likely to share certain distinctively Catholic or Jewish norms.

SOME SPECULATIONS

If one might venture for a moment into the realm of speculation, it could be suggested that virtually all the traits listed in Tables 2 and 3 could be attributed to past social history of the two groups as filtered through the immigration experience. What would happen, for example, to a Catholic group which had a "middle class tradition" like that which Glazer attributes to the Jews? Or what would happen to a Jewish group whose tradition had been that of peasant farmers? Would Armenian or Lebanese Catholics, for example, have scores in this survey more like Jews or the main sample of Catholics? Where would some of the Asiatic Jewish groups who are migrating to Israel fit into the picture? What would come from a study of the various Orthodox Christian groups which have migrated to America? Their ideology, one would take it, is probably more like the Catholic than the Protestant or Jewish creeds. Would it be possible that the Ukranian Orthodox, for example, would have scores not dissimilar from that of the Polish Catholics while the Greek Orthodox, coming from a tradition of mercantilism at least as old as that of the Jews, might have scores close to the Jewish scores? Even within the Catholic group there are possibilities that might be explored. Did the Irish, because of their command of the language, have an advantage in the struggle to become middle class Americans over, let us say, the Poles? Is it possible that the score of the Irish group on our in-

THE ORIGINS OF RELIGIOUS DIFFERENCES 31

dicators might be closer to that of the Jews? Is it possible that, even with the grosser social and economic variables controlled, those from an Irish cultural background might be more likely to go into self-employment than those from a Polish or Italian background? Would cross-cultural research show us that in some countries the occupational values of the three religious groups are arranged in different constellations?

It is time to call the preceding orgy of speculation to an end. The avenues of research suggested in the last paragraph would not be easy ones on which to journey. The precise meaning of ethnicity is by no means clear. One has the feeling that for all the books written on the assimilation—or acculturation if you will—of the immigrant groups we still know very little about the process, either about where it started, or where it has come to, or how it has got there. One also has the disturbing feeling that with each passing year the task of unraveling all the twisted threads will grow more difficult. Indeed, one might be forgiven for suggesting that if sociologists do not soon put aside the outmoded melting pot assumption and return to the study of what *is happening* to the ethnic groups, then what may well be the most significant sociological experience that

has gone on in America—or indeed anywhere anytime—will be forever beyond our comprehension.

SUMMARY

In this note we have attempted to offer some explanation of the origins of traits that were specific to the three religious groups of June, 1961, college graduates. We found that the traits did not vary directly with religiosity, but did decrease among those members of the given group who existed on the social margins of the group. This led us to suggest that the religious groups are indeed communications networks which provide their members with norms and role images, but that these norms and images do not necessarily flow from religious ideology; in some instances at least, they may rather be the result of the past cultural experience of the group which had no direct connection with the theology (official or popular) of the group. We then pointed out that all the existing differences between the minority religious groups and the main body of American college graduates could be explained in terms of the differential effects of the immigration experience on the Jewish and Catholic groups. We concluded by offering some possible methods of investigating this hypothesis.

PETER H. ROSSI

ANDREW M. GREELEY

National Opinion Research Center
University of Chicago

The Impact of the
Roman Catholic Denominational School[1]

I. INTRODUCTION

There are many ways that denominational schools affect our society. To begin with, these school systems were designed to further the goals of the churches involved and therefore have an effect on American religious life. The denominational schools also exist in the presence of a state-supported school system and compete in some sense with the public schools. Finally, there are effects on the structure of local communities and the larger society in which these communities are imbedded. We shall take up in turn these three types of effects, providing firm information where such was available to us and at least intelligent speculation where we do not have much information.

The dimensions of private religious schooling in this country are well enough known. Although several denominations provide elementary and secondary education to their members,[2] the vast majority of students attending parochial[3] schools are attending schools established and run by the Roman Catholic church. More than five and a half million pupils attend close to ten thousand elementary parochial schools, accounting for a little less than 15 per cent of all students in the elementary grades. Roman Catholic high schools account for a smaller proportion of the total high-school population. American parish priests are required by church rules to provide parochial schools for their parishioners, and Roman Catholics are required to send their children to parochial schools.[4] However, two out of every five parishes do not provide such schools. About half of Roman Catholic adults have obtained their education through the parochial schools, and perhaps as many as 60 per cent of Roman Catholic children of elementary-school age are enrolled in the parochial schools.[5] In addition, 45 per cent of the Catholics in the June, 1961, college class graduated from Catholic colleges.[6]

Schools and school systems designed to accommodate large numbers and run by churches are not unusual in the contemporary Western world. What is unique about the American Roman Catholic school system is that it operates without significant amounts of state financial support. This is a school system that is financed to some small degree by tuition charges but largely by voluntary donations. Elsewhere in the Western world, Roman Catholic schools are either heavily supported out of state funds, as in Canada and Holland, or designed primarily to serve an elite and operated substantially out of tuition charges, as in France and England.

The size and organizational vigor of the Roman Catholic schools are a tribute to the dedication of Catholic laymen, priests, and members of the religious orders who together have managed to provide mass education side by side with a free and usually relatively good public school system. When we consider further that American Catholics have been until fairly recently primarily working class, this accomplishment is one to be even further admired, if only for the financial sacrifices involved.

The Roman Catholic schools are perhaps most properly seen as part of the Counter Reformation. The American public schools established in the nineteenth century were in many cases dominated by particular Protestant denominations, and even when church and state were more clearly separated in the latter half of the nineteenth century, the schools were Protestant in tone and often curriculum, if not tied to any particular denomination. The American Catholics reacted strongly to the Protestant character of the public schools

36 | THE SCHOOL REVIEW *Spring 1964*

by enacting in 1884 the church laws, referred to earlier, setting up the parochial schools.

The bulk of the Catholic component of our population was among the later arrivals to our shores; Catholics differed from the rest of the population in ethnic background as well as religion. This ethnic difference reinforced the separatist tendencies of the church and its adherents. The parochial schools began to serve the triple purpose of providing proper religious instruction, preventing exposure to potentially alienating Protestant ideology, and welding together the members of recent newcomers from a foreign culture.

It is obvious that time has changed many of the key elements we have mentioned. First, the public schools have become more and more secular and cannot be considered even vaguely Protestant today. Second, the Counter Reformation seems to be drawing to a close with ever greater Catholic interest in the ecumenical movement.[7] Third, the Catholic population is no longer at the bottom of the occupational and economic heap and has lost through assimilation much of its ethnic flavor.[8] These three developments taken together have produced a mild crisis in the American church with respect to the parochial school system, discussion of which we shall postpone until later in this paper.

II. EFFECTS ON INDIVIDUALS

The basic rationale behind the establishment of a denominational school system was to provide for the proper religious instruction of the young and to insulate them from unorthodox influences in the public schools. At the same time, the parochial schools are designed to provide instruction in the same sorts of skills and information that is typically imparted in the ordinary elementary- and secondary-school system.

It is most difficult to evaluate the effectiveness of the denominational schools in achieving these ends. The major difficulty in making such an evaluation lies in the self-selective character of enrolment. Catholic families who send their children to parochial schools are different by that fact from other Catholics who do not. Hence, to compare parochial and public school Catholics is in part to compare persons with different levels of adherence to the teachings and rules of the church, a factor which may affect the outcome of parochial schooling as much as the fact of schooling itself.

By gathering data from a variety of sources, we are able to show that Catholics who had gone to parochial as opposed to public schools were more likely to be more observant of certain religious duties.[9] Thus parochial school attenders were more likely to be steady churchgoers and to perform their Easter duties, but they were not any more likely to marry within their faith than were public school attenders. Catholics who have gone either to a Catholic high school or a Catholic college are much less likely to apostasize than those who have not been in the Catholic system at either of these levels. In the June, 1961, college graduating class, 77 per cent of the Catholic apostasy took place among those who went to non-Catholic high schools and colleges. However, even among this group, 82 per cent of the graduates who were reared as Catholics were still Catholics at the time of graduation. The recent fertility studies would also suggest that Catholics who attended Catholic schools are considerably less likely to engage in forms of family planning that are opposed to Catholic doctrine.[10] However, so slight are the differences in religious observance (often being overshadowed by differences among the sexes and economic levels) that one must come to the conclusion that the parochial schools are not very efficient as far as this aspect of religious behavior is concerned. Were this the sole purpose of the parochial schools, one could question strongly whether the considerable investment of energy and resources in the system is justifiable in terms of end results.

But there are other, more striking effects.

First, parochial school Catholics are much more likely to be tied into the formal and informal social networks that involve the church and Catholics as a social group. Thus, French-Canadian Catholics who have attended parochial schools are much more likely to speak

38 | THE SCHOOL REVIEW   *Spring 1964*

French as a household language than those who have not. Similarly, parochial school Catholics are more likely to look to religious leaders to provide ideas and opinions concerning secular matters. Parochial school Catholics are more likely to be tied into church organizations and social circles that are predominantly Catholic.[11]

In short, while the parochial schools do not appear to have been particularly effective in producing a large increment in religious orthodoxy, they do appear to have been an effective means of furthering the integration of Catholics as a solidary social group. We may speculate on the reasons for this effect as follows: Catholics with their children in parochial schools may become much more involved in the organized social life of the parish, while for the youngsters, especially those in secondary schools, the schools themselves provide a matrix for sociability in which friendships are formed that last into adulthood.

A second important type of effect concerns opinions on educational issues. Parochial school Catholics are much more likely to take the official Catholic "line" on such matters as financial aid to church schools, released time for religious instruction, and the like. In short, the alumni of the parochial school systems constitute a group who are interested in furthering the interests of the system.

Denominational schools have, of course, larger goals than keeping people in the organization, guaranteeing certain moral or religious practices, and obtaining a modicum of in-group sentiments. We have little in the way of evidence to prove that the graduates of the Catholic school system excel their coreligionists who have not gone to Catholic schools in the practice of the virtue of charity, that they are any more opposed to racial injustice, any more concerned with the suffering people of new nations, any more inclined to agree with the teachings of the papal social encyclicals (especially the recent *Mater et magistra*). To say that we have little of such evidence does not mean that evidence cannot be found but merely that to date it has not been produced. Certainly those within the church who wish to evaluate the denominational schools in light of the highest ideals of the church ought to ask whether such evidence can be found.

Finally, one may raise the question of the quality of education being given in the parochial schools. Here one can point to very little in the way of firm data that are properly analyzed. Several studies have shown that parochial school students average slightly higher on achievement tests than public school students, especially at the high-school level. But we must remember that parochial schools, especially high schools, are selective in their admissions policy, while the public schools must accommodate all who apply in some educational context. Before we make such comparisons we need to know how well public and parochial schools do with the kinds of pupils that are enrolled in each type of school. It is probably safe to say that there is great variation from school to school in the parochial school system but that this variation is not as great as that to be found in the public schools because of the selective admissions policies of the parochial schools. It should be borne in mind, however, that of the twenty high schools that have had the best records of producing Ph.D.'s, none is a parochial school, although almost all these schools are located in the Northeast and Middle West.

Apparently the Catholic colleges are in a period of transition. The Knapp studies[12] of a decade ago and the self-criticism of certain Catholic scholars[13] had indicated that the graduates of Catholic colleges were not interested in scholarly careers. However, by June, 1961, no evidence of this was to be found. Indeed, graduates of the Catholic colleges were more likely to choose such careers than the national average.[14] The Catholic colleges ranked behind the Ivy League schools and behind a group of high-quality private colleges, but ahead of the Big Ten universities and the middle-western liberal arts and science schools. Nor was there any indication that Catholics were disinclined to go into the physical sciences. It appeared that this transition was in part at least the result of a conscious plan on the part of the faculties of Catholic colleges. The

40 | THE SCHOOL REVIEW *Spring 1964*

same processes were apparently at work in the small Protestant denominational colleges.

A few words of caution ought to be inserted at this point, lest the impression be given that these generalizations are very firmly rooted in empirical knowledge. The studies whose results we have referred to (with the exception of the college study) are limited in scope and generality, being based rather heavily on New England communities where relations between Catholics and Protestants have not been very good over the past century.

III. EFFECTS ON PUBLIC EDUCATION

Although in the nation as a whole only three of every twenty elementary-school pupils are enrolled in denominational schools, this proportion varies widely from place to place. American Catholics are concentrated in the industrial and urbanized areas in the Northeast and Middle West. Indeed, in some communities, the parochial school systems have larger enrolments than the public school systems, and in all the major cities in those two regions from one fifth to one half of the elementary-school population may be enrolled therein.

What are the effects on public education in communities that have sizable proportions of their children in parochial schools? This is not an easy question to answer, for a proper reply awaits much more firm data than we have now at hand. For example, it is often pointed out that in cities with very high proportions of parochial school children, public education is not of the best. But it should be remembered that in terms of average scores on achievement tests, the worst elementary and secondary education in this country is to be found in our southern states where there are few Catholics, and that the best is to be found in the urban Northeast and Midwest where there are many Catholics. Educational quality varies more with the general socioeconomic status of the community than with its religious composition.

In a direct sense, public education in this country relies on public support in the local community. School systems raise their support through local taxation supplemented by grants from state and federal governments. The existence of a large proportion of the population oriented to a parochial school system, it is often argued, must have some considerable effect on the ability of the public schools to mobilize support. On this score we have some small bits of information: In a study conducted in a small-sized New England city, we found that parents with children in the parochial schools had comparatively little "interest" in public school matters, paying little attention to issues involving the schools. If we assume that interest is necessary for support and that support is necessary to produce the best of public education, then the existence of a parochial school system will tend to produce less support for public education than otherwise. Of course, it should be borne in mind that, where there is an extensive parochial school system, less support is necessary for the public school system, since so much of the economic burden of educating Catholic children is taken care of by the parochial schools.

Another type of effect on the public schools stems from the fact that at the present time the parochial schools can accommodate only a little more than half of the Catholic children of school age, and the shortage of places is especially acute on the high-school level. This has meant that the parochial schools have been able to be selective in their admissions policies and have left to the public schools the hard-to-educate and "problem children." Although the Catholic "central" high schools do have "business" and "secretarial" courses, their main emphasis is normally college preparatory. There are few Catholic "vocational" high schools, since the financial outlay for manual-trade programs is so great; nor are there many "comprehensive" high schools that are designed to provide four years of secondary-school experience for anyone no matter how poor his ability. Hence Catholics who seek manual-trades training are likely to go to public schools.[15]

These selective admissions policies plus the tuition charges have

42 | THE SCHOOL REVIEW *Spring 1964*

meant that middle-class Catholics are much more likely to send their children to parochial schools, and the parochial schools are much more likely to accept them. Thus, in a study of the New Haven high schools, Strodtbeck found that the more talented among the Catholic children of high-school age were in the parochial high schools while the least talented were in the public schools.[16] Similarly, we found that the small public elementary school serving a French-Canadian neighborhood contained a high proportion of "problem children."[17]

It does not seem likely that the parochial schools will expand to the extent necessary to accommodate all Catholic children, if only because to do so would place an intolerable financial drain on the Catholic community. Hence, the presence of an extensive parochial school system in a community will usually mean that the public schools will bear the burden of providing the more expensive vocational education on the high-school level and the unpleasant task of providing education for the less gifted among Catholic children. As we indicated before, the burden would be very much greater if the public schools were to have to educate all Catholics.

Perhaps one of the most important effects on a public school system of the presence side by side with it of a denominational school system lies in an area much more difficult to pin down and for that reason probably containing large elements of myth mixed with fact. In New England cities school administrators are sensitive to their "competition" and to the fact that there is a large component of the local community whose stake in the public schools is slight. This has meant, it is said, a more conservative curriculum, less expansionist building programs, lower salary scales for teachers, and a general policy of moving slowly and cautiously. Neal Gross's study of the school superintendents in Massachusetts, for example, finds that these administrators consider the Catholic clergy one of the most important pressure groups with which they have to contend.[18] He also finds that the same group believes that opposition to increased financial support for the schools comes largely from this source.

It is hard to evaluate how accurately the superintendents see the world about them in this respect. For one thing, it would seem that in the Midwest school administrators are less nervous about their "competition," leading one to suspect that the reactions of the New England administrators reflect more the long-standing Protestant-Catholic tension in that region than anything else. Concerning the support for bond issues and increased tax rates, studies made on voting in such elections indicate that, by and large in this historical period, such measures are supported more heavily by the upper- than by the lower-income groups, a generalization which holds whether Catholics or Protestants are in the lower-income groups. In New England, where Catholics are still in the majority on the blue-collar levels of the local community, opposition to bond issues stemming from class reasons may be misinterpreted as opposition along religious lines.

In fact, a large part of the behavior of both the public and the parochial school officials can be interpreted as the avoidance of direct and open competition. A case might be made that the cause of better education might best be served by much more direct and open competition, especially in those areas where both systems are trying to accomplish the same ends. We have in mind particularly competition in academic achievement—how well the products of the two systems do on the College Entrance Examination Board examinations or in the National Merit Scholarship competition. Such competition might strengthen the thrust toward academic excellence in both systems. The danger in such competition, of course, lies in the fact that in all competitive struggles someone must lose. But we suspect that the two systems would be so evenly balanced that the result will be more like the competitive struggles between our two political parties rather than the uneven battles between giants and pygmies.

44 | THE SCHOOL REVIEW *Spring 1964*

IV. EFFECTS ON COMMUNITY AND SOCIETY

The progress of the discussion in this paper has been from the hard to the soft, from better documented matters to areas in which there appear to be fewer hard facts. We move now to a topic for which there are virtually no firm data but, as is usual in the social sciences, a topic of greater importance: How does the existence of a parochial school system affect the community and society in which it is imbedded?

There is a tension in every democratic society between the need for sufficient integration to provide consensus on values and goals and the need to provide for the existence of diversity. We want neither so much conflict that the society is in a state of civil war nor so much uniformity that we have completely undercut the meaning of democracy. To accomplish the integration of our society, we need institutions that bind regions, classes, and kinship groupings together, and to accomplish the goal of diversity we need to allow to exist separatist institutions wherein persons of one class, region, or kinship grouping can foster their separate identity.

This means that a democratic society can tolerate separatist institutions provided that they do not become total communities. This is the meaning of democratic pluralism. We would not want to see a society in which there were separate Catholic, Protestant, and Jewish communities, each with its complete set of organizations and institutions so that there was no crosscutting of memberships in organizations and institutions along religious lines. Several Western nations approximate this sort of "vertical pluralism," as Moberg has termed it, in which there is almost complete separation between several religious groups, as for example, in French Canada, Holland, and Algeria. The danger in vertical pluralism is the hardening of conflict to the extent that the society as a whole becomes paralyzed.[19]

Incidentally, this is the danger that Conant saw in the independent schools—that they would produce separate communities, while the public school system provided a setting that would bring classes and religious groups together in the same institutional setup.[20]

To what extent do the parochial schools represent such a separatist organization? What little information we do have indicates
that the separatist inclinations of parochial school Catholics are
slight. In our study of a New England city they are no less attached
to their communities, no less interested in politics, slightly more
likely to be Democrats, and slightly more likely to vote for Catholics
in local elections (as compared with Catholics who had gone to the
public schools). While data from other communities are missing,
the best guess is that we would find the same tendencies in other
cities.

It seems highly unlikely that the parochial schools represent as
much of a threat to democratic pluralism as, for example, Conant
suggests. For one thing, as long as the capacity of the parochial
schools remains as far below the potential demand as it is at present,
a *majority* of American Catholics will continue perforce to attend the
public schools. Second, the creation of a separate Catholic community would require more than a religious segregated school
system; it would require that other important areas of life also be
segregated, especially work, residence, and leisure activities, an
eventuality that is unlikely to occur unless the Catholics were to
set themselves up in a separate region of the nation. Finally, the
most recent ecumenical tendencies within Catholicism argue against
such a separatist movement. With the rise of the Catholics into the
middle classes in the past three decades, the separatist institutions
which grew up around the church of the immigrant groups seem to
have lost their distinctive flavor. It seems very likely that divisive
factionalism is more often the result of past historical experiences
than the present organization of education. Thus one has the impression that even though a far higher proportion of Catholics is in
parochial schools in Chicago than in Boston, the relations between
Catholics and non-Catholics are considerably more peaceful, if
not more cordial, in the former city than in the latter. There was
never a Brahmin class in Chicago for the Catholic population to
dislike, antagonize, and imitate.

46 | THE SCHOOL REVIEW   *Spring 1964*

V. THE CRISIS IN THE PAROCHIAL SCHOOLS

The recent rise in agitation for public support of the parochial schools argues for the existence of a kind of crisis for the parochial school systems in this country. This crisis has four main roots: first, now that the immigrant generations and their immediate descendants are disappearing from the scene and Catholics have moved into the middle classes in significant numbers, the parochial schools are being pressured into ever higher standards. Catholic parents want their children to have at least as good an education as their neighbors in the suburbs who send their children to the best of suburban schools. Furthermore, Catholic intellectuals are disturbed and upset over the apparent failure of American Catholics to contribute their proportionate share to American science and letters. (The NORC college study cited above would suggest that there is less reason for this disturbance than there was a decade ago.) Higher standards for the parochial schools mean more expensive schooling—better buildings, better equipment, and better-prepared teachers.

A second root of the crisis lies in the parochial schools' increasing reliance on lay teachers, a trend apparently produced by the failure of the orders to attract sisters and brothers in sufficient numbers to man the school systems.[21] Lay teachers require more funds, and if the teachers are to have the same level of preparation as those of the neighboring public schools, salaries have to be comparable and reach a level that is considerably above what is now paid.

The third root of the crisis lies in the expansion of the Catholic population both in numbers and location. As the Catholics have risen out of the working class, so have they spread throughout the city and especially toward the suburbs. To meet the needs caused by these shifts, new parochial schools have to be built and older ones abandoned as their constituents leave them behind.

A fourth source of difficulty is that from one point of view the proponents of Catholic education have done their job too well. The proportion of the Catholic population demanding such education for their children seems to be constantly increasing. Thus the percentage of Catholics seeking admission into Catholic high schools in Chicago has steadily increased since the 1930's and is currently at an all-time high. One rarely hears sermons in Catholic churches about the obligation incumbent on parents to provide a Catholic education for their children. Indeed in many suburban parishes in the Midwest one gets the impression that the Catholic laity are impatient with the slowness with which the clergy are expanding or improving the educational facilities. The complaint is not that there are Catholic schools but that there are not enough of them. In the absence of any conclusive data, there is some reason to suspect that large numbers of the Catholic laity are convinced that their "private" school system does have something more to offer. The image of a reluctant laity sending children to parochial schools under dire threats from the clergy is a stereotype that may provide emotional release for certain elements of the American population, but it would scarcely prove amusing to the suburban pastor who is trying to pay off a half-million-dollar debt on a new school while his parishioners clamor for ten new classrooms. One suspects that a good many Catholics view their church as primarily an educational center and their clergy as primarily school administrators. Whether such an image is good for a church is a question that is beyond the scope of this article.

In short, the maintenance of a parochial school system at the level of excellence demanded by today's needs is placing an increasing strain on the resources of the church. To relieve this strain, many Catholics are looking to a change in our traditional policy of non-support for church-related schools. Despite some attempts to give the impression of unanimity on the subject of federal aid to denominational schools, it is clear enough that within the laity, the clergy, and the hierarchy there are strong differences on the subject, with a militant lay group such as the Citizens for Educational Freedom going much further in its quest for public aid, one is inclined to think, than many bishops would be disposed to go.

48 | THE SCHOOL REVIEW   *Spring 1964*

The rethinking of policy is not limited to the question of public help. There is a substantial amount of discussion about various kinds of shared time, released time, or other co-operative ventures. Suggestions have been made that certain grades be eliminated from the parochial system so that efforts can be concentrated on other, presumably more crucial, grades; there is little agreement, however, as to which grades are the ones to be eliminated. Still other voices are heard urging that the extracurricular approach of the Confraternity of Christian Doctrine or the various Catholic action organizations such as the Young Christian Students or the Young Christian Workers be viewed as possible tools for a new kind of Catholic education.

One of the major difficulties in the present reshaping of policy is that policy-makers have so little in the way of empirical data on which to base their decisions. As we have said before, there are very few studies that provide much information on how well the Catholic schools achieve the purpose for which they were founded, and there is practically no information on how other agencies might possibly achieve the same results as are now being obtained. Neither is there much data on how the Catholic laity, who are the ones who must continue to support the schools financially, would view adaptations of the sort being discussed. Studies of the Catholic school system, such as the one now being undertaken by the University of Notre Dame with funds from the Carnegie Corporation, are thus of considerable moment not only to policy-makers in American Catholicism but also to the entire American society.

VI. CONCLUSIONS

In this paper, we have tried to spell out the effects of the existence of parochial schools upon those who attend them, upon the church which maintains them, and upon the community and society in which they exist.

The most clear-cut effects are upon those who attend these schools: Parochial school Catholics are "better" Catholics than those who attend public schools, but the differences are not over-whelming and, indeed, are so slight that we might raise the question whether the investment is worth the return if the main purpose of the investment is to produce better religious practice. The effects on public schools lie in two areas: first, in the erosion of public support for the public schools, and second, in the sensitivity of public school administrators to what they perceive to be a "rival" school system.

Finally, we considered the effects of separate schools on the community and society as a whole. We examined the parochial schools as a move in the direction of a separate Catholic community, but a realistic evaluation would have to be built on a much wider base of separatist institutions than parochial schools alone.

It is clear that the parochial schools of this country are at some sort of important decision point, and the nation as a whole faces part of this decision with them. The parochial schools can pursue their traditional policy of providing a "Catholic" education for every Catholic only by cutting educational quality, by seeking public support, by restricting their educational mission to dimensions that are within their abilities in resources and manpower to provide, or by developing some new educational procedures that would imply closer co-operation, formal or informal, with the public school system. It is difficult to see how decisions can be made without far more empirical data than are now available.

NOTES

1. A revised version of a paper presented by the senior author to the Public Affairs Forum of the Minnesota Citizens Committee on Public Affairs, April 13, 1962.

2. Up-to-date comprehensive histories of denominational schooling in this country are apparently still to be written. Such general works as Theodore Roemer, *The Catholic Church in the U.S.* (St. Louis: B. Herder Book Co., 1950) and Walter H. Beck, *Lutheran Elementary Schools in the U.S.* (St. Louis: Concordia Press, 1939) may be consulted.

3. By no means are all denominational schools "parochial" in the sense of being connected with a given parish, though most elementary schools are pa-

50 | THE SCHOOL REVIEW   *Spring 1964*

rochial. At the secondary level the trend seems to be toward "central" high schools serving several parishes or an entire community; thus in Chicago more than two-thirds of the ninety Catholic high schools are central in fact even though they may have begun as parochial schools. Colleges, of course, are not parochial, although some of them may have begun in connection with a parish as did Chicago's Loyola, which grew out of St. Ignatius College, which in turn was part of Holy Family parish.

4. Third Plenary Council of Baltimore, *Acta et decreta* (1882), p. 104.

5. These estimates are only approximations, since statistics on church membership in America are notoriously unreliable.

6. Andrew M. Greeley, *Religion and the College Graduate* (a National Opinion Research Center report [New York: Free Press of Glencoe, 1962]).

7. For an example of the kind of thinking marking the end of the Counter Reformation see Hans Kung, *The Council, Reunion, and Reform* (New York: Sheed & Ward, 1962).

8. For a summary of data available on the social and economic position of American Catholics see Andrew M. Greeley, "The Present Condition of American Catholics," *Social Order* (forthcoming).

9. The generalizations in the next six paragraphs are based on data presented in Peter H. Rossi and Alice S. Rossi, "Some Effects of Parochial School Education in America," *Daedalus*, Spring, 1961, pp. 300–328. These data in turn are from five major sources: (*a*) The "Bay City Study," conducted at the Graduate School of Education at Harvard University by J. Leiper Freeman, James Shipton, and the Rossis; (*b*) The Arlington-Somerville Study of forty-one Catholic families with children of school age as reported in Bernard Portis, "An Empirical Analysis of Catholics: Choices between Public and Parochial Elementary Schools" (unpublished Bachelor's honor thesis, Harvard University, 1956); (*c*) The New Haven High School Study, conducted by Fred L. Strodtbeck and reported in David C. McClelland *et al.*, *Talent and Society* (Princeton, N.J.: D. Van Nostrand Co., 1958); (*d*) The Diocese of St. Augustine Study, a survey of 50,000 persons reported in Msgr. George A. Kelly's *Catholics and the Practice of the Faith* (Washington: Catholic University Press, 1946); (*e*) The St. Luke's Study in Joseph H. Fichter, *Parochial School* (Notre Dame, Ind.: University of Notre Dame Press, 1958).

10. Charles W. Westoff, Robert G. Potter, Philip Sagi, and Elliot G. Mishler, *Family Growth in Metropolitan America* (Princeton, N.J.: Princeton University Press, 1961), and Ronald Freedman, Pascal K. Whelpton, and Arthur G. Campbell, *Family Planning, Sterility and Population Growth* (New York: McGraw-Hill Book Co., 1959).

11. Cf. A. M. Greeley, "Religious Segregation in a Suburb," *Social Compass*, IX (1962), 39. Catholics in the parish studied seemed more inclined to view the parish school as a social center than the parents of public school children viewed the public school.

12. R. H. Knapp and H. B. Goodrich, *Origins of American Scientists* (Chi-

cago: University of Chicago Press, 1952), and R. H. Knapp and Joseph J. Greenbaum, *The Younger American Scientist: His Collegiate Origins* (Chicago: University of Chicago Press, 1953).

13. Msgr. John Tracey Ellis, "American Catholics and the Intellectual Life," *Thought*, Vol. XXX (Autumn, 1955); Thomas F. O'Dea, *American Catholic Dilemma: An Inquiry into the Intellectual Life* (New York: Sheed & Ward, 1958); and Gustave Weigel, "American Catholic Intellectualism," *Review of Politics*, Vol. XIX (July, 1957).

14. Full data on this study can be found in the NORC research report by Greeley previously cited. The entire survey of which the report was a part was conducted on a grant from the National Institutes of Health, the U.S. Office of Education, and the National Science Foundation. Some 33,000 graduates from 135 randomly selected colleges and universities are participating in this project. A brief summary of the report is to be found in Andrew M. Greeley, "Influence of the 'Religious Factor' on Career Plans and Occupational Values of College Graduates," *American Journal of Sociology*, May, 1963.

15. Training in accounting, secretarial work, and home economics was much more common in Catholic high schools when the Catholic population was still predominantly lower class. Many of the smaller "parochial" high schools (in the sense of being part of a particular parish) still are mainly commercial schools.

16. McClelland *et al., op. cit.*

17. Neal Gross, Ward S. Mason, and Alexander McEachern, *Explorations in Role-Analysis* (New York: John Wiley & Sons, 1958).

18. Sometimes these perceptions are not wholly accurate. There was a tendency on the part of some administrators to whom the senior author talked to see Catholics voting for a given political party because that was the way their priests voted. However, in many instances the truth of the matter was that the priests voted for the other party.

19. Moberg has recently compared the situations in Holland and the United States (David Moberg, "Religion and Society in the Netherlands and in America," *Social Compass*, IX [1962], 11–21). The similarities seem to the present writers to be less than dramatic. It is worth noting that, although in many ways vertical pluralism is far developed in Holland, the ecumenical movement is perhaps more advanced in that country than anywhere else in the world. Obviously "vertical pluralism" can mean many different things in different social and historical contexts.

20. James B. Conant, *The Child, the Parent, and the State* (Cambridge, Mass.: Harvard University Press, 1959).

21. The major reason for the shortage of priests, brothers, and nuns is demographic; those coming out of seminaries or novitiates now were born during the low-birth-rate years of the depression, but must service schools that have been inundated by the postwar baby boom.

Reprinted from SOCIOLOGICAL ANALYSIS, Vol. 25, No. 1, Spring, 1964

The Protestant Ethic: Time for a Moratorium*

Andrew Greeley

National Opinion Research Center

American sociologists continue to use the Protestant Ethic hypothesis as a theoretical framework in studying the presumed differences between Catholics and Protestants in this country. However, a review of recent studies indicates that this hypothesis is anything but fruitful. It is suggested that the survival of the Protestant Ethic as a testable theory is due to a misunderstanding of Weber, an oversimplification of history, an ignorance of the pluralistic nature of Catholicism, and a refusal to be persuaded by empirical data. It is doubtful that sociological study of American religion will make much progress until a moratorium is proclaimed on further use of the current simplistic version of the Weberian theory.

It will be the contention of this paper that the Protestant Ethic hypothesis has no relevance to the study of contemporary American society. It will be further contended that many of the efforts to make this hypothesis relevant have been poorly conceived and even more poorly executed and that these efforts represent a misunderstanding of Protestantism, of Catholicism, and indeed of Max Weber.

We shall begin by commenting on a group of studies which have attempted to test the Protestant Ethic hypothesis and then proceed to an analysis of the peculiar phenomenon of the persistence of the hypothesis in the face of consistently negative findings. We shall not at this point attempt to formulate the hypothesis since the various authors of whom we will speak have somewhat different formulations. However, we can at least describe it by saying that those who look for empirical confirmation of the hypothesis tend to assume that Protestants will be more economically ambitious than Catholics because of the different orientations of the theology and the polity of the two religious bodies.

The first work we will comment on is that of Mack, Murphy, and Yellin.[1] The three authors summarize the theory as follows: "The Catholic ethic propounded a culturally established emphasis on otherworldliness; the rationale for the performance of earthly tasks was otherworldly; reparation for sins and purification through humility. Luther and Calvin sanctified work; they made virtues of industry, thrift and self-denial. Wesley preached that the fruits of labor were the signs of salvation. The culmination of the Protestant Reformation, then, was

* Paper presented at the meetings of The American Catholic Sociological Society, August, 1963.

[1] R. W. Mack, R. J. Murphy, and S. Yellin, "The Protestant Ethic, Level of Aspiration and Social Mobility," *American Sociological Review*, 21 (June, 1956), pp. 295-300.

to give divine sanction to the drive to excel."

The three authors then point out that "the theoretical question which remains unanswered is whether the Catholic and Protestant faiths in contemporary American society exert a potent enough influence on behavior" to substantiate the operation of the Protestant Ethic in modern society. They, therefore, proceed to test the null hypothesis, "no significant differences will be found either in social mobility patterns or in aspiration level between samples of Protestant and Catholic Americans in several occupations." Using a non-random sample of 2,205 white males in three white-collar professions, the authors could find no evidence which would destroy their null hypothesis. In income goal, job orientation, intergenerational and intragenerational occupational mobility, there were virtually no differences between the two religious groups (out of 36 chi square tests, only two provided significant differences). They concluded that "whatever influence these two religious subcultures have upon their adherents in our society, so far as the Weberian thesis is concerned, is overridden by the general ethos." In short if there was any difference between Protestants and Catholics in their economic ambitions, the three authors could not find it.

We next turn to the work of Bernard Rosen[2] who was concerned with independence training of children and achievement and aspiration levels. He found that Greek, Jewish and Protestant children reached independence earlier and had higher achievement motivation than did French Canadian and Italian children. Rosen strove to explain this phenomenon in terms of ethnographic

material about the native countries of the groups in question. He does refer to Weber and to the "puritan ethic" as a partial explanation of the difference and also to the strong influence of the Catholic Church on Italians and French Canadians (an influence which will be most encouraging news to the Church at least in the case of the former group). He further combines the scores of the French and the Italian groups on some items to form a "Roman Catholic score" but does not contend that religion is the sole cause of the differences he observed. Before his findings could be adduced to confirm any version of the Protestant Ethic hypothesis they would have to be replicated among the German, Polish and Irish Catholic ethnic groups. Rosen is apparently very well aware of this because he has written recently of the need to control for ethnicity when comparing Protestants and Catholics and has affirmed that Catholic ethnic groups often tend to differ more among themselves than does the Catholic average differ from the Protestant average.[3] Thus even though Rosen found different child-rearing practices and different motivational levels between certain Catholic ethnic groups and Protestants, he does not attribute these differences exclusively to a "Protestant Ethic" but more to the national background of the specific groups.

Also concerned with the influence of ethnicity are Seymour Martin Lipset and Reinhard Bendix.[4] Reanalyzing data collected by Stouffer in his civil liberties study (1955) they discovered, "That there is little or no difference between

[2] Bernard C. Rosen, "Race, Ethnicity, and the Achievement Syndrome," *American Sociological Review*, 24 (February, 1959), pp. 47-60.

[3] In his review of Lenski's book in *American Sociological Review*, 27 (February, 1962), p. 111.

[4] Seymour Martin Lipset and Reinhard Bendix, *Social Mobility in Industrial Society*, Berkeley: University of California Press, 1960, pp. 48-57.

the occupational status achieved by third generation Catholics and Protestants, except that more Protestants than Catholics are farmers. On the other hand, among those with a recent immigrant background, Protestants are in higher positions than Catholics. Thus the occupational differences between the two religious groups disappear once the ethnic factor declines. . . . To put it another way, the Protestant immigrants come from ethnic groups with high status while the Catholics are members of ethnic groups with low status. The Protestants come from countries where educational attainment is high, the Catholics from poor countries in which the lower classes receive little education. Hence the difference between Catholic and Protestant immigrants may be related to ethnic rather than to religious factors, an interpretation that is given support by the fact that there is relatively little difference in the occupations of first and second generation German-American Catholics and Protestants."[5]

With the work of Lipset and Bendix being as well known as it is, one wonders why there was no attention paid to the ethnic factor in more recent works. It is also worth noting, though it does not pertain directly to our topic, that Lipset and Bendix report that no trace of an effect of the Protestant Ethic can be found in England, Germany, and the Netherlands and that therefore Weber was probably right when he said that the effects of the Protestant Ethnic on the Spirit of Capitalism had ceased to be important.[6]

RELIGION AND NEED ACHIEVEMENT

Now to McClelland's fascinating and ingenious book, *The Achieving Society*.[7]

Having reviewed the available materials on need-achievement in Germany and the United States, McClelland concludes: "(1) More traditional Catholics do appear to have some of the values and attitudes that would be associated with lower N Achievement and (2) Other groups of Catholics exist at least in the United States and Germany which have moved away from some of these traditional values toward the 'achievement ethic.' Catholicism, while is may have been associated with attitudes promoting low N Achievement, is today a complex congeries of subcultures, some of which are traditional and others modernist in outlook."[8] He asks, "Which are the truly 'representative' Catholics? Which for that matter are the truly representative Protestants? . . . Predominantly traditionalistic, devout Catholic groups like the French Canadian almost certainly have a lower average N Achievement level than the general average among the white Protestant population. Similarly, upwardly mobile, rapidly assimilating Catholics almost certainly have higher N Achievement than the general white Protestant population. But general over-all differences are very small and depend almost entirely on the exact composition of the two groups compared."[9] Whether the Irish will like the implication that they are not as devout as the French Canadians (or the Italians) is a question which we will, for the present, pass over.

McClelland apparently based his conclusions in part on the work of Veroff, Feld and Gurin which was published, however, after *The Achieving Society*. Like McClelland they were interested in need-achievement, but unlike all previ-

---

[5] *Ibid.*, pp. 50-51.
[6] *Ibid.*, p. 55. The reference is to Weber, *The Protestant Ethic*, pp. 181-182.

[7] David C. McClelland, *The Achieving Society*, New York: Van Nostrand, 1961.
[8] *Ibid.*, p. 361.
[9] *Ibid.*, p. 363.

ous investigators they had national sample data based on the TAT tests gathered in the Survey Research Center's study of American mental health.[10] Much to their surprise they discovered that while 48 per cent of the Protestants scored high in N Achievement, 57 per cent of the Catholics did (and 68 per cent of the Jews). They adduce several explanations for this difference, the most important of which has to do with the fact that they have a representative national sample. Some of their other explanations have to do with the size of Catholic families and the pressure on lower-class Catholics to support their families and the situation which Catholics find themselves in when they are isolated from the larger Catholic body in regions of the country which do not have many Catholics. Most of these speculations, while interesting, are based on rather small N's and in any case do not salvage the Protestant Ethic hypothesis. The three authors comment, "The hypothesis does seem to work simply only at the upper status positions of a well integrated, fairly prosperous economic structure in the established northeastern parts of the United States. Perhaps this region is more typical of the European structure Weber originally observed."[11] In any case, they conclude, "change in the tempo of capitalism in America, change in the Calvinist ideology in Protestant groups, change in direction of Catholic living in a highly mobile society, may all contribute to making the Protestant Ethic less generally discernible and outstanding as a way of life geared to achievement in modern America."[12] Indeed, so indiscernible as to be just about invisible.

Mack, Murphy, and Yellin; Lipset and Bendix; McClelland; and Veroff, Feld and Gurin—none of these works either as individual research projects, nor as a body of knowledge offers the slightest confirmation for the theory that Protestants are more achievement-oriented than Catholics in American society. It ought to be sufficient to report these findings and then forget about the whole business if we did not have two more recent works which claim to have saved the Protestant Ethic for contemporary society.

"WORLDLY SUCCESS"

The first such work is reported in an article by Mayer and Sharp[13] in the same issue of the *American Sociological Review* as the Veroff article. They begin with the usual description of Catholics: "The powerfully reinforced and traditional Roman Catholic Church tends to orient its members toward the hereafter; succesful performance in the market place and the acquisition of symbols of economic achievement are of relatively little importance as an indication of the Catholic's status after death." To test the hypothesis they have available a large number of respondents from the Detroit Area Survey—9,000 respondents from five years of surveys. It would appear that on the measures of achieved status—income, self employment, high status occupations, median education, and median school years completed, Catholics are behind some Protestant denominations and ahead of others. But, the authors argue, this is not a fair picture since one must control for the status with which a given group begins. We would then expect a control for parental

[10] Joseph Veroff, Sheila Feld, and Gerald Gurin, "Achievement, Motivation and Religious Background," *American Sociological Review*, 27 (April, 1962), pp. 205-217.
[11] *Ibid.*, p. 217.
[12] *Ibid.*

[13] Albert J. Mayer and Harry Sharp, "Religious Preference and Worldly Success," *American Sociological Review*, 27 (April, 1962), pp. 218-227.

24   SOCIOLOGICAL ANALYSIS

occupation, parental education, and parental income. But apparently the data available do not permit such a control and therefore the authors are forced to make up an index which will measure the "ascribed status" of each group. Such an index is based on the following indicators: per cent with no farm background, per cent born in cities of 50,000 or more, per cent not born in the rural south, per cent with native born fathers, per cent with fathers of northwest European stock, per cent born in the United States or Canada, per cent born in the Detroit area, per cent in Detroit before age 15. The reader will note that six of these nine indicators are functions of whether one was born in Detroit. Since each indicator counts equally in the weighted index (except the last two which count for one and a half), it follows inevitably that the mere fact of having the largest per cent born in Detroit will put a group near the very top of the ascribed status index *regardless of anything else in its background*— including the occupation, education, and income of its forebears. Since Catholics were most likely to be born in Detroit, their ascribed status is very high—only slightly behind the Episcopalians in fact. However, their achieved status is only medium so therefore their "net status" is very low indeed—just behind the white Baptists and just ahead of the Negro Baptists.

It is difficult to see how the authors can be satisfied with a status indicator which ranked Catholics equal to Episcopalians in ascribed status (and both behind Lutherans), which indicated that Catholics were strongly downwardly mobile—in the face of overwhelming evidence to the contrary—and which finally is based on indicators which are not only not independent, but which in great part are the function of one factor, a factor on which Catholics would be

certain to score high no matter what their real SES background was. Instead of putting all denominations on an "equal footing" as they claim to do, the authors weighted the dice against the Catholics —one hopes unintentionally. As a result their analysis, which is at variance with most similar research, is hardly very useful.

The Religious Factor

The final work we will discuss is Gerhard Lenski's *The Religious Factor*.[14] If one goes through these pages, inspecting the data but not looking at Lenski's interpretations, the following facts emerge: (1) Passage from the working class to the middle class is no more common among Protestants than among Catholics.[15] (2) There is virtually no difference in ambitions between Protestants and Catholics.[16] (3) Negative attitudes toward work are no more common among Catholics than among Protestants (though Catholics are seven per cent more likely to have "neutral" attitudes and seven per cent less likely to have "positive" attitude, N = 111 and 106).[17] (4) There is no difference between Protestants and Catholics in the percentage self-employed.[18] (5) There is only a small difference (four per cent) between Catholics and Protestants in disapproval of installment buying and Catholics have a slight lead (two per cent) in keeping budgets.[19] (6) Catholics and Protestants are equally likely to approve saving.[20] (7) Catholics are just as likely to see God as

14 Gerhard Lenski, *The Religious Factor*, Garden City: Doubleday, 1961. My comments will be reserved to the data contained on pages 76-102.

15 *Ibid.*, p. 79 (Table 8).

16 *Ibid.*, p. 81.

17 *Ibid.*, p. 85.

18 *Ibid.*, p. 92.

19 *Ibid.*, p. 97.

20 *Ibid.*, p. 99.

endorsing economic effort as Protestants.[21]

Despite these findings, Lenski nevertheless concludes, "With considerable regularity Jews and white Protestants have identified themselves with the individualistic, competitive patterns of thought and action linked with the middle class and historically associated with the Protestant Ethic . . . . By contrast Catholics and Negro Protestants have more often been associated with the collectivistic, security-oriented working class patterns of thought and action . . . ."[22]

We may well ask how he is able to draw such a conclusion. For example even though there is no difference in the attitude toward saving in the two religious groups, he notes that Protestants are more likely to check more than one reason for saving and hence he argues that they are more favorably disposed to saving—a contention which to say the least is somewhat thin. However, his basic technique is to submit the similarities to multivariate analysis which will make the similarities go away. Now there is nothing wrong with this except that we must remember that Lenski's N's are very small and the multivariate framework he uses differs from item to item. Anyone who has worked with IBM cards knows that if you have small differences to begin with and a small N, you can prove almost any theory if you make enough cross tabulations. There is enough sampling variation to make anything look significant after a while—even the first letter of a person's name. An example can be found in the treatment of the similarity in self-employment:[23] "Differences between white Protestants and Catholics were generally quite small,

until an effort was made to limit comparisons to persons raised in similar settings. [His italics] . . . When immigrant generation and region of birth were held constant, larger differences emerged. Among first and second generation immigrants, Protestants were twice as likely to be self employed as Catholics (15 per cent versus five per cent). Among third generation Americans raised outside the southern states, Protestants were three times as likely to be self-employed (12 per cent versus four per cent)." The N's on which these comparisons are based were 39, 71, 42, and 24—hardly enough to exclude sampling variation especially since we do not know how many other cross tabulations were attempted.

Another example: "Among college trained persons in middle class families where the head of the family earned $8,000 or more a year, 85 per cent of the Protestants (N = 20) perceived God as endorsing striving, but only 62 per cent of the Catholics (N = 13) shared this belief."[24]

One hesitates to be too severe on Lenski's use of small numbers, yet the worth of his book is often vitiated by it. There can be little objection to cross tabulations with small N's if the purpose is to explain away differences which appear in marginal tabulations. However, when one begins with 111 male Catholics and 116 male Protestants, it seems that detailed analysis of similarities displayed in marginal tabulations is extremely risky and can at best be reported with extreme caution, a caution which one does not always find in *The Religious Factor*. By not limiting himself to description and by attempting analysis with inadequate data, Lenski weakens the value of an otherwise important book. However, if we inspect his marginals, we can only conclude that they do not support the

[21] *Ibid.*, p. 95.
[22] *Ibid.*, p. 101.
[23] *Ibid.*, p. 92.

[24] *Ibid.*, p. 95.

Protestant Ethic hypothesis and that the more subtle ventures of the author into analysis must be judged as "not proven" until he collects more respondents—preferably from a national sample.[25]

RELIGION AND UPWARD MOBILITY

A word ought to be said about the work of Lenski's pupil, Weller. In his dissertation Weller reanalyzed more than 1,000 males from various phases the Detroit Area study and found that Protestants were more upwardly mobile in occupation (though not so much in income) than Catholics. The relevance of this study (though not its sophistication in the handling of data—which is unassailable) is vitiated, however, by a flaw in design. Weller argues that the relevant question is the extent to which urban industrialism has narrowed the differences between Protestant and Catholic and that therefore a valid comparison would necessitate comparing only those that were born and raised in a large urban center. Thus all respondents born out of the metropolitan area were excluded from analysis. In effect, this excluded foreign-born Catholics and southern-born white Protestants. There were far more Protestants excluded than Catholics since Catholics were 34 per cent of the original sample and 52 per cent of the final sample, while Protestants were 58 per cent of the original and 48 per cent of the final. There are two flaws in this procedure. First of all, the question is not whether urbanism makes Catholics equal in mobility to Protestants but whether they are unequal at all; those Protestants who are excluded are precisely those who would be most likely to pull down the Protestant mobility rate, so that the effect of urbanism on them would be to make them more mobile and thus less like Catholics who according to Weller's hypothesis are the ones who ought to be benefiting from urbanism. Thus urbanism is used to prevent Protestants who might have a lower rate than Catholics entering into the analysis. However, the Protestant Ethic, if it has any effect, ought to have brought to the city precisely those southern whites who are most upwardly mobile.

Secondly, this procedure says in effect that children of native-born white Protestants have the same psychological and physical opportunities as do the children of foreign-born Catholics and hence must be included in the same sample while foreign-born Catholics and southern whites are equally disabled by not being born in the big city and hence must be excluded. However, in reality the southern white probably could be more fairly compared with the second generation Catholic rather than the first, because both have the advantage of speaking the language as a native and the disadvantage of coming from a cultural system (the south and the ethnic ghetto) which is part American and yet not part of the main stream of American society. If southern whites are to be excluded from the analysis, then so ought second generation Catholics.

Clearly it is not certain what a fair comparison ought to be, but until we know more regarding cultural backgrounds and how they affect mobility, it is not reasonable to arbitrarily exclude some groups from analysis and not others, especially when the exclusion is certain to work in favor of the hypothesis.

---

[25] The only solid differences that Lenski can find between Protestants and Catholics which might fit the Protestant Ethic hypothesis is that Catholics are much more oriented toward trade unions. Whether this is the result of Catholic "otherworldly" orientation is doubtful however. Indeed it might be more plausibly argued that it flows from an entirely different element in Catholic belief—an element promoted by the various social encyclicals.

A NATIONAL SAMPLE STUDY

To conclude with a final investigation of the Protestant Ethic hypothesis, we will report two series of findings based on a large national sample of college graduates, studied by the National Opinion Research Center. As will be noted in Table 1, Catholics and Protestants show little difference on "security" items (slow sure progress and avoidance of pressure) while Catholics actually lead Protestants on the desire to make money.[26] (And Jews lead Catholics which make the Jews the most "Protestant" and the Protestants least "Protestant.") Further, Table 2 shows that while Catholics are more likely to choose large corporations as employers (which might fit the security quest), they also are more likely to choose small companies and equally

[26] Whether the desire to make money is a manifestation of the Protestant Ethic or not has been debated. That it is at least required (though not sufficient) does not seem to be doubted by Weber, c.f., *The Protestant Ethic and the Spirit of Capitalism*, New York, Scribners, 1958, p. 53.

likely to choose self-employment. The Protestant lead is in primary and secondary education. These findings do not disappear under a control for sex, SES (an index based on parental income, education and occupation) and size of hometown. For example, Protestant males from large cities with a high SES background still overchoose primary and secondary education as careers which is hardly in keeping with the Protestant Ethic hypothesis. Nor does the Catholic inclination to self-employment undergo any major change under a similar control apparatus.

THE HYPOTHESIS CONTINUES

Thus in eight separate studies done in the last decade we have nothing even remotely approaching a confirmation of the Protestant Ethic hypothesis. Yet it seems safe to say that the hypothesis is still very much alive and undamaged and will continue to generate research—and frustration—for some time to come. One might well wonder why.

At least one of the explanations seems

TABLE 1

OCCUPATIONAL VALUES AND RELIGION[*]

Occupational Value	Protestant	Catholic	Jewish	P-C	P-J	C-J
				Statistical Significance		
Making a lot of money	21	27	38	01	01	01
Chance to be creative	50	50	64	no	01	01
Helpful to others	68	61	60	01	01	no
Avoid high pressure	15	17	15	no	no	no
World of ideas	39	35	50	no	01	01
Freedom from supervision	18	17	21	no	no	no
Slow and sure progress	33	32	25	no	05	no
Leadership	34	40	40	01	no	no
Same area	4	8	9	05	05	no
New area	10	11	11	no	no	no
Work with people, not things	57	55	56	no	no	no
N =	2,007	833	272			

[*] Answer to question: "Which of these characteristics would be important to you in picking a career?"

28 SOCIOLOGICAL ANALYSIS

TABLE 2
RELIGION AND EXPECTED EMPLOYER

Expected Employer	Protestant	Catholic	Jewish
Large company	25	33	26
Small company	7	11	21
Family business	2	3	4
Self-employed	7	8	14
Research organization	7	7	10
College	12	12	11
Educational system	36	27	27
Other education	—	—	—
Federal government	14	14	15
State or local government	5	7	4
Hospital, church, or welfare	9	6	4
Other	3	3	3
Total	127	131	139
N =	2,007	833	272

to be that sociologists are often tempted to an oversimplified approach to history and especially to that form of socio-economic historical analysis which Max Weber used. Indeed if one reads Weber carefully, one cannot escape a feeling of helplessness in the face of the naïveté which thinks his analysis would predict that there would be a difference in upward mobility between contemporary Catholics and contemporary Protestants. Weber—and his theory—are much too sophisticated for that.

The clearest statement of his ideas on the precise nature of the relationship between the Protestant Ethic and the Spirit of Capitalism are to be found in the author's Introduction in the edition of *The Protestant Ethic* translated by Talcott Parsons.[27] This appeared as the first pages of a final edition of the work shortly before Weber died. The essay may well have been the last thing he ever wrote on *religions-sociologie*. In any event it represented a re-examination of *The Protestant Ethic* in light of the years of research (including the work on Eastern

religions) and controversy which had passed since its original publication.

The most important fact about this essay is that now Weber puts capitalistic rationalism and its Puritan ethic in perspective against the rationalizing tendency which had gone on in occidental society long before the Reformation. Only in the West, according to Weber, is there to be found a rational natural science, the rational historical scholarship begun by Thucydides, the rational harmonious music based on the harmonic third, the rational use of the Gothic vault as a means of distributing pressure and of roofing spaces of all forms, and the rational organization of legal and political systems.

Thus, argues Weber, it is not surprising that in the West there should develop a rationalized economic system complete with the separation of business from the household, the systematic keeping of books, the separation of corporate from personal property and, above all, the rational organization of the labor force.

What Weber seems to be saying in this Introduction is that capitalism represents

[27] *Ibid.*, pp. 13-31.

TIME FOR A MORATORIUM 29

an economic manifestation of a factor which has been at work in occidental society for a long time. Protestantism did not cause this factor to work in the economic order; rather Capitalism and Protestantism both are manifestations of the factor and hence related through a common antecedent cause. The similarity between the two should not be surprising. It was inevitable that certain forms of Protestant rationalism should be so congruent with certain forms of capitalistic enterprise that the Protestant Ethic would inevitably give considerable encouragement to capitalistic development and allow it to reach its logical conclusions.

One says, "What Weber seems to be saying" because he does not say this in so many words—he never says anything quite that clearly. However, it would appear that in this introductory essay—perhaps because of the controversy the earlier edition had stirred up—he was leaning over backward to insist that he did not claim that Calvinism had "caused" capitalism. He makes quite clear his position that capitalism can trace some of its causes to elements in the occidental spirit which long antedated the Reformation.

If one might hazard a comment, it seems that too much is made of the difference between the Calvinist ethic and the Medieval ethic as represented by the Scholastics. These latter were not nearly as otherworldly as some modern sociologists would have us believe. Certainly the dogmatic and moral conclusions of, let us say, Thomas Aquinas and John Calvin were different. But one wonders if the fact that the two of them were part of a common western intellectual tradition reaching back to Aristotle (at least) has not too often been overlooked. The confidence that one can understand reality and organize it in a rational manner did not enter the West-

ern intellectual tradition in the 16th Century. The rationalist spirit of Calvin is not really so different (save in its conclusions) from that of Peter Abelard. If one reads Calvin in the original Latin, one is struck by the fact that he is very much a product of the Schools. R. H. Tawney may be wrong when he announces in typically dramatic fashion that the last of the Schoolmen was Karl Marx. A good case might be made for the claim that the last of the Schoolmen was John Calvin.

Whatever is to be said for the assumption by some sociologists that there is (or ought to be) a one-to-one relationship between Protestantism and economic rationalism, it should be clear that such an asumption is a drastic oversimplification of the theorizing of Max Weber.

Nor does this assumption show much comprehension for what Weber intended with his ideal-typical methodology. In his view, it is impossible for a social scientist to develop concepts which fit a given kind of conduct or a given form of domination in all instances and all particulars. But since he must have such concepts, he must construct ideal types at the cost of simplifying the complexity of historical data and exaggerating their uniformities. Such ideal types are just as scientific in sociology as the model of economic man is in economics. They are not descriptions of reality but rather abstract models against which reality can be judged. They are not generalizations but conceptual tools. Thus Weber's theory of the relationship between Protestantism and Capitalism would not, in his terms, be taken as a generalization for describing exactly what happened in the early centuries of our era, but rather as a concept, a model against which the events of those years in all their complexity could be examined. Weber did not deny pluralistic causation; quite the contrary, it was because of the fact of pluralistic causation that he found it necessary to insist on "atomistic isolation" of the ideal type method. One could not proceed scientifically, in Weber's view, unless one isolated one conceptual tool and analyzed all its implications. To try to describe the totality of pluralistic causation would be to run the risk of becoming bogged down in an "unscientific" morass of conflicting trends and countertrends. One had to abstract, but abstraction did not at all mean that one was insisting on just a single cause. It was the very multiplicity of causes which made abstraction inevitable.

It is obvious then that much of the criticism of Weber's work is irrelevant, at least within the framework he set for himself. He insisted time and time again both in the *Archiv* (as Fischoff tells us[28]) and in his later works that there were a multiplicity of causes at work in the development of capitalism and a multiplicity of relationships possible between religion and society. Weber had no intention of saying that Protestantism "caused" capitalism. Indeed in the revision of the *Protestant Ethic* he does not even claim that it was one of the "causes." In Fischoff's happy expression Weber was merely interested in the "congruency" between the two.[29] From the ideal typical viewpoint this is the best that can be expected.

As Yinger observes: "We may say that the essay establishes the fact that on a rather 'low' level of causation, the Calvinist ethic is properly seen as *a* cause of the capitalist spirit. Whatever the cause of Calvinism's interpretation of worldly activity, it is clear that it sponsored even

in the beginning but especially after the middle of the 17th Century the activities of the new middle class. Although it did not create the new opportunities for trade and enterprise, it did furnish businessmen with an ideological weapon and a spiritual justification which were not unimportant in helping them come to power and in conditioning the nature of their activities."[30]

But it is one thing to say that Calvinism furnished spiritual justification to the middle class of the 17th Century and quite another to say that Protestantism makes for differential upward mobility patterns in the 20th. Such a conclusion may be correct (though as we pointed out, there is little data to suggest that it is) but it hardly follows logically from anything in Weber.

A second set of assumptions behind the survival of the Protestant Ethic theory represents an incredibly oversimplified approach to Catholicism. If sociologists tend to be naive about history, they are unbelievably uninformed about Catholic theology. Indeed anyone who knows something about Catholicism cannot help but writhe uncomfortably when he reads statements like, "The Catholic ethic propounded a culturally established emphasis on otherworldliness" or "The Powerfully reinforced and traditional Roman Catholic Church tends to orient its members toward the hereafter." The blunt fact is that most sociologists are uninformed about Catholicism and hence when they try to summarize what they take to be Catholic theology or practice end up with distorted cliches and caricatures which become truth if they are repeated often enough. (For examples of this that are especially disturbing, see the work of

[28] Ephraim Fischoff, "The Protestant Ethic and the Spirit of Capitalism: The History of a Controversy," *Social Research*, 2 (1944), pp. 61-77.
[29] *Ibid.*

[30] In the introduction to the Talcott Parsons translation of *The Protestant Ethic*, p. 9.

Reiss[31] on Catholic marriage teaching and the textbook of Hoult.[32]) This would not be so bad if the sociologists in question were aware of their ignorance, because then they would try to have someone check their statements for accuracy —as they would if they were dealing, let us say, with Islam. However it is to be very much feared that they do not even know that they are uninformed and hence continue to talk about Catholicism the way the proverbial blind men described the elephant.

David McClelland states, as though he had just discovered it, that Catholicism is a congeries of subcultures; but of course, one feels like saying, this ought to have been obvious to everyone. Within the Church of Rome there is and has been room for all kinds of divergent and paradoxical emphases to such an extent that simple statements about its position are extremely risky. But the prevailing mythology in social science has not yet adjusted to this fact; the massive monolith myth dies hard. So sociologists still think that if they find one manual that says, for example, that Catholics ought not to be interested in worldly gain, they have uncovered the official Catholic position as well as the practical orientation of most "good" Catholics. When someone tells them this is not so, they feel that the rules of the game have been violated.

On the particular subject of the Protestant Ethic, there can be no question that there is an eschatological, an otherwordly, a "Christ above culture" element in Catholic doctrine which would de-emphasize worldly striving. But there is also—and the sociologists in question seen quite unaware of it—an incarna-

tional, humanistic, "Christ in culture" orientation which would support worldly striving and which indeed springs from the same humanistic rationalism as does the Calvinistic ethic. Such doctrine can be found in Aquinas, in the ethics of Antonino, in the ascetics of Frances De-Sales, and in whole approach to life which has been characteristic of the followers of Ignatius of Loyola. Indeed the rationalization of human striving attributed to the Calvinists can with equal justice be attributed to the Jesuits. Ignatius of Loyola was the last of the Calvinists (or the first of the Methodists).

One hopes that the recent dramatic shifts of emphasis within the Catholic community will persuade sociologists that Catholicism is a very complex phenomenon and will lead them, when they are of a mind to summarize "the Catholic ethic" in two sentences, to have someone familiar with the Catholic tradition read over the sentences and perhaps suggest a qualifying clause or two.

A third inexplicable element of the mystery of the Protestant Ethic myth is the inattention to sociological information which goes against its assumptions. For example, one looks in vain in the writings on the subject for references to the survey materials on Catholic social class. It still seems to be an article of faith among sociologists that Catholics are concentrated in the lower economic classes—despite the survey materials made available by Bogue,[33] Lazerwitz,[34] and the Gaffin[35] studies. One sees fre-

---

[31] Ira L. Reiss, *Premarital Sexual Standards in America*, Glencoe: The Free Press, 1960, pp. 49-53.

[32] Thomas F. Hoult, *The Sociology of Religion*, New York: The Dryden Press, 1958; see especially pp. 230-234 and 282-285.

[33] Donald Bogue, *The Population of the United States*, Glencoe: The Free Press, 1957.

[34] Bernard Lazerwitz, "A Comparison of Major United States Religious Groups," *Journal of the American Statistical Association*, 56 (September, 1961), pp. 568-579.

[35] Originally reported in the *Catholic Digest*, but now available in John L. Thomas, *Religion in America*, Westminster, Maryland: Newman Press, 1963.

quent reference to Liston Pope's article,[36] but nothing at all about the Bogue-Feldman data which suggest a dramatic change in the social position of Catholics since the Pope article was published. Indeed the fact that the section on religion in Bogue's *Population of the United States*[37] is not mentioned in any of the literature I have discussed is indeed mystifying, especially since an inspection of the tables which Feldman prepared for this chapter would suggest that within educational and occupational levels, Catholics make more money than Protestants—a finding which casts doubt on the Protestant Ethic hypothesis before any more data is collected.

A very recent large sample (12,000 households) studied by NORC enables us to get a close look at the relative economic positions of Catholics and Protestants. The marginal percentages reveal practically no difference in income, occupation, or education between the two groups. However, it could be argued quite properly that the marginal comparisons are not altogether valid since they do not take into account the fact that Negroes and non-city dwellers pull down the Protestant averages. Thus a valid comparison would be between whites from cities. I would add that a valid comparison would also control for age so as to eliminate the effect of the more recent Catholic migration to this country. Table 3 presents the effect of these three controls. It is to be noted that the same percentage of Catholics and Protestants earn more than $8,000 (the limen of the upper middle class) in the age brackets under 40. Thus among younger white males from metropolitan areas there is no difference in

[36] Liston Pope, "Religion and The Class Structure," *Annals of the American Academy of Political and Social Science,* 256 (March, 1948), pp. 84-91.
[37] *Op. cit.,* pp. 688-710

TABLE 3
INCOME OF PROTESTANT AND CATHOLIC MALES IN METROPOLITAN AREAS BY AGE

Per Cent Over $8,000 a Year

Age	Protestant	Catholic
20–29	24 (559)	25 (350)
30–39	33 (621)	34 (498)
40–49	48 (567)	38 (439)
50–59	40 (438)	36 (265)
Over 60	26 (599)	20 (260)

earning power between Protestants and Catholics.

It might be argued that the dissimilarity in the older levels results from the fact that the Catholic ethic leads to a reduction in drive during the later years. A more plausible explanation would be that the high performance of younger Catholics is the result of a gradual fading of the immigration experience in the Catholic population. Table 4 suggests

TABLE 4
COLLEGE EDUCATION OF PROTESTANT AND CATHOLIC MALES IN METROPOLITAN AREAS BY AGE

Per Cent College Graduates

Age	Protestant	Catholic
20–29	17 (601)	15 (375)
30–39	21 (669)	15 (531)
40–49	15 (609)	10 (491)
50–59	12 (484)	7 (312)
Over 60	10 (613)	5 (290)

that such a social change has in fact occurred and that the improving economic performance of Catholics is connected with the higher educational achievement of the younger Catholic population. We might remark, by the way, that the equality in education and income achieved by young Catholics from big cities would indicate that they are more upwardly mobile than Protestants because their parents (as represented to some extent by the older levels of the tables) had less.

It is further incredible that some authors ignore the obvious ethnic differences within Catholic groups such as that between Irish and Polish Catholics. Yet American sociology has ignored ethnic groups within religions for two decades and there is no reason to think that this is going to change in the near future, despite the criticisms leveled at Lenski's work by Rosen[38] and Donovan.[39]

Yet one might ask why? I fear the answer has something do to with the need for "theory." Unfortunately there

[38] *Op. cit.*
[39] In a review of the Lenski volume in the *Catholic Reporter* of Kansas City.

is not much theory in the sociology of religion. Instead of plunging into research that will enable us to fashion new theory, we turn to the past and obtain antecedent theory from the few people who seem to have fashioned it for the sociology of religion—which is to say Max Weber, Emile Durkheim, and Ernst Troeltsch. Even when the categories which these men devised have ceased to be fruitful in research projects, we continue to use them because they are "theory" and "theory" we must have. Thus the Protestant Ethic hypothesis as fashioned by contemporary sociologists is preserved—so that sociologists of religion will have some theory. It is high time for a moratorium.

Reprinted from: *Journal for the Scientific Study of Religion* Vol. V, 1, 1965

THE RELIGIOUS BEHAVIOR
OF GRADUATE STUDENTS

ANDREW M. GREELEY
National Opinion Research Center, Chicago

Interest in the relationship between science and religion is perennial. Men have committed themselves to both of these activities with singular passion. For many centuries science and religion were so interlocked as to be practically identical. During more recent centuries they have been separated and quite frequently at war. In the last decades there have been considerable attempts at rapprochement —not, it must be confessed, altogether successful, yet the attempts are likely to continue. For, in the words of Alfred North Whitehead,

When we consider what religion is for mankind and what science is, it is no exaggeration to say that the future course of history depends upon the decision of this generation as to the relations between them. We have here the two strongest general forces (apart from the mere impulse of the various senses) which influence men, and they seem to be set one against the other— the force of religious intuitions and the force of our impulse to accurate observation and logical deduction.[1]

It is not the purpose of this note to attempt to set guidelines for the decision of which Whitehead speaks, but rather to focus on a somewhat narrower question: Is it possible to be a man of religion and a man of science simultaneously? Can one be a scientist and a believer? Whatever theoretical arguments can be made on either side of the question, it is clear that in the past the practical answer has been "no." Although no conclusive evidence is available, one has the general impression that the pre-eminent scientists as well as the vast majority of journeymen scientists could at best be described as agnostics. The upper reaches of academia in this country, while perhaps not explicitly anti-religious, have been secularist. Religion is sometimes treated as an amusing curiosity, but more frequently regarded as something quite unimportant. The academician who is active in a church is surely at no social or economic disadvantage, since academia is liberal enough to permit all kinds of deviants, but his colleagues are tempted to think of him as a fascinating peculiarity. Even though Roman Catholics are no longer warned by departmental chairmen that they will not be able to continue to submit to the discipline of their church and expect to be competent positive scientists, the vast majority of academicians are still not sure how one can make a commitment to some kind of "supernatural" belief system and still be committed to scientific investigations —unless one engages in a mammoth effort at compartmentalization.

Historically, the reasons for this situation are obvious enough. Science emerged as an independent discipline only by breaking with religion. Old battles around names like Galileo and

---

[1] Alfred North Whitehead, *Science and the Modern World*, p. 260, Macmillan, 1926.

THE RELIGIOUS BEHAVIOR OF GRADUATE STUDENTS 35

Darwin are not forgotten. Even though recent philosophers of science like Michael Polanyi have suggested that the "scientific method" is largely a myth, most scientists still have slightly guilty consciences if they admit that there is a form of human knowledge that transcends the empirical. And while Pere Teilhard and others have tried to demonstrate the profound religious implications of scientific theories such as evolution, it is no secret that Teilhard did not receive a warm welcome within his own church during his lifetime, even though he has now become something of a folk hero.

Although there is considerable discussion about the nature of the so-called "revival of interest in religion" during the years after World War II, it seems safe to say that organized religion now finds itself in much better repute in our republic than it was in the 1930's. So it becomes crucial to ask whether this "revival" is affecting academia to any notable extent—whether the battles of the past are being forgotten in a new age of harmony, or at least of more effective compartmentalization. NORC's ongoing study of June, 1961

college graduates furnishes an opportunity to begin an investigation of this question. It was assumed that the most significant group to watch in an investigation of the relationship between academia and religion would be those students who were enrolled in Ph. D. programs in the top twelve[2] graduate schools. It is from these schools that the elite academicians of the future will surely come. It is further in these schools where the secular academic ethos can be presumed to be the strongest. Finally, these are the schools where the most gifted of the college graduates are to be found. It seems safe to say that in past years these schools would be the ones where the greatest conflicts would arise between traditional religious beliefs and the canons of modern scholarship. If the religious revival has affected these schools, one might presume that its influence on academia may be something more than marginal.

---

[2] The schools were Harvard, Chicago, Columbia, California (Berkeley), Yale, Princeton, Cornell, Michigan, Illinois, Wisconsin, Cal Tech and MIT.

TABLE I

RELIGIOUS AFFILIATION OF ARTS AND
SCIENCES GRADUATE STUDENTS IN TOP 12 UNIVERSITIES

	Original Religion	Current Religion
Protestant	54	38
Catholic	17	16
Jewish	19	15
Other	5	6
None	5	25
Total	100	100

N = ... 908

36   THE RELIGIOUS BEHAVIOR OF GRADUATE STUDENTS

Table 1 presents the original and current religious affiliations of the 1961 graduates who are in Ph. D. programs in the top twelve graduate schools. The net apostacy rate is 20 per cent, most of it being from the Protestant group, with the Jewish loss being small and the Catholic loss practically non-existent. Three-quarters of the graduate students still have a religious affiliation in their first year of graduate school; although this is a smaller proportion than that discovered in most national population samples, it hardly indicates that re-ligion is being routed on the graduate school campus.[3]

[3] There is a possibility that church affiliation will decline through the years of graduate school, but a previous NORC study suggests that there is rather a u-curve phenomenon at these schools with a decline in religious activity during the middle years of graduate school and an increase during the final years. There is also considerable reason to believe that religious apostacy correlates with factors at work before a person enters college.

TABLE II

CHURCH ATTENDANCE OF GRADUATE
STUDENTS BY RELIGION (ORIGINAL RELIGION)

	Protestant	Catholic	Jewish
Weekly	21	78	1
2 or 3 a month	14	4	3
Monthly	12	5	7
2 or 3 a year	26	9	38
Yearly	12	0	14
Never	15	4	38
	100	100	100
	(510)	(158)	(180)

Mere church affiliation does not make a person "religious." In Table 2 we investigate the level of church attendance among the arts and science Ph. D. students in the top twelve schools. Approximately one-fourth of all the students are weekly churchgoers with Catholics overrepresented in the active participants and Jews underrepresented. It is interesting to note that for Catholics and Protestants the rate of weekly church going is not substantially different from that reported for Catholics and Protestants in the national population (and indeed higher for Catholics).[4] Thus a Catholic or a Protestant in the top arts and science graduate schools is no less likely to go to church on Sunday than is a coreligionist in the general population. If there is a conflict between science and religion in these young people, it is not obvious in their church attendance.[5]

[4] The following table is based on the Gaffin-

Thomas National Study and NORC data on June, 1961 graduates. It is to be noted that only among Protestants are the students in the top twelve schools appreciably different from all graduates.

[5] While we are not at liberty to report data for individual schools, it should be noted that the variation in church attendance among

THE RELIGIOUS BEHAVIOR OF GRADUATE STUDENTS   37

TABLE III

CHURCH ATTENDANCE BY RELIGION BY FIELD

	Protestant		Catholic		Jewish	
	Sci	A-L	Sci	A-L	Sci	A-L
Weekly	16	24	89	68	1	1
2 or 3 a month	17	13	-	7	4	3
Monthly	14	11	2	7	7	8
2 or 3 a year	26	25	5	13	30	41
Yearly	16	10	-	-	12	17
Never	11	17	5	4	45	31
	100	100	100	100	100	100
	(198)	(310)	(64)	(94)	(73)	(107)

One might suspect that the graduate students in the "hard" sciences would be the most likely to have problems between their religion and their science. Table 3 indicates that no such clear relationship exists across the three major religious groups. The Catholics in the "hard" sciences (physical science and biological science) are more likely to be weekly churchgoers than Catholics in the arts and letters, while the reverse is true for Protestants. The Jews in the "hard" sciences are also the most likely to be among those who never attend church services. The reason for the difference among the Catholics may simply be sampling variation or may have to do with the fact that Catholicism has made its peace with Galileo and Darwin but not yet with Kant, Freud, and Compte.

The picture that emerges from these first three tables is that of a graduate student population of which one-fourth belong to no denomination and one-fourth go to church every week. If there is a conflict in the minds of these young people between scholarship and religion, it would be presumed that those who are religious would be the most likely to have problems with the academic environment in which they are studying and that therefore they would score lower on academic values, lower on plans for careers in academia, lower on self-rating as intellectuals, and higher on dissatisfaction with the schools which, by hypothesis, should stand for values they cannot reconcile with their religious faith.

Table 4 shows that while there is some slight support for such expectations, the "religious" students (Catholics who go to church every week, Protestants who go two or three times a month and Jews who go once a month)[6] are less likely to plan an academic career (73 per cent vs. 79 per cent) and less likely to choose "working in the world of ideas" as a career value (78 per cent to 89 per cent). However, there is no difference in the choice of "opportunity to be original and creative" and in the self-conception as "intel-

the twelve schools is not great. Hence the findings reported in this note are not a function of very high rates of churchgoing at a few schools.

[6] This is a rather rigorous definition of the "religious" student; however it was felt that the "most religious" third were the crucial group in this section of the analysis.

38   THE RELIGIOUS BEHAVIOR OF GRADUATE STUDENTS

TABLE IV

RELIGION AND ATTITUDES TOWARDS ACADEMIA

	Religious* (320)	Non- Religious (564)
Occupational Values		
Original and Creative	85	86
World of Ideas	78	89
College or University		
as Career Employer	73	79
Rating School as "Excellent" in		
Research Facilities	72	63
Curriculum	43	43
Students	38	38
Faculty	77	78
Self Description		
"Intellectual	45	47
"Happy"	24	17
"Liberal"	32	37
Average Number of Worries	3.0	3.5
Per cent GPA "A"	10.0	8.0

* Catholics going to church weekly, Protestants two or three times a month, Jews once a month. (Those whose original religion was "other" are excluded. N = 24)

lectual" nor is there any difference in their evaluations of the schools. Further, the religious students show no particular signs of emotional strain in their position: They are more likely to describe themselves as happy and have less worries than their non-religious counterparts. There is only a very slight difference in the proportion reporting an "A" average.

On two of the items, therefore, there is a negative correlation between religion and academia, but the strength of the correlation is rather weak and does not establish any major conflict for the vast majority of religious students.

To some considerable extent the existence of an apparent religious revival among the potential members of Upper Academia may be related to the appearance on the campuses of large numbers of Catholic graduate students, apparently for the first time in the history of American higher education. This is not to argue that Catholics have increased the level of Church attendance among other students; it is quite possible, however, that the religious participation levels for Jews and Protestants are about what they always were but that infusion of many Catholics has substantially affected the proportion of future academicians who are also religious. This shift may well represent the beginning of a major change in the composition of American academia, if churchgoing Catholics should in the future hold as many major university appointments as Jews.

Table 5 indicates that the churchgoing Catholics are not very different from the other graduate students in their values and career plans. They

THE RELIGIOUS BEHAVIOR OF GRADUATE STUDENTS   39

TABLE V

RELIGIOUS CATHOLICS AND ATTITUDES TOWARDS ACADEMIA

(N = 121)

Values	
Original and Creative	86
World of Ideas	68
College or University Career	79
Self Description	
"Intellectual"	54
"Happy"	24
"Liberal"	47
Per cent GPA "A"	8

are more likely to consider themselves as intellectuals than nonreligious of all faiths, more likely to describe themselves as politically liberal, just as likely to plan academic careers, just as likely to value originality and creativity, and less likely to value "working in a world of ideas." The last fact is the only evidence that there is any conflict between the ideals of academia and fervent Roman Catholicism, yet it is rather slender evidence to sustain a theory which has stood unchallenged for so many years. The performance of the Catholics is especially surprising because these young people must accept not only the doctrines of their church, substantially unaffected by modernism, but also the disciplinary regulations of Canon Law and an ethical system which, while it may be liberal on matters such as smoking, drinking and card playing, is most rigorous in its sexual morality.

The rather sketchy data reported in this note hardly suffice to do more than open up for further discussion the question of a possible religious revival[7] on the graduate school campus. The basic question at issue would have to

do with how the traditional conflict between science and religion has been resolved by the young people being studied. One could postulate two ideal type solutions—compartmentalization and resolution. A student could refuse to admit the possibility of conflict or ignore its existence after he had recognized it. Or he could face the problems involved and work out some kind of resolution which satisfactorily harmonizes his religion and his scholarship. In all probability most students have combined both methods, though there is a chance that large numbers of them are not even aware that a conflict exists and that there has been nothing in their class work which would make them aware of it. Thus the war between science and religion ends not with a bang, not with a whimper, but with a polite refusal even to mention the possibility of the problem.

In addition, we must learn about the religious orthodoxy of the graduate students: It is not clear from our tables the extent to which their religious practice is merely conformity to community pressures or to ingrained customs and to what extent it represents some kind of decisive existential commitment to a system of beliefs and values. In the case of the Catholic students we will want to know more about how they

---

[7] Of course there is far more to being "religious" than going to church. However, the point of this paper is that one would not have expected even the church attendance.

40   THE RELIGIOUS BEHAVIOR OF GRADUATE STUDENTS

reconcile the claim of their church to be a custodian and promulgator of revealed truth with the demands for unimpeded scientific research. It would also be of interest to know in greater detail why the Jewish students are less able to reconcile religion and scholarship than members of the other two religions. We will finally ask whether religion leads them to any differential attitudes toward their personal life which might affect their scientific productivity as the years go on.

SUMMARY

Even though one-quarter of the June, 1961 graduates who were in Ph. D. programs in the top twelve schools a year after their graduation did not list any religious affiliation, another one-quarter were weekly church attenders and better than half went to church at least every month. As far as weekly church attendance, Protestant and Catholic graduate students were little different from their coreligionists in the larger society. Although there were some slight negative correlations between religiosity and academic values, there was no major evidence that the students perceived any serious conflict.

PER CENT REPORTING WEEKLY CHURCH ATTENDANCE

	Protestant	Catholic	Jewish
National . . .	25	62	12
All Graduates	30	81	4
Top 12 Schools	21	78	1

Reprinted from AMERICAN SOCIOLOGICAL REVIEW, Vol. 31, No. 3, June, 1966

PAROCHIAL SCHOOL ORIGINS AND EDUCATIONAL ACHIEVEMENT

SEYMOUR WARKOV AND ANDREW M. GREELEY

National Opinion Research Center
University of Chicago

Data from the Post-Censal Survey of Scientific and Technical Personnel are used to explore the relationship between educational attainment beyond the high school level and exposure to public, parochial and other private elementary and high school education. Among scientists and engineers, 25–54, exposure to parochial schools is related to lower attainment of advanced academic levels. However, the conditional probabilities of moving on to the next academic level, given completion of the previous stage, suggest greater similarity of attainment for those from different types of school. Because the similarity is greatest for respondents 45–54, it is suggested that scientists and engineers with parochial school backgrounds may take longer to secure their highest academic degrees. For age group 20–24, parochial school training among 1960 engineers and scientists makes advancement no less likely than other school backgrounds. These findings support the hypothesis that the earlier lack of scientific achievement among Catholics reflected economic rather than religious factors.

THIS research note contributes to the current debate [1] on the effects of attendance at parochial elementary or high schools by reporting an investigation of subsequent educational advancement among American scientists and engineers. Data were taken from the Post-Censal Survey of Scientific and Technical Manpower, a sample survey employing mail questionnaires which secured usable responses from some 50,000 persons in 45 scientific, engineering, technical and other professional occupations in 1960.[2] To determine whether graduating col-

[1] For example, Gerhard Lenski, *The Religious Factor,* New York: Doubleday, 1961; Thomas F. O'Dea, *American Catholic Dilemma,* New York: Sheed and Ward, 1958; John Tracy Ellis, "American Catholics and the Intellectual Life," *Thought,* Autumn 1955; Peter H. Rossi, and Andrew M. Greeley, "The Impact of the Roman Catholic Denominational School," *The School Review,* 72 (1964), pp. 34–51; John D. Donovan, *Academic Man in Catholic Colleges,* New York: Sheed and Ward, 1964.

[2] The scope of the survey is described in Seymour Warkov, "Census-Related Studies of Scientific and Technical Personnel," in National Science Foundation (NSF 62–22), *Scientific Manpower, 1961,* Washington, D.C., U.S. Government Printing Office, 1961, pp. 21–24. Some preliminary results for two occupations are given in Warkov, "Physi-

ORIGINS AND EDUCATIONAL ACHIEVEMENT   407

lege seniors who had attended Catholic high schools go on for advanced study in the sciences and engineering as frequently as their non-parochial counterparts, data were also taken from the National Opinion Research Center's longitudinal survey of career choice.[3]

TYPES OF SCHOOLING AND SUBSEQUENT EDUCATIONAL ATTAINMENT

The following item in the Post-Censal Survey questionnaire permitted us to investigate the extent to which persons of varied high school experience differ in their educational attainment.

Which of the following types of elementary and high schools did you attend? (Check as many as apply)
      Public
      Parochial
      Other Private

Tabulations are presently available for five broad occupational groups: Engineers, Physical Scientists, Biological Scientists, Mathematicians and Social Scientists.[4] Between 90

and 95 per cent of persons in these occupational groups attended a public elementary or secondary school and from 12 to 15 per cent attended a parochial school at some time during their childhood or adolescence (except for the biological scientists, of whom only 8 per cent reported attending this type of school).[5] Although no information on religious origins or present religious affiliation was secured in this study, there is evidence that all but a small minority of the parochial-school attenders were in Catholic elementary or high schools.[6] The former "Other Private" school students were more varied. Twelve per cent of the social scientists reported this type of schooling, and 10 per cent of the mathematicians, while the physical and biological scientists and the engineers were least likely to have gone to private school (7 to 8 per cent).

Now, were the scientists and engineers who had ever attended a parochial school as likely to hold the bachelor's degree, enter graduate school, receive the master's or take the doctorate as respondents who reported any public or private schooling? The tabulations now available do not allow us to distinguish those with mixed educational experience from those whose early education was entirely public or entirely parochial, but we can compare those who had *any* of one type of exposure with others who had any of another type.

Intra-occupation group comparisons (not shown) [7] indicated that respondents in engineering, physical science, life science or mathematics who had attended a *private* ele-

---

cists and Mathematicians in the Post-Censal Survey of Scientific and Technical Personnel," *1963 Proceedings of the Social Statistics Section of the American Statistical Association*, pp. 163–179. For the first report of this survey, see Seymour Warkov, *America's 1960 Scientists and Engineers*, forthcoming, and Seymour Warkov and John F. Marsh, *The Education and Training of America's Scientists and Engineers*, Chicago: National Opinion Research Center, Report No. 104, 1965 (litho.).

The field work, sampling procedures and take rates per occupation are described in Stanley Greene and David Kaplan, "The Post Censal Study— Data Collection, Processing and Tabulating," *1963 Proceedings of the Social Statistics Section of the American Statistical Association*, pp. 154–162.

[3] See James A. Davis, *Great Aspirations*, Chicago: National Opinion Research Center, Report No. 90, 1963 (litho); and Norman Miller, *One Year After Commencement*, Chicago: National Opinion Research Center, Report No. 93, 1963 (litho).

[4] In preparing tabulations for this research, we asked the Bureau of the Census to group the detailed occupations given by the three-digit occupation code as follows:

Engineers: Professors and Instructors of Engineering, Civil Engineers, Electrical Engineers, Mechanical Engineers, Industrial Engineers and Other Engineers.

Physical Scientists: Profs. and Instr. Physics, Chemistry, Geology and Other Physical Sciences, Physical Scientists.

Biological Scientists: Profs. and Instr. Biological

Sciences, Biological Scientists, Profs. and Instr. Agricultural Sciences, Agricultural Scientists.

Mathematicians: Profs. and Instr. Mathematics, Profs. and Instr. Statistics, Statisticians, Actuaries.

Social Scientists: Psychologists, Profs. and Instr. Psychology, Economists, Profs. and Instr. Economics, Profs. and Instr. Social Sciences, Misc. Social Scientists.

[5] See Warkov and Marsh, *op. cit.*, Ch. 3.

[6] This assumption is supported by a recent national survey conducted at the National Opinion Research Center. Among a Sample of 7,901 children aged 7–16, 13.7 per cent were enrolled at "parochial-religious" school and among the 1,084 children enrolled at a "parochial-religious" school, 85.8 per cent were Catholic. See John W. C. Johnstone, *Volunteers for Learning*, Chicago: NORC Report No. 89, 1963.

[7] See Warkov and Marsh, *op. cit.*

mentary or high school were at an advantage in subsequent educational attainment. At the same time, *parochial* school experience was systematically related to under-representation in the physical, life, and social sciences and in mathematics. Perhaps attendance at "other private" schools reflects higher socio-economic standing, or perhaps it indicates superior scholastic ability or stronger curricular offerings. On the other hand, Catholic parochial schools allegedly transmit values that deflect their students from scientific and intellectual pursuits. But evidence is available that Catholic education has been changing in such a way as to promote the disappearance of religiously-based occupational differentiation.[8] If this is true, then *younger* engineers and scientists who had attended parochial elementary or secondary school should approximate their non-parochial peers in educational achievement, and to a greater extent than older engineers and scientists.

Within the five occupational groups, the three age groups comprising the bulk of the sample were compared on their educational attainment as of 1960, taking into account the nature of their elementary and secondary school experiences. Comparisons were made on rates of (1) completion of the bachelor's program, (2) entry to graduate school, (3) receipt of the master's degree, and (4) receipt of the doctorate. (Too few of the engineers had doctorates to permit comparisons at that level of attainment.) Of the total of 57 possible comparisons, 52 indicate that persons with public elementary or high school experience attain higher levels of subsequent education than their parochial school counterparts. Thus, the evidence is overwhelming in support of the proposition that exposure to parochial schools at the elementary or high school level inhibited the frequency with which 1960 incumbents of scientific and engineering occupations had attained advanced levels of academic proficiency. There is little indication, if any, that the younger (i.e., the 25–34 age group) scientists and engineers with any parochial school experience were more likely to catch up with their non-parochial fellows.

A related proposition, not tested by these cumulative percentage distributions, is that even when parochial-school scientists and engineers complete the bachelor's program, they do not enter graduate school as frequently as the others; when in graduate school, they are less likely to complete the master's program; and even when they take the intermediate graduate degree, they have lower rates of completion of the doctorate. In other words, motivation to scale the academic heights is unequally distributed, and those who were exposed to parochial schools are at a disadvantage. We subjected this argument to empirical test by transforming the data into conditional probabilities. That is, assuming that one cannot advance to the next level of education without completing the previous level, cumulative percentage distributions can be expressed as conditional probabilities. For example, master's recipients are treated not as a proportion of all scientists or engineers but as a proportion of those who entered graduate school.[9]

We will spare the reader a detailed exposition of the contents of Table 1.[10] It is evident, though, that these tables show a different pattern of achievement. In the previous comparisons based on cumulative percentages, public-school attenders consistently outranked their parochial-school counterparts. Here, at every level of achievement within each occupation group, and in each age group, the parochial-school attenders equalled or outranked public school attenders in at least one comparison. More important, the *older* the age group the greater the probability that parochial-school scientists and engineers equal or outrank those with public-school backgrounds.

In the 25–34 age group, parochial school engineers and scientists equal or outdo those from public school in only three of 15 possible comparisons; at the next age level, six

[8] Andrew Greeley, *Religion and Career,* New York: Sheed and Ward, 1963.

[9] For an example of the application of conditional probabilities to data on educational attainment, see James A. Davis, "Higher Education: Selection and Opportunity," *The School Review,* 71 (1963), pp. 249–265.

[10] In preparing tabulations, the Bureau of the Census weighted and expanded each occupation sample up to its 1960 universe representation in the experienced civilian labor force. We wish to acknowledge the assistance of Sanford Abrams in preparing the tables for this paper.

ORIGINS AND EDUCATIONAL ACHIEVEMENT   409

TABLE 1. CONDITIONAL PROBABILITIES FOR ATTAINING THE HIGHEST ACADEMIC DEGREE, BY AGE GROUP AND EXPOSURE TO PRIVATE, PUBLIC AND PAROCHIAL ELEMENTARY AND SECONDARY SCHOOLS

Age	Type of School	Total Number of Persons	Probability of Having Attained the Next Highest Academic Degree, Given the Previous Level		
			Entered Graduate School	Master's Degree	Doctorate
Engineering					
25–34					
	Private	17,753	.66	.35	.13
	Public	249,064	.47	.28	.11
	Parochial	42,569	.47	.23	.00
35–44					
	Private	15,350	.58	.34	.00
	Public	266,543	.45	.32	.13
	Parochial	37,666	.46	.26	.17
45–54					
	Private	11,001	.59	.33	.13
	Public	136,375	.48	.32	.17
	Parochial	16,118	.51	.28	.00
Physical Scientists					
25–34					
	Private	3,851	.76	.60	.51
	Public	41,766	.70	.54	.45
	Parochial	7,497	.68	.53	.36
35–44					
	Private	2,922	.79	.72	.67
	Public	38,890	.71	.64	.54
	Parochial	5,674	.63	.64	.46
45–54					
	Private	1,758	.80	.66	.54
	Public	18,697	.71	.67	.48
	Parochial	1,971	.73	.55	.33
Biological Scientists					
25–34					
	Private	639	.82	.66	.59
	Public	8,832	.79	.72	.45
	Parochial	980	.73	.64	.26
35–44					
	Private	688	.89	.85	.61
	Public	9,815	.83	.83	.61
	Parochial	681	.87	.75	.27
45–54					
	Private	404	.91	.79	.68
	Public	5,053	.83	.82	.58
	Parochial	402	.89	.69	.58
Mathematicians					
25–34					
	Private	1,292	.84	.60	.44
	Public	10,436	.73	.55	.25
	Parochial	2,282	.73	.49	.95
35–44					
	Private	777	.82	.65	.20
	Public	8,411	.77	.76	.34
	Parochial	1,344	.76	.82	.31
45–54					
	Private	571	.89	.82	.34
	Public	5,614	.77	.73	.46
	Parochial	590	.98	.76	.34

410 AMERICAN SOCIOLOGICAL REVIEW

TABLE 1. CONDITIONAL PROBABILITIES FOR ATTAINING THE HIGHEST ACADEMIC DEGREE, BY AGE GROUP AND EXPOSURE TO PRIVATE, PUBLIC AND PAROCHIAL ELEMENTARY AND SECONDARY SCHOOLS—*Cont.*

Age	Type of School	Total Number of Persons	Probability of Having Attained the Next Highest Academic Degree, Given the Previous Level		
			Entered Graduate School	Master's Degree	Doctorate
Social Scientists					
25–34					
	Private	1,787	.85	.91	.36
	Public	16,189	.87	.73	.38
	Parochial	2,506	.87	.72	.26
35–44					
	Private	2,037	.98	.93	.54
	Public	18,923	.92	.90	.52
	Parochial	2,210	.84	.91	.46
45–54					
	Private	1,598	.90	.91	.54
	Public	12,731	.92	.88	.54
	Parochial	1,205	.95	.88	.51

comparisons favor parochial school attenders (including ties). *In the oldest group, ages 45–54, parochial school engineers and scientists equal or outrank their public school counterparts in eight of 15 possible comparisons.* Among the several possible interpretations of this finding a plausible one is that ultimately the 1960 scientists and engineers with parochial school backgrounds do as well as those from public elementary or high schools, *but they take longer to secure their highest academic degrees.* Information on the *date* of each degree was secured so that later in the analysis we shall be able to validate this interpretation empirically.

Analyzing data from the NORC longitudinal study of career choice, Greeley showed that Catholics who received bachelor's degrees in June, 1961, at American colleges of arts and science, including those who attended parochial high schools, did not differ from Protestants in the extent to which their long-run career aspirations were directed toward the scientific occupations.[11] It is possible that this phenomenon is so recent that data on scientists and engineers no younger than 25 in 1960 would not reflect it. For this reason, we now consider the scientists and engineers in the 20–24 age group.

Table 2 shows that the pattern of academic attainment reflected in the cumulative percentage distributions for the three older age groups no longer prevails: events have taken a new turn. Parochial school training among 1960 engineers and scientists in the age group 20–24, makes advancement no less likely than does a public elementary or high school background. The data even suggest that parochial school origins may be advantageous. Considering all three types of academic background in each of the five occupation groups, private-school attenders generally maintain their lead in terms of entry to graduate school and completion of the master's degree. (It is, of course, too soon for this age group to have completed the doctorate save in very exceptional cases.) Comparisons between the *parochial-* and *public-*school engineers and scientists show a striking change, however. Although the correlation between type of early academic background and rank order on rates of academic attainment was almost perfect, in the three *older* groups, parochial-school attendance in this younger group was related to higher rates of completion of the bachelor's program, in every occupational group except social science. At the entry-to-graduate-school level, engineers, physical scientists and biological scientists with parochial school backgrounds outranked those with public school experience, while at the next level, completion of the master's degree, public and parochial origins each yielded the higher rate of completion in two occupation groups, being tied in the fifth.

[11] *Op. cit.*

Table 2 also shows the conditional probability of moving on to the next academic level, given completion of the previous stage. In seven of the ten comparisons, private-school attenders in the 20–24 age group had higher rates of attainment than those from public or parochial schools, as in the older groups. But in comparisons between public and parochial attendance, those from parochial schools had higher rates of completion in six cases, and there was one tie.

These data suggest, then, that in the past few years the influence of attendance at parochial elementary or high schools on subsequent educational attainment has changed. If one were to rely solely on the Post-Censal Survey, one could argue that it is precisely *because* they are parochial-school Catholics that these 20–24 year-olds in the 1960 experienced civilian labor force show higher rates of educational attainment: their non-

parochial school counterparts were *not* in the 1960 experienced civilian labor force, but were still enrolled for full-time graduate study and working toward their doctorates. To evaluate this interpretation, let us turn to the NORC survey of career choice, a panel study that tells us whether those in a national sample of 1961 college graduates who had graduated from Catholic parochial high schools dropped out of school more frequently than other students.

PAROCHIAL SCHOOLING, ADVANCED STUDY AND CAREER PLANS

In the sample of 1961 college graduates, those planning arts and science or engineering careers who had graduated from Catholic parochial high schools were actually *more* likely to enroll in graduate school during the year after graduation than those who had

TABLE 2. CUMULATIVE PERCENTAGES AND CONDITIONAL PROBABILITIES FOR ATTAINING THE HIGHEST ACADEMIC DEGREE FOR PERSONS IN THE AGE GROUP 20–24, BY OCCUPATION GROUP AND EXPOSURE TO PRIVATE, PUBLIC AND PAROCHIAL ELEMENTARY AND SECONDARY SCHOOLS

Occupation Group	Type of School	Total— All Types of Schools Number of Persons	Per cent having attained at least to the ... Bachelor's Degree	Entry to Graduate School	Masters Degree	Probability of having attained the next highest academic degree, given the previous level Entered Graduate School	Masters Degree
ENGINEERING							
	Private	1,990	.66	.49	.07	.74	.14
	Public	38,838	.51	.23	.01	.45	.04
	Parochial	9,336	.72	.39	.02	.54	.05
PHYSICAL SCIENCES							
	Private	671	.58	.44	.05	.76	.11
	Public	9,008	.64	.33	.03	.52	.09
	Parochial	2,300	.73	.39	.04	.53	.10
BIOLOGICAL SCIENCES							
	Private	117	.74	.54	.06	.73	.11
	Public	2,363	.60	.37	.06	.62	.16
	Parochial	382	.67	.45	.01	.67	.16
MATHEMATICS							
	Private	348	.74	.38	*	.51	*
	Public	3,817	.54	.35	.05	.65	.14
	Parochial	869	.66	.28	*	.42	*
SOCIAL SCIENCES							
	Private	470	.53	.48	.26	.91	.54
	Public	2,365	.65	.51	.13	.78	.25
	Parochial	819	.62	.37	.13	.60	.35

* Indicates no cases.

412   AMERICAN SOCIOLOGICAL REVIEW

TABLE 3. PERCENTAGE WHO ATTENDED GRADUATE
SCHOOL THE YEAR AFTER GRADUATION, AMONG
THOSE PLANNING ARTS AND SCIENCE OR ENGINEER-
ING CAREERS: 1961 GRADUATES

Parochial High School	All Other High Schools
56 (85)	46 (700)

attended other high schools (Table 3). This
finding is not especially surprising in itself,
since the Catholic high schools are concentrated in the northeastern cities where graduate school attendance is more likely than in
other parts of the country. It does, however,
represent an apparent reversal of trends
reported in previous literature as well as in
the preceding paragraphs of this note. Graduates of Catholic high schools have evi-
dently begun to take advantage of the
favorable academic opportunities in their immediate environment. And these parochial
high school graduates are as likely as the
others to have enrolled in the top 12 graduate schools (Table 4).[12]

TABLE 4. PERCENTAGE WHO ATTENDED THE TOP 12
GRADUATE SCHOOLS, AMONG THOSE WHO ATTENDED
GRADUATE SCHOOL THE YEAR AFTER GRADUATION:
1961 GRADUATES

Parochial High School	All Other High Schools
23 (47)	19 (316)

Of course, it is too early to tell whether
those students will continue toward the Ph.D
in comparable proportions, but at least their
announced intentions give no indication that
they will not. Proportionately more of them
expect higher academic degrees than their
contemporaries from other high schools
(Table 5). If they fulfill these intentions,
they will be the harbingers of a major social
change.

CONCLUDING COMMENTS

A substantial literature supports the proposition that American Catholics have not
contributed to the scientific and intellectual
life of the country in proportion to their
numbers in the population. The usual explanation for this phenomenon is that the

[12] These are the top ten graduate schools as
ranked in the Keniston Study, plus M.I.T. and
Cal. Tech.

cultural values and social organization of
American Catholics impede intellectual and
scientific achievement. The tight hierarchical
authority of the Church, as well as its emphasis on the present life as a preparation
for the hereafter encourages the attitude that
intellectual pursuits are not very important
and may even be dangerous.

Such an explanation seems plausible
enough, but it has never been tested empirically. Nor does it answer a prior question:
why did the American Church—clergy and
laity—adopt an organization and a set of
values which tended to deny the validity of
intellectual achievement? Our answer to this
question may be very prosaic, but it explains

TABLE 5. HIGHER ACADEMIC DEGREES EXPECTED,
AMONG 1961 GRADUATES PLANNING ARTS AND
SCIENCE OR ENGINEERING DEGREES

	Next Degree Expected		Highest Degree Expected	
	Parochial High School	Other High School	Parochial High School	Other High School
	%	%	%	%
None beyond Bachelor's	7	20	8	19
Professional	7	16	4	11
Master's	77	56	44	30
Doctorate	9	8	44	41
Total	100	100	100	100
(N)	(85)	(700)	(85)	(700)

the previous underrepresentation of Catholics
among scientists as well as the apparent
change recorded here. American Catholics
were too poor, and had immigrated too recently, to be concerned with much beyond
economic survival, and the Church was too
fearful of the destruction of the immigrants'
faith to worry about intellectual endeavor.
With rare exceptions intellectualism is a luxury that is sacrificed when life itself—that of
individuals or that of an organization—is
threatened.

Ordinarily, a man does not become an intellectual unless he goes to college; nor does a
group produce eminent scientists unless a substantial proportion of its members have gone
to college. Higher education was quite beyond
the imaginative powers of most immigrants,[18]

[18] Ten per cent of the Catholics in the U.S. are
immigrants, and 40 per cent are the children of

ORIGINS AND EDUCATIONAL ACHIEVEMENT   413

TABLE 6. SOCIOECONOMIC STATUS BY RELIGION AND AGE

Per Cent:	Age 23–29 Protestant	Catholic	Age 30–39 Protestant	Catholic	Age 40–49 Protestant	Catholic	Age 50–59 Protestant	Catholic
Attending College	29	28	34	26	29	19	25	12
In Duncan Categories 6–10 *	32	30	40	32	36	19	40	31
Earning More than $8000.	29	25	40	36	51	39	40	29
(N)	(907)	(352)	(167)	(653)	(169)	(691)	(97)	(352)

* See Otis D. Duncan, "A Socioeconomic Index for All Occupations," in Albert J. Reiss, Jr., *Occupations and Social Status,* New York: Free Press, 1961, Ch. 6.

and in any case it was economically unfeasible. Development of intellectual and scientific concerns among Catholics had to await the preparation of an adequate social and economic base, and this did not occur until the late 1940's.[14] As Table 6 demonstrates,[15] the younger generation of Catholics has now come abreast of white Protestants from the same sections of the country on various measures of economic and social status,[16] and as their economic situation changes, the immigrants' defensive attitude of separatism has declined, while a liberal, self-critical orientation has become more common in certain crucial segments of the Catholic community. Having "made it" economically,

immigrants. Cf. Andrew M. Greeley, Peter H. Rossi and Leonard J. Pinto, "The Social Effects of Catholic Education," Chicago: NORC Report No. 99, 1964.

[14] Comparisons between Catholic and Jewish immigrants are not especially helpful since their European backgrounds were so different. Being barred from land ownership, Jews were city or village dwellers or commercial men; they had to live by wit, intelligence, and economic striving. Their adjustment to the New World necessarily differed from that of peasant farmers who were still but a step away from feudalism. The scientific achievements of Catholic migrants—from the farms of Ireland, Italy and Poland—or their children should instead be compared with those of German or Norwegian Missouri-Synod Protestant migrants.

[15] This table is reproduced from Greeley, Rossi and Pinto, *op. cit.*

[16] The Protestants in this sample were distributed in the same proportions in the NORC primary sampling units as were Catholics, so that a control was built into the sampling for both area of the country and size of municipality.

American Catholics could turn to "making it" intellectually; or, in less journalistic terms, not until the middle 1950's did the grandchildren of the peasant immigrants have the economic and social means for serious academic pursuits.

However persuasive this explanation may seem in its broad outlines, it does not account for the apparent suddenness of the change. One might reason that the "ghetto" mentality declined steadily through the 1930's and 1940's, but economic stagnation and military conflict retarded the development of a more positive approach to American life in general and academic effort in particular. To break out of the insecurity, that seems to be typical of the Catholic academicians Donovan describes, may require not only economic affluence in one's family background, but also the confidence that affluence will continue. Such confidence may not have become widespread among Catholics until the middle 1950's. One might say that the big change in American Catholicism occurred during the ten years that began with the G.I. Bill and ended with Sputnik.

Nor can one overlook the influence of the tight communication networks within the Catholic community. A shift in emphasis can be communicated to school administrators, high school instructors and college faculty rather quickly by an article in *The Commonweal* or an editorial in *America,* or by a Sheed and Ward publication such as O'Dea's *American Catholic Dilemma.* There was some indication in Greeley's material that Catholic college teachers were in fact making special efforts to persuade their most promising students to enroll in graduate school immediately.

We have suggested that the earlier lack of scientific achievement among Catholics is not due to religious factors but primarily to economic conditions, and that the change in Catholics' economic condition explains their increased interest in scholarship in recent years. This explanation is partially confirmed by the Post-Censal data for the older age levels, showing that those trained in parochial school tend to "catch up" in their attainment of degrees—precisely the kind of behavior one would expect from an economically underprivileged group. As Alice Rossi has pointed out to us, this late age of degree attainment may have also contributed to the lack of scientific productivity among Catholics, for major scientific contributions are usually made by people under 40. If Catholics in the younger age groups are now completing their advanced training at earlier ages, we may expect more scientific contributions from this group in years to come.

Reprinted from: **Sociological Analysis**, v. 27, no. 3, Fall, 196

After Secularity: The Neo-Gemeinschaft Society: A Post-Christian Postscript*

Andrew M. Greeley

National Opinion Research Center

The Roman Catholic Church is seen as traveling down the same road from gemeinschaft to gesellschaft as the rest of Western society has traveled, but in recent years at a very rapid pace. It is suggested that Catholic sociologists can contribute to the Church's self-awareness of the meaning of this pilgrimage while, at the same time, broadening the general sociological understanding of growth and change in formal organizations. In addition, the Catholic sociologists can play an important role in the evaluation of the neo-gemeinschaft community which seems to represent one of the major directions that modern society is taking.

I intend to make three principal points in this paper. The first is that the Catholic Church as it moves from the post-Tridintine counter-Reformation stance to the post-Vatican ecumenical stance is going through the same transition that the whole of Western society has undergone since the beginning of the nineteenth century, a change from *gemeinschaft* to *gesellschaft*.

Secondly, I will contend that among the other contributions he makes to mankind, the Catholic sociologist can provide both the theory and the research to make this transition more fruitful for the Church of Rome and can, at the very same time through his studies of the Catholic Church in transition, contribute a not inconsiderable increment to more general sociological understanding.

Thirdly, I would further contend that just as the Catholic Church is getting

something of a late start in its transition into the modern world, it will travel the pilgrimage from *gemeinschaft* to *gesellschaft* much more quickly than did the rest of Western society. So, too, it will tend to evolve more quickly those post-*gesellschaft* institutions by which modern secular man strives to maintain some of the advantages and supports of *gemeinschaft* society in a *gesellschaft* world. It will be of great interest both to the Church itself and to the rest of the human race to see what new forms of fellowship and community are evolved by the Catholic Church as it proceeds into the post-secular age, the age after the post-Christian age.

PROPOSITION I

The Catholic Church is becoming secularized, secularized not in the sense of secularism as it was condemned repeatedly by the American bishops but rather secularized in Harvey Cox's sense of the word. From the point of view of the sociologist, the Vatican Council represents the Church's definitive break with the

* Presidential address given at the Annual Meetings of the American Catholic Sociological Society, August, 1966.

styles and patterns of behavior of a feudal and renaissance world and its assumption of the styles and patterns of behavior of the modern world. It should be made clear from the beginning that one can make the statement without necessarily implying that the modern styles are better than the feudal styles, that rather one can be content with saying that the patterns of the age of the post-Vatican Church are more appropriate for the Church in its work in contemporary society. In becoming secular it is putting aside the static, tribal, highly symbolic, ritualistic relationships that with some minor changes have been typical of it for half a millenium, and it is taking on the dynamic, rationalized, flexible, and technological relationships of the contemporary world. Just as the organization of the Church in the middle ages reflected the styles of organization to be found in the secular society (or perhaps vice versa) so the Catholic Church in the modern world can be presumed to take on the organizational style which is characteristic of any large corporate body in the modern world.

In short, the Catholic Church is on a pilgrimage from one end of the continuum of the Parsonian pattern variables to the other. It is moving from particularism to universalism, from ascription to achievement, and from diffuse to specific relationships. The Church is moving from familialism to professionalism, from paternalism to collegiality, and from feudalism to functionalism. It would perhaps be wise, in passing at least, to define these terms. By a feudal society I mean that style of behavior in which one man relates to the other with the totality of his person and belongs to the other in every element of his life. In a functional society, one man's relationship to another is limited entirely to a specific social function for which

the relationship has come into being; when this function is not being fulfilled, the relationship either changes completely or ceases to exist. Thus, an employer has authority over his employee in a functional society merely insofar as it contributes to the production of the particular goods or services for which they have come together. When they meet on the golf course, for example, the employer has no rights or prerogatives *vis à vis* his employee (save in feudalistic organizations like the military). In a feudal society a given type of behavior becomes virtuous if it contributes to the perfection of the relationship between a superior and a subject. Thus, for example, the virtues of poverty, chastity, and obedience are taken to be good because they symbolize the subordinance of one man to another or of a group of men to God. In a functional society, on the other hand, these virtues are taken to be good simply because they contribute to the particular goals which have brought a group of men together, and are taken to have no particular value in themselves save insofar as they contribute to these specific sets of goals.

A classic example, one would suppose, is the relationship between pastor and curate. At the present time the relationship is familialistic, paternalistic, and feudal. The curate is assigned not with specific tasks or even to a specific parish; he is assigned to a specific man. This man is assumed, at least in theory, to be the only one who is capable of making a decision and one who by his wisdom and experience is constituted a teacher and regulator of the curate in all his behavior. He is the father of the family, his power is absolute, his word is law, and the curate engages in only that kind of behavior which is specified and authorized by his feudal superior. Further, the pastor is assumed to have responsibility over almost the totality of the curate's life; to determine at what hours he may leave the parish house or return to it; whom he may see in his office; to whom he may speak on the telephone; how he spends his day off; when he takes his vacation; indeed, virtually everything he does.

Such patterns of behavior are rapidly becoming obsolete. In years to come the priests who work together will be independent professionals, men who are highly skilled in their work who will come together to share the responsibilities of a particular mission, with one of their number perhaps acting as a chairman or as a senior colleague but only with highly limited and specified authority over the others and the right to give instructions only after some kind of consensus has been realized. The authority that the senior colleague has and the extent of relationships among colleagues will be determined purely by the nature of work at hand and not by any ideal principles on how a subject and superior should relate to each other. At that point, when the relationship among priests has become factual, professional, and highly specified, it can be said that the relationship is no longer feudal or tribal but secularized.

In the secularized Church, or the post-tribal Church, the same pattern of relationships will be presumed to exist among religious superiors and the other members of the community, between bishops and their priests, between priests and people, and between pope and bishops. Let us make no mistake about it, there will be many among us who will view this secularized Church as being somehow or other unchristian, since they will have identified the transitory feudal forms in which the relationships among Christians have taken place for the last millenium with the essence of Christianity. Make no mistake about it further,

there are a good number of the traditionalists among us who did not realize that the Vatican Council, and particularly its affirmation of the principle of collegiality, involved such changes. Yet, on the other hand, those of us who have studied human society and understand the inevitability of the shift from *gemeinschaft* to *gesellschaft* will realize that the traditionalists, those who resist the emergence of a post-feudal Church, are fighting their last desperate rearguard action.

THE AMERICAN EXPERIENCE

It should be noted also that this transition from *gemeinschaft* to *gesellschaft* is accentuated in American society because at the same time the American Church is moving from the immigrant ghetto to the suburbs. The whole nature of this peculiarly American transition can be summed up by two propositions. First of all, about half of adult American Catholics are either immigrants or the children of immigrants. Secondly, American Catholics are every bit as likely to graduate from college and to go on to graduate school as American Protestants, and the average income of Catholics under forty is slightly higher than the average income of Protestants in the same age bracket even when the size of city and region of country is controlled. American Catholicism, now a full if still junior partner in the American experiment, stands with one foot in the old neighborhood in the central city and the other foot in the college educated suburb. The results of this somewhat ambivalent situation are not surprising to the Catholic sociologists. We would cheerfully predict, even if empirical data were not all around us, that this would be a time of great fluidity in the American Church, of inevitable friction, of potentially revolutionary situations, a time of fashions and fads, of mercurial movements, of great hopes and rapid dissolutions, of superficiality and divisiveness, of clericalism and anticlericalism, of laicism and antilaicism. It will be a time when, in the absence of profound and mature scholarship, our theories will be served up to us by journalists, and our controversies will tend often to be noncontroversies in which serious questions such as clerical celibacy or Catholic education will be solved in the Catholic press mainly on the basis of what "I and my friends" happen to think now.

Nor will it be hard for the sociologists to prescribe what is desperately needed by a Church caught in the intersection of two transitions—*gemeinschaft* to *gesellschaft* and ghetto to suburbia. American Catholicism needs now much more self-consciousness than it ever has in the past. It needs to understand who and what it is; where it has come from and where it is going. It seems to me that American Catholicism has moved much further towards the flexible, experimental, rationalized *gesellschaft* church than has Catholicism anywhere else in the world. We have understood through our own experience for more than a century what it means to be a church in an open society. Unfortunately, while our practice has often been the practice of a church in an open society, our theory, our rationalizations, our justifications, and sometimes our internal organization have been based on the ideology of the past, an ideology which not only has no relevance to what we have done in practice in the present, but has often been a handicap to us both in executing our authentic insights and in understanding the good which we have done.

An astonishing example of this I think can be found in a school called Carroll College in Helena, Montana. Carroll is the only coeducational seminary I know in the world in which the divinity students and the pre-divinity students are integrated completely into the student body save only that they do not date the co-eds at the school. They live in the same residence hall, play on the same athletic teams, sing in the same choruses, perform in the same plays, go to the same classes, play cards in the same student union, and eat in the same dining room with the other students at the college. The traditional theory of Catholic seminaries would say that priestly vocations would hardly survive in such a worldly and secular atmosphere. It would be most unlikely, according to the theory, that some of the vocations could be developed in a situation where young women were physically present with the seminarians for most of the waking day.

But the truth about the seminary at Carroll College is that it is, as far as I know, the only seminary in the country with a negative defection rate which has more seminarians at graduation time than it did in the first year of college. Furthermore, well over three-quarters of the Carroll seminarians persevere in their vocations through theology, and defections after ordination are apparently almost nonexistent. Finally, if one talks to the young people at Carroll College, seminarians and non-seminarians, young men and young women, one can find a profound and mature understanding of the priestly and lay vocations as well as the meaning of the celibate state. While the seminarians will laughingly say that the reason more young men enter the seminary than leave it through the college years is the absence of good looking girls on the Carroll campus, I am prepared to say from very limited and biased observation that such an accusation is calumny. I would suggest, rather, that the seminarians are a far more important influence on the campus than anyone else and because they are so attractive and so admired many of the non-seminarians have a much greater insight into what the priestly life means and find themselves attracted towards the priestly vocation.

The co-ed seminary at Carroll College emerged for sheerly practical reasons. The Helena diocese could not sustain a separate college and a seminary and then as time went on, the admission of co-eds became a financial necessity. Despite all the theories that said it shouldn't work, it worked admirably well, but only now, after years of soft-pedaling the Carroll experience, has it begun to dawn on people that perhaps the pragmatic American instinct has discovered something about training young men for the priesthood and young men and women for the lay state in contemporary American society that is profoundly important not only for the United States but for the whole Catholic world. It could just be that in a society like the United States, in a time like ours, the best way to train the people for the priesthood is to keep them as close as possible to young men and women of their own generation who constitute the Catholic laity of the future and it could just be that this is the best possible way not only for the future clergy but also for the future laity. It could be that the whole world can look at Carroll College for a profoundly new and important understanding of the meaning of growing up as a Catholic and growing up as a celibate Catholic.

Our increasing self-consciousness and our increasing understanding of what the American Catholic experience has meant will make us much more confident of our own insights, much more secure as we proceed to the development of ecclesiastical styles pertinent to the American environment, and much more positive as we point to the American way as most appropriate for the whole Church in the modern world. Just as the American bishops and American theologians like John Courtney Murray seem to have taught the rest of the Church the meaning of religious freedom at the Vatican Council, it could be that there are many more elements of the American way that could be of immense help to the rest of the Church. In any event, the transitions we are in will certainly be rough and rocky until we become much more self-conscious about who we are and what we are doing.

PROPOSITION II

It should be perfectly clear that the sociologist whose overriding theoretical concern for decades has been the change from *gemeinschaft* to *gesellschaft* should be of great help to the American Church in this time of transition. To those who are impatient for more rapid change and fearful that the present change may be aborted, sociologists can say that transition is inevitable once it has begun as is the setting of the sun once it has risen. To the openminded traditionalist, sociologists can point out that the transition through which we are now going need not mean the end of the old values in the Church but merely their transformation into more relevant values in the contemporary world. To the disturbed decision-maker who doesn't know quite how to behave in the awkward times in which he finds himself burdened with responsibility, the sociologist can offer explanations derived from the experience of other institutions and the whole of society during the journey from one end of the Parsonian continuum to the other. To the Church, looking for new structures in which to institutionalize new patterns of behavior, the sociologist can propose serious research and experiments which will ease the transition and make it a more fruitful one. To American Catholicism seeking to understand itself, the sociologist can offer his tools for analysis and explanation.

It is lamentable that the institutional church and the sociologist have not been engaged in dialogue nearly to the extent that they might. There has been much less done in the sociology of American Catholicism than one could have reasonably expected at this point in the development of sociology. Nor have the decision-makers turned to the sociologists for advice and research nearly to the extent that they might have. The last lingering suspicions of the behavioral sciences have not yet completely disappeared from the land; as far as I am aware, not a single American Catholic sociologist was a consultant at the second Vatican Council. I think I can make this observation with some grace since when the Council was being organized I was not a sociologist and hardly a candidate for the role of peritus. There were of course sociologists at the Council, most of them European, most of them not nearly as well trained as their American counterparts. It may be chauvinistic on my part to observe that I think that both the Church universal and the American hierarchy would have been much better served if at least some of the sociological advice offered at the Vatican Council had been proffered by American sociologists. But the past is the past and there is no point in lamenting it at great lengths. Nor is there any point of trying to analyze the reasons for the *détente* between the Catholic sociological fraternity and ecclesiastical administrators. Whatever the past was, there are surely more than enough hopeful signs for us to conclude that the *détente* is over.

But what is to be said of those who somehow or other feel that it is narrow and provincial for Catholic sociologists to be interested in the study of the

Catholic Church. What is to be said to those who contend that the Catholic sociologist who concerns himself with the sociology of Catholicism is living in a ghetto world. One would have thought that Everett Hughes had answered that charge long ago when he wrote, "Nearly everything sociologically speaking has happened in and to the Roman Catholic Church."[1] As non-Catholic sociologists become increasingly fascinated by the vast variety of sociological phenomena that is to be observed within the Church of Rome it ill behooves Catholic sociologists to pretend that when they study their own church they become incapable of making a contribution to the broader concerns of sociological theory. Indeed, where else in the world can one find such a magnificent laboratory to study the transition from *gemeinschaft* to *gesellschaft?*

THE NEO-GEMEINSCHAFT SOCIETY

But *gesellschaft* society is not like the Marxist classless society—the end of the evolutionary process. If anything is clear to sociologists at this state of the game (though it does not at all seem to be clear to the theologians who read the more popularized sociological books) it is that *gemeinschaft* has not died, that the family group, the ethnic community, the extended family, the religious denominations are still terribly important pillars in the social structure. Indeed, it has become clear that if we so rationalize and formalize the social structure so that a man's old intimate, primary group relationships seem to be taken away from him, a man will then proceed to build new primary groups for himself whether it be in the factory, the neigh-

[1] "The Early and Contemporary Study of Religion: Editorial Foreword," *The American Journal of Sociology* 50 (May, 1955) p. 4.

borhood community, the law office, the military establishment, or even the church. Anonymous man, in the face of the lonely crowd, living in miserable (or if you are a disciple of Harvey Cox, splendid) isolation in a rationalized, formalized, mechanized, technological world is largely a figment of the sociological and, more recently, the theological imagination. Modern man, as we know him from our research experience (often opposed to our theoretical speculation) still wants all the *gemeinschaft* he can find, be it in the extended family, the informal group on the job, or the religio-ethnic community which shields him from the impersonality of the larger society. It would be a mistake to feel that modern man wishes to return to the feudal. What he wants, rather, is to have the best of both possible worlds. He wishes to enjoy warm, intimate support of *gemeinschaft* at the same time as he enjoys the freedom, the rationality, and the technological flexibility of a *gesellschaft* world. Modern man wants to put aside irrelevant myths and the obsolescent sacred symbols of the past but only so he might devise relevant and exciting new sacred symbols. Modern man wishes to put aside the primary groups in which his grandfathers were imprisoned and replace them with primary groups which enable him to enjoy even greater personal development and freedom. Modern man wants Community in the midst of his Associations. Modern man, in short, wants to be able to establish by free contract a new clan, a new tribe.

The surest sign of this hunger for new *gemeinschaft* in the post-secular world is the tremendous vigor of personalism in contemporary America. The modern American is convinced that his happiness will emerge essentially out of human relationships and if the modern American is young what he wants

is "deep and meaningful relationships." Indeed, the modern young American, as fantastic an offspring of a marriage between *gemeinschaft* and *gesellschaft* as the mind of man could imagine, wants even to establish a deep and meaningful relationship with the bus driver. As a matter of fact, I someday expect to see the new breed arrive with picket sign in front of the bus terminal announcing, "We love the bus driver; why doesn't he love us?"

The personalist revolution is a revolt against the detribalized society. It is a desire to reestablish once again in the human community the bonds of what Edward Shils calls "premordial ties," bonds that at least at one time were furnished by such things as blood, land, soil. If there is any premordial relationship which serves the same purposes today and which may eventually replace all the other premordial relationships, it is that of friendship. Indeed, to those of us who put aside our theoretical blinkers and take a hard empirical look at the modern world, the question is no longer whether the primary group will survive, but exactly what kind of primary groups will result from man's desperate longing for community. For it seems to me to be still in doubt that the post-secular community will rather replace the oppression and tyranny of the old *gemeinschaft* society with a more subtle and more sophisticated *neo-gemeinschaft* society.

For the Catholic Church, the question is the same. Will the old unfreedom of irrelevant, feudalistic forms be replaced by an authentic and free fellowship of the people of God or is it to be approached instead by a new form of unfreedom, all the worse because it is described in terms of personalist philosophy and reinforced by all the subtle methods of manipulation that modern social psychology has revealed to us? Have we learned in fact that brainwash is brainwash whether you call it brainwash or whether you call it participatory democracy or a cursillo? Have we learned that tyranny is tyranny even if it is called freedom? Have we learned that men can be quite convinced they are free even though they are in fact subtly manipulated slaves? It is by no means clear that the new fellowship within the Church, the new community of which I have written elsewhere, will destroy or reinforce freedom. It is by no means clear that the more intimate personalist groups which seem to be emerging all over the country will turn in upon themselves and rigidly restrict the freedom of their members or whether they will turn out on the rest of the world in a burst of love and trust and enthusiasm which could mark one of the great milestones in the development of human society. As the Catholic Church completes its transition from *gemeinschaft* to *gesellschaft* there will emerge inevitably within it the small, subparochial, or transparochial fellowships of believers which will give new depth and meaning to the collegial and functional Church resulting from the Vatican Council. Whether the new functional Church really is able to appeal to the profound longings in the heart of modern man depends on the success or the failure of these informal communities and fellowships of believers.

If we can say that phenomenologically, original sin leads to the tragic inability on the part of man to love and to trust his fellow man, then we could affirm that the theological and philosophical personalism of our time, coupled with sophisticated social and psychological insights into the nature of human behavior, have made it possible for contemporary man to make a major and significant leap forward towards a more loving and more humanly fulfilling society.

If contemporary sociology and psychology (as well as theology, literature, and philosophy) have accomplished anything, they have taught us a much more profound understanding of the meaning of human relationships and how a community at the same time free and intimate, flexible and yet bound together by powerful forces, providing strong emotional support and yet open-ended, can be constructed. Unfortunately, misunderstood and inadequately understood group dynamics can readily turn what might have been a promising and free new community into a subtle form of tyranny. If Catholic sociologists and social psychologists cannot engage in intensive study of the new communities that are emerging and if they do not provide meaningful generalizations as to crucial differences between free communities and tyrannies masquerading under the name of freedom, then the responsibility they must bear for this failure will be great indeed.

It would be my conclusion that historians of the future will look back at our time—the post-post-Christian world and the post-secularist society—as an era when man, at least Western man, had acquired freedom and abundance by leaving behind the *gemeinschaft* world and moving into the technological *gesellschaft* world; then man determined that it was humanly and psychologically possible to have the best of both, to combine the freedom and affluence of a technological society with the warmth and fellowship of a tribal society. Of course, whether historians of the future will also say that modern man, while he knew from social science that such community was possible, actually only discovered it in practice when the Roman Catholic Church, a relative newcomer in the pilgrimage to the *gesellschaft,* was able to produce its own free human fellowships in the midst of a functional and secularized church, still is unclear. But, if the historian of the future is able to make such an affirmation then at least in one of his footnotes it seems to me that he will have to concede that a small albeit important part in this great leap forward towards the omega point was made by the Catholic sociologists who combined a sophisticated understanding of the dynamics of human society with a faith that at least in Christ Jesus modern or secular man is capable of loving.

Reprinted from THE AMERICAN JOURNAL OF SOCIOLOGY
Vol. 72, No. 6, May 1967
Copyright 1967 by The University of Chicago
Printed in U.S.A.

Religion and Academic Career Plans

A Note on Progress[1]

Although there is a long history of debate about the relationship between religion and the intellectual life, the most recent developments of the debate within the social science fraternity have generally been limited to the issue of whether membership in the Roman Catholic church is a barrier to serious intellectual concerns—at least in the American environment. Lenski,[2] for example, has suggested that scholarship and Roman Catholicism may be incompatible both because of the general "overt conflict between the churches and modern scientific movement" and because of the "basic intellectual orientation which Roman Catholicism develops: an orientation which values obedience above intellec-

tual autonomy." Several Catholic writers[3] have taken the same stand, attributing the intellectual deficiencies of American Catholicism to the absence of a scholarly tradition, clerical domination, fear of modern science, lack of concern for temporal values, materialism among the Catholic laity, low valuation on curiosity and initiative in Catholic training, and the tendency to encourage talented youth to enter the religious life. The findings of Knapp and his associates on the poor productivity of scholars by Catholic schools apparently confirm these conclusions.[4]

However, data from NORC's 1961 study of college graduates did not confirm[5] the

---

[1] The data considered in this article were originally collected under a grant from the National Institutes of Health, the National Science Foundation, and the U.S. Office of Education. The analysis reported in this paper was made possible by a grant from the Carnegie Corporation. The author is indebted to Peter H. Rossi, Michael Schiltz, and Joe L. Spaeth for their helpful suggestions.

[2] Gerhard Lenski, *The Religious Factor* (Garden City, N.Y.: Doubleday & Co., 1960).

[3] E.g., Thomas O'Dea, *American Catholic Dilemma* (New York: Sheed & Ward, 1958).

[4] Robert H. Knapp and H. B. Goodrich, *Origins of American Scientists* (Chicago: University of Chicago Press, 1952); and Robert H. Knapp and Joseph J. Greenbaum, *The Young American Scholar: His Collegiate Origins* (Chicago: University of Chicago Press, 1953).

[5] Andrew M. Greeley, "Influence of the 'Religious Factor' on Career Plans and Occupational Values of College Graduates," *American Journal of Sociology*, LXVII (May, 1963), 658–71.

assumption of antiscientism among Catholics. Members of the Catholic church were as likely to go to graduate school, to choose an academic career, to specialize in the physical sciences, and to plan a life of research as were Protestants (though Jews were more "scholarly" in their inclinations than either gentile group). While it was carefully noted that such indicators did not support an assumption of Catholic antiscientism, neither were they strong enough

from the fact that what was being analyzed was the graduate school and academic career plans of college graduates at the time of graduation.[6] It was argued that with the passage of time it could reasonably be expected that Catholic graduate students would not persevere in their plans for graduate school and for academic careers.

Such intention is not at all implausible since there is every reason to believe[7] that the movement of large numbers of Catholics

TABLE 1

GRADUATE SCHOOL EXPERIENCES BY RELIGION OF JUNE, 1961, COLLEGE GRADUATES (ONLY WHITE MALES FROM UPPER HALF SES BACKGROUNDS WHO GREW UP IN NEW ENGLAND OR MIDDLE ATLANTIC CITIES WITH A POPULATION OF OVER 500,000)*

Graduate School Experiences	Protestants	Catholics from Catholic Colleges	Catholics from Other Colleges	Jews
Percentage still in graduate school (spring, 1964)	45	46	44	60
Percentage with M.A.	12	15	11	24
Percentage expecting Ph.D.	21	20	15	26
Percentage expecting academic careers	20	19	15	43
Percentage in arts and sciences graduate programs	20	22	18	30
Percentage of those in graduate school who attend full time	58	57	38	55
Of those expecting Ph.D., when it is expected (percentage):				
By 1965	38	28	26	26
By 1967	78	79	62	89
Percentage of Ph.D. topics chosen	65	70	55	68
N	163	510	316	121

* Subsample includes all respondents whose original religion was Catholic and one of every six whose origianl religion was not Catholic.

to definitively refute the assumptions. It was observed that mere enrolment in graduate school did not guarantee a Ph.D., much less promise excellent or eminent scholarly work.

This note is intended to serve as a progress report on the relationship between religion and academic career plans of the June, 1961, graduates, in which it can be indicated whether the careers of the June, 1961, graduates in the postcollege years necessitate any revision of the findings previously reported. Some commentators have observed that similarities between Catholics and Protestants might well result

into the graduate schools and academic profession is quite recent. Fortunately, the NORC survey is a panel study, and data are now available on these June, 1961, graduates three years after they received their undergraduate degrees. Table 1 would suggest that none of the major conclusions reported in the previous article needs to be modified at the present time.

[6] Donald P. Warwick, "Letter to the Editor," *American Journal of Sociology*, LXIX (November, 1963), 295; and Gerhard Lenski, *op. cit.*

[7] See Seymour Warkov and Andrew M. Greeley, "Parochial School Origins and Educational Achievement," *American Sociological Review*, XXXI (June, 1966), 406–14.

It should be noted that the percentages in Table 1 are based only on white males from the upper socioeconomic half of the population in the New England and northeastern section of the country who were raised in cities with a population over a half-million. Thus, there is built into the table control for race, sex, socioeconomic status (SES), region of the country, and size of city of origin.

While Jews still are considerably different from Gentiles, the differences between Protestants and Catholics who attended Catholic colleges are almost non-existent. Better than two-fifths are still in graduate school, close to three-fifths are attending school full time, between one-sixth and one-seventh already have their M.A., and about one-fifth are expecting to obtain a Ph.D. Almost four-fifths feel that their doctoral work will be finished by 1967, and better than two-thirds have already chosen a topic for their doctoral dissertation, while two-fifths of those who have chosen their doctoral topics report that they have done so independently and not at the urging of a particular advisor. Finally, one-fifth of both these groups expect academic careers and are specializing in arts and sciences disciplines while they are in graduate schools.

The deviant groups, insofar as there is any deviancy in Table 1, are the Jews and, to some extent, the Catholics who attended non-Catholic colleges. The former are much more likely to be in graduate school, to obtain their M.A., to expect their doctorate before 1967, to expect academic careers, and to be specializing in the arts and sciences. The latter are considerably less likely to be going to school full time and are somewhat less likely to expect the doctorate or to plan academic careers; and among those in this group pursuing the Ph.D., there is less of an expectation of finishing the doctorate by 1967.

The Jewish differential, of course, is not difficult to explain, given the traditional commitment of the Jewish community to advanced education and to scholarly efforts. But the fact that the non-Catholic school Catholics are more dissimilar from their Catholic school coreligionists than the latter are from Protestants is not so easily explained. However, there is an increasing body of data which suggests that this phenomenon occurs rather consistently and ought to be the object of further research.[8] (Controls for socioeconomic status, generation, and ethnicity are not successful in explaining the phenomenon.

The mere fact of attending graduate school and planning an academic career, or even of finishing school the same time as others, would not necessarily establish that there could be some expectation that Catholics were beginning to assume a major role in American academia. It could, of course, be quite possible that the Catholic graduate school students were going to inferior universities or, if they were going to the best graduate schools, were doing poorly in these schools. However, of those going to graduate schools in the arts and sciences, among the three gentile religious groups being analyzed, approximately one-fifth of each group is attending one of the top twelve graduate schools.[9]

Table 2 provides information on how the graduate students in these quality graduate schools are faring in the pursuit of their Great Aspirations. While the case base in Table 2 is admittedly relatively small, at least the proportions in the table provide grounds for interesting speculation. None of the four analytic groups is likely to have dropped out of school since the spring of 1962. The Catholic students, if anything, are slightly more likely to report that they have an A grade-point average. Only the Catholics who went to non-Catholic undergraduate colleges are different from the others in reporting plans for the doctorate, and the Catholic school Catholics do not lag behind the Jewish or Protestant groups in

[8] See Andrew M. Greeley and Peter H. Rossi, *The Education of Catholic Americans* (Chicago: Aldine Press, 1966), chap. v.

[9] The top ten of the Kenniston list plus California Institute of Technology and Massachusetts Institute of Technology.

their plans to obtain their Ph.D. by 1965 or 1966. Protestants and Catholic school Catholics are much more likely to have had their theses topics approved. Even though the small number of respondents represented in Table 2 make it impossible to use more detailed socioeconomic controls, there surely is no evidence to be found in the table for the notion that Catholics (at least if they have gone to Catholic colleges) are unsuccessful in the high-quality graduate schools.

Only the Catholics who did not go to Catholic colleges seem to have delayed their decision to leave Catholicism until graduate school.

Thus, there is no evidence from data available to us that American Catholics are disinclined to enter the top-quality arts and sciences graduate departments, nor that they do poorly in their academic efforts in these departments (especially if they have attended Catholic undergraduate colleges).

TABLE 2

GRADUATE SCHOOL EXPERIENCE BY RELIGION OF ARTS AND SCIENCES STUDENTS
FROM THE JUNE, 1961, CLASS WHO IN THE SPRING OF 1962 WERE AT-
TENDING TOP TWELVE GRADUATE SCHOOLS (WHITES ONLY)*

Graduate School Experiences	Protestants	Catholics from Catholic Colleges	Catholics from Other Colleges	Jews
Percentage still in graduate school (spring, 1964)...................	95	100	100	88
Percentage with A grade-point average.	10	16	17	14
Percentage planning Ph.D............	97	98	66	100
Of those expecting Ph.D., when it is expected (percentage):				
By 1965.....................	59	56	33	24
By 1966.....................	79	96	47	86
Percentage having thesis topic *approved*.	50	59	22	19
Percentage still in religion in which they were raised.....................	55	85	52	71
Percentage still in religion in which they belonged at college graduation......	81	98	54	79
N..................................	40	54	27	21

* Subsample includes all respondents whose original religion was Catholic and one of every six whose original religion was not Catholic.

Half of the Protestant graduate students and half of the Catholic graduate students who did not attend Catholic undergraduate colleges are no longer members of the religion in which they were raised, while some 15 per cent of the Catholic school Catholics have defected, and almost 30 per cent of the Jews no longer consider themselves Jews. However, for all but the non-Catholic school Catholics, these decisions seem to have been made before the graduate training began. The vast majority of the other three analytic groups reports that their religious preference after three years of graduate school is no different from their religious preference at the time of graduation.

Finally, those who had Catholic undergraduate training do not seem to find any conflict between their religious faith and their academic pursuits.

As we have noted in previous papers, attendance at graduate school, or even the possession of the Ph.D., does not guarantee that a young person will become a scholar, much less a distinguished scholar. However, the data presently available in the NORC panel study of June, 1961, graduates show no signs that, at least thus far, the Catholic graduate students have defected from their Great Aspirations for the academic life. Only the test of time will tell whether they will in fact be the ones to disprove definitively the notion that in the United States, at least, there need be a conflict between serious scholarship and membership in the Roman Catholic church.

In conclusion, we must take into account the possibility raised by one writer that the findings reported of 1961 graduates must be explained in terms of sampling variation.[10] Ordinarily, a major social research center would not be expected to be called upon to defend its sampling methodology. Although it is surely possible to establish the validity of the June, 1961, sample, in the present instance it is not necessary to do so. For

The Schiltz data merely confirmed what has already been reported. At least among American Gentiles, there are precious few differences in career plans or values which cannot be explained by factors other than the religious one.

The new data reported in this note in no way force a revision of earlier findings: On the indicators available to us, there is to be found no evidence of conflict between scholarship and membership in the Roman Catholic church. The absence of such scholarship in the past may very well be the result of the traumas of the immigration experience,

TABLE 3

DEGREE AND CAREER PLANS OF 1964 GRADUATES BY RELIGION AND SCHOOL BACKGROUND (UPPER SES, UPPER API, MALES ONLY)

DEGREE AND CAREER PLANS	NON-CATHOLICS	CATHOLICS			
		Catholic High School, Catholic College	Catholic High School, Non-Catholic College	Non-Catholic High School, Catholic College	Non-Catholic High School, Non-Catholic College
Percentage aspiring to "higher degree"*.....	57	55	52	53	48
Percentage planning academic careers........	15	13	8	9	11
N...................	3,619	255	198	78	217

* Ph.D. or professional degree.

there exists that *rara avis* in social research, a replication. In June of 1964, NORC replicated the 1961 survey with a completely independent sample. While a forthcoming work by Schiltz[11] will confirm the findings of the 1961 sample concerning the relationship between religion and career plans, it is proper at the present time to reproduce one of Schiltz's tables (Table 3).

With a control for sex and SES and undergraduate academic performance, it is clear that there are no substantial differences between Catholics and non-Catholics either in their aspirations for the doctorate or in their plans for academic careers.

[10] Gerhard Lenski, Book Review, *American Journal of Sociology*, LXXI (September, 1965), 200.

[11] Michael Schiltz, *Seniors: '64* (in preparation).

rather than any specifically credal or ecclesiastical influence. It remains to be seen, of course, whether Catholics from the June, 1961, class will earn by their scholarly work the title "scientist" or "intellectual"; but at this point in their careers, we could find little reason to think that they are losing their enthusiasm for the academic life. It is therefore not beyond the realm of possibility that within the next quarter-century Catholics will be as visible in the senior ranks of the major university faculties as Jews are today. Whether such faculty positions are the ultimate indicator of scholarly achievement is a question beyond the immediate concern of this note.

ANDREW M. GREELEY

University of Chicago

Reprinted from THE AMERICAN JOURNAL OF SOCIOLOGY
Vol. 75, No. 3, November 1969
c 1969 by The University of Chicago All rights reserved.
Printed in U.S.A.

Continuities in Research on the "Religious Factor"

Andrew M. Greeley

University of Chicago

Analysis of the attitudes and behavior of graduates of Catholic colleges seven years after graduation indicates that the experience of attending a Catholic college caused no economic, educational, or intellectual handicaps for the alumni of such schools. They are also likely to score higher than other Catholics on measures of religious behavior and on measures of political and social liberalism.

The purpose of this brief note is to report on certain continuities in research on the question of the influence of religion and religious education on adult attitude and behavior. Among the relevant publications are those by Greeley (1963a, 1963b), Greeley and Rossi (1966, chap. 5), Knapp and Goodrich (1952), Knapp and Greenbaum (1953), Lenski (1960, 1965), O'Dea (1958), Warkov and Greeley (1966), and Warwick (1963).

Three major conclusions about the impact of the Roman Catholic educational system in the United States can be drawn from previous research: (1) Those who attended Catholic schools are more likely to be religious in adult life than those who did not, even when the religiousness of the family of origin is held constant; (2) there is no evidence of economic, educational, or intellectual handicaps affecting those who have attended Roman Catholic schools; and (3) those who have attended Roman Catholic colleges seem more politically and socially liberal than those Catholics who did not attend such colleges, particularly if the former had also attended Catholic grammar school and high school.

However, there were a number of weaknesses in the data gathered in earlier studies. The sample interviewed by Greeley and Rossi in their *Education of Catholic Americans* (1966) was made up of adult Catholics between twenty-three and sixty years old. Many of the older respondents in the sample were immigrants or the children of immigrants, and the impact of Roman Catholic schools on them might have been very different from the impact on younger and more assimilated Catholics. Furthermore, the major social class differences between the older immigrants and the younger assimilated Catholics could easily be blurred in a national sample of the adult population.

The other major data concern June 1961 college graduates and labor under two sets of weaknesses: First of all, the graduates filled out their questionnaires in the years immediately after graduation from college, when the influence of the college experience might still have been very strong on them. Second, there were no questions about political or social attitudes which would enable researchers to examine in greater detail, with a larger

American Journal of Sociology

sample, the conclusion about the greater liberalism of the graduates of Catholic colleges reported by Greeley and Rossi with a relatively small number of respondents.

However, the fifth phase of the National Opinion Research Center's (NORC's) ongoing study of June 1961 college graduates (commissioned in this instance by the Carnegie Foundation Commission on the Future of Higher Education) makes it possible to reexamine the conclusions of previous research in a sample that is adequate in size, youthful in age, and similar in social class (as all are college graduates). In addition, measures of political and social attitudes were included in the study so that the third and most dubious conclusion of previous research could be more carefully investigated.

Those who have attended Catholic schools are more religious seven years

TABLE 1

RELIGIOUS BEHAVIOR AND EDUCATION OF CATHOLICS IN 1968
(PERCENTAGE JUNE 1961 COLLEGE GRADUATES)

| | | CATHOLIC EDUCATION | | | |
ITEM	All Catholic	Catholic College Only	Catholic Primary Only	Catholic Primary and Secondary	ALL NON-CATHOLIC EDUCATION
Percentage still Catholic...	96	93	91	92	84
Percentage in Catholic marriage................	87	59	77	79	77
Percentage attending church weekly...........	81	83	71	70	52
Weighted N............	459	132	235	101	449

after they have graduated from college than those who have not attended Catholic schools (table 1); almost any attendance at Catholic schools correlates with remaining in the Church, while attendance at a Catholic college is positively correlated with frequent church attendance. But, curiously enough, those who went to Catholic colleges without attending Catholic grammar schools or high schools are the most likely of all to enter religiously mixed marriages—perhaps because they come from sections of the country where the Catholic population is not large. Even for the younger Catholic population, there remains a positive relationship between Catholic education and religious behavior in adult life

Catholic education does not seem to interfere with educational or financial success or with the choice of an academic career (table 2). The Catholics who had all their education in Catholic schools are twice as likely as those who had all their education in public schools to have either a terminal professional degree or a Ph.D. They are also considerably more likely to have such a degree than the non-Catholic respondents in the survey. Only those Catholics who went to Catholic colleges without attending Catholic gram-

Research on the "Religious Factor"

mar schools and high schools are less likely to have a terminal degree than the typical 1961 alumnus. Furthermore, the respondents who received all their education in Catholic schools are also the most likely to have the arts and sciences Ph.D. and the most likely to be working for a college or university or for a research organization, though the differences among the six groups are too small to be important.

Those who had all their education in Catholic schools are more likely to score high on the reading index[1] than are any other respondents in the sample, although Catholics with partial Catholic education score lower on this measure than do non-Catholic respondents.

Finally, with the exception of those who went to Catholic colleges after public grammar school and high school, there is a positive relationship between Catholic education and earning more than $11,000 per year.

TABLE 2

CATHOLIC EDUCATION AND ACHIEVEMENT IN 1968
(PERCENTAGE JUNE 1961 COLLEGE GRADUATES)

EDUCATION AND ACHIEVEMENT	CATHOLICS					NON-CATHOLICS
	All Catholic	Catholic College Only	Catholic Primary Only	Catholic Primary and Secondary	All Non-Catholic Education	
Ph.D. or professional degree..	18.0	10.0	15.0	14.0	9.0	12.0
Ph.D.	5.8	0.0	2.1	1.9	3.7	3.8
Earning more than $11,000...	37.0	27.0	40.0	45.0	32.0	27.0
High on reading scale.......	28.0	18.0	19.0	7.0	16.0	23.0
Choosing academic careers...	29.0	20.0	17.0	13.0	19.0	27.0
N.....................	459	132	235	101	449	6,289

Thus, there is no evidence that attending Catholic schools interferes with one's intellectual, educational, or financial achievement—quite the contrary. If anything, Catholic school attendance seems positively to facilitate such achievements. It may be that those who have attended Catholic schools come from families where there was more emphasis on upward mobility and educational achievement than there was in other families (a curious reversal of the Protestant ethic). It also may be, as Greeley and Rossi (1966) suggested, that they are more successful because, in Rosenberg's terms, they enjoy greater "emotional well-being" inside the subculture than they would outside the subculture. Finally, it may also be that the faculty and administrators of Catholic colleges, in particular, put strong emphasis on academic and economic achievement in the training of their students. There is some evidence of this (see Greeley 1963b). However, it now seems quite clear that the suggestion of Lenski (1960), Trent (1967), and others,

[1] Based on reported ownership of books and frequent reading of nonfiction and poetry.

American Journal of Sociology

that the rather surprising scores of Catholics on measures of "intellectualism" in NORC's June 1961 sample was a function of great aspirations that would not be carried to fulfillment, must be definitively rejected. The graduates of Catholic colleges, in particular, cannot be written off as "anti-intellectual."

But the most striking data to be reported in this note may be observed in table 3. Attendance at Catholic college, particularly after attendance at Catholic grammar school and high school, correlates quite strongly with liberal, not to say radical, political positions. Those who have attended Catholic colleges (independent of their primary and secondary education)

TABLE 3

SOCIAL ATTITUDES AND CATHOLIC EDUCATION IN 1968
(PERCENTAGE JUNE 1961 COLLEGE GRADUATES)

SOCIAL ATTITUDES	CATHOLICS					NON-CATHOLICS
	All Catholic	Catholic College Only	Catholic Primary Only	Catholic Primary and Secondary	All Non-Catholic Education	
Percentage liberal Democrat..	23	36	17	14	18	16
Percentage thinking Negro protests healthful for America..............	63	68	53	47	53	53
Percentage blaming riots on white racism..........	47	41	33	28	33	33
Percentage supporting student political involvement......	31	16	21	24	23	28
Percentage supporting student militancy................	29	20	17	13	19	27
N......................	459	132	235	101	449	6,289

are more likely to describe themselves as liberal Democrats, though the differences on this item are much less striking than they are on the other four items of the table. Those who attended Catholic colleges are considerably more sympathetic to black militants and also substantially more likely to accept the conclusion of the Kerner report that riots are caused by white racism. Even more surprisingly, those who have attended Catholic colleges after Catholic grammar school and high school experience are far more sympathetically disposed toward student militancy than are other Catholics who have graduated from college, and they are slightly more favorably disposed toward militancy than the typical American college graduate.

The conclusion, therefore, of the Greeley-Rossi report, that the graduates of Catholic colleges are more socially liberal than either Catholics who went to non-Catholic colleges or the general population, seems to be confirmed. Differences between the graduates of Catholic colleges and all others on items measuring racism may not be surprising, for the Roman Church

Research on the "Religious Factor"

in recent years has taken a strong theoretical stand on the race issue; but that those who had all their education in Catholic schools would be more sympathetic to student militancy than other Catholics is not so easily explained. One might suggest that the reason for their support of militancy is that they were dissatisfied with their own college education, but other data to be reported elsewhere would indicate that exactly the opposite was the case.

Another possible explanation is that there is a strong relationship between Irish ethnic background and attendance at Catholic schools and that Irish Catholics tend to be more liberal than the other three major ethnic groups, but a good deal of this difference vanishes among college graduates.

It may be possible that there is some sort of preselection factor at work. Catholics with more liberal political and social inclinations may selectively overchoose to attend Catholic colleges; but if this were true—and there is some slight indication of this in yet unpublished material by other writers—the mystery would be even deeper: why would politically and socially liberal Catholics be more likely to choose to go to Catholic colleges, especially when such colleges do not have a reputation for political and social liberalism?

No definitive conclusions, therefore, can be reached as to the reason for this apparent greater liberalism among the graduates of Catholic colleges until more detailed research becomes feasible on attitudinal trends through the four years of college experience. It might be suggested that, as a tentative hypothesis for investigation, the faculty of Catholic colleges, particularly the younger members of the religious orders, have strong commitments to certain kinds of social liberalism and push these commitments perhaps a bit more strongly than do the younger faculties of typical American colleges.

REFERENCES

Greeley, Andrew M. 1963a. "Influence of the 'Religious Factor' on Career Plans and Occupational Values of College Graduates." *American Journal of Sociology* 67 (May): 658–71.
———. 1963b. *Religion and Career.* New York: Sheed & Ward.
Greeley, Andrew M., and Peter H. Rossi. 1966. *The Education of Catholic Americans.* Chicago: Aldine.
Knapp, Robert H., and H. B. Goodrich. 1952. *Origins of American Scientists.* Chicago: University of Chicago Press.
Knapp, Robert H., and Joseph J. Greenbaum. 1953. *The Young American Scholar: His Collegiate Origins.* Chicago: University of Chicago Press.
Lenski, Gerhard. 1960. *The Religious Factor.* Garden City, N.Y.: Doubleday.
———. 1965. "Book Review." *American Journal of Sociology* 71 (September):200.
O'Dea, Thomas. 1958. *American Catholic Dilemma.* New York: Sheed & Ward.
Trent, James. 1967. *Catholics in College.* Chicago: University of Chicago Press.
Warkov, Seymour, and Andrew M. Greeley. 1966. "Parochial School Origins and Educational Achievement." *American Sociological Review* 31 (June):406–14.
Warwick, Donald P. 1963. "Letter to the Editor." *American Journal of Sociology* 69 (November): 295.

[Reprinted from SOCIOLOGY OF EDUCATION, Vol. 42, No. 1, Winter, 1969]

A Note on Political and Social Differences Among Ethnic College Graduates

ANDREW M. GREELEY, *National Opinion Research Center, University of Chicago*

THE PURPOSE OF this essentially descriptive note is to report on data which indicate that even among young people with a college education, ethnic background continues to be a strong predictor of attitudes and behavior. It is reasonably well known that religion correlates with attitude and behavior, even among the well educated; but in this note we will present evidence that there were wide divergencies among the ethnic groups within the Protestant, Catholic, and Jewish religious traditions, and that in many instances the differences among groups within the traditions are greater than the differences among the religions themselves.

In the spring of 1968 the National Opinion Research Center, under commission of the Carnegie Foundation Commission on the Future of Higher Education, mailed questionnaires to the subsample of its June, 1961 College graduation class population. The response rate to the mail questionnaire was 81 percent (89 percent of those '61 graduates whose addresses could be located seven years after graduation). The sample was of such a size that 11 ethnic groups could be investigated within the respondent population. At the present time both our theory and methodology for the study of ethnic groups are not sufficiently advanced to enable us to do more than present the basic findings of differences across ethnic lines. But that the differences should persist, even among young college graduates, is, we think, sufficiently contrary to expectations to cause social scientists to re-examine their idea that ethnicity is no longer an important variable in American society.

In the first table we observe that the blacks, Polish Jews, Irish Catholics, and Polish Catholics are the most likely to consider themselves Democrats, whereas Protestant Germans and Protestant Scandinavians are the most likely to describe themselves as Republicans; and German Jews most likely to think of themselves as political Independents. With the exception of the Polish Jews, religious differences seem to be more important than ethnic differences, with Protestants least likely to be Democrats and Polish Jews most likely among the white population.

But if one turns to whether the respondents describe themselves as Liberals (Table 2), ethnic variations begin to be important. The blacks and the Jews are most likely to say they are liberals, with the Catholic Poles, Italians, and Irish following close behind. But German Catholics are the least likely of all to describe themselves as liberals, and, in fact, ally themselves in this respect with Protestant Germans, at the very bottom of the liberal rank order.

On an item measuring attitudes toward race—the conclusion of the Kerner report that white racism is the cause of Negro riots in American cities—an

A Note on Political and Social Differences 99

TABLE 1

POLITICAL AFFILIATION BY FATHER'S ETHNIC BACKGROUND

(Percent for June, 1961 College Graduates)

Political Affiliation	Protestant				Catholic				Jewish		Black
	English	Irish	German	Scandi-navian	Irish	German	Italian	Polish	German	Polish	
Democrat	25	28	21	22	41	37	37	48	36	49	80
G. O. P.	48	45	56	49	30	35	38	24	21	14	..
Independent	24	22	25	25	26	23	31	26	40	34	17
New Left	1	2	2	2	2	1	1	0	2	1	1
Other	2	3	6	2	1	4	3	0	2	2	1
Weighted N	1,775	304	1,059	360	366	336	199	111	60	333	76

TABLE 2

PERCENT LIBERAL, IN RANK ORDER, FOR JUNE,
1961 COLLEGE GRADUATES

Rank Order by Religion and Ethnicity	Percent
Black	83
German Jew	82
Polish Jew	69
Catholic Pole	62
Catholic Italian	56
Catholic Irish	55
Protestant Irish	53
Protestant Scandinavian	51
Protestant English	49
Protestant German	45
Catholic German	44

interesting pattern develops. Outside of the blacks, only the German Jews and the Catholic Irish are willing to give a majority vote to such an assertion; after them, the Catholic Poles and the Polish Jews (surely a strange combination), and then the Protestant Scandinavians would support the Kerner Commission report. A number of interesting facts emerge from Table 3. First of all, it is surprising that the Catholic Irish, who had never been thought of as being particularly pro-black, are the only ones besides the German Jews who would accept, in majority, the Kerner Commission report. Secondly, the Catholic Poles, who at least in the general population have scored very high on measures of racism, take second place among the Catholic college graduates to the Irish in their support of the Kerner report conclusion, and stand substantially ahead of other Catholic and Protestant groups. Third, the Scandinavians are the most liberal on racial matters of the Protestant respondents, and indeed, fall within the "Catholic" spectrum on the rank order continuum. Finally, the Germans are the least sympathetic to the Kerner report conclusion, both inside the Catholic and the Protestant groupings.

TABLE 3

RACIAL ATTITUDES OF JUNE, 1961 COLLEGE GRADUATES
Percent Agreeing (in Rank Order) with Statement:
White Racism Cause of Negro Riots in City

Rank Order by Religion and Ethnicity	Percent
Black	84
German Jew	54
Catholic Irish	51
Polish Jew	43
Catholic Pole	43
Protestant Scandinavian	37
Catholic Italian	35
Catholic German	34
Protestant English	30
Protestant Irish	28
Protestant German	28

TABLE 4

PERCENT OF JUNE, 1961 COLLEGE GRADUATES HIGH ON
SUPPORT OF STUDENT MILITANCY

Rank Order by Religion and Ethnicity	Percent
German Jew	50
Polish Jew	45
Black	39
Protestant Scandinavian	33
Catholic Irish	29
Protestant Irish	28
Catholic Pole	28
Catholic German	24
Protestant English	23
Protestant German	21
Catholic German	20

Turning from racism to another measure of attitudes on contemporary social problems—an index devised to measure sympathy for student militancy, one finds a not dissimilar pattern. The Jews and the blacks are most sympathetic, though here the Jews are the first and the blacks second; the Irish are the most sympathetic of the Catholics, only slightly ahead of the Poles; the Scandinavians the most sympathetic of the Protestants, and indeed, ahead of all Catholic groups; and the Germans, both Catholic and Protestant, are the least sympathetic within their own religious traditions.

One can summarize these two tables, then, by observing that on both issues, Jews tend to be more "liberal" than Catholics and Catholics more "liberal" than Protestants, with German Jews more liberal than Polish Jews, the Irish Catholics the most liberal of the Catholics, and the Protestant Scandinavians so liberal that they fall into the Catholic spectrum and not the Protestant. Germans, both Catholic and Protestant, are the least liberal within their own religious traditions.

A similar pattern is manifested in Table 4 and in Table 5 (which presents

TABLE 5

PERCENT OF JUNE, 1961 COLLEGE GRADUATES HIGH ON
FEDERAL AID TO COLLEGES

Rank Order by Religion and Ethnicity	Percent
Black	56
Polish Jew	41
Catholic Irish	32
German Jew	30
Catholic Pole	30
Catholic Italian	27
Protestant Scandinavian	26
Protestant English	22
Protestant German	20
Protestant Irish	18
Catholic German	17

an index of sympathy toward federal support for higher education). The blacks, Jews, and Catholic Irish are most sympathetic, and Catholics, with the exception of the Germans, tend to be more sympathetic than Protestants; the Scandinavians are the most favorable to higher education of all the Protestants, though in this matter they fall somewhat behind the Catholic Poles and Catholic Italians (but the latter only by one percentage point). The Catholic Germans are the least likely of all to support federal aid for higher education.

In Table 6 two cultural measures are used—an index of interest in art and

TABLE 6
ARTISTIC AND READING HABITS OF JUNE, 1961 COLLEGE GRADUATES

High on Art Scale		High on Reading Scale	
Rank Order by Religion and Ethnicity	Per- cent	Rank Order by Religion and Ethnicity	Per- cent
German Jew	39	German Jew	37
Polish Jew	31	Polish Jew	25
Protestant Irish	30	Protestant Irish	23
Black	27	Protestant Scandinavian	23
Protestant Scandinavian	24	Protestant English	23
Protestant English	21	Catholic Irish	23
Protestant German	19	Catholic Pole	22
Catholic Irish	19	Black	20
Catholic Italian	19	Catholic Italian	18
Catholic Pole	17	Protestant German	17
Catholic German	13	Catholic German	16

an index of interest in reading, to determine what ethnic differences may exist in respondents' intellectual orientations. One can conclude from these tables that Jews are notably more interested in art and reading than are Protestants or Catholics, and that Protestants are very slightly more concerned about art than are Catholics. But the Scandinavians are the most "cultural" of the Protestants, and the Irish, the most "cultural" of the Catholics. The Catholic Germans are again at the bottom of the list.

Table 7 investigates the question of whether there is a relationship between ethnicity and career choice. Somewhat surprisingly, Catholic Poles are the most likely to choose a career in a college or a research institution, and Catholic Germans and Italians are the least likely. Catholics are also most likely to work for a large business corporation, unless they happen to be Irish, and the Protestants are the least likely to work for such large companies, particularly if they are Scandinavian or Irish or black.

Regional differences, as well as differences in size of locality in which they live may very well explain many of the differences reported in this note. Nevertheless, the distribution of, let us say, the Irish Catholic, the Italian Catholic, and the Polish Catholic population is such that differences among these three groups cannot be explained away in terms of region or locale (or social class, since all the respondents are college graduates). The sociali-

TABLE 7

CAREER CHOICES OF JUNE, 1961 COLLEGE GRADUATES BY RELIGION AND ETHNICITY

Academic Career Choice		Private Business Corporation Career Choice	
Rank Order by Religion and Ethnicity	Per-cent	Rank Order by Religion and Ethnicity	Per-cent
Catholic Pole	23	Catholic Pole	41
German Jew	17	Catholic German	41
Protestant Scandinavian	17	Catholic Italian	36
Catholic Irish	16	Protestant English	30
Protestant Irish	15	Protestant German	30
Black	14	Polish Jew	30
Protestant English	13	German Jew	28
Polish Jew	11	Catholic Irish	22
Protestant German	11	Protestant Scandinavian	22
Catholic German	8	Protestant Irish	21
Catholic Italian	5	Black	9

zation experience of higher education has not eliminated ethnically linked differences in attitudes and behavior, even among groups whose geographic dispositions are similar, such as the Scandinavians and the Germans, or the Catholics—Irish Catholics, Italian Catholics, and Catholic Poles. The present stage of our very sketchy knowledge about the late stages of the acculturation process of American ethnic immigrant groups is such that we cannot assert flatly that there are cultural and social psychological variables at work within ethnic communities that explain these different behaviors and attitudes, but it is high time that we began to investigate these differences, for if among college graduates, most of them under thirty, differences persist among American ethnic groups, it is quite likely that they will persist for a long time to come.

[Reprinted from SOCIOLOGY OF EDUCATION, Vol. 43, No. 1, Winter, 1970]

Research Note

Political Change Among College Alumni*

Andrew M. Greeley

National Opinion Research Center and University of Illinois at Chicago

Joe L. Spaeth

National Opinion Research Center

A longitudinal study of 1961 alumni shows that in the years since graduation, they have moved away from Democratic political affiliation towards "independence," while the net loss among Republicans was quite small. However, the alumni were far more likely to describe themselves as "liberal" than they were to describe their parents with the same term. The "independents" were more likely to be sympathetic with both black and student movements than were either the Democrats or the Republicans. Even "conservative independents" were more "radical" than conservative Democrats or Republicans. Change from Democratic preference among one's parents to "Independence" corre-lated with attendance at elite universities and liberal arts colleges.

THE VARIOUS STUDIES of the impact of college education on political attitudes are conflicting. (For example, see Corey, 1940; Edelsten, 1962; Educational Reviewer, 1963; Nogee and Levin, 1958–59; Newcomb and others, 1967.[1]) College is presumed to have a "liberalizing" effect on its graduates, although it is reasonably clear that there are many different and not necessarily correlated dimensions to liberalism. On the other hand, college graduates are also likely to be Republicans, and hence to be affiliated with a more conservative political party.

Recent national survey data indicate a considerable increase in the number of Americans who describe themselves as "Independent," and the college educated are especially likely to be in

---

* The research reported herein was supported through the Cooperative Research Program of the Office of Education, U. S. Department of Health, Education, and Welfare, under contract SAE-9102, by the National Institute of Mental Health under grants M5615, M5615–02, M5615–03, M5615–04, and M5615–05, and by a contract with the Carnegie Commission on Higher Education.
[1] For a schematic presentation of the literature on the subject, see Feldman and Newcomb (1969:19–24).

107   *Political Change Among Alumni*

this category. But the category "Independent," in itself, is amorph-
ous. In popular American mythology, the Independent is the
"mugwump"—the man who thinks for himself and refuses to be
caught by any ideological party line. Research findings however,
indicate that among the so-called independents are those who are
not deeply involved in the political process and lack any kind of
coherent system of political symbols.

A recent study, conducted by the National Opinion Research
Center, of alumni who graduated from college in 1961 enables us
to shed some light on these issues.[2] In Tables 1 and 2, we trace

TABLE 1

Party Affiliation and Political Orientation of Alumni and Their Parents
(Per Cent)

		Alumni		Changes		Net Change
				Parent to	1964 to	Parent to
Affiliation	Parents	1964	1968	1964	1968	1968
A. Party Affiliation						
Republican	44	38	43	—6	+5	—1
Democratic	44	36	29	—8	—7	—15
Independent	8	24	26	+16	+2	+18
Other	3	2	2	—1	0	—1
Total	99	100	100			
B. Political Orientation						
Liberal	40	56	52	+16	—4	+12

changing party affiliations of the 1961 alumni by comparing the
affiliations that they reported for their parents with the affiliations
that they reported for themselves in 1964 and again in 1968.[3] Approximately the same proportion (43 per cent) reported themselves
as Republicans in 1968 as came from Republican families (44 per
cent). However, Democratic affiliation declined dramatically from

[2] The methodology and sampling design of the NORC study of college alumni
are reported in Davis (1964) and Spaeth (forthcoming). In the original 1961
phase of the study, 35,000 graduates of 135 colleges and universities responded to a
self-administered questionnaire. The fifth wave, on which this note is based, consisted of a self-administered questionnaire mailed in 1968 to a subsample of 5,000
members of the original sample. A detailed description of the fifth wave is reported
in Spaeth and Greeley (1970).

[3] Parental affiliation is measured by responses in the 1964 wave to the second
part of the following question: "Which of the following comes closest to (A) your
own political leanings at the present time, and (B) those of your parents when you
were in high school?" The response categories were: "Conservative Republican,"
"Liberal Republican," "Conservative Democrat," "Liberal Democrat," "Conservative
Independent," "Liberal Independent," "Other."

108   *Greeley and Spaeth*

44 per cent in the parental generation to 29 per cent in the respondent generation. All of the loss of the Democrats was to the benefit
of the "Independents," who were more than one-quarter of the
alumni in 1968 and only 8 per cent of the parental generation.

However, there were interesting shifts between 1964 and
1968, with an upswing for the Republicans of 5 per cent and a
downswing for the Democrats of 7 per cent; thus the Republican
curve from high school (parental preference) through 1964 to 1968
is U-shaped, but the Democratic curve is a downward slant and the
Independent curve an upward slant. To what extent the confused,
frustrating, and bitter 1968 presidential campaign contributed to

TABLE 2

Political Leanings of Alumni, 1964 and 1968
(Per Cent)

Political Leanings	1964	1968	Net Difference
Conservative Republican	18	22	+4
Liberal Republican	20	21	+1
Conservative Democrat	13	12	−1
Liberal Democrat	23	18	−5
Conservative Independent	11	12	+1
Liberal Independent	13	14	+1
New Left	..	1	+1
Other	2	1	−1

this change remains to be seen. The data for the study were
collected after President Johnson's withdrawal and before the
assassination of Senator Robert Kennedy.

Table 1B shows that while the alumni were considerably
more likely to describe themselves as political liberals than they
were to describe their parents as such, nonetheless, there has been
a decrease (4 percentage points) of liberalism and a corresponding
increase of conservatism since 1964.

Table 2 indicates that when party affiliation and political
orientation are combined, the principal losers between 1964 and
1968 were the liberal Democrats, and the principal gainers, the
conservative Republicans. The alumni were at least as Republican
and much less Democratic than were their parents, and they were
more likely to think of themselves as "liberal" than they were to
describe their parents as having been "liberal." They were also
more likely to think of themselves as "conservative" in 1968 than
they were four years previously.

Liberalism more or less held its own, but the Democratic
party did not. The strength of the trend away from the Democrats
in 1968 is shown in Table 3, in which are considered not only

109   *Political Change Among Alumni*

TABLE 3

1968 Party Affiliation by 1964 Party Affiliation and Parental Party Affiliation
(Per Cent)

1968 Party Affiliation	Parental Party Affiliation								
	Democratic			Republican			Independent		
	1964 Party Affiliation			1964 Party Affiliation			1964 Party Affiliation		
	Democratic	Republican	Independent	Democratic	Republican	Independent	Democratic	Republican	Independent
Democratic	73	8	20	53	4	8	58	2	14
Republican	9	74	21	22	85	39	18	63	32
Independent	18	17	58	26	11	54	25	35	54
N	(1,894)	(577)	(663)	(446)	(2,072)	(686)	(163)	(161)	(376)

110   *Greeley and Spaeth*

the respondent's party affiliations in 1964 and 1968, but also the
party affiliation of the respondent's parents. The Democratic party
was not able to attract back into the fold more than a handful of
those children of Democratic families who had become Republicans by 1964, and, though it regained 20 per cent of those who
were Independents in 1964, it lost more than one-quarter of those
who in 1964 were Democrats. The principal gainers, however,
from the Democratic defections were the so-called "Independents,"
and not the Republicans.

On the other hand, almost nine-tenths of those whose parents
were Republicans and were themselves Republicans in 1964 were
still Republican in 1968; 22 per cent of those from Republican
backgrounds who were Democrats in 1964 and 39 per cent of those

TABLE 4

1968 Political Orientation by 1964 Political Orientation and Parental
Political Orientation
(Per Cent)

	Parental Political Orientation			
	Liberal		Conservative	
	1964 Political Orientation		1964 Political Orientation	
1968 Political Orientation	Liberal	Conservative	Liberal	Conservative
Liberal	69	37	67	33
Conservative	31	63	33	67
N	(1,999)	(799)	(2,042)	(2,198)

who were Independents in 1964 reported Republican affiliation
in 1968. Finally, the Republicans made strong inroads into the
ranks of those who came from Independent family backgrounds,
and even into the ranks of those whose backgrounds were Independent and who themselves were Independent in 1964 (32 per
cent).

Perhaps the erosion of Democratic strength indicated in Tables 1 through 3 was part of a natural change in the economic
and social perspective of college alumni or was related specifically
to the confusing political situation of 1968. In any event, the
changes between liberal and conservative orientation do not seem
to be very striking (Table 4) when the political orientation of parents is held constant. Thus the "liberalization" of college students
reported by Spaeth (forthcoming:ch. 3) and others does not seem
to have been affected either by the passage of time or by the
political events of 1968.

111   *Political Change Among Alumni*

TABLE 5

Attitudes on Student and Negro Protests by Political Leanings
(Per Cent Agree)

| | Political Leanings | | | | | | |
| | Republican | | Democratic | | Independent | | |
Attitude	Conservative	Liberal	Conservative	Liberal	Conservative	Liberal	New Left
Student protests a healthy sign for America	30	55	36	64	43	77	97
Negro protests will be healthy for America	33	58	44	73	50	78	97
N	(1,638)	(1,595)	(899)	(1,292)	(914)	(1,031)	(89)

The Democratic party lost strength, but more of it to Independents than to Republicans, though the Republicans made gains; but there has been only a minor erosion of "liberalism." When the alumni are compared with their parents, one can say that a college education produces substantial gains for both liberals and Independents, substantial losses for Democrats, and a "break even" for Republicans. The critical question, however, is: What do these shifts mean in terms of concrete political issues? Is a liberal Republican less "liberal" than a liberal Democrat? Is a conservative Independent more "conservative" than a conservative Republican?

Table 5 enables us to provide answers to these questions for the issues of protests by students and blacks. The striking finding in Table 5 is that on both issues, the Independents, whether they be conservative or liberal, were more "liberal" than their counterparts in either the Democratic or the Republican party. Liberal Independents were more "liberal" than liberal Democrats, who were, in their turn, more "liberal" than liberal Republicans. In addition, conservative Independents were more "liberal" than conservative Democrats or Republicans, and only somewhat less likely to be "liberal" than were liberal Republicans.

One therefore can argue that, at least for the June, 1961, college graduates, the trend toward Independency has been a trend to the left in regard to the racial and student protest issues. For this population, the experience of passing through college produced a movement both toward liberalism and toward Independency, and the move to Independency, in itself, was "liberal."

One important question remains to be answered: Can the political change reported in this note in any way be attribtuted to the educational experience of the alumni? An attempt to answer

such a question labors under the handicap of the twin problems
that plague all research on the sociology of higher education: Is
the change recorded a generational change that has little to do
with whether one went to college? Can enough input variables
be held constant to generate confidence that there is a college
effect that cannot be attributed to background variables of these
young people who attended college?

The first question cannot be answered with the present data,
since no strictly comparable information is available for the age
peers of the 1961 alumni who did not go to college. A number of
other studies, however, suggest that youth who did not go to
college have moved to the right instead of to the left politically.
(See, for example, Lipset and Raab, 1969.)

One still cannot eliminate the possibility that those who
went to college were the ones most likely to be disposed to a left-

TABLE 6

Net Changes in Party Affiliation of Alumni by Type of College Attended (Own
Affiliation in 1968 Compared with Parental Affiliation when
Respondent Was in High School
(Per Cent Change)

Type of College	Party Affiliation		
	Republican	Democratic	Independent
Elite	−6	−13	+19
Liberal arts	−10	−13	+23
State	+2	−14	+12
Catholic	+4	−19	+15

ward political drift. But it is possible to ask whether this leftward
drift is more likely to occur at certain kinds of colleges than at
others. One would anticipate that the high quality liberal arts
colleges and universities, with their greater faculty concern for
political and social liberalism, would be institutions whose alumni
would be more likely to move towards Independency. Table 6
gives some confirmation for such an assumption. The alumni of
all four types of colleges represented in the table were substantially more likely to describe themselves as Independents than they
were to describe their parents as Independents. But the graduates
of the elite universities and colleges moved much more strongly
towards Independency than did the alumni of Catholic colleges or
state colleges. In fact, the gain of Independents among the alumni
of liberal arts colleges is almost twice the gain of Independency
among the alumni of state colleges.

Furthermore, even though the Democrats lost among all four
groups of alumni, the Republicans made slight gains among the

113   *Political Change Among Alumni*

alumni of state colleges and Catholic colleges and suffered some loss among the graduates of the elite universities and liberal arts colleges. One concludes, therefore, that a drift towards the political left was most visible among the alumni of elite institutions, a drift which was perhaps a prophecy of how the undergraduates of these institutions would behave in the last half of the 1960s.

But the finding must be hedged. It is altogether possible that the elite schools recruited students who were more likely to be disposed to a leftward political drift. (One must wonder how much predisposition there was in this direction in 1957 when most of the 1961 graduates enrolled in college.) We must be content with the typical conclusion of all input-output research in higher education; there is a *correlation* between leftward political movement and attendance at elite liberal arts colleges and universities.

References

Corey, S. M.
   1940   "Changes in the opinions of female students after one year at a university." Journal of Social Psychology 11:341–351.
Davis, J. A.
   1964   Great Aspirations: The Graduate School Plans of America's College Seniors. Chicago: Aldine.
Edelsten, A. S.
   1962   "Since Bennington: evidence of change in student political behavior." Public Opinion Quarterly 26(Winter):564–577.
Educational Reviewer.
   1963   "Survey of the political and religious attitudes of American college students." National Review 15:379–301.
Feldman, K. A., and T. M. Newcomb.
   1969   The Impact of College on Students, Vol. II. San Francisco: Jossey-Bass.
Lipset, S. M., and E. Raab.
   1969   "The Wallace whitelash." Transaction (December):23–35.
Newcomb, T. M., K. E. Koenig, R. Flacks, and D. P. Warwick.
   1967   Persistence and Change: Bennington College and Its Students after 25 Years. New York: Wiley.
Nogee, P., and M. B. Levin.
   1958–59 "Some determinants of political attitudes among college voters." Public Opinion Quarterly 22(Winter):449–463.
Spaeth, J. L.
   forth-   Recent College Graduates.
   coming
Spaeth, J. L., and A. M. Greeley.
   1970   Recent Alumni and Higher Education: A Survey of College Graduates. New York: McGraw-Hill.

Reprinted from THE AMERICAN JOURNAL OF SOCIOLOGY
Vol. 75, No. 6, May 1970
c 1970 by The University of Chicago. All rights reserved.
Printed in U.S.A.

Religious Intermarriage in a Denominational Society

Andrew M. Greeley

National Opinion Research Center and *University of Illinois at Chicago Circle*

Data from the 1957 Current Population Survey of Religion and from the NORC study of June 1961 college graduates indicate that denominational homogeneity in marriage exists for at least three-quarters of the major religious denominations, including the various groups within Protestantism.

The United States is a denominational society, that is, a society in which membership in religious denominations plays a considerable role in determining patterns of interaction which establish the social structure. It was indeed a religiously pluralistic nation before it became a politically pluralistic one, and one of the reasons the founding fathers were constrained to keep it politically pluralistic was the denominational heterogeneity of the various liberated colonies.

While sociologists have argued about and refined considerably Will Herberg's notion of religion as a provider of "social location" in the United States, few have questioned the validity of his basic insight. This paper has two modest goals: (1) to suggest that Herberg's categories of Protestant, Catholic, and Jew are not comprehensive enough—the various denominations within the category "Protestant" still constitute important subcollectivities in the larger society; and (2) to suggest that, if denominational intermarriage is used as an indicator, there does not seem to be an appreciable decline in denominational membership.

Most research done on religious intermarriage lumps all Protestant denominations together, if only because it requires very large samples to make possible the distribution of Protestants into the various denominations. The evidence in these studies seems to indicate that Jews are the least likely to marry members of other faiths, Catholics most likely, and Protestants somewhere in between. However, the release of the tabulations of the 1957 Current Population Survey of Religion enables us to determine rates of religious intermarriage for a number of the Protestant denominations. The first row in table 1 provides the rather striking information that approximately four-fifths of the members of each of the four Protestant denominations are married to people whose present religious affiliation is the same as their own. Not only are Protestants married to other Protestants, as previous studies have shown, but they are married to Protestants who share the same denominational affiliation. And the ratio of mixed marriages *does not vary much across denominational lines.*

American Journal of Sociology

The 1957 census data contained information for the whole population. If there had been some decline in homogeneity of denominational affiliation, one would expect to find evidence of it among the young and the better educated. Furthermore, one would expect that the date gathered after 1957 would show such a change.

In 1968, eleven years after the national census of religion, NORC collected data on original and present religious denominations of both the respondent and spouse, as part of its ongoing study of June 1961 college

TABLE 1

DENOMINATIONAL INTERMARRIAGE (%)

Denominational Intermarriage	Catholic	Baptist	Lutheran	Methodist	Presbyterian	Jew
Proportion of U.S. population married to member of same denomination in 1957..	88	83	81	81	81	94
Proportion of 1961 alumni married to member of same denomination in 1968..	86 (1,130)	84 (355)	83 (354)	86 (712)	78 (402)	97 (353)
Proportion of alumni in which marriage took place between two people whose original denomination was the same and who currently belong to that denomination..	75	35	34	30	15	94
Proportion of alumni whose original denomination has remained unchanged and whose spouse has converted to that denomination........	11	14	22	16	15	2

graduates. The second row in table 1 shows the proportions of the major denominations who are presently married to spouses who share the same religious affiliation. There is virtually no difference between the endogamy ratios for young college alumni in 1968 and the general population in 1957. The tendency to seek denominational homogeneity in marriage does not seem to have weakened in the slightest.

The first two rows in the table represent data indicating present denominational affiliation of both respondent and spouse, but they do not tell us whether the denominational homogeneity in marriage has been attained by marrying within one's own denomination, or by substantial conversions at the time of marriage (or at least in relation to the marriage).

Religious Intermarriage

However, the third row in table 1 shows the proportion of respondents who married a spouse whose original religious denomination was the same as their own, with both now practicing that religion. It becomes clear that denominational homogeneity is maintained by Catholics and Jews through the process of marrying within one's own denominational boundaries, whereas it is maintained by other religious groups largely through considerable shifting of denominational affiliations. For Catholics and Jews it is important that one marry within one's own denomination (and far more important for Jews than for Catholics). When Catholics marry into other denominations, the non-Catholic is likely to convert. Protestants may marry across denominational lines, but then denominational change occurs in order to maintain religious homogeneity in the family environment.

It also appears from the fourth row in table 1 that those of Lutheran background are able to attract a considerable proportion of their non-Lutheran spouses to join their own Lutheran denomination; thus one-fifth of the Lutherans have married people who have converted to Lutheranism, but none of the other three major Protestant denominations seem to have any special relative strength in the game of denominational musical chairs that is required to maintain the family religious homogeneity.

We do not know, of course, whether the patterns of denominational change to maintain homogeneity observed in the college population is the same as the pattern in the more general population, since the 1957 census did not provide information about original denominational affiliation. However, further research on the subject is clearly indicated.

In summary, then, one may say that America is still very much a denominational society to the extent that denominational homogeneity in marriage exists for at least three-quarters of the major religious denominations.[1]

One may speculate that the strain toward denominational homogeneity is rooted in the American belief that religious differences between husband and wife are not good either for the marriage relationship or for the children of the marriage. This belief is probably reinforced by the fact that it is simpler and more convenient that everyone in the family belong to the same denomination. For example, one need not worry about two sets of contributions to the support of one's church. Whether the maintenance of high levels of denominational homogeneity in marriage has any specifically religious or doctrinal significance may be open to question. Nevertheless,

[1] Denominational homogeneity in marriage seems equally important in another denominational society, Canada. In 1967, 69 percent of the marriages which took place in Canada were between members of the same denomination, a slight dip from the 71 percent of 1957. It should be noted that this statistic represents homogeneity at time of marriage. Presumably some postmatrimonial conversions would push the Canadian statistic even closer to the one for the United States (cf. 1968, p. 284).

American Journal of Sociology

it is still extremely important in American society that one's spouse be of the same religious denomination as oneself.

REFERENCES

Tabulations of data on the social and economic characteristics of major religious groups. In *1957 Current Population Survey of Religion.* n.d. Washington, D.C.: Government Printing Office.
Canada Year Book. 1968. Ottawa: Dominion Bureau of Statistics.

SOCIOLOGY AS AN ART FORM

ANDREW M. GREELEY

National Opinion Research Center of The University of Chicago

The American Sociologist 1971, Vol. 6 (August):223–225

One of the latent advantages of the development of path analysis as a major tool of social research is that the graphic models this form of analysis produces may make it difficult for us to ignore the obvious fact that sociology is an art form. One need only observe or experience the aesthetic pleasure the path analysts experience when admiring the elegance of their models to realize that path analysis has progressed beyond mere rational science, and path analysts are dealing with both an artistic activity and an artistic experience. As anyone who has engaged in constructing a survey questionnaire has known all along, social science is, if not an art, at least a rather artistic craft. But model building and model modification go beyond mere craftsmanship.

After one has developed a model of path analysis, or when one is in the process of reconstructing such a model in the light of empirical data, one should read Lévi-Strauss's famous description of mythology as *bricolage*, a word that one English writer happily translates as "puttering." Like the mythmaker, the model builder has at his disposal a definite and finite number of components which he arranges and rearranges and then rearranges again, endlessly searching for the most elegant way of displaying his handicraft. Having read Lévi-Strauss on puttering, one can overcome one's guilt feelings about having engaged in such nonscientific activity by reading Watson's (1968) account of the development of the double helix which is certainly a description of *bricolage* with a vengeance.

Even if one is not persuaded by Thomas Kuhn's (1970) description of paradigm construction or Michael Polyani's (1958) account of the tacit dimension and personal knowledge, even if one does not believe that the scien-

tific enterprise is, in effect, an attempt to prove that which one already tacitly knows is true, one still must recognize, having constructed a path diagram, that one is engaged in something quite different from an exercise in discursive reasoning reinforced by the experimental method. Discursive reasoning and the experimental method are present, but also present are instinct, passion, compassion, conviction, philosophy, and theology—all involved in headlong, perhaps even violent, artistic endeavor. As Professor Harrison White, with a secure perspective obtained from having Ph.D.s in both physics and sociology, once remarked to his statistics class at Harvard University, "Science is man pursuing truth, no holds barred."

The distinction, then, between art and science is probably both invalid and deceptive. Artistic creation depends to some extent at least on discursive reasoning, and the scientific enterprise necessarily involves man's artistic instincts even if he tries to pretend that it does not. Sociology is a craft, an art, a game, and an exercise in creative playfulness, and it may very well be time for us to admit this fact and explore its implications.

The sociological act is the act of the whole man. Even if we try, we cannot suppress from that act our hunches, our instincts, our passions, our commitments, and our convictions. Discursive reasoning may reign over the sociological act but it does so not as a dictator with monopoly rights but as a constitutional monarch that coordinates the operations of other dimensions of the human personality.

We might like to persuade ourselves, for example, that our religion—herein defined à la Clifford Geertz (1970) as our convictions about the nature of the Real—can be excluded from our sociology, but if we pause for but a moment and consider the implication of Geertz's definition of religion, we realize that it is impossible to exclude our convictions about the Real from any of our endeavors. The best we can do, and all we ought to try to do, is to take those convictions into account.

"What makes us scientists, I suspect, is . . . that we have carefully developed and maintained the ability to test not only the explanations toward which our personalities and our convictions incline us but the ability to listen carefully to the positions of persons whose passions, convictions, and sympathies are different from our own."

The young radicals among us insist, I believe quite correctly, that passion, compassion, and conviction must be part of the sociological endeavor. If one is to fault them it is not so much for having Marxist convictions as for being on occasion shallow Marxists, not so much for having no compassion but for on occasion being very selective about who is a legitimate object of compassion, and not so much for approaching their work without compassion and enthusiasm but for being unable on occasion to sustain that enthusiasm for very long.

What makes us scientists, I suspect, is not that we exclude conviction, passion, and compassion from our activities, but that we have carefully developed and maintained the ability to test not only the explanations toward which our personalities and our convictions incline us but the ability to listen carefully to the positions of persons whose passions, convictions, and sympathies are different from our own. If we are to fault the young sociologists, it is not for arguing that the whole person should be engaged in the sociological act but for not taking seriously or testing on occasion explanations that are contrary to their convictions and sympathies. We ought not to criticize our junior colleagues for being explicitly religious when we ourselves are implicitly religious (in the Geertzian sense, of course), but we ought to criticize them when their religion makes them sectarian and deprives them of the capacity to dialogue with those who have other religions. Unfortunately, ecumenical dialogue is a difficult art, acquired only through discipline and practice.

The radical young among us, then, are not to be criticized when they announce that they have an ideology, for having an ideology is an inescapable aspect of the human condition; rather, they are to be criticized when they talk or act as though their ideology is the only ideology that men of sincerity, good will, and compassion should be permitted to express.

We have observed that the most creative of our colleagues do not seem to work according to the strict rules of the scientific method. They form explicit hypotheses only when they are ready to write up the account of their work, and generally they worry about specifying their formal theory only as they try to figure out how to begin their article. I am not suggesting that theories or null hypotheses are absent from their works but that theories,

hypotheses, scholarly footnotes, and familiarity with the literature are present in implicit and fundamentally unimportant fashion. What the creative scholars are doing when they are working in a project has nothing to do with anything that fits in the neat paradigm of scientific method. What they are doing is dreaming, speculating, playing with the variables in the model, following their hunches and instincts, and puttering with their raw materials. None of these activities get into sociological reports because they are not "science." However neat and precise the professional tone of articles, papers, and monographs, are they really honest descriptions about how our colleagues went about their work? No, they are using the approved literary form for communicating with each other and can escape the charge of dishonesty with the plea that nobody really believes that the analytic process described in an article is in fact the one that went into its preparation.

I can recollect only one account of a sociological enterprise that violated the rules of "scientific formalism"—the account by Davis (1964) in *Sociologists at Work*. Davis is one of the rare sociologists who permit their playfulness to break through the mask of professionalism. He once even managed to get the words "frog pond" in a title of an article in the *American Sociological Review*. What is the reaction to Davis's wit? People shake their heads in puzzlement and ask, "He isn't serious, is he?"

The last thing in the world that is to be tolerated in the writings of a sociologist is wit, either in the modern or the Elizabethan sense. Ours is a "serious enterprise," and since it is serious, there is no reason for humor or playfulness as we describe what we are about. Even the slightest sign of anything but the most somber prose style is viewed with bafflement and suspicion. I once violated the canons of sociology to the extent of writing an article for the *New York Times Magazine* and, to make matters worse, I suggested in the article that intellectuals were an ethnic group. One of my younger colleagues wrote a particularly nasty letter to the *Times* suggesting that either I was serious and, hence, quite wrong or I was joking and, hence, quite irresponsible. I presume that if I had begun the article by saying, "It is sometimes useful to use the model of a religio-ethnic group as a tool for examining the phenomenon to be observed among American academics," the young man would have had no problem. Oh, I was using a "model." Well, then, it is all right because it is "serious" to use a model. I would have preferred to say that I was using a "conceit," that is, in the Elizabethan sense, an exercise in wit; but the poor young man was witless and couldn't be expected to understand.

I think the day may come when men are astonished that there was a generation of scholars that rigorously excluded wit from their work. These scholars of the future will simply not be able to comprehend why wit, such a marvelous attribute of the human personality, was considered unscientific and unprofessional. I am arguing that the sociological act is an exercise in artistic playfulness and that sociologists have all entered into a mammoth conspiracy to hide the fact. Our papers are obscure, our journal articles are dull and frequently unintelligible, and our meetings are sluggish and wearisome (save when John Barleycorn or, recently, marijuana takes effect) precisely because we have persuaded ourselves that this is the only way to establish our professionalism. Despite our serious efforts to turn off all other modalities of knowing and expressing, our work, if it is worth anything at all, goes far beyond discursive reasoning. Indeed, the really good social scientists are made of the same stuff that novelists and poets are made of; in fact, if they were a little more talented they might be poets instead of social scientists.

We are all born poets in the sense that our first cognitive activities involve the arrangements of symbols. We have to learn to write prose, and it takes a good deal of effort for us to learn how to think exclusively in prose. This, of course, is what graduate education in the social sciences is designed to teach, and it must be confessed that we are quite successful. Whatever trace of the poet is left in a student after primary and secondary and higher education we successfully eliminate in his professional socialization—and then we find it difficult to understand why his work is dull and uncreative.

By the time a person is a graduate student, his work is frequently illiterate, too. Part of this can be attributed to the fact that the student never learned to write a decent sentence in his prior education and part of it can be attributed to his personal insecurity, but I think much of the inarticulateness of the dissertation writer results from the fact that he is trying to write "scientifically." I have known very literate students to turn out gibberish in the first draft of their dissertations because they believed that to be scientists they had to suppress in themselves precisely those skills that would have enabled them to write literate prose. With such students one can usually get a second draft that is not gibberish by instructing them to forget about being scientists and tell their story. They do so, but feel guilty about it: their paper seems so unscientific and unprofessional.

> "The requirement that we listen to other men's perspectives and the requirement that we test explanations other than our own seem to me to guarantee that reason will exercise effective discipline over our emotions, passions, convictions, and commitments as we use our sociological imaginations."

Will we not be subject to error if we abandon our pose of professionalism and pursue knowledge "with no holds barred"? If we give free rein to our instincts, our institutions, our passions, and our convictions, will we not be more likely to make mistakes, be more prone to error, and deceive ourselves as to what our data really say? One need only review the last quarter of a century of social science to become aware that the mask of scientific professionalism has by no means preserved us from mistakes, errors, and self-deceptions.

An additional advantage of acknowledging the fundamentally artistic and playful nature of our enterprise is that we might become more respectful of other forms of social knowledge than those we ourselves possess. It is the nature of our enterprise that we deal with reality in

a formal and abstract way, but it should not follow that we cannot learn from persons whose approach to social reality is more specific and concrete. There are political leaders in our large cities whose concrete knowledge of the city is probably far more extensive than that of all the social scientists in the city put together. It is fashionable among many of my colleagues to be amused by Mayor Daley's diction and his malapropisms, but the mayor is, I suspect, a more astute student of social reality than any of us are. The modality of the approach of the sociologist is distinct, and properly so, from the modality of the approach of the politician, and while we are only too ready to rush in and offer to the politician our advice, our theories, our perspectives, and our recommendations, only a few of us are willing to consider the possibility that we might learn something from him.

I am not calling for the abandonment of reason in the social science enterprise; I am too much of an Aristotelian for that. It would not be appropriate for the annual ASA meeting to become a group encounter, much less a liturgy. I am not suggesting that the *American Sociological Review* come out with a psychedelic cover or even that it have cartoons or poetry in its somber pages. The requirement that we listen to other men's perspectives and the requirement that we test explanations other than our own seem to me to guarantee that reason will exercise effective discipline over our emotions, passions, convictions, and commitments as we use our sociological imaginations. What I suggest is that we abandon the pretense that we have stripped ourselves of everything but pure reason as we grapple with social reality. The pretense is not and cannot be true, and to the extent that we distort our personalities to make it true, we weaken, if we do not destroy, the capacity of the sociological act.

It may well be too late. Graduate school, regular reading of sociological journals, and dutiful attendance at prescribed meetings may have accomplished our professional socialization so successfully that we have become permanently half-human, at least as far as our sociology is concerned. We may well have become scholastics— scholastics of the age of Occam rather than Aquinas—in which case we can of course continue with our work. We shall still receive research grants, we shall still write articles and make reports, and students will still enroll in our courses, but persons who are interested in understanding the full richness of human society will turn to the novelists, the poets, and the politicians.

References

Davis, J .A.
    1964   "Great books and small groups: an informal history of a rational survey." Pp. 212–234 in P. E. Hammond (ed.), Sociologists at Work: Essays on the Craft of Social Research. New York: Basic Books.
Geertz, Clifford
    1970   Islam Observed. New Haven: Yale University Press.
Kuhn, Thomas
    1970   Structure of Scientific Revolution. Chicago: University of Chicago Press.
Polyani, Michael
    1958   Personal Knowledge. Chicago: University of Chicago Press.
Watson, James
    1968   Double Helix. New York: Atheneum.

The Rediscovery of Diversity

BY ANDREW M. GREELEY

Reprinted from  Fall 1971, Vol. XXXI, No. 3

The Rediscovery of Diversity

BY ANDREW M. GREELEY

For those of us who read serious newspapers, magazines and books, the most important conflict that has divided man in the last quarter-century has been ideological. The critical question for us is where one stands in relationship to Karl Marx. Is the man a capitalist or socialist? Is he "a citizen of the free world" or does he live "behind the Iron Curtain?" Is he on the side of the "imperialists" or of the "people's democracies?" But in fact, the conflicts that have occupied most men over the past two or three decades and which have led to the most horrendous outpourings of blood have had precious little to do with this ideological division. Most of us are quite unwilling to battle to the death over ideology, but practically all of us, it seems, are ready to kill each other over really important differences: which is to say, differences of color, language, religious faith, height, food habits, and facial configuration.

Many millions have died tragically in what are purported to be ideological conflicts in Korea and Vietnam, but many more millions, perhaps as many as twenty million, have died in conflicts that have to do with far more ancient divisions than that between the capitalists and the socialists. One need only think of the Hindus and Moslems at the time of the partition of India, of Sudanese blacks and

Arabs, of Tutsi and Hutu in Burundi, of Kurds in Iraq, of Nagas in India, of Karens and Kachins in Burma, of Chinese in Indonesia and Malaysia, of Khambas in Tibet, of Somalis in Kenya and Ethiopia, of Arabs in Zanzibar, of Berbers in Morocco and Algeria, of East Indians and blacks in Guiana, of Ibos in Nigeria, and, more recently, of Bengalis in East Pakistan to realize how pervasive is what might be broadly called "ethnic" conflict and how incredible the numbers of people who have died in such "irrational" battles. Two million died in India, five hundred thousand have perished in the "unknown war" in the Sudan, and two hundred thousand more in the equally unknown war in Burundi. The numbers may have been over a million in Biafra and over a half million in Malaysia and Indonesia, and as high as one hundred thousand in Burma and Iraq.

The ethnic conflicts have not been so bloody in other parts of the world, but tens of thousands have died in the seemingly endless battle between those two very Semitic people, the Jews and the Arabs. The English and the French glare hostilely at each other in Quebec; Christian and Moslem have renewed their ancient conflicts on the island of Mindanao; Turk and Greek nervously grip their guns in Cyprus; and Celt and Saxon in Ulster have begun imprisoning and killing one another with all the cumulative passion of a thousand years' hostility.

And, even when there is practically no violence, tension and conflict still persist as the old nationalisms of Wales, Scotland, Brittany, Catalonia and Navarre, Flanders, and even of the Isle of Man are reasserted. Even in the world of socialism, Great Slav and Little Slav do not trust each other, and Slav and Oriental have renewed their ancient feuds. Moreover, the rulers of the Slavic socialist states are troubled by internal conflict. What, for example, are the Great Russians to do about the Little Russians, much less about the Volga Germans or the Kahsacks, to say nothing of the Crimean Tartars? The new masters of Czechoslovakia still struggle with the ancient conflict between Prague and Bratislava. Finally, the old partisan leader Marshal Tito spends his last years trying desperately to hold his polyglot peoples' democracy together.

In a world of nuclear energy, the jet engine, the computer, and the rationalized organization, the principal conflicts are not ideological but tribal. Those differences among men which were supposed to be swept away by science and technology and political revolution are as destructive as ever.

Indeed, if anything, the conflicts seem to be increasing rather than decreasing. Just as the collapse of the Austro-Hungarian empire increased tension in central Europe, so the collapse of the old colonial empires has opened a Pandora's box of tribal, linguistic, religious, and cultural conflicts. It may be also the "turning in on oneself" which follows the relinquishing of imperial power that has given rise to the new nationalisms in Western Europe. Finally, it seems that the failure of both capitalism and socialism to deliver on their promises of economic prosperity for all is responsible for the tensions both in Eastern Europe and between black and white in the United States. Men were promised affluence and dignity if they yielded their old primordial ties. They now suspect that the promise was an empty one and are returning to those primordial ties with a vengeance.

HOMICIDE BEGINS AT HOME

The differences over which we kill each other are relatively minor. It is not those who are tremendously different from us that we slay or hate; it is rather those similar to us. Punjabi and Bengali share the same religion; they differ only in geography and to some extent in skin color. A Canadian would be hard put to tell the difference between an Ibo, a Hausa, a Fulani, and a Yoruba. The difference between a French and English Canadian would escape all but the most sophisticated Yorubas. A Kurd could not tell a Flem from a Walloon on a street in Brussels. Most Africans would be struck by the similarity in everything but skin color between American blacks and American whites. An American black, in his turn, would find it very difficult to tell the difference between Catholic brogue and Protestant brogue in Ulster. An Indonesian would be properly horrified at the thought that he looked rather like a Filipino, but he would not understand how a Greek could distinguish another Greek from a Turk, or even how one could tell the difference between a Jew and an Arab. The differences over which we human beings take arms can be very minor indeed.

I sometimes speculate that the incredible diversity of the human race is a great joke of a humorous God; He finds it hilarious, but we have not quite gotten around to laughing.

But what is the nature of this primal diversity over which we so eagerly do battle? The question is easy to ask but extremely difficult to answer. With his characteristic elegance, Clifford Geertz observes:

> When we speak of "communalism" in India we refer to religious contrasts; when we speak of it in Malaya we are mainly concerned with racial ones, and in the Congo with tribal ones. But the grouping under a common heading is not simply adventitious; the phenomena referred to are in some way similar. Regionalism has been the main theme in Indonesian disaffection, differences in custom in Moroccan. The Tamil minority in

Ceylon is set off from the Sinhalese majority by religion, language, race, region, and social custom; the Shiite minority in Iraq is set off from the dominant Sunnis virtually by an intra-Islamic sectarian difference alone. Pan-national movements in Africa are largely based on race, in Kurdistan on tribalism; in Laos, the Shan, and Thailand, on language. Yet all these phenomena, too, are in some sense of a piece. They form a definable field of investigation.

*That is they would, could we but define it.**

But Geertz at least attempts a definition. Leaning on a concept introduced by Edward Shils,**** Geertz suggests that what we are dealing with is "primordial attachments."

By a primordial attachment is meant one that stems from the "givens"—or more precisely, as culture is inevitably involved in such matters, the "assumed" givens—of social existence: immediate contiguity and kin connection mainly, but beyond them, the givenness that stems from being born into a particular religious community speaking a particular language, or even a dialect of language, and following particular social patterns. These congruities of blood, speech, custom, and so on, are seen to have an ineffable, and at times overpowering, coerciveness in and of themselves. One is bound to one's kinsman, one's neighbor, one's fellow believer, ipso facto, as a result not merely of one's personal affection, practical necessity, common interest, or incurred obligation, but at least in great part by the virtue of some unaccountable absolute import attributed to the very tie itself. The general strength of such primordial bonds, and the types of them that are important, differ from person to person, from society to society, and from time to time. But for virtually every person, in every society, at almost all times, some attachments seem to flow more from a sense of natural—some would say spiritual—affinity than from social interaction.†

It is the primordial tie, then, a "longing not to belong to any other group," according to Geertz, that is essential to what is broadly defined as "ethnic" behavior.

Following Geertz, Professor Harold Isaacs speaks of "basic group identity," which is not merely related to a need to be special,

---

Clifford Geertz, "The Integrative Revolution," in Old Societies and New States *(Glencoe, Ill., 1963).*

**Edward Shils, "Primordial, Personal, Sacred, and Civil Ties," British Journal of Sociology, *June 1957, pp. 130–145.*

†Geertz, op. cit. pp. 109–110.

or unique, or different from others; but is fundamental to an individual's sense of *belongingness* and to the level of his *self-esteem*.

> *In my own mind, I picture group identity as looking more like a cell of living matter with a sprawlingly irregular shape. It is a part of a cluster of cells making up the ego identity, sharing elements and common membranes with that other elusive quarry, the "individual personality." In it, floating or darting about, are specks and flecks, bits and pieces, big shapes, little shapes, intersecting each other or hanging loose or clinging to one another, some out at the margins, some nearer the middle, some in wide orbits around the edges, some more narrowly moving deeper inside, but each one impinging upon, drawn to or repelled by a nuclear core that exerts its gravity upon them all and fixes the shape and content of the messages that go out along the tiny meshes of the nervous system. The arrangement and mutual relationship of these elements differ from cell to cell and the nature of the nuclear core differs not only from cell to cell but can change within any one cell, all of these interactions having a fluid character and subject to alteration under the pressure of conditions that come in upon them from the outside.*
>
> *Here, I think, in the inwardness of group identity is where we can learn more than we know now about the interactions of the individual, his group, and the larger politics of his time and place, and, more therefore, about the nature of our common contemporary experience.**

As am I, both Isaacs and Geertz are deeply indebted to Edward Shils for his ideas of primordial ties. In his famous 1957 article in the *British Journal of Sociology*, Shils comments:

> *Man is much more concerned with what is near at hand, with what is present and concrete than with what is remote and abstract. He is more responsive on the whole to persons, to the status of those who surround him and the justice which he sees in his own situation than he is with the symbols of remote persons, with the total status system in the society and with the global system of justice. Immediately present authorities engage his mind more than remote ones.·.... That is why the ideologist, be he prophet or revolutionary, is affronted by the ordinary man's attachment to his mates, to his pub, to his family, to his petty vanities in his job, to his vulgar gratifications, to his concern for the improvement of his conditions of life. That is also why the ideologist dislikes the politician, who aspires to do no*

---

*Harold Isaacs, "*Group Identity and Political Change*," Bulletin of the International House of Japan, *April 1964, pp. 24-25.*

*more than to help keep things running and to make piecemeal
changes, and of course, the businessman, the manager, the tech-
nologist who works on a limited front. . . .**

The striking thing about the comments of Isaacs, Geertz, and
Shils is that they all use a rhetoric which is uncommonly poetic for
the social sciences. Part of the poetry is no doubt the result of the
fact that the three men are students of English style, but part of it
too, I suspect, comes from the fact that they are dealing with something so basic and so fundamental in the human condition that prose
is not altogether adequate in dealing with it.

And since the primordial tie has to do with something which
is so extremely basic in man's life, it is not at all a mystery that man
is willing, indeed, almost eager, to die in the defense of it. As Harold
Isaacs pointed out at the September 1971 meetings of the American
Political Science Association, much of what is evil in the human condition—as well as much of what is good—flows from a man's primal
sense of *belonging* to something that makes him a *somebody*.

When we consider all the evil that flows from ethnic diversity,
we are strongly tempted to conclude that such diversity should be
done away with. Peace and harmony will come to the world
through rational, liberal, scientific, democratic homogenization.
There was a time when such optimistic liberal faith did not seem
naive. It must be confessed that many illustrious Americans still subscribe to that faith: "ethnicity" is part of man's primal, primitive,
and prerational (which of course means irrational) past, a past out
of which he is supposed to be evolving. With more faith in science,
with more experience in political democracy, with more of the advantages of economic progress, with more replacement of the sacred
by the secular, man will finally, to use Dietrich Bonhoeffer's phrase,
"come of age." He will not need the tribal ties, and all the parapher-
nalia of his old prerational, superstitious, unscientific past can safely
be cast off.

When Professor Harvey Cox wrote his now-famous *Secular
City*, such a liberal optimistic faith seemed justified. But Professor
Cox himself has made a pilgrimage from *The Secular City* to *The
Feast of Fools*, a medieval feast that takes place in a festive and
fantastic Camelot. The mood of American academia today is one of
massive apostasy from liberal rationalism.

One need not swing quite as far as Professor Cox and others
have—from the dialectics of the rational to the irrational—to recognize that man does not live by reason alone. The collapse of the
empires, and modernization, both of which were supposed to bring
liberal democracy and rational secularism to the uttermost parts of

Edward Shils, op. cit., *pp. 130-131.*

the earth, have instead produced a resurgence of the tribe and the clan. Under such circumstances, every man must reconsider the possibility and the desirability of homogenization. At a time when many in the American academy rigorously support what they take to be black separatism—and at times enforce such separatism on blacks who might not be inclined in that direction—it is hardly possible or logical to insist that everybody else be homogenized.

But we are dealing with far more than the abandonment of one fad for another, or an over-hasty and naive apostasy of a naively held scientific faith. Serious scholars like Shils, Geertz, Isaacs, Glazer, and Moynihan have offered persuasive evidence of the persistence of diversity. The profound and ingenious work of Chomsky in linguistics and Lévi-Strauss in anthropology suggests that diversity might be "structured into" the human experience. Man has no other way to cope with the reality in which he finds himself, including the reality of his own relationship network, than by differentiating it. Such a view of things suggests that the hope of unity through homogenization was not just naive and premature but also betrayed a profound misunderstanding of the human condition. Diversity may lead to hellish miseries in the world, but without the power to diversify—and to locate himself somewhere in the midst of the diversity—man may not be able to cope with the world at all.

To descend briefly from the cosmic level of macro-social theory to the grubby data of survey research, my colleagues, Norman Nie and Barbara Currie, and I have discovered that among American ethnic groups there is a positive correlation between sympathy for integration and identification with and involvement in the ethnic community. The more "ethnic" a southern and eastern European Catholic is the more likely he is to be pro-integration—and, incidentally, the more likely he is to be a "dove" on the Vietnam war. This finding, which flies directly in the teeth of the well-nigh unanimous conventional wisdom about southern and eastern European Catholics, raises the interesting possibility that diversity in "basic group identification" may under certain sets of circumstances be more than just a heavy burden for society; it may even be on occasion a positive asset.

With such a theoretical backdrop, let us now turn to the more specific question of religious, racial, geographic, and ethnic* diver-

---

*"Ethnic" is now used in the sense of "nationality." In the nominalism of American survey research, there are ten basic religio-ethnic groups in American society, a number based not on any astrological mysticism nor any complex theory, but simply on the number of respondents available for analysis in an ordinary-sized national sample. They are: Anglo-Saxon Protestants, German Protestants, Scandinavian Protestants, Irish Catholics, German Catholics, southern European Catholics, eastern European Catholics, Jews, blacks, and Spanish speaking people.

sity in American society. There are four major observations that can be made about the subject of diversity in the United States.

PORTNOY'S COMPLAINT?

Most Americans feel ambivalent about the fact of diversity and also about their own particular location in ethnic geography. We are torn between pride in the heritage of our own group and resentment at being trapped in that heritage. (An ambivalence which is surely not absent from this issue of *The Antioch Review*.) This ambivalence is probably the result of the agonies of the acculturation experience in which an immigrant group alternately felt shame over the fact that it was different and unwanted and a defensive pride about its own excellence, which the rest of society seemed neither to appreciate nor understand. It is that ambivalence which produced the superpatriotism that Daniel P. Moynihan neatly epitomized in his remark about the McCarthy (Joseph) era: "Harvard men were to be investigated and Fordham men were to do the investigating." The superpatriot is the man who is proud of his own uniqueness and yet simultaneously wants to be like everyone else, only more so.

The ambivalence about one's own specific contribution to diversity is clear in both the Irish and the Jewish novels written in America. Jewish authors, it has always seemed to me, achieve a much better balance of self-acceptance and self-rejection than do their Irish counterparts. One need only compare Farrell with Malamud and Saul Bellow with Tom McHale to discover that the Jewish writers are much more at ease with who and what they are than are the Irish. (Or to take a more extreme case: Philip Roth is surely ambivalent about being Jewish; John O'Hara was not ambivalent about being Irish, he was ashamed of it.) Perhaps the years of persecution of Jew by Christian did not have nearly the impact on Jewish self-respect that the millennium of political oppression of the English by the Irish had on the Irish self-respect.

The Anglo-Saxon Protestant may be free of this ambivalence, though if he is, there are enough strains towards guilt in the American Protestant consciousness to even the score. But whatever is to be said of the WASP, all those who came after him wanted to be different, yet feel uneasy and guilty about being different. We praise the melting pot out of one side of our mouths and honor cultural pluralism out of the other.

NEGLECTED ROOTS

Precisely because of this ambivalence about American cultural pluralism, *there has been in the last quarter of a century relatively little in the way of serious research on the subject, despite the fact that the later stages of the acculturation of the immigrant groups should have been considered a fascinating subject for social science.* One can look through the indices of the various sociological and psychological journals for the last three decades and find practically nothing on the subject of American ethnic groups—a vacancy even more perplexing when one understands that there is a vast market for such research. (Nathan Glazer and Daniel Patrick Moynihan's *Beyond the Melting Pot* has sold over a half million copies.) Until a year or two ago, practically no survey questionnaires had an ethnic question. Even today, the Gallup organization does not routinely ask about ethnicity, and probably a majority of survey questionnaires still contain no such item. During the 1960s, those of us who maintained some sort of interest in the subject periodically had to explain to skeptical colleagues that what we were concerned about was a legitimate field of research. The presumption seemed to have been that there was nothing there to study, or that even if there was something to study, it was somehow immoral to be concerned about it. Even today, there is a considerable residue of skepticism on the subject of ethnic diversity. (A skepticism which coexists, incidentally, with an incredible flow of anecdotes about ethnic diversity, a flow which is released when the ethnic researcher persuades his colleagues that it is, after all, legitimate to discuss the subject. Indeed, many a conversation which begins with one social scientist politely but firmly suggesting that the ethnic researcher might be a charlatan ends up with collective nostalgia about respective ethnic childhoods.)

In addition to our generalized ambivalence about diversity, there are a number of more specific explanations for the lack of serious research on the subject.

Research acknowledges that diversity has persisted and that it is likely to continue to persist. Such an assumption is at odds with the still dominant assimilationist ideology, an ideology that is, if anything, more important to those who are being assimilated than to those who are doing the assimilating. The idea that it is an admirable goal for all Americans to become alike is deeply rooted in our collective unconscious, reinforced by the mass media, emphasized by the ideology of public education (one remembers Dr. Conant's notion that it was only the public high school which could eliminate the divisiveness and provide the common culture to integrate the society—the common culture, of course, was to be white Protestant), and honored by many of the symbols of our political rhetoric. The assimilationist assumptions, though rarely stated explicitly in recent years, were institutionalized in the immigration laws recommended by the famous Dillingham Commission. Nobody says any more—as the Dillingham Commission virtually did—that Anglo-Saxon culture is superior to southern and eastern European culture; nobody says that American society had a very difficult time "Americanizing" the Italian, Slavic—and, yes, even the German and Irish—immigrant groups. But the idea that "Americanization" means the conversion of later immigrants into something that looks very much like a white Protestant (and as Peter Rossi has remarked, someone who speaks radio-standard English) has yet to be exorcized from the collective unconscious.

It is very difficult to deal with the assimilationist mentality, particularly because it is usually implicit and especially in circumstances when the assimilationist is someone who himself is in the process of assimilation. Anyone who lectures, even to scholarly audiences, on the subject of ethnic diversity is almost certainly to be asked whether, after all, the emphasis on diversity is not dangerous, since it stresses those things which separate men rather than those things which unite them. He is also likely to be cornered before he leaves the lecture hall by an eager questioner who wonders whether it isn't true that, after all, the Irish (for example) have become "just like everyone else." What makes it even more difficult to cope with these questions is that those who ask them frequently bear names that indicate they were scarcely born white Protestants. The last one who wants to hear that diversity is now acceptable is he who has embarked, perhaps irrevocably, on the process of liquidating his own diversity. The sociologist Paul Metzger has appropriate comments to make on "liberal assimilationism" in a recent article in the *American Journal of Sociology*:

1. The belief that racial assimilation constitutes the only democratic solution to the race problem in the United States should be relinquished by sociologists. Beyond committing them to a value premise which compromises their claim to value neutrality, the assimilationist strategy overlooks the functions which ethnic pluralism may perform in a democratic society. . . . The application of this perspective to the racial problem should result in the recognition that the black power and black nationalist movements, to the extent that they aim at the creation of a unified and coherent black community which generates a sense of common peoplehood and interest, are necessarily contrary neither to the experience of other American minorities nor to the interests of black people. The potential for racial divisiveness—and in the extreme case, revolutionary confrontation—which resides in such movements should also be recognized, but the source of this "pathological" potential should be seen as resting primarily within the racism of the wider society rather than in the "extremist" response to it on the part of the victimized minority.

2. To abandon the idea that ethnicity is a dysfunctional survival from a prior stage of social development will make it possible for sociologists to reaffirm that minority-majority relations are in fact group relations and not merely relations between prejudiced and victimized individuals. As such, they are implicated in the struggle for power and privilege in the society, and the theory of collective behavior and political sociology may be more pertinent to understanding them than the theory of social mobility and assimilation. Although general theories of minority-majority relations incorporating notions of power and conflict can be found in the writings of sociologists . . . it is only recently, . . . that such perspectives have found their way into sociologists' analyses of the American racial situation.

3. To abandon the notion that assimilation is a self-completing process will make it possible to study the forces (especially at the level of cultural and social structure) which facilitate or hinder assimilation or, conversely, the forces which generate the sense of ethnic and racial identity even within the homogenizing confines of modern society. On the basis of an assessment of such forces, it is certainly within the province of sociological analyses to point to the possibilities of conscious intervention in the social process (by either the majority or the minority group) to achieve given ends and to weigh the costs and consequences of various policy alternatives. These functions of sociological analysis, however, should be informed by an awareness that any form of intervention will take place in a political context—that intervention itself is in fact a political act—and that the likelihood of its success will be conditioned by the configuration of political forces in the society at large. Without this awareness—which is nothing more than an awareness of the total societal context within which a given minority problem has its meaning—sociological analysis runs a very real risk of spinning surrealistic fantasies about a world which is tacitly believed to be the best of all possible worlds. Whether the call of sociologists for racial assimilation in American society as it is currently organized will fall victim to such a judgment remains to be seen.*

Metzger's implication is inescapable: while it is now appropriate and perhaps even obligatory for blacks to explore and enjoy their own cultural heritage, there is no reason why other Americans should

---

*L. Paul Metzger, *"American Sociology and Black Assimilation: Conflicting Perspective,"* American Journal of Sociology, *Vol. 76 No. 4, January 1971, pp. 643-644.*

not do the same thing—though for some of us, like the Irish, it may be almost too late.

Furthermore, in the implicit Marxism which is so powerful among Western intellectuals, there is an assumption that the only meaningful differences among human groups are social class differences—even black militancy and women's liberation are justified as class movements. In such a perspective, differences of language, religion, or national background are either irrational and ought not to be taken seriously or are a disguised attempt of the oppressor class to justify continuing oppression. A society divided along class lines and along lines of essentially economic political issues is an acceptable society, but there is no room there for divisions on issues that are primordial, ethnic, particularistic, and personal. Such issues and divisions are "irrational," which is to say that they are not to be found in the Marxist paradigm. In the words of Mr. Justice Goldberg, "I think ethnic politics are degrading."

Most American social scientists are profoundly influenced by the basic insight of the sociological tradition of Tönnies, Weber, and the other giants of the late nineteenth and early twentieth centuries, which sees the Western world shifting from *gemeinschaft* to *gesellschaft*, from folk to urban, from particularistic to universal, from sacred to profane. To Weber and the other giants, this evolution was descriptive rather than normative—and descriptive, indeed, with a considerable nostalgia for *gemeinschaft*. One suspects that it has become normative for many modern observers, not only for those who engage in the pop sociology of exercises like *Future Shock*. To such observers, it is a good thing for men and women to give up their ethnic ties, not merely because ethnicity is un-American and not merely because it is politically irrational but also because it is "tribal" and "pre-modern." The persistence of ethnic identification is a form of collective regression to a prerational past which ought to be unacceptable to educated and civilized men. In other words, since we are civilized and educated, we don't give a damn what kind of an accent our grandmother had.

Finally, there may be a further political explanation for the absence of serious research on ethnic pluralism and diversity. Most of those who might do such research prefer their politics to be ideological. They place themselves on the "liberal" end of the ideological spectrum. As they perceive the rest of the world, those groups which are especially likely to be labeled "ethnic" not only reject ideological politics but in fact are opposed to precisely those liberal social changes that American scholars support. It is no accident that *Beyond the Melting Pot* was written by two political deviants.

As one intellectual on the staff of a government agency remarked to me, "I suppose those people have problems of their own.

The only way I can think of them is as an enemy to social progress." Such a view of things is reinforced by the fact that the geographical location of many of the "ethnic" communities puts them
in immediate competition with blacks for jobs and housing. Hence,
their reaction to black militancy is obvious grist for the mills of the
mass media. The hard-hat ethnic, on the one hand, and the militant
black—plus his student supporters—on the other, represent for many
American intellectuals the most obvious conflict in society, and the
intellectual has no doubt as to which side he wants to be on—the side
where all the virtue is to be found.

The data to refute this myth are overwhelming, but the myth
refuses to die. One can cite survey after survey after survey which
shows that the ethnics are more pro-integration and pro-peace than
the American population in general. One can even point out that the
Irish, in some ways the most hated of all the ethnics (they *do* include George Meany and Richard Daley among their number), are
second only to the Jews in their support for "liberal" political re-
forms. It does no good, however, to assert that the ethnics are still
very much a part of the liberal coalition, for they have been
drummed out of it—to be replaced, apparently, by the young, who
are expected to provide nearly unanimous support for liberal causes.

Two comments must be made about this mythology: First, those
who preached the new coalition from which the ethnics will be excluded cannot count—or worse, are content never to win an election, and second, they are simply incapable of admitting that ethnicity is an asset to liberalism. The facts are still there: ethnics are
more likely to be politically "liberal" than Anglo-Saxon Americans
of comparable social class, and the more ethnic a person is, the more
likely he is to be "liberal."* It is, one presumes, much more satisfy-
ing to lose the election than to have to cope with such disconcerting
phenomena.

The net results of all these factors is that most of us who write
about politics and society and who read the important journals in

*A number of readers of the early draft of this article have expressed astonish-
ment at these statements and wondered whether I have proof for them. There
is considerable proof from many different surveys—enough to leave the matter
in little doubt. It would not be appropriate in this article to present statistical
tables since the article is designed as a general overview rather than an exercise in
fact grubbing. However, the skeptical reader is referred to Andrew M. Greeley
and Paul B. Sheatsley, "Changing Attitudes On Racial Integration," The Scientific American, December 1971; Andrew M. Greeley, "Political Attitudes of
White Ethnics," Public Opinion Quarterly, Winter 1971; and Andrew M.
Greeley, Norman Nie and Barbara Currie, "Ethnics and the Coalition," unpublished paper, National Opinion Research Center, 1971. It is much to be
feared that the truth about the political attitudes of white ethnics will make
an even shorter trip than normal from being what everyone knows is not true
to what everyone knew all along was true.

which articles about politics and society are presented know practically nothing about large segments of the American diversity. Few of our professional colleagues grew up in ethnic communities; only a handful of our students are from these communities, and they are, frequently with considerable encouragement from us, quite alienated from their background. Works of literature that are concerned with these communities are not widely accepted in our society, and until very recently no one has written dissertations or novels about them. Indeed, the suggestion that they might be worth writing about has been viewed as "divisive" and "separatist." Most of us may know more about what goes on in certain tribal communities of Africa and Asia than we do about what occurs in Hamtramck, Queens, or Avalon Park. This is an extraordinary phenomenon. American society is one put together only yesterday from a great variety of immigrant groups, yet our scholars, artists, and journalists seem only marginally interested in these immigrant groups. Black diversity is good, Jewish diversity is palatable, but all other forms of diversity, even if they should exist, which is unlikely, are unimportant.

AN OUTRAGEOUS ASSUMPTION

It must be said that, on the whole, American social and cultural pluralism has worked rather well. Such a statement is a dangerous one to make, for in the present climate of scholarly opinion even the most modest compliment to American society is taken as a sign of immorality and racism. Everything about the United States must be bad, and the lightest suggestion that American society may be successful at anything must be rejected out of hand.* It ought to be possible, however, to steer a middle course. We ought to be able to say that there have been serious injustices done in the American society and that they are still being done; and, on the other hand, to also assert that the United States has probably coped more ef-

---

**For an almost biblical vision of America as the new Babylon and the young as a messianic nation, see Kenneth Keniston's graduation address of last June at Notre Dame. Also see the anguished cries of American reviewers in response to Jean-Francois Revel's claim that there is more toleration for dissidents in American society than anywhere else in the world. Of course Revel's claim is self-evidently true. He does not claim, as reviewers would dearly like to believe, that there is total toleration for dissidents; simply that there is more of it in the United States now than at any time in its past history and than in any other nation of the world. One just has to realize that, as Revel points out, Frenchmen can be sent to jail merely for being around when a riot occurs, and in both Canada and the United Kingdom, those eminently civilized countries so envied by intellectual Americans, men have been interned in the last year without trial. The Chicago Seven trial is cited as counter-evidence, oblivious to the fact that the Seven are not in jail and probably not likely to be. The Quebec separatists are definitely in jail and, in case nobody noticed, so is the IRA.*

fectively with ethnic, religious, racial, and geographic diversity better than any large and complex society in the world.* Indeed, when one considers the size, geographic diversity, heterogeneity of the population, and the sheer newness of the society, the astonishing thing is that the nation has survived at all.

It is fashionable in some circles to make unfavorable comparisons between the United States and, let us say, Britain or Sweden. (For example, see Professor Titmuss' recent book on blood donation.) But rarely in such comparisons is it asked whether there might be differences in the countries that make comparison invalid. Britain has behind it a thousand years and more of cultural and legal heritage. It solved its major religious problems in 1689 and its major ethnic and frontier problems with the pacification of the Highlands in the middle 1700s (assuming, as the English certainly did, that the Irish were not part of their ethnic problem). It has had only minor immigrations (again, save for the Irish, who really don't count for the British), and since the Norman invasion virtually all of its people speak the same language. Its political and civil symbols are ancient and universally honored. It is geographically compact and less than a third the size of the United States in population. That Britain is more civilized under such circumstances is not at all surprising. It is surprising, however, that a society of such diverse components as the United States has stitched together in so short a time has not come apart at the seams; and that, despite the alleged crises of the present moment, the seams remain relatively strong. One gets into serious trouble in many American circles for even suggesting that this phenomenon might be worth investigating. What counts is not careful analysis of American society but rather vigorous and virtuous denunciation of its immorality. The fact that Americans live in relative peace with one another in the midst of great diversity, when in other parts of the world men are swatting each other for ethnic reasons, is quite irrelevant.

But irrelevant or not, there are at least some of us who think it might be worth studying. Obviously, the country's richness of natural resources and its resultant economic prosperity has had something to do with the success of its pluralism. One might be less inclined to go after one's neighbor with a rock, club, or knife when one has just consumed a succulent steak from the backyard bar-

*For example, one American reviewer dismissed Revel's observation that a higher proportion of American blacks go to college than do citizens of France with the statement that American blacks frequently receive a poor education. Some do and some don't. Presumably some French young people also receive very poor educations; but Revel's point—ignored by the reviewer—was that America has made greater progress towards universal higher education than has France—a major accomplishment for which we are apparently not to be awarded any points.

becue. It may well be that the ultimate answer to primordial conflict around the world is universal affluence.

But perhaps more than economics are involved, for the immigrants of the early middle and middle nineteenth century were
not affluent. The Irish, for example, were impoverished and diseased
fugitives from famine. Yet, while they were not particularly welcomed, and did not in their turn profess too much affection for their
hosts, the riots between Irish and WASPS were limited in number
and extent.

THE CHURCH OF THEIR CHOICE

My own hypothesis is that the cultural matrix that has made American diversity possible is denominational pluralism. The United
States was a religiously pluralistic society even before it became a
politically pluralistic society. The pluralism which was institutionalized in the Constitution antedated that document. It developed in
the previous half-century mostly because Virginia Episcopalians and
Massachusetts Congregationalists learned that they had to get along
with one another despite their serious religious differences. The Congregationalists, the Quakers, the Episcopalians, and the Methodists
all shared one English cultural tradition; but they shared it in di-
versified styles, styles which were shaped by their denominational
affiliations. By 1789, such diversity was so obvious to the framers
of the Constitution that they did not even have to advert explicitly
to it; denominational differences among the various states had to be
respected.* The Constitution, then, specified for the political dimension of society a heterogeneity which was already taken for granted
in the common culture.

This heterogeneity was broad enough to absorb the later immigrant groups when they swarmed ashore. Many native Americans
may not have wanted the immigrants, and many assumed that the
only appropriate behavior for the immigrants was for them to become native Americans as quickly as possible. Nevertheless, the
pluralistic culture of the society was such that it would be a century before the country could bring itself to act against its own self-
image of diversity and begin systematically to exclude certain kinds
of immigrants. Without understanding how it had been accomplished, America had arrived at a political, cultural, and social style
which had made it possible for vastly diverse groups to live together
with at least some harmony and if not with justice, still at least
with the conviction that justice was a reasonable expectation. By
our own very high standards, there was still much injustice, but at

*And of course the fact that the economies of these denominationally different
states were also different reinforced the religious pluralism.

least one question that ought to be asked by those who will hear not a word in defense of American pluralism is, how come the standards are so high?

Horrendous injustice has been done and is being done to American blacks. Considerable injustice was done to other American groups. The Japanese were locked in concentration camps, and the Germans, only too willing to fight and die for the United States against their native land, were forced to yield much of their culture and language. (In some American cities after the First World War it was impossible even to play Beethoven's music.) Those with Slavic and Italian names are still systematically excluded from important corporate offices. Jews are still subject to subtle social discrimination. There is only one Catholic president of any major American university. The Irish have become respectable—something they always desperately wanted—at the price of losing any sense of their own history or culture. But despite all these injustices, three things still must be said: First, our incredibly variegated society has survived. Second, minority groups are treated better in the United States than they are in any other large nation of the world—and many of the small ones besides. (The American black, a tragic victim of injustice, is still in much better political, economic, and social condition than is the Catholic in Ulster.*) Third, the ideology of cultural diversity to which most Americans are more or less committed makes it impossible for us to be complacent at the continuation of injustice. In the three decades since Myrdal gave a name to the American dilemma, immense progress has been made.** It is considered almost treasonable in some circles to point to the fact of progress. In these circles, progress is thought to be an excuse from further effort; what escapes me is why progress cannot also be conceived of as a context for further efforts.

WE THOUGHT YOU'D NEVER GET HERE

For a number of different reasons there has been a dramatic increase of interest in America's cultural heterogeneity in recent years. To some very considerable extent, this new interest in Isaacs' "basic membership group" is a black contribution to American society. For the blacks have legitimated definitively the idea of cultural pluralism. The mainline American society may have endorsed pluralism in theory, but in fact its basic tendencies were always assimilationist. It has now, however, become official: it is all right for blacks

---

See Professor Richard Rose's comparison in Governing Without Consensus (Boston, 1971).
**For an account of changing attitudes on racial integration in the three decades, see Andrew M. Greeley and Paul Sheatsley, "Attitudes Toward Desegregation," Scientific American, December 1971.*

to have their own heritage, their own tradition, their own culture. If it is all right for the blacks, then it ought to be all right for everyone else.* Some blacks seem ambivalent about this contribution, and even on occasion dismiss the resurgence of interest in other heritages as a form of racism, but one cannot have it both ways. Once pluralism is legitimated for one group, it has become legitimated for everybody; or, as the ancient political adage puts it, what is sauce for the goose is sauce for the gander.

In addition, the loss of faith on the part of many younger Americans in the optimistic, liberal rationalist vision of their predecessors and teachers has once again opened for these young people the question of "who am I?" (For example, the young Catholic scholar, Michael Novak, having written extensively on global political, religious, and philosophical issues, is now exploring the meaning of his own Slovak heritage. See his recent article in *Harper's*.) It has been my experience that many if not most of the graduate students who have suddenly appeared in faculty offices all over the country clutching proposals for ethnic research are motivated by highly personal reasons. In the process of doing their dissertations, they want to find out who they are.

Both on the college campuses, then, and within the bosom of middle America, the new, or at least newly manifested, interest in diversity is part of a cultural identity crisis. That the question, "Who am I?" can arise after so many years of pretending that it is either unimportant or that it has already been solved is some evidence of how persistent and powerful the issue may be.**

There are two major thrusts of the new interest in diversity. The first is the "rediscovery of middle America." The social, cultural, and intellectual elites of the country have discovered that

---

*Interestingly enough, despite considerable statistical evidence to the contrary, many Americans are persuaded that what the blacks want is not cultural pluralism but separatism. In other words, the black problem is seen as the same as the Polish or German problems sixty years ago; the alternatives are either assimilation or separation. The Poles and the Germans were compelled to assimilate; the blacks are permitted to be separate. However, in fact, research evidence leaves little doubt that most blacks want exactly what most Germans and Poles wanted—not separatism but a subculture of their own within a larger social and cultural context.

**William Harwood of the Washington Post has recently suggested that the new interest in ethnicity is already out of fashion. We who were interested in those things six months ago are now no longer interested in them, so they are not important. It is this sort of arrogance on the part of those who have established themselves as the cultural arbiters of the nation that makes some people listen sympathetically to the Vice President's tirades. Unquestionably, there was a journalistic fad on the subject of ethnicity, but apparently it never occurred to Mr. Hardwood that such fads do not cause social reality, and there just might possibly be something "out there" of which the fad is but a pale imitation.

there is a substantial segment of the population living somewhere between them and the poor and the nonwhites who view social reality from an entirely different perspective. They are still patriotic Americans and for some unaccountable reason, they are afraid of crime and violence. Some of this rediscovery of middle America (or blue collar workers, or white ethnics, or whatever name one chooses to use) is modish and patronizing; some of it is moralistic and self-righteous; but a good deal of it is honest and open and sympathetic. As this thrust is represented by such agencies as the Ford Foundation and the American Jewish Committee, it represents a sensible and realistic comprehension that social reform and indeed social harmony in the United States is impossible if some groups are deliberately or inadvertantly excluded from the consensus. However, there is a tendency for some of these rediscoverers to view middle Americans as a "problem," or at least as people with "problems." As empirical data begin to become available which indicate that the ethnic component of middle America is not all that hawkish or all that racist, this emphasis on problems is beginning to change. (It is still difficult, however, to persuade some of those concerned with the rediscovery of middle America that not all blue collar workers are ethnics and not all ethnics are blue collar workers. The majority of American blue collar workers are, of course, native American Protestants, and many ethnics have become upper middle class and even college professors. In fact, some data available to us at the National Opinion Research Center would indicate that college graduates with an Irish background are now more likely to pursue careers in the sciences than are graduates of Jewish background. And the Irish, like the Jews, are twice as likely to graduate from college as is the general American population. Blue collar indeed!)

One sub-emphasis in the rediscovery of middle America is the notion that the ethnics ought to be "organized." It is argued that "ethnic militancy" can be socially positive and constructive, particularly if it is presided over by the right sort of leader. The most extreme form of the "organize the ethnics" approach suggests that the ethnics ought to "get their thing together" just like the blacks have done. Then militant blacks and militant ethnics can solve the cities' problems jointly. (By which I suspect it is frequently meant that alliances between the Poles and the Italians on the one hand and the blacks on the other can dispense with the Irish middlemen who have governed American cities for such a long time. On the whole, it might be a good idea, but the Irish will be excused for not thinking so.) The consistent triumphs of Steve Adiuabato, a Newark Italian politician who maintains good relations with both Mayor Gibson and LeRoi Jones while trouncing Tony Imperiale, are cited as an example of what ethnic militancy can accomplish.

I must confess grave reservations about this "organize the ethnic" ideology. First of all, I think the militant political style is becoming passé in American society, despite the broad media coverage it still receives. Secondly, the pretense of organizing the ethnics strikes me as absurd. The ethnics are already organized and scarcely need social worker messiahs who arrive on the scene to "build community" among them. Adiuabato's success is unquestioned and admirable, but he is an extraordinarily skillful ward political type and not a community organizer, though he obviously has no objections to being considered one when such a definition provides him with more resources for his work. It is probably my own corrupt Irish heritage, but if I am given a choice between ward politicians and community organizers, I will always pick the former, if only because they tend to win. In terms of the people who live in the neighborhoods, winning is better than losing.

The other major thrust of the concern about ethnic diversity is what I would call the "rediscovery of pluralism." It is a thrust manifested by most of the writings in this issue of *The Antioch Review* and obviously so by this particular article. It is, I suppose, more ordered toward thought and reflection than it is toward immediate ends, but it asks a fundamental question which ought to precede any action: What in the hell makes a society tick?

The cultural pluralist attitude has a limited interest in immediate social action to alleviate problems, though it certainly applauds and supports such action and makes whatever contribution it can to it. It is more concerned about figuring out how cultural diversity persists along primordial lines in the United States and what contributions this persistence makes to the American social structure. It is an extraordinarily difficult task and one which I must confess has led to more failures than successes up to the present time. There is so little in the way of social history for the ethnic groups. There is quite an extensive literature on American Jews and a small but consistent literature on American Italians, but there is nothing in the way of social theory to provide a perspective for investigating ethnicity. No empirical data from past studies exists, nor even agreement among survey researchers as to how questions ought to be asked, nor any clear indicators as to what research and analytic methodologies are pertinent.

HOW TO TALK ETHNICS

There are, as I see it, three different approaches to the problem: the social class approach, the political approach, and the cultural approach. In the first, ethnic differences are equated with social class differences. Thus, Herbert Gans in his *Urban Villagers* explains the behavior of Italians in Boston threatened by urban renewal as a class rather than a cultural phenomenon.* Secondly, Daniel Patrick Moynihan and Nathan Glazer in *Beyond the Melting Pot* argue that, at least in New York City, the ethnic collectivities are essentially giant political interest groups without too much in the way of a correlated cultural heritage. Finally, such observers as Edward Laumann and Peter Rossi argue that there is persuasive evidence that the ethnic collectivities do indeed act as bearers of differential cultural heritages; Rossi suggests that the heritage may have to do with subtle but important differences of expectation in one's most intimate personal relationships.

The burden of the evidence that we have been piling up at the National Opinion Research Center for the past several years is strongly in support of the third position. Indeed, data we now have on the differential personality constellations of eight American white ethnic groups seem to me to offer conclusive evidence that even when social class is held constant, immense differences of personality have persisted between these groups.

But theoretical problems persist. Is everyone ethnic? (*The Christian Century* has recently suggested that even WASPS are ethnic.) Does one have to be an ethnic whether he wants to or not? For example, are Appalachian whites an ethnic group? Or are Texans? Are some basic "membership groups" in American society based on nationality, racial, or religious factors while others are based on geographical or social class or organizational or professional factors? Are intellectuals, as I not altogether facetiously suggested, an ethnic group? What happens in an ethnically mixed marriage? Does one select one's basic membership group or does one absorb it from the parents of the same or opposite sex?

Indeed, to what extent is basic group membership a matter of choice? Does it matter whether you consciously identify with a group or not? For example, it seems reasonably clear that most of the American Irish know very little about their own Irish heritage and think of themselves explicitly as Irish only on rare occasions. Nevertheless, our data indicate very strong correlations between Irishness and patterns of attitudes and behavior. And once we have established such patterns, are they a part of the heritage that the group brought with it from the Old World or are they a function of its experiences when it arrived in American society, experiences which in turn were functions of the shape of American society at that time? Or, finally, are they the result of where the group is in American society at the present time?

About all one can say in response to these thorny questions is

One wonders if lower class Irish in Boston would have responded in the same way.

that no one knows, and it is extremely difficult to sense even where one ought to begin.

Within such theoretical obscurity, methodological difficulties are inevitable. The survey researcher can, of course, fall back on his beloved nominalism: American society is divided into ten major ethnic collectivities on the basis of where one's grandparents came from or what one considers to be one's principal ancestry. Then the scale of ethnic diversity is correlated with all the independent variables that happen to be on the questionnaire. The astonishing thing about such a crude procedure is that it seems to work, at least to the extent that it confirms the persistence of great diversity across ethnic lines even when social class, religion, and region of the country are held constant. Unfortunately, there is no way in which ethnicity can be registered on even a pseudo-linear scale, and as the mathematically-oriented readers of this article will perceive, that makes it very difficult indeed to sort out the relative influences of religion, social class, and ethnicity on human attitudes and behavior. Dummy variable multiple regression models are of some use in such situations, but they would be much more help if we were able to clarify our theoretical problems.

It is an interesting if embarrassing position for a social scientist to be in. The more we probe the question of primordial bonds, the more obvious it becomes that they are pervasive in American society, despite and perhaps because of our ambivalence about them. One is not going to be able to understand American society without first coping with the phenomenon of primordial bonds. But at the present state of our knowledge, we don't know quite what to do with them. Man may have traveled a long way indeed from one end of the continua represented by Parsons' pattern variables to the other, from the particularistic to the universalistic, from ascription to achievement, from the diffuse to the specific; but he still seems to have kept one foot on the particularistic, diffuse and ascriptive end of the continua, and not just in his family relationships. It will take some years to be able to understand just how this has occurred, and perhaps some more years to be able to make intelligent suggestions to social policy-makers concerning what, if anything, they should do about the extraordinary survival of primordial diversity.

In the meantime, however, it has become possible for men and women to talk about it, as this issue of *The Antioch Review* demonstrates. We can recall our heritage and even enjoy it, if not altogether without guilt, at least with the feeling that there are some others who will understand* It has even become possible for us to

*I would have much preferred an article in which I recalled the memories of growing up Irish. But the editor rightly insisted that someone had to engage in analysis. It is a terrible thing to grow up Irish—till one considers the other possibilities.

The
Rediscovery
of
Diversity

begin to understand and appreciate and enjoy other people's heritages, which may be the beginning of an evolutionary step of extraordinary moment.

Celts and Saxons are killing each other once again in Ulster as they have for centuries. In the United States, however, Scotch-Irish Presbyterians and Celtic-Irish Catholics get along with each other moderately well. They do not feel constrained to shoot at each other from behind the hedges or out of the windows of slums. Given the history of the two groups, that is not inconsiderable progress.

Occasionally Celts are even permitted to write for *The Antioch Review.*

And that's real progress.

SCIENTIFIC
AMERICAN

Established 1845   December 1971   Volume 225   Number 6

Attitudes toward Racial Integration

*The third in a series of reports spanning nearly three decades shows
a continuing advance in the support of desegregation by U.S. whites.
The trend has not been affected by the racial strife of recent years*

by Andrew M. Greeley and Paul B. Sheatsley

We present herewith the third report in these pages on the findings of the National Opinion Research Center concerning the attitudes of white Americans toward the position black Americans should occupy in American society. Together the reports cover a period of almost 30 years, which is the length of time the Center has been sampling these attitudes. In that time the trend has been distinctly and strongly toward increasing approval of integration. For the most part the trend has not been slowed by the racial turmoil of the past eight years. We believe these findings have significant political implications.

Our sample usually consists of about 1,500 people, chosen to represent a spectrum of the population of adults in the U.S. About 1,250 of the people in the sample are white, and it is with the attitudes of whites that this article is concerned. With a sample of this size we are able to test for opinion by age, region, income, occupation, education, religion and ethnic origin.

Since the last report [see "Attitudes toward Desegregation," by Herbert H. Hyman and Paul B. Sheatsley; SCIENTIFIC AMERICAN, July, 1964] the U.S. has experienced what is probably the most acute crisis in race relations since the end of the Civil War. City after city suffered racial violence, with Watts, Detroit and Newark only the most conspicuous among them. Martin Luther King, the apostle of nonviolence, was assassi-

nated and another spasm of riots shook the nation. King was replaced on the television screen by a far more militant brand of black leader. Stokely Carmichael, H. Rap Brown, Eldridge Cleaver, Bobby Seale and LeRoi Jones became nationally known. Newspapers carried accounts of blacks arming for guerilla warfare. The Black Panthers appeared on the scene, and in several cities there were gunfights between the police and the Panthers. Columnists, editorial writers and political analysts worried publicly about the "backlash." George Wallace did well in several primaries, and in the presidential election of 1968 he made the most successful third-party showing in many decades.

Concurrently with these dramatic events the attitudes of white Americans toward desegregation continued to change almost as though nothing was happening. The data do offer a certain amount of evidence of a negative reaction to black militancy; we shall return to this point. Even so, the negative reaction has not impeded the steady increase in the proportion of white Americans willing to endorse integration.

Two questions have been asked throughout the period covered by the National Opinion Research Center's surveys, which were conducted in 1942, 1956, 1963 and 1970. One question is: "Generally speaking, do you think there should be separate sections for Negroes in streetcars and buses?" The other ques-

tion is: "Do you think white students and Negroes should go to the same schools or separate schools?"

In 1942 some 44 percent of the white population was willing to endorse integrated transportation [*see top illustration on next page*]. By 1970 the proportion had doubled, reaching 60 percent in 1956 and 88 percent in 1970. In the South the change has been even more pronounced. Only 4 percent of white Southerners accepted integrated transportation in 1942; by 1970 the proportion was 67 percent.

Integrating transportation, then, is no longer a significant issue. In retrospect it may well be said that the right of blacks to sit where they wish in public vehicles is not a very important right, since obtaining it does not notably improve the welfare of black people. From the perspective of 1971 such an assertion is certainly correct, but when one recalls what the attitudes were in 1942 or even in 1956, the change is striking. In less than 15 years—since Martin Luther King's historic boycott in Montgomery, Ala.—integrated transportation has virtually disappeared as an issue.

The integration of schools, however, is still an issue, even though in the North the idea is now endorsed by eight of every 10 respondents. In 1942, 2 percent of whites in the South favored school integration. By 1956 the proportion had increased to only 14 percent. Since 1956—two years after the U.S. Supreme Court's decision in *Brown* v.

3

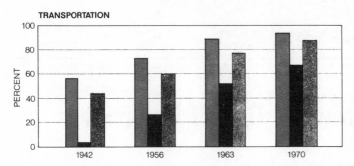

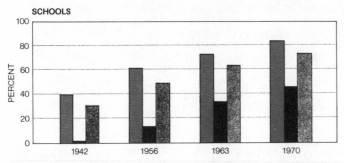

TREND OF WHITE OPINION on integration of transportation and schools is traced for 28 years in surveys by the National Opinion Research Center. For each of the four surveys cited the percentage of people giving an integrationist response is shown for the North (*gray*), South (*dark gray*) and nation (*color*). Questions were identical in each survey.

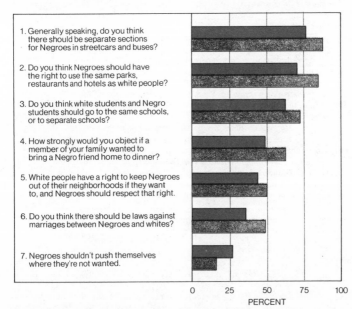

SCALED QUESTIONS were employed in 1963 and 1970 to test white opinion. The property of the scale is such that if a respondent has rejected one item, the likelihood is that he also rejected all the succeeding items. The bars at right reflect the percentage of integrationist responses elicited by each question in 1963 (*gray*) and seven years later (*color*).

Board of Education—the proportion of Southern whites accepting school integration has increased sharply. Now almost half of them favor it. Nationally the support of whites for integrated schools is 75 percent.

An interesting pattern emerging in the successive surveys is that the proportion of the Northern white population supporting integration at one point in time is quite close to the proportion of the total white population accepting it at the next point in time. If the trend continues, one can expect a majority of the white population in every region to accept integrated schooling by 1977. Perhaps 60 percent of Southern whites will be willing to accept it. One could then say that desegregating schools had ceased to be a significant issue.

In 1963 the National Opinion Research Center employed in its survey a "Guttman scale" prepared by Donald Treiman of the Center's staff. The properties of a Guttman scale (named for Louis Guttman, now of the Israeli Institute of Public Opinion, who devised it) are such that if a respondent rejects one item on the scale, the chances are at least 90 percent that he will also reject all the items below it [*see bottom illustration at left*]. We used a similar scale in 1970. It has seven questions, relating successively to integrated transportation; integrated parks, restaurants and hotels; integrated schools; having a member of the family bring a black friend home for dinner; integrated neighborhoods; mixed marriages, and blacks intruding where they are not wanted.

The first six items on the scale show a consistent increase in support of integration between 1963 and 1970. Indeed, on transportation, public facilities, schools and having a black guest to dinner a large majority of whites respond favorably. Only neighborhood integration and mixed marriages still divide white Americans about equally. If present trends persist, it seems likely that both neighborhood integration and racial intermarriage will be accepted by 60 percent of the white population at the time of the next report by the National Opinion Research Center in about seven years.

Only on the last item of the Guttman scale does one find any evidence of a backlash response to events of the period from 1963 to 1970. In 1963 about 25 percent of the white population rejected the idea that "Negroes shouldn't push themselves where they're not wanted." By 1970 the proportion taking

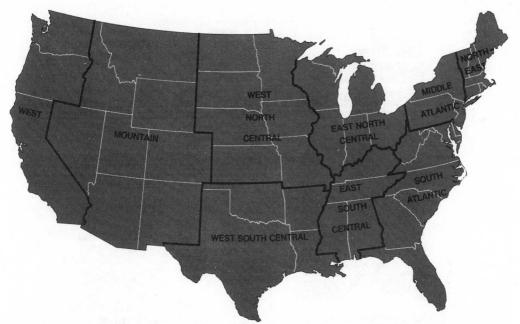

NINE REGIONS of the U.S. appear in evaluations by the National Opinion Research Center of responses to the scaled questions. The regional designations are the ones employed by the U.S. Bureau of the Census. Alaska and Hawaii were not included in the sampling.

an integrationist stand on this issue had dropped to 16 percent. One can surmise that this change is a response to black militancy, but even if that is so, the change has not interfered with increasing support for specific aspects of racial integration.

The seven items of the Guttman scale comprise a "pro-integration scale" on which each respondent can be assigned a score ranging from 0 to 7 depending on the number of pro-integration responses he gave: 0 if he gave none and 7 if he favored integration in all his responses. From there it is a small step to compute mean scores for various population groups to see where the strongest integrationist and anti-integrationist positions are. The mean score for all white Americans in 1970 was 4.2, indicating that the typical American accepts at least four of the seven integrationist attitudes. The mean score in 1963 was 3.57 [see illustration on next page]. Another way of putting it is that the average white American in 1963 could live with integrated transportation, integrated education and integrated parks, restaurants and hotels; he could accept, although just barely, a black dinner guest. In 1970 he was no longer concerned about having a black dinner guest and was no longer ready to totally

reject the possibility of integrated neighborhoods.

As one might expect, the greatest differences are regional. The typical Southerner accepts completely only the first two items on the scale, although he leans toward the third. The typical Northerner accepts the first four items and is strongly disposed toward the idea of accepting neighborhood integration. The net change of mean score, however, has been somewhat larger in the South than in the North: .77 compared with .6.

Also as one might expect, the highest pro-integration scores are among people aged 25 and under, both in 1963 and in 1970. As one might not have expected, the most dramatic increase in any age group is among the young: the mean score for people under 25 has increased by 1.08. It is even more striking that young Southerners manifest the largest net rise in integrationist scores: from 2.35 to 3.87. In other words, Southerners under 25 were as likely to be integrationist in 1970 as Northerners aged 45 to 64, whereas in 1963 young Southerners were less likely to be integrationist than Northerners over 65. Moreover, Southerners at each of the three older age levels had higher pro-integration scores than the people at the next-younger age level had had in 1963. Thus one can say that the changing attitudes in

the South entail not only the influx of a new generation but also an actual change of position by many older white Southerners.

The mean scores of the various groups can be summarized by saying that there is an increase in integrationist sympathies in all segments of the white population, with the most notable changes at present taking place among people whose scores in the past were the lowest. The net result is that groups at the extremes seem to be moving toward a more central position. For example, the Jewish score is still higher than the Protestant score, but the Protestant score is catching up. People who have been to graduate school still score higher than people who went no further than grammar school, but the difference between the two groups is narrowing. Similarly, whites in large cities continue to be more likely than whites in rural areas to endorse integration, but again the difference is declining. Finally, unskilled workers and service workers now have scores closer to the scores of professionals.

To a certain extent this catching up is a statistical artifact. People with high scores in 1963 did not have much room for improving the scores by 1970. Nonetheless, the diminishing differences indicate that the turbulence of the past

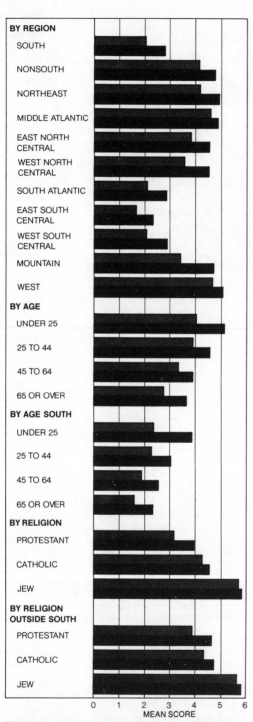

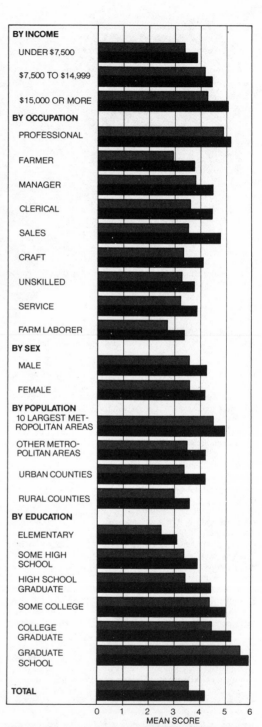

CHANGING SCORES on the pro-integration scale are depicted by various groupings for 1963 (*gray*) and 1970 (*color*). The range of scores is obtained by assigning each respondent a rating of 0 to 7 depending on the number of pro-integration responses he gave to the scaled questions. His score was 0 if he gave no pro-integration replies and 7 if he took an integrationist position on all the questions. The individual scores were used to compute the mean scores shown here for the various regions and groups and for the nation.

few years has not interfered with increasing sympathy for integration, even among people who were least likely to have been sympathetic in the early 1960's. Their scores on the integration scale can increase more rapidly than the scores of people who sympathized with integration in 1963 because there is more room for improvement in their scores. It is not a statistical artifact that the scores continue to increase. That phenomenon reflects changing attitudes in the midst of turmoil and conflict.

Popular mythology would lead one to believe that if there is a backlash, it would be most likely to appear among the "white ethnic" groups, because they are less securely established in American society and also are the people most likely to be in direct conflict with newly militant blacks over such issues as jobs, education and housing. No ethnic-background question was asked in 1963, so that we are unable to compare the attitudes of white ethnics in 1963 and 1970. The 1970 scores alone, however, provide little evidence for the existence of a white backlash [see top illustration at right]. When the ethnics are compared with white Protestants in the North (the only comparison that is valid since most ethnics live in the North), it turns out that Irish Catholics and German Catholics have a higher average score on the integration scale than the typical white Protestant Northerner does. Catholics of southern European origin (mostly Italian) and Catholics of Slavic origin (mostly Polish) scored only slightly below Anglo-Saxon Protestants. Whatever direct confrontations there may be between blacks and Catholics of southern European and eastern European origin, they have had only a marginal effect on the integrationist sympathies of these two groups. It is also interesting to note that Irish Catholics are second only to Jews in their support of integration.

Considering the integrationist sentiments of ethnic groups by educational background, one finds that insofar as there is a white ethnic backlash it seems to be limited to people who have not finished high school [see bottom illustration at right]. (The sample here is small, so that the finding is at best suggestive.) Among people who have graduated from high school, only Slavic Catholics have scores lower than the white Protestant mean (and not much lower). Irish Catholics, German Catholics and southern European Catholics have scores that are higher than the Anglo-Saxon Protestant mean.

One of the most sensitive issues in

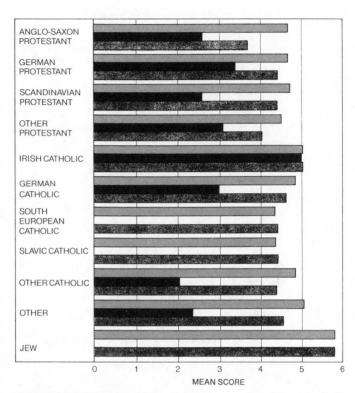

RELIGIOUS DISTRIBUTION of integrationist responses to the scaled questions is depicted by region for the questions asked in 1970. The distribution also reflects certain ethnic groupings. In each case the mean scores are shown for the North (gray), the South (dark gray) and the entire country (color). Three groups had little representation in the South.

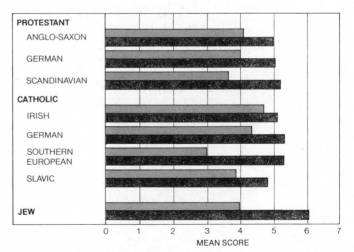

EDUCATIONAL BACKGROUND of Northern whites responding to the scaled questions is shown by religious and ethnic groupings. Mean scores are shown according to whether the respondents had less than a high school education (gray) or had at least been graduated from high school (color). Many respondents in the second group went beyond high school.

Northern urban politics is open-occupancy legislation, which forbids racial discrimination in housing. An item measuring attitudes on this subject was included in the 1970 survey [see upper illustration below]. Three of the four ethnic groups—the Irish, the Germans and the largely Italian southern Europeans—are slightly more likely than Northern Anglo-Saxon Protestants to support such legislation. Only among the Slavic Catholics is there less inclination to be in favor of open-housing laws.

The question of the relation between blacks and white ethnics is a complicated one, lying largely beyond the scope of this article. On the basis of the data available to us, however, there seems to be no evidence of racism among white ethnics except in the Slavic Catholic group. To the extent that a backlash exists even in that group, it seems to be concentrated among the less educated people. The other three Catholic ethnic groups are, if anything, even more integrationist than the typical Northern Protestant white—although less so than the typical Northern Jew.

Why, then, is the popular image of the "hard hat" ethnic racist so powerful? Our colleague Norman Nie has suggested that the reason may well be that the ethnics, particularly those from southern and eastern Europe, are "next up the ladder" from blacks and are most likely to be in competition with them for jobs and housing. We were able to put this hypothesis to a crude test by dividing the respondents to our survey into two groups, one comprising people who live in places where fewer than .5 percent of the residents are black and one comprising people who live in places with a higher proportion of blacks. Our supposition was that ethnics would be more likely to be in the latter group and that scores on the integration scale would be lower in that group.

Although the number of respondents is small, the findings indicate confirmation of Nie's suggestion [see lower illustration at left]. Every ethnic group in an integrated area had a lower integration score than members of the same ethnic group in nonintegrated areas except the Irish Catholics, the German Catholics and the Jews. The differences between Anglo-Saxon Protestants and southern Europeans were slight when the comparison was made among people living in nonintegrated areas. Thus there does seem to be a correlation between lower scores and feeling "threatened." It is interesting to note that living close to blacks raises the level of Jewish support for integration. German support rises slightly with propinquity, but the Irish score is unaffected.

In the light of our various findings one inevitably asks: Where is the backlash? It could be said to appear in the responses to the item on blacks intruding where they are not wanted. The decline between 1963 and 1970 in the proportion of whites willing to reject the item is, however, fairly evenly distributed in the white population, although it is somewhat less likely to be observed among the young and among the better educated [see illustration on opposite page]. It is also somewhat less likely to be observed among Catholics than among Jews and Protestants. (Here is further evidence against the validity of the notion that there is a "white ethnic racist backlash.") In short, if the extent to which whites are now somewhat more likely to say that blacks should not intrude where they are not wanted is a measure of negative response to black militance, the response is fairly evenly distributed among the Northern white population.

Two important observations are in or-

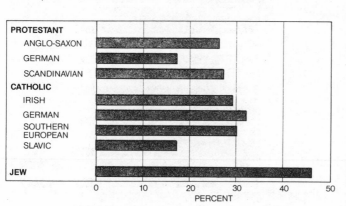

ATTITUDES ON HOUSING appear in the percentages of Northern whites who gave integrationist responses to the question, "Would you favor or oppose making it against the law to refuse to sell or rent houses and apartments to Negroes?" Eight groups are shown.

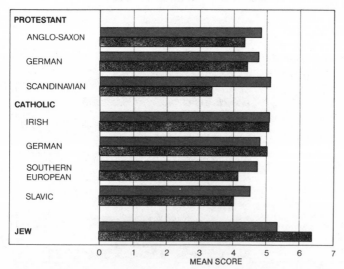

ETHNIC VIEWS are portrayed according to the residential situation of the respondents. The bars show the mean scores on the list of scaled questions of Northerners living in neighborhoods with a black population of less than .5 percent (gray) and people in more integrated areas (color). The analysis was made to test the assumption that proximity to blacks might lower the scores of ethnics who are in competition with blacks for housing and jobs.

der. First, attitudes are not necessarily predictive of behavior. A man may be a staunch integrationist and still flee when his neighborhood is "threatened." A man with segregationist views may vote for an integrationist candidate if the key issues of the election are nonracial.

Second, responses to the interviewers from the National Opinion Research Center may reflect what the white American thinks he ought to say rather than what he believes. Nonetheless, even a change in what one thinks one ought to say is significant. In any case, no one can measure another person's inner feelings with full confidence. If someone asserts that notwithstanding our evidence white ethnics are racists, it seems to us that a claim is being made to some kind of special revelation about what the white ethnic really thinks.

Although a change of attitude does not necessarily predict a change in behavior, it does create a context in which behavioral change becomes possible. Increasing support for school integration, for example, makes it somewhat easier for official policies of school integration to be pursued. The increase in support for integrated neighborhoods may facilitate at least tentative solutions to the vexing problem of changing neighborhoods in Northern cities. In sum, changing attitudes—even the dramatic ones monitored by our group over the past 30 years—do not by themselves represent effective social reform, but one can see them as a sign of progress and as creating an environment for effective social reform.

It is not our intention to argue that the data point to a need for more militant or less militant action by blacks. The appropriate strategy for blacks is also beyond the scope of this article. To note that American attitudes have changed is not to suggest that all is well in American society; it is merely to note that there has been change. Presumably no one will argue that the fact of change should go unrecorded because it will diminish the motive to work for further change.

It has been argued recently that American politics are politics of the center, albeit a floating center. We do not want to deny the utility of such a model, but we would point out that at least on the matter of racial integration the center has floated consistently to the left since 1942. We would also note that the shift has not been impeded (or accelerated either) by the racial turmoil of recent years.

The political significance of these conclusions is twofold. On the one hand,

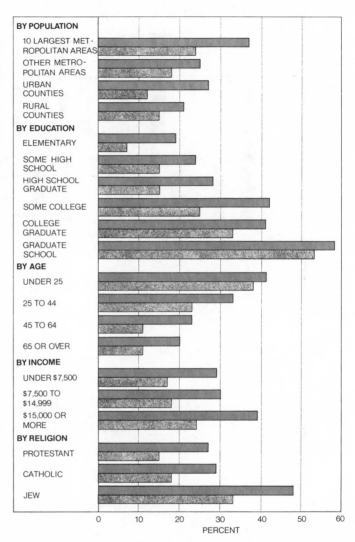

BY POPULATION / BY EDUCATION / BY AGE / BY INCOME / BY RELIGION

EVIDENCE OF BACKLASH appears in a uniform decline between 1963 (*gray*) and 1970 (*color*) in rejection by Northern whites of the proposition that blacks should not intrude where they are not wanted. Even this change of attitude, however, did not alter the prolonged trend toward greater acceptance of integration by whites on more specific issues.

the political leader who adjusts his style to an anti-integration backlash is, on the basis of our data, adjusting to something that does not exist. On the other hand, the leader who thinks social conditions are suitable for leading the center even further to the left on the subject of racial integration would find strong support for his strategy in the findings made by the National Opinion Research Center.

We cannot say with measurable precision that sustained pressure by the national leadership is the reason for the increasing support for integration since 1942. It does seem reasonable to argue, however, that if every president since Franklin D. Roosevelt had not endorsed an integrationist position, the change of attitude monitored by our surveys might not be anywhere near as impressive as it is. By the same token it is reasonable to argue that if the present Administration and future ones put forward the case for integration more forcefully, they will find basic attitudinal support among the nation's white people.

A REPRINT FROM:

THE Public Interest

NUMBER 28, SUMMER 1972. PRICE: $2.00

American Catholics—
making it
or
losing it?

ANDREW M. GREELEY

American Catholics— making it or losing it?

ANDREW M. GREELEY

I N YEARS to come, it seems very likely that historians will shake their heads in disbelief over many of the events that occurred between 1960 and 1975. Among the things which will dismay them is the fact that during the era when Americans became concerned to the point of obsession about minority groups—Puerto Ricans, Chicanos, blacks, American Indians, Appalachian whites, homosexuals, prisoners, old people—there was virtually no interest shown in our largest minority group, Roman Catholics.

Defense attorneys pleading the case for our era before the tribunal of history will argue that there was no reason to be concerned about Catholics, because "the Catholic problem" was solved in 1960 when John Kennedy was elected to the presidency. The prosecuting attorneys will respond—after noting that Kennedy won by only a little over a hundred thousand votes—that there was, after all, not much real evidence that the Catholic problem was solved in the 1960's; and even if it had been, the acculturation of the Catholic immigrants, or at least the acceptance of the immigrants and their offspring by the larger society, ought to have been a phenomenon of major importance to those who sought to understand the strengths and the weaknesses, the mechanisms and the processes of the American republic.

The only answering plea available is that in the 1960's and the early

1970's nobody was really much interested in understanding how the American republic worked. Indicting, denouncing, and raging were thought to be suitable alternatives to understanding. To admit that the acculturation of Catholics was something worth investigating would have been to admit that something good could have happened in American society. It would also, perhaps, have been to admit that from the past successes of American society something might be learned about dealing with present problems. But this latter admission would have required a pragmatic stance in an era when only an apocalyptic stance was thought to be legitimate.

Yet the facts of the case are striking. Roman Catholics form slightly over one quarter of the American population. They are concentrated to a considerable extent in cities in the northeast and north central parts of the country, where they are frequently close to, if not in excess of, one half the population. Most Catholics came to America as rather unwelcome immigrants—poor, uneducated, and ignorant of the language, customs, and styles of the new country.[1] They were originally viewed by the larger society as superstitious, inferior, and, frequently, uneducable, and they have long been the objects of intensive nativist prejudice, which denied Al Smith the presidency, almost denied it to John Kennedy, and, as I will argue in this paper, has not yet dissipated altogether. Yet notwithstanding substantial pressure and a not inconsiderable social disadvantage, most Catholics have maintained an intense loyalty to the Church of Rome (even though at this point in time it is less clear exactly what the Church of Rome stands for than it was a decade ago).

The facts stated above are common knowledge. What is less well known is that Catholics, despite the barriers of history, culture, and religion, have now "made it" in American society. Catholics under 40 are as likely to be college graduates and to be economically successful as are comparable American Protestants.[2] In addition, as the recent

---

[1] It is generally thought that the Irish were an exception to this because they at least knew the language. However, as Professor Emmet Larkin has pointed out to me, large numbers, quite possibly a majority, of the Famine Irish were Irish-speaking rather than English-speaking. The Irish language died out as the first language in the west of Ireland—whence came most of the Famine immigrants— only after 1850. There is little doubt that by 1870 most of the Irish immigrants spoke English as their first language, but the earliest immigrants were not only uneducated, contentious, terribly impoverished people; many of them probably could not speak English with any degree of fluency.

[2] That is to say, Protestants whose geographic distribution is similar to that of Catholics. It is inappropriate to compare Catholics with the general Protestant population because so many American Protestants are southern and rural that the general "score" of Protestants on socio-economic indicators is substantially lower than that of the largely urban Catholics.

research of Lipset and Ladd has demonstrated, Catholics have even begun to "make it" in the sheltered groves of the academy: Approximately one fifth of the faculty members under 30 at elite colleges and universities are Catholic. Another interesting bit of evidence is that in 1960 one quarter of the nation's college students were Catholics; today one third are—a fantastic shift in a brief period of time.

Although there are such unmistakable indications that a dramatic change has occurred in the social status of the Catholic population in the last 20 years, virtually nothing is known about the dynamics of this change and even less is known about its differential impact on the various components of the Catholic population. In other words, an extraordinary phenomenon has taken place in American society in the last two decades, having a major effect on one quarter of the population, and yet few people are even aware of its occurrence, only a handful have tentative explanations for why it happened, and the overwhelming majority of the American intelligentsia are not even remotely interested.

In the shadow of the Church

There is, of course, great interest in the Roman Catholic Church. While the Church has not been very impressive in its spiritual capacity, it has been splendid theater and, as such, has managed to get front page coverage in the *New York Times* and most of the other papers in the country with greater frequency than any other religious body. In fact, one can encounter at any major university social science professors who consider themselves experts on Catholicism because they regularly follow Church politics in the popular press. Yet, when one gently suggests that most of the change in the Church's organization is not so much the result of the Vatican Council as its cause, and that in the last 20 years there have been profound, pervasive, and dramatic changes in the Catholic population which have had nothing to do with Daniel Berrigan, John XXIII, or John Kennedy, these learned social scientists look mystified.

Their mystification is understandable, for the image of Catholicism has been, and to a considerable extent still is, that of a massive monolith. Word comes down from Rome through the Vatican Council that now is the time to be flexible, and we become flexible as all hell. That changes could go on in the Catholic population which influence the Church as an organization far more than the Church influences the population is contrary to what most social scientists, deep down in their consciousness, *know* to be true about Catholicism.

These kinds of preconceptions for the most part are allowed to go unchallenged. There is little serious research being done on American Catholics, either by Catholic scholars or by others. If one approaches government or private funding agencies with the suggestion that something fascinating and perhaps very important has happened in American society in the acculturation of the Catholic population and that major research projects are in order, one is greeted with an expression that suggests one ought to consult a competent therapist or perhaps retire to a monastery for prolonged prayer and contemplation. More recently, it has become possible to do research on "ethnics," but the implication of most of the research on ethnicity is that ethnics are a "problem." When one discovers that the ethnics are not really discontented at all and are still the backbone of the American liberal coalition,[3] the reaction in many quarters is a mixture of disbelief and the feeling that, well, after all, there's not much left to study about them.

Yet the relative contentment of the Catholic population is in itself a noteworthy phenomenon which reveals a great deal about our nation. For the success of American Catholics is less a credit to Catholics themselves (though it obviously does them some credit, one supposes) than to American society. Even though native Americans did not like Catholics and were not especially pleased at their arrival, they let them into the country and permitted them to become part of it. This is a fact which most Americans, intellectuals or not, take for granted, but one realizes how astonishing it is when one looks beyond the borders of our republic.

The success of pluralism in America

The plight of the Italian and Yugoslav "guest workers" in countries like Austria, Switzerland, Germany, and Sweden, of the Algerians in France, and of the Indians and Pakistanis in England makes it quite clear that none of these allegedly enlightened and progressive European societies are at all willing to tolerate ethnic diversity. The guest workers are not permitted to become citizens, or if they are, it is only after many serious obstacles are overcome. More important, the opposition to their becoming part of the culture of the society where they are working is such that in many cases they are not even permit-

---

[3]In its views on most items of current political and social interest, the Catholic population is substantially to the left of the comparable American population as a whole. Irish Catholics are second only to Jews in their scores on indicators of political and social "liberalism."

ted to bring their families with them. The guest worker is the European equivalent of the *bracero,* who comes for a year or two to work in the host country and then returns to his own family and culture. His labor is wanted, but he and his family are not. They are considered a threat to the purity of the host culture.

Perhaps the enlightened and progressive European social democracies should not be criticized too strongly for such behavior. After all, such exclusiveness has been typical of most societies throughout human history. Suspicion of the foreigner—even if he lives just across the river—is much more typical than an enlightened pluralism which not only permits the foreigner to cross the river but welcomes him. But the most striking point about comparisons of the American attitude towards cultural pluralism and, let us say, the German or the Swedish is that they are rarely if ever made. I am unaware of a single American scholar who has pointed out, perhaps with some modest pride, that the United States did, after all, let the immigrants in and, however grudgingly, did permit them to become full-fledged Americans. As the record of the human race in dealing with diversity goes, this is no small achievement.

The Catholic immigrants (Jewish immigrants too, for that matter) were accepted as potential Americans and were given the opportunity to practice their faith and maintain their own identity—at least up to a point. All the pressures on them were, of course, assimilationist, despite occasional nods to the ideal of cultural pluralism. But the assimilationist pressures were relatively gentle and did not prevent the persistenct of unofficial cultural pluralism. You could, after all, "make it" in the United States and remain a Catholic. You could not make it everywhere (and you still can't), but you could in most places and, indeed, you might be rather strongly urged to try.

The easy Marxist explanation for this is that the United States desperately needed unskilled workers as the economy expanded. But Sweden and Germany need unskilled workers today, too, which is precisely why they bring in Italian and Yugoslav immigrants. A more sophisticated Marxism would contend that the rapid economic, technical, and territorial expansion of American society made it economically profitable for American capitalism to try to absorb the immigrant groups. But all this argument proves is that it was economically profitable to let the immigrants in. There were no particular *economic* reasons to let them move to the suburbs, much less to let one of them become president of the United States.

The truth of the matter is that we don't really know why a country whose citizens until 1820 were so predominantly white Protestant[4] was able in a relatively short span of time to become one of the most pluralistic societies the world has ever known—so pluralistic that one may suppose that Thomas Jefferson and James Madison would have feared for the country's survival if they had known it was going to happen. Nor do we have any clear idea why there has been relatively so little violence as the tremendously diverse groups in American life adjusted to one another. There has been only one Civil War, and that was fought essentially between two Anglo-Saxon groups. In other words, if one wishes to understand the relative success of American pluralism, the acculturation of the Catholic population ought to be a fascinating and informative test case. Alas, no one seems interested.

My own hunch is that the native Americans became pluralists in spite of themselves, because they were caught in an ideology which legitimated pluralism. Much of the writing about the founding of the American republic stresses the geographic and economic diversity of the various states. But if one reads the documents of the time, one becomes aware that the states were also denominationally diverse and that the founding fathers had to cope with a Congregationalist New England, a Quaker Pennsylvania, an Episcopalian Virginia, and a Free Church Georgia. Indeed, the country was denominationally pluralistic before it became politically pluralistic. The republic had to establish structures flexible enough to include Boston Congregationalists and Unitarians, Virginia Anglicans, Georgia Methodists, and backwoods Baptists; hence it was ill-equipped both ideologically and structurally to say "no" when Irish Catholics arrived on the scene. And once it had let in Irish Catholics, it was too late to refuse the Poles and

---

[4]Professor Arthur Mann has pointed out to me that at the time of the Constitutional Convention one half of the non-Indian population of the United States was Anglo-Saxon, one fourth was non-Anglo-Saxon white—mostly the so-called Scotch Irish (they did not call themselves this at the time) and Palatinate Germans—and one fourth was black.

According to Professors Ronald Greene and Albert Outler, there were really four different groups of Irish migrations to the United States—the Ulster Irish, mostly before 1800; the Celtic Protestants (mostly townsfolk who had converted to Protestantism during the penal times in Ireland), most of whom came through Philadelphia to the South; the German Irish (Palatinate Germans who had dwelled in Ulster for a time before migrating to the Colonies), who also settled mostly in the South and were active in the beginnings of Methodism; and finally the "mere Irish," who began to come in considerable numbers after 1820 and in very great numbers at the time of the Famine. It was to distinguish themselves from the "mere Irish" that the Ulster Irish (who had previously called themselves "Irish" and had founded St. Patrick societies) began to use the term "Scotch-Irish" which others had attached to them. It is interesting to note that in national sample surveys more American Protestants than Catholics claim Irish national backgrounds.

the Italians. The "American dilemma" that Gunner Myrdal saw in white attitudes towards blacks was merely one instance of a larger American dilemma: Native Americans did not particularly like diversity, but their ideology gave them little option in the matter.

"The Americanization process"

One can make some educated guesses as to why the Catholic immigrants were tolerated and even encouraged to become full-fledged Americans. One can say much less, however, about the dynamics of "the Americanization process." The official model has assumed that the individual immigrant and his children and grandchildren learned the language, went to school, worked hard, and eventually became "as American as anyone else." But this official model ignores the fact that the mobility of the Catholic populations has been a group mobility: The Germans, the Irish, and now the Italians and the Poles have made it into the upper-middle class as collectivities, and ethnic and cultural diversity continues to flourish in the upper-middle-class suburbs. The Irish are still Irish, Italians still Italians, Poles still Poles.

Unquestionably, there was a good deal of individual effort at education and achievement, but it now seems probable that this effort went on within a context of important group processes that we only dimly understand. First of all, there was the "internal mobility pyramid": One can become a success in American society, as Peter Rossi has observed, by serving the members of one's own constituency—not merely as a politician but as a doctor, lawyer, dentist, psychiatrist, undertaker, construction contractor, or clergyman. While it is possible to fall into a mobility trap—the Italian surgeon who makes it as the number one surgeon in the Italian community has little prestige in the non-Italian medical profession—even those who are caught there enjoy considerable economic success with all the material accoutrements that come with it. The Mafia don or the corrupt Irish politician may not be able to get his daughters into the elite debutante ball, but his home, automobile, and clothes will compare favorably with those of the native American elite. And from his point of view, that may be all that matters.

Second, in the large cities there are networks of intra-group client-professional relationships. The Italian doctor sees an Italian lawyer when he wants legal advice, both of them have their expensive suburban homes built by an Italian contractor, and all of them vote for an Italian political leader to represent the interests of their community at city hall or the state house. Thus an exchange of goods and services goes on within the religio-ethnic collectivity which may well have a multiplier effect in contributing to the economic well-being of this community as a whole.

Finally, there is the process of group conflict, a process symbolized by the balanced political ticket but which also includes much broader areas of contention over homes, neighborhoods, schools, churches, and jobs. Again, what is astonishing is not that this group conflict persists, but that it so rarely turns into violence. A whole series of rituals and protocols have been devised which enable American groups to keep their disputes at the level of rhetoric while working out adjustments and accommodations more or less responsive to their respective power in the particular context. I sometimes wonder if the ritualized conflict of collective bargaining isn't merely a formalization of a much more general process that goes on in many different types of group conflict situations in American society.

Obviously, my comments on these three modalities of "group mobility" can only be the sheerest sort of speculation, for no one has bothered to devote the time or energy or research resources necessary to move beyond speculation. The conventional wisdom suggests that if Catholics have made it in American society (the conventional wisdom is still somewhat dubious about the fact), it is because they have worked hard and because native Americans have been gracious enough to reward them for it. Catholics have indeed worked hard, and the native Americans have grudgingly been willing to accept them; but no one who thinks seriously about American cities for very long will believe that this is the whole story.

Nor should it be assumed that the price the immigrants and their children and grandchildren have had to pay has been a small one. There is much that the ordinary American Catholic has given up. As one of my students commented recently in a discussion of the splendor, ingenuity, precision, and wit of political rhetoric in the Republic of Ireland, "It is a long way from West Clare to Bridgeport."[5] The poetry, music, wit, mysticism, and passion of Celtic culture at its best has been lost by most of the American Irish, and that is a considerable loss for them and for the rest of American society too. Similarly, the cultural riches of the other ethnic communities are still locked up within the ethnic neighborhoods and are not shared with the rest of society, in part because the nativist American doesn't

---

[5]The Bridgeport in question is not the city in Connecticut but that district on the south side of Chicago whence came Chicago's last several mayors. Mr. Daley's malaproprisms would be terribly embarrassing in the Dail in Dublin. His political skills, however, might be appreciated in that worthy parliamentary body.

think there are any such riches and in part because the ethnic communities are afraid to share them for fear of being ridiculed. The example of the American Jews, who have made immense contributions to the common culture, has not been successfully imitated by other groups (with the possible exception of the blacks). The Irish, and probably the Germans, have abandoned their folk heritage; the Italians, the Poles, and the other Eastern European groups keep theirs carefully hidden. This is a misfortune, it seems to me, for all concerned.

The acceptance—indeed the encouragement—by elite Americans of cultural pluralism for blacks has probably legitimated cultural pride for the white ethnic groups; but it is too late for the Irish[6], and it is not clear whether the elite groups in the society are willing to take seriously the possibility that Poles and Italians have something important and valuable to contribute to the rest of American culture.

The Catholic ethnics have not stopped being Catholic ethnics. Our research data would indicate, though, that to a considerable extent they are ethnic only in an implicit and frequently unconscious way. Behavior characteristics, attitudinal constellations, relational styles persist without awareness on the part of many Catholic ethnics that their behavior is different from that of others in the society. This forced repression of diversity, while perhaps a small enough price to pay for admission into American society, is nonetheless unfortunate both for the people involved and for the rest of the country. The present writer can hardly be optimistic about any dramatic changes in this area. When the *New York Review of Books* becomes as enthusiastic about Polish-American writers as about black-American writers, then the new fashion of cultural pluralism ought to be taken seriously indeed—but not until then.

The Catholic intellectuals

The problem for the Catholic intelligentsia is much more serious, because intellectuals by their very nature cannot, like most of the rest of the Catholic population, spend most of their time with their fellow Catholics. They must interact with the mainstream intelligentsia if they are to achieve any prestige at all. And if they are to be accepted by the mainstream intelligentsia, they must, if anything, overacculturate. Just as rank-and-file American Catholics had to be-

---

[6] I personally don't believe that it is too late for the Irish, but the only way to make an Irishman do anything is to tell him that it's already too late.

AMERICAN CATHOLICS—MAKING IT OR LOSING IT?   35

come super-patriots (and assist Mr. Moynihan's Fordham man in his investigation of Harvard men), so Catholic intellectuals who wish to make it must become almost caricatures of the ideal types of American intelligentsia. Being a Catholic is no longer, I think, an obstacle to acceptance among intellectual elites, so long as you are the "right kind" of Catholic—not too pushy, not too militant, in other words, not too Catholic. I recently remarked to a colleague concerning some implacable enemies of mine on the university campus, "When I first came here they were very friendly."

"Sure," he replied, "they were friendly then because they thought of you as a possible deserter. When they found out that you weren't, you could hardly expect them to keep on being friendly."

It is all right, then, to be a Catholic priest at the University of Chicago, though it is probably more acceptable if you are an ex-priest; but to be a priest who has no intention of turning away from his own heritage, who, on the contrary, rather enjoys being a part of that heritage, is to make yourself very unpopular. As one social scientist remarked about me during a recent unsuccessful campaign by some of my colleagues to get me a certain position, "He's nothing but a loudmouthed Irish priest." I hope that phrase ends up on my gravestone, but the man who spoke it certainly did not intend it as a compliment.

No one who has spent any time in the upper echelons of the American academy and is sensitive to the nuances of acceptance and rejection can doubt that to be an active, committed Roman Catholic is to be thought a very queer fish indeed. The anti-Catholicism of the upper academy is subtle and frequently unconscious, but it is pervasive nonetheless. It cannot be explained away simply by denying that it exists, for, of course, if there is one thing we have learned recently about prejudice, it is that the unconscious kinds of sexism and racism are the worst. And the same is true of unconscious or barely conscious anti-Catholicism.

I recently heard it seriously argued at a national symposium that although the absence of blacks and women from upper-level faculty positions at the great universities was a sign of discrimination, the absence of Catholics was merely a sign of their intellectual inferiority. Nobody in the audience stirred in the slightest at such an incredible assertion. If there is any concern in American universities about the absence of Catholic presidents, deans, department chairmen, and full professors, it is one that has been very well hidden; and if the elite universities are concerned about the absence of Polish and Italian students in their undergraduate and graduate programs, they have not let it get too far out of their presidential offices or faculty clubs. If there is anyone who wonders whether graduates of Catholic liberal arts colleges are given fair treatment by graduate school admissions committees (and in my experience they are not), this wonder has been spoken only in whispers. Finally, in the whole lengthy debate about the absence of Catholics in intellectual life, I am unaware of a single writer (myself included, incidentally) who ever questioned whether one of the reasons for this absence might be a subtle anti-Catholic bias in the academy. Strange behavior indeed for a profession that prides itself on questioning all assumptions.

Younger Catholic scholars, almost by sheer weight of numbers, have now made it into the academy, and, as data from the recent Carnegie research on college faculty indicate, they are publishing articles and obtaining tenure in the same proportion as Protestants. The academy can heave a sigh of relief: Catholics have finally become bright enough and intellectual enough to merit entrance—but of course they are not yet bright enough or intellectual enough to merit prestige appointments, deanships, chairmanships, and university presidencies. What disturbs me about all this is not that the exclusion of Catholics from such positions is necessarily the result of bigotry (for it may very well be that a later phase of the acculturation process will be required before there will be enough Catholics to occupy such positions), it is the complacent assumption that bigotry couldn't possibly play a part in the situation. Anyone who knows anything about the human condition knows that a Ph.D., a full professorship, or a deanship does not necessarily contribute anything at all to the development of toleration or the enjoyment of diversity. I begin to believe that any group of human beings may not be biased on that day when they begin to examine seriously the possibility that they are biased.

The limits of cultural pluralism

But the Catholic intellectual is not only required to be something less than committed to his Catholicism if he wants full acceptance; he also should not become too concerned about the explicit study of Catholic matters. He will probably be disinclined to do this, in any case, because it involved considerable emotional stress for him to break out of the Catholic subculture and move into the larger society. When someone suggests to him that something in that subculture might be worth analyzing and interpreting for the rest of society, he is not particularly disposed to take such advice seriously.

Thus, among the official American Catholic intelligentsia, only Michael Novak has shown much concern about the new interest in ethnicity and cultural pluralism. When you have just left the ghetto behind, it is difficult to believe that you ought to go back into it to administer a questionnaire or to write a novel that implies something good might be going on there.

There is, then, not the slightest chance of the emergence of a Catholic militancy or pride. Such attitudes will occur in any group only when the larger society legitimates it. The larger society is not about to say to Poles (as it has said to blacks), "Why aren't you militant and proud?" Until the day comes when the American elites begin to demand pride and militancy from Polish and Italian and, yes, even Irish intellectuals, the Catholic intelligentsia will remain a very tame and docile crew, taking out its frustrations by flailing away at the hapless and incompetent ecclesiastical authority structure, which hasn't been able to mobilize its resources to do a great deal of harm to anybody for most of the last decade.

One of my Jewish colleagues put his finger on the whole problem when he said, "The difference between the Jews and you Irish is that we know that we have a self-hatred problem, take it into account, and even occasionally turn it to profit in our literature." The problem may be aggravated by the fact that, while it's pretty hard for Jewish novelists and intellectuals to become very angry at their rabbis, the Irish intelligentsia, for reasons far beyond the scope of this essay, find it difficult to control their ambivalent feelings towards priests.

The larger American elite culture is at present willing to tolerate a Catholic intelligentsia as long as its Catholicism is quiet, restrained, and devoid of all militancy and enthusiasm. One may, of course, wonder whether such an intelligentsia is really Catholic at all.

In this respect, the treatment accorded Catholics by the American intellectual community is in no way unique. Jews, for example, have undoubtedly achieved a central role in American intellectual life. But where among our leading intellectual figures is there an Orthodox Jew? The situation of blacks merely represents the opposite side of this same coin. Black pride has been granted the intellectuals' seal of approval—so black militants are immediately welcomed, but black moderates are ignored. The "diversity" of American intellectual life extends no farther than the prevailing ideological climate will allow. Pluralism seems to be much less successful in our universities than in our politics. So while the Catholic ethnics may have "made it" in socio-economic terms, their intellectual and cultural traditions continue to be despised or ignored by most of the American intelligentsia.

Offprint from THE PUBLIC OPINION QUARTERLY
Volume 36, Summer 1972
© 1972 by Columbia University Press

POLITICAL ATTITUDES AMONG AMERICAN WHITE ETHNICS

BY ANDREW M. GREELEY

Data from a variety of sources are brought to bear on the "proposition" that white American ethnic groups are composed of bigots and hawks. The data fail to conform with the model, raising some interesting questions about the origins of the stereotype and the functions—and dysfunctions—it serves in contemporary society.

The author is director of the Center for American Pluralism of National Opinion Research Center of the University of Chicago. This article is based on a paper presented to the American Political Science Association Meetings, September 10, 1971.

THE TERM "white ethnic" is used frequently, and generally loosely, in contemporary writing as a synonym for "hard hat" or "racist." Obviously, not all members of American ethnic groups are hard hats, and the extent of their racism is, we assume, a question for research rather than for a priori definition. In most instances, one can legitimately suppose that subsumed under the label "white ethnic" are the children and the grandchildren of the eastern and southern European immigrant groups who managed to get into American society before nativism was at last successful in slowing down appreciably, if not completely stopping, the flow of immigrants. To be more blunt about it, "white ethnic" usually means "Polish and Italian." Whether the Irish are a white ethnic group in this usage of the phrase is open to question, but it is worth noting that Joe, in the movie of the same name, representing as he did the quintessence of what the American elite defines as white ethnic, was Irish.

It is generally assumed in much of the popular and serious writing on the "resurgence of ethnicity" that the American ethnic—that is to say, Polish Catholics, Italian Catholics, and Irish Catholics—are both racist and hawkish. It is also assumed that even though they are nominally members of the Democratic party, the ethnics are strongly attracted to George Wallace—despite the fact that there is considerable evidence that the "ethnics" were no more likely to vote for Wallace than any other northern white group.

A number of explanations are given for this "conservatism" of the white ethnic. They are more recent recruits to American society, they are thought to be still insecure and threatened by social change,

214   ANDREW M. GREELEY

they are the ones most likely to be in competition for jobs and neighborhoods with the various nonwhite groups in the large cities of the Northeast and North Central parts of the country. Their Catholicism is said to dispose them to an "anti-Communist" and hence "conservative" political response. Thus, in any discussion of the emergence of new political coalitions, it is generally assumed that the conservative, racist, hawkish white ethnics will not be part of the coalition. On occasion, at least, the new coalition sounds like the old New Deal coalition, minus the ethnics. It is the purpose of this article to see whether there is sufficient evidence available to us to justify the portrait of the white ethnic as conservative, racist, and hawkish.

Survey research is constrained by the size of the sample and distribution of the American population to deal under normal circumstances with no more than eight "white ethnic" groups. The largest is the WASP or American Protestant, and the smallest is Jewish. In between are Germans, both Protestant and Catholic, with the former outnumbering the latter about two to one, Scandinavians, Irish Catholics, South European Catholics (mostly Italians), and East European Catholics (mostly Poles, but including other Slavic groups, and such non-Slavic Catholics as the Lithuanians). Obviously Italian Protestants, Serbian Orthodox, and Slovak Lutherans do not fall into any of these categories and in any analysis which is not based on an extremely large sample must be excluded.

Let me concede all the weaknesses of survey research. Let me concede further that the evidence pulled together for this paper is sketchy and incomplete almost to the point of being random. Nevertheless, I think it legitimate to assert that there is almost no evidence in this paper to support the image of the racist, hawkish white ethnic, and considerable evidence suggesting that there is still substantial support for social change and for the liberal political tradition among American ethnic communities—particularly, I might note, in that group which is frequently despised as politically amoral—the Irish.

ATTITUDES TOWARD THE VIETNAM WAR

Blue-collar workers, including Protestants as well as Catholics, were more likely than the national average to favor withdrawal from Vietnam within eighteen months in February of 1970. It is also worth noting that white-collar Catholics were substantially more likely to be in favor of withdrawal than were white-collar Protestants, and that Catholic professionals and executives were the most likely of any group shown in Table 1 to be opposed to the war.

The data in Table 1 were collected in 1970, when it was permissible

POLITICAL ATTITUDES OF AMERICAN ETHNICS   215

TABLE 1

ATTITUDES TOWARD THE WAR, FEBRUARY 1970

(Percent in favor of immediate withdrawal or within 18 months)

Occupational Group	Northern Whites Protestants	Catholics
Blue collar	50% (195)	47% (114)
Clerical, sales, service	32% (73)	38% (60)
Professional and executive	39% (160)	52% (101)
National average	46%	

and even fashionable to be against the war. I have been told when I cited this datum that the ethnics were recent converts to the cause of peace. However, on the dove scale constructed by Sidney Verba and his colleagues at Stanford in their 1967 study of attitudes on the Vietnam War (Table 2), they were substantially more likely to be at the dove end of the scale than were native American Protestants. Only the eastern European Catholics were lower on the dove scale than were native American Protestants. In other words, three of the four ethnic groups were not only *not* more hawkish in 1967, they were in fact less hawkish than native Americans. One wonders why so few of the leaders of the peace movement were aware of white ethnic antipathy toward the war, and why so many were eager to write off white ethnics as hard-hat hawks. As I have noted elsewhere, you cannot expect second- and third-generation immigrants to hate a society which has made possible for them a kind of life that their predecessors in the old world would never have dreamed possible. A position toward the war that might have been effective among such groups would have appealed to patriotism instead of ridiculing it.

ATTITUDES ON CONTEMPORARY POLITICAL ISSUES

We turn next to the attitudes of ethnics on several critical contemporary political issues. Unfortunately, the Gallup survey in question

TABLE 2

ATTITUDES OF AMERICAN WHITE ETHNIC GROUPS
TOWARD THE VIETNAM WAR, 1967

Group	Percent Dove[a]
Jewish	48% (47)
Western European Catholic	29% (149)
Southern European Catholic	26% (60)
Western European Protestant	17% (499)
Native American	15% (104)
Eastern European Catholic	7% (42)

[a] Adapted from a forthcoming paper by Norman Nie and Barbara Currie.

216   ANDREW M. GREELEY

does not ask an ethnic question.[1] Therefore, we have been forced to assume that northern, white, blue-collar Catholics are, for all practical purposes, ethnics. In Table 3, therefore, we ask how blue-collar ethnics compare both with Protestant blue-collar workers and with national averages on certain critical political issues. There is little difference in sympathy for the eighteen-year-old vote, or on the welfare reform that bases welfare on the cost of living. However, Catholic blue-collar workers are more likely than Protestant blue-collar workers and the national average to be in favor of a guaranteed annual wage, to say they would vote for a black president, and to be deeply concerned about pollution. They are also less likely than the two comparison groups to say that integration is moving too fast. In other words, if American liberals are looking for groups in the population that are more likely than other groups to support action on pollution, integration, welfare reform, and electing blacks to political office, it is precisely among Catholic blue-collar workers that they should look.

This conclusion is further supported by data in a forthcoming paper by Norman Nie and Barbara Currie. Table 4 presents the proportion of each ethnic group that is high on a scale indicating sympathy for government support for the poor. Contrary to what might have been expected, the southern and eastern European Catholics are the most likely to be sympathetic to government on behalf of the poor, second only to the Jews.

RACIAL ATTITUDES

For thirty years, NORC has been collecting data on the changing attitudes of Americans on racial integration. Unfortunately, it was

TABLE 3

ATTITUDES ON CERTAIN POLITICAL ISSUES

	Northern White Blue-Collar Workers		
Attitude	Protestant	Catholic	National Average
In favor of 18-year-old vote			
1968	62% (217)	65% (150)	66%
1969	62% (221)	64% (129)	61%
In favor of basing welfare on cost			
of living	79% (191)	79% (136)	77%
In favor of guaranteed annual wage	29% (228)	47% (134)	32%
Would vote for a black president	72% (193)	78% (142)	67%
Integration moving too fast	57% (280)	42% (127)	48%
Deeply concerned about pollution	50% (258)	55% (110)	51%

* SOURCE: Gallup Polls.

[1] The Harris survey does, but we are still in the process of analyzing the data made available to us by Harris.

POLITICAL ATTITUDES OF AMERICAN ETHNICS　　　217

TABLE 4

ATTITUDES OF AMERICAN WHITE ETHNIC GROUPS
TOWARD GOVERNMENT INTERVENTION IN
AID TO POOR[a]

Group	Percent Favoring Intervention	
Jewish	55%	(32)
Southern European	47%	(115)
Eastern European	44%	(110)
Western European Protestant	27%	(1175)
Western European Catholic	26%	(300)
Native American	19%	(315)

[a] Adapted from a forthcoming paper by Norman Nie and Barbara Currie.

only in the most recent of these surveys (in 1970) that an ethnic question was asked. Hence, no longitudinal data on changing racial attitudes of white ethnic groups can be adduced, although the fact that there is little difference in the rate of change of racial attitudes among the various religious groups would suggest that the ethnics are not becoming more favorable toward integration at a slower rate than anyone else.[2]

The NORC racial integration scale is the Guttman scale composed of the following seven items:

1. Generally speaking, do you think there should be separate sections for Negroes in street cars and buses? ("No")
2. Do you think Negroes should have the right to use the same parks, restaurants, and hotels as white people? ("Yes")
3. Do you think white students and Negro students should go to the same schools, or to separate schools? ("Same schools")
4. How strongly would you object if a member of your family wanted to bring a Negro friend home to dinner? ("Not at all")
5. White people have a right to keep Negroes out of their neighborhoods if they want to, and Negroes should respect that right. ("Disagree slightly" or "disagree strongly")
6. Do you think there should be laws against marriages between Negroes and whites? ("No")
7. Negroes shouldn't push themselves where they're not wanted. ("Disagree slightly" or "disagree strongly")

Thus, in Table 5, a score of 5.79 for the Jewish respondents means that the typical American Jew accepts the first five items on the

[2] It is interesting, by the way, to observe that despite the tumult of the years from 1963 to 1970, and despite the alleged "backlash," Americans continue to become more favorable toward racial integration by about the same rate according to which they had changed their attitudes in the previous seven years. See Andrew M. Greeley and Paul B. Sheatsley, "Attitudes toward Desegregation," *Scientific American*, Vol. 225, December 1971, pp. 13-19.

TABLE 5

Score of American White Ethnic Groups on NORC's
Pro-Integration Scale (1970)

	Mean Score[a]			
Group	Total Group	Non-South	Less than H. S. Grad.	H. S. Grad.
Jewish	5.79	5.79 (24)	—	6.05 (21)
Irish	5.02	5.02 (48)	4.72 (11)	5.11 (37)
German Catholic	4.62	4.85 (41)	4.35 (20)	5.33 (21)
German Protestant	4.42	4.67 (137)	4.02 (50)	5.04 (87)
Scandinavian	4.41	4.72 (29)	3.66 (9)	5.20 (20)
Italian	4.41	4.34 (38)	3.00 (16)	5.31 (22)
Slavic	4.41	4.37 (43)	3.88 (25)	4.82 (29)
WASP	3.71	4.68 (220)	4.11 (79)	4.99 (139)

[a] High score = favorable attitude on integration.

NORC scale and, in all likelihood, accepts the sixth item, too; whereas a score of 3.71 for American WASPS indicates that a typical American Protestant accepts the first three items of the NORC scale and is more than likely also to be ready to approve someone in his family bringing a Negro friend home to dinner.

The first column of Table 5 clearly shows that all the ethnic groups are more pro-integration than native-born, white Protestants. However, since only small numbers of white ethnics live in the South, it would be more informative to compare ethnics with non-Southern WASPS. Even outside the South, as Column 2 shows, Irish and German Catholics and Scandinavian Protestants are more pro-integration than WASPS.

Columns 3 and 4 control for education rather than region. Because so few are now in each cell, all conclusions are highly tentative. (Column 3 shows no Jewish score because only three Jews in our sample did not graduate from high school.) Still, we may note the apparent effect of having graduated from high school. Among those who did not, both Irish and German Catholics are more pro-integration than WASPS. Among those who did, only Slavs are less favorable to integration than WASPS.

Another source of data available to us is NORC's ongoing study of the 1961 college graduation class. In the spring of 1968, a questionnaire was administered to these college alumni (still for the most part under thirty) in which, among other things, their attitudes on racial and student militancy were measured. In Table 6, we note that Jewish, Slavic, and Irish alumni have higher scores of sympathy for militancy than typical American alumni do, while German and Italian Catholics have lower scores. Even though the number of Slavic respondents is

POLITICAL ATTITUDES OF AMERICAN ETHNICS   219

TABLE 6

SYMPATHY OF AMERICAN WHITE ETHNIC GROUPS
FOR BLACK AND YOUTHFUL MILITANCY
AMONG 1961 COLLEGE GRADUATES
(AS MEASURED IN 1968)

Group	Average Score[a]	
Jewish	11.9	(100)
Irish	10.6	(269)
Slavic	10.5	(54)
All other alumni	9.5	(4324)
German Catholic	9.2	(280)
Italian	8.3	(168)

[a] High score = pro-militant.

quite small, the data in Table 6 suggest an interesting change in attitudes among young college-educated Slavs. Instead of being at the
bottom of the scale of sympathy for Negroes, they are now just behind
the Irish, and substantially *ahead* of typical American alumni.

Furthermore, while students are very likely to describe themselves
as politically "independent" (as apparently student respondents of
past decades have also done) it is still clear from Table 7 that the
young alumni from ethnic backgrounds are more likely than old-line
Americans to declare their loyalty to the Democratic party.

One might ask, and not unreasonably, why the stereotype of the
white ethnic to be found among so many American liberals is at such
variance with the data reported in this paper. A number of explanations might be advanced. One might, for example, agree with Michael
Lerner that there is a tendency toward snobbery on the part of one
social class toward the social class immediately below it on the SES
ladder. Most liberals are members of the upper middle class; most

TABLE 7

AMERICAN WHITE ETHNIC GROUP AFFILIATION
WITH DEMOCRATIC PARTY AMONG 1961
COLLEGE GRADUATES
(AS MEASURED IN 1968)

Group	Percent Democratic
Eastern European Jew	49
Polish	48
Irish	41
German Catholic	37
Italian	37
German Jew	36
WASP	25
Scandinavian	22
German Protestant	21

ethnics are members of the lower middle class. In Lerner's paradigm, then, the attitude of some liberals and intellectuals toward ethnics may not be all that dissimilar to the attitude of some ethnics toward blacks and other nonwhite minority groups.

It also may be that society needs some justification for taking from the white ethnics and giving to the blacks. Thus, for example, in a city like Newark, when it is decreed that scores in merit exams are no longer the only criterion for promotion in the public school system, it follows inevitably that higher places in the educational bureaucracy will be taken from Italians and given to blacks, since these are the only two groups that are involved in competition for such positions. The Italians, who may well feel that they have not gotten a fair shake from American society, are understandably outraged. The elite groups who decree that such departures from the traditional norms of merit promotion are appropriate must have some justification for taking from one group and giving to another. If the group from which one is taking is a group that is committed to immoral or socially undesirable attitudes, it is somewhat easier to do the taking.

However, I think that while there may be some merit to these two explanations, they are of minor importance compared to a third explanation. Most of those of us who write about politics and about society and who read the important journals in which articles about politics and society are presented know practically nothing about American ethnic communities. We may know more about what goes on in certain tribal communities in Africa and Asia than we do about what occurs in Hamtramck, Queens, or Avalon Park.

This is an extraordinary phenomenon. America is a society put together only yesterday from a great variety of immigrant groups and yet our social and political scientists seem only marginally interested in these immigrant groups, and most of our national survey questionnaires do not even think that immigrant background is important enough to merit an item on a questionnaire. The reasons for this phenomenon are beyond the scope of this paper, but it may be advisable for those of us who are part of the liberal and intellectual communities to ponder the fact that we know virtually nothing about very large segments of the American population, and that when we generalize about these segments, our generalizations run the risk of being dramatically wrong.

The "Religious Factor" and Academic Careers: Another Communication

Andrew M. Greeley
University of Chicago

Strong evidence indicates that, despite social, economic, historical, cultural, and perhaps religious obstacles, many more Catholics are electing academic careers. Little is known about either the facts or the dynamics of this change, and there seems to be little interest among sociologists or the funding agencies to inquire about it. While these changes occur, the long-standing assumption that the absence of Catholics in scholarly careers is a proof of Catholic intellectual inferiority remains essentially unchallenged.

During the last decade a polite controversy has raged in the pages of this *Journal* on the relationship between the "religious factor" and the choice of an academic career. It is the purpose of this brief communication to add one more—and perhaps a final—word to the continuity.

The term "religious factor" is a euphemism; no one has ever suggested that a Jewish or a Protestant background are obstacles to making the choice of an academic career. The real issue has always been whether a Roman Catholic background interfered with such a career choice.

The evidence was fairly persuasive that at one time it did. The literature reporting this evidence included Knapp and Goodrich (1952), Knapp and Greenbaum (1953), Ellis (1955), O'Dea (1958), and Lenski (1963). Two reasons given for the underrepresentation of Catholics in the academy were summarized by Lenski (1963). Catholicism develops an intellectual orientation which values obedience above intellectual autonomy, and Catholicism values family and kin group relations above other relations. Hence, "membership in the Catholic group is more likely to inhibit the development of scientific careers than is membership in either Protestant or Jewish groups. The implications of this for the future of American society are not difficult to discover" (p. 255). Catholic authors like Ellis and O'Dea (1958) argued that clerical domination, the absence of a scholarly tradition, fear of modern science, lack of concern for "temporal" values, and low respect for curiosity and initiative in Catholic training also contributed to the presumed intellectual inferiority of Catholics.

However, beginning in 1963, a series of reports on the NORC college graduate study, contained in Greeley (1963, 1967, 1969) found little empirical support for the argument that younger Catholics were not choosing academic careers. In 1961, Catholic graduates were as likely to graduate

American Journal of Sociology

from college, to go to graduate schools, to choose academic careers, and to manifest "intellectual" values as Protestants. By 1965, they were at least as likely to still be in graduate school, to be attending high-quality universities, to have acquired the M.S., and to be expecting the Ph.D. By 1968 they were more likely than the typical 1961 graduate to have received the Ph.D. and to have committed themselves to a permanent academic career.

There was considerable criticism of the NORC findings. Warwick (1963), Lenski (1963, 1965), Trent (1967), and Carr and Bowers (1968) all expressed doubt about the validity of the findings. There were two principal criticisms:

1. The NORC sample was deficient.

2. In Lenski's (1963, p. 284) words, the NORC data dealt "with the aspirations and intentions of young people on the verge of graduate school whereas the other studies which have so troubled Catholic educators and intellectuals deal with established men of science. . . . the aspirations of Catholics are as high as those of non-Catholics. Contrary to the popular understanding of the Protestant ethic, Catholics are ambitious and hard working. If they fail to get ahead in certain areas, it seems to be due more to the influence of other factors." In other words, Lenski—and the other critics—expected the Catholic graduate students to "drop out" at some point en route to becoming "established men of science."

The first criticism was based on a misunderstanding of the NORC sample design and was quickly dropped when other surveys based on different samples reported identical findings. However, even the most recent NORC report (Greeley 1969) did not provide data on the performance of Catholics as faculty members. Furthermore, the NORC data, while assuming a change from the situation reported by previous authors, did not make it possible to specify when the change occurred. Finally, despite the large size of the initial NORC sample, there were not enough respondents who had chosen academic careers to provide the 1969 NORC report with the size of case bases that would make possible confident assertions about the fate of Catholics who had chosen academic careers.

However, the recent research commissioned by the Carnegie Commission on American Higher Education has made possible a new analysis of the religious background of American academics. This analysis is reported in Lipset and Ladd (1971) and is primarily concerned with the contributions of Jews to American academia. However, a reanalysis of their data enables us to trace the careers of the contemporaries of the 1961 Catholic graduates in the academic life and to give some hint as to when the "turnaround" took place in Catholic decisions about academic careers.[1]

[1] In a footnote, Lipset and Ladd (1971, p. 92) describe the design of the Carnegie study. We are grateful to Lipset and Ladd for providing new tabulations: "In 1969 the Carnegie Commission on Higher Education initiated several large-scale national

"Religious Factor" and Academic Careers

In this communication we will limit ourselves to those with Catholic backgrounds on the faculties of the "elite" universities because it is precisely in those universities that the "distinguished men of science" are likely to be concentrated and because it is precisely in those universities from which Catholics have presumably been absent.[2]

TABLE 1

RELIGIOUS BACKGROUND (RELIGION IN WHICH RAISED) OF AMERICAN PROFESSORATE
IN 1969 BY AGE—ELITE COLLEGES AND UNIVERSITIES ONLY

	N	Protestant (%)	Catholic (%)	Jewish (%)	Other and None (%)	Total* (%)
65 and over ...	439	75	9	9	7	100
60–64	1,012	73	9	10	7	99
55–59	1,317	70	10	14	6	101
50–54	1,756	66	11	16	7	101
45–49	2,425	58	12	20	10	100
40–44	2,749	55	12	23	11	101
35–39	3,322	54	15	20	11	100
30–34	3,398	54	15	20	10	99
29 and under ..	2,673	52	19	21	9	101

SOURCE.—Adapted from Lipset and Ladd (1971, p. 93).
* Totals are not always 100% because of rounding errors.

Table 1 indicates that Catholics are about one-fifth of the faculty under 30 at "elite" colleges and universities,[3] approximately equal numerically

surveys of students, faculty, and administrators. These studies were administered by the Survey Research Center of the University of California, Berkeley, with advice and technical assistance from the Office of Research of the American Council on Education. Financial support was provided by the Carnegie Commission and the United States Office of Education, Department of Health, Education and Welfare. A disproportionate random sampling procedure was used to select colleges and universities, to obtain adequate numbers of institutions of various types and characteristics. The 303 schools thus chosen included 57 junior colleges, 168 four-year colleges, and 78 universities. Next, a six-in-seven random sample of faculty was drawn from the rosters of the included institutions, yielding a sample of 100,315. A very high return of 60,028 completed questionnaires (60 per cent) was achieved. The returned questionnaires, finally, were differentially weighted, adjusting the data for the disproportionate sampling of institutions and the unequal rates of response. Tabulations from the weighted data of this survey, then, may be taken as reasonably representative of the entire population of teaching faculty at colleges and universities in the United States."

[2] The universities were scored by Lipset and Ladd (1971) on a three-item index: SAT scores required for admission, revenue per student, and research expenditure per student. Approximately one-third of their 60,000 respondents were on the staffs of the institutions they rated as "elite."

[3] Catholics are 22% of the faculty under 30 at nonelite colleges. Since Catholics are one-fourth of the total population and one-fifth of the elite faculty under 30 it may be argued that this is, after all, not the last "continuity" and that the case will be closed only when Catholics are represented in the elite faculties (at least the younger component of such faculties) in their exact proportion in the national population.

American Journal of Sociology

to the Jews and approximately equal proportionately to Protestants (with relation to the respective proportions in the total American population). The "breakthrough" for Jewish faculty members at the elite schools apparently took place with those faculty members who in 1969 were between 45 and 60—that is to say, for those who were in graduate school between 1935 and 1950. Since that time, Jews have been consistently about one-fifth of the "elite" faculties. The "breakthrough" for Catholics has occurred for those under 40—that is, those who were in graduate school from 1955 to the present. There is no evidence that the Catholic increase has stopped.[4]

To say that Catholics are now present on the elite faculties in equal numbers with Jews does not say that Catholics have—or can ever—"catch up" with Jews in proportional representation. Since Jews are about 3% of the American population and Catholics about 25%, the Catholics would have to occupy over 125% of the faculty positions in the American universities to have the same proportional representation as Jews do. But the data in table 1 do strongly suggest that a Catholic background is no longer an obstacle to academic career at a major American university.

Nor are the Catholic faculty under 35, whether at elite or nonelite colleges (table 2), inferior to the Protestant faculty in either the acquisition of tenure or the publication of five or more scholarly articles—though both groups are substantially behind the Jews in both these respects (for a discussion of the reason for this finding see Lipset and Ladd [1971]). As a matter of fact, the faculty with Catholic backgrounds differ from their Protestant colleagues only in frequency of church attendance and are similar in their attitudes, self-definition, and values at both elite and nonelite colleges.

Lenski's (1963) prediction, then, that the aspiring Catholic academics would "drop out" remains unfulfilled and it seems legitimate at this time to wonder whether even Lenski would seriously maintain that at some unspecified date in the future the "Catholic intellectual orientation" will catch up with these Catholic faculty members.

A more appropriate strategy might be to ask what happened to the

---

However, it is to be noted that Protestants constitute about two-thirds of the total population and only a little more than half of the elite faculties under 30. Thus, the ratio of "actual" to "expected" elite faculty members for Catholics is .8 and for Protestants, .79. In other words, Catholics under 30 are no less likely than Protestants to be faculty members at elite colleges. (The ratio of "actual" to "expected" for Jews is 7.00—a figure which would be statistically impossible for either Catholics or Protestants ever to match.)

[4] In 1961, Catholics were 25% of the college population—about their proportion in the total American population. In 1971, according to the annual norms published by the American Council on Education, Catholics were 33% of the college population—a very dramatic increase in a 10-year span. In addition, in 1961, Irish Catholics were twice as likely to graduate from college as were typical Americans.

"Religious Factor" and Academic Careers

TABLE 2

PERCENTAGE OF YOUNGER PROFESSORS IN COLLEGES AND UNIVERSITIES BY RELIGION
HAVING CERTAIN ATTITUDES AND BEHAVIOR

	29 AND UNDER			30–34		
	Protestant	Catholic	Jew	Protestant	Catholic	Jew
	ELITE					
With tenure	2	3	3	23	22	31
5 or more professional articles published	15	14	17	40	39	51
Describing self as "intellectual" (strongly agree) ..	22	23	34	23	27	33
Supporting Vietnam withdrawal	28	30	43	24	22	31
Sympathetic with student protest ...	61	58	69	56	54	61
Attending cultural event 2 or 3 times a month	34	33	37	31	30	36
"Left" politically ...	12	13	21	11	10	14
Church attendance at least monthly ..	32	52·	8	35	53	8
	NONELITE					
With tenure	3	2	2	20	19	21
5 or more professional articles published	1	1	1	5	5	12
Describing self as "intellectual" (strongly agree) ..	13	16	26	14	14	31
Supporting Vietnam withdrawal	20	20	39	14	17	35
Sympathetic with student protest ...	46	50	57	43	49	61
Attending cultural event 2 or 3 times a month	26	31	36	26	26	35
"Left" politically ...	6	8	20	5	5	16
Church attendance at least monthly ..	49	63	11	57	70	13

Catholic population. It will not do to say as Lenski did recently (1971) that Catholicism has changed. For such an assertion is merely a repetition of the data in table 1. Somthing obviously changed. Nor will it do to cite the Second Vatican Council which had not even begun in 1955 when the change in academic career decisions among Catholics apparently started.

American Journal of Sociology

Nor can the decisions of the 1961 graduates be attributed to the council which was only just beginning when they went off to graduate school.[5]

There obviously have been major changes in the American Catholic Church in the last decade, but these changes may well be as much a cause of the Vatican Council experience as a result.

It might be argued that a certain level of parental education is required before a large number of young people begin to choose academic careers. However, table 3 does not support such an argument. Catholic scholars at

TABLE 3

PARENTAL EDUCATION OF YOUNGER FACULTY IN
ELITE COLLEGES AND UNIVERSITIES BY RELI-
GION (PERCENTAGE OF FATHERS WHO
ATTENDED COLLEGE)

	29 and Under	30–34
Protestant	62	58
Catholic	44	43
Jew	57	48

the elite schools come from a lower educational background than do either Protestants or Jews. Nor does the figure for frequent church attendance cited in table 2 indicate that Catholics pursue academic careers at the price of ceasing to be Catholics.

One might argue that an "acculturation process" has taken place in which the Catholic immigrant groups have become part of the larger society. In such a perspective, the earlier Catholic groups ought to be further along in the process than the more recent immigrants, and the Irish ahead of the rest. Table 4 gives some confirmation of this suggestion. (Unfortunately, there was no ethnic question asked in the Carnegie study —itself an interesting fact for the sociologists of knowledge to consider. Hence, table 4 is based on a reanalysis of the 1968 NORC data.) Not only are the Irish scientists ahead of the other Catholic ethnics in the percentage having Ph.D.'s choosing academic careers and in describing themselves as intellectuals, but they are also ahead of everyone else on all these items on the table (and 73% of them go to church every week). Whether "the implications of this for the future of American society are not difficult to discover" had best be left to observers other than the present writer.

[5] Other NORC research by Davis (1962) and Warkov and Greeley (1966) confirm the fact of the change in the middle 1950s. The former found that by 1958 Catholics were about one-fourth of the graduate student population—approximately their proportion in the general American population. The latter writers indicate that in the middle 1950s the proportion of Catholic secondary school graduates going on for the B.A. jumped dramatically.

"Religious Factor" and Academic Careers

TABLE 4

ATTITUDES AND BEHAVIOR OF YOUNGER AMERICAN SCIENTISTS BY
RELIGION AND ETHNICITY*

	Ph.D. (%)	Career in University or Research (%)	Expecting Major Satisfaction from Career (%)	High on "Reading Frequency" Index (%)	Describing Self as Intellectual (%)	Weekly Church (%)
Protestant:						
Anglo-Saxon (295)	19	24	28	15	47	28
German (181)	15	21	31	10	48	33
Scandinavian (27)	22	29	28	10	52	44
Catholic:						
Irish (40)	43	58	51	32	75	73
German (66)	29	12	40	12	65	58
Italian (31)	10	6	15	4	33	51
Polish (34)	23	37	6	2	44	91
Jewish (27)	27	30	25	25	64	10

* Those who in 1968 reported that their long-range career would be in the physical, chemical, or
biological sciences or in mathematics.

Something has clearly happened to the American Catholic population and
in all likelihood is still happening. But we have only the vaguest notion
of what it is, why it is occurring, and what is likely to come of it. The
debate of which this communication is part might be wisely called to a halt.
One can, of course, wait till the Nobel prizes are awarded to those who
were in graduate schools in the late fifties and early sixties to concede
finally that a Catholic background does not inhibit a successful academic
career. But it would probably be much more profitable for social scientists
to accept the fact as being reasonably well established and begin to try
to explain the change.

When the debate over Catholic "intellectualism" began it was assumed
that the absence of Catholics in scholarly careers was a proof of a Catholic
problem of intellectual inferiority. More recently, the absence of blacks
and women has been seen as proof of discrimination. At a conference in
1971, I heard it seriously argued—without any evidence being adduced—
that the Catholic absence from academia in the past was the result of
intellectual inferiority but that the absence of women and blacks was a
result of discrimination. A study of the possibility of anti-Catholic feelings,
past and present, at elite schools is beyond the scope of this communication
—but it is not beyond the scope of social research. That there has never
been—as far as I know—any such study and that the possibility of subtle
forms of discrimination was never raised during the debate about Catholic

American Journal of Sociology

intellectualism, must at least be described as an interesting phenomenon, especially in a discipline that prides itself on testing assumptions.

There is strong reason to believe that an extraordinary and exciting change has occurred in one-fourth of the American population during the last 20 years. Among the aspects of this change has been a dramatic increase in the choice of academic careers by young people in this group—despite social, economic, historical, cultural, and (perhaps) religious obstacles to such career decisions. This change may say much about American society's capacity to absorb diversity and indeed about the whole structure of that society. Yet precious little is known about either the facts or the dynamics of the change. When asked about it most sociologists begin to sound like the religion sections of *Time* and *Newsweek*. Even Catholic scholars (and Catholics now are slightly overrepresented in sociology according to Lipset and Ladd [1971]) have done rather little to attempt to explain a striking phenomenon of which they are so clearly the products. One looks in vain in the professional journals for articles on the subject—save for the present, by now tiresome, debate. And if one approaches funding agencies with the suggestion that someone ought to be looking at the acculturation of the Catholic population as a model for understanding American society, one is given a look reserved for those who ought to be on the funny farm—if not sequestered in a monastery.

None of this is persuasive evidence of discrimination. But neither is it persuasive evidence of good sociology.

REFERENCES

Carr, Andrea, and William J. Bowers. 1968. "Letter to the Editor." *American Journal of Sociology* 73 (May): 768.
Davis, James A., David Gottlieb, Jan Hadja, Carolyn Huson, and Joe L. Spaeth. 1962. *Stipends and Spouses: The Finances of American Arts and Science Graduate Students*. Chicago: University of Chicago Press.
Ellis, John Tracy. 1955. "American Catholics and the Intellectual Life." *Thought* (Autumn).
Greeley, Andrew M. 1963. "Influence of the 'Religious Factor' on Career Plans and Occupational Values of College Graduates." *American Journal of Sociology* 68 (May): 658–71.
———. 1967. "Religion and Academic Career Plans: A Note on Progress." *American Journal of Sociology* 72 (May): 668–72.
———. 1969. "Continuities in Research on the 'Religious Factor.'" *American Journal of Sociology* 75 (November): 355–59.
Knapp, Robert H., and H. B. Goodrich. 1952. *Origins of American Scientists*. Chicago: University of Chicago Press.
Knapp, Robert H., and Joseph J. Greenbaum. 1953. *The Young American Scholar. His Collegiate Origins*. Chicago: University of Chicago Press.
Lenski, Gerhard. 1963. *The Religious Factor*. Rev. ed. Garden City, N.Y.: Doubleday Anchor.
———. 1965. Review of *Religion and Career: A Study of College Graduates*, by A. M. Greeley. *American Journal of Sociology* 71 (September): 200–201.

"Religious Factor" and Academic Careers

———. 1971. "The Religious Factor in Detroit: Revisited." *American Sociological Review* 36 (February): 48–51.

Lipset, Seymour Martin, and Everett C. Ladd. 1971. "Jewish Academics in the United States: Their Achievements, Culture and Politics." In Michail Wallace, *Jewish Year Book*. Hartford, Conn.: Prayer Book.

O'Dea, Thomas. 1958. *American Catholic Dilemma*. New York: Sheed & Ward.

Trent, James. 1967. *Catholics in College*. Chicago: University of Chicago Press.

Warkov, Seymour, and Andrew M. Greeley, 1966. "Parochial School Origins and Educational Achievement." *American Sociological Review* 31 (June): 406–14.

Warwick, Donald P. 1963. "Letter to the Editor." *American Journal of Sociology* 69 (November): 295.

ANDREW M. GREELEY

Making It in America: Ethnic Groups and Social Status

If the Republican party is ever to become the "New Major-ity"—which the dreams of Kevin Philips and Richard Nixon sug-gest that it might—it will have to capture the "Catholic ethnics." For this group seems to be the most vulnerable component of the old New Deal coalition; indeed, it is a component that many of the theorists of the "New Politics" were willing to write off in 1972 on the grounds that the "minorities" and the "young" would more than compensate for the loss of the ethnic hard-hats.

Just as Jean Westwood quickly closed down the "ethnic" desk at Democratic headquarters when she ushered the New Politics into the now safely debugged Watergate headquarters, the Republicans went out of their way to cultivate the "nationali-ties" operations in their campaign. Mr. Nixon had been very at-tentive to the "nationality" leadership during his first three years in office, even after Kevin Philips, routed by the California Ger-man-Americans and decamped from the Justice Department, set himself up as an entrepreneur in the knowledge industry. Nor is there any reason to doubt that in 1974 and 1976 the "blue-collar ethnics" are going to be a favorite target for Republican bush-beaters and a group to be treated with tender loving care by those trying to put back together the battered Democratic coalition.

But both those New Politics Democrats who wrote off the eth-nics in favor of Gloria Steinem and Jesse Jackson and the Re-publican theorists of the New Majority shared a common as-sumption about the ethnics—that they were blue-collar workers caught in a bind between high taxes and inflation and deeply

ANDREW M. GREELEY is Director of the Center for the Study of American Pluralism at the National Opinion Research Center. The material on which this article is based has been extracted from NORC research monograph "The Demography of Religio-ethnic Identification."

resentful of the attention and assistance being given the Blacks. Kevin Philips might not have used the work "racist" but he shared with his left-liberal foes the assumption that the ethnics were both blue-collar and racist.

Occasionally I would try to persuade a colleague that there were ethnics who were not blue-collar workers. Indeed, I had worked for a whole decade in a neighborhood of well-educated Irish Catholics who were not all firemen or policemen or bailiffs in Mr. Daley's court system. The response was skeptical: "You mean they have money like the Kennedys?" It was inconceiv-able that there could be a massive Irish upper-middle class somewhere, existing between police sergeants and Cape Cod millionaires. Nor did it seem believable that there could be Polish Ph.Ds, Italian city planners, Lithuanian television writ-ers, and Slovak philosophers. The ethnics were blue-collar workers, and that was that. Research efforts, summarized briefly in the accompanying tables, are an attempt to explore, if not to explode, the myth of the blue-collar ethnic.

ETHNIC GROUP STATUS

Even though the data referred to in this article are inadequate when compared with the decennial United States Census or even the monthly Current Population Surveys, they are the best available on the subject of American ethnic groups. Indeed, they are almost the only ones available. Census materials are not of much value in estimating the demographic distributions of American religio-ethnic groups, because the U.S. Census cannot ask questions about religion and religion is an essential part of ethnic self-definition for some groups. As far as we know, the analysis that the National Opinion Research Center (NORC) has undertaken, which is based on a composite of seven NORC samples and a composite of twenty samples from the Survey Research Center (SRC) at the University of Michi-gan, is the only attempt in recent years to go beyond guessing about the demography of American ethnic groups.

Two-fifths of the American population are white-collar workers.[1] Jews and British-Americans are the most likely to be white-collar workers, followed by Irish and German Catholics and Scandinavian Protestants. Italian Catholics are on the national average and Polish Catholics only five percentage points behind it. The Irish are just behind the Jews in mean years of education, and Italian, Polish, and Slavic Catholics are only a fraction of a year beneath the American mean. Finally, the Irish are second only to the Jews in annual family income, and the Italians, Poles, and Slavs are all above the national average. In short, in terms of education, income, and occupational prestige, two of the Catholic ethnic groups,—the Irish and the German— are substantially above the national mean, the Italians are about on the national mean, and the Poles and the Slavs just slightly beneath it. The adjective "blue-collar" is no more appropriate before the descriptive noun "ethnic" than it is before "American." The ethnics are no more "blue-collar" than anyone else.

With the exception of the French, the Catholics are predominantly metropolitan dwellers, with the Italian and the Spanish-speaking the most likely (44 and 45 percent respectively) to be in the great cities of over two million population. (Presumably, the Italians are especially likely to be found in New York and the Spanish-speaking in Los Angeles.) The most rural Gentile ethnic group is the French Catholic (32 percent), followed by the Irish Protestant (29 percent), the "Other Protestant" (28 percent), and the German Protestant (25 percent). The Jews, of course, are the least rural of all—in fact, none of the 240 Jews in the NORC composite sample reported rural residence. The Spanish-speaking Catholics, the Italian Catholics, Polish Catholics, and Irish Catholics also report less than 5 percent of their population to have rural residence.

The Jews, those with no religion, and "other religion" are the most likely to have attended graduate school; but among the Gentiles, the Irish Catholics are both the most likely to have attended graduate school (3 percent) and the most likely to have gone to college at all (40 percent as opposed to 37 percent for the British Protestants). Among the English-speaking white Gentiles, the Polish are the least likely to have gone to college (15 percent), followed by the Slavic group (16 percent) and the Italians (17 percent). The eastern and southern European Catholics, in other words, have not yet caught up to the national average in college attendance, though their German coreligionists are slightly ahead of the national average and their Irish coreligionists are substantially above the national average.

On the other hand, the Italians have reached the national average in the percentage of those who have become managers or owners, or professional or technical workers (26 percent). However, the Poles and the other eastern European Catholics are still substantially beneath that average (17 and 19 percent respectively). The Jewish groups, as one might expect, are the most likely to be found in these two categories, and the Blacks and the Spanish-speaking the least likely. Among English-speaking white Gentiles, British Protestants have a minuscule advantage over Irish Catholics in the proportion in these two top categories (36.5 percent as against 36.2 percent). It is interesting to note that the occupational distribution of the Irish Protestants is virtually the same as the national average. The Germans and the Scandinavians are the most likely to be farmers; the Italians, Spanish-speaking, Blacks, and Orientals most likely to be service workers; the Poles and the Slavs the most likely to be skilled or craft workers; the Spanish-speaking, Blacks, and French the most likely to be operatives or unskilled factory workers (though the Poles are also disproportionately represented in this group).

"Kevin Philips might not have used the word "racist" but he shared with his left-liberal foes the assumption that the ethnics were both blue-collar and racist."

---

1 In the American Pluralism program at the National Opinion Research Center we use "ethnicity" in the broad sense of the word, including differences of race, religion, language, and national origin. However, in this article the principal focus will be on diversity based on religion and national origin. Data will be presented about "Spanish-speaking" and "Black" for the sake of completeness of our tables. Because there is census data of much higher quality than ours on Black and Spanish-speaking Americans, I shall refrain from detailed commentary on the demography of those collectivities. I wish to emphasize that this decision is based on the limited nature of our data, not on any lack of interest in or concern for the so-called nonwhite ethnics.

Jews, Orientals, and those with no religion are the most likely to be earning more than $15,000 a year. Among white Gentiles the Irish Catholics and the German Catholics (16 percent and 12 percent respectively) are the most likely to be in the $15,000-plus category, with the British Protestants (11 percent) right behind them. The Blacks and the Spanish-speaking are most likely to be under $4,000 a year in income (with 48 percent of the Blacks in this category). Among the white English-speaking groups, 30 percent of the Irish Protestants earn less than $4,000, as do approximately one-fifth of the Italian, Polish, Slavic, and French Catholics.

In summary, then, American society has bestowed economic, occupational, and educational success on its Jewish, British-Protestant, and Irish-Catholic populations. German and Scandinavian groups have done moderately well. The southern and eastern European Catholic groups have done less well, and the Blacks and the Spanish-speaking, quite badly. Surprisingly, the Irish Protestants are on most measures in last place among the white English-speaking groups, in part, perhaps, because of their heavy concentration in the South and in rural areas. It is the purpose of this article to report these phenomena; data are not available in this analysis to sort out the social, cultural, psychological, historical, and racial discrimination factors that may be responsible for these differences. We can, however, in a crude sort of way take into account differences of region and city size as they affect education and income.

Education

Based on the national average of 10.9 years of education, we note that the Jews, the British Protestants, and the Irish Catholics have the greatest educational advantage, while the Blacks and the Spanish-speaking have the greatest educational disadvantage. The two German groups and the Scandinavian Protestants are virtually at the educational mean. Among English-speaking white Gentile groups, the Poles are almost a year beneath the national average, and the Slavs and the French Catholics are almost a half-year beneath the national average. But the performance of the southern and eastern European Catholics may be even worse than may appear, because these groups excluding the French) tend to be concentrated in large cities and in the North where there is more opportunity for education and educational achievement is higher. Hence let us see how these groups do in a situation in which geographic and metropolitan distribution are held constant.

Standardizing for region and size of place does not affect the mean scores of the British, German, and Scandinavian Protestant groups very much. However, the deviation from the educational mean of the Irish and Other Protestants is eliminated in the former case and substantially reduced in the latter. The lower educational scores of these two groups, in other words, result from their rural and southern locations.

On the other hand, the low scores of the Italian, Polish, Slavic,

French, and Spanish-speaking Catholics grow even lower when region and city size are held constant. If the southern and eastern European Catholics are compared with those who live in the same size places and the same regions, they are at even more of an educational disadvantage. The Poles, for example, have a minus deviation of 1.1 years of school—the same as the Blacks.

The high scores of the Irish Catholics and the Jews are diminished somewhat by standardizing for region and size of place, but the educational success of these two groups cannot be explained merely by their nonsouthern and metropolitan locations.

Income

Surprisingly, the educational disadvantage of the eastern and southern European Catholics is not translated into income disadvantage. While the Jews, the Irish Catholics, and the German Catholics have the highest gross incomes, the Italian, Polish, and French Catholics are all above the national average. The Irish Protestants are substantially ($566) beneath the national average, and the Other Protestants are somewhat ($313) beneath the national average. Indeed, Polish and Italian Catholics have higher annual incomes than do any of the Protestant groups, with the exception of the British Protestants. The incomes of the Black and Spanish-speaking groups are deplorably beneath the national average.

When education, region, and city size are all held constant, Irish, German, Italian, and Polish Catholics all have higher net incomes than do any of the Protestant groups under these circumstances (such for the Protestant ethic!). Further, even when we asked what the difference in educational attainment would be if all ethnic groups had the same regional and metropolitan distributions, the income disadvantage for Spanish-speaking Catholics was cut in half and for Blacks it was reduced from $2,163 to $1,437. But here again the phenomenon of the Irish Protestants continues to be surprising. In fact, they make on the average $500 less than the national average, and the standardization only slightly reduces that deficit. There is every reason to assume that the Blacks and the Spanish-speaking have been the objects of discrimination, but one wonders whether there has been any discrimination against Irish Protestants.[2] Equally surprising is the finding that both in the real world and the world created by standardization techniques the southern and eastern European Catholic groups earn more money than the national average and in many cases more than their native-born American counterparts.

One is led to wonder whether the surprising income levels of the Catholic ethnics may be the result of an acculturation process by which the children and grandchildren of these immi-

---

2 I am reminded of Arnold Toynbee's essay on the success of the Protestant ethic among Scotch Presbyterians who migrated to Ulster and its failure among the Ulster Presbyterians who migrated to the United States.

"The English-Protestant Americans, then, are substantially ahead of the national average for their age group during the 1950s, and remain ahead in the 1960s. . . ."

grants have not only achieved some sort of rough parity in American society but have actually managed to fight their way to the middle of the pack, if not to the top of the heap as the Irish Catholics have nearly done.

Intergenerational Mobility

Since the SRC data include both the 1950s and the 1960s, they enable us to explore from a different perspective the question of the recent economic history of cohort religio-ethnic groups. We assume that those who were in their twenties during the 1950s are a representative sample of those born between 1931 and 1940, and those who were in their thirties in the 1960s are a representative sample of that same group ten years later. Thus by looking at those who were in their twenties in the 1950s and in their thirties in the 1960s, we are able to see how a specific segment of the population changed its income over the course of a decade. The technique of cohort analysis is elementary and used often. But even though we are dealing with a sample of 15,000 respondents, our analysis has a basic weakness: the cross-tabulation by age, decade, and ethnic group leaves us with rather small numbers of respondents for each ethnic cohort. Thus the most we can say is that we are dealing with very tentative and speculative data.

The figures in Table I, A-K represent deviations in income from a cohort mean which is shown below.[3] Thus to say that the English Protestants in Cohort I (between twenty and thirty years old during the 1960s) have a score of -16 is to say that they earned $16 less than the mean for their cohort during that de-

[3] *Mean Income in Dollars for Age Cohorts in the 1950s and 1960s (SRC Composite Sample)*

	1950s	1960s	Change
Cohort I (Born 1941–1950; in its twenties during the 1960s.)		$7,723	
Cohort II (Born 1931–1940; in its twenties during the 1950s and its thirties during the 1960s.)	$4,837	9,345	$4,508
Cohort III (Born 1921–1930; in its thirties during the 1950s and its forties during the 1960s.)	5,633	9,459	3,826
Cohort IV (Born 1911–1920; in its forties during the 1950s and its fifties during the 1960s.)	5,888	8,136	2,248
Cohort V (Born 1901–1910; in its fifties during the 1950s and its sixties during the 1960s.)	5,222	5,478	256

cade. The mean for Cohort I during the 1960s (see footnote 3) is $7,723, which makes the mean for English Protestants $7,707. By looking down the columns in each panel of Table I, one can see the income differences among various age groups in the specific ethnic groups during each of the decades. Thus during the 1950s, English Protestants in their twenties made $631 more than the average of all Americans at the same age level. Those in their thirties made $1,997 more than their age-level average, those in their forties made $1,781 more, and those in their fifties made $1,060 more than their age-level average. Similarly, as one looks down the second column (1960s), one can see that except for the English Protestants in their twenties, each age level among the English-Protestant ethnic collectivity made more than the mean for the national cohort at that age level.

If one looks at the rows in the table, one can see how a specific age cohort improved its relative position in the decade between the 1950s and 1960s. Thus those English Protestants (Table IA) who were born between 1931 and 1940 made $631 more than the national cohort mean in the 1950s and $1,360 more than the national cohort mean in the 1960s. They not only improved their absolute level of income—as did every ethnic group—but also improved their relative position. They were even more ahead of the mean for their age peers in the 1960s than they were in the 1950s.

The English-Protestant Americans, then, are substantially ahead of the national average for their age group during the 1950s, and remain ahead in the 1960s except in Cohort I where they fall slightly beneath the national average for those who were in their twenties during that decade. It may well be that the reason for the $16 deficit in Cohort I during the 1960s is that a substantial segment of the English-American population was still in college or graduate school while in their twenties. However, it is also worth noting that in Cohorts III and IV the relative advantage of English-Protestant Americans over the national mean diminishes considerably.

A very different picture is presented by the Irish Protestants (Table IB). While they are above their respective cohort averages in three of the four levels in the 1950s, they are below the national average in three of the five levels in the 1960s; and in all four cases they experience a negative change in deviation from the mean in the two decades. It is true that the Irish Protestants in their twenties during the 1960s are substantially above the national mean for that cohort. However, it should be noted that their predecessors, who were in their twenties during the previous decade, slipped badly ($1,569) in the 1960 decade. This

"If there are any ethnic groups, then, that have suffered in the last two decades, they are the older groups, those who have been here since the beginning of the Republic."

Table I *Income Deviation in Dollars of Ethnic Groups in the 1950s and the 1960s by Cohort (SRC Composite Sample)*

	1950s	1960s	Net Change in Deviation from Cohort Mean		1950s	1960s	Net Change in Deviation from Cohort Mean
A. English Protestants				**H. Polish Catholics**			
Cohort I	$	$− 16 (193)	$	Cohort I	$	$− 345 (24)	$
Cohort II	+ 631 (51)	+1,360 (168)	+ 729	Cohort II	+ 706 (19)	+ 446 (15)	− 260
Cohort III	+1,997 (106)	+ 748 (217)	−1,252	Cohort III	− 226 (28)	− 245 (33)	+ 20
Cohort IV	+1,781 (138)	+1,443 (193)	− 338	Cohort IV	− 517 (35)	− 429 (20)	+ 88
Cohort V	+1,060 (139)	+1,384 (155)	+ 324	Cohort V	−1,745 (13)	− 342 (13)	+1,403
B. Irish Protestants				**I. Italian Catholics**			
Cohort I	$	$+2,260 (99)	$	Cohort I	$	$+1,036 (46)	$
Cohort II	+1,326 (39)	− 243 (65)	−1,569	Cohort II	− 338 (36)	+ 426 (46)	+ 764
Cohort III	+ 741 (51)	+ 127 (79)	− 614	Cohort III	+ 102 (61)	+ 256 (48)	+ 154
Cohort IV	− 67 (39)	− 957 (79)	− 890	Cohort IV	− 152 (50)	+1,073 (37)	+1,225
Cohort V	+ 699 (32)	− 101 (67)	− 800	Cohort V	+ 595 (26)	+2,437 (21)	+1,842
C. Scandinavian Protestants				**J. Jews**			
Cohort I	$	$+ 663 (46)	$	Cohort I	$	$+2,804 (40)	$
Cohort II	+ 548 (38)	+2,160 (65)	+1,612	Cohort II	+2,444 (24)	+2,382 (41)	− 72
Cohort III	+ 748 (34)	+ 670 (53)	− 78	Cohort III	+1,681 (42)	+3,769 (37)	+2,088
Cohort IV	+1,054 (43)	+2,859 (37)	+1,779	Cohort IV	+2,265 (51)	+2,910 (26)	+ 645
Cohort V	+ 37 (49)	+ 329 (33)	+ 292	Cohort V	+1,522 (40)	+1,358 (22)	− 164
D. German Protestants				**K. Blacks**			
Cohort I	$	$+ 75 (200)	$	Cohort I	$	$−2,258 (148)	$
Cohort II	+ 308 (93)	+ 977 (152)	+ 699	Cohort II	−1,495 (192)	−3,613 (148)	−2,118
Cohort III	+ 530 (113)	+ 629 (156)	+ 99	Cohort III	−2,556 (148)	−4,198 (121)	−3,826
Cohort IV	+ 449 (128)	+ 683 (143)	+ 234	Cohort IV	−2,923 (119)	−5,291 (106)	−2,998
Cohort V	+ 380 (85)	− 144 (83)	− 524	Cohort V	−2,712 (77)	−2,633 (69)	− 79
E. Other Protestants ("American")							
Cohort I	$	$− 134 (325)	$				
Cohort II	− 155 (475)	− 874 (287)	− 719				
Cohort III	− 28 (606)	−1,093 (305)	−1,125				
Cohort IV	− 195 (457)	−1,311 (263)	−1,506				
Cohort V	− 456 (339)	−1,111 (186)	− 655				
F. Irish Catholics							
Cohort I	$	$+1,148 (50)	$	KEY:			
Cohort II	+ 928 (24)	+1,006 (44)	+ 78	Cohort I	Born 1941–1950; in its twenties during the 1960s.		
Cohort III	+1,821 (49)	+1,046 (51)	− 775	Cohort II	Born 1931–1940; in its twenties during the 1950s and		
Cohort IV	+ 274 (40)	+ 680 (34)	+ 406		its thirties during the 1960s.		
Cohort V	+ 288 (30)	+2,349 (34)	+2,061	Cohort III	Born 1921–1930; in its thirties during the 1950s and		
G. German Catholics					its forties during the 1960s.		
Cohort I	$	$+ 296 (52)	$	Cohort IV	Born 1911–1920; in its forties during the 1950s and		
Cohort II	+ 750 (27)	− 172 (46)	− 922		its fifties during the 1960s.		
Cohort III	+ 640 (49)	+2,145 (29)	+1,501	Cohort V	Born 1901–1910; in its fifties during the 1950s and its		
Cohort IV	+ 122 (32)	+ 990 (30)	+ 968		sixties during the 1960s.		
Cohort V	+ 140 (20)	− 139 (30)	− 273	NOTE: Numbers in parentheses are respondents.			

suggests that the income advantage of the Irish Protestants in their twenties in both decades may be the result of the fact that they began their occupational lives early, so that in their twenties they earned more than their age peers of other groups who may still have been in college. However, by the time they reached their thirties, this initial advantage was canceled out by the college education of other groups. Thus while English-Protestant Americans display a picture of maintaining economic superiority, though perhaps with some erosion, Irish Protestants present one of a rapid erosion of economic superiority. The SRC data, then, like the NORC data, indicate that the Irish Protestants—an ethnic group that seems to lack consciousness, organization, and visibility—are downwardly mobile.

Just the opposite is true of the Scandinavian Protestants (Table IC). In all cohorts in both decades the Scandinavians are higher than their cohort mean, and in three of the four cohorts they improved their relative position in the decade of the 1960s. Twenty years ago Scandinavians were already above the national income average, and in the course of the two decades they improved their position even more. The most notable improvements are among those who were in their twenties in the 1950s and those who were in their forties in the same decade. Cohort III of the Scandinavian Protestants did not improve that much, possibly (and this is extremely speculative) because they were born or spent their childhood years during the worst years of the Great Depression.

Another group that has made the most of the last two decades is the German Protestants (Table ID). They are above the national average at all age cohorts in the 1950s and at four of the five age cohorts in the 1960s. Only in Cohort V during the 1960s does one German age group fall beneath the national mean. The $520 loss in relative position among German Protestants in their sixties during the 1960s may possibly be the result of the fact that this group is heavily composed of farmers, and a deterioration of farm income among people in their sixties may be more serious than among other groups in the population. The relative improvement in the economic condition of German Protestants is not as strong as that among Scandinavian Protestants. Nonetheless, the former group continues to improve its relative position in the decade between 1960 and 1970 vis-à-vis the rest of American society.

But the Other Protestants (for the most part, those who re-

GEORGE W. GARDNER

sponded that they were "American" to the SRC ethnic question) are the major losers among the white groups. All four age cohorts of Other Protestants are beneath their respective means in the 1950s and even further beneath those means in the 1960s. In two of the cohorts (III and IV) they suffer a loss in relative position of more than $1,000. Granted that the Other Protestants tend to be rural and farm people, Table IE establishes that not only does a population segment concentrated in rural areas earn less than more urban population segments but also that its relative position is deteriorating. In each age cohort in the 1960s, income is even further from the cohort mean than it was in the 1950s. Neither the Irish Protestants nor the Other Protestants are ethnic groups in the sense that the Polish or the Italian Catholics are. Neither of the two Protestant groups have much self-conscious ethnic identity nor are they so identified by the rest of American society. It just so happens that they include the element in the white American population that is not keeping pace with the general increase in income level. Precisely be-

the Great Depression may have had some impact on this cohort's capacity to take advantage of the opportunities of the last twenty years. Let it be noted, however, that Cohort III is well above the national average for that cohort during the 1960s for both the English-Protestant and Irish-Catholic groups. It is not as far above as one might have expected based on their performance in the 1950s.

German Catholics (Table IG) like German Protestants suffer a decline beneath the cohort mean at the level of Cohort V (those who were in their fifties in the 1950s and in their sixties in the 1960s). In addition, German Catholics suffer a decline in Cohort II (those who passed from their twenties to their thirties during the last two decades). NORC data for the same age cohort do not indicate the same phenomenon. German Catholics improved their relative position in American society during the 1950s and 1960s but not as much as the Irish Catholics did.

The Polish-Catholic performance (Table IH) indicates a slow upward movement of that population, however, the number of

" . . .the upward mobility system, which worked extremely well for the Jews, the Irish, and the Italians, reasonably well for the Germans, and has at least begun to work for the Poles, has not yet worked at all for the Blacks."

cause they do not identify themselves as a group and are not so identified by others, their deteriorating position is not obvious to the rest of society and perhaps not even obvious to many of them.

Irish Catholics, on the other hand, are the most successful of the white immigrant groups. In all age cohorts in both the 1950s and 1960s, the Irish Catholics are very substantially ahead of the national average in their respective age cohorts (see Table IF). Indeed, in five cases they are more than $1,000 ahead and in one case, more than $2,000. Furthermore, the Irish who were under thirty in the 1960s are $1,000 ahead of the cohort mean for that group, indicating that the movement upward of Irish Catholics continues unabated. In only one age cohort (III) was there a decline in relative advantage of the 1960s over the 1950s. Interestingly, it is this same Cohort III in which a $1,252 decline in deviation from the mean was also recorded among the English-Protestant Americans. We may speculate, just as we did in reporting on this phenomenon for the Scandinavians, that

respondents are sufficiently low that judgments should be made cautiously. The three oldest age cohorts of Poles were beneath the national mean for those age cohorts in both the 1950s and the 1960s, although they improved their relative position somewhat during the two decades. Cohort II was the first Polish cohort to be above the national mean, but its relative advantage slipped somewhat between the 1950s and the 1960s. Polish Catholics, then, seem to be improving their relative position in American society, but much more slowly than the earlier Catholic immigrant groups.

The Italian Catholics (Table II) are doing much better than the Poles. They are substantially above the mean for their respective age levels, and all of them improved their relative position notably since the 1950s. The Italians are in fact the only group to have improved their position in all four age cohorts between the two decades. Only the Jews have scored a greater increase in income between the 1950s and the 1960s. Thus, while the evidence about the upward mobility of Polish-Americans is unclear, there is no doubt at all that the Italians are moving very rapidly into the upper-middle class of American society.

The Jews (Table IJ) are already solidly in the upper-middle class. At all but the oldest age cohort, the relative Jewish advantage over the cohort income mean in both the 1950s and the 1960s is in excess of $2,000, and while Jews in Cohort II slipped a little ($72) in their relative advantage over the cohort mean between the 1950s and 1960s, they are still almost $2,400 ahead of the average for their age level in the 1960s. Finally, Jews in their twenties in the 1960s have the greatest advantage ($2,437) over their age peers of any ethnic group. It is twice that of their nearest competitor, the Irish Catholics.

The last panel (Table IK) is extremely depressing. While much better evidence can be made for the case with data more reliable than ours, and while perhaps in the late 1960s and early 1970s there has been some change, still one is forced to conclude that in the two decades between 1950 and 1970, the upward mobility system, which worked extremely well for the Jews, the Irish, and the Italians, reasonably well for the Germans, and has at least begun to work for the Poles, has not yet worked at all for the Blacks. Whether it may have begun working since 1965 is beyond the scope of this presentation.

CONCLUSION

To return to our initial question of whether the ethnics are "blue-collar" or not, the evidence in the NORC and SRC composite samples on which this presentation is based leaves little doubt that the Irish Catholics, Germans, Scandinavians, and Italians have moved rapidly into the upper-middle class of American society during the last two decades. Furthermore, despite fears that these groups would become alienated, there is no evidence that between 1950 and the late 1960s any of them suffered appreciable decline in their relative incomes. Whatever the inflationary income squeeze of the 1960s may have been, it does not seem to have affected these ethnic groups disproportionately. The English Protestants have managed to hold their own in American society, although they seem to have been displaced as the second richest group by the Irish Catholics. The Polish-Catholic situation is uncertain. While there is some evidence that the Poles are leaving their blue-collar status behind and are moving upward relatively as well as absolutely, the speed of their movement seems to be considerably less than that of the Italians, who entered American society at approximately the same time. The mobility system did not work at all for the Blacks between the 1950s and the 1960s. It seems to work to the disadvantage of the Irish Protestants and Other Protestants or "Americans," who have slipped even further beneath the cohort means despite an income increase in absolute terms. If there are any ethnic groups, then, that have suffered in the last two decades, they are the older groups, those who have been here since the beginning of the Republic.

Let us observe in conclusion that while the data presented in this article represent the best information we have on the demography of American religio-ethnic groups, they are still extremely tentative. Even in dealing with samples of more than 10,000 respondents, one ends up with very small subsamples of American religio-ethnic groups. Therefore, while we can be quite confident of the general picture of upward mobility of American ethnic groups, we must exercise considerable reservations about the details of such a picture.

Regarding the assumption shared by liberals and conservatives alike that ethnics are predominantly blue-collar workers, the data presented here suggest that both are wrong in their assumption. Only the Poles are still disproportionately blue-collar and are not moving rapidly out of that status. Yet the Polish vote for Democratic candidates has been over 70 percent since 1952 and it is very likely that of all American groups only the Blacks were more inclined to support McGovern in 1972. One could argue that as new members of the middle class, the ethnics are most likely to be the victims of "status anxiety" and hence most likely to react unfavorably to those beneath them on the status ladder. But while the Catholic proportion voting Democratic in 1972 declined some 12 percentage points (from 60 to 48 percent), Catholics were still more likely to vote for McGovern than the national average. Over 50 percent of both Poles and Irish voted for McGovern. In other words, for all his "ethnic" activity, Mr. Nixon was not able to make any greater inroads on them than on the whole American population. On the contrary, there is every reason to think that in congressional voting in 1972, the ethnics were as Democratic as they ever were—which is very Democratic indeed.

In the era between 1950 and 1970, then, the Catholic ethnic groups, with the possibe exception of the Poles, moved from the lower-middle class and working class into the upper-middle class. Not all of their members, of course, enrolled in the white-collar world, but they were as likely to be in that world—and in most cases, more likely—than the American average. Those critics who label ethnics as hard-hats and racists will concede, if pressed, that they have made dramatic social progress since the end of World War II. But the critics will add that the ethnics show singular unconcern about the lack of success of other Americans. They will assert that the Catholic ethnics, once the backbone of the liberal coalition, have slipped away from that coalition because their upward mobility has made them conservative. The ethnic, it seems, can't win. But it may well be that the most fascinating political phenomenon of the 1970s is that the white-collar ethnics are remaining Democrats. Dogmatic ideology should not be permitted to obscure the possibilities for building a social-change coalition in which the ethnics would be a prime component. There is substantial evidence that during the past two decades the ethnics have turned to the left, not to the right. But that is another story and perhaps another article.

Reprint from

Social Research

New School for Social Research

Religion in a Secular Society / BY ANDREW M. GREELEY

An incredible amount of written material is produced each year on the subject of American religion. Indeed, only politics, sex, and money seem to merit more attention. Yet very little is known about the condition of religion in the United States today. There are two reasons for this deficiency: (1) The consumers of information about American religion—journalists, scholars, religious functionaries—are content with inferior information, and (2) the proliferation of religious trends and fads has been presented by the media as a confusing array of new movements and theologies, all misrepresented as having a disproportionate impact on American religious behavior.

If the data offered on American politics, sex, and money were as inferior as the religious data available, there would be cries of outrage. But in the matter of religion those who are either proreligion or antireligion seem to be content with third-rate information. It is quite possible that both sides are wary of what first-rate data might reveal.

Seven Models of Religious Sociology

It is not unfair to suggest that virtually all the research done on the sociology of American religion can be subsumed under one of the following seven models. These models are narrow and unfruitful even for a discipline not noted for producing insightful models.

1. *The Protestant ethic model.* This tradition of research takes its cue from Max Weber and attempts to establish that Protestants

are more achievement-oriented than Catholics. There are often nativist overtones to this research tradition and it evidences a very shallow and superficial reading of Weber. The quintessential exercise in the Protestant ethic tradition is Gerhard Lenski's *The Religious Factor* (1961).[1]

2. *The decline of religion or the secularization model.* In this view people are not as religious as they used to be. The precise time of "used to be" is not altogether clear. Hampered by the fact that there were no research data collected by social scientists a hundred years ago, the purveyors of the secularization hypothesis are forced to postulate some mysterious Golden Age in which everyone was more religious than they are now. Much of the work of Glock and his colleagues [2] is in the secularization tradition, as is some of the theoretical writing of Peter Berger.[3] Indeed, the secularization model has become almost dogma among American intellectual and cultural elites, although recently some have suggested that those who criticize it are knocking down a straw man.

3. *The conflict between science and religion model.* A more limited version of the secularization model, this one argues that the conflict between rational empirical science and "nonrational" and "superempirical" religion is inevitable. Glock's student, Rodney Stark,[4] has argued that those who discuss the end of the conflict between science and religion do not understand the nature of the inevitability of that conflict.

4. *The church-sect model.* A good deal of ink has been spilt in an attempt to apply the Weber-Troeltsch church-sect dichotomy to American religious organizations. That the dichotomy is unsatisfactory is clear from the fact that virtually every author tries to establish intermediary states between church and sect. One

---

[1] Gerhard Lenski, *The Religious Factor* (Garden City, N.Y.: Doubleday, 1961).

[2] Charles Y. Glock and Rodney Stark, *Religion and Society in Tension* (Chicago: Rand McNally, 1965).

[3] Peter L. Berger, *A Rumor of Angels* (Garden City, N.Y.: Doubleday, 1969).

[4] See chap. 14, "On the Incompatibility of Religion and Science," in Glock and Stark, *Religion and Society in Tension*, pp. 262–306.

unpublished paper developed a typology with sixty-four cells of religious organizational style devolving from the church to the sect, many of which were, alas, unoccupied. The controversy between N. J. Demerath and Erich Goode is an example of the persistence of this tradition of discussion.[5]

5. *Clergy-laity conflict model.* Writers like Jeffrey Hadden [6] have suggested that American churches are in the process of being torn by a liberal, socially activist clergy confronting a conservative, frequently racist laity. A close reading of Hadden's book, however, might as well lead one to conclude that there are surprising similarities between the attitudes of most clergy and most laity.

6. *The generation gap model.* While this perspective has produced no formal research studies, there is still a tendency among some writers concerned with the youth culture to see a notable decline in religious behavior among young people as compared with the religious behavior of their parents.

7. *The social class or economic model.* Much energy has been expended on this approach to religion. The Goode-Demerath controversy as well as Estus and Overington [7] attempt to explain levels of religious participation in social-class terms either by using very simple correlations of education, income, and occupation with church attendance or by using more elaborate social-class models in which different class processes are seen at work in different denominational contexts. It is rarely noted in such discussions that a tiny proportion of the variance in religious behavior is in fact explained by social-class variables.

Protestant ethic, decline of religion, clergy-laity conflict, church-sect, the generation gap, science and religion, religion and social class—all these may be interesting and even occasionally useful

[5] Erich Goode, "Some Critical Observations on the Church-Sect Dimension," *Journal for the Scientific Study of Religion*, VI (Spring 1967), 69–77; N. J. Demerath III, "In a Sow's Ear: A Reply to Goode," *ibid.*, pp. 77–84.

[6] Jeffrey Hadden, *Gathering Storm of the Churches* (Garden City, N.Y.: Doubleday, 1969).

[7] Charles Estus and Michael Overington, "The Meaning and End of Religiosity," *American Journal of Sociology*, LXXV (March 1970), 760–778.

analytic tools, but they don't tell us what religion means in the lives of most Americans, and their predictive value is very small indeed. My own work in the middle sixties,[8] Schuman's [9] recent replication of Lenski, and a lengthy review of Protestant ethic literature in the *Journal for the Scientific Study of Religion* [10] all indicate that the Protestant ethic is as dead as a doornail. (Indeed, on many measures of the so-called Protestant ethic, the Jews are the most "Protestant" and the Protestants the least "Protestant" of the three major American denominations.) Survey evidence indicates fluctuations but no extended decline of religious practice in American society. The rise of new forms of superstition and the revival of old superstitions on college campuses make Rodney Stark's evidence of the persistence of conflict between science and religion look dubious. McCready [11] has demonstrated that while social class may explain a few percentage points of the variance in religious behavior, religious socialization (the religiousness of one's parents) explains over half the variance in religious behavior among adults and only slightly less among adolescents. Research in which McCready and I are currently engaged shows that young people may be somewhat less likely to go to church than their parents (and this may be a life-cycle and not a generational phenomenon), but they are no different from their parents in holding the convictions that there is purpose in human life, that the universe is not governed by chance, that man survives death, and that God's love is behind everything.[12] In fact, young people are slightly more likely to endorse such

[8] Andrew M. Greeley, "The Protestant Ethic: Time for a Moratorium," *Sociological Analysis*, XXV (Spring 1964).

[9] Howard Schuman, "Religious Factor in Detroit: Review, Replication, and Reanalysis," *American Sociological Review*, XXXVI (Fall 1971), 30–50.

[10] Gary D. Bouma, "Recent 'Protestant Ethic' Research," *Journal for the Scientific Study of Religion*, XII (June 1973), 141–155.

[11] William C. McCready, "Faith of Our Fathers: A Study of the Process of Religious Socialization," unpublished Ph.D. dissertation, University of Illinois Circle Campus, 1972.

[12] William C. McCready and Andrew M. Greeley, "American Religion: A Report to the Henry Luce Foundation," in preparation.

propositions than any other age group. They are also slightly more likely to report psychic experiences.

In summary, then, we are likely to get little help from sociology in our attempt to discover what is happening in American religion. We are tempted to conclude in all charity that the serious study of religion in American society has not even begun.

The Theological Marketplace

Turning from the sociologist to the theologian, we discover a plethora of fads and fashions. We were told in the middle sixties that God was dead. Then we were told that first it was necessary to play, then to be hopeful. More recently, theologians have unfurled the banners of "political" theology and "liberation" theology, and now just this last summer special issues of *World View* and the *Journal of Current Issues* have suggested that these banners are being struck and furled once again. The most recent theological fad has to do with the counterculture, the ecological movement, the resurgence of superstition, and what one unintentional theological wit calls "countersecularization." (The premise behind this label is that if it turns out that people are not secularized this doesn't mean that the secularization trend was a myth, only that a countertrend has just set in.) In the most recent issues of the theological and religious journals we discover that there is a "neofundamentalist" (particularly Pentecostal) trend in American society. We can only conclude from reading such theological and religious commentaries that the state of American religion is as volatile as the love life of a Hollywood starlet.

In fact, of course, such trends are mostly a function of the need for assistant professors to disagree with full professors in order to find cause for tenure, the need of journalists to find story leads that are different from last year's, and the need of publicity copywriters of major publishing companies to find grounds for persuading a potential reader to buy yet another book by a professional theologian.

The volatility of the theological marketplace may come as a surprise to those who thought it was the role of the theologian to explicate and of the minister to preach the Scripture. Unfortunately, explicating and preaching the Scripture is not all that exciting when the Good News seems to have become old hat. It should not be assumed, however, that the waving antennae of the "with it" theologians pick up nothing but static. Unquestionably, there has been powerful movement within the fundamentalist churches, a movement which has affected some nonfundamentalist denominations. There is also a wide array of counterculture religious forms, distinct not so much in their originality as in the fact that they have found their way into upper-middle-class behavior. There is new interest too (mostly psychedelic in origin) in mysticism and ecstasy, particularly of the Oriental variety. Professor Theodore Rozak is not the only tenured faculty member who has acquired enough personal and financial security to proclaim his agnosticism as Truth manifested in a Rousseauian return to nature (a return whose bible is the *Whole Earth Catalog*).

Two observations must be made about these theological and religious "trends." First, despite the wide publicity accorded them, they are novelties that attract only tiny fractions of the population. Most young people are not in the counterculture and most of the counterculture is into ecstasy only intermittently. Furthermore, what is proclaimed as new turns out not to be new at all, just newly discovered. Astrology was a multimillion-dollar industry long before it was discovered on the university campus. Mysticism is certainly not new to the world, and recent research [13] indicates that mystical experiences are widespread in the population. It is as frequent in square, nonpsychedelic adults as it is in young people. (For what it's worth, mystics are happier than

---

[13] William C. McCready and Andrew M. Greeley, "The Sociology of Mystical and Psychic Experiences," paper presented at the meeting of the Society for the Scientific Study of Religion, San Francisco, October 25–28, 1973.

most people and are also less racially prejudiced. They are also much more likely than the general population to have attended college.) What is surprising is not that mysticism in American society has been rediscovered but rather that it was so long undiscovered.

Problems of the Study of American Religion

We need only read the magnificent religious histories produced in recent years by Sydney Ahlstrom and Martin Marty [14] to see that in comparison with these men contemporary social scientists and social theologians are virtually illiterate on the subject of religion in contemporary America.

There are two underlying causes for the inability of contemporary American scholarship to address itself seriously to the question of religion in American life. First, most of those who write on the subject have gone through a painful alienation from their own religious backgrounds. This alienation has generated in them complex ambiguities and ambivalences. They are nostalgic about the security, peace, and warmth they left behind but angry at its narrowness and rigidity. They love the past but they hate it; and since most Americans are not yet religiously alienated, such scholars are caught in a profound love-hate situation vis-à-vis the ordinary believer and the ordinary Sunday (or Saturday) churchgoer. The religious scholar both envies their security and despises their ignorance. It is of course taken for granted that one cannot be a scholar without being alienated. The divinity schools and the social-science divisions of the country are, after all, designed to alienate a student from his heritage. What earthly good would a sociologist or a theologian be if he could in fact "go home again," if he could live in a neighborhood, or commute from

[14] Sydney Ahlstrom, *A Religious History of the American People* (New Haven: Yale University Press, 1972); Martin Marty, *Righteous Empire: The Protestant Experience in America* (New York: Dial Press, 1970).

RELIGION IN A SECULAR SOCIETY   233

a small town or a rural congregation? Paradoxically, it is all right to set up communes that attempt to achieve the atmosphere of small towns or neighborhoods, but such behavior becomes legitimate only when one has been first thoroughly and decisively alienated from his own *gemeinschaft* origins.

I am not making the debatable point that one can write about religion or study it seriously only if one is religious. It seems to me that both the thoroughly religious and the thoroughly unreligious have their own distinctive advantages and disadvantages when they engage in the serious study of religion. Both the third-generation agnostic and the convinced believer are at least free from internal conflict and ambivalence. They are not fighting their churchgoing fathers or their parish pastors. They do not feel guilty about leaving the neighborhood or the home town. They are not so self-consciously on an open-ended pilgrimage from belief that they cannot respect those whose religious concerns are much less marked by *angst*. One can read three autobiographical works by distinguished American religious scholars [15] to discover how strains of nostalgia and repulsion war with one another on the subject of the religious world these scholars left behind. It is fair to suggest that they have merely made explicit an ambivalence that affects most other religiously interested academics of their generation—and perhaps also a substantial number of those who do not write about religion but still think and argue about it. Dispassion may be impossible to achieve in scholarly discourse, and if it were achieved it might well prove counterproductive; but passionate ambivalence is a serious obstacle to objective understanding of that world which was left behind.

Does graduate school need to be an alienating experience? Can alienation be transcended? Should it be? Should the healthy and mature person be able to arrive at a critical yet sympathetic under-

---

[15] Robert Bellah, *Beyond Belief* (New York: Harper & Row, 1970); Sam Keen, *To a Dancing God* (New York: Harper & Row, 1970); Harvey Cox, *The Seduction of the Spirit* (New York: Simon & Schuster, 1973).

standing of that part of his personality that has been shaped by his heritage? These are all questions beyond the scope of this paper. It seems fair to observe, however, that our understanding of American religion will be greatly facilitated when the religious phenomena of our society are approached by scholars not constrained to attack or defend either the religious phenomena or the society.

The second problem with much of the contemporary religious analysis is that it proceeds from an implicit evolutionary perspective. This perspective may have been derived from Marx or Darwin or, more likely, from the high sociological tradition of Tönnies, Weber, and Durkheim. It may be rooted ultimately in Plato and Augustine, as Robert Nisbet has suggested. It surely owes something to August Comte and perhaps to Joachim of Flora. Whatever its origins, such a perspective sees us locked into a period of dramatic social change which is about to produce the Third Age of the world. Most of those who implicitly view reality from such an evolutionary perspective view that Third Age as benign, thus being true to Joachim, Augustine, and Comte. Others, perhaps understanding their Weber better, have begun to wonder whether the Third Age might be apocalyptic rather than messianic. Whatever the expectations, most comment on contemporary American religion (and on all other contemporary social phenomena) makes the assumption that our time is the hinge of history; that decisive changes are taking place in religion, sex, the family, politics—whatever is important at the time. Indeed, this "picture" of the present as an eschatological time is so powerful and so pervasive that it is rarely questioned and almost never denied. Ethnocentrism can be temporal as well as racial and geographic.

Such a change-obsessed perspective has been given its quintessential statement in Alvin Toffler's *Future Shock,* its most foolish statement in Margaret Mead's *Culture and Commitment,* and its most manic statement in Charles Reich's *The Greening of*

America.[16] One need not deny that change occurs or even that there might be some rough direction to change to recognize the immense power of continuity and consistency in human society and in human religious behavior. The fact that McCready can explain more than half the variance of religious behavior of adults in terms of the religious behavior of their parents is of immense importance to all discussions of religion. That the transmission of religious behavior seems closely linked to sex roles suggests further that religious consistency takes its origin from early childhood experiences. John Kotre [17] found that self-definition in or out of the church is largely a function of early childhood experience, which would indicate that psychological rather than intellectual strains may explain much of the variation and change in religious behavior that does occur across generational lines.

One of the reasons that it is difficult to study religious consistency is that, in the peculiar ideological climate of contemporary American intellectual life, he who studies it will be dismissed as conservative. Those who can explain 3 percent of the variation in religious behavior in social-class terms somehow are the "good guys" and appropriately radical, while those like McCready who explain half the variation in terms of intergenerational influence are somehow "bad guys" and inappropriately conservative. It is an approach to scholarship that the Supreme Sacred Congregation of the Holy Office (recently renamed the Congregation for the Faith—a rose is a rose is a rose) would have no trouble understanding.

Yet there is a massive continuity in American religious life. One need only read de Tocqueville's comments on American religion to see how persistent religious styles have been. Large numbers of people go to church; large numbers affiliate with denominations. Levels of membership and attendance fluctuate

16 Alvin Toffler, *Future Shock* (New York: Random House, 1970); Margaret Mead, *Culture and Commitment* (New York: Natural History Press, 1970); Charles Reich, *The Greening of America* (New York: Random House, 1970).
17 John Kotre, *View from the Border* (Chicago: Aldine Press, 1971).

in response to external social stimuli, but the churches are never deserted. Most Americans continue to agonize, sometimes at least, on fundamental life problems: purpose or absurdity, life and death, love and hate, good and evil, tragedy and comedy. Most of them still respond to these life problems through interpretations of the historical symbol system that began on Sinai. Superstition, occultism, mysticism are not new; neither is fundamentalism, the social gospel, the quest for relevance, the religions of peace of mind and national unity. Atheists, agnostics, true believers, sinners, saints, mystics, prophets, visionaries, charlatans, crackpots, hypocrites, and, above all, the lukewarm exist in substantial numbers in American society. Whether the distribution of these various population groups is any different than it was in 1874 or 1774 or A.D. 74 is a question very difficult to answer. One could assert with some confidence at least that there have never been very many saints and there have always been a hell of a lot of the lukewarms.

I submit that the prime requisites for the study of American religion are a skepticism about the pervasiveness of change and doubt about the utility of virtually all existing models.

A Program

Let me suggest some testable hypotheses and some areas of research about American religion.[18]

1. Religious symbols and religious organizations are important at least intermittently to an overwhelming majority of Americans. What one would want to know is how the symbols are interpreted at certain times in the lives of Americans.

2. Churches will be "successful" (by which we mean organizationally successful) to the extent that they respond to what their memberships feel are their fundamental religious needs. Social

[18] And this is about as good a point as any to acknowledge my profound debt to the work of Clifford Geertz and his definition of religion as a cultural system.

RELIGION IN A SECULAR SOCIETY   237

activism will be more acceptable when it is perceived as a consequence of responding to religious needs, not as a substitute for it.

3. There will be much less conflict between laity and clergy if the laity are not forced to accept the vocabulary and rhetoric of the liberal ideology that the clergy absorbed in the seminaries and divinity schools.

4. There is a close relationship between religion and sexuality. One's fundamental world view is acquired in the process of acquiring one's sexual identity. This world view in its turn will have a profound effect on one's sexual behavior in later life. A more generalized statement of this hypothesis would be that man creates himself in the image and likeness of God, which image he acquires in childhood. World view, basic belief system, religious symbols —call it what we will—shapes the personality as well as being shaped by it.

5. In a society with more leisure time, with the vocabulary to raise questions about self-fulfillment, and with active competition in the marketplace of belief systems, religious issues become more important and more explicit.

There are several general areas that I think might be explored profitably.

1. *Religious socialization.* Granting the importance of the McCready finding of the power of parental religious behavior in explaining the adult religious behavior of their children, we need to know much more about how religious traditions are passed on —particularly why the father is critically important as a religious socializer.

2. *Religion and life cycle.* There is some evidence in the research in which McCready and I are currently engaged that religious problems, religious needs, and religious questions vary considerably at different times in the life cycle. What interests an adolescent or a young person will not necessarily interest one in the middle years, and the interests of the elderly may be very different from those two or three decades younger. (In some respects those interests may be more like those of teenagers.)

Investigation of the relationship between basic belief system and life cycle has not even begun seriously.

3. *Religious experience.* Sociologists have ignored mysticism, and psychologists have tried to "explain" it as being "like" schizophrenia or a regression to infancy relationships with reality. More recently, the human potential movement and the wide variety of related phenomena have tried to persuade us that ecstasy (frequently drug induced) is good for you, a suggestion that Abraham Maslow made some time ago. Our own preliminary research indicates that most ecstatics are extraordinarily happy people who do not need drugs to achieve either ecstasy or health. The ecstatic argues that he *knows* something, that he has had a cognitive experience which has enabled him to *see* things the way they *really are*. It might be useful to take him at his word to see what causes and consequences such a cognitive experience might have. Thirty-seven percent of the American public reports at least one mystical experience (and perhaps ten million of our fellow citizens have such experiences frequently). It hardly seems appropriate to write mysticism off as deviant behavior.

4. *Use of interpretation of religious symbols.* Paul Tillich defines religion as "ultimate concern," Thomas Luckmann as "primary interpretive scheme," and Clifford Geertz as "ultimate cultural system." Critics contend that these definitions are so broad as to include almost everything. In fact such a contention indicates their failure to understand what Tillich, Luckmann, and Geertz are saying. (Most of those critics, incidentally, are much more interested in arguing about the "decline" of American religion than they are in even "trying on for size" the ultimate-concern approach.) But if one concedes—as I believe one must—that everyone has some sort of fundamental symbol system on which he falls back at critical points in life, the question then becomes what are the decisive (or to use Paul Ricoeur's word, "privileged") symbols in the lives of Americans and how are these symbols interpreted? Such a task is clearly complex and difficult but not therefore to be denied investigation.

5. *Religion and intimacy.* I have suggested in earlier paragraphs that there seems to be a close relationship between religion and sexuality, but it may well be that there is a close relationship between religion and all forms of intimacy. Students of the commune movement have reported how quickly communards fall back on some kind of world view to interpret, underpin, and reinforce the intimacy they believe they have created—and also to provide sanctions against those who want to break the bonds of intimacy. Is there a challenge in intense interpersonal relationships which almost demands religious or quasi-religious symbols to underpin such relationships?

6. *Religion and tolerance.* While Gordon Allport's "intrinsic"–"extrinsic" distinction and the scale purporting to measure these dimensions may still be a matter of controversy, it is now reasonably well established that certain kinds of religious persons are very high on prejudice scores (at least as prejudice is defined by researchers who are themselves quite free from it). Other kinds of religionists seem to be low indeed on prejudice scales. It might be useful to leave aside those research projects that are designed to prove that "the churches" are responsible for racism, anti-Semitism, pollution, and whatever else the pretext for scapegoating is and find out which religious symbols and which approaches to these symbols are most likely to produce pluralistic tolerance.

7. *Roman Catholics.* Roman Catholics constitute one-quarter of the American population. Most American scholars are content with ignorance bordering on prejudice when it comes to the subject of the Roman Catholic population. The companion volume to Martin Marty's *Righteous Empire* in the "Bicentennial History of the United States" was not written by a historian but a journalist, John Cogley. It was an inoffensive book but scarcely comparable in depth or breadth with Marty's brilliant work. In the meantime the younger generation of Catholic history scholars find it impossible to get their works accepted by university presses because "no one is interested in American Catholics," as one editor commented. (One-quarter of the population and no one is inter-

ested!)   Unfortunately, much of America's cultural elite is content to accept Gary Wills and Daniel Berrigan as authentic interpreters of what is going on in the Catholic population.   Furthermore, there is a systematic refusal to accept the fact that nativism persists in American society—and this in the face of serious evidence that anti-Catholic feeling is increasing among Jews and Protestants (while, paradoxically, anti-Jewish and anti-Protestant feeling is declining among Catholics).   If the stereotyping of ethnics as racists and hawks continues along with the easy dismissal of those of us who are interested in research on ethnic groups as racists is not evidence of cryptonativism, then no evidence would be persuasive.

I conclude this article on a melancholy note.   I have argued that we know practically nothing about contemporary American religion, yet neither sociologists, theologians, nor journalists seem particularly interested in understanding it.   I have seen no evidence that the situation is likely to change.   There are many things about American religion worth studying, and they are far more interesting and important than whether religion is "declining" or not.   But that question is an "Enlightenment" one, and it will continue to be asked, however mindlessly, until a new generation of scholars arrives on the scene which is willing to acknowledge that the Enlightenment is over.

Political Participation among Ethnic Groups in the United States: A Preliminary Reconnaissance[1]

Andrew M. Greeley
National Opinion Research Center

Religioethnic background is a meaningful predictor of political participation in American society. Its impact does not go away when social class is held constant, and it has an independent explanatory power that compares favorably with social class. Different causal models for political participation seem to apply for different ethnic collectivities, and the diversity among such collectivities is of similar magnitude to the diversity found in various nations in cross-national studies. Irish Catholics and Jews are the most active groups; Irish Protestants and blacks, the least active. The importance of ethnicity as a predictor variable can no longer be ignored by American social research.

Considerable work has been done recently (most of it cross-national) on the subject of political participation or political "mobilization," as it is sometimes called. Nie, Powell, and Prewitt (1969) spelled out the relationship among economic growth, attitudinal change, and political participation in six nations, using for the most part data from the civic culture study (Almond and Verba 1965). Verba, Nie, and Kim (1971) developed causal models to explain political participation in five countries, using data from the political participation study (Verba and Nie 1972). These models were generally satisfactory in explaining four different kinds of political participation in the five countries. Verba, Ahmed, and Bhatt (1971) have traced the similarities and differences in political participation models to be observed among blacks in the United States and Harijans in India.

These three studies are based on an explanatory model that is described in its simple form by Verba et al. (1971, p. 55): "According to this model, rising levels of socioeconomic status—in particular increased education, but also higher income and higher-status occupations—are accompanied by increased civic orientations such as interest and involvement in politics, sense of efficacy, and norms that one ought to participate. This leads to participation. The model looks something like the following:

$$\text{socioeconomic status} \longrightarrow \text{civic attitudes} \longrightarrow \text{participation.}"$$

[1] I wish to acknowledge the assistance generously offered by Sidney Verba, Norman Nie, William McCready, David Greenstone, Norman Bradburn, Bernice Neugarten, John Petrocik, and Shirly Saldanha in the preparation of this paper.

Political Participation among American Ethnic Groups

The last-named work addresses itself not only to between-system variation but to within-system variation. It not only discusses the similarities and differences in political participation in the United States and India but also compares white and black political participation in the United States and the participation of the Harijans and caste Hindus in India. In large societies like the United States the division of the society into "nonoppressed" and "oppressed" groups, however useful it may be for asking certain questions, does not exhaust the possibilities for exploring within-system variations. The present paper is intended to explore within-system variation in political participation among the white religioethnic groups in American society.[2] (Data on blacks are included for comparative purposes.)

We shall address the following five questions:

1. Are there differences in levels of political participation among the major religioethnic groups in American society?

2. Do these differences persist when controls for social class, region, age, and sex are applied?

3. How important as a predictor of political participation behavior is ethnicity?

4. Are there differences in political participation "style" as well as in levels of participation among American religioethnic groups?

5. Is there a relationship between the degree of ethnic identification and political participation or nonparticipation?

The present analysis labors under two major weaknesses: first, this will be, for the most part, a descriptive paper. The normal method of social research is to use data to test hypotheses that have been derived either from general theory or from previous research. However, there is presently no theory of ethnic diversity in the United States, and there has been practically no empirical research done on many of the major religioethnic collectivities. For example, the only major work done on the Poles, a group that is extremely interesting in its modes of political participation, is *The Polish Peasant in Europe and America,* published over a half-century ago (Thomas and Znaniecki 1918).

---

[2] Respondents answered these questions:
In what country were you born?
  A. In what country was your mother born?
  B. In what country was your father born?
  C. If both parents were born in the U.S.:
      What is the nationality of most of your ancestors?
What is your religion?
  Protestant
  Catholic
  Jewish
  Other (specify)
  None

American Journal of Sociology

In a subsequent paragraph we shall list certain "expectations" about various ethnic groups. This paper was deliberately entitled "A Preliminary Reconnaissance" because such "expectations" are hardly hypotheses as the word is normally understood.[3]

Second, even though the national sample used in the political participation study (which we are reanalyzing in the present paper) had a weighted size in excess of 3,000 respondents, many of the more interesting American ethnic groups have a relatively small number of respondents, as table 1

TABLE 1

DISTRIBUTION OF MAJOR RELIGIOETHNIC GROUPS IN POLITICAL PARTICIPATION SAMPLE

Religioethnic Group	N
Anglo-Saxon Protestant	591
Scandinavian Protestant	110
German Protestant	333
Irish Protestant	188
Other Protestant	447
Irish Catholic	95
German Catholic	97
Italian Catholic	109
French Catholic	40
Polish Catholic	56
Slavic (other Eastern European) Catholic	41
Spanish-speaking Catholic	89
Other Catholic	182
Jews	72
Blacks	406
Other	230
Total	3,095

makes clear. Hence, material presented in this paper must be considered not as a definitive study of the Irish, the Italians, the Poles, or the French, but a tentative initial investigation.[4]

[3] There are many complicated theoretical and substantive problems in defining ethnicity. Max Weber thinks of it as "consciousness of common origin." Clifford Geertz (leaning on Edward Shils) speaks of "primordial group attachment." Harold Isaacs writes of "basic membership group." While it is important that our theoretical thinking on the subject of "ethnicity" be clarified, the word is being used very loosely for the purposes of this paper and includes such "nonsocial class collectivities" as those created by diversities of religion, race, and national origins. A purely nominalistic definition was used in selecting the groups included in this analysis. There are a sufficient number of cases in our data for each of these groups to enable us to speak about them without a total absence of confidence. We hope that future research will be based both on a more clearly specified theoretical definition of ethnicity and on larger case bases. For example, to combine all Anglo-Saxon Protestants in one category is a dangerous oversimplification. A Yankee is not a Texan and neither can be termed Kentucky "country folk." But a good deal more theoretical clarity and much larger samples will be necessary before knotty problems of this sort can be resolved.

[4] It can be seen in table 1 that there are three principal residual groups: "other"

Political Participation among American Ethnic Groups

The descriptions presented in this paper have two principal goals: (1) we wish to assert that ethnicity is an important predictor of political behavior in American society and ought not to be excluded from any serious analysis of such behavior, and (2) we argue that in the United States cross-cultural research can deal with within-system variation as well as with cross-system variation.

Given the paucity of research done on American ethnic groups, it is impossible to generate any hypotheses about their political participation. We may, however, list certain "expectations" based on folklore, impression, journalistic commentary, and the occasional research document available.

Anglo-Saxon Protestants.—Because they are the largest group in the country, their political behavior will constitute the statistical norm. It also seems not unreasonable to assume that as first arrivals and as those who created the American republic, their behavior will also constitute the cultural norm.[5]

Germans.—There are two reasons for assuming that German political participation will be rather like that of the Anglo-Saxons. Their immigration to the United States has been spread over the longest time, and they are part of the northern European cultural heritage. On the other hand, it may well be that the traumatic experience of two world wars will lead to slightly lower political participation among them.

Scandinavians.—One would expect that the Scandinavians will show high levels of political participation because of the long tradition of political democracy in the Scandinavian countries and because of the general reputation of civic-mindedness attributed to members of the Scandinavian-American community.

Protestant Irish.—The Protestant Irish—perhaps for the most part the so-called Scotch-Irish—can be expected to be rather like the Anglo-Saxons

---

Protestants, "other" Catholics, and "others." Those who have been assigned to these three groups were unable to describe their ethnic background (which was the case in most of the "other" Protestants who simply described themselves as "Americans"), or were from ethnic groups too small to include in our analysis (Greeks, Lebanese, Armenians, etc.), or had such a complicated ethnic background that they were unable to say what their main ethnic identification was. Finally, the "Slavic" group in our analysis is a combination of all the non-Polish Eastern European Catholics. Clearly, the three "other" groups pose complicated theoretical and methodological problems. They are excluded from the present analysis because we wish to simplify what should be considered only a first step in research on ethnic political behavior and because the sample is not large enough to cope with the many possible combinations of ethnic background that are to be observed in American society. Hence, it could be said that have little trouble in placing themselves within one such group. Such a concern limits us to dealing with approximately three-quarters of the American population.

[5] In the forthcoming figures and tables the Anglo-Saxon scores will tend to be somewhat higher than the mean, and more groups will have positive scores than negative ones. The reason is that the "other" Protestants (a substantial proportion of whom are from the South) tend to have negative scores.

American Journal of Sociology

because of their early arrival in the United States and because they have been the main partners of the Anglo-Saxons in the American enterprise for so long that they have become almost indistinguishable from them.

Irish Catholics.—It seems safe to assume that the Irish—by reputation a highly political people—will be more involved in political behavior than any of the other Catholic groups (with the possible exception of the Germans) if only because they came first, understood the language, and developed in the penal time of Ireland a high level of political sophistication and skill. The Irish, like all the Catholic groups, may very well end up low on the communal activity variable because civic-minded traditions, so much a part of the Anglo-Saxon culture, may not yet have had time to develop among the Catholic groups.

French.—About the French-American community very little is known.

Italians.—Given the findings of a number of authors indicating that the Italians are low on social trust and proclivity for cooperation, it might be expected that they will score low on most political participation measures, though perhaps high on the particularized contact scale.[6]

Slavs and Poles.—Very little is known about the Polish and other Eastern European Catholic groups. However, given their more recent arrival, their lack of English language skills when they came, and the absence of a tradition of political democracy in Eastern Europe, it may well be that Eastern European Catholic groups will be low in political participation, save on the particularized contact scale.

Jews.—The Jews could easily be the most active political participants in America since American Jews generally appear to be politically and socially active. But it may well be that just as the Catholic groups are high on particularized contact, the Jews will be low on this variety of political behavior.

DIFFERENCES IN POLITICAL BEHAVIOR

Political participation scale.[7]—In figure 1 we see that there are very considerable differences in the general participation scores of American ethnic collectivities. (Figs. 1–10 show political participation for American ethnic groups on different scales; numbers shown in parentheses represent deviations from the mean.) The Protestant-Irish, the Italian Catholics, and blacks have scores substantially below the mean, with blacks having a slightly larger negative score than the Protestant-Irish. ("Substantial" will

[6] Particularized contact scale measures whether the respondent attempts to contact either personally or in writing a government representative outside of the local community.

[7] The generalized participation score is a combination of the four particular participation scores to be discussed subsequently.

Political Participation among American Ethnic Groups

be used in this discussion to indicate a difference from the mean in excess of 10 standardized units.) On the other hand, the highest scores in political participation are registered by the Irish Catholics (41 standardized units), the Scandinavian Protestants (32 units), and the Jews (19 units). Polish Catholics, German Catholics, and Anglo-Saxon Protestants are all slightly above the score of 10 units.

A number of observations are pertinent for figure 1.

First, there are major differences within religious groups. The highest scores are registered by a Catholic group—the Irish—and a Protestant group—the Scandinavians. On the other hand, the two lowest scores for white groups are also registered by a Catholic group—the Italians—and a Protestant group—the Irish. Second, there is almost no difference between the scores of German Catholics and German Protestants, but there are very substantial differences between the scores of Irish Catholics and Irish Protestants. Finally, the expectation that Italian Catholics and French Catholics might score low on political participation is upheld. On the other hand, both the Eastern European and Polish Catholics have positive scores.

Voting scale.[8]—In figure 2 we observe that the two Eastern European Catholic groups, Slavs (non-Polish Eastern Europeans) and Poles, are the most likely to score high on the voting scale. The Irish Catholic and Scandinavian Protestants are slightly behind them with scores still in excess of 30 units. The only negative scores on the voting scale are registered by Irish Protestants and by blacks with −24.9 occupying the lowest range. The following observations are pertinent: all the Catholic groups score higher on the voting scale than do the non-Scandinavian Protestants. Thus it seems safe to conclude that high voting scores tend to be a Catholic phenomenon even though Scandinavians also rank high on this scale.

Among the Catholic groups, the French and the Italians have the lowest scores; this result suggests that even in this "Catholic" modality of participation they do less well than the other groups.

The differences between the Irish Catholics and the Irish Protestants are substantial, but there is also a difference of 19 units between the German Protestants and the German Catholics; this finding indicates perhaps that as far as voting is concerned, Catholicism is more important than "Germanness."

Campaigning scale.[9]—As is perhaps appropriate for a group that is reputed to have mastered the art of being precinct captains, the American

[8] Voting score represents the respondents' participation in the 1960 and 1964 presidential elections and the 1966 congressional election.

[9] The campaigning scale is composed of four items: whether the respondent had worked for a party or a candidate in an election, whether he had attended political meetings, whether he had contributed money to a political party or candidate, whether he had ever tried to persuade others to vote for a candidate or a party.

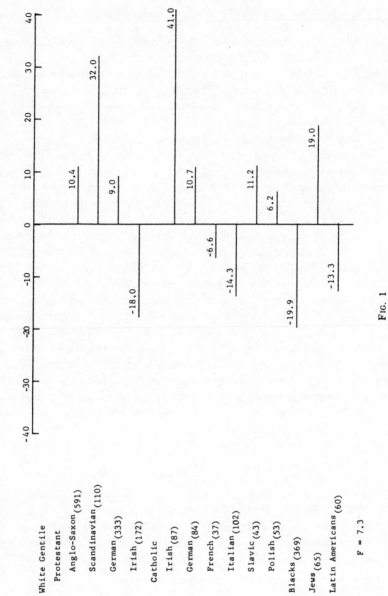

FIG. 1

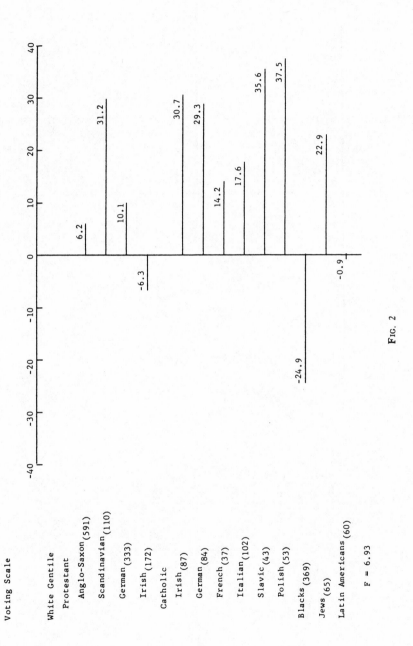

Fɪɢ. 2

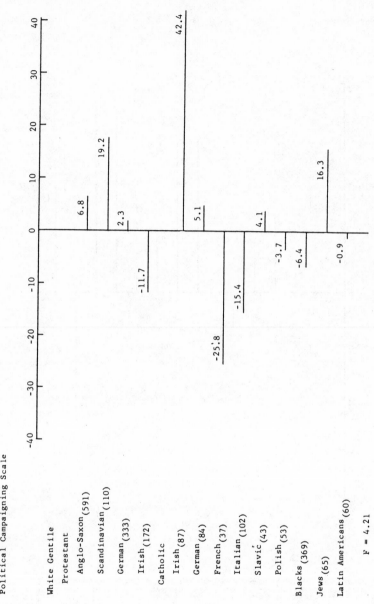

Fɪɢ. 3

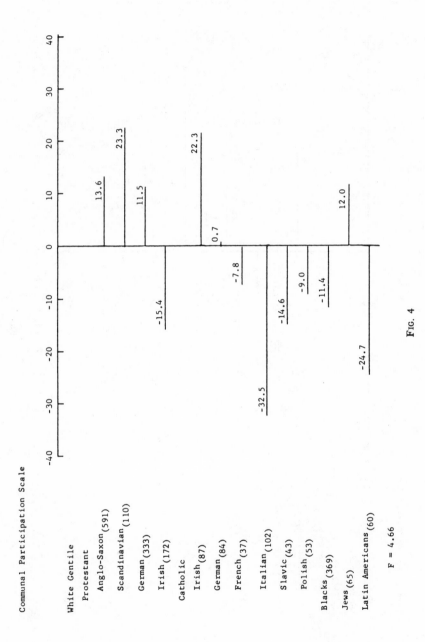

FIG. 4

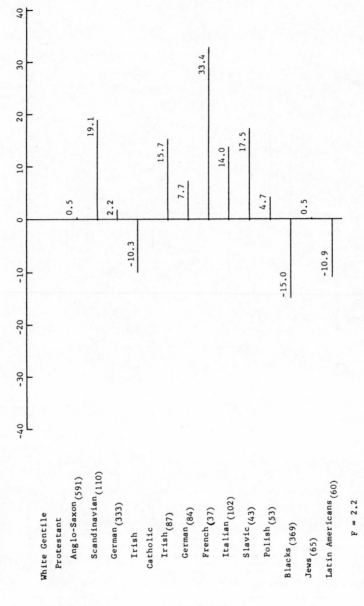

Fig. 5

Political Participation among American Ethnic Groups

Irish Catholics have the overwhelming lead on the political campaigning scale of figure 3. Indeed, their score is more than twice as large as that of the nearest group, the Scandinavian Protestants. The French and Italian Catholics and the Irish Protestants have substantial negative scores, while the Jews have a substantial positive score (as they also do on the voting scale). There is very considerable difference between Irish Catholics and Irish Protestants and relatively little difference between German Catholics and German Protestants.

Communal participation scale.[10]—Verba and Nie (1972) have observed in a forthcoming monograph that communal participation is a specifically Protestant form of political participation. There is some verification of this observation (made from the same data, of course) in figure 4. Three of the four Protestant groups have positive scores on the scale and four Catholic groups have negative scores (the Italians show a very considerable —32.5). The Scandinavians have the highest positive score (23.3), followed by the Anglo-Saxons (13.6), the Jews (12.0), and the German Protestants (11.5).

We may make some additional observations:

Irish Catholics and Irish Protestants continue to be different. German Protestants score somewhat higher on the communal participation scale than do German Catholics, a reversal of the finding on the voting scale. Voting is an especially Catholic mode of political participation, and German Catholics lead German Protestants in it. On the other hand, communal participation is an especially Protestant form of political participation, and German Protestants lead German Catholics on this measure.

The black score continues to be negative as it has been in all previous figures. The Jewish score continues to be positive.

Particularized contact scale.[11]—The French, who were low on both communal participation and campaigning, score very high (33.4) on this measure (fig. 5). The non-Polish Eastern Europeans, the Irish Catholics, and the Italians also have scores above 10. On the other hand, the second highest score on the particularized contact indicator is registered by the Scandinavian Protestants (19.1).

The following comments are appropriate: as on all previous scales, the scores of the Irish Protestants and the blacks are negative. As on all previous scales, the score of the Jews is positive, but only very slightly so. Irish Protestants and Irish Catholics continue to be quite different; German Catholics and German Protestants, relatively similar.

The picture that emerges from the five figures presented so far would

[10] The communal participation scale measures membership in a "civic" organization, working with others to solve community problems, forming a community organization, or trying to influence somebody in the community on a matter of community concern.

[11] See n. 6 for a definition of the particularized contact scale.

American Journal of Sociology

indicate that, not only on the general participation scale but also on all of
the specific scales, the Irish and the Scandinavians are most active
politically. The Irish Protestants and the blacks tend to be low, and in
most instances the Jews are in third position behind the Irish Catholics
and the Scandinavians. French, Italian, Slavic, and Polish Catholics are
positive on voting and particularized contact and negative on political
campaigning and communal participation. The Italians and the French
are lowest on campaigning and participation. The Poles and other Eastern
Europeans are highest on voting, and the French are highest on particularized contact. The Spanish-speaking are on the mean on both voting and
political campaigning, though substantially below the mean in communal
participation and somewhat below it on particularized contact.

DIFFERENCES WITH SOCIAL CLASS AND REGION CONTROLLED

In figures 6–10 we leave behind the real world of actual collectivities and
ask what the scores of various groups would be like if their social class
and region were the same. It is worth noting that this analysis does not
assume that ethnic differences are caused by social class. On the contrary,
a persuasive case might be made that the differences in behavior recorded
in the previous five figures may represent dimensions of cultural heritage
which are the cause rather than the effect—or at least a partial cause as
well as a partial effect—of social class differences.

By comparing figure 6 with figure 1 we see that the Irish and the
Scandinavians continue to be the most active participants. The scores
for the Eastern Europeans go up. The negative scores of the blacks and
the Irish Protestants become slightly positive. Perhaps the most interesting
comparison between figures 6 and 1 is that the relatively high Jewish score
on figure 1 becomes negative on figure 6. In other words, in the abstract
model created by holding region and social class constant, the Irish
Catholics, the Eastern European Catholics, and the Scandinavian Protestants emerge as exceptionally active political participants, while the Jews
emerge as the least active of all the groups. One might then conclude that
at least as far as the Jews are concerned, the reason for their high level of
general political participation is their social class.

When social class and region are held constant, the differences in voting
behavior also decline somewhat (fig. 7). Although the non-Irish Catholic
groups continue to have the highest scores and the Irish Catholic and
Scandinavian Protestants still score higher than the rest of the Protestant
population, the Protestant Irish negative score becomes slightly positive,
the black negative score is reduced almost to the mean, and the positive
Jewish score becomes negative.

Control for social class and region does rather little to deprive the Irish

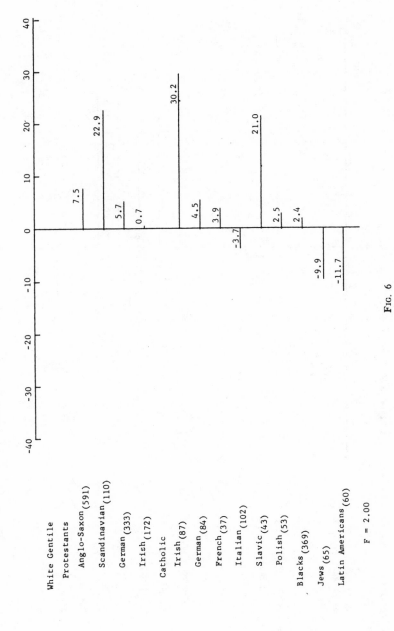

Fig. 6

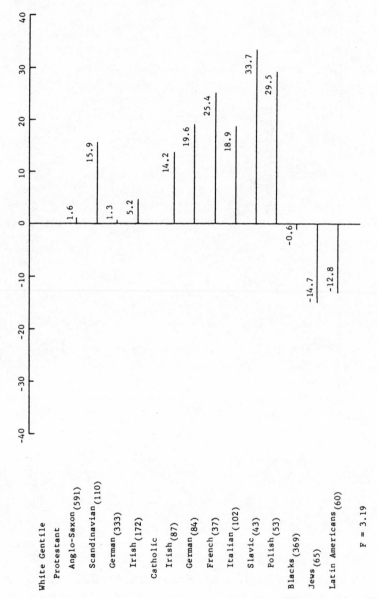

FIG. 7

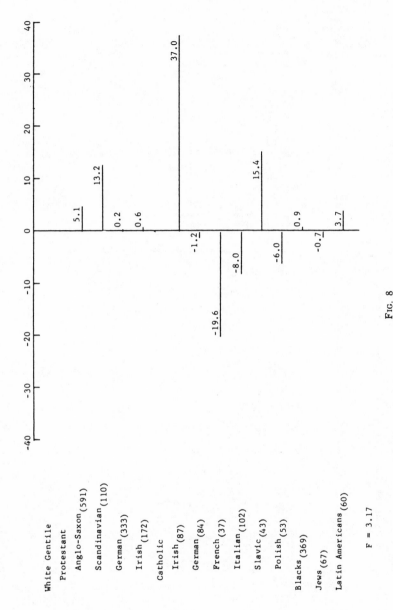

Campaigning Scale with Region (South) and Social Class Held Constant

White Gentile
  Protestant
    Anglo-Saxon (591)
    Scandinavian (110)
    German (333)
    Irish (172)
  Catholic
    Irish (87)
    German (84)
    French (37)
    Italian (102)
    Slavic (43)
    Polish (53)
  Blacks (369)
  Jews (67)
  Latin Americans (60)

F = 3.17

Fig. 8

185

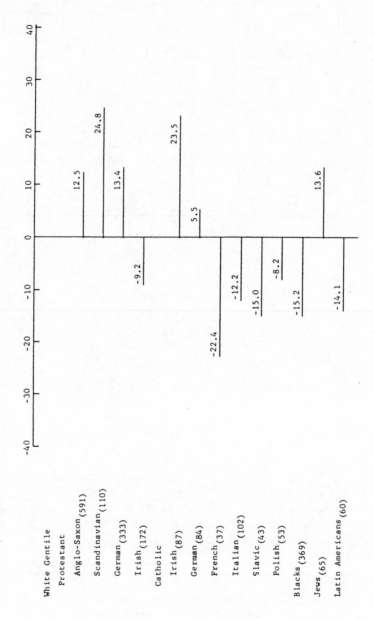

Communal Activity Scale with Region and Social Class Held Constant

White Gentile
  Protestant
    Anglo-Saxon (591)   12.5
    Scandinavian (110)   24.8
    German (333)   13.4
    Irish (172)   -9.2
  Catholic
    Irish (87)   23.5
    German (84)   5.5
    French (37)   -22.4
    Italian (102)   -12.2
    Slavic (43)   -15.0
    Polish (53)   -8.2
Blacks (369)   -15.2
Jews (65)   13.6
Latin Americans (60)   -14.1

Fig. 9

186

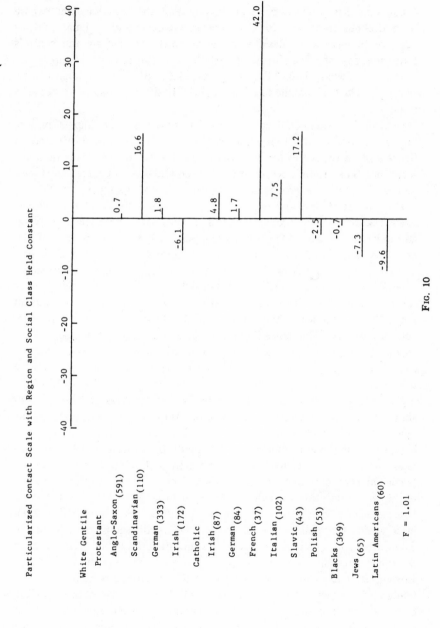

Fig. 10

American Journal of Sociology

Catholic of his rating as a campaigner par excellence (comparison of fig. 8 with fig. 3). The score of 42.4 in figure 3 declines to 37.0 in figure 8, a much smaller proportional loss than that of the Scandinavians, whose score declines from 19.2 to 13.2. The social class and regional controls improve the scores of Slavs, who in the world created by the controls forge ahead of the Scandinavians. All the negative scores in figure 3 are reduced somewhat, though the French (-19.6) still have the largest negative score. Once again, the fairly substantial positive Jewish score becomes negative.

Control for region and social class has practically no impact on the pattern of communal activity that was reported in figure 4. As we note in figure 9, negative scores of the Italians and the Latin Americans diminish somewhat. The negative scores of the French increase, but there is virtually no change among the groups on the positive side of the scale (fig. 9).

Holding social class and region constant creates a situation in which the French score goes up (comparing figs. 5 and 10). The French score on particularized contact (42.0) is more than twice as large as that of the Scandinavians. Furthermore, the Italians' score is cut almost in half, suggesting that if there is an Italian tendency to appeal to the *padrone,* or "godfather," it is one which is substantially reduced when social class is taken into account. The large negative score for blacks is reduced in figure 10 to practically the mean, and the slight positive Jewish score becomes negative. The Irish Protestant's negative score declines somewhat. In four of the five figures generated to describe a world where the effect of region and social class is removed, the Jewish score moves from positive to negative.

We may summarize the results of holding social class and region constant as follows: even under such controls, the Irish Catholics remain the most active political participants in American society. Not only are they high on voting and campaigning, as might be expected, they are also moderately high on communal participation and relatively low only on particular contact, which is the "Catholic" modality of political behavior in the sense that other Catholic groups tend to be high on it. Scandinavian Protestants are the second most active political group in America, even in a world where differences of social class and region are eliminated. The Catholic groups that are not Irish continue to have higher scores than do the Protestant groups (except the Scandinavians) on voting; the French, Italians, and other Eastern Europeans are also higher on particularized contact. The negative scores of the Irish Protestants and the blacks are substantially reduced, if not eliminated, when region and social class are held constant. The positive scores of Jews become negative when social class is held constant.

In summary, then, the Irish and the Scandinavians are not only the

Political Participation among American Ethnic Groups

most politically active, they are also the ones who deviate the most from the behavior characteristics of their coreligionists. Blacks and Irish Protestants would not be much different in their political participation from the American mean if differences of region and social class were eliminated. Finally, the high level of Jewish political participation seems to be almost entirely a social class phenomenon. (This is not to say that it is "caused" by social class.)

POLITICAL STYLES

The next step in our strategy was to attempt to determine whether there were "styles" of political participation that were unique to the various ethnic collectivities. To do this, a higher-order factor analysis was prepared for each of the American ethnic groups. A differential distribution of factor loadings would suggest differential political styles.[12]

In table 2 we present the results of the higher-order factor analysis. In

TABLE 2

POLITICAL "STYLES" OF AMERICAN ETHNIC GROUPS
(HIGHER-ORDER FACTOR ANALYSES)

	Voting	Campaigning	Communal Activity	Particularized Contact
White gentile:				
Protestant:				
Anglo-Saxon	.65	.82	.80	.17
Scandinavian	.46	.89	.85	.29
German	.60	.80	.69	.41
Irish	.64	.80	.80	.05
Catholic:				
Irish	.67	.88	.80	.07
German	.71	.79	.73	.55
French	.29	.90	.83	.42
Italian	.56	.87	.87	.01
Slav	.37	.90	.89	.03
Poles	.39	.87	.81	.32
Blacks	.72	.74	.67	.31
Jews	.65	.85	.79	.15

our discussion of it we will assume that the loadings on the Anglo-Saxon factor are the basis for comparison. The following comments may be made on table 2.

[12] The given factor loading tells the relationship between, let us say, voting for a given group and an underlying dimension of political behavior for the group in question. A high loading means that the scale in question relates at a high level with the dimension that is characteristic of the particular group.

American Journal of Sociology

There are relatively few differences among the various groups in loading on either campaigning or communal activity. The highest loading on campaigning is .9 for the French Catholics, and the lowest (among whites) is .79 for German Catholics. (The black loading of .74 is lower.) Similarly, eight of the collectivities have loadings in the .80s on communal activity. Somewhat lower scores are to be observed for the German Protestants (.69), German Catholics (.73), and blacks (.67).

But while there is relatively little variation in the loadings on these two items, there are considerable variations in loadings on voting and particularized contact. German Protestants, Irish Protestants, Irish Catholics, German Catholics, Italian Catholics, blacks, and Jews have relatively high loadings, while Scandinavian Protestants and Polish and Slavic Catholics have relatively low loadings. French Catholics have a very low loading (.29).

If the Anglo-Saxon loading of .17 is considered "typical" for particularized contacts, then the Scandinavian, German Protestants, German Catholics, French Catholics, Poles, and blacks have high loadings, while Irish Catholics, Irish Protestants, Italians, and Slavs have very low loadings.

Another way of looking at the data in table 2 is to observe that the three British Isles groups and the Jews have very similar political "styles," with the principal difference that the two Irish groups score relatively lower on the particularized contact item and the Jewish and Anglo-Saxon groups score relatively higher. Similarly, the German Catholics and German Protestants have relatively similar "styles," both of them substantially higher than most other groups on particularized contact. They are similar to the Jews, the Irish, and the Anglo-Saxons on the other three items.

One of the more deviant groups in their political "style" is the French Catholics, who have a lower loading on voting than they do on particularized contact. The Poles, whose loading on voting is only slightly higher than their loading on particular contacts, are also noteworthy. The Scandinavians are lower than most in their loading on voting and relatively high on their loading on particularized contact. The blacks, finally, tend to be lower than other groups on the first three items and higher than some other groups on their loading on particular contacts.

In summary then, insofar as political "styles" are accurately described in table 2, the Jews are the most like the Anglo-Saxons and the Germans (Catholic and Protestant), and the Irish (Catholic and Protestant) are relatively similar to the Anglo-Saxons and the Jews. The Germans are slightly higher than the Anglo-Saxon–Jewish "norm" on particularized contact, and the Irish Catholics and the Irish Protestants are lower than the "normal" loading on this variable.

The fact that the Irish Catholics, who are the most active political participants, and the Irish Protestants, who are the least active, are relatively

Political Participation among American Ethnic Groups

similar to each other (as well as to the Anglo-Saxon and the Jewish norm) in their political styles would seem to indicate that while there may be substantially different levels of participation among these three groups, the components of their participation are relatively similar. While the Irish Catholics may be much more active politically than the Anglo-Saxons and the Irish Protestants much less active politically, the "mix" of their political behaviors tends to be similar.

It is possible to speculate about the Irish Catholics and the Irish Protestants. Both groups had experience with the Anglo-Saxon political system in Ireland, learning both to live with it and to exploit it. (It should not be forgotten that the Ulster-Irish were dissidents against the established Church of Ireland as much as were the Celtic Catholics.) The "rotten borough" politics of the British parliament of that time was an excellent preparation for the Irish Catholics for the politics of the areas most of them settled in, large cities in the northeastern and north central part of the United States. It also provided the Irish Catholics with certain appropriate political skills for the American environment. Thus, the Irish Catholics discovered that involvement in politics in the United States was a way to respectability, power, and affluence. They became involved in party politics and in political or politically related jobs such as the fire department, the police force, and public transportation. Their children and grandchildren continued the political interest as they chose careers in law and government service. Irish Protestants, on the other hand, settled for the most part in the Piedmont area of the southeast, an environment where there was less political activity and where politics was not a path to affluence and respectability. The two groups, coming from an Anglo-Saxon political system, became either hyper-political or hypopolitical as the result of the environment into which they moved at immigration and their developmental history since.

Considerably more research must be done on the social history of the American religioethnic groups before even tentative explanations like the foregoing can be possible for the different political "styles" of the various ethnic subcomponents within American society.

ETHNICITY AND SOCIAL CLASS

We have thus far established that there is a relationship between ethnicity and political participation and that this relationship is not just a function of social class. But how important is ethnicity as a predictor variable? Even if it is distinct from social class, how much explanatory power does it have? What is the impact of ethnicity net of social class compared to the impact of social class net of ethnicity?

In social research where we deal with ordered variables, the obvious

American Journal of Sociology

technique to use for such questions is multiple regression analysis. The simple correlation coefficient (r) indicates the relationship between a predictor variable and a dependent variable, and the standardized co-efficient (β) indicates the relationship between the two net of all other predictor variables put into the equation.

Unfortunately, for our purposes, neither ethnicity nor religion is an ordered variable. However, an analytic technique called "multiple classification analysis" (MCA) has been developed at the University of Michigan Survey Research Center (1967) that enables us to analyze variables that are not ordered. The program produces η and β that are standardized measures for nonordered variables equivalent to r and β in multiple regression analysis. The MCA η is a zero-order correlation; the MCA β, a partial-order correlation.

With the assistance of John Petrocik of the NORC staff, a set of MCA equations was prepared for the political participation variable and six predictor variables—income, education, occupation, region, religion, and religioethnicity. The β's that emerged from this analysis enabled us to compare the relative impact of ethnicity on political behavior compared to those social class and religion variables that Verba and Nie (1972) found important in their analysis.

An inspection of table 3 reveals that ethnicity is a relatively important predictor of political behavior. It is stronger than religion, region, and occupation for all four of the variables, equal to or stronger than income on two variables (voting and contact), and stronger than education on

TABLE 3

A. COEFFICIENTS OF MULTIPLE CLASSIFICATION ANALYSIS FOR POLITICAL PARTICIPATION VARIABLES

Predictor Variables	Voting	Campaigning	Civic Activity	Particularized Contact
Religion	.13	.09	.10	.04
Income	.17	.15	.16	.09
Education	.14	.20	.23	.06
Ethnicity	.17	.13	.14	.10
Region	.06	.09	.10	.06
Occupation	.11	.08	.13	.07

B. COEFFICIENTS OF MULTIPLE CLASSIFICATION ANALYSIS FOR POLITICAL PARTICIPATION VARIABLES, NORTHEAST AND NORTH CENTRAL ONLY

Religion	.16	.12	.17	.08
Income	.17	.19	.15	.11
Education	.13	.21	.28	.09
Ethnicity	.20	.16	.16	.16
Occupation	.14	.06	.15	.06

Political Participation among American Ethnic Groups

two variables (voting and contact). It is the strongest predictor of both voting (though tied with income) and particularized contact, and in third place on both campaigning and civic activity. The differences among the various predictor variables are relatively small, and not much should be made of one predictor's being more powerful than another. However, it does seem safe to say that at least as far as political participation is concerned, ethnicity is not an unimportant variable compared with other predictors. One could as well omit occupation from a questionnaire as ethnicity.

Ethnic diversity in the United States is greatest in the northeast (New England and Middle Atlantic states) and north central (the Midwest and plains states) regions because the largest number of immigrants settled there. Hence, it is fair to ask whether the predictive power of ethnicity increases when only respondents from those regions are the subject of multiple classification analysis.

We note in table 3B that there is indeed a moderate increase in the predictive power of ethnicity when the analysis is limited to those in the regions where ethnic diversity is most likely to be found. However, the differences are not of such a magnitude as to appreciably change the picture presented in table 3A. Perhaps the most interesting question that might be asked cannot be answered with our data. In the big heavily ethnic cities of the "quaradcali" (to use Scammon and Wattenberg's word) does ethnic diversity become the most important predictor of political participation? One might also wonder if the various urban ethnic groups have different styles of political participation in different cities. Are the New York Irish, for example, as active as the Chicago Irish? Do the Detroit Poles vote as much as the Milwaukee Poles? The answer to such questions must await an extensive and systematic series of research projects on the relationship between ethnicity and politics in American life. The data presented in table 3, however tentative and limited they may be, suggest that such systematic research would be no more out of place than systematic research on the relationship between social class and political participation in the United States.

CAUSAL MODELS OF POLITICAL MOBILIZATION

Nie et al. (1969), Verba, Nie, and Kim (1971), and Verba, Ahmed, and Bhatt (1971) all insist on the importance of social class (as usually measured by educational level) as a cause of higher levels of political participation. Verba, Nie, and Kim (1971, p. 59), for example, present models showing that campaign activity, voting, and communal activity are strongly related to education in the United States. It is therefore legitimate to ask whether this general correlation persists among the various religioethnic

American Journal of Sociology

TABLE 4
CORRELATIONS BETWEEN POLITICAL PARTICIPATION AND EDUCATIONAL LEVEL FOR
MAJOR AMERICAN RELIGIOETHNIC GROUPS

	Voting	Campaigning	Communal Activity	Particularized Contact
White gentile:				
Protestant:				
Anglo-Saxon	.22	.29	.32	.06
Scandinavian	.20	.28	.23	.06
German	.19	.29	.33	.03
Irish	.29	.24	.27	.04
Catholic:				
Irish	.23	.25	.30	.06
German	.06	.27	.02	.02
French	.00	.33	.33	.09
Italian	.13	.13	.23	.16
Slavic	.20	.33	.53	.06
Polish	.03	.02	.07	.23
Spanish-speaking	.00	.21	.35	.24
Blacks	.21	.14	.22	.00
Jews	.07	.50	.44	.00

groups with the American social and political system. The data in table 4 would indicate that while the picture is complicated, the educational level does not affect all the ethnic groups' political behavior in the same way. Thus, there are virtually no differences in the correlations between voting and educational level for the first five groups. However, among the German Catholics, the French, the Italians, the Poles, the Spanish-speaking, and the Jews, the relationship between voting and education is much lower than it is among other groups. This cannot be described as a Catholic-Jewish phenomenon because the correlation between education and voting for the Irish and Slavic Catholics is virtually the same as that for the Anglo-Saxon Protestants.

Similarly, while there is a strong correlation (in the neighborhood of .3) between education and political campaigning for most American religio-ethnic groups, this correlation does not exist at all for the Poles and is substantially below .3 for the Italians and the blacks. On the other hand, the relationship between education and political campaigning for Jews is .5.

For two groups there are very low correlations between education and communal activity. For German Catholics the relation is .02; for the Polish Catholics, .07. On the other hand, for Jews (.44) and for Slavic Catholics (.53), the correlation is much higher than that of the Anglo-Saxons (.32). Finally, while education in the United States correlates in general at a very low level with particularized contact, it is substantially higher both for the Poles and the Spanish-speaking (.23 and .24, respectively) and somewhat higher than the average for the Italians (.16).

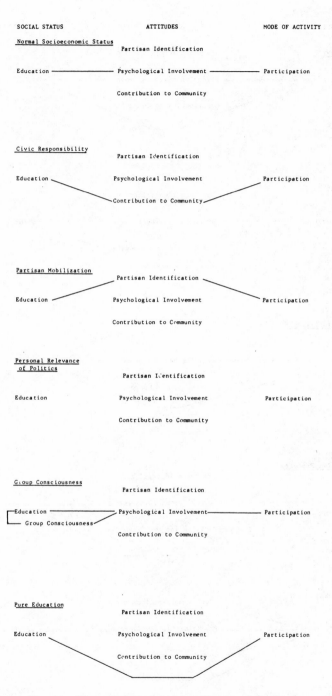

Fɪɢ. 11.—Theoretical models of political mobilization

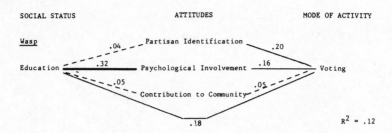

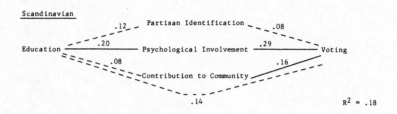

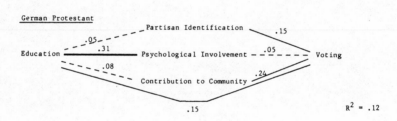

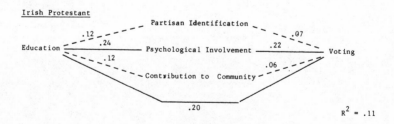

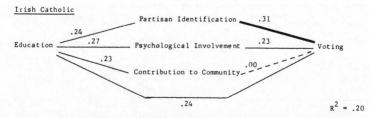

Fig. 12.—Paths to voting participation: American ethnic groups

SOCIAL STATUS ATTITUDES MODE OF ACTIVITY

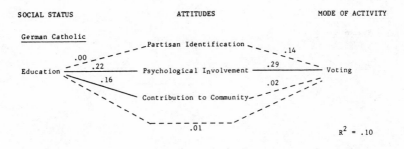

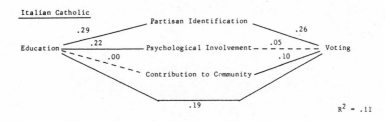

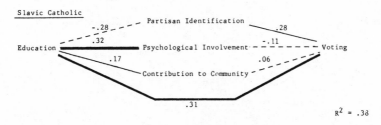

FIG. 12 (*Continued*)

197

SOCIAL STATUS   ATTITUDES   MODE OF ACTIVITY

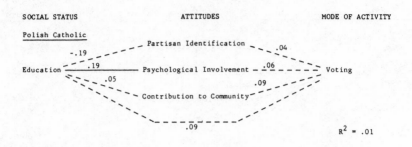

Polish Catholic

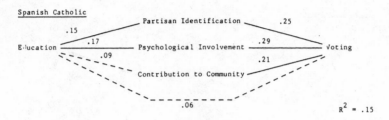

Spanish Catholic

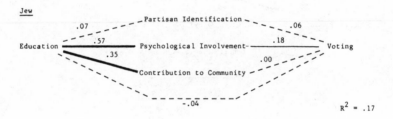

Jew

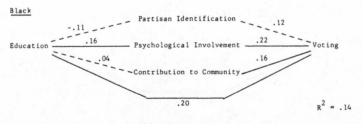

Black

FIG. 12 (*Continued*)

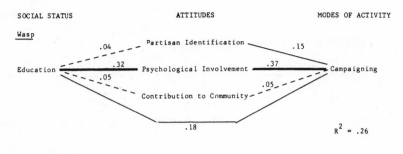

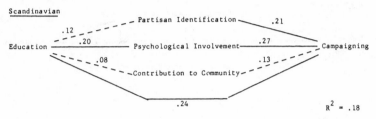

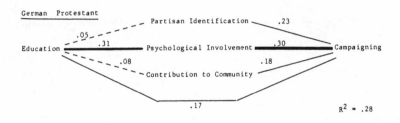

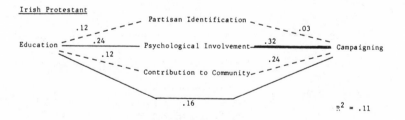

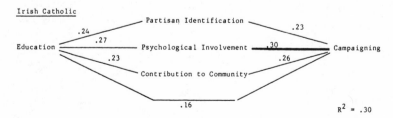

Fig. 13.—Paths to campaigning participation: American ethnic groups

199

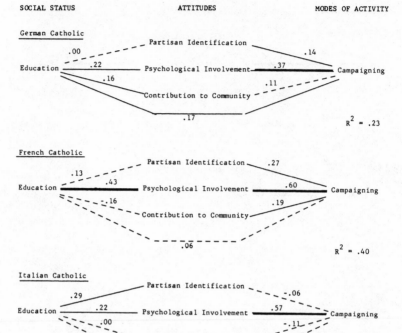

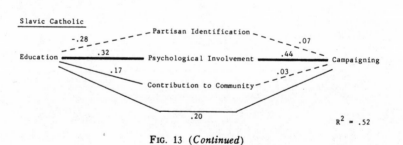

FIG. 13 (*Continued*)

SOCIAL STATUS   ATTITUDES   MODES OF ACTIVITY

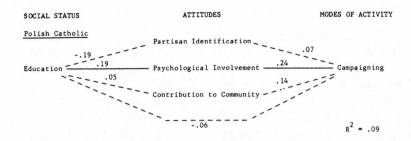

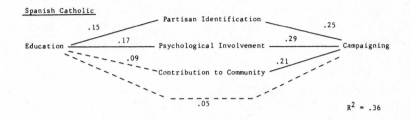

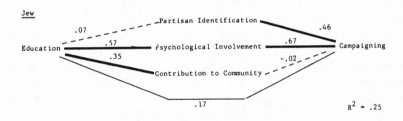

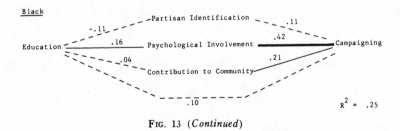

FIG. 13 (*Continued*)

201

American Journal of Sociology

To summarize the data in table 4, the blacks and the French depart from the ordinary pattern of relationship between education and political participation once. German Catholics and the Spanish-speaking depart from the pattern twice. The Jews and the Italians depart from the pattern three times, and the Poles four times, displaying practically no correlation between education and political behavior for voting, campaigning, and communal activity and a relatively high correlation between education and particularized contact. Education does correlate with political participation in American society, but not for all ethnic groups. One ethnic group in particular, the Poles, seems to represent a phenomenon completely at variance with that described by Nie et al. (1969) in their study of six nations.

DEGREE OF ETHNIC CONSCIOUSNESS AND
POLITICAL PARTICIPATION

While it is impossible to test Verba, Ahmed, and Bhatt's (1971) group consciousness model of political participation with these data, we may still ask whether some sort of an ethnic identification does influence those particular kinds of political behavior that seem to be especially characteristic of certain groups. For example, if ethnic identification does reinforce a particular kind of political behavior to which an ethnic group is predisposed, we could predict a positive correlation between ethnic identification and voting for the Poles and the Slavs; a positive correlation between ethnic identification and campaigning for the Scandinavians, Jews, and Irish; and a negative correlation between political participation and ethnic identification for Italians. In table 5 we see that there is modest support

TABLE 5

CORRELATION BETWEEN ETHNIC IDENTIFICATION AND
CERTAIN FORMS OF POLITICAL PARTICIPATION

Polish voting	.19
Slavic voting	.16
Scandinavian campaigning	−.03
Jewish campaigning	.13
Irish campaigning	.14
Italian political participation	−.11

NOTE.—Ethnic identification items:

1. What proportion of your friends are of your own nationality? All, Most, About half, Less than half, None.

2. Do you or your family observe any customs connected with the country from which your family originally came such as cooking special food or observing particular holidays or anything like that?
   Do you observe a lot of such customs? Some, Only a few, No such customs at all.

3. Could you tell me if you belong to any nationality groups? (In the context of the questionnaire, "nationality groups" means nationality-based membership organizations.)

Political Participation among American Ethnic Groups

for five of these six expectations. Ethnic identification does indeed lead to higher levels of voting for Poles and Slavs, and to higher levels of campaigning for the Jews and the Irish (though not for the Scandinavians). Finally, among the Italians, whose political participation is low, identification as Italian leads to an even lower level of political participation.

One could speculate that since, for the Irish, political campaigning was a way to upward mobility, it is not unreasonable that those who are still conscious of their Irishness would be even more interested in that path to power and affluence. It is even more interesting to speculate that if the vote is a symbol of Americanism for the Poles, then it is precisely those Poles who are most conscious of being Polish who find the greatest need to manifest this American symbolism.

CONCLUSIONS

The descriptions presented in this paper would seem to support a plausible case for the two basic arguments being made: ethnicity is still an important variable in American society and cross-cultural research can be done not only among nations but among diverse groups within large nations. Unfortunately, we need to know much more than we presently do about American religioethnic groups to be able to fully exploit the possibilities of such research. If the findings reported in this paper can be substantiated in research with a much larger sample (and clearly such research is of the first order of importance), we will have conclusively established that the levels, the "styles," and the causes of political participation among the major ethnic groups in American society are different. Being able to define these differences is of course an important accomplishment, but serious scholarly research cannot be content with differences that are unexplained.

It may be that the diversity of political behavior among American ethnic groups can be explained by any one of three (or any combination of three) possible causes:

Cultural heritage from the Old World.—Were there events in the historical, cultural, and social heritages of the Irish and the Poles that predisposed one group (the Irish) toward becoming active campaigners and the other (the Poles) toward becoming enthusiastic voters?

Experience at the time of immigration.—The Irish were the first of the Catholic ethnic groups to move into the large American cities in numbers great enough to seize control of the political mechanism. Having control, they were in a position to block access to the mechanism to subsequent Catholic groups. Or at least they blocked access to the amount of power the Irish already had.

The "natural history" of each group since the immigration experience. —The very fact that the Irish moved almost unrivaled into politics pre-

American Journal of Sociology

disposed them to political jobs and government service, a predisposition that was handed down from generation to generation even after they found other channels to affluence and respectability.[13]

With data currently existing it is impossible to examine the relative impact of these three factors on the different political behaviors of American ethnic groups. Clearly, a considerable amount of cooperative effort on the part of historians and social scientists is in order. Researchers need not fear that there are no longer any social puzzles left to be explained within the boundaries of the United States.

It may be time for American social scientists to begin to attempt explanations for such puzzles. Less is known about Polish Americans than about many African tribes. Surely the study of African tribes ought not to be abandoned, nor has there necessarily been conscious discrimination against Polish Americans. However, on the basis of data presented in this paper it would be foolish for researchers to continue to ignore them—or indeed any of the other fascinating groups that make up the American nation.

REFERENCES

Almond, Gabriel, and Sidney Verba. 1965. *The Civic Culture.* Boston: Little, Brown.
Nie, Norman, G. Bingham Powell, and Kenneth Prewitt. 1969. "Social Structure and Political Participation Developmental Relations." *American Political Science Review* 63 (June): 361–78; and (September): 808–32.
Scammon, Richard W., and Ben J. Wattenberg. 1970. *Real Majority.* New York: Coward.
Thomas, William I., and Florian Znaniecki. 1918. *The Polish Peasant in Europe and America.* Chicago: University of Chicago Press.
University of Michigan Survey Research Center. 1967. *Multiple Classification Analysis: A Report on a Computer Program for Multiple Regression Using Categorical Predictors.* Frank M. Andrews, James N. Morgan, John A. Sonquist. Ann Arbor: Institute for Social Research, University of Michigan.
Verba, Sidney, Bashirubdin Ahmed, and Anil Bhatt. 1971. *Caste, Race, and Politics: Comparative Study, India and the United States.* Comparative Politics Series. Beverly Hills, Calif.: Sage.
Verba, Sidney, and Norman H. Nie. 1972. *Participation in America: Political Democracy and Social Equality.* New York: Harper & Row.
Verba, Sidney, Norman H. Nie, and Jae-on-Kim. 1971. *The Modes of Democratic Participation: A Cross-national Comparison.* Comparative Politics Series. Beverly Hills, Calif.: Sage.

[13] Research done at NORC indicates that in the 1960s young men and women of Irish background graduating from college were one and a half times more likely than typical Americans to choose careers in government service and three and a half times more likely to choose careers in law.

Ethnicity and Racial Attitudes: The Case of the Jews and the Poles

Andrew M. Greeley[1]
National Opinion Research Center

Data from a survey in 1968 of a sample drawn from the population of 15 U.S. cities that had experienced racial unrest revealed clear differences in racial attitudes among members of 10 ethnic groups. The Poles were the least sympathetic to black militance, the Jews the most sympathetic. A model incorporating educational attainment and two measures of general predispositions toward racial problems, called "support" and "avoidance," was used to explain variation of attitudes toward election of a black mayor, civil rights legislation, interracial contact, and repressive riot control. Of the two predispositions, "avoidance" had the stronger effect on acceptability of interracial contact, "support" the stronger effect on attitudes toward riot control and civil rights legislation. There was no direct effect of educational level on any of the four specific racial attitudes. The model successfully explains most of the observed differences between Jews and Poles in these four attitudes. To some extent the differences between these two ethnic groups seem to be related to stronger feelings of alienation among Poles.

It is widely assumed that the so-called ethnic groups are politically conservative, racist, and resistant to social change despite their Democratic voting record (see Litt 1970; Myrdal 1969; Campbell 1971). Research has indicated that the matter may not be so simple (see Greeley 1972; Greeley and Sheatsley 1971; Nie, Currie, and Greeley 1974). In many respects the Catholic ethnics may be at least as "liberal" as their native American counterparts. Thus for 1970 and 1972, data (summarized in table 1) from the National Opinion Reseach Center's monitoring of national attitudes toward racial integration show that Irish Catholics were in both years the most prointegration of all but the Jewish religio-ethnic groups in the North. Even the Slavic Catholics, the lowest scoring of the Catholic groups in 1970 and 1972, had a somewhat higher prointegration score in 1972 than did the German Protestants. Furthermore, the largest positive change in mean score on the NORC Integration Scale

[1] Another version of this article appears as a chapter in *Ethnicity in the United States: A Preliminary Reconnaissance* (New York: Wiley, 1974). The data utilized in the article, exclusive of table 1, were made available by the Institute for Social Research (ISR) Social Science Archive. They were originally collected by Dr. Angus Campbell and Dr. Howard Schuman of the Survey Research Center, Institute for Social Research, University of Michigan. Neither the original collectors of the data nor the archive bear any responsibility for the analyses or interpretations presented here.

American Journal of Sociology

TABLE 1

FAVORABILITY TOWARD RACIAL INTEGRATION BY ETHNICITY
(NON-SOUTH ONLY)

	1970	1972	Change 1970–72
All Northerners	2.88	3.16	.28
Anglo-Saxons	2.80 (220)	3.18 (148)	.38
German Protestants	2.81 (137)	2.70 (142)	—.11
Scandinavian Protestants	2.82 (29)	2.98 (65)	.16
Irish Catholics	3.06 (48)	3.46 (63)	.40
German Catholics	2.97 (41)	3.18 (44)	.21
Italian Catholics	2.65 (38)	3.14 (63)	.49
Slavic Catholics (including Poles)	2.45 (53)	2.76 (49)	.31
Jews	3.79 (24)	3.67 (52)	—.12

SOURCE.—National Opinion Research Center continuing study of white attitudes toward racial integration, 1963–72.
NOTE.—Mean scores on a Guttman scale based on number of prointegration responses to five items on the NORC questionnaire (see Greeley and Sheatsley 1973). The higher the score, the greater the favorability toward racial integration. Number of cases shown in parentheses.

between 1970 and 1972 was among Italian Catholics, and the second largest was among Irish Catholics. The positive change among Slavic Catholics was about the same as the Northern average and substantially more positive than changes among either German or Scandinavian Protestants. Hence, as far as NORC's scale is concerned, there was no "white ethnic backlash" between 1970 and 1972.

But table 1, like most research that attempts to analyze diversity among religioethnic groups, is seriously deficient in the number of respondents on which the statistics in each cell are based. To generalize about American Slavs on the basis of 49 cases or American Irish Catholics on the basis of 63 cases is a risky enterprise. Unfortunately, the typical national survey sample of 1,500 respondents does not provide many respondents for the individual religioethnic groups.

In 1968, however, the University of Michigan Survey Research Center surveyed 15 cities affected by urban unrest. Because it was conducted in cities where much of the "ethnic" population is concentrated, this survey provides a substantial number of respondents for each of the major ethnic groups in the U.S. population.

Ethnicity and Racial Attitudes

The Michigan survey developed 12 measures of attitudes toward racial issues, each based on from one to five items in their questionnaire. In this paper I first use four of these 12 measures to compare the racial attitudes of several white religioethnic groups. Next I describe and apply a general model to explain these attitudes, and finally apply this model in a more specific analysis of differences in racial attitudes between two urban ethnic groups, the Polish Catholics and the Jews. The four scales concern riot control, interracial contact, civil rights legislation, and black mayoral candidates. Since scales can easily derive meanings from their labels that have little connection with their content, Appendix A lists the questionnaire items that comprise each of these scales. In the analysis, the attitude scale scores are Z-scores; in other words, measures of the percentage of a standard deviation away from the sample mean of the score of a given subpopulation. A Z-score of 100 indicates a score 1 SD from the mean of the score distribution.[2] I comment only on Z-scores of 10 points or more.

DIFFERENCES IN RACIAL ATTITUDES AMONG ETHNIC GROUPS

In figure 1, 10 religioethnic groups are compared according to their views on riot control. We note that the Poles, followed closely by the German Catholics, were most inclined to support a repressive response to riots, while the Jews and the Irish Catholics were least likely to support such a response. Jewish liberalism is not surprising, but the liberalism of the Irish Catholics may startle some readers.

Comparison of figure 2 with figure 1 shows that there was greater variation in religioethnic attitudes toward interracial contact than toward riot control. Again, however, the Jews are the most "liberal" and the Poles the most "illiberal." The Irish Protestants are considerably below the sample mean on support for interracial contact, and the Italian Catholics somewhat below it, while the Scandinavian Protestants are 10 points above it. The Jews, though, are farther above the sample mean than the Irish Protestants are below it, and the Poles rank markedly farthest below the mean.

The same pattern emerges with respect to support for civil rights legislation (fig. 3). The Jews rank highest by far and the Poles quite low. Slavic and German Catholics are also rather low on this scale.

In figure 4, willingness to support a black mayor is represented by Z-scores. Jews and Irish Catholics are above the mean, while British Protestants, Scandinavian Protestants, Irish Protestants, and Polish Cath-

[2] Thus, for example, the Irish Catholic Z-score of −10 on attitude toward repressive riot control indicates that the score is 10% of a standard deviation below the mean of the entire sample.

911

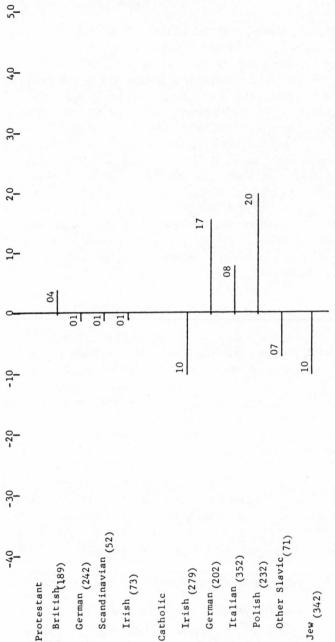

FIG. 1.—Attitude on riot control of American religioethnic groups in 15 cities affected by riots in 1967 (Z-scores), a positive score indicating support for repression of riots.

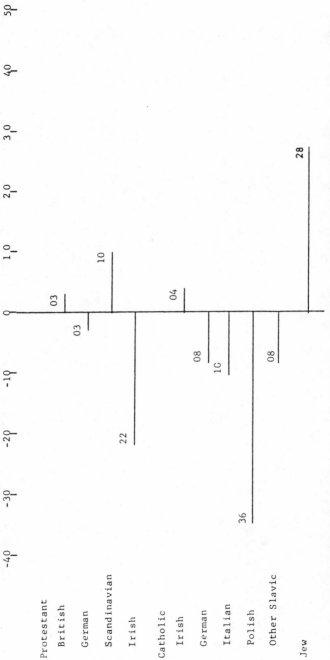

Fig. 2.—Estimation of amount of interracial contact that is desirable for American religioethnic groups in 15 cities affected by riots in 1967 (Z-scores), a positive score indicating support for interracial contact.

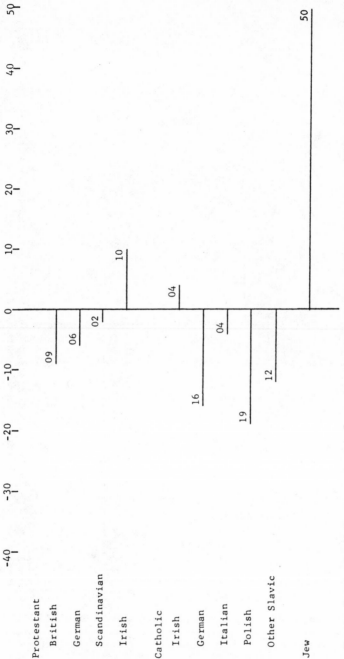

FIG. 3.—Support for civil rights legislation among American religioethnic groups in 15 cities affected by riots in 1967 (Z-scores), a positive score indicating support for legislation.

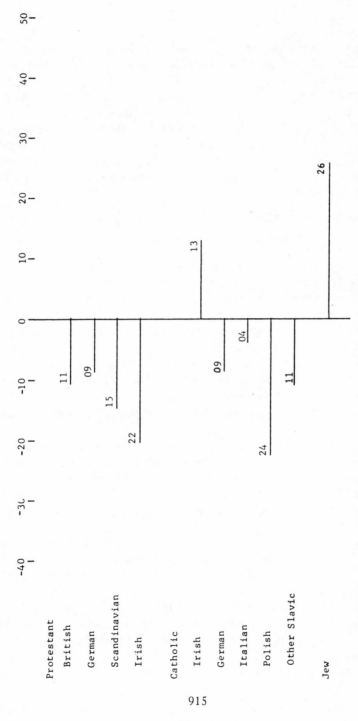

Fig. 4.—Willingness to vote for black mayor among American religioethnic groups in 15 cities affected by riots in 1967 (Z-scores), a positive score indicating willingness to vote for black mayor.

American Journal of Sociology

olics are all below the mean. There seems to be greater diversity among the religioethnic groups in their willingness to support a black mayor than there is in attitudes toward the other three issues.[3]

To summarize, among respondents in the 15 cities affected by the 1967 riots, the Jews are clearly the group most favorably disposed to the blacks, and the Poles are the group least favorably disposed. Except for the Jews, the Irish Catholics are the most favorable. Italian Catholics differ very little from the 15-city mean, while German Catholics, Slavic Catholics, other than Poles, and Irish Protestants are sometimes favorable and sometimes not.

A MODEL TO EXPLAIN RACIAL ATTITUDES

Having discovered substantial differences between Polish Catholics and Jews on the four major racial issues we are investigating, one might be content to conclude that Poles are "racist" and Jews are not, or that in comparison with the Jews (and, on two issues, the Irish Catholics) the Poles are more likely to be racist. It is surely the case that a good deal of analysis, both popular and serious, of American racial problems is content with such conclusions. It seems appropriate, however, for serious researchers to try to explain the reasons for such differences among major population categories. An explanation of this diversity might be of use to those policymakers who must deal with ethnically heterogeneous urban situations.

As social research moves gingerly toward causal explanations, it has become clear that in most cases longitudinal studies are required to test the models that are proposed. In the absence of longitudinal research, the models remain at best tentative and speculative. Still, such models may force us to look at a phenomenon analytically and to make explicit the causal assumptions that are hidden in correlational analysis.

Why do people vary in the strength and direction of their racial attitudes? The social science and humanistic literature suggests a number of explanations. Those who are "enlightened" on the race question may be better educated, they may have more frequent contact with blacks, they may have a keener perception of the amount of racial injustice in the country and greater sympathy with the protests of those who are its victims. On the other hand, those who are threatened by racial progress may have more intolerant personalities and may be frightened by "real" threats to what they perceive as their own welfare (for example, increase

---

[3] There is, however, majority support from all groups for a qualified black mayor, the 15-city average being 66%. Eighty percent of the Jews would vote for such a candidate, 72% of the Irish Catholics, 66% of the Italians, and 58% of the Poles.

Ethnicity and Racial Attitudes

in crime or deterioration of property values in their neighborhoods with the advent of racial integration).

The Michigan survey data provide good indicators of five of these six variables: education, "black friends," "sympathy with black protest," "perception of racial discrimination," and "intolerant personality." Unfortunately, there was no good item to tap the dimension of "real" fear. As a surrogate, I use a questionnaire item that indicates whether a respondent thought that there ought to be some sort of limitation on the number of black families living in a given neighborhood.[4] Of course one reason for responding positively to this item might be a belief that after a certain "tipping point" had been reached, an entire neighborhood would turn black, thus making racial integration impossible. The "fear for neighborhood" item, then, is not an entirely adequate surrogate for "real" fear, but it was the only one available.

The model emerging from consideration of these variables may be exemplified as follows:

education → black friends → response to urban unrest.

I assume that those with more education will be more likely to have black friends (or to sympathize with racial protest or to perceive discrimination) and that this intervening variable will link their higher educational attainment to their racial responses. Conversely, as our model suggests, ethnic groups with less education will be less likely to have black friends (or to sympathize with racial protest or to perceive discrimination) and hence more likely to respond with hostility to urban racial disturbances.

Because there was a moderate level of intercorrelation (table 2) among

TABLE 2

INTERCORRELATIONS AMONG POTENTIAL PREDICTORS OF RACIAL ATTITUDES

	1	2	3	4
1. Black friends	...	...	...	...
2. Fear for neighborhood (neighborhood racial quota)	.25	...	...	...
3. Sympathy for black protest	.18	.33	...	...
4. Perception of discrimination	.09	.29	.45	...
5. Intolerance	.14	.21	.34	.26

five of the items (excluding education, for the moment), a factor analysis was done. Two significant factors[5] emerged after rotation (table 3, A). The heaviest loadings on the first factor were sympathy for black protest and

[4] See Appendix B for measures of the six variables discussed in this section.
[5] An eigenvalue greater than .01 was used as the criterion of significance.

American Journal of Sociology

TABLE 3

FACTOR LOADINGS AMONG PREDICTOR VARIABLES

	I	II
A. Rotated Factors		
Intolerance	.155	.115
Sympathy for black protest	.523	.236
Perception of discrimination	.302	.002
Black friends	.030	.296
Fear for neighborhood	.112	.383
B. Support and Avoidance Factors		
Intolerance	.173	...
Sympathy for black protest	.274	...
Perception of discrimination	.586	...
Fear for neighborhood	...	.497
Black friends	...	.497

perception of discrimination. Black friends and the "neighborhood fear" items loaded most heavily on the second factor. Two scales were then constructed based, respectively, on factor analyses for the first three variables and for the last two (table 3, B). The first factor, with heavy loadings for sympathy and perception of discrimination and a less heavy loading for the intolerance scale, has been labeled the "support" factor because tolerance for diversity, perception of discrimination, and sympathy for black protest indicate a disposition toward positive support for blacks. The second factor has been called the "avoidance" factor because fear for neighborhood (represented by the desire to impose a quota on the number of blacks that could live in one's neighborhood) and absence of black friends seem to indicate both past avoidance and desire for future avoidance.

As can be seen in table 4, the three predictor variables—amount of education and scores on the support and avoidance scales—correlate quite well with the four dependent variables—support for a black mayor, support for civil rights laws, attitudes toward riot control, and support for interracial contact. Education is the least powerful of the three predictors. It is interesting to note in passing that education seems to have had little impact on people's feelings about how riots ought to be handled.

Both the avoidance and support variables correlated at reasonably high levels with the four dependent variables. Only one coefficient is under .20 (.15 between the avoidance factor and riot control). Another coefficient is .28 (between the support factor and riot control), but all the

Ethnicity and Racial Attitudes

TABLE 4

INTERCORRELATIONS OF PREDICTOR AND DEPENDENT VARIABLES

	1	2	3	4	5	6
1. Education	...	...	...	...	...	...
2. "Support" factor	.34	...	...	...	...	...
3. "Avoidance" factor	.27	.34	...	...	...	...
4. Would vote for black mayor	.21	.32	.38	...	...	...
5. Support for civil rights legislation	.17	.41	.35	.31	...	...
6. Riot control	.06	.28	.15	.13	.16	...
7. Interracial contact	.19	.39	.34	.42	.47	.16

others are above .30. Thus the hypothesis implicit in the previous paragraphs seems to have been supported: education, sympathy, perception of discrimination, "intolerant personality," and interaction with black friends all seem to have some impact on response to urban unrest.

It would be most helpful if there were some way to establish a causal relationship between the avoidance factor and the support factor (they correlate .34). However, there is no way to do this with the available data base. Thus, in the general model presented in figure 5, I assume that

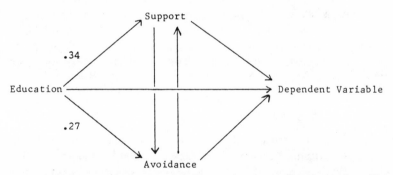

FIG. 5.—General model of the causal impact of education, support, and avoidance factors on racial attitude variables. Depending upon the data being analyzed, the dependent variable may be support for black mayor, civil rights legislation, repressive riot control, or interracial contact (coefficients with a β of less than .10 are omitted).

education has a causal impact on both support and avoidance. These in turn have causal impacts on the dependent variable, but I make no assumption about the causal relations between support and avoidance. It may well be that having black friends leads one to be more tolerant, more perceptive, and more sympathetic. But it may also be true that tolerance, perception, and sympathy generate a greater propensity to have black friends.

As shown in table 5, the model is moderately successful in explaining

American Journal of Sociology

TABLE 5

EDUCATION, SUPPORT, AND AVOIDANCE IN RELATION TO RACIAL ATTITUDES
(β'S AND R^2S)

Support for	Education	Support	Avoidance	R^2
Black mayor	...	.19	.29	.18
Civil rights legislation	...	.32	.24	.22
Repressive riot control	...	−.27	...	.09
Interracial contact	...	.25	.39	.30

NOTE.—All coefficients under .10 were eliminated from the table.

the variance in support for a black mayor, for civil rights legislation, and
for interracial contact. It is much less powerful in explaining variation
on the riot control scale. Perhaps civil rights laws, election of black mayors,
and sympathy for interracial contacts were less salient questions in the
15 cities studied in 1968 than control of riots.

   The avoidance factor is stronger than the support factor in explaining
sympathy for interracial contact and for a black mayor. The support
factor is stronger than the avoidance factor in explaining variation in attitudes toward civil rights laws, and it alone significantly influences attitudes toward riot control. People, then, appear to be against interracial
contact and a black mayor because they are afraid of or wish to avoid
blacks, but against civil rights laws and permissive riot control because
they cannot sympathetically support blacks. It is also worth noting that
there is no direct path between education and any of the dependent variables.

THE CASE OF THE JEWS AND THE POLES

In figures 1–4, the Jews and the Poles were most clearly differentiated in
their racial attitudes; they were in fact consistently opposed. Will the
explanatory model presented above assist us in specifying sources of the
observed differences between Jews and Poles on the four interracial scales?
Can the differences between Jews and Poles be traced to differences in
education, avoidance, and support? Table 6 presents, in the first row of
each panel, the raw differences in Z-scores between Poles and Jews and,
for comparison, between Poles and Irish Catholics, who, except for the
Jews, display the most liberal racial attitudes. The three succeeding rows
of each panel show how the raw differences are affected by standardizing
first for education, then for education and avoidance, and, finally, for
education, avoidance, and support.

   One can see at a glance that with one exception the variables of the
model do not completely convert the differences among the ethnic groups
to differences among racial attitudes. They do, however, make substantial

Ethnicity and Racial Attitudes

TABLE 6

Differences in Racial Attitudes between Jews and Poles and between Poles and Irish Catholics: Raw Differences between Z-Scores Followed by Successive Standardization for Education, Avoidance, and Support

	Poles and Jews	Poles and Irish Catholics
	A. Support for Black Mayor	
Raw difference	50	37
Standardized for education	37	32
Standardized for education and avoidance	55	21
Standardized for education, avoidance, and support	11	10
	B. Support for Civil Rights Legislation	
Raw difference	69	23
Standardized for education	59	19
Standardized for education and avoidance	53	14
Standardized for education, avoidance, and support	34	00
	C. Support for Repressive Riot Control	
Raw difference	30	30
Standardized for education	26	27
Standardized for education and avoidance	14	23
Standardized for education, avoidance, and support	08	16
	D. Support for Interracial Contact	
Raw difference	64	40
Standardized for education	51	34
Standardized for education and avoidance	47	26
Standardized for education, avoidance, and support	26	15

headway in that direction. The differences between the Poles and each of the other groups are cut in half at least, and in most cases they are cut to a third, a fourth, and even a fifth. Poles are more likely to be opposed to blacks than are Jews because the Poles have less education and have higher scores on the avoidance scale and lower scores on the support scale. To put the matter differently, Jews are more favorable to blacks than Poles are because they have better education, score lower on avoidance of blacks, and show higher support predispositions.

In the comparison between the Poles and the Jews, the greatest decline in difference occurs between the third and fourth rows in table 6 (with the exception of the riot control item in panel C). That is, even when the effect of education and the avoidance factor are taken into account, the most powerful explanation of differences between Poles and Jews has to do with the support factor.

American Journal of Sociology

The explanatory model eliminates most of the diversity among American ethnic groups on the four attitude scales (table 7). The Jews continue to be the strongest supporters of civil rights laws and interracial contact. The Slavic Catholics emerge as the strongest supporters for a black mayor,

TABLE 7

Z-Scores for Certain Ethnic Groups on Racial Attitudes, Controlling for Education, Avoidance, and Support

	Vote for Black Mayor	Civil Rights Laws	Riot Control*	Interracial Contact
British Protestants	—17	—04	00	03
Irish Catholics	07	04	—07	00
Italian Catholics	04	01	07	—02
Polish Catholics	03	03	10	—09
Other Slavic Catholics	25	—06	00	07
Jews	08	31	02	16

* High score indicates support for repression.

and the Irish Catholics as those most opposed (though not by very much) to oppressive riot control. Only two scores for negative racial attitudes reach or exceed 10, the 17-point English Protestant opposition to a black mayor and the 10-point Polish support for repressive riot control.

CAUSAL MODELS FOR THREE ETHNIC GROUPS

In this section I shall estimate the effect parameters of the model for each of the three ethnic groups with which I have been principally concerned: the Poles, the Jews, and the Irish Catholics (tables 8–11).

There is relatively little difference between the Poles and the Jews in the first portion of the model. Education correlates with the support factor at approximately the same level, and the correlation between the two factor scores is .42 for the Poles and .34 for the Jews. The Irish model, however seems substantially "looser." Education has relatively slight impact on avoidance for the Irish, and avoidance and support are more weakly related among them than among either the Poles or the Jews. Is this evidence of a political pragmatism among the Irish that inclines them to be less consistent than the other two groups?

For both the Jews and the Poles, only the avoidance factor is correlated above .10 with support for a black mayor (table 8), a pattern that is very different from the parameter estimates for the total sample presented in table 5. Jews are more inclined to support a black mayor because they do not fear blacks and they have black friends. Poles are less inclined to support a black mayor because they are afraid of blacks

Ethnicity and Racial Attitudes

TABLE 8

ESTIMATED EFFECT PARAMETERS FOR GENERAL MODEL (FIG. 5):
SUPPORT FOR BLACK MAYOR

	Education	Support	Avoidance	Mayor*
	A. Polish Catholic			
Education	...	†	.32	†
Support	...	...	.42	†
Avoidance	...	...	...	.42
Mayor	...	...	...	$R^2 = .20$
	B. Jewish			
Education	...	†	.28	†
Support	...	...	.34	†
Avoidance	...	...	...	.31
Mayor	...	...	...	$R^2 = .37$
	C. Irish Catholic			
Education	...	.24	.10	.28
Support	...	...	.22	.17
Avoidance	...	...	...	.16
Mayor	...	...	...	$R^2 = .18$

* The coefficients of correlation with the dependent variable are β's.
† Coefficients under .10 are eliminated. Coefficients which are irrelevant because of a less than .10 subsequent path (general model, fig. 5) are also eliminated.

and do not have black friends. In both cases, support for the black cause is less important than it is in the general population. But for the Irish, the strongest direct effect is from education, a finding that makes them, like the Poles and Jews, different from the total sample. Approximately half the explained variance in Irish support for a black mayor is a result of direct influence of education. Again, it may be that, for a group alleged to be politically pragmatic, such attitudes as are measured by the support and avoidance scales are not nearly as important as they are for other groups.

On the question of civil rights legislation (table 9), the Poles differ from the Jews and indeed from the general population. There is a direct effect of education on sympathy for civil rights laws, and the effect of avoidance on the latter variable is much stronger than that of support. The Irish and the Jews are basically similar to one another and similar to the national population in the causes of sympathy for civil rights legislation. Both differ from the Polish Catholics.

The estimated effects on attitudes toward riot control, however, differ across the three subsamples (table 10). For neither the Poles nor the Jews does avoidance have a significant effect on this variable. In this

American Journal of Sociology

TABLE 9

ESTIMATED EFFECT PARAMETERS FOR GENERAL MODEL (FIG. 5):
SUPPORT FOR CIVIL RIGHTS LEGISLATION

	Education	Support	Avoidance	Laws*
		A. Polish Catholic		
Education	...	.39	.32	.14
Support	...	...	.42	.15
Avoidance	...	...	...	.34
Laws	...	...	...	... $R^2 = .16$
		B. Jewish		
Education	...	.36	.28	†
Support	...	...	.34	.21
Avoidance	...	...	...	.23
Laws	...	...	...	... $R^2 = .15$
		C. Irish Catholic		
Education	...	.24	.10	†
Support	...	...	.22	.32
Avoidance	...	...	...	.31
Laws	...	...	...	... $R^2 = .25$

* The coefficients of correlation with the dependent variable are β's.
† Coefficients under .10 are eliminated. Coefficients which are irrelevant because of a less than .10 subsequent path (general model, fig. 5) are also eliminated.

respect they are like the total sample. Education has a significant effect on the riot-control variable for the Poles but not for the Jews. For the Irish, unlike the other two groups and the total sample, avoidance has a significant effect on support for repressive riot control.

Finally, as might be expected, there are for all three groups strong effects of avoidance on support for future interracial contact (table 11). Among the Poles, however, there is no effect of support on the latter variable. For the Jews the effect is moderate (.15), and for the Irish Catholics somewhat stronger (.24). In addition, for the Irish, education also has an effect on contact.

What is one to make of the intricacies and complexities of the relationships presented in tables 8–11? In most respects the Polish and Jewish results are more alike than those for either Poles or Jews and Irish Catholics. Indeed, were it not for the relationships between education and the dependent variables in tables 9 and 10, one might conclude that the antecedents of racial attitudes among the Poles and Jews were virtually the same. The Irish Catholics—the most "enlightened" on race of the non-Jewish groups—seem to respond to racial issues for a different mixture of reasons. More secure, perhaps in their American identity than the Poles but less committed to ideological liberalism than the Jews, the

Ethnicity and Racial Attitudes

TABLE 10

ESTIMATED EFFECT PARAMETERS FOR GENERAL MODEL (FIG. 5):
SUPPORT FOR REPRESSIVE RIOT CONTROL

	Education	Support	Avoidance	Riot Control*
		A. Polish Catholic		
Education	...	.39	.32	.19
Support	...	...	.42	—.28
Avoidance	...	...	...	†
Riot control	...	...	...	$R^2 = .08$
		B. Jewish		
Education	...	.36	.28	†
Support	...	...	.34	—.23
Avoidance	...	...	...	†
Riot control	...	...	...	$R^2 = .09$
		C. Irish Catholic		
Education	...	.24	.10	†
Support	...	...	.22	—.15
Avoidance	...	...	...	—.16
Riot control	...	...	...	$R^2 = .06$

* The coefficients of correlation with the dependent variable are β's.
† Coefficients under .10 are eliminated. Coefficients which are irrelevant because of a less than .10 subsequent path (general model, fig. 5) are also eliminated.

Irish may have developed a pattern of racial attitudes that is distinctly their own, different not only from that observed for the Poles and Jews but also from that found for the total sample.

No one who must deal with the complexity of ethnic diversity in the urban milieu can afford to act as though all population groups were alike. Not only were the religioethnic groups different from each other in their racial attitudes, they appear also to have differed in the sources of those attitudes.

THE ALIENATION OF THE POLES?

The model does not account fully for the different responses of the Poles and Jews to racial issues. Notably, years of education provide a very limited explanation of why Poles are high on avoidance and low on support and Jews are high on support and low on avoidance.

There are at least two explanations to fall back on. Perhaps there was something in the heritage that each group brought to the United States that predisposes its members distinctively toward what I have labeled support and avoidance of blacks. Perhaps something in each group's experiences in this country has made it either more or less suspicious of

American Journal of Sociology

TABLE 11

ESTIMATED EFFECT PARAMETERS FOR GENERAL MODEL (FIG. 5):
SUPPORT FOR INTERRACIAL CONTACT

	Education	Support	Avoidance	Contact*
A. Polish Catholic				
Education	...	†	.32	†
Support	...	...	.42	†
Avoidance	...	...	...	.65
Contact	...	...	...	... $R^2 = .43$
B. Jewish				
Education	...	.36	.28	†
Support	...	...	.34	.15
Avoidance	...	...	...	.49
Contact	...	...	...	... $R^2 = .31$
C. Irish Catholic				
Education	...	.24	.10	.13
Support	...	...	.22	.24
Avoidance	...	...	...	.44
Contact	...	...	...	... $R^2 = .35$

* The coefficients of correlation with the dependent variable are β's.
† Coefficients under .10 are eliminated. Coefficients which are irrelevant because of a less than .10 subsequent path (general model, fig. 5) are also eliminated.

other groups in the society (Thomas and Znaniecki 1918; Wytrwal 1961; Radzialowski 1974). Most probably there has been a complex interaction of the two explanations. There is a long Polish history of oppression and betrayal by strangers; but then there is nothing in Jewish history that would dispose that group to be very trusting either. Furthermore, the family structures of the two groups seem to be different (McCready 1973). The mother tends to be a much stronger figure in the family life of Jews than of Poles. It remains to be seen, though, whether or how family structure produces different responses to racial problems.

It is worth noting that the ancestors of most American Jews came from the same areas of eastern Europe as did the ancestors of most American Poles (Landes and Zborowski 1958). Furthermore, recent research indicates that, until the middle of the last century, Polish and Jewish elites worked together for the liberation of Poland from foreign rule. On the other hand, Polish immigrants did not come to the United States with a radical or socialist tradition like that of many Jewish immigrants, perhaps because Polish immigrants came predominantly from the farms and fields of southern Poland, while a far greater number of Jewish immigrants had urban backgrounds. So, the differences between the Poles and the Jews

Ethnicity and Racial Attitudes

in their racial attitudes may be rooted in the peasant origins of the one group and the more urban origins of the other. Both the Irish and Italian Catholics, however, also have peasant origins, and they react very differently from the Poles to racial questions.

The Jews have been much more successful in the United States than the Poles. Indeed, recent demographic research indicates that the Poles are lagging behind other Catholic ethnic groups in the pursuit of affluence (Greeley 1973). As a group, they may feel less accepted in American society. Less upwardly mobile than other ethnic groups, perhaps they are more disposed to be suspicious of those beneath them. Even a control for education would not eliminate such feelings; one may be educated and still feel one's group has not received an equal chance. The "other Slavic" group (non-Polish eastern European Catholics) is very different from the Poles in its response to racial questions. But then Slovaks, Slovenes, Czechs, and Lithuanians in the United States have not, as have the Poles, been special objects of derogatory jokes and opprobrium.

Are the Poles, then, especially prone to feelings of alienation? Three measures in the riot study are relevant to such feelings. They are measures of personal efficacy, citizen competence, and trust of government.[6] On all three, the Poles score substantially below the mean (table 12). The Irish

TABLE 12

Measures of "Alienation" for Certain Ethnic Groups (Z-Scores)

	Efficacy	Competence	Trust of Government
British Protestant	11	16	−12
Irish Catholics	−08	−15	26
Italian Catholics	−22	06	09
Polish Catholics	−11	−21	−14
Other Slavic Catholics	−04	−07	02
Jews	02	07	00

Catholics are somewhat low on efficacy and competence but high on trust in government (perhaps because in some cities they are the government). Italians are low on feelings of efficacy but above the mean on competence and trust. The scores for the Jewish subsample are quite close to the mean on all three items. Hence one might make a fairly persuasive case that there is an alienation syndrome among American Polish Catholics. But, unfortunately for our purposes, there does not seem to be much correlation between the efficacy, competence, and trust measures and the four measures of racial attitudes (table 13).

[6] See Appendix C.

American Journal of Sociology

TABLE 13

CORRELATIONS BETWEEN ALIENATION MEASURES AND
RACIAL ATTITUDES: TOTAL SAMPLE

	Trust	Efficacy	Competence
Vote for black mayor	.04	.04	.08
Civil rights legislation	.04	.05	.01
Riot control	.02	.01	.01
Racial contact	.02	.01	.02

Nevertheless, do these alienation measures correlate with racial attitudes among the Poles (see table 14)? In the Polish subsample, lack of

TABLE 14

CORRELATIONS BETWEEN ALIENATION MEASURES AND RACIAL ATTITUDES:
POLISH CATHOLICS ONLY

	Trust	Efficacy	Competence
Vote for black mayor	.20	.15	.16
Civil rights legislation	.08	.00	.21
Riot control	.31	.12	.23
Racial contact	.08	.02	.00
Support	.17	.07	—.06
Avoidance	.12	.12	—.12

trust in government correlates .20 or above with attitudes toward a black mayor and riot control; feelings of competence correlate above .20 with attitudes toward civil rights laws and riot control. For the Poles, there are certain modest relationships between alienation and racial attitudes. The relatively small correlations between the alienation variables and scores on the avoidance and support scales suggest that any influence of alienation on Polish attitudes is not channeled through our model. The concept of alienation would not greatly improve our capacity to explain why Poles are high on avoidance and low on support.

Clearly, the correlates of Polish racial attitudes and, indeed, the comparative analysis of these attitudes and their antecedents among the American religioethnic groups are fascinating and socially important questions that merit much further research.

CONCLUSION

The effort reported here is both tenuous and tentative. It attempts to offer some preliminary suggestions as to why different ethnic groups respond differently to urban unrest. Such explanations are not absent from

Ethnicity and Racial Attitudes

ordinary conversation about the cities of the United States. If the speculations in this paper have any merit at all, it lies in their having been submitted to a more precise sociological analysis than is the case in ordinary conversational speculation. Unfortunately, the tools for this analysis, while they are the best currently available, are far from adequate.

There is a strong tendency in contemporary social policy and even social research to assume that once the magic word "racism" is uttered all need for further understanding—to say nothing of compassion—has been eliminated. There may be every reason to suspect that bigotry lurks in every human personality (although the object of bigotry may vary); it may be that some of the fears of certain segments of the population have a basis in reality; it may be, indeed, that the very term "racism" has become broad enough to include so many different meanings that it now means nothing. However, it is only pragmatic wisdom that if one is going to have to deal with certain ethnic groups, one must attempt to understand the causes of the responses of those groups to racial issues. To write them off as racist and be done with them may well be socially and politically counterproductive.

APPENDIX A

Michigan Survey Questionnaire Items Used as Indicators of Racial Attitudes

RIOT CONTROL

Summative index based on first, second, and third choices in response to the question: what is the most important thing a city can do to prevent riots? (O. Other; 1. End discrimination; 2. Get tough.)

INTERRACIAL CONTACT

Cumulative index based on these items:

1. Suppose you had a job where your supervisor was a qualified Negro. Would you mind that a lot, a little, or not at all?

2. If a Negro family with about the same income and education as yours moved next door to you, would you mind a lot, a little, or not at all?

3. Who do you feel you could more easily become friends with—a Negro with the same education and income as yours, or a white person with a different education and income from yours?

4. If you had small children, would you rather they had only white friends, or would you like to see them have Negro friends too, or wouldn't you care one way or the other?

American Journal of Sociology

CIVIL RIGHTS LEGISLATION

Summative index based on these items:

1. Do you favor or oppose laws to prevent discrimination against Negroes in job hiring and promotion?

2. How about laws to prevent discrimination against Negroes in buying or renting houses and apartments? Do you favor or oppose such laws?

VOTE FOR CAPABLE BLACK MAYOR

Based on answers to the question: if a capable Negro of your own party preference were running for mayor of (central city), would you vote for him or not?

APPENDIX B

Michigan Survey Questionnaire Items Used as Basis of General Model

EDUCATION

Based on answers to the question: what is the highest grade of school you completed (from kindergarten through graduate or professional degree)?

BLACK FRIENDS

Summative index based on these items:

1. Are you friends with any of them (Negroes) who live around you?

2. Have you ever known Negroes outside this neighborhood with whom you were friends?

SYMPATHY WITH BLACK PROTESTS

Cumulative index based on these items:

1. Some people say these disturbances which occurred in Newark and Detroit in the summer of 1967 are mainly a protest by Negroes against unfair conditions. Others say they are mainly a way of looting and things like that. Which of these seems more correct to you?

2. Do you think the large disturbances like those in Detroit and Newark were planned in advance, or that there was some planning but not much, or weren't they planned at all?

3. If that (orderly marches to protest racial discrimination) doesn't help, do you think Negroes are justified in protesting through sit-ins?

4. Some Negro leaders are talking about having nonviolent marches

Ethnicity and Racial Attitudes

and demonstrations in several cities in 1968 to protest lack of opportunity for Negroes. Do you think such demonstrations are different from riots, or that there is no real difference?

5. Some say that Negroes have been pushing too fast for what they want. Others feel they haven't pushed fast enough. How about you—do you think Negroes are trying to push too fast, are going too slowly, or are moving at about the right speed?

PERCEPTION OF RACIAL DISCRIMINATION IN RESPONDENT'S CITY

Cumulative index based on these items:

1. It is sometimes said that the things we have just been talking about, such as unnecessary roughness and disrespect by the police, happen more to Negroes in (central city) than to white people. Do you think this is definitely so, probably so, probably not so, or definitely not so?

2. On the average, Negroes in (central city) have worse jobs, education, and housing than white people. Do you think this is due mainly to Negroes having been discriminated against, or mainly due to something about Negroes themselves?

3. Do you think that in (central city) many, some, or only a few Negroes miss out on jobs and promotions because of racial discrimination?

4. Do you think that in (central city) many, some, or only a few Negroes miss out on good housing because white owners won't rent or sell to them?

INTOLERANT PERSONALITY

Modified F-scale based on these items:

1. When you read about the long-haired hippies and people like that, do you feel some curiosity about their ideas, or do you feel mostly distaste for such people?

2. In schools do you think it's more important for children to learn about many different countries of the world or to concentrate on our own country's history and geography?

3. Do you favor trying out new ways of teaching subjects like arithmetic in schools, or do you think it's better to stick with the well-tried methods of the past?

NEIGHBORHOOD RACIAL QUOTA

Based on answers to the question: suppose there are 100 white families living in a neighborhood. One white family moves out and a Negro family moves in. Do you think it would be a good idea to have some limit on the

American Journal of Sociology

number of Negro families that move there, or to let as many move there as want to?

APPENDIX C

Michigan Survey Questionnaire Items Used as Basis of Alienation Measures.

PERSONAL EFFICACY

Cumulative index based on these items:

1. Have you usually felt pretty sure your life would work out the way you want it to, or have there been times when you haven't been sure about it?

2. Do you think it's better to plan your life a good way ahead, or would you say life is too much a matter of luck to plan ahead very far?

3. When you do make plans ahead, do you usually get to carry out things the way you expected, or do things usually come up to make you change your plans?

4. Some people feel they can run their lives pretty much the way they want to; others feel the problems of life are something too big for them. Which are you most like?

CITIZEN COMPETENCE

Summative index based on these items:

1. If you have a serious complaint about poor service by the city, do you think you can get city officials to do something about it if you call them?

2. Have you ever called a city official with a complaint about poor service?

TRUST OF GOVERNMENT

Summative index based on these items:

1. Do you think the mayor of (central city) is trying as hard as he can to solve the main problems of the city, or that he is not doing all he could to solve these problems? (If not doing all he could) do you think he is trying fairly hard to solve these problems, or not hard at all?

2. How about the state government? Do you think they are trying as hard as they can to solve the main problems of cities like (central city), or that they are not doing all they could to solve these problems? (If not doing all they could) do you think they are trying fairly hard to solve these problems, or not hard at all?

Ethnicity and Racial Attitudes

3. How about the federal government in Washington? Do you think they are trying as hard as they can to solve the main problems of cities like (central city), or that they are not doing all they could to solve such problems? (If not doing all they could) do you think they are trying fairly hard to solve these problems, or not hard at all?

REFERENCES

Campbell, Angus. 1971. *White Attitudes toward Black People*. Ann Arbor: Institute for Social Research, University of Michigan.
Greeley, Andrew M. 1972. "Political Attitudes among American White Ethnics." *Public Opinion Quarterly* 36 (Summer) 213–20.
——. 1973. "The Demography of Ethnic Identification I and II." Lithographed. Chicago: Center for the Study of American Pluralism, National Opinion Research Center
Greeley, Andrew M., and Paul B. Sheatsley. 1971. "Attitudes towards Desegregation." *Scientific American* 225 (December): 13–19.
——. 1973. "Attitudes toward Racial Integration: The South 'Catches Up.' " Pp. 240–50 in *Social Problems and Public Policy: I. Inequality and Justice*, edited by Lee Rainwater. Chicago: Aldine.
Landes, Ruth, and Mark Zborowski. 1958. "Hypotheses concerning the Eastern European Jewish Family." Pp. 58–76 in *Social Perspectives on Behavior*, edited by Herman D Stein and Richard A. Cloward. Glenview, Ill.: Free Press.
Litt, Edgar. 1970. *Ethnic Politics in America*. Glencoe, Ill.: Scott, Foresman.
McCready, William C. 1973. "Ethnic Family Structures: Styles of Intimate Relationship." Lithographed. Chicago: Center for the Study of American Pluralism, National Opinion Research Center.
Myrdal, Gunnar. 1969. *An American Dilemma*. New York: Harper & Row.
Nie, Norman H., Barbara Currie, and Andrew M. Greeley. 1974. "Political Attitudes among American Ethnics: A Study of Perceptual Distortion." *Ethnicity* 1 (December): 317–43.
Radzialowski, Thaddeus. 1974. "The View from the Polish Ghetto: Some Observations on the First Hundred Years in Detroit." *Ethnicity* 1 (July): 125–50.
Thomas, William I., and Florjan Znaniecki. 1918. *The Polish Peasant in Europe and America*. Chicago: University of Chicago Press.
Wytrwal, Joseph A. 1961. *America's Polish Heritage: A Social History of the Poles in America*. Detroit: Endurance.

ANDREW M. GREELEY
University of Chicago

A Model for
Ethnic Political Socialization*

A model is presented to analyze the transmission of political values across generational lines. The variables within the model are social class, parental value, family
structure, and "ethnic heritage" (a residual variable). Political values do differ among
ethnic groups both in the parental and adolescent generation. Ethnicity tends to be a
stronger predictor of adolescent values than parental education. Some groups are more
effective in transmitting values than others. While family structure does not shape the
political values of the whole population, it does influence the transmission of values
within certain ethnic groups.

In the present paper we address two great debates current in American
social science: that of the family and political socialization, and that of the
nature and importance of ethnicity in American society.

The debate on ethnicity is complicated by the fact that it is not clear what
constitutes an ethnic group in American society, and until the terms of the
theoretical controversy are clarified we must be content with saying that an
ethnic group is one defined by race, religion, nationality, language, or some
combination of those that is generally recognized as a distinctive group in
American society and is large enough to provide adequate numbers of
respondents for analysis in the typical representative national survey sample.

We asked five questions about the political socialization of American
ethnics:

1. Are the political values of young people influenced by their ethnic
background?

2. If such an influence exists, to what extent is it the result of direct
parental socialization, and to what extent does it seem to be a function of an
ethnic subculture that operates independently of the young person's propensity to imitate his parents' values?

*I wish to thank Norman Nie, M. Kent Jennings, William McCready, John Petrocik,
and Shirley Saldanha for their help in writing this paper.

188 *Andrew M. Greeley*

3. If indeed there is such a thing as an ethnic political subculture, is it in fact merely a social status subculture that results in a correlation between ethnicity and social class?

4. Are there differences in family structure among certain American ethnic groups, differences which are predictable from the existing literature?

5. Finally, if such differences in family structure exist, do they correlate with differences in political values?

The issues raised in these questions can be stated in the five-variable model in Figure 1. The first variable, ethnic subculture, is a residual variable not specified in the present analysis. It represents those traits, values, and experiences and predispositions which a given ethnic collectivity carries both because of its Old World background and its experiences since arriving in the United States (the Irish predisposition to political careers, for example). Operational measures for the other four variables—social class, family struc-

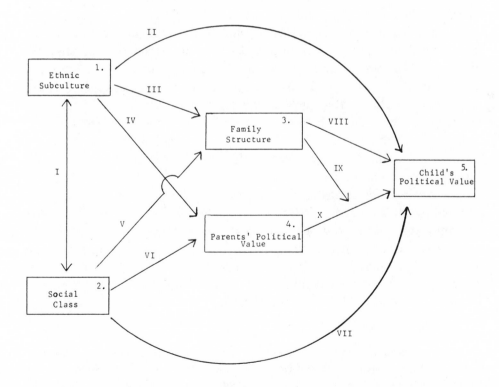

FIGURE 1

A Model for Political Socialization within an Ethnic Collectivity

A Model for Ethnic Political Socialization   189

ture, parent's political value and child's political value, are available in the data we will analyze.

Of the ten paths in the model, path I (ethnicity-social class) will be assumed. Social class-parents' political value (VI) has already been established by the research of Jennings and his colleagues (Jennings and Niemi, 1968a,b; Jennings and Langton, 1969). The other eight paths will be examined here. We note that path IX, leading from family structure to the line connecting parents' political value and child's political value, represents an interaction term, that is, the propensity of certain forms of family structure to facilitate or impede direct transmission of a political value from parent to child.

The model hypothesizes four direct paths of political socialization within an ethnic collectivity. A child's political value may be influenced directly by the political value of his parents (X), by the family structure that is peculiar to his ethnic collectivity (VIII), by the social class background of his family (VII), and by those aspects of the ethnic subculture which are not mediated through either family structure or parents' political values (II). We also hypothesize that both family structure and parents' political value are influenced by ethnic subculture and by social class (III, IV, VI).

There is no reason why numbers could not be put on the paths of our model (whether they come from parametric or nonparametric analysis) save that in the data set we are analyzing there are simply not enough cases in any ethnic group to justify a serious attempt to fit the data to the model. The somewhat complex strategy used in this paper has been imposed upon us by the limited size of each ethnic group in our sample. We think that for those interested in ethnic political socialization, to obtain information about a much larger number of respondents within the given ethnic groups is of the highest order of importance.

The data we used to answer our questions were taken from the 1965 study directed by M. Kent Jennings (1971). In Table 1 we present the distribution of family (one parent and one adolescent child) by major ethnic groups. In our analysis we are concerned particularly with four ethnic groups, the Irish and Italian Catholics, Scandinavian Protestants, and Jews.[1] The theoretical perspectives gained from family structure literature (to be discussed later) inclined us to expect structural and behavioral differences among these four groups.[2]

[1] Both parents and children were asked their religion. In those cases where there was a different religion between parent and child, the respondent was excluded. In the ethnicity question, the parent was asked what country he was born in; if the U.S. he was asked what country his parents were born in; if the U.S. he was asked what country his father's ancestors came from.

[2] There were two reasons for *not* including blacks in this analysis:

190   *Andrew M. Greeley*

TABLE 1

Distribution of American
Religioethnic Groups in Jennings'
Intergenerational Survey

Ethnic Group	Number
White	
Protestant	
British	268
Irish	77
Scandinavian	65
German	200
"American"	502
Catholic	
Irish	49
German	57
East European	45
Italian	62
Spanish-speaking	25
Jewish	76
Black	183

Ethnicity and the Political Values of Two Generations

Table 2 gives the correlation between parental value and adolescent value for each ethnic group and the rank order correlations of the groups in the first and second generations.[3] As Jennings and his colleagues indicated in their own publication (Jennings, 1971), it is clear that there is only a low to moderate correlation between parental political values and adolescent politi-

---

(a) Given the nature of our approach it seemed necessary to hold race constant so that a racial variable would not confound the religioethnic variable. Indeed, if there were enough groups within one denominational category (Protestant or Catholic) it would have been appropriate to hold denomination constant also.

(b) The literature on the black family, while more extensive than that on the Irish or Scandinavian families, is inconclusive. It would be hard to predict where the black families would fall on measures being used.

An auxiliary publication is available from the author which provides information on the scores of blacks of both generations (which indicates, incidentally, that when educational level is held constant they are rather like the American mean). For a review of the available literature on the socialization of blacks and other minority groups, see Young (1969). For black socialization experience specifically, see Marvick (1965).

[3] The auxiliary publication available from the author contains a description of the times used in the scales, the sampling techniques, and the detailed tables from which Table 2 is constructed. A description of the scale is also available in the ICPR codebook of the Jennings (1971) study.

TABLE 2

Political Values among Four American Ethnic Groups by Generation

Political Value	Irish					Italians					Scandinavians					Jews				
	Parents		Children			Parents		Children			Parents		Children			Parents		Children		
	Score[a]	Rank[b]	Score	Rank	r*	Score	Rank	Score	Rank	r	Score	Rank	Score	Rank	r	Score	Rank	Score	Rank	r
Social trust	24	3	07	6	.05	-16	9	02	9	.27	39	1	18	3	.02	-12	7	-08	10	.24
Civic tolerance	24	3	07	6	.17	-26	12	-02	8	.28	43	1	10	5	.28	35	2	16	4	.15
Political efficacy	13	5	33	3	.08	-08	8	-04	7	.04	35	1	10	5	.01	24	3	35	2	.21
Ego strength	21	2	26	2	.07	-22	10	-43	12	.03	09	4	43	1	.09	-36	11	11	4	.12
Cosmopolitanism	27	3	25	3	-.03	21	4	-01	9	.28	14	6	41	1	.37	35	1	35	2	.11
Political cynicism	-40	12	-10	7	.39	-38	11	-18	10	.22	08	4	-16	8	.22	11	3	-06	6	.04
Political activity	14	5	28	1	.15	-06	9	-11	11	.24	50	1	10	4	.04	39	2	25	2	.24
Political knowledge	51	2	28	2	.14	08	7	-17	10	.39	26	4	19	4	.12	63	1	65	1	.37
Ideology	-30	10	-12	10	-.02	24	3	01	4	.36	-31	11	-12	10	.27	-47	12	-11	9	.45

*Correlation between parental score and adolescent score in each ethnic group.

[a]Scores represent standardized points deviating from mean for generation. 1.00 = 1 standard deviation. Scores are the percentage of standard deviation above or below the mean.

[b]Rank is the rank of the group within its own generation among the twelve major groups.

192 *Andrew M. Greeley*

cal values, but it is also clear that the various ethnic groups sort themselves in relatively the same order in both generations. Only one of the rank order correlations was not significant. Thus on the ego-strength scale (the scale might be considered to measure "stubbornness") Irish Catholics are second in both generations, but the correlation between parent and adolescent on this variable is only .07. Ego strength seems to be part of the Irish Catholic subculture, but it does not seem to be handed on directly from parent to child. There is then, some reason to believe on the basis of Table 2 that there are ethnic political subcultures which are transmitted to a considerable extent independently of the direct influence of parental values on child values.

Of the four groups we are particularly interested in, Irish Catholic adolescents are substantially above the mean on political efficacy, ego strength, cosmopolitanism, political activity, and political knowledge. They are substantially below the mean on cynicism and on the perception of sharp ideological differences between the parties. In all cases the scores of the Irish Catholic adolescents reflect more or less similar positions on the same scales for their parents, although only on the scale of political cynicism is there a strong correlation between parental and adolescent position. The Irish appear to be political sophisticates in both generations, with a strong sense of political efficacy, high level of cosmopolitanism, a low level of cynicism, and a high level of political activity and knowledge.

Their adolescent Italian coreligionists are beneath the mean on political efficacy, civic tolerance, ego strength, political activity, and political knowledge. In each case they reflect scores beneath the mean of their parents. Italians of both generations seem to be neither political activists nor political sophisticates.

Jews of both generations are beneath the mean on social trust but substantially above it on political efficacy, civic tolerance, cosmopolitanism, political activity, and political knowledge. Indeed, Jews of both generations have the highest rank on the political knowledge scale and the second highest rank on the political activity scale. Jewish teenagers are also second on the cosmopolitanism scale (their parents rank number one) and second on the political efficacy scale (their parents rank third). Like the Irish, the Jews seem to be both political participators and political sophisticates.

Finally, Scandinavians of both generations are above the mean on social trust, civic trust, ego strength, cosmopolitanism, political activity, and political knowledge. They are below the mean on perception of sharp ideological differences between the two parties. Scandinavians, like the Irish and the Jews, are political sophisticates and activists, but they are more likely than Jews and Irish of either generation to be high on social trust and, with the exception of the second generation of Jews, to be high on civic tolerance. Thus the Scandinavian political culture seems to involve not only political activism and sophistication but also a certain civic-mindedness, which is less likely to be found among the Irish and the Jews.

Ethnicity, Parental Values, and Social Class

There are apparently ethnic political subcultures which are passed on from generation to generation, with direct parental influence playing only a limited role in the transmission of such political values. But to what extent are these ethnic subcultures in fact social status subcultures? To answer this, we attempted a multiple classification analysis in which the dependent variable was the adolescent's political value and the three predictor variables were the political value of the parent (measuring the impact of direct socialization), the education of the head of the family (measuring roughly the family's social (status), and the father's religioethnic identification. Table 3 presents the unadjusted and the standardized etas for each of nine dependent variables.[4] The relationship between education and political value is statistically significant seven of the nine times (only social trust and political cynicism seem to be independent of social status as measured by education). The influence of parental values, controlled for education and ethnicity, is significant eight times, with only adolescent civic tolerance being immune from the influence of the parental value. Finally, ethnicity, controlled for the effects of education and parental attitude, is statistically related to the adolescent political value eight times, with only the perception of ideological differences between the parties not significantly related to ethnicity.

Ethnicity, then, is a stronger predictor of adolescent values than is the social status of the family (as measured by the head of the family's education) six of the nine times, and education is a stronger predictor than ethnicity only two of the nine times (civic tolerance and ideology). Ethnicity is a stronger predictor than parental score on the same value five times, though it is less strong than parents' score on the same value four times. It would surely seem that there are ethnic political subcultures that are not the same as social class subcultures and which are transmitted across generational lines, in part at least, independent of direct influence of parents on children. The mean adjusted eta for ethnicity is 13.7, for education, 12.5, for parental value, 12.3. All three factors influence adolescent behavior to some extent, and ethnicity is by no means the weakest of the three.

[4] The multiple classification analysis is described in Andrew, Morgan, and Sonquist (1967).

194   *Andrew M. Greeley*

TABLE 3

Adolescent Political Values by Education of Parent,
Parental Ethnicity, and Parental
Political Value: A Multiple Classification Analysis

Political Value	Unadjusted Eta			Adjusted Eta		
	Education	Parental Value	Ethnicity	Education	Parental Value	Ethnicity
Social trust	.07	.12	.21	.04	.08	.19
Civic tolerance	.28	.13	.19	.25	.06	.12
Political efficacy	.18	.14	.18	.13	.08	.15
Ego strength	.13	.14	.19	.09	.12	.17
Cosmopolitanism	.15	.21	.16	.10	.19	.12
Political cynicism	.02	.16	.12	.02	.16	.12
Political activity	.14	.11	.13	.13	.08	.13
Political knowledge	.29	.33	.18	.16	.21	.18
Ideology	.23	.20	.11	.19	.14	.08

Ethnicity and Family Structure

In a review of the family structure literature, Straus (1964) argues that much of the research he reviews on family structure indicates that two "reference axes" may be used to array patterns of interaction or personality. Relying on the work of many authors, he contends that the two principal axes in family structure are "power" and "support." He defines *power* as "actions which control, initiate, change, or modify the behavior of another member of the family" (Straus, 1964, p. 18). *Support* is "actions which establish, maintain, or restore, as an end in itself, a positive affective relationship with another family member" (Straus, 1964, p. 18). A two-by-two model like the one developed by Straus is presented in Figure 2. Straus suggests that the most effective transmission of parental values will take place in the upper left quadrant, where both power and support are the strongest. He does not suggest, although it seems to follow logically, that the second most effective direct socialization will take place in the upper right quadrant, where if power is low, support is still high. Young people are not forced by power to imitate their parents. but are won by the relaxed and democratic styles of the family. They imitate their parents voluntarily. It would also suggest that the least effective direct socialization will occur in the lower left-hand corner, because in a situation where power is strongly concentrated

A Model for Ethnic Political Socialization   195

in the family and support is weak, there will be a propensity to rebel against explicit parental values. Finally, in the lower right, where both support and power are low, socialization will be more effective than it will be in the rebellious lower left quadrant, but less effective than in the upper half of the diagram. The numbers we have placed in the quadrants indicate our expectations of the relative effectiveness of direct socialization.

The literature on ethnic family structures in the United States is not extensive. However, the Italians (about whom the literature is the most extensive) clearly belong in the upper left-hand quadrant. The Italian family is warm and affectionate, but power is concentrated in the hands of a strong, paternal personage (Tomasi, 1972). The Jewish family has traditionally been

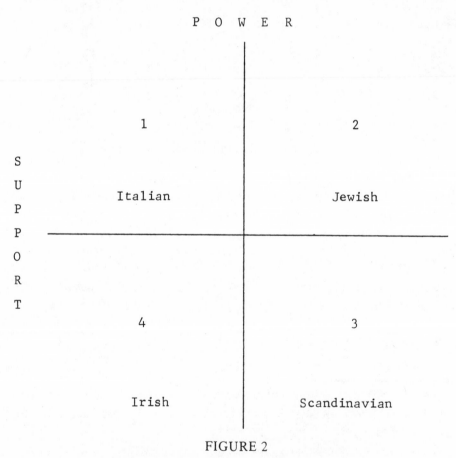

FIGURE 2

Power, Support, and a Hypothesized Ranking of
"Value Transmission Effectiveness" with the Hypothesized
Distribution of Four American Ethnic Groups

196   *Andrew M. Greeley*

both strongly affectionate and democratic, if only because of the relative strength of the Jewish mother (Landes and Zborowski, 1958; Wolfenstein, 1955). Thus the Jewish family seems to belong in the upper right quadrant. The Irish family is ordinarily described as both unaffectionate and undemocratic, with a very strong father in rural Ireland and an autocratic mother who overwhelms both father and children in urban Ireland and urban United States (Stein, 1972; Greeley, 1972). The Irish would fit in the lower left-hand quadrant. Finally, the Scandinavian family, about which much less is known than the other three, seems to belong in the lower right-hand quadrant. The Scandinavian, or at least the Swedish, family is relatively democratic and low on explicit support and affection.

To confirm our hypothesized distribution of the four ethnic family structures and to see whether they can in fact be ranked in the effectiveness of direct political socialization, we looked at a number of questions in Jennings' study (1971) which could measure both the concentration of decisionmaking power and the levels of affection in a family. Since his questions were asked of both generations, it was possible to view the family structure from the perspectives of both parents and adolescents. An oblique factor analysis with Kaiser normalization was attempted on a number of these items, and two factors did emerge which seemed to measure roughly support and power.[5] The first factor (power) loads heavily on items measuring the young person's perception of his influence in the decisionmaking of the family, hence the democratic structure of the family.[6] The second factor (support) loads heavily on items measuring the student's perception of his closeness to his parents and the parents' perception of closeness to their parents when they were children.

---

[5] The word "roughly" here is important since, as in most attempts to fit secondary analysis to concepts derived from other research, there is a different shading of meaning. In Straus' paradigm a high-power family is one in which decisionmaking is concentrated in the hands of parents; the "control, modification, initiation" of behavior tends to be from parent to child. Our factor taps the young person's perception of his influence on decisionmaking. A high score on this factor implies that power is not concentrated solely in the parental generation. One would of course like to know much more about the initiation and control of behavior by both generations among various ethnic groups. To what extent, for example, do adolescents control the behavior of their parents, and does this differ among groups?

[6] The items loading on the "power" factor were student influence on family decision (.668), student freedom to complain about family decisions (.732), and effectiveness of complaint (.799). On the support factor the items were student closeness to father (.577), student closeness to mother (.563), parent closeness to own father (.525), parent closeness to own mother (.554), parent closeness to child (.686).

A Model for Ethnic Political Socialization   197

TABLE 4

Rank Order of Four American Ethnic Groups on the
Support and Power Scales
(Standardized Points)

Support		Power	
Ethnic Group	Score	Ethnic Group	Score
Italian Catholics	33	Italian Catholics	19
Jews	14	Irish Catholics	08
Irish Catholics	−19	Scandinavian Protestants	−09
Scandinavian Protestants	−24	Jews	−32

We would expect the Irish and the Italians to be high on the power factor, the Jews and the Scandinavians low. The Jews and Italians should be high on the support factor, the Irish and the Scandinavians low. In Table 4 we note that more than half a standard deviation separates the Italians and the Scandinavian Protestants on the support scale and the Italians and Jews on the power scale. (We should note here, incidentally, that there is no correlation between either the support scale or the power scale and the social status of the family as measured by the education of the head of the family.)

Does family structure as measured by power and support factors predict the effectiveness of direct parent-child political socialization? Are the Italians the most effective in transmitting political values to their children and the Irish the least effective? Table 5 indicates that the predicted ordering does exist in reality. The average intergenerational correlation on the nine political value scales is .215 for the Italians, .213 for the Jews, .146 for the Scandinavians, and .122 for the Irish Catholics. The Italians and the Jews are virtually tied for first place of the twelve religioethnic groups, and the Scandinavians and the Irish Catholics are at the bottom of the list, with their average intergenerational correlations being higher only than that of the German Protestants There are not only ethnic political subcultures, there are also ethnic family structures, some of which are much more favorably disposed than others to the direct transmission of political values.

The question arises: Might it be that in addition to facilitating or impeding the effectiveness of the family as a direct agent of political socialization, the structure of the family itself may be involved in the transmission of political values? For example, are Italian adolescents less likely to be politically involved not only because their parents are less likely to be involved but also

198   *Andrew M. Greeley*

TABLE 5

Rank Order of American
Ethnic Groups on Average
Correlation of Nine Political
Value Scales between Parents
and Adolescents

Ethnic Group	Score
Italian Catholic	.215
Jewish	.213
East European Catholic	.183
Irish Protestant	.172
German Catholic	.163
Spanish-speaking	.163
American Protestant	.160
Black	.152
British	.151
Scandinavian	.146
Irish Catholic	.122
German Protestant	.105

because there is something in the dynamic of Italian family life which leads of itself and independent of parental values to lower levels of political interest or concern? We have come full circle in our argument. While there is little evidence in the general American society (as noted by Jennings and his colleagues) that family structure influences political values, perhaps within certain ethnic groups family structure influences political values. We are clearly within a very speculative area, and we are using measures designed for purposes other than those for which we use them here. Hence this phase of our analysis must be considered extremely tentative.

First of all. there is in the general population only one correlation between the two family structure scales and the nine political value scales we are using that is higher than .1, and that is a correlation of .12 between the power factor and the perception of sharp ideological differences between political parties. Thus, although our measures are different from Jennings', we come to the same conclusion—that for the national population family structure does not seem to influence the political values of adolescents.

But does family structure exercise such influence within the various ethnic subcollectivities? The Italian family is the best test case, because Italian political participation is low and the Italian family is strong on power and support, which might be thought to lend the family a self-sufficiency that

A Model for Ethnic Political Socialization   199

would obviate the need for adolescents to involve themselves in other institutions.

Table 6 generally confirms this expectation. The stronger family support is in the Italian family, the weaker is trust, tolerance, cosmopolitanism, and political knowledge. Tolerance and political knowledge also correlate negatively with power in the Italian family, although political activity correlates positively with power. Its strong support mechanisms, then, incline the offspring of Italian families to be less concerned about the outside world (low on both cosmopolitanism and political knowledge) and also more suspicious of the outside world (low on trust and tolerance). Furthermore, the strong concentration of power in the Italian family also correlates negatively with interest and positively with suspicion—though it is in those Italian families where power is most strongly concentrated that somewhat higher levels of political activity are likely to be found.

For the Jewish family one might expect just the opposite. Political participation and the absence of suspicion might be heightened by the democratic style of the family and perhaps reinforced by its strong internal cohesion and warmth. It indeed turns out to be the case that the more democratic the Jewish family is (that is, the lower on the power scale), the more tolerant the adolescent and the more likely he is to be involved in political activity. Furthermore, ego strength (stubbornness), on which Jewish adolescents are much more likely to score high than are their parents (see Table 2), also correlates negatively with power (and hence positively with democratic style). The more democratic the family, the stronger the ego strength of the Jewish adolescent. Power in the Jewish family correlates positively only with cosmopolitanism, and there are no correlations between political values and family support for the Jewish family.

It is somewhat harder to elaborate expectations for the Irish family. But one might predict that interest in politics for the Irish could result from strong family power constraints. The Irish young person is so busy calculating the implicit, unspoken conflicts over power in his family that he has a predisposition to be interested in the exercise of power wherever it occurs. However, it would only be in the Irish families where there is some encouragement and warmth that children could work up enough courage to be actually involved in politics.

It is precisely in the high power-concentration Irish families that one is most likely to find higher scores of political knowledge—and also more cynicism, weakened ego strength, and weaker social trust. Furthermore, while the support level is low in the Irish family, still it is in those families where there is more support than the average that the higher level of political

200   *Andrew M. Greeley*

TABLE 6

Correlations between Family Structure Scales and Political Values

Political Value	Scandinavian		Irish		Italian		Jewish	
	Support	Power	Support	Power	Support	Power	Support	Power
Social trust	-.16	—	—	-.37	-.27	—	—	—
Tolerance	—	—	—	—	-.45	-.15	—	-.25
Efficacy	—	—	—	-.29	—	—	—	—
Ego strength	—	—	—	—	—	—	—	-.18
Cosmopolitanism	—	—	—	—	-.31	—	—	.26
Political cynicism	—	—	—	.24	-.21	—	—	—
Political activity	—	—	.20	—	—	.21	—	.20
Political knowledge	-.19	—	-.33	.16	-.18	-.27	—	—
Ideology	—	—	—	—	—	-.23	—	—

Note: Only correlations larger than .15 are shown.

A Model for Ethnic Political Socialization 201

activity is to be found, as well as a lower propensity to see sharp ideological cleavage between the parties.

Finally, one might ask whether the stronger "civic-mindedness" of the Scandinavian adolescents might relate to the democratic structure of the Scandinavian family. In fact, however, the opposite seems to be the case. Civic trust (and political knowledge) relate negatively not to power but to support in the Scandinavian family. One finds higher levels of trust and of political knowledge precisely in the Scandinavian families where affection seems to be the lowest. In three of the four cases, then, our tentative expectations about the relationship between family structure and political values were at least partially confirmed. Only with the Scandinavians could we find no support for our expectations.

It is interesting to note in Table 6 the different relationships that family structures have for various ethnic groups on political knowledge and political activity. For the Italians political activity correlates positively with a strong concentration of power in the family; for the Jews it correlates negatively. For the Irish there is a positive correlation between political activity and the support factor. Political knowledge correlates positively with power concentration for the Irish and negatively with power concentration for the Italians. It correlates negatively with support for both the Scandinavians and the Italians. The Irish who are the most likely to be politically knowledgeable come from power-concentrated families. The Scandinavians who are the most likely to be politically knowledgeable come from weak-support families. The Italians with high political knowledge come from families with weak power concentration and weak social support. The activist Italians come from high-power families, activist Jews from low-power families, and the activist Irish from high-support families.

We conclude, then, that while the fit is not perfect and many uncertainties and obscurities remain, there is a relationship between family structure and political values in various ethnic collectivities. These relationships run one way in some ethnic groups and in the opposite direction in others.

There are ethnic subcultures which transmit different political values to the children born within these cultures. The ethnic subcultures have different family structures. These family structures affect the strength of the direct parent-child political socialization, with the family structures in some ethnic subcultures being much more successful at passing the explicit values of parents to the children. But, in addition, the family structure itself, quite independently of specific values of the parents, is also a socializing institution that transmits the ethnic culture independently of explicit parental values. Italians, for example, are likely to be low political participators because their

202   *Andrew M. Greeley*

TABLE 7

Differences between Italian and Jewish Adolescents
in Two Political Values
(Jewish "Lead" in Standardized Points)

	Political Activity	Civic Tolerance
Raw differences	43	21
Net of parental value	41	16
Net of parental value and parental education	24	− 9
Net of parental value, education, and power factor	23	−11
Net of parental value, education, power factor, and support factor	24	−16

Note: Scores were obtained by multiple classification analysis
with two categories (above and below the mean) for the value and
factor scores, and three categories for education (grammar, high
school, and college).

TABLE 8

Differences between Irish and Jewish
Adolescents in Social Trust
(Irish "Lead" in Standardized Points)

	Social Trust
Raw differences	13
Net of parental value	10
Net of parental value and parental education	11
Net of parental value, education, and power factor	12
Net of parental value, education, power factor, and support factor	11

A Model for Ethnic Political Socialization   203

parents are low political participators, because the strength and warmth of the Italian family more effectively communicates low participation values across generational lines, and because the structure itself—independent of specific parental attitudes—produces lower levels of political interest and higher levels of political suspicion.

The Jews are high political participators in part because of higher social status, in part because Jewish parents are more likely to be high participators, in part because Jewish family structure facilitates the direct transmission of parents' participation values to their children, and finally because the democratic structure of the family itself, independent of specific parental values, creates a higher propensity for political activism.

Ethnic political cultures, then, are handed on in part directly through children imitating their parents, in part both directly and indirectly because family structure increases the amount of imitation, and in part indirectly because family structure acts as an independent variable with an impact of its own for some ethnic groups on some political values.

What happens to our socialization model when various controls are introduced for selected political values on which differences between two groups are considerable? Tables 7 and 8 illustrate two examples.

Jewish adolescents and Italian adolescents are rather different from each other, both in their scores on political activity and civic tolerance, with the Jews in both cases having higher scores than the Italians. The difference in political activity is diminished by 17 points by a control for parental education. None of the other factors in the model seem to have much impact. When parental education is taken into account, Jewish adolescents are still more likely to be politically active than Italian adolescents, though the difference has been narrowed somewhat.

However, on the subject of civic tolerance the model operates in another manner. Jewish adolescents are 21 points higher on civic tolerance than Italians. When parental values are taken into account, the difference diminishes to 16. When parental education is taken into account the Italians actually become 9 points more tolerant than the Jews; and when the two family factors are taken into account the Italian lead is increased to 16 points. Social class, in other words, accounts for a change of 25 points, and the other variables in the socialization model account for 16 additional points in the change.

Then there are some variables on which the model has almost no impact. The Irish are somewhat more likely than the Jews to score high on social trust (Table 8), but none of the controls introduced affect the difference very much. The slight propensity of Irish adolescents to be more trusting than

204   *Andrew M. Greeley*

Jews is not a function of education or parental values or family structure, and
to the extent that it represents a meaningful difference at all, it must be
attributed to some residual cultural difference not accounted for by our
model.

Summary and Concluding Remarks

To return to the model in Figure 1, only one of the paths (V) has not been
confirmed. There appears to be no relationship between social class and
family structure as measured by our two factors. Path II, measuring the direct
relationship between ethnic heritage and adolescent behavior, independent of
both parental value and family structure, is confirmed in some cases and not
confirmed in others. In the matter of the differences between Italians and
Jews in political activity, there is a substantial difference between the two
groups when the effect of all the variables in the model has been taken into
account, as we saw in Table 8. Thus ethnic heritage seems to have an
independent influence outside the family socialization environment. On the
other hand, the differences between Italians and Jews on civic tolerance is
eliminated by our model, and indeed it is turned in the opposite direction.
One could then conceive of path II either being eliminated from the application of our model to civic tolerance, or the ethnic heritage having the
opposite effect of the one that first appears. Pure ethnic heritage—net of the
socialization model—seems to make the Italians more tolerant than Jews
rather than less.

We shall conclude with four comments:

1. The model presented in this paper does not require ethnic "consciousness." Insofar as the model explains differences in values among adolescents
in the various ethnic groups it does so in terms of the socialization process.
For example, the diminution and then reversal of the difference between
Jews and Italians in civic tolerance (see Table 8) can be explained quite
independently of whether Jewish adolescents are particularly conscious of
being Jewish. Ethnic self-consciousness might, of course, modify the findings
presented in Table 8, but it is not required to explain it; the differences are
explained and then reversed by variables already built into the model.

2. Given the persistence of moderate differences in political values among
the adolescents in the various ethnic subcultures that results from the impact
of socialization and family structure, it becomes justifiable to raise the
question about differences in other areas of values and behavior besides the
political. The model presented in this paper could easily be used to explore
other dimensions of ethnic socialization.

A Model for Ethnic Political Socialization   205

3. Because the ethnic socialization model does explain some or all of the differences between some ethnic groups, it does not follow that the transmission of ethnically linked values and behaviors across generational lines is purely a matter of the family socialization experience. Path II, in other words, will in some cases be the only one on which one can expect to find a strong coefficient; and since it is, in effect, a residual path, under such circumstances the model would not work at all.

The Irish are an ethnic group concerning which one would have to turn almost completely to a nonfamilial explanation for the transmission of ethnic culture. There is a very low intergenerational correlation in political values, and, while family structure does have some impact on the effectiveness of direct parental transmission of values to children, it is nowhere near a large enough impact to explain why in both generations the Irish are political activists. Thus variables must be at work in the Irish subculture, distinct from the immediate family socialization experience, that transmit a high propensity to political activism across generational lines. For example, the Irish propensity to seek political related careers might lead to high levels of activism regardless of the behavior of one's own parents.

4. It would appear that ethnic subcultures are useful areas for research in value socialization. Phenomena not found in the larger society may occur within ethnic groups. However, much larger samples of the various ethnic subcultures would be required if the research is to be anything more than tentative.

Manuscript submitted March 28, 1974.
Final manuscript received July 19, 1974.

REFERENCES

Andrew, Frank; Morgan, James N.; and Sonquist, John A. 1967. *Multiple Classification Analysis: A Report on a Computer Program for Multiple Regression Using Categorical Predictors.* Ann Arbor: Survey Research Center, University of Michigan.

Greeley, Andrew M. 1972. *That Most Distressful Nation: The Taming of the American Irish.* New York: Quadrangle Books.

Jennings, M. Kent. 1971. *The Student-Parent Socialization Study.* Ann Arbor: The University of Michigan Inter-University Consortium for Political Research.

Jennings, M. Kent, and Langton, Kenneth P. 1969. "Mothers Versus Fathers: The Formation of Political Orientations among Young Americans," *The Journal of Politics,* May 1969, pp. 329–358.

206 *Andrew M. Greeley*

Jennings, M. Kent, and Niemi, Richard G. 1968a. "Patterns of Political Learning," *Harvard Educational Review,* Summer 1968, pp. 443–467.

_____. 1968b. "The Transmission of Political Values from Parent to Child," *American Political Science Review,* March 1968, pp. 169–184.

Landes, Ruth, and Zborowski, Mark. 1958. "Hypotheses Concerning the Eastern European Jewish Family," in Herman D. Stein and Richard A. Cloward, eds., *Social Perspectives on Behavior.* Glencoe, Ill.: The Free Press.

Marvick, Dwaine. 1965. "The Political Socialization of the American Negro," *The Annals of the American Academy of Political and Social Science,* 369 (1965), pp. 112–127.

Straus, Murray A. 1964. "Power and Support Structure of the Family in Relation to Socialization," *Journal of Marriage and the Family,* August 1964, pp. 318–326.

Tomasi, Lydio F., ed. 1972. *The Italian in America: The Progressive View, 1891–1914.* New York: Center for Migration Studies.

Wolfenstein, Martha. 1955. "Two Types of Jewish Mothers," in Margaret Mead and Martha Wolfenstein, eds., *Childhood in Contemporary Cultures.* Chicago: University of Chicago Press.

Young, Donald R. 1969. "The Socialization of American Minority Peoples," in David A. Goslin, ed., *The Handbook of Socialization Theory and Research.* New York: Rand McNally.

WHO CONTROLS CATHOLIC EDUCATION?

ANDREW M. GREELEY
Center for American Pluralism
University of Chicago

The question that constitutes the title of this paper is unanswerable. If one is forced to it, the best answer would be "no one." The next best would be "everyone."

A more operational question would be, "Who controls this particular Catholic school?" It is in principle answerable, but in practice it may take a considerable amount of study to determine who, indeed, controls this particular school.

The question of who *owns* the Catholic schools is somewhat easier to answer. Most of the elementary schools are owned by the bishop of the diocese, incarnated as a "corporation sole" (a legal form that seems almost to have been designed with the Roman Catholic Church in mind). Many high schools are owned the same way, either directly by the bishop or through a parish that in its turn is owned by the corporation sole. Other high schools and many colleges and universities are owned by religious orders that have their own forms of civil incorporation. Oftentimes, in the case of universities, this takes the form of a legal board of trustees. In the last decade, some of these boards have become partially or even totally lay, so that a legal distinction does

EDUCATION AND URBAN SOCIETY, Vol. 9 No. 2, February 1977
©1977 Sage Publications, Inc.

exist in fact between the trustees of the university and the officers of the corporation, which is the religious order. (Though the bylaws of the college or university may still require, as does Notre Dame, for example, that the president be chosen from the religious community.)

Legally, then, the matter is relatively straightforward (though it is only relatively so, because in the Church of Rome nothing ever manages to stay simple for long). But legal ownership does not necessarily guarantee control, and I take it that my assignment here is to try to chart a path through the mysteries of how de facto decisions get made in and about Catholic schools.

And, of course, the answer to the question of how decisions get made about Catholic schools is an echo of our first answer to the title question of this paper, "Often they don't."

The non-Catholic who wishes to journey with me through the tangled web of Catholic educational control will have to begin by disabusing himself of two myths about the Roman Catholic Church: (1) The Catholic church is a highly centralized, monolithic, bureaucratic structure administered throughout the world on the basis of policy decisions made in Rome and executed by a Roman-controlled civil service. (2) Long years of administrative experience made the Roman Catholic Church wise in the ways of corporate bureaucracies, and therefore its key positions are manned by smooth, able, and sophisticated leaders who are able to translate central directives into effective policies and programs.

In fact, neither of these myths is even remotely true.

The analogy between the Catholic church and a corporate enterprise—in recent years most frequently stated as an analogy with the multinational corporations—is simply not valid. The Catholic church may well be the most decentralized, not to say chaotic, large human organization in the world. Many decisions (to the extent that they are made at all) are made at the farthest limits of the grass roots; and centralized decisions, when they are made, do not necessarily have any impact on lower levels of the organization. Part of the reason for this decentralization is the incompetence and indifference of the upper-level bureaucrats. However, the Catholic social theory (Greeley, 1976) has been committed historically to the principle of subsidiarity—the notion that nothing should be done by a higher or larger body that could be done just as well by a lower or smaller body. This principle is not always honored in practice by the church and, while much of the decentralization is the result of drift rather than conscious and explicit policy, it is also the case that the almost anarchic decentralization of power in the Catholic church is not nearly as offensive to the Catholic world view as it would be to other world views.

Furthermore, the Peter Principle does not apply in the Catholic church—at least not in the United States; one can be promoted far, far above the level of one's own incompetence. For almost a half-century, those responsible for appointing bishops in the American church (principally the apostolic delegate, the representative of the pope in Washington) have been passionately concerned about "safe" bishops. By that they meant that no risks would be taken to repeat the mistake of the late nineteenth century, when a collection of dazzlingly brilliant, if sometimes erratic, American bishops graced the American scene and momentarily captured the imagination of Europe. A "safe" bishop was one who did nothing "dangerous," but was also one who did nothing he didn't absolutely have to do. The result was the appointment of men who did nothing but continue what had been done before them. Until the early 1960s, this policy was only partially successful, however: the unexpected courage and vigor of the American hierarchy at the Second Vatican Council horrified the curialists in Rome, who thought they saw the ghosts of the late nineteenth century rising from the

[150] EDUCATION AND URBAN SOCIETY / FEBRUARY 1977

dead to haunt them once again. So in the years between the end of the Council and the arrival in 1974 of the present apostolic delegate, Jean Jadot, a renewed effort was made to appoint only "safe" men to the major archdioceses in the United States. Since safety meant mediocrity, the level of competence in the American hierarchy has sunk to an all-time low in the two-hundred year history of American Catholicism in America.[1] Mediocre men do not like intelligent men around them; indeed, they are only at ease with even more mediocre men. Bishops tend to be selected from men on the staffs of bishops. The best way to win the approval of your bishop is to not make any mistakes, and the best way to not make mistakes is to not do anything at all. Since the Catholic school administrator operates in areas where decisions can have important implications outside the paperwork world of the chancery office, he must be particularly cautious if he does not want to offend his bishop. Therefore, the school administrator will lean over backward to avoid making any decisions he does not absolutely have to make.

Timidity, passivity, fear of mistakes, pervasive incompetence—all of these might be counterproductive in a business enterprise. However, the church is not a business enterprise, but in fact a world-wide collection of local congregations. When relatively few decisions are made by the men above the congregation level, there can be a good deal of freedom at the level of the congregation. If one wants to learn, therefore, who controls a particular Catholic school, one begins not with the pope, but with the parish where the school is located.

When one combines decentralization of power and timid and inept administration, one has a situation in which personalities and circumstances can have enormous influence on the course of events—far more than in a rigid, "efficient," "rational" centralized bureaucracy. The de facto decision-making power in Catholic schools, then, varies greatly not only from country to country, but from city to city, from parish to parish. A strong-willed bishop may make all his school principals toe the mark—but he's only likely to get away with it for a short time and only if he has a small diocese where he can keep an eye on each of his principals. In large cities, the bishops have far more to do with their time than to harass principals.

A brilliant school administrator may have tremendous impact on the professionalization of teaching within his responsibility, but he is not analogous to the public school superintendent, for the public school superintendent does not have several score or several hundred independent power entities (called "pastors") intervening between his office and the principals of his schools. Even the most dedicated and talented Catholic school superintendent must be an adroit diplomat if he is not to lose the confidence of the pastors of his diocese. In almost any struggle between the pastors and the superintendent, the bishop will probably come down on the side of the pastor.

Similarly, in some parishes a strong-willed pastor with educational ideas of his own may effectively dominate his school. (Though this happens much less frequently now than it did in the years before the Second Vatican Council.) In other parishes the pastor may delegate this responsibility to one of his curates, who may choose to rule with an iron hand (running the risk of having the principal go over his head to the pastor, of course). In still other schools, the clergy will delegate (with a sigh of relief) the responsibility to the principal, who is often, in addition, the superior of the religious community that teaches in the school. The principal will determine what actually goes on in the school—until recently, quite free of any obligation to consult with parents

or faculty. Finally, in the years since the Second Vatican
Council, parish councils or parish school boards have emerged
in many parishes where they have been able to move into a
power vacuum created by an uncertain principal and a passive
pastor, and exercise considerable power and authority over
the school. Tuition, for example, is almost always set at the
parish level. In the past it was typically set by the pastor, but
on the instruction of the principal-superior. More recently,
however, the parish council and/or the school board set the
tuition. In many parishes they may even establish the budget,
hire the principal, and review the qualifications of the
teachers. Usually the pastor will have veto power over the
decisions of the school board, but if it has tough, articulate,
and determined leadership, it stands a good chance of forcing
the pastor into line. In many inner-city black parishes, the
elected parish school boards are especially powerful; they
may well set tuitions higher than any pastor would dare set
them.

Figure 1 is a rough road map of the maze of Catholic
school administration. Since it is impossible to generalize
about the direction of the flow of authority among most of
the boxes on the figure, I have drawn connecting lines only
where there is clearly established *appointive* power. (Difficulties arise even in this area because it so depends on what
the relationship is between the bishop of a given diocese and
his school board—if there is a school board. This depends
almost entirely on the personality of the bishop and the
quality of leadership of the school board.) The pope appoints
the heads of both the Congregation of Religious and the
Congregation of Education, the two pertinent Roman "cabinet" offices. He also appoints the local bishop, who in his
turn appoints both the superintendent of schools and the
pastor. (Though in many dioceses, the appointment of the
pastor is on the recommendation of a semi-elected personnel

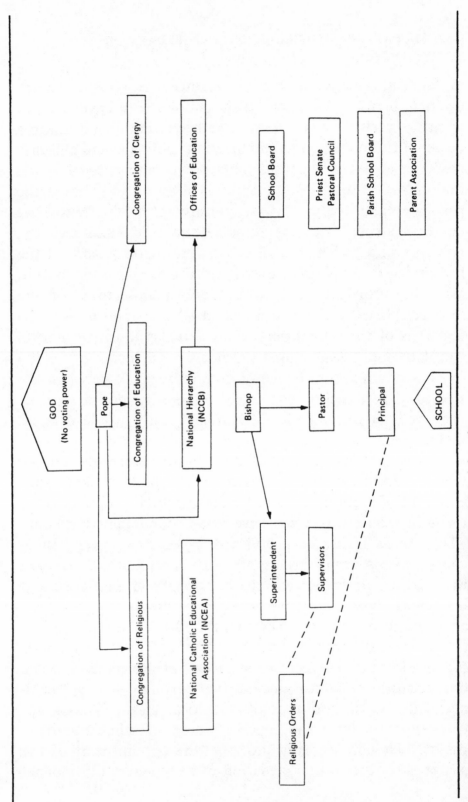

Figure 1: Schematic Description of Catholic School Administration.

WHO CONTROLS CATHOLIC EDUCATION?361

board, which in its turn may or may not be related to the priests' senate of the diocese.)

In large dioceses, the superintendent may appoint—though usually at the recommendation of the various religious orders—"supervisors" who have some investigative power over teaching in the schools. The religious orders in their turn sometimes appoint principals. (Formerly they did so on almost all occasions, although if a pastor objected, the individual would be eventually removed. On the other hand, a pastor who objected too often might begin to lose some of the faculty religious from his schools.) In more recent years, however, parish councils and school boards, as well as the pastor, have directly chosen the principal and in some cases have even appointed lay principals.

Thus the accompanying figure ought not to be taken too seriously. Indeed, it is even less a description of what actually goes on than is the ordinary formal organizational chart. Theoretically, the pope could make a ruling tomorrow—pass it down through the Congregation of Education to the national hierarchy, to the bishop, to the pastors, and to the principals—that mandated a change in every Catholic school in the world to take place on the day after tomorrow. Such a decision has never been made, and in the unlikely eventuality that it ever would be made, there is every reason to suppose that by the time it passed from the pope to the classroom teacher, it would have changed completely beyond recognition.

Theoretically, the Roman Congregation of Education could exercise great power over what goes on in Catholic schools, particularly at universities and seminaries. In fact, it does not do so—partly because of the magnitude of trying to run a world-wide church, partly because of the ineptitude of the Roman administrators, partly because you can't get all that much done when you generally work until one in the afternoon,[2] and partly because of a realistic comprehension that more than a little interference would be counterproductive. The Congregation of Education has issued rulings on the granting of honorary degrees at Catholic universities, the kinds of courses that should be taught at seminaries, and appropriate norms for theology teachers. Before the Vatican Council such regulations were sometimes taken seriously, though rarely outside the United States and Italy. Presently, however, Catholic colleges and universities even in the United States are jealous of their prerogatives and freedom, and resolutely resist Roman interference.

The Congregation of the Clergy is also responsible for "catechetics" (religion teaching). It may issue general "directories" about the teaching of religion, but it makes little attempt to monitor whether such directories are honored. It is realistically aware that out beyond the Tiber River ("west of the Pecos," so to speak), there isn't all that much respect for canon law any more.

There is always the possibility, of course, that the Congregations of the Religious, Education, and the Clergy may intervene in Catholic schools. Or, if the issue is deemed to be a matter of "faith," one may even risk the intervention of the Congregation of the Faith (still called by almost everyone, the "Holy Office"). The fact of a possibility of such intervention—often seemingly arbitrary and capricious—acts as some restraint on what happens at lower levels. After a while you learn the art of pushing about as far as you can go without stirring up trouble at some higher level. But in the demythologization of authority that has taken place in American Catholicism in the wake of the Second Vatican Council, lower levels are likely to push a lot harder and a lot further toward limits than they did in the past. Upper levels are much less confident now of their ability to impose limits. Such weakening is going on at every level from the curial congregations all the way down to the classrooms. The result is more decentralization, more chaos, more confusion, and, of course, more local autonomy and freedom of decision-making.

As a result of the Second Vatican Council, the national hierarchies of the various countries have been formally organized along lines generally anticipated in the previously informal National Catholic Welfare Conference in the United States. (This was an early twentieth-century American innovation that survived annihilation by Rome only through a brilliantly executed battle plan by its supporters.) Thus the Catholic bishops in the United States are organized into two formal bodies, the United States Catholic Conference (USCC) and the National Conference of Catholic Bishops (NCCB).[3] The bishops have a "Committee on Education" that oversees an "Office of Education" with a permanent staff at the USCC-NCBB headquarters in Washington. The Committee and the Office issue statements occasionally or prepare statements to be voted on at the semiannual meetings of the hierarchy; the Office provides educational advice to the Committee and to the hierarchy, as well as engages in relationships with governmental bodies in office (often called by the uncharitable name "lobby"). Neither the Committee nor the Office, however, has any authority to lay down national policy on Catholic educational matters. The statements prepared for debate and endorsement by the bishops at their meetings are of a sufficiently high level of generality and obscurity as to impose no obligation on anyone—not even the bishops—to read them.

Parallel to the National Education Office of the bishops is the National Catholic Educational Association (NCEA), a professional association of Catholic teachers and administrators. Technically the NCEA is independent of the hierarchy, although its president (now chairman of the board) has always been a bishop, and its general secretary (now president) at one time was also the secretary of the Educational Department of the old National Catholic Welfare Conference. In recent years, however, the NCEA, which runs an annual national convention, publishes journals, issues policy statements, lobbies with the government, and presides over a national data archive, has been prone to show more independence and assertiveness. Its annual Easter meetings are likely to be ingenious and creative—as well as being splendid carnivals of exhibition for almost everyone who could possibly sell anything to schools.

The level of competence of these national organizations is not ordinarily very high. The head of the bishops' Office of Education not infrequently will become a bishop himself, and that means he must be very careful not to step on the toes of any bishop—an act which makes walking on eggshells look like a recreational pastime for water buffaloes. The NCEA staff has more independence in theory, but it has often been unwilling to take the chance of offending its neighbors further down Massachusetts Avenue by using that independence very much.

However, inefficiency is sometimes not efficient at maintaining itself, and mediocrity can become mediocre at supporting its own survival. So able men and women do rise to positions of power and influence in the Catholic educational structure and, indeed, in the broader administrative structure of the church. Not everyone who is appointed to a position of power turns out to be as "safe" as he was thought to be. (Remember Pope John?) Sometimes very feisty and difficult characters step on all kinds of episcopal toes and still become bishops—though if you are ambitious, it is not a route to be recommended. As the American Catholic Church is presently constituted, intelligence, creativity, and competence are not assets to recommend one for promotion; indeed, they are likely to be liabilities. Still, the system is flexible enough, or one might say disorganized enough, that

[158] EDUCATION AND URBAN SOCIETY / FEBRUARY 1977

people of both ability and integrity manage to live and work in the interstices, occasionally winding up with effective decision-making power.

Nevertheless, Catholic educational administrators at both the national and local levels are rarely paragons of either ability or integrity. Two incidents in 1976 illustrate this fact. (1) The higher educational branch of the NCEA, together with the University of Notre Dame, decided that the "nonrelationship" between the bishops and the Catholic universities of the United States ought to be ended. (Hardly any Catholic university faculty, for example, were on the staffs of expert advisors who served the American hierarchy at the Second Vatican Council. The bishops would never have thought to look to the universities for such advice, and the universities had never thought to ask.) So they summoned a meeting of university presidents and prominent and moderately progressive hierarchs to discuss the present state and future prospects of the American church and the role the universities could play in supporting the church and its work. Unfortunately the meeting was innocent of any historical, social scientific, or economic expertise on the present, past, and future of American Catholicism and of Catholic education. The papers presented rarely reached even the level of banal pieties. It was a nice idea, though.

(2) When the NORC report, *Catholic Schools in a Declining Church* (Greeley, McCready, McCourt, 1976), appeared with evidence that (a) the birth control encyclical and not the Vatican Council was responsible for the deterioration of American Catholicism; (b) in the present transitional time, Catholic schools are more important than they were in the more stable period of the past; (c) there continues to be widespread support for Catholic education among the laity, the NCEA[4] convened a symposium of experts and wise persons on the subject of Catholic education to consider the implications of the report. Unfortunately, with one or two

exceptions the papers presented were of the quality of college freshman book reviews—in part because the "experts" apparently were afraid to offend the hierarchical leaders by saying too much one way or another about a report which had already acquired the fatal label "controversial."

While the national organizations, then, may do some moderately effective lobbying, they have virtually no control over what goes on in Catholic schools. Indeed, the decision made by bishops to discontinue the construction of Catholic schools in the late 1960s was probably made at their national meeting. It was not made on the floor of any specific meeting and seemed to have resulted more or less implicitly from informal conversations. Even those who will acknowledge, somewhat sheepishly, that there is such a decision, more or less, will not be able to point to an exact time when it was made. Many more bishops will vigorously deny that a decision to discontinue the construction of Catholic schools was ever made. It just "happened" that almost everyone stopped building schools more or less at the same time, they will say. One begins to understand the dynamics of American Catholicism when one grasps that such an assertion may not be altogether false.

There is one occasion when the bishop's legal control of the local elementary or secondary school becomes critically important: when the school needs money. If a given school is paying its own way, then the bishop is likely to leave it alone; but given the self-image of the many American hierarchs as a financial administrator above all, they are most likely to be directly concerned with the schools when there is a question of debt. (Not unreasonably so, after all, for financial incompetence is one of those things for which bishops occasionally get removed—though never any cardinal; by definition cardinals are incapable of financial maladministration.)

[160] EDUCATION AND URBAN SOCIETY / FEBRUARY 1977

Debt can normally arise under two sets of circumstances: (1) when a school is being built or expanded, and (2) when the clientele is moving out of the neighborhood and being replaced by non-Catholic population groups (in most cases, those with a dusky skin color). In these circumstances it must be noted that the bishop's control has nothing to do with what is taught in school, but merely whether the school comes into existence or ceases to exist. In the first case, the bishop determines whether to make a loan so that a school may be built; in the second, he determines whether a subsidy is to be paid from the central office of the diocese to make up for the subsidy that is no longer available from the Sunday parish collections. The bishop's power, in other words, is merely that of life and death when the school cannot provide for itself. In recent years this power has normally meant death.

In line with the ancient principle of handling crises not by doing good but by doing what you think you do well, bishops have tended to act more and more like conservative financial administrators in response to the current crisis in Catholicism. The "safe" thing, in other words, is not to build new schools and to close down the older ones as quickly as you decently can—all the while protesting your commitment to Catholic education.

A word should be said about the influence on decision-making of research and educational faculties. Not much more than a word is required, because there is no such influence. Indeed, there is virtually no research and planning anywhere in the Catholic educational apparatus on national, local, or university levels. The Catholic hierarchy as a body does not believe in research, since it has discovered that research findings cannot be controlled and might turn out to be embarrassing in Rome. There is a research secretariat in the U.S. Catholic Conference, but no research is done there, and the data collection section of the NCEA merely collects data.

The education faculties at Catholic universities train teachers but engage in very little scholarship. Professors in such faculties have no influence whatsoever on the theory or practice of Catholic education. But then no one else has much influence either, except for the editorial writers on certain liberal Catholic journals who establish what the current fad is among the Catholic elites. This is in turn often translated into informal curriculum material. Research and scholarship have very little impact on Catholic schools, since they are neither valued nor recognized by Catholic school administrators and teachers.

The two principal studies of Catholic education in the last decade were done at the National Opinion Research Center (NORC) and were funded by the Carnegie Corporation in the first instance (Greeley and Rossi, 1966) and the National Institutes of Education in the second (Greeley, McCready and McCourt, 1976). The reaction of Catholic educators and administrators to both projects was distinctly hostile even though the results of the surveys were rather more favorable than not to Catholic education.

The amount of control over Catholic schools possessed by the diocesan educational offices varies greatly from diocese to diocese and from administrator to administrator. In some cities, central administrative units are little more than a set of addressograph plates and a small staff to produce the mail the addressograph labels. In other dioceses, the central office is administrated by skilled and able professionals who have been able to impose a considerable amount of curriculum uniformity and teacher-training requirements and even contractual standards throughout the schools of the diocese. The quality of the diocesan educational office is often merely a matter of historical accident determined sometime in the past by the choice of a man to "go away" for a year to obtain an advanced degree in education (usually an M.A.) so he could "run the schools for the bishop." If such a man were

[162] EDUCATION AND URBAN SOCIETY / FEBRUARY 1977

ingenious enough and diplomatic enough, he could build up an effective central unit and then maintain it in the face of episcopal change, because most bishops, in line with the usual policy of "safe" men, would not want to disturb an existing status quo.

Since the Second Vatican Council, diocesan school boards, often with some lay members, have come into existence in many dioceses. (They are usually appointed. After two hundred years' experience of representative democracy in the United States, the Catholic church is still quite uneasy about returning to the representative democracy it practiced in the Middle Ages.) Such school boards may be rubber stamps for the bishops or for the school administrator, or they may exercise very real decision-making power. Again it is the random accident of history, as well as the personalities of those involved, that usually determines how much power such "new" bodies in the church like school boards, priests' senates, and pastoral councils (made up of both priests and laity) actually have, and how representative of the clergy, laity, and parents of the diocese they may be.

But whatever is to be said about the central administrative bodies of the Catholic school "systems," they are surely inexpensive. The most sophisticated, the most professional, and the most able of the central offices serves the Archdiocese of Chicago. It is able to run one of the largest school systems in the country quite effectively with about 30 professional personnel and a tax of $5.00 per student per year. (Twenty-five years ago, when I worked for this office in the summertime, it was doing quite nicely with three professionals, three secretaries, and a couple of people to pack books in boxes.) It has been estimated that in other large cities, the administrative costs are no higher than $.75 per student—often compared with many hundreds of dollars in the parallel public school system. The central administrative offices of the Catholic school systems may not be very effective, but neither are they very expensive; and apparently, while most of them don't do much good for the schools, neither are they able to do very much in the way of harm.

Thus the practical and effective control of most of what happens in a given Catholic school is still at the parish level, doubtless influenced (to some extent positively and to some extent negatively) by the policies, programs, and decisions at higher levels, but still maintaining considerable amounts of freedom for innovation, creativity, and freedom of choice. Again, however, it is often very difficult to find where the principal control power is in the school, since in practice control is usually exercised by a rather fluid coalition of clergy, women religious, and, increasingly, parish councils and school boards (which, unlike their diocesan counterparts, are usually elective and representative bodies).

If one were seeking to specify the principal difference between the control of Catholic schools and the control of public schools in the United States, one would probably end up by pointing to the very considerable amount of "politics" that can occur at the level of the individual Catholic school. In most public schools, relatively little control power exists at the lowest level, so there is relatively little room for politics. What exists is normally institutionalized in the PTA or in the now highly ritualized confrontation politics of some inner-city school situations—rituals that are designed to bring pressure on higher levels of the system. However, in the Catholic schools, there is relatively less control at higher levels and relatively more political forces at work at the lower level (parents, local school board, pastor, in addition to faculty and teachers); so there is more room for fluid and dynamic political processes to work. Usually such "politics" are implicit and consensual, but the observer who wishes to know who controls a given Catholic school must be sensitive to the nuances of the particular political dynamics at work

[164] EDUCATION AND URBAN SOCIETY / FEBRUARY 1977

there. There is no reason in the world for him to think that the processes in this school are the same or even remotely similar to those at work in the school over in the next parish.

One of the forces at work, perhaps the main one, toward greater centralization in Catholic schools is the development of unionization of Catholic school teachers. The unions find it difficult if not impossible to negotiate with each separate school; they insist on some sort of citywide bargaining. However, they are usually told—not inaccurately—that the central office really has no control over the bargaining process in the individual school. While such an argument is in part a tactic for stalling the union, it is also substantially the truth. It would be ironic indeed if unionism forces on Catholic schools the centralization that the schools themselves have successfully resisted in the face of internal pressures.

While the trend toward unionization of Catholic schools is strong, and while the unions might achieve more control power than they would know what to do with because of the resultant power vacuum, the future of unions in Catholic education is not clear at the present writing. Despite its strong support for unions in principle, the Catholic church vigorously resists the unionization of its own employees. In many dioceses presently the church is engaging in many classical techniques of union-busting, going so far as to argue in the courts that teachers in the Catholic schools have no rights under the National Labor Relations Act. It is unlikely that the courts will uphold this bizarre and unedifying thesis, but it may be an extremely effective delaying tactic.

Who controls Catholic schools? As we said at the beginning, no one and everyone. Who controls this particular Catholic school? The answer to that question must be discovered by empirical investigation, and it won't be easy.

The reader may well conclude that it's a hell of a way to run a school system. Doubtless. But then running a school system may have relatively little to do with educational outcome. By almost all standards of output presently available to us, Catholic schools do at least as well and usually better than their public counterparts. Young people learn to read and write and occasionally even to think and to express themselves; they acquire a certain amount of information (some of them can even tell you approximately when the French Revolution occurred and who their U.S. senator is). Most depart from the schools with at least marginally improved skills at interacting with other human beings.

The chaos of organization, the obscurity of control, the general structural "messiness" of Catholic education doesn't seem to do much harm to anybody except to those tidy personalities who like neat organizational charts with consistent flow lines showing clearly the direction of power and authority.

Messy it certainly is; but in the midst of the mess there is probably more room for initiative, innovation, and creativity than there is in the public schools—indeed, in the years after the Vatican Council, much more room than ever before. Catholic schools ought to be excellent experimental laboratories for American education. Virtually everything that one can imagine has happened in and to them. They stand as powerful witnesses that schools can function well with little administration and almost no clearly established control.

Or to paraphrase the man who went to Moscow, "We have seen the past and it doesn't work any worse than anything else."

NOTES

1. Fortunately, the latest recommendations for appointment made by Archbishop Jadot seem to have reversed this trend.

2. When asked how many people work in the curia, Pope John XXIII was supposed to have responded, "About half of them." He might have added, "And even they work only half the time."

3. If the reader is interested in trying to ascertain the difference between the two groups and to puzzle out the interconnecting links, he should contact the two offices directly. Both the United States Catholic Conference and the National Conference of Catholic Bishops are at 1312 Massachusetts Avenue, N.W., Washington, D.C. As far as I can figure out, the NCCB is the formal bishops' organization that relates directly to Rome; the USCC is a national Catholic organization that addresses itself to problems in the United States. But since the upper-level administrative staff of both organizations is the same, I am not at all sure even they are able to untangle the two sets of functions.

4. An organization whose top leaders, president, and chairman of the board are able and adroit men.

5. In one archdiocese the archbishop made it quite clear when the school board was created that it worked for the superintendent and not vice versa.

REFERENCES

GREELEY, A. M. (1976) No Bigger than Necessary. (unpublished manuscript)
——— , W. C. McCREADY, and K. McCOURT (1976) Catholic Schools in a Declining Church. Kansas City, Kansas: Sheed & Ward.
GREELEY, A. M. and P. H. ROSSI (1966) The Education of Catholic Americans. Chicago: Aldine.

Religious Musical Chairs

Andrew M. Greeley

The literature of religious disidentification generally offers three different kinds of explanations for the phenomenon of people withdrawing from the religious denomination in which they were raised:

The secularization model. In the form advanced by Charles Y. Glock and his students, *secularization* means that the more sophisticated, the better educated, the more cosmopolitan people become, the less likely they are to maintain their ties with their traditional religious affiliations or with any religious affiliation at all. Robert Wuthnow has reexamined this explanation and found it deficient in many respects. A more popularized form of the secularization model can be found in the thinking of many religious leaders. Whatever factors lead people to the fringe of a denomination will lead them out of the denomination when they become powerful. A person will drift into the low levels of religious devotion because, let us say, of dissatisfaction with the sexual ethic or racial stance of his denomination, and then when his dissatisfaction grows stronger will drift across the line separating the identifier with the disidentifier.

The family strain model. Most serious research done on religious disidentification (by John Kotre, Joseph Zelan, David Caplowitz, and Andrew M. Greeley) emphasizes the powerful influence of family background in the decision to disidentify religiously. The church, as Kotre has pointed out, is an institution which emits many stimuli. Which stimulus one chooses to focus on in determining to identify or disidentify is a function of the psychological perspective one brings from the family experience to one's encounter with the church. Living apart from one's family, coming from a broken family, a family in which there is conflict, or a family in which there is unusual strain between a person and his parents are powerful predictors of religious disidentification. Similarly, the religious disidentifiers are likely to be dissatisfied and unhappy personally and to take strong liberal stands on political and social issues. Zelan and Caplowitz suggest that an ideology of political liberalism may become a substitute religion for them.

The religious intermarriage or "musical chairs" model. This explanation, contained in one essay by the present author and much of the research literature on Jewish intermarriage, recognizes that the American population plays a game of religious musical chairs at the time of marriage. Men and women rearrange their religious affiliations to minimize the strain and conflict which might exist in a family because of different religious loyalties. In such a game of musical chairs, religious conviction, faith and unbelief, devotion and loyalty are less important than minimizing family conflict. The conversion will usually be in the direction of the more devout of the two marriage partners.

There has been relatively little research done on either religious disidentification or religious exogamy in recent years. Caplovitz's monograph on disidentification is concerned basically with young people who graduated from college in the early 1960s. The Jewish exogamy studies focus on that denomination and show mixed and conflicting findings. However, the National Opinion Research Center (NORC) General Social Survey has asked questions about present and past religious identification for four of its five annual surveys as well as a number of other questions which enable us to test each of the three explanations offered above for religious disidentification.

Questions about age and education will enable us to examine the Glock model of secularization. Questions about sexual attitudes and belief in life after death will permit us to examine the variant of the secularization model which sees disidentification as a continuous behavior logically linked with low levels of religious practice. Questions about whether the respondent lived with both parents at age 16, about trust, psychological well-being, and political disaffiliation will enable us to examine the family strain/disaffiliated personality model. Finally, questions about the religious affiliation of spouse at 16 and the present time will enable us to investigate the musical chairs model.

The most plausible explanation for the religious disidentification phenomenon is religious exogamy—an especially powerful explanation for Catholics. There is also some support for the other explanation, though virtually none for the Glock secularization thesis. It is true that both the young and the better educated are more likely to disidentify religiously, but this can be explained by increased exogamy and an increase in the level of general societal disaffiliation.

To say that disidentification is connected with exogamy does not mean that one has a clear notion of how the two relate to one another. Not all disidentifiers marry out of their denominations and not all participants in exogamous marriage disidentify. Where the two phenomena do occur, one does not know whether disidentification came before the marriage or after it, and whether if it came before it was a time immediately before the marriage, taking place with the marriage in mind, or was an earlier event which might have

0147-2011/78/0515-0010$02.50/1
© 1978 Transaction, Inc.

been accounted for by either of the other two explanatory models. In the present analysis we find that there are a substantial number of young unmarried people whose disidentification can be accounted for by an alienation/disaffiliation model. These young people are part of a special phenomenon that occurred in the late 1960s. There may have been among older generations a similar disidentification based on anger or disbelief; but if this disidentification occurred prior to a religiously mixed marriage, very little trace of it can be found among those who entered religiously mixed marriages and then disidentified. It would appear that musical chairs is one way out of a denomination—a response to the religious convictions of one's spouse—while religious alienation, for reasons either of conviction or a general tendency toward disaffiliation, is another way out with relatively little linkage between the two. Nonetheless, since we are dealing with a phenomenon that occurred sometime between the sixteenth birthdays of our respondents and the present, the most we will be able to do here is to speculate about the connections. A much more detailed study of the religious maturation process between the late teens and the late twenties would be required for more precise information and precise explanations of the complex link between religious identification and marriage. There is substantial evidence to believe that young people make up their minds about their religious affiliation at about the same time they make up their minds about their political affiliation—sometime between 17 and 30 (the generation that grew up in the 1960s tends to have suspended ultimate decision about both these affiliations).

The questions in the General Social Survey pertinent to our analysis are at least as good as items ever available for the study of disidentification and exogamy in the past. Nonetheless, they leave something to be desired. In a study explicitly designed to study disidentification better operational indicators would surely have been designed.

For the present analysis the following variables were routinely built into the mathematical models: age, sex, respondent's education, respondent's spouse's education, respondent's parents' education, geographic region, city size, personal psychological well-being, marital adjustment, whether one lived with one's mother and father at 16, belief in life after death, church attendance, approval of extramarital sex, premarital sex, the distribution of birth control information to teenagers, belief that most people can be trusted, support for prayer and bible reading in public schools, confidence in religious leadership, support for the legalization of marijuana, and certain anomie items about whether people can be trusted to be fair, whether life is exciting or dull, and marital status.

The issues explored here are extremely complicated. For purposes of simplicity of presentation, correlational analysis is used most of the time. One of the disadvantages of using correlation/multiple regression is that when the distribution of respondents is skewed (for example, only one-sixth of our respondents have disidentified religiously), the correlation coefficients are likely to be relatively small and to obscure

important relationships that nonparametric statistics would reveal. The problem is even more serious when the distribution on the second variable (area of the country in which the respondent lives) is also badly skewed. Thus evidence was found to sustain the conviction that religiously mixed marriages are more likely for Catholics who live in the South and West than for those who live in the Northeast and North Central regions of the country. However, since only a relatively small proportion of the Catholic population lives outside of the Northeast and North Central regions, the regional variable is not a powerful explanation of religious disidentification (because most religious disidentification for Catholics still occurs in the North where most Catholics live). Similarly, disidentification rates are high among those who were not living in an intact family at age 16. Again, only a relatively small proportion of the population did not live in intact families; therefore, an unintact family is not an important explanation for religious disidentification. Most religious disidentification occurs among those who came from intact families. When one chooses between parametric and nonparametric statistics in an analysis like the one here, one realizes that there are costs and advantages to both techniques. The costs in a decision to use parametric statistics here are a loss of some interesting and useful information; but the benefits include a much clearer, orderly, and systematic presentation of a subject matter which is complicated enough to begin with.

The critical question is not why people enter religiously mixed marriages, but rather why some of those who do, disidentify with their denomination

---

Ten percent of those who were Protestants at age 16 are no longer Protestants, while 16.5 percent of Catholics and 16 percent of Jews have disidentified with their denominations. (Jews are omitted from this analysis because 150 respondents are not sufficient for generalizations in an area in which there is intensive research being carried on by other scholars. There is not sufficient numbers for most Protestant denominations to permit detailed analysis—though, as we will note later, Baptists alone have a lower mixed marriage rate than other Protestant denominations. The Baptist/non-Baptist dichotomy, however, was not statistically significant in any other of the models constructed).

Sixteen percent of those who were Protestant at age 16 contracted marriages with spouses who were also Protestant at age 16. (It does not follow necessarily that either was still Protestant at the time of marriage.) Thirty-nine percent of Catholics contracted such exogamous marriages, as did 15 percent of Jews. However, when one looks at the present endogamy rates, one notes that they fall to 11 percent for Protestants, 23 percent for Catholics, and 10 percent for Jews. In other words, the game of religious musical chairs, by which spouses reduce exogamy rates by religious change, cuts by one-third Protestant and Jewish exogamy rates and cuts almost in half Catholic exogamy rates.

Two-fifths of those who were Catholic at 16, in other words, married people who were not Catholics; but only about one-fourth of those who are Catholics today are married to people who are not Catholics today. Some of those who were Catholic at 16, in other words, have become non-Catholic; others remain Catholic and their spouses who were non-Catholic at 16 have become Catholic. The net result of the rearrangements of religious affiliation in association with exogamous marriages is a 2 percent loss in total membership for Protestants and a 7 percent net loss for Catholics. In other words, while 9 percent of those born Protestant disidentify, 7 percentage points of that disidentification is compensated for by conversions—most in association with religiously mixed marriages—and while 16.5 percent of those who were born have disidentified, 10 percentage points of that change is compensated for by converts—again, most of them in association with religiously mixed marriages.

Disidentification is closely related to exogamy. For both Catholics and Protestants, only 6 percent who married a spouse who was the same religion as they were at 16 have disidentified, while 30 percent of those who married out of their denomination have disidentified. Disidentification, in other words, is five times higher in exogamous marriage as it is in endogamous marriages. About one-fifth of both denominations who were never married have disidentified. Whether in conjunction with marriage such respondents will reidentify with their old religion, identify with a new one, or remain disidentified is at best a matter of conjecture. However, most of the unmarried disidentifiers are young, and, as we shall suggest later, there seems to be a special dynamism at work among the disidentifying young.

Exogamy accounts for 50 percent of Catholic disidentification and 34 percent of Protestant disidentification. One-fourth of Protestants married to other Protestants have disidentified, while only 13 percent of the Catholics married to other Catholics have disidentified. Approximately four-fifths of the married Catholics who have disidentified entered religiously exogamous marriages, as opposed to 56 percent of the disidentifiers among married Protestants in religiously mixed marriages. Among Protestants and Catholics, then, an absolute majority of the married disidentifiers are in religious mixed marriages—more than half the Protestants and almost four-fifths of the Catholics. The exogamy explanation of disidentification is clearly the most powerful. But the question remains as to whether there are dynamics at work which lead to both disidentification and mixed marriage. Do people enter mixed marriages because they have disidentified, or are there two separate paths out of religious denominations—one through mixed marriage and one that may lead to mixed marriage but would operate independently of mixed marriage?

The musical chairs model works as follows: Eighty percent of those who were Protestant at 16 married others who were Protestant at 16; four percent married spouses with Protestant identification at 16 but have themselves disidentified (a disidentification independent of marriage). Five percent entered religiously mixed marriages and now disidentify; another 4 percent have entered religiously mixed marriages, but their spouse became Protestant so that now the marriage is endogamous. Finally, 7 percent of the Protestants entered marriages which then and now are religiously exogamous, in which neither the respondent nor the spouse changed religious identification. It is the third and fourth categories, then, which represent the religious musical chairs—5 percent of the Protestants marry out of the denomination and move out of it, 4 percent move out but the spouse moves into the Protestant denomination—a net loss of 1 percent.

For Catholics the mixed marriage rates are much higher—44 percent of American Catholics marry persons who were not Catholics at 16. Twelve percentage points of this group disidentify with the church, but another 8 percentage points are in marriages in which the spouse has converted to Catholicism, making it a net loss of 4 percentage points to American Catholicism because of religious intermarriage. Twenty percent of those Catholics who entered religiously mixed marriages are still in religiously mixed marriages with no change in spouse or self. Conversion as a result of mixed marriages among Catholics is more likely than disidentification, and a continuation of the marriage as mixed is more likely.

There are almost a bewildering number of possibilities: (1) Why do people disidentify if they are not in mixed marriages? (2) Why do people enter mixed marriages? (3) Why do some of the exogamously married disidentify? (4) Why do some "convert" their spouses, and why do some remain in marriages which continue to be religiously mixed? (5) What impact does "marriage conversion" have on denomination? (6) Are those who were recruited in association with marriage as devout as the born members of the denomination? The answer to each question assumes a different comparison, one that is logically designed to provide an answer.

The first question has to do with that minority of disidentifiers whose decision is not related to a religiously exogamous marriage. The analytic variables available to us enable us to explain 14 percent of the disidentification of Protestants and 17 percent of the disidentification of Catholics—when one compares the unmarried respondents or endogamously married respondents who disidentify with the unmarried respondents and the endogamously married respondents who do not disidentify. For Protestants there are no statistically significant relationships in the multiple regression model between nonmarital disidentification and demographic variables, such as age, education, sex, and region. Three of the predictors of disidentification have to do with religion—confidence in religious leaders, belief in life after death, support for prayer and Bible reading in the classroom—while three have to do with "moral" issues—premarital sex, extramarital sex, and legalization of marijuana. A generalized disaffiliation as measured by being a political "independent" also relates to Protestant disidentification, but only indirectly through the two "blocks" or religious and moral issues. Nonmarital disidentification for American Protestants, then, insofar as it can be explained by the tools available to us, seems to be a rather straightforward religious and moral disenchantment. There are other factors at work, but as far as our theories and analytic tools are able to be used on the question of nonmarital disidentification, it would seem that Protestants disidentify for religious and ethical reasons.

By far, the largest number of those who have disidentified from the Roman Catholic church . . . are happily married, devoutly practicing, believing members of Protestant denominations

---

Among Catholics, the religious and ethical reasons are also at work—somethat more strongly. There is a − .21 relationship between confidence in religious leaders and disidentification and .17 between support for the legalization of marijuana and disidentification. There are also direct relationships between disidentification and age (− .1), education (− .11), general disaffiliation (.10), and divorce (.18). The three most powerful predictors of disidentification among Catholics whose disidentification is not related to religiously mixed marriage are a previous divorce, low confidence in the clergy, and political liberalism as represented by support for the legalization of marijuana. Our rather complex model has two separate subsystems, a religious subsystem at the bottom of the model that involves divorce, belief in life after death, and confidence in religious leadership; and a "secular" subsystem at the top of the model that involves age, education, "unaffiliation," and support for the legalization of marijuana. Younger Catholics, better educated Catholics, Catholics who are political independents, and Catholics who support the legalization of marijuana are more likely to disidentify, as are Catholics who have been divorced, who have a low level of confidence in religious leadership, and who do not believe in life after death. Among that minority of Catholic disidentifiers whose disidentification is not marriage associated, both the first and second models described in the beginning (the secularization model and the alienation model) seem to apply. The secularization model applies in two forms—age and education on the one hand and a continuation of problems with the clergy and religious conviction on the other. (Confidence in religious leadership can be taken as a rough equivalent indicator of attitudes toward clerical performance, and life after death as a rough equivalent indicator of attitudes toward doctrine. Sexual attitudes while tested, were not strong enough in their influence on Catholic disidentification to be included in this model—or any of the models presented here for Catholics, save that a

previous divorce may in some indirect sense represent an indicator of sexual attitudes.)

The data available do not provide much illumination on the question of why young people choose to marry outside of their religious denomination. For Protestants intermarriage is more likely to occur among the young and in the metropolitan area of the North, and less likely among Baptists. The Catholic picture is more complicated. Polish, German, French, and English Catholics are more likely to enter religious intermarriage than Irish Catholics, Italians, and Spanish-speaking. They are also more likely to enter religiously mixed marriages if they are from the South and if there is a previous divorce in their marital experience. There is no connection between their own education and religious intermarriage, but both their mother's and spouse's education correlate positively with religious intermarriage. Thus the better educated the mother is and the more education the spouse has, the more likely one is to enter an exogamous marriage if one is Catholic. Perhaps if one has a better educated mother one is more likely to be in a social environment in which there is more mixing between Protestants and Catholics and perhaps also, better educated women as potential marriage partners. Region plays a part for both Protestants and Catholics. Denomination for Protestants and ethnicity for Catholics are roughly parallel factors for both groups.

We can only give a meager answer to the question of why people enter religiously mixed marriages, even though such marriages are in turn a substantial answer to the question of why people disidentify from the denomination in which they were raised. The data available provide virtually no information on the childhood, familial, or religious experiences of our respondents, and it ought not to be expected that we would be very successful in explaining choice of marriage partners. The critical question is not why people enter religiously mixed marriages, but rather why some of those who do, disidentify with their denomination. One must compare those who entered exogamous marriages and remained in their denomination without their spouses converting and those who enter religiously exogamous marriages and disidentify with their own religion.

For Protestants this identification correlates positively with education. The better educated a Protestant is in the exogamous situation, the more likely he is to disidentify. Also, there is a surprisingly high correlation between not living with both parents at age 16 and disidentifying (.23). Finally, those Protestants who have left their own denomination in association with a mixed marriage are much more likely to report a higher level of marital happiness than those who remain Protestant in religiously mixed marriages. Respondents who had rather unhappy and troubled childhoods seem to find happiness in the marriage they have entered. It is possible that this combination of unhappy childhood and deep satisfaction in a relationship with a spouse leads one to disidentify with one's original religion and join that of the spouse. It could also be that the sharing of values that results from religious conversion in this particular case (not in any other comparisons) leads to a higher level of marital happiness.

The model explaining Catholic disidentification in exogamous marriages is completely different. There is a large negative correlation of − .20 with being Irish. (Thirty-eight percent of those Catholics in religiously mixed marriages whose spouses have not converted disidentify with Catholicism. However, only 15 percent of the Irish in such marriages disidentify, the only group that is statistically different from any of the others. The Irish are less likely to enter mixed marriages, and once they have entered them, they are much less likely to disidentify.) There is also a − .14 relationship between belief in life after death and disidentification for Catholics, and a .12 between personal psychological well-being and disidentification. Catholic disidentifiers, in this particular set of circumstances, are no more likely to describe their marriages as happy than those who do not disidentify, but they are more likely to describe themselves as personally happy—a phenomenon which may be roughly parallel to the marital happiness described by Protestant disidentifiers.

In the introduction we raised the possibility that there may be two different systems of disidentification at work among Americans, one applying to those who entered religiously mixed marriages and the other applying either to the unmarried or those who entered endogamous marriages. We have presented, on the one hand, a picture of religious and moral crisis for Protestants and alienation and disaffiliation for Catholics. On the other hand, we have a picture of personal and marital psychological well-being, ethnicity for Catholics, and broken family for Protestants. While we still can explain only a relatively small amount of the variance, there seems little overlap in the reasons why the exogamously married disidentify and the reasons why others disidentify. Religiously mixed marriages do not seem to produce the kind of disidentification that can be considered a religious crisis, while the disidentification of the unmarried and the endogamously married does seem to correlate with a set of variables that could be described as religious crisis. This explanation is disappointingly weak given the fact that religiously mixed marriage is the most important explanation of religious disidentification. One would still like to know more of why some people in mixed marriages disidentify and others do not. One possibility would be that the explanation for disidentification lies less with the respondent himself than in the respondent's spouse. Might it not be that the musical chairs at time of exogamous marriage is a response to the religious needs, demands, or convictions of the spouse with the stronger religious commitment? Perhaps one should look at the matter the other way around, looking not at those who disidentify but rather at the spouses of those who convert.

We are not able to look at the spouses of the disidentifiers in our sample since the sample is not a study of families but of individuals. However, there are individuals in the sample whose spouses have disidentified with their religion of origin

and joined the respondent's religion. It is therefore possible to ask how those whose spouses convert differ from those in mixed marriages in which the spouse does not convert—the two people continuing to live together with two religious commitments. The spouses of the converts are far more devout than the spouses of those who do not convert—a beta of .41 with church attendance for the spouses of those who converted to Catholicism and one of .32 for spouses of those who converted to Protestantism. Those outside the metropolitan North are more likely to have spouses who converted to Protestantism; older Catholics and female Catholics are more likely than younger Catholics and male Catholics to report their spouses have converted.

The model explaining Catholic disidentification in exogamous marriages is completely different from the Protestants

---

We do not know whether the high level of church attendance reported by the spouses of converts was a cause or a result of the conversion, since all we know is church attendance at the present time and not church attendance at the time of the marriage. It could be that the mutual and self-conscious reinforcement of religious values that comes from a "marriage conversion" leads the spouse to higher religious devotion than he/she would otherwise have had. However, it is certainly valid to speculate that the high level of religious practice observed among the spouses of converts reveals a deep religious commitment which existed also at the time of the marriage and which balanced the game of musical chairs in favor of the more devout partner. One may tentatively conclude that in religious disidentification associated with mixed marriage the important variables are less those to be found relating to the marriage partner who disidentified and more relating to the marriage partner with whose denomination the spouse comes to identify. One converts to the religion of the more devout spouse. The religious crisis of a mixed marriage which leads to disidentification is not so much the crisis of lack of faith or commitment in one's own denomination as it is a crisis of stronger faith and commitment of the other person to his/her denomination.

It should not be thought, however, that the conversion is unauthentic or hypocritical, that the spouse merely goes along with the religion to which he/she has converted in order to keep the more devout member of the pair happy. There are little differences between those who were born Protestant or Catholic and convert when it comes to religious behavior. Catholic converts are even more likely than born Catholics to believe in life after death (though Protestant converts are less likely to believe in it than born Protestants). In terms of confidence in the clergy, church attendance, and sexual attitudes, converts and born members of denominations do not differ from one another at a level which achieves statistical significance. Converts are no less devout and, save for the

Catholic belief in life after death, no more devout than those born in a denomination. However, those who have converted to Catholicism are not only more likely to report that they are happy in their marriages than those who have remained in religiously mixed marriages, they are also more likely to report that they are more happy in their marriages than are born Catholics married to other Catholics. Marital happiness among Catholics is more strongly affected by conversion than it is by initial endogamy.

If one compares those Catholics who converted to Protestantism with those who remained Catholics, the converts are about as religious as those who remain Catholic. There is no statistically significant difference in church attendance. (Because of the small size of the number of converts, the 9 percentage point difference in weekly church attendance between converts to Protestantism and Catholics is not statistically significant.) Nor is there any significant difference in belief in life after death, and the marriage converts to Protestantism are significantly more likely to say they are very happy than Catholics who are still practising Catholics. Those Catholics who have converted to Protestantism and Protestants who have converted to Catholicism because of religiously mixed marriages, in other words, have not become unbelievers or undevout; they have simply shifted the locus of their religious belief to another denomination—in all likelihood because the religious convictions of their spouse were stronger. The switch means greater marital happiness for those who convert to Catholicism and greater personal happiness for those who convert to Protestantism.

The greater marital happiness for converts to Catholicism seems to be confined—at least as far as statistical significance goes—to Protestant men who have converted to the religion of their Catholic wives. Nine-tenths of such men described their marriages as "very happy." The same is not true of Catholics, men and women, who have converted to the Protestantism of their spouses.

Does this phenomenon of greater marital satisfaction among men who converted to the Catholicism of their wives correspond to a higher level of satisfaction for their wives, that is to say, for the women whose husbands have converted to Catholicism because they (the wives) are Catholic? We are not dealing with the same couples but rather with national samples—and by now with a very small number of cases—of the two different categories, that is, male converts to the Catholicism of their wives and Catholic women whose husbands have converted to Catholicism. The data show, as one might expect if the higher level of satisfaction is shared by husbands and wives, that Catholic women whose husbands have converted to Catholicism report a higher level of marital satisfaction than Catholic women married to husbands who were always Catholic. But the difference (69 percent saying "very happy" for the former and 65 percent for the latter) is not statistically significant even though it is in the hypothesized direction. One can therefore say only tentatively that religiously mixed marriages which end up as Catholic marriages because of the conversion of the male

partner to Catholicism produce the highest level of satisfaction (as perceived and reported by the respondent) of any marriages in the country.

To summarize our findings we will provide tentative answers to the six questions asked earlier.

1. *Why do those who are not in religious mixed marriages disidentify?* Protestants, insofar as our data provide answers, disidentify for religious and moral reasons; Catholics for religious reasons such as divorce, belief in life after death, anger at the clergy, and also more general reasons of alienation, as measured by political nonidentification.

2. *Why do people enter religiously mixed marriages?* Baptists are less likely than other Protestants to do so; Irish, Italian, and Hispanic Catholics are less likely than other Catholics to do so. Younger Protestants and higher status Catholics (as measured by their mother's and spouse's educational achievement), as well as divorced Catholics are more likely to enter exogamous marriages.

3. *Why do some exogamous marriages correlate with disidentification?* Marital happiness for Protestants and personal happiness for Catholics correlates with disidentification. Leaving the church of one's origin gives Protestants higher levels of marital happiness and Catholics higher levels of personal happiness. Those who grew up Irish Catholics are much less likely to disidentify in mixed marriages, and those Protestants who were raised in broken families are much more likely to disidentify as Protestants.

4. *Why do other exogamous marriages correlate with conversion of the spouse to self's religion?* The principal correlate of marrying a spouse who converts is one's own high level of church attendance—perhaps a reflection of the situation at the time of marriage in which the self was perceived as by far the more religious of the two and hence the one who determined the religious course the family would take.

5. *How religious are marriage converts in the new denomination?* Generally speaking, they are at least as religious as those who were born in the denomination.

6. *How religious are married converts compared to those in the denomination they left behind?* The answer seems to be that marriage conversion may lead to a shift in affiliation, but it does not lead to a change in religious devotion.

The last question provides an appropriate way to begin a final discussion of the various models proposed to explain religious disidentification. Quite clearly, mixed marriages are the major cause of religious disidentification. They have relatively little impact on the personal religious behavior of the people involved. Rather, they change the denominational situation in which religious behavior occurs. A mixed marriage, in other words, may lead to a crisis of religious affiliation but not to a crisis of religious conviction or devotion. However, that kind of religious disidentification which occurs in a nonmarital and nonmixed marital context seems to involve for both Protestants and Catholics a religious and moral crisis, which for Catholics, at any rate, seems to have some connection with a more general alienation.

Is disidentification, then, merely a continuation of dynamics that are already at work in leading to low levels of religious practice? Does one drift to the fringes of the church and then if the factors affecting drift grow stronger, eventually drift out? The answer seems to be that such a process is indeed one way out, but a way out for only a minority of the disidentifiers. The other way is followed by the majority of Catholics who enter religiously mixed marriages in which faith and devotion do not change but affiliation does.

Finally, let us turn to the secularization explanation. Is it true that both youthfulness and education lead to higher rates of religious disidentification, which suggests that society is tending toward a higher level of religious nonaffiliation and indifference? The data show that those with college education and those under 30, both among Protestants and Catholics, are more likely to disidentify. For Catholics under 30, the disidentification rate is 21 percent, for Catholics over 30, 15 percent. For Protestants under 30, the disidentification rate is 15 percent, and over 30, 8 percent. Virtually the same percentages apply to the difference between college attenders and nonattenders. However, when one holds religious intermarriage constant, all statistically significant difference among age groups disappear. If Protestants and Catholics under 30 are more likely to disidentify, the reason is that they are more likely to enter religiously mixed marriages. We have suggested before that since religiously mixed marriage represents a crisis of denominational affiliation and not one of religious conviction, the secularization trend, insofar as it is measured by higher youthful rates of disidentification is a trend which may affect denominational affiliation but not religious devotion.

A control for exogamy also eliminates statistically significant differences between Catholic college attenders and nonattenders, though a difference does remain among exogamous Protestants (36 percent of the college attenders disidentify, as opposed to 16 percent of those who did not attend college).

Among those who enter religiously mixed marriages there are no differences between Protestants and Catholics and between those under and over 30—about three out of 10 in all four categories of exogamous marriages disidentify.

Is the higher level of religious disidentification among the young part of a more general alienation syndrome that was the result of disturbances in American society in the late 1960s and early 1970s? It is well known that a large number of young people under 30 have not yet made a choice between the two political parties and continue to be political independents. Nie, Petrocik, and Verba have raised the question of whether this group will ever be politically mobilized. A parallel question is whether they will ever be religiously mobilized. The important question here is whether those who are unmobilized politically are also unmobilized religiously. Are the political nonidentifiers the same ones as the religious disidentifier? Our data suggest that for Catholics, at any rate, they are. The politically affiliated Catholics under 30 are no more likely than those over 30 to disidentify religiously.

However, it is precisely among those Catholics who are both under 30 and politically disaffiliated that one finds a rate of religious disidentification twice that of both their affiliated age peers and their fellow disaffiliates over 30. A similar pattern appears for Protestants. The highest disidentification rate is among disaffiliates under 30. Among the affiliates, there is a statistically significant but very small (3 percentage points) difference between the younger and the older group.

Is mixed marriage or a more general nonaffiliation syndrome the more important predictor of religious disidentification for those under 30? Exogamy continues to be the strongest predictor, even for those under 30, of religious disidentification. But for Catholics there is also an independent contribution of college education (.09) and an independent contribution of societal nonaffiliation, as measured by lack of political affiliation. Alienation from societal institutions, in other words, does not seem to be a particularly pertinent factor in explaining disidentification of the young Protestants, but it does seem to be an influence on the disidentification of young Catholics—perhaps a sign of the acute institutional crisis which afflicted Roman Catholicism in the late 1960s and early 1970s.

By far the largest number of those who have disidentified from the Roman Catholic church have done so in association with religiously mixed marriages. They are happily married, devoutly practicing, believing members of Protestant denominations. They may have gone through a crisis of institutional affiliation but they do not seem to have suffered any acute crisis of religious conviction. Attempts to "reclaim" them are not likely to be very successful or even advisable.□

READINGS SUGGESTED BY THE AUTHOR:

Caplovitz, David. *The Religious Dropouts: Apostasy among College Graduates*. Beverly Hills, Calif.: Sage Publications, 1977.

Glock, Charles Y., and Stark, Rodney. *Religion and Society in Tension*. Chicago: Rand McNally, 1965.

Kotre, John. *View from the Border: A Social Psychological Study of Current Catholicism*. Chicago: Aldine, 1971.

Greeley, Andrew M., McCready, William C., and McCourt, Kathleen. *Catholic Schools in a Declining Church*. Kansas City: Sheed and Ward, 1976.

Wuthnow, Robert. "Recent Pattern of Secularization: A Problem of Generations?" *American Sociological Review* 41 (October 1976): 850-67.

Andrew Greeley is director of the Center for the Study of American Pluralism at National Opinion Research Center, a sociologist, journalist, and Catholic priest. His syndicated column is in more than eighty newspapers. His recent catechism, The Great Mysteries, has become a best seller in the United States. His other recent books include The Mary Myth: On the Femininity of God and The American Catholic: A Social Portrait.

SCIENTIFIC
Established 1845 ## AMERICAN   June 1978   Volume 238   Number 6

Attitudes toward Racial Integration

*The fourth in a series of reports on racial attitudes shows that U.S.
whites have increased their support of integration at a steady pace,
with a striking period of more rapid change between 1970 and 1972*

by D. Garth Taylor, Paul B. Sheatsley and Andrew M. Greeley

The 1970's are generally characterized as being years of disgruntled reaction to the rapid social, economic and political changes of the 1960's. In some areas of American life that may well be a correct assessment, but it does not seem to have been the case in race relations. The continuing monitoring of racial attitudes conducted by the National Opinion Research Center (NORC) makes it clear that since

1970 white Americans have moved steadily toward approval of racial integration. The most striking fact to emerge from our analysis of the surveys is that the years between 1970 and 1972 were an extraordinary interlude in U.S. history: just when the "white backlash" was thought to be taking effect there was instead a leap forward in racial tolerance—or, to be more specific, in the verbalized attitudes of white Americans

with regard to the integration of blacks into U.S. society. The early 1970's were marked also by an increased rate of change in several other measures of support for civil or personal liberties, equality between the sexes and tolerance (some call it permissiveness) in general. The years since 1972 have seen not a reversal of the liberal trend in racial and other matters but rather a return to the slower, but nevertheless steady, rate

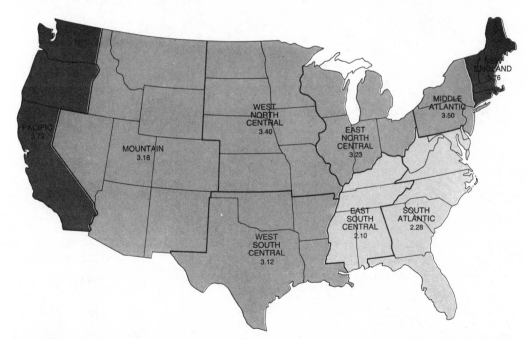

GEOGRAPHIC DISTRIBUTION of white Americans' 1976 scores on a scale of attitudes toward integration is displayed for the U.S. Census regions. The average scale score was highest in the Pacific Coast region and in New England and lowest in the Southern states.

of change that has been recorded by NORC surveys for the past 35 years.

The changing racial climate revealed by the response of white Americans in those surveys has been described in these pages in a series of articles [see "Attitudes toward Desegregation," by Herbert H. Hyman and Paul B. Sheatsley; SCIENTIFIC AMERICAN, December, 1956, and July, 1964, and "Attitudes toward Racial Integration," by Andrew M. Greeley and Paul B. Sheatsley; SCIENTIFIC AMERICAN, December, 1971]. Since 1963 the surveys have been based on a particular scale of racial tolerance and in 1976 the scale was again included in NORC's General Social Survey. (The survey is conducted by interviewing a nationwide sample of about 1,500 people; the questions constituting the scale were put to the approximately 1,350 whites in the sample.)

The purpose of this article is to report the results of that study, to highlight the continuities and the striking discontinuity in the rate of improvement and to examine some of the causes of the trends we observe. We find that some of the movement can be accounted for by the entry into the population of younger people and by the rising level of educational attainment, but that a good deal of the trend represents actual modification of attitudes on the part of older people. Moreover, our analysis indicates that the change in attitude on racial matters is part of the broader movement toward what can be considered a more liberal position on a range of other social issues.

The five items of the scale, which was devised by Donald J. Treiman, are selected and arranged in order of what might be called increasing stringency, that is, people are more likely to give the "liberal," or prointegration, response to the first item than to the second one, to the second item than to the third one, and so on [see upper illustration at right]. For each question the percentage of the white population giving the prointegration response is recorded. In addition, each respondent is assigned a score ranging from 0 to 5 depending on the number of his prointegration responses. Mean scores can then be computed for the total white population and for various subgroups of the population. Almost every item shows a substantial change in the integrationist percentage from 1963 to 1970, 1972 and 1976. As for the mean score for all white Americans, it was 2.09 in 1963, indicating that the average white American then gave the prointegration response to just over two of the five integrationist questions. By 1976 the score had increased to 3.17.

Two observations should be made with regard to the scale questions. One is that the first item is coming to elicit such broad agreement that it will soon not be useful in discriminating racial opinion.

Three of the items in the original eight-question Treiman scale had to be "retired" for just that reason. They had to do with the integration of public facilities, an issue that was problematic not so many years ago but then became so settled in the public mind that it was difficult to find whites who would not endorse the principle. If the racial climate continues to improve, other questions in the scale will presumably become less effective and will have to be dropped as new items, reflecting current issues such as busing for school integration, are added to the bottom of the scale.

The second observation is that not all the items show the same pattern of change. The last question, about blacks

pushing themselves "where they're not wanted," elicited a more negative response in 1972 than in 1970, and its integrationist percent is about the same now as it was in 1963, whereas the other items show unambiguous trends in the prointegration direction. We believe the last question may not measure the same dimension of racial attitude as it was measured when the scale was first administered, but rather other dimensions or values such as politeness and conventional social behavior. For example, a person might decide that whites do not have the right to exclude blacks from a neighborhood without necessarily deciding that blacks should "push" into the neighborhood. (Indeed, an otherwise

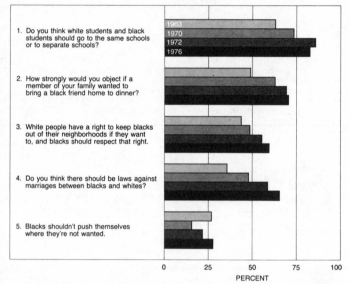

TREIMAN SCALE of questions on racial attitudes was administered to a nationwide sample of about 1,350 whites in 1963, 1970, 1972 and 1976. The bars show for each year the percentage of respondents giving what is considered to be a prointegration response to each question.

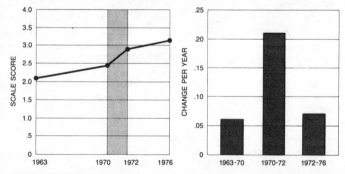

SCORE ON TREIMAN SCALE is the number of questions to which a respondent gives an integrationist response. The curve (left) shows how the mean scale score of the U.S. white population increased in successive surveys, with a sharper rise between 1970 and 1972. The bars (right) show the amount of change per year during the intervals between nationwide surveys.

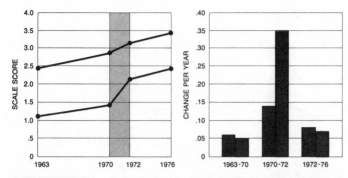

RATE OF CHANGE in scale score has been about the same in the North (*gray*) and the South (*color*) except during the 1970–72 period, when the mean score in the South rose more rapidly.

quite liberal person might believe that no one, including a sociologist, should push in where he is "not wanted.")

The different periods of change in white racial attitudes since 1963 are revealed if one compares the annual rates of change in the scale score during the several intervals between surveys. Between 1963 and 1970 the score moved in the liberal direction at the rate of six-hundredths of a question, or .06 point, a year. Between 1970 and 1972 the rate of change was .21 point a year, more than three times as high. For 1972–76 it declined to just about the pre-1970 level. A number of studies of U.S. attitudes on other issues show a similar pattern: slow but steady change through the 1960's, a quick spurt in the early 1970's and then a return to a stable, slower pattern of change. For example, analyses by James A. Davis and his colleagues at NORC show this pattern of change in the population's support for legalizing abortion under certain circumstances, for expansion of various rights of women and for some other measures of liberalism. In the last part of this article we shall attempt to interrelate some of these patterns of change in an effort to understand the reasons for the modification of white American racial attitudes.

Comparing the changes in scale scores for various subgroups of the population provides a fuller description of the trends we have noted and also some clues to factors that may account for the different periods of change. The causes of the steady long-term trend could include demographic changes, such as the succession of new age groups and the increasing educational level, or other persistent kinds of forces, such as the expansion in scope of civil-rights legislation. The accelerated movement of the early 1970's, however, will have to be explained in terms of more rapid introduction and acceptance of new values within the population or within regional or other subpopulations.

Regional differences persist, and there is little evidence to suggest that they will disappear in the near future. The most liberal regions are the Pacific Coast states and New England. The Middle Atlantic region, the Middle West and the Mountain and West South Central regions are grouped at a level fairly close to the national average. In the Deep South the verbally expressed level of toleration of interracial contact remains substantially below the level in other regions. The gap between the South as a whole (the three southern regions) and the rest of the country (the North) did close substantially during the period between 1970 and 1972; in those years the rate of change in the South increased by a factor of seven while the rate in the North about doubled: otherwise the rates of change have been about the same in the North and the South. Whatever forces caused the increased liberalization of the early 1970's apparently hit with particular force in the South.

Why did that happen? And as a matter of fact has the apparently similar long-term pattern of steady change actually been the same in the North as in the South? To answer these questions we turn to a more detailed breakdown of the trends in regional differences [*see illustrations on opposite page*]. Before 1970, in both the South and the North, the youngest age group became liberal faster than other age groups; the older age groups changed a little faster in the North than in the South; there were no appreciable differences among educational groups in rate of change. In other words, there was some increase in North-South polarization and there was rapid polarization by age within each region.

Between 1970 and 1972 the rate-of-change pattern is quite different. In the North the three older age groups became substantially more liberal, whereas the youngest group (which by 1970 had become quite distinctive in outlook) changed hardly at all; as a result, by 1972 age differences were smaller in the

North than they had been in 1970. As for education, it was those who had finished high school or finished college and those who had not entered high school (those, in other words, who had been able to achieve what they had striven for in education) whose scale scores rose most sharply. Those who had started high school or started college but had not finished also moved in the integrationist direction, but at slower pre-1970 rates.

In the South between 1970 and 1972 the age gap widened instead of narrowing. In general, the younger a person was the faster he changed; the two youngest groups changed at the rate of .43 point a year and the oldest group changed at the rate of .12 point a year, about the same rate as the older groups in the North. This age-group pattern was reflected in, and partly responsible for, the educational-level differences in the South during this period: the rates of change increase with education. The pattern of age and educational differences in the South during those two years was what one might expect of a region undergoing modernization and increasing acceptance of the dominant values of a society. This modernization pattern is observed only in the South, and there only between 1970 and 1972.

For many years the history of racial prejudice in the U.S. has been influenced by religious and ethnic considerations and the movements of religious and ethnic subgroups. Since World War II the distribution of such groups in the population has changed very little, and so shifts in ethnic composition cannot account for changes in racial attitudes of the kind we have described. Examining patterns of change within various groups, we find that in each of the four survey years the three major religious groups differed in their average scale score. The differences have been narrowing, however. In the period between 1963 and 1970 almost all the country's increase in racial liberalism was accounted for by the Protestant population, the least integrationist of the three religious groups. (The rate of change was .07 point per year for Protestants, .02 for Catholics and .03 for Jews; the figure for the U.S. population as a whole was .06.) During the period of rapid liberalization in the early 1970's the Protestant and the Catholic mean scores rose sharply at about the same rate, and they both continued to increase at lower rates between 1972 and 1976. Jews, historically the most liberal of the religious groups in verbal expression of racial tolerance, have had the lowest rate of liberalization over the entire period since 1963; indeed, their mean score actually decreased from 1970 to 1972. The reason for the slow rate of long-term change among Jews may be that their prointegration level has been so high that further change has become difficult to discern. Such an explanation would not, however, account for the apparent retrogression in the early 1970's. (The small size of the Jewish subgroup in our sample somewhat reduces our confidence in our ability to measure trends in the group.)

Differences among various ethnic groups within the northern Protestant and Catholic populations can be identified for the period since 1970. (It is only in the past decade or so that social researchers have "rediscovered" ethnicity as a factor in public opinion, and ethnic-identity questions were not included before that.) The highest rates of change between 1970 and 1972 were experienced by Anglo-Saxon Protestants and by Irish, Italian and Slavic Catholics (even though Catholics from eastern and southern Europe are popularly considered to be most resistant to racial change). The most resistant group appears to have been the German Protestants, who had the smallest increase over the six-year period.

The differences in the 1976 scores of various income and occupational groups are about what one might expect on the basis of educational and ethnic differences: the higher the income and the higher the occupational prestige are, the more favorable a white person is to the integration of his neighborhood and social relationships [see illustration on page 47]. There is a distinct gap between the white-collar and blue-collar occupational groups, and the gap is larger than can be accounted for by the income and educational differences between those groups. There is no significant sex difference on the racial tolerance scale.

The data we have cited can be summarized very briefly. The facts do not support the common assumption that the pace of liberalization in racial matters has been slowed by a white backlash. Instead the rate of change toward a more integrationist attitude has been rather constant since 1963, with a short period of faster change in the early 1970's. In the remainder of this article we shall attempt to "decompose," or account for, the changes in the Treiman scale, parceling out the total change into component changes brought about by various demographic factors and what can be termed a cultural factor: the general movement toward a liberal position on several measures of personal and civil liberties.

Our problem was to find an index of that general change in liberal values, such as responses given by Americans to some question that measures liberalization and that was posed, in the same form, at the right times to be incorporated in a statistical model explaining the racial data. We found one such question: "If your party nominated a woman for president, would you vote for her if

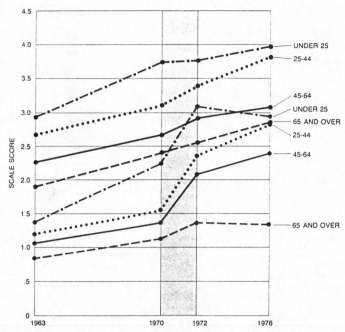

BREAKDOWN OF SCORES BY AGE GROUP shows that in the North (*gray*) and the South (*color*) younger groups had higher scores and scores increased more rapidly. During 1970–72 younger groups in the South changed particularly rapidly, tending to close North-South gap.

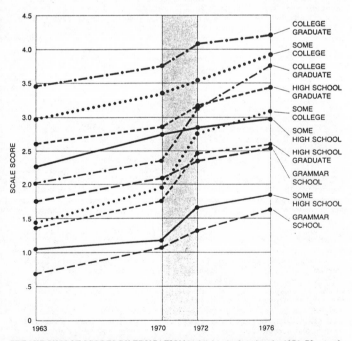

BREAKDOWN OF SCORES BY EDUCATION highlights the fact that the 1970–72 rate of change in the South (*color*) increased linearly with education. Together with the age-group variation, this pattern is a characteristic of a region that has been undergoing rapid modernization.

45

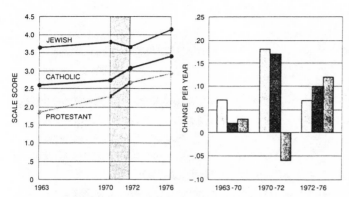

BREAKDOWN BY RELIGION shows gaps between the scores of Protestants, Catholics and Jews are narrowing. Protestants and Catholics changed at about same rate, Jews more slowly.

she were qualified for the job?" It was included in Gallup surveys in almost exactly the same years as our earlier racial surveys, and it appeared in our General Social Survey along with the Treiman scale in 1972 and 1976. The level of support for a woman as president rose with the same dynamic as the racial-liberalism scale. A "yes" answer was given by 54 percent of the population in 1963 and

then by an estimated 59 percent in 1970. Between 1970 and 1972 there was a dramatic increase to 69 percent. The trend continued after 1972, but at a slower pace, with 78 percent giving the positive response in 1976.

We adopted this variable as an index of a general shift in the society toward support for the expansion of civil and personal liberties. It is far from being a

perfect indicator, to be sure, since attitudes on a woman as president must have been affected by the changing climate with regard specifically to women's rights and roles. Moreover, it would have been better to have several indicators rather than one. Because we had only the one indicator whatever role we ultimately assign to the general cultural movement toward liberalism must necessarily represent a lower limit for the role of that cultural factor.

A somewhat similar analysis, also aimed at allocating responsibility for change in liberal values to various determinants of change, was performed in 1975 by Davis and his colleagues. The sociologist Samuel A. Stouffer had predicted in 1955 that support for liberal values would increase with increases in education and with the succession of new cohorts, or age groups, whose members were more educated and more open-minded. Davis found that by 1975 the level of support for measures of liberalism Stouffer had devised had indeed increased, by an average of 28 percent, and that the dynamics of cohort succession and increasing educational attainment alone accounted for more than half of that change. We could not expect demographic changes to account for that much of the change we sought to analyze in racial attitudes because our time span was only 13 years rather than 20. On the other hand, the explanatory power of the model we devised should be increased by our inclusion of another explanatory variable: support for a woman as president.

The logical basis of our analysis is an assumption that changes in the Treiman scale result from changes in a number of "predictor variables" related to racial liberalism, which themselves change over time. The predictor variables are cohort succession, rising educational level and the general liberalization of values. (There are other variables that tend to predict racial attitude but that are ineffective for explaining changes because they themselves do not change much over time. Region of residence is a good example.) We defined four cohorts—"old" (born before 1907), "middle" (born from 1907 through 1923), "young" (1924–39) and "new" (1940–58)—and tracked them through the population with data from a number of NORC surveys. Three educational groups (those with at least some college, high school graduates and nongraduates) could be established within each cohort on the basis of another question on each racial-attitude survey. And support for a woman as president, of course, was our measure of general liberalization.

Having specified the important predictor variables, we arrange them on what is called a linear flow graph that indicates their presumed causal relation

ETHNIC SUBGROUPS among Northern Protestants and Catholics have been separately recorded since 1970. The most rapid change was in mean score of Italian Catholics between 1970 and 1972. Irish and Slavic Catholics increased score rapidly, as did Anglo-Saxon Protestants.

[*see top illustration on page 49*]. The next step is to determine the quantitative relation between each predictor variable and the dependent variable: a person's score on the racial-liberalism scale. This is a problem in multiple regression analysis. The numbers (the path coefficients) on arrows near the right side of the flow graph show the extent to which each characteristic of a respondent tends to raise or lower his racial-liberalism score—after controlling for the other characteristics. For example, young people are more liberal on racial matters in part because they are better educated, and so we need to control for educational differences before making statements about "pure" cohort effects. The path coefficient (.56) on the arrow from "new cohort" to "racial liberalism" is the difference in score between the new cohort and a base group (the middle cohort), after adjustment for the differences between those cohorts in educational attainment and support for a woman as president. In other words, controlling for differences in education and in support for a woman as president, people in the new cohort score, on the average, .56 point higher on the Treiman scale than do people in the middle cohort. The young cohort scores .23 point higher than the middle cohort, the old cohort .30 point lower than the middle cohort.

Again, within any cohort and whatever the opinion on a woman as president, a person who has finished high school scores .49 point higher on the Treiman scale than someone who has not finished high school; a person with at least some college scores 1.01 points higher than someone who has not finished high school. And people who would vote for a woman as president score .68 point higher, no matter what their age or educational level, than those who would not vote for a woman. The other paths in the flow graph show how the variables that predict the racial liberalism score are themselves interrelated. They show how age cohorts differ in attaining a particular educational level and in supporting a woman as president.

The flow graph, then, shows the structure of the relations between the variables. In order to determine how much of the total change in the score (the dependent variable) is explained by changes in each of the prior variables, we first need to determine the amount of change over time—the delta (Δ)—for each of the prior variables. The new cohort, for example, came to constitute a much larger proportion of the population over the years and the old cohort accounted for a much smaller percentage. The young cohort's percentage did not change significantly. Specifically, the percent of the population in the new cohort increased by 12.85 percent between 1963 and 1970, by 11.95 percent between

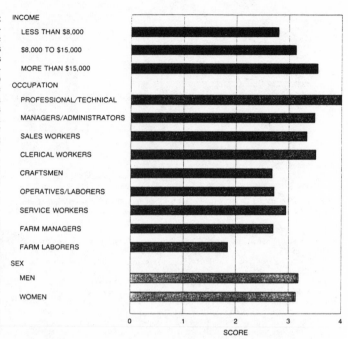

INCOME

LESS THAN $8,000

$8,000 TO $15,000

MORE THAN $15,000

OCCUPATION

PROFESSIONAL/TECHNICAL

MANAGERS/ADMINISTRATORS

SALES WORKERS

CLERICAL WORKERS

CRAFTSMEN

OPERATIVES/LABORERS

SERVICE WORKERS

FARM MANAGERS

FARM LABORERS

SEX

MEN

WOMEN

0   1   2   3   4

SCORE

1976 SCALE SCORES are shown here for various income and occupational groups and by sex. The occupational groups are listed here in the order of decreasing perceived "prestige," as determined by a public-opinion survey conducted by National Opinion Research Center.

1970 and 1972 and by 9.99 percent between 1972 and 1976.

These numbers provide change coefficients for the new cohort, or delta 1, for the three periods [*see illustration on next page*]. The deltas measure the amount of change in each variable that is not accounted for by a change in a prior variable. Deltas 2 and 3 are the change coefficients for the young and the old cohorts. Deltas 4 and 5 are zero because we find that just about all of the increase in educational level is a by-product of the succession of better educated cohorts; there is no significant net change, or increase in educational level within cohorts (by a back-to-school trend, for example). As for support for a woman as president, again some of the change is attributable to the succession of younger and better educated cohorts, but a significant amount of change is still not accounted for. This delta 6, the net change in our liberalism indicator, was small before 1970 and large thereafter—particularly large, in terms of change per year, between 1970 and 1972.

The final step is to multiply the changes in prior variables, the deltas, by the path coefficients linking the prior variables to the dependent variable, which we want to explain. The change in racial attitude that is attributable to the direct effect of the increase in the new cohort during a particular period, for example,

is found by multiplying the change for that period (delta 1) by the direct path linking the new cohort to the racial-liberalism scale. For the period from 1963 to 1970 that means multiplying .1285 by .56. The product, .0719, is the fraction of a point by which the mean U.S. Treiman-scale score increased between 1963 and 1970 because of the direct effect of the succession of the new cohort; it comes to 18 percent of the gross change (.40 point) in the scale score for that period [*see bottom illustration on page 49*]. There are other, indirect effects of new-cohort succession, as the flow graph arrows make clear. One of them is the effect of the new cohort's increased probability of being a high school graduate, graduates in turn tending to have higher Treiman scores. That effect is calculated by multiplying .1285 by .26 by .49. In the same way the change attributable to the independent effects of the liberalization measured by support for a woman as president can be seen to be .0207 multiplied by .68, or .0141.

What can an examination of these numbers reveal about the process of change in racial attitudes? For one thing, the results illuminate the two kinds of effect of cohort succession. One is indirect. Younger cohorts are better educated and more supportive of other liberal values in addition to racial integration. As these cohorts loom larger, the population as a whole becomes better educated and more attached to liberal values, and those changes in turn have implications for racial liberalism. There is also a direct effect of cohort succession. Quite apart from their higher level of education and their increasingly liberal stance in general, younger white people have been exposed to different values in race relations. They are more likely to go to school with blacks, serve with them in the Army and work with them. The impact of recent advances in race relations has been age-specific in many respects. If a segment of a population is changed by certain events, then that change is preserved as a cohort effect. As the proportion of the population exposed to these change-generating events becomes larger, U.S. society will move in the liberal direction.

For the entire period from 1963 to 1976 the increase of the new cohort accounted directly for 18 percent of the total amount of change in the white racial-attitude score. Another 19 percent of the change was an indirect effect of the same increase: the new cohort was better educated and more liberal—and therefore more prointegration. In other words, the succession of the cohort of whites born between 1940 and 1958 has been tremendously important; it accounted, directly or indirectly, for 37 percent of the total change in racial liberalism from 1963 to 1976. (The result is similar to Davis' finding that the direct and indirect effects of cohort succession accounted for 32 percent of the increased support he found for unpopular political and religious minorities.) The impact of the new cohort is particularly impressive for the period 1970–72. It accounted for an increase in the Treiman score of almost .07 point per year, thus explaining at least part of the sharp increase in integrationist support during that period. The decline of the oldest

cohort had much the same effect as the increase of the new one, both directly and indirectly, but it accounts for much less of the change (particularly after 1972, by which time most of its members had died). Nevertheless, its effect was far from trivial.

We come finally to the question of how much of the change in racial liberalism can be explained by a broad shift in the society's evaluation of personal and civil rights and liberties. We believe that some of the contribution of that factor is measured by the direct effect of the change in the percentage of the population who would vote for a woman as president (only a lower limit of what might be explained by the broad liberalization factor, as we pointed out above, because we have only the one indicator). For the period as a whole, increased support for liberal values, as measured by the woman-as-president indicator, accounted for 10 percent of the increase in the racial-attitude score. What is most interesting is the variation of this factor over time, which helps to explain the difference between the 1970–72 period and the other periods. Before 1970 the woman-as-president issue accounted for only 4 percent of the change in the Treiman-scale score. Between 1970 and 1972 the influence of this factor was much greater; it accounted for 12 percent of the total change. In absolute terms, the liberalization factor contributed .025 point per year in those two years. Meanwhile, as we pointed out above, the effects of cohort succession also increased sharply. The result was a rapid change in the two-year period, much of it accounted for by these two factors. After 1972 the amount of change attributable to broad liberalization declined along with that attributable to the other variables, but the relative importance of this variable increased.

When all the changes explained by

these variables in the flow graph are added up, the sum is less than the gross change in the Treiman-scale score. That means there are other sources of change that are not accounted for by our model. The model does account for between 53 and 65 percent of the change in each time period, which suggests that we are doing a respectable, but by no means complete, job of accounting for the trend in racial attitudes.

Our data do not allow us to do more than speculate about the meaning of the liberal leap of the early 1970's, one that has been hitherto invisible to observers of U.S. politics and society. We note that most of the change must have been generated during the time of the Kent State and other disturbances arising from the invasion of Cambodia. We also know it was during the two years just before this period that the majority of the American public turned against the war in Vietnam, as was shown in a study by John E. Mueller of the University of Rochester in 1973. Is it possible that the process of deciding that the leadership of the country had been wrong about the war—and had deceived the people about the war—was a radicalizing experience for a substantial segment of Americans, an experience that made people reexamine their beliefs on a variety of related subjects? Is it possible that even though they disapproved of student radicals and vigorously rejected Senator George McGovern as a presidential candidate a substantial number of Americans were willing to accept some of the ideology of the McGovern wing of the Democratic party? May the antiwar Democrats have been more successful than they thought, precisely when they thought they had begun to fail?

To be even more speculative, could a more adroit liberal leadership have taken advantage of this unperceived trend in the early 1970's to build new coalitions with the people they had unknowingly influenced? Were those who talked about such coalitions in the early 1970's right about the possibility and wrong about the strategy? May they not have offended their most likely recruits by adopting strategies designed to please those who were already in their camp?

The fact that our evidence even raises such questions suggests that both conventional public-opinion polls and the traditional "feel" of politicians and political activists for shifts in public attitudes are imperfect instruments for shaping political strategies. To the sociologist our results may suggest that more carefully designed and more elaborate time-series measurements of public attitudes are needed if we are to document and understand social change in America and challenge the myths that become history because there are no data to refute them.

Δ	VARIABLE	1963 – 1970	1970 – 1972	1972 – 1976
1	NEW COHORT	.1285	.1195	.0999
2	YOUNG COHORT	0	0	0
3	OLD COHORT	– .0948	– .0562	– .0078
4	HIGH SCHOOL	0	0	0
5	COLLEGE	0	0	0
6	WOMAN AS PRESIDENT	.0207	.0718	.0727

CHANGE COEFFICIENTS, or deltas, give the change in the course of each period for "predictor variables" (*see top illustration on opposite page*). Deltas 1, 2 and 3 give the increase in age cohorts as a percent of the total population; the young cohort did not change significantly. Deltas 4 and 5 are zero because the effect of increasing education is fully measured by the succession of new cohorts. Delta 6 is the net change, after controlling for cohort succession, in the support of a woman as president. Deltas are multiplied by "path coefficients" in the final step.

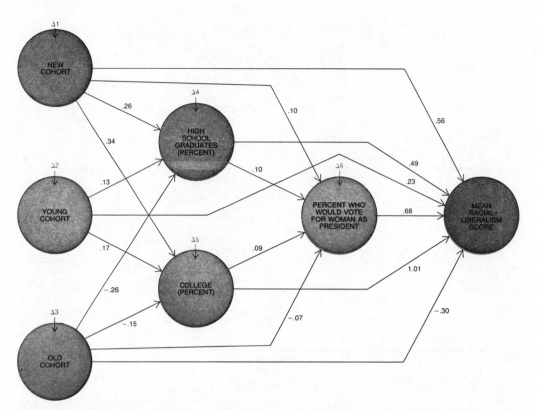

LINEAR FLOW GRAPH shows the relations between predictor variables (*light color*) and the dependent variable (*dark color*), which is the racial-liberalism score. The numbers (path coefficients) on the paths from the predictor variables to the score state the extent (in fractions of a point) to which a given variable raises the score of a respondent above that of a member of the appropriate base group (the middle cohort, those with less than a high school education or those who would not vote for a woman as president), controlling for other variables; other paths, at the left and center, show the interrelations of the predictor variables. For example, a member of the old cohort is 15 percent less likely to have gone to college than a member of the middle cohort, and people who have gone to college tend to score 1.01 points higher than those who have not graduated from high school. The short arrows labeled delta (Δ) refer to the change coefficients.

	1963–1970		1970–1972		1972–1976		TOTAL, 1963–1976	
GROSS CHANGE IN SCALE	.40		.42		.26		1.08	
	AMOUNT	PERCENT	AMOUNT	PERCENT	AMOUNT	PERCENT	AMOUNT	PERCENT
COHORT SUCCESSION, DIRECT:								
INCREASE OF NEW COHORT	.0719	18	.0668	16	.0559	22	.1946	18
DECLINE OF OLD COHORT	.0284	7	.0168	4	.0023	1	.0475	4
COHORT SUCCESSION, INDIRECT:								
INCREASE OF NEW COHORT	.0742	19	.0690	16	.0577	22	.2009	19
DECLINE OF OLD COHORT	.0330	8	.0195	5	.0028	1	.0553	5
VALUE CHANGE:								
NET CHANGE ON WOMAN AS PRESIDENT	.0141	4	.0489	12	.0495	19	.1125	10
TOTAL CHANGE ACCOUNTED FOR	.2216	55	.2210	53	.1682	65	.6108	57

CHANGES IN SCALE SCORES are "decomposed," or parceled out, to show the contribution of each of the predictor variables. The gross change in score for each interval is shown at the top. Then the amount of change contributed by each variable (the product of the appropriate path coefficient and delta) is listed, along with the percent of the gross change that it accounts for. At the bottom the various contributions are summed to show how much of the gross change in mean score can be accounted for by demographic and cultural variables.

Varieties of Apocalypse in Science Fiction

Andrew M. Greeley

The science fiction "little magazines" (*Analog, Galaxy*, etc.) have been distinctly ambivalent about *Star Wars* and *Close Encounters of the Third Kind*. On the one hand, they are delighted to see science fiction forms appeal to a broad range of consumers of popular culture. On the other hand, like all cultists, the SF purists who review for the science fiction journals are appalled at how disrespectful both of the films were of the solemn and sacred Forms which currently reign in "authentic" science fiction. Heroic sagas of the *Star Wars* sort, particularly those with reasonably happy endings (living happily ever after for Luke Skywalker and Pricess Leia must mean at least several fights a week) were abandoned by the SF purists long ago and the thought that the wee folk on the flying saucers might be benign (even Cherubic) is enough to send the canonists of SF off to the local office of their Inquisition to demand that Orthodox Doctrine be enforced. For one knows that the saucer folk are either callously indifferent to us lesser mortals here on earth or ultimately impatient with our stupidity and bent upon either reforming us despite ourselves or simply eliminating us from the universe as a dangerous lower life form which does not deserve to exist. The smiling little fellows from *Close Encounters* are not apocalyptic visitors at all.

Apocalypse, ah, that's the word! Science fiction was born from an apocalyptic vision, and currently flourishes on another apocalyptic vision, but does not seem to understand what apocalypse really is.

In the Christian scriptures there is the Book of Revelation (once called by the papists such as the present writer, "Apocalypse") which is filled with falling stars, suns going out, moons disappearing from the heavens, blasting trumpets and the general dissolution of the world. The book represents in a sense an extended reflection on the descriptions of the final days of the world given by Jesus in the gospel stories.

The apocalyptic literary style, it turns out, was the most popular religious literary form in the Middle East, and particularly, in Palestine during the Second Temple era. If you wanted to communicate religiously with Jews and proselytes (fellow travelers of Jews who did not practice the full rigors of the Mosaic law)—who may have been one-quarter of the citizens of the Roman Empire—the apocalyptic religious mode of expression was almost essential. Hence, its popularity with the writers of the Christian scriptures.

It is very difficult for those of us who live in a different era to penetrate back into the minds of the apocalyptic writers and preachers. Were they speaking "literally" or "poetically"? Did they really think the stars were going to fall from the heavens and that the world was going to be consumed by fire? Or were they rather describing in striking imagery the human condition and particularly the human religious condition? The best answer to that question seems to be that if we asked it of an apocalyptic

280   Journal Of American Culture

preacher or writer he would not have the faintest notion of what we were talking about. If we could explain our terms he would probably say that his style was somewhere between poetry and literal description and would be baffled as to why anybody would be interested in a question such as ours.

Later Christians' piety, however, became quite literal and rigid in its interpretation of apocalypse and identified the apocalyptic imagery with the "end of the world" or "Judgment Day," a specific event with which history was to terminate, and at which all the imagery described in the apocalyptic literature would *physically* occur. The medievel Latin hymn *Dies Irae* is the epitome of the extreme literalization of apocalyptic imagery as it has found its way into the Western imagination (think, for example, of the wild music of Verdi's *Dies Irae* in his *Requiem*). The end of the world, and its possible renewal, then, is a major theme in the Western creative imagination although destruction of the cosmos has always seemed far more important to popular Christian piety and to elite artistic and literary imaginations than the renewal which may come afterwards. One need only think of the horrors of Michelangelo's Last Judgment in the Sistine Chapel (horrors which never seem to terrify the College of Cardinals all that much when it assembles to elect a new pope) to realize that what fascinated Michelangelo's genius was destruction, not reconstruction.

One of the curious anomalies of the development of the apocalyptic/eschatological imagery in the Western imagination is that those literary scholars who have very skillfully attempted to reconstruct the style and the imagination of Jesus himself are now pretty well persuaded that he personally avoided almost entirely the apocalyptic imagery and that apocalypse in the New Testament is an adaptation of the message of Jesus to a popular literary and oratorical style carried on by his followers. Jesus himself, it would seem, much preferred to shatter people's preconceptions with parables instead of with falling stars, exploding suns, vanishing moons and great conflagrations sweeping across the earth. But if we wish to understand the importance of the apocalypse in the Western imagination and in the science fiction segment of popular culture we must go back beyond the Christian scriptures to the origins of apocalypse in the post-exilic, pre-Second Temple era of Judaism. As good a place as any to start is the fourteenth chapter of the book of Zechariah.

See, a day is coming for Yahweh when the spoils taken from you will be divided among you. Yahweh will gather all the nations to Jerusalem for battle. The city will be taken, the houses plundered, the women ravished. Half the city will go into captivity, but the remnant of the people will not be cut off from the city. Then Yahweh will take the field; he will fight against these nations as he fights in the day of battle. On that day, his feet will rest on the Mount of Olives, which faces Jerusalem from the east. The Mount of Olives will be split in half from east to west, forming a huge gorge; half the Mount will recede northwards, the other half southwards. And the Vale of Hinnom will be filled up from Goah to Jasol; it will be blocked as it was by the earthquake in the days of Uzziah king of Judah. Yahweh your God will come, and all the holy ones with him. When that day comes, there will be no more cold, no more frost. It will be a day of wonder— Yahweh knows it—with no alternation of day and night; in the evening it will be light. When that day comes, running waters will issue from Jerusalem, half of them to the eastern sea, half of them to the western sea; they will flow summer and winter. And Yahweh will be king of the whole world. When that day comes, Yahweh will be unique and his name unique. The entire country will be transformed into plain, from Geba to Rimmon in the Negeb. And Jerusalem will be raised higher, though still in the same place; from the Gate of Benjamin to the site of the First Gate, that

Apocalypse in Science Fiction 281

is to say to the Gate of the Corner and from the Tower Hananel to the king's winepress, people will make their homes. The ban will be lifted; Jerusalem will be safe to live in.

And this is the plague with which Yahweh will strike all the nations who have fought against Jerusalem; their flesh will moulder while they are still standing on their feet; their eyes will rot in their sockets; their tongues will rot in their mouths. And such will be the plague on the horses and mules, camels and donkeys, and all the animals to be found in that camp. When that day comes, a great terror will fall on them from Yahweh; each man will grab his neighbour's hand and they will hit out at each other. Even Judah will fight against Jerusalem. The wealth of all the surrounding nations will be heaped together; gold, silver, clothing, in vast quantity.

All who survive of all the nations that have marched against Jerusalem will go up year by year to worship the King, Yahweh Sabaoth, and to keep the feast of Tabernacles. Should one of the races of the world fail to go up to Jerusalem to worship the King, Yahweh Sabaoth, there will be no rain for that one. Should the race of Egypt fail to go up and pay its visit, on it will fall the plague which Yahweh will inflict on each one of those nations that fail to go up to keep the feast of Tabernacles. When that day comes, the horse bells will be inscribed with the words, "Sacred to Yahweh," and in the Temple of Yahweh the very cooking pots will be as fine as the sprinkling bowls at the altar. And every cooking pot in Jerusalem and in Judah shall become sacred to Yahweh Sabaoth; all who want to offer sacrifice will come and help themselves from them for their cooking; there will be no more traders in the Temple of Yahweh Sabaoth, when that day comes. (from the *Jerusalem Bible*)

Leaving aside the references to Yahweh, and the bizarre Middle Eastern names, the images are not all that foreign to the addicted reader of science fiction. Indeed, Zechariah might be giving a brief synopsis of *Lucifer's Hammer* by Larry Niven and Jerry Purnelle (an account of a comet colliding with earth). What did Zechariah have in mind?

Contemporary research on the apocalyptic literature (see, for example, Paul D. Hansen, *The Dawn of Apocalyptic: The Historical and Sociological Roots of Jewish Apocalyptic Eschatology*. Fortress Press, 1975) are reasonably persuaded that apocalyptic literature is fundamentally Jewish in its origins and influenced only very slightly by the neighboring pagan literary styles. Jewish literature of the immediate pre-exile era was prophetic, heavily concerned with moral striving, humanist in obligation in Yahweh's name to create a just and moral society. It would remain free and powerful, not by force of arms, but because of its fidelity to him, and the moral excellence which characterized the lives of its people. The moral and religious visions of the prophets, of course, are the core of the Jewish and Christian religions and represent one of the major breakthroughs in religious consciousness of all human history. However, the prophetic vision of a just and religious messianic age was not achieved and later prophets such as Jeremiah wrestled with an explanation. Had Yahweh's promise been misunderstood or had the people been faithless? In any event, the kingdom was destroyed, the people carried off into captivity, and the messianic hopes dashed. Upon return from exile the Israelite elites, discouraged, disheartened and oppressed, fell back on the older creation symbols which their religious heritage shared with the rest of the Middle East—images of the struggle between cosmos and chaos, between good and evil, between light and darkness. Creation was the ordering of the universe by Yahweh (or by demigods in other Eastern religions). The fires were put out, the darkness was illuminated, disorder and conflict was held at bay, and life became possible in the world though sometimes only tenuously and barely possible. If the first creation had not inaugurated a process which led to fulfillment, so argued some of the post-exilic elite, most notably Zechar-

282   Journal Of American Culture

iah and the author of the second part of Isaiah, then perhaps what was needed was a dissolution of the old world back into its primal chaos and a recreation of the cosmos by a new and decisive act of the Ordering Principle. The notion of a new beginning, of the destruction of the old and the creation of the new, was apparently widespread in ancient times—widespread in the era after the exile. The old kingdoms and empires were breaking up and new were being born. It was, for those who followed the stars, the end of Taurus the Bull and the beginning of the Age of the Fish. If the apocalyptic literary style was Jewish and even prophetic in its formation, it reached backwards into the creation images of the Middle Eastern nature religions and sideways into the conviction that a new era was beginning which was prevalent in Meditterranean Hellenism (when the Emperor Augustus closed the door to the Temple of Mars the event was hailed as the beginning of a new era of peace, not totally dissimilar to the messianic eras hailed in the Jewish scriptures—given the enormous influence of Judaism in the Roman Empire at the time of Augustus, of course, it is quite possible that most of the in-flow of imagery was from Judaism to Roman Hellenism instead of vice versa).

Note well that in its origins, as described in the passage from Zechariah, apocalypse is more reconstruction than destruction, more of a beginning of a new than an ending of the old, more of a vision of hope than a vision of dissolution. Even by the time of the Christian scriptures, however, the fascination of writers and preachers with dazzling accounts of destruction was already well under way The *Dies Irae* would take thirteen more centuries to write but the raw material was already there.

The apocalypse image, as such, is unique to those cultural environments where Yahwehism—in its Jewish and/or Christian forms— has had an impact. Both eschatological themes are muted, or nonexistent, in other religious traditions. We so take for granted the apocalyptic theme, it is so much part of the unconscious cultural environment, the literary air we breathe, that we hardly distinguish it and are hence quite unaware of its special impact, particularly on the Western imagination. Still, it is not unreasonable to assert that if it were not for apocalypse there would not be science fiction because there would not be a vision of a future that is better than the past nor of a decisive intervention of a saving force which leads to a recreation, a reconstruction, a renewal of the world.

In the nineteenth century, philosophy believed that science could eliminate human misery and suffering, and the literary imagination strove to construct scientific paradises in which the good life, guided by a benign (if mildly totalitarian) science, was possible. The work of the American Ignatius Donnelly and the Englishman H.G. Wells testified to that bright scientific vision. It was science as a reconstructing agent that was intervening in a more or less gentle apocalypse to renew the earth.

The vision has faded. We are now in post-exilic times and the Second Temple has yet to be constructed. It is an era of pessimism, not to say fatalism, which makes Zechariah seem like a naive optimist. The SF imagination no longer constructs scientific utopias but either partial or total apocalypses in which the bad we know is wiped out and replaced by something worse or, alternatively, something every bit as bad. The positive component, then, of the apocalyptic imagination has been lost and the science fiction writer of the day has more in common with Thomas of Celano (the author of the *Dies Irae*) than he does with Zechariah.

Much of the science fiction literature simply assumes that there has been a nuclear war. Even the benign *Star Trek* series operated on such an assumption, and so do the future histories of Isaac Asimov, Poul Anderson (in his Nicholas van Rijn series), and Robert Heinlein. The world which has evolved is almost invariably at least as bad as the one that antedated the catastrophy and oftentimes much worse—humankind sinking back into barbarism and savagery, made even worse by the presence of mutants produced by radioactive fallout.

Thus, in *Lucifer's Hammer,* life goes on after the collision with the comet but it is a life much like that of the Dark Ages with the ruthless war lords presiding over small territorial kingdoms locked in endless combat with their neighbors. Human nature is, the writers say, following the popularizers of primate research, basically evil, aggressive, destructive. All the apocalyptic events do is strip away the veneer of civilization and turn us back into savages.

(The serious scholarly research in comparative primatology doubts that there is any such thing as an aggressive instinct and suggests that our pre-hominid and protohominid ancestors had to develop abilities at both cooperation and love before we could evolve into human beings—far too benign a view of human nature for the currently fashionable pessimism.)   In addition to the manmade holocausts, which usually end with the human race badly damaged but struggling on, and the extraterrestrially induced holocausts in which human nature is sometimes renewed but other times virtually eliminated (in one science fiction series, recently serialized in a magazine, genetic experiments produce god-like creatures who oppress and virtually destroy the descendants of the original human species), there are also the cataclysmic apocalypses which sound in their descriptions much like those in the scriptures but which result (like the comet collision in *Lucifer's Hammer*) from the blind working of astronomical fate—not infrequently ending completely the world and the human race (though somehow or other, accounts manage to get written after the apocalypse, often in ways never explained by the author). For example, in Isaac Asimov's classic, *Nightfall,* darkness descends. "This was the dark—the dark and the cold and the doom. The bright walls of the universe were shattered and their awful black fragments were falling down to crush and squeeze and obliterate him...on the horizon outside the window...a crimson glow began growing, strengthening in brightness that was not the glow of the sun...the long night had come again."

Thomas of Celano would really have liked that.

And in Arthur Clarke's *The Nine Billion Names of God,* the Mark V computer, programmed by Tibetan monks, does indeed speak the nine billion names of God. The universe has had its purpose and "overhead, without any fuss, the stars were going out."

Sometimes, however, while destruction is induced by fates, the agent of the fate is human, as in L. Sprague DeCamp's *Judgment Day,* in which Wade Ormont, a "mad scientist," who has been persecuted by other human

284   Journal Of American Culture

beings all his life, is pushed to the breaking point by "mischief night" (the night before Hallowe'en when the local kids raise hell). The kids had "soaped the windows and scattered the garbage and spread the toilet paper around...they had also burgled my garage and gone over my little British two-seater. The tires were punctured, the upholdery slashed, the paint scratched and the wiring ripped out of the engine...to make sure I knew what they thought, had lettered a lot of shirt cardboards and left them around, reading: 'Old lady Ormont is a nut; beware of the mad scientist!'

"That decided me. There is one way I can be happy during my remaining years and that is by the knowledge that all these bullies will get theirs. I hate them, I hate them, I hate everybody; I want to kill mankind; I'd kill them by slow torture if I could; if I can't blowing up the earth will do."

Why are the current science fiction apocalypses almost totally gloomy and destructive events, why is the pessimism even worse than at the time of Zechariah, and even more gloomy than that of the time of Thomas Celano, who managed in the last couple of stanzas of the *Dies Iraes* to breathe a few words of hope?

The modernist approach in literature, of course, precludes the possibility of hopefulness or happiness in serious novels. Science fiction writers aspire to be serious novelists and therefore they have become more pessimistic, or as they strive to achieve something beyond what they consider merely pulp popularity (so as mystery writers come to be more "serious" they give up the mythological conflict between good and evil, in which good as represented by the detective tends to win, and either have the detective defeated or identify the detective ambiguously with the forces of evil—such are the requirements of literary modernism). Furthermore, in the years since the 1945 bombings of Hiroshima and Nagasaki, and in particular since the discovery of the apocalyptic possibilities of pollution, science has become another one of the gods that failed and is perceived now by many American intellectuals as a malign and destructive force. (One writer has observed that evolution made a mistake when it produced humankind and human reflective self-consciousness because it produced a force which would eventually terminate the evolutionary process—Manichaeism which would make St. Augustine look like a flaming Pelegian optimist!) As destructive apocalypse has become part of the mythology and the imagery of the wider national intelligentsia (Robert Heilbruner, in his *On the Human Prospect,* asks whether there is hope for humankind and responds vigorously in the negative), then that segment of the elite or would-be elite which produces science fiction is necessarily driven to apocalypse, but always, of course, the apocalypse of destruction, and rarely the apocalypse in which destruction is a prelude to reconstruction.

There is, however, one fascinating exception, a writer who continues to practice the apocalyptic tradition in a style that would please Zechariah and Deutero Isaias. His name is Raphael Aloysius Lafferty, and he was born in Neola, Iowa, in 1914, of Irish immigrant parents. A self-educated electrical engineer (for thirty-five years before he turned to writing full-time), Lafferty has a literary style which reminds one of Gilbert Keith Chesterton, and a creative imagination filled with light, fire and divine lunacy.

For Lafferty, apocalypses, even savage ones, are gracious and often comic.

In his novel *Past Master,* Thomas More is rescued from the headman's block by a people who are able to reach back into history and brought him into another era in which he is charged with saving a world that is coming apart at the seams. More does brilliantly and ends up on the headman's scaffold once again. After having been world president and king for nine days, he's doomed to die again. His allies, led by a marvelous young woman named Evita (and a boy named Adam, who dies repeatedly only to be born again), storm the scaffold but are driven back. "The boy Adam, in particular, died magnificently, as he always did." Evita destroys More's enemy, but More himself is executed—*possibly*—though a stranger does appear on the platform and speaks with him. "Thomas seemed both excited and pleased."

"Will it work, do you think?" he cried loudly, with almost delight. "How droll. Can a man have more heads than two? I'll do it, I'll go with you."

But then there is apocalypse.

But one thing *did* really happen at that moment. At the moment that life flickered out of the beheaded corpse, *the worlds came to an end.*

All life and heat and pulse went out of the world. It died in every bird and rock and plant and person of it, in every mountain and sea and cloud. It died in its gravity and light and heat, in its germ-life and in its life-code. Everything ceased. And all the stars went out.

Was it for a moment? Or a billion years? Or forever? There is no difference in them, when the world is ended, when there is no time to measure time by.[1] (Author's emphasis)

But all of this is not yet quite the end; in fact it might not be the end at all for, as Lafferty concludes the book:

Remember it? Then it happened?
Be quiet. We wait.
The spirit came down once on water and clay. Could it not come down on gell-cells and flux-fix? The sterile wood, whether of human or programmed tree, shall it fruit after all? The Avid Nothingness, the diabolically empty Point-Big-O, is it cast away again? Is there then no room for life? Shall there be return to real life?
Well, does it happen? Does the reaction become the birthing? What does it look like?
Will we see it now, in fact and rump, the new-born world?
Be quiet. We hope. (pp. 247-8; author's emphasis)

In the book *Apocalypses*[2] (oh, yes, Lafferty is well aware of what he's up to), there is a long novella called "The Three Armageddons of Enniscorthy Sweeny," in which a long chronology is presented of the life and times of the picaresque genius Enniscorthy Sweeny, 1894 to 1984—including the election of Robert Taft as president of the United States in 1948 and Douglas MacArthur in 1952, John XXIII as pope in 1958 and Richard Nixon as president in 1960. In 1984, Enniscorthy Sweeny himself dies (and the year is no accident) and his opera, *Armegeddon Three,* is performed, apparently beginning the process that leads to the end of the world. The final entrance in the chronology is 1984, "the situation worsens." After the chronology, the world may or may not end, but one is not quite clear because, as one preacher, warning of the end of the world, says in the tale, "...when the

286   Journal Of American Culture

world is finally destroyed will it *act* as though it is destroyed? Or will it be the most casual and nonbelieving cinder ever?" (p. 361)

It is quite clear that "just at the winddown of the years, the world and its people have gotten mighty mean. They were the meanest and the rottenest people that anyone ever saw." Enniscorthy Sweeny may not have been dead either; he may simply have been sitting in the tree like Mad Sweeny, the king in ancient Irish legend, and his wife Mary Margaret, who stood beneath the tree and crooned, "Aw, c'mon down, Sweeny." It would appear that some people set Sweeny's tree on fire to roast him to death and that began the final fire of the world.

> So Final Armageddon was burning and raging out of control, and the World was ending.
> That's funny. The people didn't *act* as if the world were ending. But they didn't act quite as if it were going to continue either.
> They behaved as though they didn't very much care whether it ended or not (p. 374).

Thus, the end of the world and the end of Enniscorthy Sweeny—maybe, and then, maybe not, because it would appear that Sweeny had been killed many times before and kept coming back.

But the wildest of Lafferty's apocalypses is in his brilliant story— perhaps his masterpiece—*And Walk Now Gently Through the Fire,* a tale about the Ichthyans, or queer fish, a group of people who keep alive a strange version of Christianity after "The Great Copout."

> ...the Day of the Great Copout was worldwide. As though at a given signal (but there had been no signal) people in every city and town and village and countryside of earth dropped their tools and implements and swore that they would work no more. Officials and paper shufflers ceased to officiate and to shuffle paper. Retailers closed up and retailed no more. Distributors no longer distributed. Producers produced nothing. The clock of the people stopped although some had believed that the hour was still early.
> The Last Day had been, according to some.
> "The Last Day has not been," said a prophet. "They will know it when it has been." (pp. 45)

The leading characters of *And Walk Now Gently Through the Fire* are the Thatcher family—Judy, the young mother, and her two early teenage children, Trumpet and Gregory. The head of the family, one John Thatcher, had been one of the Twelve, a leader of the Ichthyans, but he had been killed. However, he rose from the dead for a brief period of time to pass on his leadership function to his wife, who casually jots off Epistles, such as the Epistle to the Church of Omaha in Dispersal.

Judy was a Queer Fish. She was also, according to the story, "a young and handsome woman of rowdy intellect." Her son Gregory, who clearly has an important role to play, is early in the novel tempted by a minor devil. "His name was Azazel. He wasn't the great one of that name but one of his numerous nephews. There is an economy of name among the devils." Azazel asks Gregory to "command that these stones be made bread." "Does it always have to start with those same words?" Gregory asks in response. He is then instructed to cast himself down from a height because, "if you are one of the elect you will not be dashed to pieces." Gregory dodges the temptation. "I'll not be dashed to pieces yet. It's high but not really steep, not a good selection." And finally Azazel offers him the "world and all that

Apocalypse in Science Fiction 287

is in it." Greg Thatcher grins, "It really isn't much of a world you have to offer. . .really, where is the temptation?" However, Gregory does not give the devil the traditional dismissal. "I'll not say, 'get them behind me, satan,' for I wouldn't trust you behind me for one stride."

Trumpet and Judy, alas, are killed in a fierce battle and Gregory and a certain Levi Cain band together with a group of other young people named Simon Canon, Tom Culpa (his name meant Tom Twin), Joanna Gromova (daughter of Thunder), Andy Johnson, Mattie Miracle, and Peter Johnson—who seems to be their leader.

Then, "events have gathered into constellations" and the big fire begins, though it is an acre of fire, fire through which the young Ichthyans must walk.

One may be offended by Lafferty's playful manipulation of the Christian symbols in this episode, offended because one believes that the symbols are too sacred to be manipulated, or alternately, offended because one believes the symbols are too false to be discussed. Still, one has to say that the apocalypses of R.A. Lafferty are the closest things in science fiction to Zechariah, who started the whole thing, because Lafferty's apocalypses are apocalypses of rebirth, renewal and beginnings again.

He may, in other words, be right or wrong about the nature of reality, but he certainly is right about the nature of apocalypse.

With one exception, Zechariah was not a humorist. R.A. Lafferty imagines wild, renewing, destructive, manic, recreating apocalypses just as Zechariah did, but R.A. Lafferty's apocalyses are also comic—a phenomenon which might well have offended Zechariah and certainly would have offended Thomas of Celano.

But then, neither of these two worthies was Irish.

Notes

[1]Raphael A. Lafferty, *Past Master*, New York: Ace Books, 1968, p.246.
[2]Raphael A. Lafferty, *Apocalypses*, Los Angeles: Pinnacle Books, 1977.

Andrew Greeley is professor of sociology at the University of Arizona and Senior Study Director at the National Opinion Research Center. His sociological specialty is the study of ethnic diversity. His *Making of the Popes 1978* was a book of the month club feature and was serialized in *Playboy*, his first novel *The Magic Cup*, based on the Irish version of the Grail Myth (in which the grail is found) will be published by McGraw Hill for Christmas 1979.

Ann. Rev. Sociol. 79. 5:91–111
Copyright © 1979 by Annual Reviews Inc. All rights reserved

THE SOCIOLOGY   ❖ 10572
OF AMERICAN CATHOLICS

Andrew M. Greeley

Department of Sociology, University of Arizona, Tucson, Arizona 85721

INTRODUCTION

1978 was the twentieth anniversary of the election of Pope John XXIII, the fifteenth anniversary of the election of Pope Paul VI, and the tenth anniversary of the issuance of the encyclical letter on birth control, *Humanae Vitae*. It is an appropriate time to review the social science literature on American Catholicism.

Few Catholics who were adults when Angelo Guiseppe Roncalli ascended the papal throne twenty years ago would have imagined in their wildest moments the changes that have occurred in the Catholic Church in the ensuing decades. Few Catholic moderates and progressives, who cheered enthusiastically at the election of Giovanni Batista Montini fifteen years ago, could have anticipated in the euphoria at the end of the first session of the Vatican Council (but six months before Montini's election) how quickly Paul VI would dissipate that euphoria; and virtually no one would have anticipated in 1968 the subtle and sophisticated response of American Catholics to the birth control encyclical.

Catholicism in the United States finds itself caught in the intersection of two major transition processes: (*a*) the change from the immigrant church, which reached its flowering in the 1940s and 1950s, to the middle and upper middle-class suburban church of the 1960s and 1970s; (*b*) the transition from the narrow, defensive garrison church of the counter-reformation to the informal, voluntaristic, open-ended Catholicism of the years after the Second Vatican Council. Either of these transitions would have produced major shifts in the shape and the dynamics of American Catholicism; the convergence of the two has created an extraordinarily rich and variegated condi-

91

0360-0572/79/0815-0091$01.00

92   GREELEY

tion in a church once thought of (understandably, though mistakenly) as monolithic and unchanging.

Two main sections of this review deal with the socioeconomic change and the religious change within American Catholicism. Everett Hughes said long ago that, sociologically speaking, everything has happened in and to the Roman Catholic Church. Since Professor Hughes wrote those lines (just twenty years ago), everything seems to have happened once again.

ECONOMIC, SOCIAL, AND INTELLECTUAL CHANGE

Since the publication of Lenski's (1961) *The Religious Factor,* the notion has been widespread in American social science that as a group Catholics are deficient in economic, social, and academic achievement. *The Religious Factor* seemed to confirm the self-criticisms of Catholics such as Ellis (1955), O'Dea (1958), Donaven (1964), and Weigel (1957). Even though Schuman (1969) was unable to replicate the Lenski findings in Detroit, *The Religious Factor* has continued to influence thinking about the economic and intellectual state of American Catholics. Recently, Hardy returned to the theme (1974:505):

> Roman Catholics are extremely low producers of scientists and scholars. . . .
>
> Highly productive groups share a certain set of values, unproductive groups hold the antithesis of these. . . . The common beliefs and value systems of high producers seem to include naturalism; intrinsic valuation of learning and the individual quest for truth; emphasis on human dignity, goodness, and competence; a life pathway of serious dedication, of service to humanity, of continual striving; humanistic equalitarianism; a pragmatic search for better ways of doing things unfettered by traditional restraints; and a focus on the relatively immediate, forseeable future which can be affected by personal effort.

Hardy suggests that his research ranks Catholics low on these value scales.

Thomas Sowell (1975) has argued that Italian Catholics have been more successful than Irish Catholics in America. He has elaborated a complex explanation for this phenomenon. But Sowell's data are based on the US Census, which combines the largely northern urban Irish Catholic population and the mostly southern rural Irish Protestant population (which virtually all national surveys show is somewhat larger than the Irish Catholic population). As we shall see subsequently, the Irish Catholics are actually the most successful Gentile ethnic group in America.

Research conducted at the National Opinion Research Center (NORC) (Greeley 1976a) calls into serious question the Lenski and Hardy assumptions. In education, annual family income, and occupational achievement Catholics have higher mean scores than do American Protestants. These differences remain when the minority groups within the two denominations are removed—black Protestants and Hispanic Catholics—and when controls are introduced for region of the country and city size. Indeed, in metropolitan areas in the North, Irish, Italian, and Polish Catholics have higher annual incomes than do white Episcopalians; and the upward mobility rate in terms of own education (as compared with parents' education) is highest among Italian and Polish Catholics of any of the religio-ethnic groups in American society. Irish Catholics are second only to Jews in income, occupational prestige, and education.

Furthermore, additional research (Greeley 1978a) enables one to trace the social mobility of the three principal Catholic ethnic groups. By use of the large combined NORC General Social Survey file for cohort analysis it was shown that Irish Catholic men crossed the national average for college attendance before the First World War; they are now as likely to attend college as Episcopalians. Italian and Polish Catholics of college-attending age crossed the national average (a non-Hispanic white population) during the 1960s. Similarly, while the proportion of American white-collar workers did not change for age cohorts in the last half century (about half the men have white-collar occupations), Italian and Polish Catholics surpassed the national average in white-collar occupations during the 1960s, and crossed the national average for professional and managerial occupations (for non-Hispanic whites) during the 1960s. This is to say that the Polish and Italian Catholic cohort that came of age in the 1960s surpassed the national average for non-Hispanic whites in their own cohort. Again, the proportion of Americans in professional and managerial occupations has not changed since the First World War. (The odds of an American's being a professional or managerial worker are somewhere between one-to-two and one-to-three.) Thus the Polish and Italian shift represents an actual change in their status. Irish Catholics have been above the national average in both white-collar and professional managerial professions since the First World War era. (The odds of an Irish Catholic's being in a professional or managerial occupation are better than one-to-two.)

The educational and occupational achievement of Irish, Polish, and Italian Catholic women in comparison with a white, non-Hispanic population of non-Catholic women is comparable to that of Catholic men in the same ethnic communities.

The NORC findings have been replicated by Kobrin & Goldscheider (1978) in studies of an extensive sample in Rhode Island. Similarly, the Hunts (1975, 1976, 1977) have argued that Catholicism is apparently compatible with both upward mobility and social militancy for black Catholics. According to the Hunts, Catholicism is a religious factor "supporting moderate mobility and status maintenance among working- and middle-class

94   GREELEY

blacks.'' Indeed, it ''may continue to be consequential for the development among blacks of a highly individualized orientation to secular achievement consistent with the success ethic of the white world'' (Hunt & Hunt 1975:605).

In a study sponsored by the National Bureau of Economic Research, Juster (1974) has reported that Catholic and Jewish family dynamics seem to facilitate economic achievement. Hill & Stafford (1974) suggest that the significant factor may be special attention to the children in their early years of life, particularly assistance with their schoolwork. However, in a study of 4,000 Minnesota adolescents, Nelson & Simpkins (1973) could find little difference in aspiration between Protestants and Catholics. Chiswick (1977) reports that the sons of immigrants earn 15% more than the sons of natives and that half of this advantage remains even when region and city size are held constant. Thus an achievement ethic may be at work among American Catholics who are the offspring of immigrants.

The history of Catholics in the last half century, then, has been one of extraordinary economic and social progress—progress of the sort that the National Immigration Commission (the so-called "Dillingham Commission"), whose research led to the restrictive immigration laws, had confidently called impossible.

It would appear that Catholic schools have facilitated this upward mobility. Greeley, McCready & McCourt (1976:196–98) report a high correlation between Catholic school attendance and educational and economic achievement even when parental educational achievement is held constant. The correlation between Catholic education and achievement seems to be especially strong for those who also grew up in heavily Catholic neighborhoods. R. Stryker (unpublished findings) reports an extraordinarily high standardized correlation between Catholic high school attendance and college graduation and first-job status, holding constant parental achievement, IQ, curriculum, and closeness to teachers. Neither Catholicism nor Catholic education appears to be a barrier to achievement in American society; indeed, for both blacks and whites it seems to facilitate upward mobility.

What, then, to make of Hardy's challenge, an update of Lenski's assertion that Catholicism and intellectual achievement are incompatible? As Schnell & Rooke (1977) observed, when the argument raged between 1955 and 1975, Catholics were as ready as non-Catholics to reject the evidence of notable change in the intellectual achievement of American Catholics. The various NORC publications of the 1960s that purported to show an increase in the percentage of American Catholics in academic careers were rejected vigorously by many Catholics; Catholic intellectuals insisted on the anti-intellectualism of their own religion. Schnell & Rooke, however, concluded that the NORC evidence was unassailable, although the development of a

Catholic intellectualism has not been paralleled by the development of high-quality graduate schools at Catholic universities. Greeley (1979: Ch. 4) summarized the fifteen-year discussion that began with the publication of his *Religion and Career* (1963) by noting that Catholics who graduated from college in the early 1960s were as likely as Protestants to choose academic careers. By the early 1970s, they were as likely to have faculty positions in the thirty top universities (as measured by Lipset & Ladd, 1971), as likely to have published five or more professional articles, and more likely to describe themselves as intellectual; they were equally likely to support withdrawal from Vietnam, to be sympathetic with student protests, to describe themselves as left-of-center politically, and to attend a cultural event two or three times a month. Half of them, at the time of the Lipset and Ladd data collection, attended church at least once a month. Steinburg (1974) came to approximately the same conclusion, though he failed to distinguish among the various Catholic ethnic groups and did not question the extent to which anti-Catholic discrimination at the elite private universities, like the anti-Jewish discrimination in a somewhat earlier era, might affect the data.

Again, how are these findings about Catholic intellectual and academic success to be reconciled with the Hardy article? The data in the Hardy (1974) study are based on research done before 1958. There is not a single reference in his article to any research done on American Catholic intellectualism since 1960. None of the NORC research is mentioned—not even to challenge or refute its claims. The possibility of change in an ethnic immigrant population, which is richly documented by numerous publications, is ignored completely by Hardy.

In summary, then, evidence of an economic, social, educational, and intellectual transformation in American Catholicism, going on for many years but reaching its fulfillment during the 1960s, is virtually indisputable. Neither Catholicism nor Catholic education seem to be a barrier to economic success or intellectual achievement, though as Schnell and Rooke (1977) point out, these changes have yet to lead to an intellectuality that will produce high-quality Catholic graduate departments. As I noted earlier in this paper, it has certainly not produced high-quality self study within the American Catholic community.

Political and Social Attitudes

Greer (1961) suggested that as Catholics moved to the suburbs they would defect from the Democratic party and become Republicans. Others, such as Kevin Phillips (1969), William Rusher (1975), and William Gavin (1975), suggested that Catholics could be easily drawn away from the Democratic party because that party no longer stands for what Catholics stand for. Still others, such as Frederick Dutton (1971), John Kenneth Galbraith (1971), and Lanny Davis (1974), described "new coalitions" in which there is apparently no room for Catholics. It was indeed the Catholic labor union leaders and the Catholic big-city bosses who were ejected from the Democratic party at the time of the disastrous McGovern nomination. In addition, the impression is widespread in the national media, though never clearly asserted in the social science literature, that Catholics are racist in their response to problems of integration (Greeley 1977b).

Nie, Currie & Greeley (1974) addressed themselves to these issues and could find no evidence of either Catholic conservatism or Catholic racism. Fee (1976) could not confirm Greer's hypothesized withdrawal of Catholics from the Democratic party as they moved to the suburbs. Four NORC articles monitoring racial integration (Hyman & Sheatsley 1964; Greeley & Sheatsley 1971; Greeley & Sheatsley 1974; Taylor, Sheatsley & Greeley 1978) have demonstrated that Catholics are more likely to support racial integration than other white groups, even outside the South. Taylor, Sheatsley & Greeley (1978) could find no evidence of the alleged white ethnic backlash against racial integration. They also found that Irish, German, and Italian Catholics outside the South continued to be above the Anglo-Saxon Protestant average in their support for racial integration. Indeed, Irish Catholics were even more likely than Jews to be willing to accept for their children a school where most of the students were black. More than 70% of the Catholic parents in the country, according to Greeley, McCready & McCourt (1976), report their children are in integrated schools. A positive correlation exists between Catholic school attendance and support for racial integration, as well as opposition to anti-Semitism.

Reviewing the present state of the literature, Greeley (1978b) concluded that on the average Catholics remain where they were a quarter of a century ago—slightly to the left of center in the Democratic coalition, less leftist on most issues than blacks and Jews but more leftist than white Protestants, even white Protestants of the North who describe themselves as Democrats. Nie, Petrocik & Verba (1976) reported the same findings.

In summary, despite conviction to the contrary in many quarters, Catholics continue to be moderate Democrats; more strongly than other Democrats and other white northern Americans, they support racial integration. Irish Catholics, incidentally, are the most politically liberal Gentile ethnic group in the country; they are the most pro-integration of any Gentile group.

RELIGIOUS CHANGE

The decline in church attendance among American Catholics has been richly documented by Gallup and Harris surveys and by Greeley, McCready &

McCourt (1976). Church attendance, support for a priestly vocation in the family, church contributions, and membership in church organizations have all declined more than 20 percentage points. Various explanations for the decline have been offered. Weigert & Thomas (1974), for example, see a long-term secularization trend. Gleason (1972) detects the impact of 1960s romanticism on American Catholicism. O'Brien (1972) describes the phenomenon as the result of the integration of American Catholicism into American society. Hitchcock (1973–1974) attributes the declines to the antagonism of the ordinary faithful toward the American Catholic left. All of these authors assume, either explicitly or implicitly, that while the second Vatican council may have accelerated the decline of traditional Roman Catholic practice in the United States, this decline would have occurred anyway.

However, Greeley, McCready & McCourt (1976) could find no evidence to support explanations based on either long-range secularization or actions of the Vatican council. Rather, using J.A. Davis' (1972a, b) d-systems, social-change model, they argue that virtually the entire change can be accounted for by the hostile reaction of American Catholics to the birth control encyclical, *Humanae Vitae*. Critics of this thesis have responded with an amalgam of the arguments put forth in the previously cited articles, speaking of secularization and sexual revolution. However, the reanalysis of data from the 1963 and 1974 NORC studies (on which the d-systems, social-change model was based) shows that while there was a Catholic sexual revolution between 1963 and 1974 [declines of more than 30 percentage points in the proportions disapproving of sex for pleasure alone, thinking a family ought to have as many children as possible, and thinking that three or more children was a desirable family (Greeley 1979)], none of these changes accounted for the decline in church attendance and other measures of religious devotion among Catholics. Indeed, these three "fertility" variables apparently do not correlate with church attendance at all. Only the declines in acceptance of both the birth control teaching and papal authority account for the devotional decline. (These two variables also predict church attendance, support for vocation in the family, church contributions, etc.)

The decline is not an evidence of long-term secularization among Catholics. Even though church attendance has declined, communion reception has increased among American Catholics; the proportion of American Catholics who believe in life after death has not changed since the 1930s (Greeley 1979: Ch. 8). About half of American Catholics in every age group pray every day, about four fifths pray at least once a week, and about one quarter have had intense religious experiences. Support for Catholic schools was as high in 1974 as it was in 1963. In addition, there are no statistically significant differences in religious behavior between those who reject the church's right to teach on both birth control and race and those who accept at least one of these teaching rights (Greeley 1979). Nor has the proportion of Catholics who disidentify with the church increased appreciably (Greeley 1979). The rate of disidentification has risen from 7 to 15%, but this can be accounted for entirely by the increase in the rate of religious intermarriage. Four fifths of disidentification among Catholics is attributable to religious intermarriage.

Between 1968 and 1978 American Catholics seem to have become more selective in their religious practices and behavior. They continue to identify with the church, but they take it much less seriously as a teaching authority; they continue to believe in the existence of God, life after death, and Catholic schools, and are even more likely to receive communion now than they were ten years ago. They continue to take that approach to the problem of evil which does not deny evil but which sees good as somewhat stronger (McCready & Greeley 1976). Yet they reject the church's sexual ethic (as we shall see in a later section), and they are skeptical about papal authority. Young Catholics, who are much less likely to go to church and much more likely to reject the church's teaching on sexual matters, still pray as frequently as do Catholics over thirty.

Ten years ago, Catholics were expected to react to the birth control encyclical either by accepting the papal ruling and giving up their birth control practices or by rejecting the papal ruling and leaving the church. In fact, however, while the Pope's teachings were rejected, with a resultant decline in some measures of religious fervor, Catholics remained in the church—a sophisticated response that few observers predicted.

The Catholic Clergy

Schoenherr & Greeley (1974) developed an eight-variable model for the decision of Catholic priests to leave the ministry. If the priest sees marriage as a desirable opportunity foregone, if the costs of loneliness outweigh the satisfactions that flow from his job, and if movement is made easier by the fact that he is relatively young, the clergyman is likely to withdraw from his role as a religious professional. Schoenherr & Perez-Vilarino (1975) compared role-commitment processes in Spain and the United States and found that "youthfulness and the costs associated with celibacy are predominatly important conditions leading to resignation for both Spanish and American priests . . . '' (Shoenherr & Perez-Vilarino 1975:15).

Recent research by Schoenherr (NORC 1971) updates the 1970 NORC study and indicates that there has been a very slight decline in the annual resignation rate. During the last decade some 11% of the diocesan clergy in the country have resigned. Losses to the priesthood through death and resignation have barely been replaced by ordination. According to Schoenherr (personal communication), the 9% retirement of older clergy represents the approximate net decline of diocesan clergy at work in American dioceses (as opposed to the foreign missions) since 1965. Schoenherr predicts that the combination of resignation (disproportionately likely among the more liberal clergy) and the decline of vocations will produce an older (average age) and more conservative clergy in years to come.

Greeley (1973) reports a sexual revolution among the Catholic clergy, with almost four fifths willing to question the church's teaching on birth control under some circumstances. More than two thirds are willing to question the church's teaching on divorce, and two fifths are ready to keep an open mind on the investigation of the abortion issue. Three fifths of the variance in sexual attitudes of the clergy (which roughly parallel the sexual attitudes of the laity to be described subsequently) can be explained by age, modern religious values, and inner direction of personality. The birth control encyclical had a negative impact on the clergy as well as the laity. A large number of priests reported that their positions shifted in the liberal direction after the encyclical.

Sex and Abortion

The study of Catholic fertility and birth control practices has been more detailed and more extensive than that of any other aspect of contemporary American Catholicism. Murphy & Erhart (1975) summarized the history of the church's response to birth control and the deliberations that preceded *Humanae Vitae*. (They noted, incidentally, that Cardinals Hume of Westminster and Doepfner of Munich, who served as vice presidents of the Papal Commission on birth control, were utterly astonished because their final report, which was axed by backstairs Vatican politics, advocated a change in the birth control teaching.) Other investigators (Wilson & Bumpass 1973; Potvin & Lee 1974; Groat, Neal & Knisely, 1975; Grindstaff & Ebanks, 1975; Westoff & Jones 1978; Bouvier 1972) report a steady increase in the use of forbidden forms of birth control by Catholics and a convergence between Catholic and non-Catholic fertility rates. So great is the convergence, in fact, that Westoff & Jones are able to speak of "the end of 'Catholic' fertility." Perhaps the most interesting table in the entire literature is Table 3 of the Westoff & Jones (1978), which shows that in the 1956–60 era, those Catholics who received communion at least monthly had a total marital fertility of 4.83, while those who received communion less frequently had a fertility of 3.99—a difference of .84. In 1971–75, the former group had a total marital fertility of 2.32 and the latter of 2.27, a difference of .05. Such was the impact of the encyclical letter *Humanae Vitae* on American Catholics.

Furthermore, the NORC General Social Survey (Greeley, 1979) indicates

100   GREELEY

that Catholics are becoming more permissive about premarital and extramarital sex.

In 1963, 69% of American Catholics thought the ideal family was more than three children; in 1974, only 39% so believed. In 1963, 29% thought that a husband and wife might have intercourse for pleasure alone; in 1974, 51% approved this practice. In 1963, 25% rejected the notion that the family should have as many children as possible; in 1974, 58% rejected that premise.

Sexual attitudes among contemporary American are diverse. Only 22% of American Jews, but 52% of the Baptists, think that premarital sex is wrong, (Table 1). Seventy-one percent of the Jews think that extramarital sex is wrong, as do 90% of (American) British Protestants. Thirty-eight percent of the Jewish respondents believe that homosexuality is always wrong; 83% of the Baptists hold this opinion. Fifty-seven percent of blacks and 48% of Jews think that divorce ought to be made easier; only 18% of (American) Scandinavian Protestants and 17% of (American) German Catholics so believe. One quarter of Jews and 27% of blacks would support a law banning all pornography, while approximately half of (American) Slavic Catholics and (American) German Protestants would support such a law. Thirty-seven percent of Jews and 34% of Hispanics have seen an X-rated movie, while only 14% of Episcopalians and 14% of (American) Scandinavian Protestants have sampled such films.

On the average, the majority of Americans still reject premarital sex and overwhelmingly reject extramarital sex and homosexuality. The majority are also against making divorce laws easier and are against banning all pornography. Only on one of seven measures of the "sexual revolution" does there seem to be a consensus: 93% of Jews, 78% of Baptists and Irish Catholics, and 79% of blacks favor the availability of birth control information for teenagers.

On most of these issues, Catholics are somewhere in the middle of the population between the Jews and the Baptists. Jews, Presbyterians, and Episcopalians tend to be the most liberal on matters of sexual permissiveness; blacks are liberal on premarital and extramarital sex, divorce, pornography, and X-rated movies but conservative on homosexuality. Italian and Hispanic Catholics tend to be at the permissive end of the list of ethnic groups, while German and Slavic Catholics tend to be in the more conservative half of the list. As in so many other areas of human behavior, the Irish prove difficult to categorize. They are slightly more conservative than the national average on premarital and extramarital sex and in their attitudes toward divorce and pornography laws. On the other hand, the Irish Catholics are more likely than all Protestant groups in the country to have seen an X-rated movie (though only slightly less likely than their Italian, Hispanic,

Table 1 Rank of ethnic groups and denominations on 7 sexuality items on the NORC General Social Survey

| Premarital sex | | Extramarital sex | | Homosexuality | | Birth control information to teenagers | |
Religio-ethnic group	Wrong (always/ sometimes, %)	Religio-ethnic group	Wrong (always/ sometimes, %)	Religio-ethnic group	Always wrong (%)	Religio-ethnic group	Yes (%)
Jewish	22(15/7)	Jewish	71(48/23)	Jewish	38	Jewish	93
Episcopalian	32(16/16)	Black	76(64/12)	Episcopalian	50	Episcopalian	92
Black	34(26/18)	Presbyterian	76(59/17)	Irish Catholic	60	Presbyterian	87
Lutheran	37(22/15)	Episcopalian	78(56/22)	Presbyterian	66	Lutheran	85
Presbyterian	38(24/14)	Hispanic	81(74/7)	Italian Catholic	68	British Protestant	83
Methodist	39(35/14)	Scandinavian Protestant	82(7/15)	Slavic Catholic	70	German Protestant	81
Italian Catholic	40(29/11)	Italian Catholic	83(67/16)	Hispanic	73	Hispanic	82
Hispanic	42(32/10)	German Catholic	86(73/13)	German Catholic	74	Methodist	80
Slavic Catholic	43(35/8)	Irish Catholic	88(69/19)	Lutheran	75	German Catholic	80
Scandinavian Protestant	44(37/17)	Slavic Catholic	88(73/15)	German Protestant	77	Slavic Catholic	80
German Catholic	46(32/14)	German Protestant	89(69/20)	Scandinavian Protestant	77	Italian Catholic	80
Irish Catholic	47(32/15)	Baptist	89(78/11)	Black	77	Black	79
German Protestant	47(32/15)	Methodist	90(74/16)	Methodist	78	Irish Catholic	78
Baptist	52(41/11)	British Protestant	90(74/16)	Baptist	83	Baptist	78
ALL	46(33/13)	ALL	85(71/14)	ALL	72	ALL	83

Table 1 (Cont.)

Table 1 (cont'd) Rank of ethnic groups and denominations on 7 sexuality items on the NORC General Social Survey

Divorce laws should be made easier		Support laws banning pornography		Have seen an X-rated movie	
Religio-ethnic group	Yes (%)	Religio-ethnic group	Yes (%)	Religio-ethnic group	Yes (%)
Black	57	Jewish	24	Jewish	37
Jewish	48	Black	27	Hispanic	34
Hispanic	36	Italian Catholic	38	Black	25
Episcopalian	35	Hispanic	38	Italian Catholic	25
Presbyterian	34	Episcopalian	41	Slavic Catholic	23
Baptist	34	German Catholic	41	German Catholic	21
Italian Catholic	34	Presbyterian	43	Irish Catholic	20
Lutheran	29	Irish Catholic	44	Methodist	18
British Protestant	27	Baptist	44	Presbyterian	18
Methodist	25	Scandinavian Protestant	44	Baptist	17
German Protestant	24	Lutheran	44	Lutheran	16
Irish Catholic	23	British Protestant	44	German Protestant	16
Slavic Catholic	22	Methodist	48	British Protestant	15
Scandinavian Protestant	18	Slavic Catholic	48	Episcopalian	14
German Catholic	17	German Protestant	50	Scandinavian Protestant	14

and Slavic counterparts). However, only Jews and Episcopalians are more tolerant on homosexuality than Irish Catholics. There is nothing in the Irish Catholic tradition, as far as this writer is aware, to explain this relative tolerance of homosexuality. The Catholic Church, at least in its American manifestation, strongly influenced by the Irish tradition, has vigorously resisted any attempts to modify the church's stern reaction to homosexual activity. However, the practice for many decades was that Irish-American clergy tended to be sympathetic in counseling homosexuals.

Catholics are not, however, among the most conservative groups in America on any issue but the easing of divorce laws, an issue in which three of the four most conservative groups are Catholics—Irish, Slavic, and German. On all other issues Methodists, Baptists, and German and British Protestants tend to be more conservative sexually than are Catholics. This despite the fact that in the church's official sexual ethic, premarital and extramarital sex, homosexuality, birth control, divorce, and pornography would certainly be condemned as seriously sinful.

In several of the Catholic groups, especially the Irish, a liberalizing trend is notable among the younger members. Four of the sexual permissiveness items were combined into a scale (premarital sex, extramarital sex, homosexuality, and birth control information for teenagers). A z-score (percentage of a standard deviation above or below the mean) was computed for each of the groups (Table 2). Since the Jewish score is the most liberal in each of the three age categories, Table 2 consists of a comparison of each of the groups with the Jewish group. One can measure change toward greater liberalism in a given group by comparing it with change within the most liberal group. Thus a $-.49$ for British Protestants in the oldest age category means that the British Protestants between 46 and 89 had a 0.23 z-score and were 49 points (about half a standard deviation) beneath the Jews of comparable age. In the 46–89 year-old category, Irish Catholics are the most conservative, being well over one standard deviation less permissive than Jews. In the 30–45 year-old category, the Irish Catholics are slightly more than a standard deviation more conservative on sexual matters than Jews. However, in the age group under 30, Irish Catholics and Slavic Catholics are second only to Jews in their permissiveness, having passed the Italians, who in the two previous age groups were the most sexually permissive of the Catholic ethnic communities.

Among the oldest group, the Italians were the most liberal of the Catholics on sexual matters. They change relatively little across age categories. Germans continue to be conservative in all three, as do the Hispanics. The Slavs were relatively liberal in the oldest group and become even more so in the youngest. For the Irish the change has been from being

104   GREELEY

Table 2 Difference from Jewish score on sexual permissiveness scale by age by ethnic group[a]

Ethnic Group	Age		
	46–89 (z-score)	30–35 (z-score)	18–29 (z-score)
(Jewish Score)	(.26)	(1.03)	(1.16)
British Protestant	− .49	.99	− .79
Scandinavian Protestant	− .56	.93	− .68
Slavic Catholic	− .56	.75	− .41
German Protestant	− .63	− 1.03	− 1.01
German Catholic	− .64	− 1.15	− 1.01
Italian Catholic	− .65	− .65	− .59
Black	− .74	− .71	− .68
Hispanic	− .74	− 1.06	− .61
Irish Catholic	− .89	− 1.05	− .48

[a]Groups ranked according to scores of 46–89 age group.

the most conservative on sexual matters among those over 30 to being the third most liberal (preceded by the Slavs and the Jews) of those under 30.

A number of observations are in order about Tables 1 and 2. (*a*) Several different sexual subcultures exist within the American Catholic community—Italians, relatively liberal; Germans, relatively conservative; Slavs and Irish, quite unpredictable. (*b*) On most matters Catholics are *not* among the most restrictive subcultures in the country. (*c*) Insofar as a study of age cohorts can simulate changing trends, it is certainly the case that most Americans and ethnic groups have become more liberal in their sexual norms through the years. But with the exception of the Irish Catholics, the rate of change among Catholics does not seem to have been any more rapid than that among other groups in the society.

Differences between Catholics and Protestants (but not between Protestants and Jews) on abortion seem to have narrowed, as McIntosh & Alston (1977) first reported. Blasi, MacNeil & O'Neill (1975) suggested that it is particularly Catholics with a devoutly religious background who are most likely to oppose abortion. Leon & Steinhoff (1975), in a study in Hawaii, found Catholics were also less likely actually to seek abortions. However, recent research at the National Opinion Research Center (Greeley 1979:Ch. 9) shows little significant difference between Catholics and white Protestants over a wide range of abortion attitudes; black Protestants are more likely to oppose abortion than white Catholics. The most recent NORC General Social Survey asked not only whether abortion were permissible, but also whether oneself or one's wife would use abortion. In cases of danger to the health of the mother and the possibility of a handicapped child, there were statistically significant differences between white Protestants and Catholics.

A less dogmatic response to the birth control pill than that recorded in the encyclical letter *Humanae Vitae* might have preserved Catholicism's distinctive sexual ethic. Now, however, both clergy and laity have rejected the birth control encyclical, and Catholics differ little from Protestants on a wide range of other sexual issues. Indeed, in some matters Catholics seem to be more permissive than Protestants. Despite the enthusiasm of the Right to Life movement, the majority of American Catholics are willing to support abortion under three sets of circumstance: danger to the life of the mother, risk of a handicapped child, and rape victimization. In other circumstances —unmarried mother, the desire not to have any more children—the majority of Catholics reject abortion. So do the majority of Protestants. It also appears that the majority of Catholics, like the majority of other Americans, oppose abortion after the first trimester.[1]

Catholic Schools

Catholic schools continue to be popular: Three quarters of American Catholics supported them in both 1963 and in 1974. They are not obstacles to economic or academic success; attendance correlates positively with favorable attitudes toward Jews and blacks. The correlation between attendance at Catholic schools and the maintenance of adult religious attitudes and behavior is stronger during times of transition than in times of stability (Greeley, McCready & McCourt 1976). These correlations are especially strong for men, for those under thirty, and for those from devoutly Catholic families. Since men are the most effective religious socializers (McCready 1972a), since those from devout Catholic families are the most likely to be Catholic activists in their adult lives, and since young people are more likely to survive than old people, the importance of the Catholic schools seems to be greater at present than earlier.

Two thirds of the decline in Catholic school enrollment can be accounted for by failure of the church to build new schools in the suburban areas. Hundreds of millions of dollars in contributions for Catholic schools are available, but no attempt has been made to raise them. Since the contributions in adult life of those who attended Catholic schools seem to offset the expense of maintaining such schools (Greeley 1977a; McCready 1976), Catholic schools are not an enormous drain on the church's financial resources.

[1] Some Catholic moral theologians, using the "Schuler Preference Principle," are willing to legitimate abortion when the life of the mother is in danger. They even may be willing (verbally, not in writing) to counsel abortion in cases of clearly and hopelessly defective fetuses.

Catholic Pentecostals

One mark of the change in Catholicism is the Catholic pentecostal movement, a religious development unthinkable a decade ago. In two excellent articles, McGuire (1974, 1977) has compared the Catholic pentecostals with the so-called "underground church," an informal Catholic community that does not emphasize the emotionalism characteristic of the charismatics. McGuire found few economic or social differences between the two groups but did uncover several important social-psychological divergences. Pentecostals are much less able than "underground church" members to cope with ambiguity and change and are more likely to display tendencies toward escapism. Furthermore, the various "gifts" of the pentecostal movement (glossalalic prophecy, interpretation, confirmation, and discernment) serve to "embody lines of stratification in the prayer group and to promote control by the leaders . . . fulfilling for many members a felt need for . . . strong authority . . . " (McGuire 1977:134). In a study of a small charismatic community, Westley (1977) emphasizes the importance of surrender to a more powerful authority as experienced in the presence of the Holy Spirit. Walker (1975) has criticized, from a methodological perspective, the sociological style used in evaluating the Catholic charismatic movement, but he does not seem to have solved the problem of how one might adequately describe such experiences. Harrison (1974) reports that those attracted to the movement were exposed to it in person, share its problem-solving perspective, have few social obligations that conflict with membership, and have or develop social relationships with members. Harper (1974) reports that social attitudes, whether liberal, moderate, or conservative, appear to be uncorrelated with adherence to the pentecostal movement because they are not allowed to intrude on the main purpose of the charismatic renewal. The pentecostals studied by Bord & Faulkner (1975), however, tended to take social-activist stands on religiously salient issues. The pentecostals studied by McGuire, on the contrary, tended to be uninvolved socially and politically and to be content with "band-aid forms of social action" (Christmas baskets to the poor, for example). Fichter (1975) finds little evidence of social activist commitment and considerable evidence of tendencies toward doctrinal heterodoxy. McCready (1972b), relying on Ann Parsons' thesis that pentecostalism is a response to social and economic transition, suggests that the charismatic renewal in the church may be a response to religious transition and ambiguity, a search to combine the certainties of the old church with the informalities of the new. This position would be consistent with that of McGuire.

The literature on the Catholic charismatics suffers methodological deficiencies. Only Fichter tried to obtain a large sample from widely distributed charismatic communities, and he, unfortunately, attempted no comparison between charismatics and the rest of the Catholic population. Five percent of American Catholics, according to the 1974 NORC Catholic school study (Greeley, McCready & McCourt 1976), have attended charismatic meetings. A comparison between them and other devout Catholics revealed only relatively minor differences, but those differences did seem to suggest that the charismatics tended toward social and political conservatism. Until more methodologically adequate research is attempted, one must be content with the conclusion that Catholic charismatics are probably a segment of already devout Catholics seeking a more emotional religion than that of their parishes and striving to regain some of the certainties they lost in the post-conciliar church.

Socialization

McCready (1972a) has pioneered in the study of religious socialization, using a multigenerational model which far more successfully accounts for the variance in religious behavior than do the usual social-class and social-deprivation approaches. Most of his models account for more than half of the variance in adolescent religious behavior, for example, by using items derived entirely from parental questionnaires. Fathers have far more impact on the religious behavior of children than do mothers (in regression equations that produce standardized betas); and the quality of the parental relationship is also an important factor in affecting the religious behavior of the adolescent. These socialization models show parental behavior affecting church attendance, prayer, sexual and racial attitudes, and even basic world views such as "hopefulness," "optimism," and "pessimism." Furthermore these models fit the grandparent-parent as well as the parent-adolescent relationship (McCready 1976). While the models have stronger explanatory power for Catholics, they are also effective in predicting the religious behavior of Protestants in both generational transitions. Within Catholicism, the dynamics of these models have not been changed by the turbulence of the past fifteen years.

McCready distinguishes two important socialization experiences in human life; the family of origin and the family of choice. In the former, father is more important than mother; in the latter, wife is more important than husband. Study of how husband and wife influence each other religiously will be important in the future of the sociology of religion, both Catholic and non-Catholic.

ANTI-CATHOLICISM

Greeley has raised the question of whether anti-Catholic nativism persists in American society. He has gathered a considerable body of evidence that

108 GREELEY

suggests it might. For example, Polish and Italian graduates suffer underrepresentation in high-occupational-prestige categories amounting to about half that suffered by black and Hispanic college graduates (Greeley 1976a). No serious attempt has been made to explore the explanations for such underrepresentation. Indeed, the American sociological profession seems systematically uninterested in the absence of Catholics from its membership. At the 1977 meetings of the American Sociological Association, for example, a report was submitted on minorities in the profession. It observed that minorities represent 20% of the population and that sociology ought to be concerned about their underrepresentation. No mention was made of the fact that Catholics represent 25% of the American population and that by all available statistics they are even more underrepresented in the sociological profession than the minorities with which the report was concerned. Furthermore, as far as the present writer is aware, no one has even suggested that the sociological profession should investigate the absence of Catholics in its ranks. The author has been told repeatedly by colleagues that one cannot be a Catholic and a good sociologist, and that while the underrepresentation of blacks and women may be attributable to discrimination, the absence of Catholics must be attributed to their intellectual inferiority. Even those sociologists who disagree with such judgments are silent in their disagreement. Recently, however, Wuthnow (1978) urged the sociology profession to be more aware of the persistence of anti-Catholicism.

Seidler (1978), however, dismisses Greeley's (1977) finding of Polish and Italian underrepresentation in the lead positions by citing as "plausible" the interpretation that they may have jobs of high pay but low status, such as garbage collection in San Francisco. No social scientist would dare advance such a glib explanation of black or Hispanic underrepresentation. Nor would any sociological journal publish such an offensive comment about blacks or Hispanics. That Seidler could make the comment and that *Social Forces* would publish it surely provide prima facie evidence of the persistence of nativism in both the sociological profession and the society that dispassionate social scientists are supposed to be studying.

SUMMARY AND CONCLUSION

Ethnic diversity within American Catholicism has been excluded from the present review since white ethnicity probably deserves a separate review of its own. One may note, however, that the transition in Catholicism has not affected the ordering of external devotional activity among the six major Catholic ethnic groups. Irish, Poles, and Germans are the more devout; Italians, Hispanics, and French are the less devout.

The grandfather of the family in the Sicilian novel, *The Leopard,* insists that one must change in order to remain the same. American Catholicism as a religious institution and as a human collectivity has hardly pursued a policy of changing in order to remain the same. Catholicism has changed enormously to become a powerful populist religious tradition in the United States, despite the necessity for coping with two transitional crises: the ecumenical age, and the massive move to the suburbs. The acceptance of ecclesiastical authority in matters of sexual morality has declined dramatically. There has been, and apparently continues to be, erosion in some forms of religious devotion; but there has been only slight erosion in basic convictions (e.g. the belief in survival after death) or in personal affiliation.

Catholics have adjusted to the dissonance created by their upward mobility on the one hand and the disillusionment following the birth control encyclical on the other by choosing to ignore those ethical and doctrinal positions that lead to dissonance; at the same time they have maintained their affiliation, their basic beliefs (e.g. in life after death), their devotional practices, and the organization loyalties (e.g. to Catholic schools) that seem to them to have religious and human value. Such a situation may be unstable. The charismatic response certainly seems to indicate instability for one segment of the Catholic population. However, those who accept the church's teaching authority on both race and sex do not differ significantly on other issues and practices from those who reject it. This suggests that for most Catholics the ambiguities are tolerable. Indeed, the new Catholicism that seems to be emerging in America appears similar to what has existed in many Catholic countries for centuries. The ordinary Catholic may decide he cannot practice "official" Catholicism; he then chooses among several alternate practices. Wisely, the official church refrains from making a particularly vigorous issue of such options. For example, the refusal of the American hierarchy vigorously to enforce the birth control encyclical suggests that they are far more flexible in their approach to pluralism and voluntarism within American Catholicism than the text of the encyclical would enjoin them to be. Even authorities in Rome have made no attempt to require the American hierarchy to impose the encyclical's injunctions. Perhaps they learned long ago from their own Italian Catholic experience that flexibility and pluralism are the price of survival.

Literature Cited

Blasi, A. J., MacNeil, P. J., O'Neill, R. 1975. The relationship between abortion attitudes and Catholic religiosity. *Soc. Sci. Winter*:34–39

Bord, R. J., Faulkner, J. E. 1975. Religiosity and secular attitudes: the case of Catholic pentecostals. *J. Sci. Stud. Relig.* 14:257–70

Bouvier, L. F. 1972. Catholics and contraception. *J. of Marr. Fam.* 34:514–22

Chiswick, B. R. 1977. The effect of Americanization on the earnings of foreign-born men. Paper presented at the Workshop on Applications of Economics, University of Chicago, September, 1977.

Davis, J. A. 1972a. *Survey Replications, Log*

110 GREELEY

Linear Models, and Theories of Social Change. Chicago: Nat. Opin. Res. Cent. (Multilithed)

Davis, J. A. 1972b. *The Goodman Log Linear System for Assessing Effects in Multivariate Contingency Tables.* Chicago: Nat. Opin. Res. Cent. (Multilithed)

Davis, L. J. 1974. *The Emerging Democratic Majority: Lessons & Legacies from the New Politics.* NY: Stein & Day

Donaven, J. 1964. Creating anti-intellectuals. *Commonweal* October 2:37–39

Dutton, F. G. 1971. *Changing Sources of Power: American Politics in the 1970's.* NY: McGraw Hill

Ellis, J. T. 1955. American Catholics and the intellectual life. *Thought* Autumn:355–88

Fee, J. 1976. Political continuity and change. In *Catholic Schools in a Declining Church,* ed. A. M. Greeley, W. C. McCready, K. McCourt, pp. 76–102. Kansas City: Sheed & Ward

Fichter, J. 1975. *The Catholic Cult of the Paraclete.* NY: Sheed & Ward

Galbraith, J. K. 1971. *The Affluent Society.* Boston: Houghton Mifflin

Gavin, W. F. 1975. *Street Corner Conservative.* NY: Arlington House

Geertz, C. 1968. Religion as a cultural system. In *The Religious Situation: 1968,* ed. D. Cutler, pp. 641–83. Boston: Beacon Press

Gleason, P. 1972. Catholicism and cultural change in the 60's. *Rev. Polit.* 34:91–107

Greeley, A. M. 1963. *Religion and Career.* NY: Sheed & Ward

Greeley, A. M. 1973. The sexual revolution among Catholic clergy *Rev. Relig. Res.* 14:91–100

Greeley, A. M. 1976a. *Ethnicity, Denomination, and Inequality.* Beverly Hills, Calif: Sage Publications

Greeley, A. M. 1976b. *Catholic Schools in a Declining Church.* Kansas City: Sheed & Ward

Greeley, A. M. 1977a. A preliminary investigation: the 'profitability' of Catholic schools. *Momentum* 8:43–49

Greeley, A. M. 1977b. *An Ugly Little Secret.* NY: Sheed, Andres & McMeel

Greeley, A. M. 1978a. Ethnic minorities in the United States: a demographic perspective. *Int. J. Group Tensions*

Greeley, A. M. 1978b. Catholics and coalition: where should they go? In *Emerging Coalitions in American Politics,* ed S. M. Lipset. San Francisco: Inst. Contemp. Stud.

Greeley, A. M. 1979. *Crisis in the Church: A Study of Religion in America.* Chicago: Thomas More Press. 261 pp.

Greeley, A. M., McCready, W. C.,

McCourt, K. 1976. *Catholic Schools in a Declining Church.* Kansas City: Sheed & Ward

Greeley, A. M., Sheatsley, P. B. 1971. Attitudes toward racial integration. *Sci. Am.* 225:13–19

Greeley, A. M., Sheatsley, P. B. 1974. Attitudes toward racial integration: the South "catches up." In *Social Problems and Public Policy: I. Inequality and Justice,* ed. L. Rainwater, pp. 186–216. Chicago: Aldine

Greer, S. A. 1961. Catholic voters and the Democratic party. *Pub. Opin. Q.* 25:611–25

Grindstaff, C. F., Ebanks, G. E. 1975. Protestant and Catholic couples who have chosen vasectomy. *Sociol. Anal.* 36:29–42

Groat, T. H., Neal, A. G., Knisely, E. C. 1975. Contraceptive nonconformity among Catholics. *J. Sci. Stud. Relig.* 14:367–77

Hardy, K. R. 1974. Social origins of American scientists and scholars. *Science* 185:497–506

Harper, L. 1974. Spirit-filled Catholics: some biographical comparisons. *Soc. Compass* 21:311–26

Harrison, M. I. 1974. Sources of recruitment to Catholic pentecostalism. *J. Sci. Stud. Relig.* 13:49–64

Hill, C. R., Stafford, F. P. 1974. Family background and lifetime earnings. Presented at Econometric Society meetings, December 1974, San Francisco

Hitchcock, J. 1973–1974. The evolution of the American Catholic left. *Am. Scholar* 43:66–84

Hunt, L. D., Hunt, J. G. 1975. A religious factor in secular achievement among blacks: the case of Catholicism. *Soc. Forces* 53:595–605

Hunt, L. D., Hunt, J. G. 1976. Black Catholicism and the spirit of Weber. *Sociol Q.* 17:369–77

Hunt, L. D., Hunt, J. D. 1977. Religious affiliation and militancy among urban blacks—some Catholic-Protestant comparisons. *Soc. Sci.* 57:821–33

Hyman, H. H., Sheatsley, P. B. 1964. Attitudes toward desegregation. *Sci. Am.* 211:2–9

Juster, F. T. 1974. *Education, Income, and Human Behavior.* NY: McGraw-Hill

Kobrin, F. E., Goldscheider, C. 1978. *The Ethnic Factor in Family Structure and Mobility.* Cambridge, Mass: Ballinger Publishing Co.

Lenski, G. 1961. *The Religious Factor.* Garden City, NY: Doubleday

Leon J. J., Steinhoff, P. G. 1975. Catholics' use of abortion. *Sociol. Anal.* 36:125–36

Lipset, S. M., Ladd, E. C. 1971. Jewish

academics in the United States: their achievements, culture, and politics. In *Jewish Year Book,* ed. M. Wallace. Hartford, Conn: Prayer Book

McCready, W. C. 1976. Financial support for church and schools. In *Catholic Schools in a Declining Church,* ed. A. M. Greeley, W. C. McCready, K. McCourt, pp. 244–62. Kansas City: Sheed & Ward

McCready, W. T. 1972a. *Faith of our fathers.* PhD dissertation, Univ. Illinois, Chicago Circle, Ill.

McCready, W. T. 1972b. American Catholic pentecostals: a social analysis. *Concilium Int. Rev. Theol.* pp. 55–60

McCready, W. T., Greeley, A. M. *The Ultimate Values of the American Population.* Beverly Hills, Calif: Sage Publications

McGuire, M. B. 1974. An interpretive comparison of elements of the pentecostal and underground church movements in American Catholicism. *Sociol. Anal.* 35:57–65

McGuire, M. B. 1977. The social context of prophecy: "word-gifts" of the Spirit among Catholic pentecostals. *Rev. Relig. Res.* 18:134–47

McIntosh, W. A., Alston, J. P. 1977. Acceptance of abortion among white Catholics and Protestants, 1962 and 1975. *J. Sci. Stud. Relig.* 16:295–303

Murphy, F. X., Erhart, J. F. 1975. Catholic perspectives on population issues. *Popul. Bull.* 30:3–31

Nelson, J. I., Simpkins, C. 1973. Family size and college aspiration: a note on Catholic-Protestant differences. *Soc. Sci. Q.* 14:544–55

Nie, N. H., Currie, B. F., Greeley, A. M. 1974. Political attitudes among American ethnics: A study of perceptual distortion. *Ethnicity* 1:317–44

Nie, N. H., Petrocik, J. H., Verba, S. 1976. *The Changing American Voter.* Cambridge, Mass: Harvard Univ. Press

Natl. Opin. Res. Cent. 1971. *American Priests.* Rep. of the Nat. Opin. Res. Cent. prepared for the US Catholic Conf. Chicago: NORC. (Multilithed) 486 pp.

O'Brien, D. J. 1972. American Catholicism and American religion. *J. Am. Acad. Relig.* 40:36–53

O'Dea, T. F. 1958. *American Catholic Dilemma: An Inquiry into the Intellectual Life.* NY: Sheed & Ward

Phillips, K. 1969. *The Emerging Republican Majority.* Garden City, NY: Doubleday Anchor

Potvin, R. H., Lee, Che-Fu. 1974. Catholic college women and family-size preferences. *Sociol. Anal.* 35:24–34

Ricoeur, P. 1967. *The Symbolism of Evil.*

(transl. E. Buchanan) Boston: Beacon Press

Rusher, W. A. 1975. *The Making of a New Majority Party.* NY: Sheed & Ward

Schnell, R. L., Rooke, P. T. 1977. Intellectualism, educational achievement, and American Catholicism: a reconsideration of a controversy, 1955–1975. *Can. Rev. Am. Stud.* 8:66–76

Schoenherr, R. A., Greeley, A. M. 1974. Role commitment processes and the American Catholic priesthood. *Am. Sociol. Rev.* 39:407–26

Schoenherr, R. A., Perez-Vilarino, J. 1978. Organizational role commitment in Spain and the United States. In *Organizations Alike and Unlike,* ed. D. Hixon, In press

Schuman, H. 1969. Free will and determinism in public beliefs about race. *Trans-Action* December:44–48

Seidler, J. 1978. Review of A.M. Greeley, *The American Catholic: A Social Portrait.* *Soc. Forces* 56: 1263–65

Sowell, T. 1975. *Race and Economics.* NY: David McKay

Steinburg, S. 1974. *The Academic Melting Pot: Catholics and Jews in American Higher Education.* NY: McGraw Hill

Stryker, R. 1978. *Religio-ethnic and Catholic school effects on attainments in the early career.* Madison, Wis: Center Demog. Ecol., Univ Wis.

Taylor, D. G., Sheatsley, P. B., Greeley, A. M. 1978. Attitudes toward racial integration. *Sci. Am.* 238:42–49

Walker, A. 1975. Sociological and lay accounts as versions of reality: choosing between reports of the "charismatic renewal movement" amongst Roman Catholics. *Theor. Soc.* 2:211–34

Weigel, G. 1957. American Catholic intellectualism: a theologian's reflections. *Rev. Polit.* 19:289–90

Weigert, A. J., Thomas, D. L. 1974. Secularization and religiosity: cross-national study of Catholic adolescents in five societies. *Sociol. Anal.* 35:1–23

Westley, F. R. 1977. Searching for surrender: a Catholic charismatic renewal group's attempt to become glossolalic. *Am. Behav. Sci.* 20:925–40

Westoff, C. F., Jones, E. F. 1978. The end of "Catholic" fertility. Paper presented at the annual meeting of the Popul. Assoc. Am., Atlanta, April 12–15, 1978

Wilson, F. D., Bumpass, L. 1973. The prediction of fertility among Catholics: a longitudinal analysis. *Demography* 10:591–97

Wuthnow, R. 1978. Review of *The American Catholic: A Social Portrait,* by Andrew M. Greeley. *Contemp. Sociol.* 7:346–47

1

RELIGIOUS IMAGERY AS A PREDICTOR VARIABLE IN THE GENERAL SOCIAL SURVEY

Plenary Session of Society for Scientific Study of Religion

October 26, 1984

Andrew M. Greeley

2

I shall propose tonight for your consideration, a simple, easy to administer, four-item measure of the religious imagination which, I will contend, can be demonstrated to be a sufficiently important predictor variable of attitudes and behaviors frequently studied in American society -- racial attitudes, political behavior, civil liberties attitudes -- as to merit inclusion in all studies of these phenomenon. Moreover, these four variables are already included in the 1984 General Social Survey and will be, God and the royalty checks permitting, part of the next three General Social Surveys. Thus, anyone who has any questions about tonight's presentation can merely call up the '84 GENSOC on his/her IBM PC-XT or mainframe computer, replicate the analysis presented tonight, and push beyond it in her/his own direction.

This scale, so simple-minded I will confess I should have thought of it long ago, is the result of almost fifteen years of searching for a sociology of religion measure that was powerful enough that no social scientist, no matter how grimly secularist or agnostic, would be able to ignore it.

This search, begun in the late 1960's, had two motivations: first of all, it seemed to me that if religion, as Clifford Geertz has suggested, is really a culture system composed of symbols which purport uniquely to explain what the world is about, which symbols become not merely categories for explaining reality but templates for shaping it, then the ordinary measures we use in research in the sociology of religion are not religious at all, or only religious in a derivative sense. Belief in God, the inspiration of the scripture, infant

3

baptism, frequency of prayer and church attendance, formal membership in a denomination, may be the results of one's religion as "culture system" (to use Geertz's words) that need not, and usually do not tell us very much about a person's organizing symbols/directing templates.

Moreover, it also seemed to me that one of the reasons most sociologists do not take religion very seriously is that it is not particularly useful as a predictor variable. Those of us who, for one reason or another, are interested in religion may study it as a dependent variable asking, especially, whether religion is eroding under the pressure of "secularization." But the variables which we monitor in the search for secularization are not very powerful predictors, if they are predictors at all, of the sorts of things of which sociologists are normally interested -- social, political and racial attitudes and behaviors, for example. There are some correlations between denominational affiliation and such attitudes and behaviors, with Jews normally more "liberal" than Catholics and Catholics somewhat more "liberal" than Protestants. Beyond this phenomenon, our measures don't seem to have much influence on social attitudes and behaviors, a fact which confirms the agnostic sociologist in his conviction that religion doesn't matter anymore.

I found myself wondering, when this exploration began back in the late 1960's, whether the two phenomena might not be related, whether the weakness of religion as a predictor variable, in other words, might be attributed to the fact that we really were not trying to measure religion as a culture system. As I would put the question now, though I would not have been perceptive enough to state it that way

4

fifteen years ago, if we can measure the religious imagination, might we not derive a presentable predictor variable which our agnostic friends and colleagues could only ignore at the price of some self-deception and intellectual dishonesty.

I will confess guilt of three false starts, false not in the sense that they were useless but rather in the sense they provided the occasion for mistakes on which my colleagues and I had to build.

First of all, in the 1972 study reported by William McCready and myself in our book, THE ULTIMATE VALUES OF AMERICANS, we attempted to measure religion as a culture system by the use of a number of vignettes in which, for example, the respondent was asked to choose among a number of propositional responses to a situation of tragedy or suffering, such as a parent's death. The trouble with the vignette approach was that, being too clever, it was also too complex. While we did find explainable relationships, it was not evident what these relationships meant and they lacked the predictive power to demand attention from others, even in the sub-specialty of religion, to say nothing of general empirical sociology.

The second attempt, in the study of young Catholic adults in 1979, abandoned the vignette and the propositional answer for the image: "When you hear the name of God, how likely (on a five-point scale), do each of the following words come to your mind -- Father, Mother, King, Lord, Redeemer, etc. etc. (the various images were chosen after consultation with theologians and reading the theological literature on the religious imagination). This approach proved to be considerably more fruitful than the vignette/proposition approach as

5

of course a moment's reflection would have prepared us to expect: if you want to find out about people's images, then you ask them about their images. The principal weakness from the point of view of the study of religion as symbol system in the young Catholic project (reported in my book THE RELIGIOUS IMAGINATION, William H. Sadlier, Inc., 1981) was that our respondents were young and Catholic and were quizzed on mostly religious matters. As an exploration the project was useful, but as evidence to which one could point with confidence it was, again, something less than persuasive.

Moreover, it contained a hidden flaw which would appear only last year when the same items, slightly reworked, were included in the 1983 General Social Survey. When the same question was administered verbally that there was a powerful "yes saying" phenomenon (the young Catholics were studied through a mail questionnaire in which they filled out replies themselves without the aid of an interviewer). Many respondents, particularly the more devout, agreed enthusiastically with every image that was presented to them. It was possible to filter out the "yes saying" dimension but what remained was a variable so elaborate and complex that it was virtually impossible to explain, often even to myself. Thus, at the suggestion of Tom W. Smith, the Guardian of the General Social Survey, we administered in the 1984 survey to two-thirds of our respondents, a forced choice question in which they were asked, as you can see from Table 1, to locate themselves on a seven-point continuum, between Father/Mother, Master/Spouse, Judge/Lover, King/Friend, Creator/Healer and Redeemer/Liberator. Incidentally, both in the pre-test and in the

6

actual survey, few if any of our respondents had difficulty in locating themselves on the seven-point scales. They did not think, in other words, that the forced-choice was irrational. Because we hedged the risk of a forced choice by administering only to two-thirds of our respondents, the number of cases available for analysis are less than that of the 1500 respondents in the '84 General Social Survey, a problem which will be corrected next year but which does, at the present, raise some questions about statistical significance in one or two tables.

Let me briefly repeat here the theoretical orientation behind this attempt to find a useful measure of religious images and correlate that measure with the less ultimate attitudes and behaviors of a person's life. Like Rudolph Otto and William James, I believe that religion takes its origin from experience, those experiences in which "accurately or falsely" (sociologists cannot say) our hope is renewed. These experiences are, in their turn, recorded in our imagination as symbols, not merely images of past experiences but images which -- because of the peculiar nature of the hope renewal experience -- interpret, organize and direct our response to ultimate phenomena of life. These images are stories or directing templates which shape not only our responses but even shape the reality to which we respond. The church or ecclesial community or worship group -- whatever -- is that community in which, at the most fundamental level, we share our experiences and images and to which we tell our stories in order that they might be correlated with the overarching stories of our heritage. Finally, the more intimate and affective, more "gracious" and

7

"graceful" our hope renewal experiences (or experiences of the Other
or our experiences of the Sacred, if you wish to use those terms) are,
the more gracious and graceful will be our template stories and the
more gracious and graceful our response to less ultimate life
situations. Briefly, the organizing hypothesis of this presentation
is that those whose religious imagination has a propensity to a
warmer, affectionate, more intimate, more loving representation of
Ultimate Reality will also be more gracious or more benign in their
response to political and social issues. Might I note in passing that
stated thus simply, the hypothesis does not seem all that extraordinary. Nonetheless, it has not been so self-evidently true that social
scientists have frantically searched for a way to measure the gra-
ciousness and the gracefulness of their respondents' religious imagination (RELIGION A SECULAR THEORY, The Free Press, 1982).

You can observe in Table One that the more traditional and perhaps less affectionate images still predominate in the religious imagination of Americans: forty-six percent of the population is at the
far end of the scale on Father, fifty-two percent on Master, forty
percent as Judge, thirty-three percent as Creator and forty percent as
Redeemer. Nonetheless, and somewhat surprisingly, thirty-six percent
of our respondents were willing to caste a vote for the androgyny of
God, placing themselves in the middle or to the left of the
Mother/Father Mother/Father scale, twenty-eight percent were to the
middle or the right of the Master/Spouse scale forty percent are on
the right of the Judge/Lover scale. Majorities, however, are willing

8

to take at least a middle ground on the images of Friend, Healer and
Liberator.

The response pattern derived in the factor analysis summarized in
Table Two is basically the same as those derived from the question
wording in the 1983 General Social Survey, without the ambiguities and
complexities of the "yes saying" dimension to the 1983 answers. In
the first factor, the heavy positive loadings (on the right-hand item
because numbers in the scale range left to right from one to seven)
are on Spouse, Mother, Friend and Lover and the heavy negative
loadings on Master, Father, King and Judge. The high score on this
factor, in other words, indicates a propensity to endorse the more affectionate, more intimate, more gracious and graceful experience of an
image and symbol for God while a low score represents the propensity
to choose Master, Father, King and Judge imagery. Note carefully what
is being said here: the majority of Americans tend in the direction
of the less intimate and more formal images of their relationship with
God. Factor one (called hereafter for the sake of convenience the
Grace factor) merely measures where in relationship to the average a
given respondent falls in the continuum between the two sets of
measures.

A second factor involves high loadings on the Creator/Healer and
Redeemer/Liberator variables with positive score indicating a propensity to lean in the direction of the Healer/Liberator image. While
these images might be more ideologically desirable from the point of
view of religious social activists, they did not correlate in any
important fashion with the variables selected for this analysis and

9

hence, factor two is omitted from the rest of this presentation. It may well be, however, that further analysis may prove that it has a more powerful effect on other attitudes and behaviors than does the Grace factor (I call the second factor, rather unimaginatively, the Healer/Liberator factor. If you use it in your own analysis, be my guest and give it whatever name you wish.)

Our first question is whether there are any social and demographic characteristics that we must take into account in our attempt to determine whether the Grace factor does affect social attitudes and behavior. In Table 3, the measure used is the so-called Z score. It represents percentage of a standard deviation above and below the mean, on a scale for which the mean is zero and the standard deviation is one. Thus, women are four percent of a standard deviation higher than men on the Grace Scale -- a very small difference, indeed.

The higher scores on the Grace Scale occur among the young, the better educated, and those who live in the north, and those whose racial designation is "Other." While none of these relationships are especially powerful, they still have to be taken into account in further analysis because, human kind being a strongly multi-variate species, even rather tiny relationships may make a correlation spurious.

I am excluding from the rest of this analysis the hundred or so Black respondents to whom the forced choice scale was administered. I have investigated the different correlation patterns in the black and the white population sufficiently to realize that religion operates rather differently in the two racial groups, but I am not going to try to describe those differences, even to myself, until I have a substan-

10

tially larger case base of Blacks. Since General Social Survey data are available to you as quickly as they are to me, anyone is free to explore the black religious imagination and its impact on attitudes and behaviors whenever that anyone is confident there are enough cases to justify such analysis. At the end of the currently contemplated funding of religious imagination questions in GENSOC, there should be perhaps seven hundred Black respondents available for analysis.

University of Chicago Divinity School theologian, David Tracy, in his study of the "classics" of the Protestant and Catholic heritage has argued (with little disagreement from Protestant reviewers, I might add) that the Catholic Imagination is more "analogical" and the Protestant imagination more "dialectical." By this he means that of the two fears -- one, a fear of uniting God too much to the world, and the other of isolating God too much from the world -- the Protestant propensity is to fear the idolatry and superstition which comes form not safeguarding adequately the "Radical Otherness" of God whereas the Catholic propensity is "sacramental," that is to say, it fears more the ill effects of denying all similarity between God and creation, between divine relationships and human relationships. Neither the analogical imagination nor the dialectical imagination is superior to the other in Tracy's formulation. Both, indeed, are essential. They merely represent tendencies and choices in both the traditions, one fearing a desacralized world, a world in which God is radically absent, and the other fearing a sacralized world in which God is imagined as so present that religion turns to superstition and idolatry.

11

From this theorizing, the accuracy of which, as I have said, Protestant reviewers do not seem to deny, one would hypothesize, perhaps, that Protestants would score somewhat more highly on images that are more formal and tend in the direction of protecting the "Radical Otherness" of God whereas Catholics might tend to choose those response patterns which more strongly emphasize the intimacy of God's presence and the sacramentality of the world as revelation of what God is like. Mother, Lover, Spouse, Friend seem to resonate with the analogical imagination; Father, King, Master and Judge more to the dialectical imagination.

Whatever one might think of this process of reasoning, it is true that a hypothesis based on Tracy's theory is supported by our data. Catholics are a third of a standard deviation higher on the Grace Scale than are Protestants. Unfortunately, there are not enough cases available for this first analysis for me even to print denominational differences among Protestants. Therefore, until the next two general social surveys are completed, I will limit myself to saying that, on the basis of the data so far available to me, none of the Protestant denominations come close to the Catholic score on the Grace Scale (and the Jewish score, based on seventeen respondents, ought not to be taken seriously).

Interestingly enough, those who describe themselves as "extremely close to God" score lower on the Grace Scale than those who are not likely to say that they are extremely close to God. Those who think of themselves as extremely close to God tend to use images which suggest less closeness while those who do not think of themselves as

12

close to God are more likely to use images which do suggest closeness.
The explanation for this can perhaps be found in the fact that those
who believe in the literal inspiration of the bible (see Table 5 for
the wording of the question) are substantially lower (about one-third
of a standard deviation) than those who do not believe in literal inspiration. It may be that if one is of a fundamentalist religious
orientation, one is skittish about religious images such as spouse,
and mother and lover for which there seems to be less justification in
the heritage strictly and rigidly interpreted. There is, of course,
ample justification in the scripture for these three images) but it
seems safe to say that the more fundamentalist religious mind -- and I
use the word fundamentalist here with a small "f" -- has not, through
the centuries given much emphasis to such images.

Table 4B suggests that such an explanation may be valid. There
is virtually no difference in Grace Scale scores between those who say
they are very close to God and those who do not claim to be very close
to God among the respondents whose view of the bible is not fundamentalist. A similar analysis, omitted here, for the sake of brevity,
also applies to the negative relationship between church attendance
and the Grace Scale in Table 4. There is a certain antipathy between
fundamentalism (with a small "f" again, I note) and religious imagery
which may seem too non-traditional to be orthodox. Nevertheless, the
puzzle remains for further exploration. Why is it true that even
among the respondents who are freed from the constraints of
fundamentalism, that those whose religious imagery suggests a more
intimate relationship, are not substantially more likely in their

13

propositional description of their relationship to God, to describe themselves as "extremely close" than are those who do not have such intimate imagery?

Table 5 presents the variables that are to be used in the central analysis of this presentation -- attitudes towards government giving special treatment to Blacks, towards the death penalty, towards Blacks pushing where they are not wanted, and towards civil liberties, and remembered voting behavior in the 1980 Presidential election -- two observations are pertinent about the dependent variables:

(1) the civil liberties scale is composed of attitudes towards five dissonant groups as college faculty members -- homosexuals (as in Table 5) communists, atheists, racists, and those who wish to turn over the government of the country to militarists. All these variables load on a single factor which is our dependent variable in the present analysis.

(2) our analysis of voting behavior is limited to those respondents who claim that they voted in 1980 and hence the number of cases available to us in this part of the analysis is diminished substantially.

The central finding of the present paper is contained in Table 6. There are positive and statistically significant correlations between the Grace Scale and attitudes towards capital punishment, civil liberties, Blacks not pushing, and the government helping Blacks and a negative correlation between the Grace Scale and a vote in 1980 for Ronald Reagan. A first glance for those not familiar with sociological analysis may think the correlations are rather thin. However,

14

those who have labored in the vineyards of sociology for a long time will recognize that they are presentable correlations indeed. As was remarked before, the human species is multi-variate. When one encounters a large univariate correlation which purports by itself to explain substantial amounts of variants in human behavior then, as Peter Rossi once remarked, the explanation is normally that the correlation is in fact a definition or there has been a computational error.

The pertinent question for the coefficients in Table 6 is not how large is their absolute size but how well they survive when standardized by the analytic variables normally used in social research and how they compare in standardizing equations with such variables.

To illustrate the dimensions of the relationships in Table 6 with a percentage cross-tabulation, Table 7 shows that those high on the Grace Scale are eighteen percentage points less likely to report that they voted for Ronald Reagan in 1980 (and thus eighteen percentage points more likely to say they voted either for Jimmy Carter or John Anderson) a difference which is statistically significant even with a case base of 506 respondents. Note, incidentally, in Table 7 that the total proportion remembering that they voted for Ronald Reagan is virtually the same as the actual election results.

Tables 8 and 9 represent an attempt to explain away the correlation between the Grace Scale and the five dependent variables. The coefficients in Table 8 are all betas, i.e., standardized coefficients emerging from multiple regression equation; each coefficient represents the relationship of the variable at the head of its column with the dependent variables, net of all other predictor variables; thus

15

the betas between Grace and capital punishment represents the relationship between Grace and capital punishment, net of age, sex, education and region and the beta for age represents the relationship
between age and capital punishment attitudes, net of Grace, sex, education and region.

If one wishes to measure the effects of the four other predictor
variables in diminishing the relationship between Grace and the dependent variables, one need merely compare the betas in Table 8 with the
R coefficients in Table 7. By way of summarizing the durability of
the Grace Scale as a predictor of attitudes and behavior, one must observe that it is the only one of the five variables in the regression
equations that relates at a level of statistical significance to the
five dependent variables. Age is is significant twice (with civil
liberties and Blacks "pushing"); sex is statistically significant
twice -- women are more likely to oppose capital punishment and more
likely to be tolerant of Black pressure. Education is statistically
significant three times -- in relationship to civil liberties, Black
pressure, and a vote for Ronald Reagan; and residence in the South is
statistically significant in attitudes towards civil liberties and
Black pressure (negatively). Moreover, the Grace Scale is tied with
sex to be the most important predictor of attitudes on capital
punishment and the most important predictor of a non-Reagan vote in
the 1980 election (education being the only other significant
predictor). Grace is a weaker predictor of civil liberties attitudes
than education and age; it's stronger than sex and region (not much
stronger than region). It is a more powerful correlate than sex in

16

attitudes towards Black pressure but a weaker correlate than age, education and region (not much weaker than region). Finally, the Grace Scale is the only statistically significant correlate of the measure of respondents' sympathy for government going out of its way to help Blacks.

There is as much reason, therefore, to include the Grace measure in surveys of social attitudes and behavior as there is for including measures of age, sex, education and region; not to use the four item Grace Scale, I would like to suggest tonight, would be as absurd as not using measures of age, sex, education and region in social surveys.

But is the Grace Scale, in fact, a religious measure or is it a surrogate for some more basic and fundamental social and political orientation? There are positive correlations, for example (.20) between the Grace Scale and political liberalism and religious liberalism (as the latter is measured by belief in biblical inspiration) (the wording for these two items are presented in Table 5). Granted that the generally tolerant and liberal orientation which lurks beneath the Grace Scale is not eliminated by measures of either education or age (which normally account for shifts in the "liberal" direction) might not the attitudes of those high on the Grace Scale be notably diminished if we took into account their political and religious liberalism?

Table 9 demonstrates, however, that the Grace Scale is not a surrogate for political or economic or social or religious liberalism or abortion liberalism as we can measure these variables from the General

17

Social Survey. The correlation between the Grace Scale and a vote
against Ronald Reagan is -.22(Table 7) It is reduced only to -.15
when the four forms of liberalism are taken into account. While it is
third to political and economic liberalism in its power to predict
1980 voting behavior (-.25 and -.20 respectively), it is a much
stronger predictor of presidential voting than either social (life
style) or religious liberalism and makes an important contribution in
its own right. Indeed it's independent effect is sufficiently close to
that of political and economic liberalism that one might as reasonably
omit the two latter measures as to omit a measure of the religious
imagination. Perhaps there is another measure of liberalism which is
not captured by political self description and attitudes towards
legalization of marijuana, goverment help to the poor, abortion on
demand (A) and the literal inspiration of the the bible. Nonetheless,
it is worthwhile, minimally, to use the Grace measure until we
discover what that something else might be because it would appear
that the ordinary variables currently possessed by the collective
unconscious of the social survey fraternity do not account for the
relationship between the Grace Scale and other measures.

   Perhaps you will say that what the Grace Scale measures is a personality orientation. Perhaps it is a psychological rather than a religious variable. Obviously, there is no way to refute such an
assertion. While it is possible in theory (Parsonian theory) to separate the culture system from the personality system) the two interact
so powerfully in an individual from the very earliest days of his life
that in practice it would be very difficult to sort them out. It may

18

be that the religious imagery questions asked in the General Social
Survey are nothing more than a kind of ink blot which merely measures
different personality orientations. One would respond in passing,
even if this were true, that it's certainly a very powerful
personality test if, through four simple items, it provides a good
deal more predictive power than do most far more elaborate personality
tests.

There is, however, one last argument that I would advance at
least as suggestive evidence that we are dealing here with a measure
that is authentically religious, however much it may also be mixed
with personality. It will be noted in Tables 10 and 11, that the
strongest negative correlation with a vote for Ronald Reagan is to be
found precisely among those who describe themselves as "close to God"
and who cannot view the bible from a fundamentalist perspective. The
most powerful political effect of the Grace Scale, in other words, can
be found in respondents in which two religious tendencies converge --
a sense of closeness to God and an openness in their attitude towards
the bible. Religious matrix, in other words, has a powerful effect on
the operation of the Grace Scale suggesting that in part, at any rate,
it does indeed measure religion as a culture system and not merely religion as a personality factor.

Tables 10 and 11 indicate that the relationship between an anti-
Reagan note and the Grace Scale is not merely a function of religious
liberalism. Table 12 demonstrates that neither is it merely a function of political liberalism. The majority of conservatives, of
course, voted for Reagan but if they were high in the Grace Scale,

19

forty-fix percent of the conservatives did not vote for him (as opposed to thirty percent of the conservatives who were low on the Grace
Scale who did not vote for him). Another way of looking at the same
phenomenon is to say that a high score on the Grace Scale cost Ronald
Reagan fifteen percentage points of the votes in each of the three political categories. The lowest Reagan vote, seventeen percentage
points, was for liberals who were high in the Grace Scale and the
highest Reagan vote, seventy percentage points, was for conservatives
who were low on the Grace Scale. A variable, we would suggest, that
can swing fifteen percentage points of the vote within ideological
categories, is a variable that should be taken very seriously indeed.

Moreover(Table 12A) there is a denominational specification for
the operation of the Grace Scale. The correlations between it and the
dependent variables are especially strong in that denomination
(Catholic) which has the highest average score on the scale and whose
high score was indeed antecedently predicted on the basis of David
Tracy's theological work. Note that the specification (or interaction,
if you wish) is the exact opposite of an explanation. The correlation
between Grace and the dependent variables is not spurious and explained by denomination. It is rather especially concentrated in the
denomination which has higher scores on the Scale.

Another approach to the question of the specifically religious
nature of the Grace Scale is the opposite of the last one. It is possible to ask whether the Scale contributes to an explanation of
attitudinal difference between Protestants and Catholics. As it was
noted earlier in this paper, these differences have been noted in pre-

20

vious research but nothing in the sociology of religion has enabled
sociologists to account for the differences. Might it be that the
higher score of Catholics on the Grace Scale, anticipated from David
Tracy's analysis of the "Classics" of Protestant and Catholic literature, might, in fact, account in part for the social and political
attitudinal differences between Protestants and Catholics. Table 13
demonstrates that this is precisely what happens. When attitudes towards racial pressure, help for Blacks, capital punishment and civil
liberties are combined into a single factor the difference (in standardized or z score) between Protestants and Catholics is twenty-nine
points. When the disproportionate representation of Protestants in
the South is taken into account, the difference diminishes to twenty-
one points and when the different scores on the Grace Scale are further taken into account, differences diminished six more points to
statistical insignificance. Even after region is taken into account,
in other words, the Grace Scale accounts for almost as much of the
difference between Protestants and Catholics in social and political
liberalism as does region. The Grace Scale, therefore, seems to measure something that is more likely to be found in the Catholic religious tradition than in the Protestant religious tradition, a
difference in the two traditions, as we have said, which one would
have derived from a consideration of David Tracy's work on the
Catholic and Protestant imaginations.

Obviously this presentation is preliminary. We have proved that
our so-called Grace Scale is a useful measure in social surveys, one
which adds explanatory power not accounted for by either demographic

21

or attitudinal measures currently in use. It seems likely, though not conclusively proven, that the Grace Scale does measure religion as a culture system in Clifford Geertz's definition -- the Grace Scale, in other words, is a set of symbols (partial, of course) which explains the Real and acts as a template for responding to and shaping reality.

One final question: since religion in the perspective used in this paper is symbol and story, do stories dealing with religious symbols affect the religious imagination of those who read them. To answer this question (and to test my own hypothesis) I persuaded the Literary Guild to include two thousand questionnaires in a random sample of those who accepted the Literary Guild's selection of my novel LORD OF THE DANCE.

The pertinent question for our purposes in this paper, however, is whether the novels affect the religious imagination of the readers. Note that it is much easier to prove that there is no such impact than to prove that there is. To prove with certainty that there is such an impact, one would have to do before and after tests. As it is, we are forced to ask whether those readers who say the book helped them to understand the relationship between religion and sex (religion and intimacy, in other words) and those who say it improved their understanding of God's love are in fact more likely to be high on the items constituting the Grace Scale. Table 14 demonstrates that those who answered Yes to the two questions do indeed demonstrate a propensity to be more accepting of intimate and affectionate images of God. The smallest difference in Table 14 in the predicted direction is seven percentage points, the largest is thirty-one percentage points. There

22

are, however, two possible conclusions one can draw from the data: the first is that, indeed, those who find more understanding of God's love and of the relationship between religion and sex in an explicitly religious/symbolic novel do undergo a development in their religious imagination in the direction of a high score on the Grace Scale.

The second explanation is that hose who already have high scores on the Grace Scale have a tendency, after reading a book such as LORD OF THE DANCE, to feel that they understand better the relationship between religion and sex and that they understand better God's love. There is little reason to choose between one or the other explanation.

Both imply a relationship between the novel and the religious imagination and even the second explanation, a greater feeling of understanding for those who have high scores on the Grace Scale, would not be unacceptable to an author interested in affecting the religious imagination of his readers in a graceful and gracious direction.

Doubtless some will say that this particular part of the paper is defensive and self-serving, surely an act of self defense. But then as Stanley Liberson might have once remarked, narcissism begins at home. The question of the effect of religious novels on the religious imagination is a valid one, no matter who analyzes it.

Besides, the readers of LORD OF THE DANCE have payed for this project and that cannot be dismissed as altogether ungracious and ungraceful on their part.

Finally in the last table I present a second set of questions about the nature of the world, the relationship between God and world, and the good person's posture vis a vis the world which will be asked

23

in the next Gensoc, courtesy of the readers of LORD OF THE DANCE and

subsequent novels. I would predict that this measure will correlate

with the God images analyzed in this paper and will enhance their pre-

dictive power.

And I thus end on the note of the old Saturday afternoon serial

movies, "Continued Next Year."

God, She being willing.

(A) It is worth observing that for all the public discussion of

the abortion issue in the current campaign, none of the seven NORC

abortion items correlate at statistically significant levels with

remembered 1980 presidential voting.

TABLE 1

IF FORMS "X" OR "Y" ASK Q. 124 FORM "Z" GO TO Q. 125.

124.   There are many different ways of picturing God. We'd like to know the
        kinds of images you are most likely to associate with God.

        Here is a card with sets of contrasting images. On a scale of 1-7
        where would you place your image of God between the two contrasting
        images?   (HAND CARD W)

        The first set of contrasting images shows Mother at 1 on the scale and
        Father at 7. If you imagine God as a Mother you would place yourself
        at 1. If you imagine God as a Father, you would place yourself at 7.
        If you imagine God as somewhere between Mother and Father, you would
        place yourself at 2, 3, 4, 5 or 6. (REPEAT EXAMPLE AS NECESSARY FOR
        EACH ITEM A-F, SUBSTITUTING IMAGES A-F FOR "MOTHER" AND "FATHER".)

        Where would you place your image of God on the scale for . . . READ
        EACH SET OF IMAGES AND CIRCLE ONE CODE FOR EACH.

HAND CARD W							TOTAL
3%	2%	3%	28%	9%	9%	46%	100%
A. Mother						Father	
01	02	03	04	05	06	07	
52%	12%	8%	19%	3%	2%	4%	100%
B. Master						Spouse	
01	02	03	04	05	06	07	
40%	11%	9%	24%	4%	3%	9%	100%
C. Judge						Lover	
01	02	03	04	05	06	07	
32%	8%	4%	28%	6%	3%	19%	100%
D. Friend						King	
01	02	03	04	05	06	07	
33%	4%	4%	46%	3%	3%	7%	100%
E. Creator						Healer	
01	02	03	04	05	06	07	
40%	8%	5%	37%	3%	2%	5%	100%
F. Redeemer						Liberator	
01	02	03	04	05	06	07	

TABLE 2

FACTOR LOADINGS (ROTATED) FOR IMAGES OF GOD

	FACTOR 1	FACTOR2
MASTER/SPOUSE	.721	.309
MOTHER/FATHER	-.665	-.119
FRIEND/KING	-.602	.245
JUDGE/LOVER	.588	.245
CREATOR/HEALER	.110	.783
REDEEMER/LIBERATOR	.106	.793

TABLE 3

GRACE SCALE AND DEMOGRAPHIC BACKGROUND

(Z SCORES)

SEX	
MALE	-.03
FEMALE	.01
AGE	
18-29	.09
30-49	.02
50+	-.06
EDUCATION	
10 YEARS OR LESS	-.10
11-12 YEARS	-.05
13 YEARS +	.10
RACE	
WHITE	.00
BLACK	-.10
OTHER	.18
REGION	
SOUTH	-.09
NORTH	.04

TABLE 4

GRACE SCALE AND RELIGION

(Z SCORES)

DENOMINATION		
PROTESTANT	-.16	(479)
CATHOLIC	.18	(214)
JEW	-.02	(17)
CLOSE TO GOD		
EXTREMELY	-.18	(254)
SOMEWHAT	.03	(512)
NOT VERY	.16	(124)
CHURCH ATTENDANCE		
NEVER	.29	(102)
YEARLY TO ONCE A MONTH	.08	(348)
MORE THAN ONCE A MONTH	-.16	(329)
BIBLE		
LITERAL INSPIRATION	-.27	(273)
INSPIRED BUT NOT LITERAL	.07	(386)
NOT INSPIRED	.09	(104)

TABLE 4B

BIBLE INSPIRATION, CLOSENESS TO GOD, AND GRACE SCALE

(ZSCORES)

	VERY CLOSE	NOT VERY CLOSE
LITERAL INSPIRATION	-.28	-.13
	(152)	(195)
NOT LITERAL	.07	.11
	(254)	(636)

TABLE 5

40. And what about a man who admits that he is a homosexual?

A. Suppose this admitted homosexual wanted to make a speech in your
community. Should he be allowed to speak, or not?

Yes, allowed...........1
Not allowed............2
DON'T KNOW.............8

B. Should such a person be allowed to teach in a college or university, or not?

Yes, allowed...........1
Not allowed............2
DON'T KNOW.............8

C. If some people in your community suggested that a book he wrote in
favor of homosexuality should be taken out of your public library,
would you favor removing this book, or not?

Favor..................1
Not favor..............2
DON'T KNOW.............8

55. Do you favor or oppose the death penalty for persons convicted of
murder?

Favor..................1
Oppose.................2
DON'T KNOW.............8

83. Here are some opinions other people have expressed in connection with
(Black/Negro)-White relations. Which statement on the card comes
closest to how you yourself feel? (READ EACH STATEMENT. CIRCLE ONE
CODE FOR EACH.)

HAND   The first one is . . .
CARD
K

	Agree strongly	Agree slightly	Disagree slightly	Disagree strongly	No opinion
A. (Blacks/Negroes) shouldn't push themselves where they're not wanted	1	2	3	4	8

TABLE 5 - continued

108. We hear a lot of talk these days about liberals and conservatives. I'm
      going to show you a seven-point scale on which the <u>political</u> views that
      people might hold are arranged from extremely liberal--point 1--to
      extremely conservative--point 7. Where would you place yourself on
      this scale?

```
┌────────┐                (1)   Extremely liberal............01
│ HAND   │                (2)   Liberal.......................02
│ CARD   │                (3)   Slightly liberal.............03
│  O     │                (4)   Moderate, middle of the road.04
└────────┘                (5)   Slightly conservative........05
                          (6)   Conservative.................06
                          (7)   Extremely conservative.......07
                                DON'T KNOW...................98
```

112. Now look at CARD S. Some people think that (Blacks/Negroes) have
      been discriminated against for so long that the government has a
      special obligation to help improve their living standards. Others
      believe that the government should not be giving special treatment to
      (Blacks/Negroes).

```
┌────────┐   I strongly                              I strongly agree
│ HAND   │   agree the                               that govern-
│ CARD   │   government              I agree          ment shouldn't
│  S     │   is obligated           with both         give special
└────────┘   to help Blacks          answers          treatment
                                                                      DON'T
                                                                      KNOW
             |_____|
             1          2          3          4          5           8
```

      A. Where would you place yourself on this scale, or haven't you made up
          your mind on this?

TABLE 5 - continued

116. In 1980, you remember that Carter ran for President on the Democratic
ticket against Reagan for the Republicans, and Anderson as an Independent.
Do you remember for sure whether or not you voted in that election?

                    Voted (ASK A)..............................1
                    Did not vote (ASK B)......................2
                    INELIGIBLE (ASK B)........................3
                    REFUSED TO ANSWER (GO TO Q.117)...........4
                    DON'T KNOW, CAN'T REMEMBER (GO TO Q.117)...8

IF VOTED:

A. Did you vote for Carter, Reagan, or Anderson?

                    Carter.....................................1
                    Reagan.....................................2
                    Anderson...................................3
                    OTHER CANDIDATE
                       (SPECIFY)_____4

                    DIDN'T VOTE FOR PRESIDENT (ASK B)..........5
                    DON'T KNOW/CAN'T REMEMBER..................8

129. Which of these statements comes closest to describing your feelings
about the Bible? READ FIRST THREE STATEMENTS [(a)-(c)] ONLY. CIRCLE
ONLY ONE CODE.

|HAND| a. The Bible is the actual word of God and is to be
|CARD| taken literally, word for word..................... 1
| Z |
           b. The Bible is the inspired word of God but not
              everything in it should be taken literally,
              word for word...................................... 2

           c. The Bible is an ancient book of fables, legends,
              history, and moral precepts recorded by men........ 3

           d. OTHER... 4

           e. DON'T KNOW.. 8

TABLE 6

CORRELATIONS WITH GOD SCALES

(R's)

	GRACE SCALE	HEAL SCALE
Capital punishment (oppose)	.11	.05**
Civil Liberties (favor)	.16	.12
Blacks should not push (disagree)	.13	.02**
Government should help blacks	.12	.02**
Reagan vote	-.22	.03**

** Not significant

TABLE 7

REAGAN VOTE IN 1980 BY GRACE SCALE

Low on Grace Scale	57%
High on Grace Scale	39%*
Total	52%
	(506)

*Significantly different from Low on scale. p=>.000

TABLE 8

STANDARDIZED COEEFICIENTS FOR GRACE SCALE AND
DEMOGRAPHIC VARIABLES

(BETAS)

	GRACE	AGE	SEX	EDUC.	SOUTH
Capital Pun	.11	-.02**	.11	.00**	.00**
Civil Lib.	.12	-.26	.03**	.27	-.11
Blacks push	.09	-.15	.07	.24	-.12
Help Blacks	.11	-.01**	.02**	.04**	-.03**
Reagan vote	-.18	-07**	-.05**	.14	.07**

TABLE 9

IMPACT OF GRACE SCALE ON PRESIDENTIAL VOTING (For Reagan)
NET OF POLITICAL, ECONOMIC, SOCIAL AND RELIGIOUS LIBERALISM

(BETAS)

Grace Scale	-.15
Political Liberalism	.-25
Religious Liberalism(1)	-.04**
Social Liberalism(2)	-.01**
Economic Liberalism(3)	-.20
Abortion LIberalism(4)	-.00**

** not statistically significant

(1)Rejection of literal inspiration of the bible

(2) Support for legalization of marijuana

(3)Support for government assistance to the poor

(4)Approves availability of abortion for any reason a woman
wishes.

TABLE 10

CORRELATIONS BETWEEN REAGAN VOTE AND GRACE SCALE BY
RELIGIOUS ATTITUDES

R's

Not close to God and Bible literally inspired	-.11**
Close to God and Bible literally inspired	-.15**
Not Close to God and Bible not inspired	-.15
Close to God and Bible not inspired	-.38

** Relationship not statistically significant

TABLE 11

REAGAN VOTE BY GRACE SCALE BY RELIGIOUS ATTITUDES

% Voting for Reagan

	Low on Grace scale	High on Grace Scale
Not Close to God and Bible literally Inspired	60 (46)	47 (17)
Close to God and Bible literally Inspired	50 (60)	31 (13)
Not Close to God and bible not Inspired	55 (171)	40* (103)
Close to God and bible not inspired	68 (45)	28** (121)

*Statistically significan p=.07

**Statistically significant p=.02

TABLE 12

PRESIDENTIAL VOTE BY GRACE SCALE BY POLITICAL
ORIENTATION

%Voting for Reagan

	Low on Grace Scale	High on Grace Scale
Liberal	32	17
	(73)	(46)
Moderate	59	44*
	(117)	(62)
Conservative	70	54**
	(155)	(46)

*p=.06

**p=.07

TABLE 12A

CORRELATIONS WITH GRACE SCALE BY RELIGIOUS DENOMINATON

	PROTESTANT	CATHOLIC
Capital Punishment	.08	.09
Black Pressure	.04	.17
Help Blacks	.05	.09
Civil Liberties	.10	.15
Reagan Vote	-.12	-.20

TABLE 13

SOCIAL LIBERALISM AND CATHOLICISM BY REGION AND GRACE

Difference between
Catholics and
Protestants
(Z score)   29

Difference net of
Region   21

Difference net of
Region and Grace
Scale   15**

*Factor compose of black pressure, government help to
blacks, capital punishment, and civil liberties.

** Not statistically significant

TABLE 14

GRACE SCALE ITEMS BY RESPONSE TO LORD OF THE DANCE

A) BOOK HELPED UNDERSTAND OF RELATIONSHIP BETWEEN
RELIGION AND SEX

	YES	NO
Mother (1-4)	35%	29%**
Spouse (4-7)	34%	19%
Lover (4-7)	46%	24%
Friend (1-3)	68%	56%

B) BOOKED IMPROVED UNDERSTAND OF GOD'S LOVE

	YES	NO
MOTHER (1-4)	35%	27%**
SPOUSE (4-7)	25%	23%**
Lover (4-7)	38%	26%
Friend (1-3)	66%	55%

** Not statistically significant

TABLE 15

TENTATIVE ITEMS FOR NEXT GENERAL SOCIAL SURVEY

1)The world is basically filled with disorder and sin.

There is much goodness in the world which hints at God's goodness.

2)The good person must be deeply involve din the problems and activities of the world.

The good person must avoid contamination by the corruption of the world.

3)For the most part human activity is vain and foolish.

Human effort helps to reveal God in the world.

4)God is almost totally removed fromt he sinfulness of the world.

God reveals himself in and through the world.

5)Human nature is fundamentally perverse and corrupt.

Human nature is more good than evil.

6)Through such things as art and music we learn more about God.

It is dangerous for humans to be too concerned about worldly goods like art and music.

172

REVIEW ESSAY: THE CULT OF THE VIRGIN MARY

Andrew M. Greeley
University of Arizona and
National Opinion Research Center

SSR, Volume 71, No. 3, April, 1987

This is a review essay concerning the cult of the Virgin Mary, prompted by two recent books, detailed in a note at the end. As Michael Carroll, Professor of Sociology at the University of Western Ontario, notes in his introduction, the general neglect of the Mary cult by sociologists of religion seems surprising given their great concern over the past ten or fifteen years with the study of religious cults.

And, one might add, given the empirical evidence (which Carroll ignores) of the persistence of that cult among Catholics in the years since the Vatican Council.

With considerable imagination and resourcefulness, Carroll attempts to locate the origins of the cult with snippets of historical information, data about parallel cults from the Standard Cross Cultural Sample files, and psychoanalytic theory. In fact, his focus is not so much on the Mary cult in all of Christianity but on the emphasis on Mary's perpetual virginity in Western (i.e., Latin) Christianity. In his own words:

the father-ineffective family produced in Roman proletarian sons a strong but strongly repressed desire for the mother than found its expression in the Cyble cult. When males of this sort began moving into the Church in large numbers during the Great Transformation of the fourth and fifth centuries, they created a demand for a goddess who was like Cybele. Although the middle-class sensibilities of the Church hierarchy forced a muting of the masochism associated with Cybele, these newcomers did get the goddess they wanted. She is Mary.

Carroll's insights are powerfully suggestive. But his research suffers under two serious handicaps.

The first is reductionism, a peril hard to escape if one uses psychoanalytic methods without restraint. I found myself thinking after I had read the quote cited that we number crunchers labor under a terrible disadvantage. We have to report the amount of variance our theories and our data explain. Those who use non-numerical methods have no such obligation. We are often gratefully content with explanations that account for ten percent of the variance. We know that reality is complex and that any explanation which accounts for most or all of the variance is suspect.

Scholars like Carroll are under no compulsion to be that cautious. Hence they offer sweeping explanations with little modesty or restraint. For how much of the variance between Greek and Latin Mary Cults does Carroll's theory account?

It would appear from his text that he thinks it accounts for all of the variance -- a most im-

modest claim. If he were content to say tentatively that his "masochism" explanation was partial, I would find no fault with his analysis.

But, come on, Chartres masochistic? Or renaissance Madonnas? Or Hopkins "May Magnificat"? Or the poem of Francois Villion?

Carroll does not seem to comprehend that symbols are both dense and multivalent (polysemious, if you wish). While they have structures of their own and are not inkblots into which any meaning may be read, they still emit many different cues within their proper structure and may have many different meanings -- or more appropriately many different stories to tell.

Among contemporary Catholics, devotion to Mary seems to correlate positively with sexual fulfillment in marriage because it acts as a "conduit" between happy relations with parents and a happy relationship with a spouse. Same symbol, but a very different story than Carroll thinks he has found during the Great Transformation.

In the second half of his study Carroll turns to the Marian apparitions in the last and the present century and analyzes, mostly from a psychoanalytic perspective, the "hallucinations" and the "illusions" of those who claim to have been visited by the mother of Jesus. While I have no vested interest in any of these apparitions (and I reject in principle the possibility that the Mother of Jesus would mouth conservative Republican propaganda), Carroll is too much the "village atheist" in this section of the book, a scholar reducing in principle to neurosis all traces of The Wonderful and all hints of an Open Universe -- thus, I think, begging the question.

At least at Lourdes, something remarkable seems to have occurred, although whether the mother of Jesus was involved may be another question. I wish that Carroll had been more restrained in his reductionism: he would have been more persuasive if he had displayed an open mind.

Thus, while his study is a ground-breaking effort and should occasion more research, he may have made a strategic mistake in choosing both his data and his tools. It seems to me that the best strategy is to study present manifestations of the Mary cult apart from the extraordinary events of alleged apparitions.

At the most general level, the Mary symbol raises the possibility that whatever (or Whatever) is the driving power of the universe loves with the tender passion of a mother holding a baby in her arms. Robert A. Orsi explores the implications of that symbol in the cult of Our Lady of Mount Carmel in Italian Harlem in the first half of this century, a cult which was brilliantly if all too briefly re-enacted in the Godfather film.

Orsi sees the festival of Our Lady of Mount Carmel as a celebration of immigrant hope -- "the street theologians proclaimed that divine and human are in a relationship of mutual responsibility and reciprocity; that the divine needs the human as the human needs the divine, that Christ's redeeming blood an intimacy between heaven and the domus." (p.230). Mary was the link between heaven and the family house and hence the reason for hope in a better life.

Orsi's work represents almost the exact opposite of Carroll's: he seeks to explain, not to explain away, to understand as best he can from the inside not from the outside. He recognizes the rich and polyvalent nature of a symbol and does not attempt to generalize beyond the particular cult that he has empirically studied.

Both approaches are necessary in any social science study of religion. It will betray my own biases if I say that I much prefer Orsi's style.

It is to be hoped that these two thoughtful, and original books are the beginning of serious study of the Mary cult. Whatever else one may think about the Madonna, she is the only mother goddess currently to be found in the market place of religious symbols.

NOTES

THE CULT OF THE VIRGIN MARY: Psychological Origins. By Michael P. Carroll. Princeton: Princeton University Press, 1986, xv + 253. $25.00.

THE MADONNA OF 115TH STREET: Faith and Community in Italian Harlem, 1880-1950. By Robert A. Orsi. New Haven: Yale University Press, 1985. xxiii + 287.$29.95.

Address correspondence to Andrew M. Greeley, National Opinion Research Center, 1155 E. 60th St., Chicago, Illinois 60637.

Manuscript was received January 16, 1987 and reviewed January 21, 1987.

THE CENTER DOESN'T HOLD: CHURCH ATTENDANCE IN THE UNITED STATES, 1940–1984*

MICHAEL HOUT
University of California, Berkeley

ANDREW M. GREELEY
NORC
University of Arizona

Theories about the secularization of society notwithstanding, basic indicators of participation in organized religion show little change over the 50 years covered by the survey research record. Among Protestants, we find that 1950 was a point of low attendance with no prior or subsequent deviation from an average of 40 percent weekly attendance. Among Catholics, attendance rates fell rapidly between 1968 and 1975 but not before or after. Since there are few other trends in the data, we focus on this period of falling attendance among Catholics. The key to falling attendance was the conjuncture of vocal defense of traditional sexual teaching by the Pope and other leaders in the face of rapidly growing opposition to that position among the church-going population. Many Catholics who disagreed with Church teachings on sexuality reduced their attendance (very few actually left the Church). Among active Catholics, opposition to the hierarchy continues to grow, but there has been no decline in attendance rates since 1975. From a latent variable analysis, we conclude that loyalty to the community and communal values is the factor that separates the active from the lapsed Catholics in the 1980s.

No celibate Bishop of Rome is going to take away my birthright.
—Christopher J. Harmon, 1969

INTRODUCTION

The thesis of secularization dominates discussion of trends in religious indicators. The basic tenet of secularization is that modern material values are replacing the traditional spiritual outlook on life. As science and reason provide ever more consistent explanations of life and the cosmos, humans make fewer references to spiritual considerations, leading to a long-term decline in religious belief and practice (esp. Wilson 1976, 1982; also see Glock and Stark 1965; Lenski 1966; Luckmann 1967; Berger 1969). The thesis focuses on consciousness and motivation more than on behavior, but a clear,

testable corollary is the prediction that church attendance will wane in the long run. We undertake a test of the hypothesis of declining church attendance using survey data on religious practice in the United States.

This paper is part of a broad and growing literature questioning the assumptions and implications of secularization theory. Greeley (1972) reviewed the empirical evidence on a long list of secularization indictors—behavioral and subjective. He found that the absolute level of religious belief and practice in the United States was much higher than the secularization thesis would lead one to suspect and that the lack of trends contradicted the secularization thesis. Subsequent work revealed substantial decline in weekly church attendance among Catholics, but the sudden decline had few of the characteristics associated with secularization (Greeley, McCready, McCourt 1976). In particular, it was a short-term decline after which half of the Catholic population continued attending weekly, about one-third substituted monthly or yearly attendance for their former weekly practice, and very few people actually left the Church.

The relatively short time series available a decade ago left open the prospect that a longer perspective might reveal some changes in religious beliefs or practices that resemble secularization. The recent Middletown III research provides that longer perspective, covering fifty years. Caplow, Bahr, and Chadwick (1983) investigated eleven indicators of religious belief and practice in Muncie, Indiana. They found that "none of these series offers

* Direct all correspondence to Michael Hout, Department of Sociology, 410 Barrows Hall, University of California, Berkeley, CA 94720 (BITNET: mikehout @ ucbcmsa).

Support for this research was provided by the University of Arizona and by the Survey Research Center, University of California, Berkeley. We are grateful to Duane Alwin, Otis Dudley Duncan, Herbert McClosky, Paul Sniderman, James Wiley, and Robert Wuthnow for useful comments on prior drafts of this paper. We have also benefitted from the unflagging research assistance of Sean Durkin. Of course, we alone are responsible for our use of their comments and assistance. This is a revision of the paper we presented to the annual meetings of the American Sociological Association in New York, August 30, 1986.

Table 1. Percent Attending Services Last Week by Religion and Year: United States, 1939–1984

Year	Religion				
	Protestant	Catholic	Jewish	Other	None
1939	40	64	12	—	1
1950 ˙	36	63	32	56	4
1959	39	72	20	49	14
1960	39	70	11	57	12
1969	39	64	8	18	0
1979	40	53	19	40	5
1980	43	47	5	16	6
1984	42	52	13	46	7
χ^2 (d.f. = 7)	14.74	111.85	13.72	27.68	17.06
N	8,629	3,501	386	340	672
p	.04	<.01	.06	<.01	.02

Source: American Institute of Public Opinion tapes.

much support for the hypothesis of secularization" (Caplow et al. 1983, p. 35). Most significantly, weekly church attendance in Muncie nearly doubled between 1924 and 1977–78, while the incidence of never attending in 1977–78 was only one-third of what it had been in 1924 (pp. 74–78).

This paper has three parts. In the first we reexamine the issues raised by Greeley (1972; Greeley et al. 1976) and Caplow et al. (1983), combining the advantages of analyzing a national population over a time span nearly as long as Middletown III. In particular, we subject the widely quoted Gallup data to statistical tests that establish the lack of trends among Catholics and Protestants.[1] Among Protestants no trends are uncovered, although the statistical power of a sample of 8,600 respondents allows us to say that the attendance rate in 1950 is significantly lower than the rates in other years. Among Catholics there is a clearly identifiable drop in weekly attendance that started in 1968 and stopped in 1975. The second part of the paper focuses on the importance of declining sexual orthodoxy and the erosion of papal authority in declining Catholic attendance (and their lack of effects on Catholic identification). The last part of the paper addresses the question of why the decline stopped and presents some quantitative conjectures on the source of persistent attendance among many who disagree with the Pope.

TRENDS IN WEEKLY CHURCH ATTENDANCE

Differences among Major Religions

The American Institute of Public Opinion has the longest national time series on church attendance in the United States.[2] From their

archives we have chosen surveys from February or March of years ending in 9 or 0 for detailed analysis. We also use the February 1984 survey because it was the most recent data available at the beginning of our project. We avoided surveys from months with religious holidays, so we could not use any of the 1970 surveys that include the church attendance question. The percentage of affirmative answers to various forms of the question "Did you, yourself, happen to attend church or synagogue during the last seven days?"[3] by year and religion are reported in Table 1.

The most striking aspect of Table 1 is the absence of a consistent trend in weekly church attendance for any group except Catholics. Although the year-to-year differences are significant in each group, these data contradict expectations based on the secularization thesis.

The question wording changes spelled out below may well have consequences that we overlook in our interpretations. All of the problems with the Gallup data serve to induce annual fluctuations in the data. Nonetheless, it is the stability of the series, not irregularity, that strikes most observers. We considered other data sources partly because of the methodological problems with the Gallup data and partly because we would have preferred a church attendance item with more than two responses. The other national series (the Michigan National Election surveys) changed its question in 1970—right in the middle of the one trend we found. Sasaki and Suzuki (1987) use the SRC data. They find that all cohorts observed after the wording change have lower attendance than previous cohorts. They interpret this as modest support for secularization. In our opinion, they have not ruled out the prospect that it is due to the wording change.

[3] The question has evolved over the years. In 1939, "or synagogue" was not part of the question. In 1950, the word "synagogue" was substituted for "church" for those respondents who identified themselves as Jews in a preceding question. The form quoted in the text has been in use at least since 1959. These variations in wording make interpreting the data on Jews difficult, as we note below. In some surveys the words "yourself" and "happen to" were not in the questions.

[1] There is some difficult-to-interpret data on Jews (presented below) that may or may not be evidence of secularization.

[2] These Gallup data are not perfect. Little is known about the sampling procedures used in the early surveys.

Among Protestants, 1950 is the year of lowest attendance; 1980 and 1984 are highest. The differences are very small departures from an overall average of 39.6 percent.[4]

Among Catholics, weekly attendance has dropped off from a high in 1959–60 to a low in 1980. This is the clearest evidence of change in church attendance in the Gallup data. As we shall make clear in the next section, even these falling rates of weekly attendance among Catholics are due to factors that cannot be described as secularization.

Among Jews, church attendance decreased after 1950, albeit not monotonically. With only 350 Jews in seven surveys, it is difficult to sort the systematic variation from the random fluctuations due to sampling error. However, there is reason to believe that the 1939 data understate Jewish attendance. If so, then these data might lend some support to secularization among Jews. The net downward trend from 1950 to 1980 looks like secularization if one is willing to attribute all deviations from the expected monotonic trend to sampling variability.[5] From a secularization perspective, the low 12 percent attendance in 1939 is an anomaly. A change in question wording between 1939 and 1950 may account for it (see note 3). If two-thirds or more of Jews who attended services in the week before the 1939 survey answered "no" to the Gallup question about "*church* last Sunday" and that measured attendance since 1959 fluctuates randomly around an underlying low rate, then these data constitute the only known support for the secularization thesis in the survey research record. If one is not prepared to accept the supposition that so many Jews answered "no" because they were not asked about synagogue,

then even these data cannot be construed as support for secularization.

Changes in the "other" and "none" categories are pronounced but uninterpretable. The composition of the heterogeneous "other" group has undoubtedly changed over 50 years covered by this series, and we cannot account for the swings evident here. Nor can we account for the observation that one-eighth of respondents who profess no religion went to church in 1959 and 1960.

Differences among Age Groups

The Long View: 1939–84. Religious participation increases with age. Some of the changes in Table 1 might be due to changes in the age composition of the population. In particular, the 1950s were a time when the proportion of young adults was low, while the 1960s and 1970s had a large young adult segment. Some of the increase in the attendance of Catholics and Protestants from 1950 to 1959 might be due to this life cycle effect.

Equally important is the prospect that cohorts who enter adulthood during eras of atypical attendance may continue to bear the mark of this socialization throughout their lives. In particular, cohorts that enter adulthood when attendance is down might never pick up the habit of weekly church attendance. If so, then the cohorts of young Catholics who failed to get involved in parish life in the late 1960s and early 1970s might not ever support the Catholic Church to the same extent that their parents and grandparents did. Significant cohort effects will also show up in an analysis of this type if recent changes affect young people more than they affect older people.[6]

The methodology of separating age, period, and cohort effects of this type is complicated (Mason et al. 1973; Fienberg and Mason 1979; Sasaki and Suzuki 1987). The mathematical identity that cohort = year-age precludes any final solution to the identification problem. Separation requires some assumptions. In this case we achieve identification by setting pairs of period effects to equality. In particular, we assume that the year effects for adjacent years (1959–60 and 1979–80) are equal. Furthermore, we define cohorts that span 15 years, so that the multiple correlation of cohort with age and year, though still large, is not unity.[7]

---

[4] Some readers have suggested that we might see more of a clear trend among Prostetants if we included more years. In fact, because the degrees of freedom proliferate faster than do departures from the overall average, filling in the years since 1958 with the percentages from Gallup (1972) and Gallup (1985) and assuming 1,000 Protestants in those surveys for which the actual count is not reported, raises χ^2 so little that it is no longer significant at the .05 level. Other readers suggest that aggregating Protestant denominations as we have hides a trend. They reason that growth of denominations like Baptists with attendance rates that are high by Protestant standards may cancel out downward trends within each denomination. Analysis of Gallup and NORC data reveals that disaggregating Protestant denominations reveals more fluctuations attributable to sampling variability, but no net trends in attendance (Greeley 1987). This finding contradicts the conclusions based on other kinds of data, but it is what the survey research record shows.

[5] Support for such a notion can be gleaned from the wide jumps in measured attendance between adjacent years (1959–60 and 1979–80).

---

[6] The statistical model that we use below will attribute to "cohort" any age-by-year interactions that affect cohorts for which we have few observations.

[7] Our model is a logit regression with dummy independent variables for age, cohort, period, and religion. The input data are from a four-way cross-tabulation of attendance by age (single years up to 69, plus a "70 or more" aggregate) by period (single years)

Table 2. Scaled Deviance (L^2) for Selected Models Based on Logistic Regression of Church Attendance (Y) on Period (P), Age (A), and Cohort (C) by Religion: United States, 1939–1984

Model	Catholics ($N = 3,501$)		Protestants ($N = 8,629$)	
	L^2	d.f.	L^2	d.f.
0. [APC][Y]	710.5	407	581.6	412
1. [APC][PY]	601.5	402	569.1	407
2. [APC][AY]	646.7	399	515.5	404
3. [APC][CY]	593.9	403	575.8	408
4. [APC][PY][AY]	544.4	394	499.2	399
5. [APC][PY][CY]	556.1	398	544.7	403
6. [APC][AY][CY]	564.1	395	505.2	400
7. [APC][PY][AY][CY]	523.8	390	492.6	395
8. [APC][PY][CY][LY]	553.6	397	—	—
9. [APC][PY][CY][QY]	546.2	396	—	—
10. [APC][PY][CY][KY]	543.4	395	—	—

Note: The input data for the logistic regressions are cross-tabulations of church attendance by age (single years up to age 69 years plus an aggregate "70 or more" category) by period (single years). For Catholics there are 408 combinations of age and period in which cases were observed; for Protestants there are 413 such combinations.

A: age group (eight categories); *C:* cohort (five categories); *K:* cubic age effect; *L:* linear age effect; *P:* period (six categories); *Q:* quadratic age effect; *Y:* church attendance.

For Catholics, the preferred model includes the effects of age, period, and cohort on church attendance (Table 2) The logit regression coefficients in Table 3 confirm the significance of the trend apparent in Table 1: a sharp drop in attendance since 1969. The variations in attendance prior to 1969 are within the (large) margin of sampling variability. Looking at the cohort effects we note that, contrary to the expectations of some observers, the post-Vatican II cohort (born since 1945) attends church at rates that are not significantly different from the rates for other cohorts born in this century (once the effects of age and period are factored in). This means that the post-*Humanae Vitea* decline in church attendance affected all Catholic cohorts proportionately. The damage done to the church attendance habits of the cohort that was young during the period of decline is no greater (and no less) than the damage done to the church attendance of the adjacent cohort. A surprising

by religion (Catholic or Protestant only). Our dependent variable is the probability of attending church in the past seven days (p_{ijk}) for each combination of age (indexed by i), period (j), and religion (k), transformed into a log-odds:

$$\text{logit } (p_{ijk}) = \log(p_{ijk}) / (1 - p_{ijk})$$

for $i = 18, \ldots, 70$ ages; $j = 1, \ldots, 7$ periods; and $k = 1$ for Catholics or 2 for Protestants. The independent variables are sets of dummy variables for eight age groups, five cohorts, six periods, and two religions, plus sets of interaction variables formed as the products of religion by each of age, cohort, and year. Parameters are estimated using the GLIM program (Baker and Nelder 1983). Preliminary analyses showed all of the interaction effects involving religion to be significant, so we present the results for Catholics and Protestants separately.

discovery concerns the attendance of the cohort born before 1900: at the ages we observe them, their church attendance falls behind that of subsequent cohorts.

Among Protestants, the year effects are significant because church attendance in 1950 was lower than it was in any of the other years. In particular, note that the .17 (logit scale) increase in attendance since 1969 is not significant.

Among both Catholics and Protestants, age affects attendance. The pattern of the age effect differs by religion, though. Catholics reach peak attendance after age 60 and Protestants in their forties. With advancing years there is a modest trend toward disengagement from the Church.

Sasaki and Suzuki (1987) find a weaker age effect than we report here. Their estimates of age and cohort effects are probably biased because they do not separate Catholics and Protestants. That omission certainly leads them to misspecify the period effect in the United States. The change in question wording right at the time of the greatest period effect probably contributes additional bias to their estimate of the period effect. Considering that cohorts are observed only once at each combination of period and age, failing to obtain unbiased estimates of period biases their estimates of age and cohort effects also.

A Period of Stability: 1975–84. The post-*Humanae Vitae* drop in attendance among Catholics came to an end in 1975. A new equilibrium established itself at a lower level of attendance. Catholics still go to church more than do Protestants. What of other kinds of differences between Catholics and Protestants? Are Life-cycle effects more similar in this new equilibrium than they were in the 1950s?

Table 3. Maximum Likelihood Estimates of the Effects of Age, Period, and Cohort on Church Attendance: United States, 1939–1984

Effect	Catholics ($N = 3,501$)		Protestants ($N = 8,629$)	
	b	s.e.	b	s.e.
Period				
1939	—	—	—	—
1950	−.209	.186	−.233	.094
1959–60	.037	.196	−.103	.076
1969	−.290	.258	−.122	.091
1979–80	−.877	.312	.037	.080
1984	−.793	.340	.050	.093
Cohort				
Before 1900	—	—	—	—
1900–14	.529	.185	—	—
1915–29	.528	.249	—	—
1930–44	.678	.347	—	—
1945–66	.382	.464	—	—
Age				
18–24	—	—	—	—
25–29	−.369	.149	.070	.106
30–34	.328	.158	.291	.104
35–39	.374	.176	.366	.101
40–44	.483	.210	.604	.105
45–49	.417	.228	.604	.106
50–54	.494	.260	.425	.108
55–59	.444	.299	.467	.108
60–64	.615	.333	.463	.089
65–69	.615	.333	.463	.089
70 or more	.615	.333	.463	.089
Constant	.054	.250	−.743	.095

Perhaps the young cohorts of Protestants and Catholics have the same (low) rates of attendance.

To address these issues we have tabulated NORC General Social Survey (GenSoc) reports of church attendance for all years from 1975 to 1984. We analyze a cross-classification of attendance by age, cohort, religion, and sex. Year is excluded because it has no significant effect on Catholic or Protestant attendance after 1975 (as shown in the next section). The GenSoc attendance question differs from the Gallup question in time reference and number of alternatives offered to the respondent. "How often do you attend religious services? (0) Never, (1) less than once a year, (2) about once or twice a year, (3) several times a year, (4) about once a month, (5) two or three times a month, (6) nearly every week, (7) every week, or (8) several times a week?"[8] We collapsed categories for our analysis: (0) never, (1–3) "yearly," (4–5) "monthly," (6–8 "weekly." We take advantage of the absence of year effects to make fine distinctions among age groups and

cohorts, giving us more precise estimates of these effects than were possible using the Gallup data (because we had to control for year in that analysis). The categories used are shown in subsequent tables. We began our analysis with a four-way table having 496 cells.[9] It turns out that sex and religion interact with both age and cohort, so for ease of presentation, we treat the analysis as if we carried out a separate analysis for each of the four combinations of sex by religion.

The dependent variable in this section is the log-odds on weekly attendance relative to each of the other three outcomes: never, yearly, or monthly. We begin with the working hypothesis that the age curves for these log-odds are equidistant, that is, although the log-odds on weekly relative to never or monthly are less than the log-odds on weekly relative to yearly, perhaps the effects of age and cohort are the same on all three. To operationalize a test of that supposition, we define three coding variables and fit them instead of the usual dummy variables for three of the four attendance categories. The coding variables are:

$A2$ = if attendance is yearly, monthly, or weekly
     = 0 otherwise
$A3$ = 1 if attendance is monthly or weekly
     = 0 otherwise
$A4$ = 1 if attendance is weekly
     = 0 otherwise.

Models that fit all three coding variables reproduce the marginal distribution of attendance. If the coding variables interact with sex and religion, they reproduce the conditional attendance distributions. However, it may be possible to model the relationships between age and attendance or cohort and attendance with only one of the coding variables. If we can delete some of the coding variables without undue increase in L^2, then the working hypothesis of equal effects will be sustained. If two coding variables interact with age or cohort, then we will conclude that two of the age curves are equidistant, but that one of them departs from the others. If all three coding variables interact with age or cohort, we will conclude that none of the age curves follows any of the others.

---

[8] In the interview, the respondent was given the opportunity to answer before the response categories were read. The categories were used as probes if the respondent did not volunteer an answer that fit unambiguously into one or another of the categories.

[9] The four-way table is not a complete $4 \times 11 \times 11 \times 2 \times 2$ ($=1,196$ cells) table because many combinations of age and cohort cannot be observed in the eight surveys between 1975 and 1984. Despite this substantial censoring, we observe each age group and each cohort at least twice; for all but the oldest and youngest groups, there are three observations. In the log-linear analyses that follow, the unobservable combinations of age and cohort are treated as structural zeroes (Fienberg 1980, pp. 140–49).

The search for a preferred model of attendance within sex and religion combinations is spelled out in Table 4. The preferred models contain the following effects of age and cohort on attendance (as transformed by the coding variables):

Catholic women:	$A2 \times$ Age, $A4 \times$ Age, $A2 \times$ Cohort
Catholic men:	$A3 \times$ Age, $A4 \times$ Age
Protestant women:	$A2 \times$ Age, $A3 \times$ Age, $A4 \times$ Cohort
Protestant men:	$A4 \times$ Age.

The fit of each preferred model is shown in the second row of Table 4. The consequences of adding and deleting terms are shown in the lower rows.

Three-way interactions involving attendance, age, and cohort combinations are not needed in any of the religion by sex subgroups. This confirms the lack of period effects in these data. Furthermore, it means that all cohorts have the same distributions of attendance by age, that is, the same age trajectories. These age trajectories differ by sex and religion. The shape of the trajectories can be seen in the parameter estimates presented in Table 5. According to these coefficients, attendance rises after age 25 in all groups. The curve is steeper among women than among men, steeper among Catholics than among Protestants. Among Catholics of both sexes, the odds on weekly attendance drop in the early twenties (precipitously among

men), rise steeply between ages 25 and 35 years, and rise again between 45 and 55 years (especially among women). For Protestants, the rate of increase in the odds on weekly attendance from any age to the next is more gradual than it is for Catholics.[10] However, the diminished attendance after age 45, evident among Protestants in the Gallup data, does not appear here.

The cohort effects are significant only among women. For Protestant women, the cohort effect is the same on each level of attendance. The parameter estimates show that the 1920–24 cohort has exceptionally low attendance. This is the cohort that grew up in the Depression and came to maturity during World War II—a period of low attendance among Protestants (Gallup 1985). Other cohort effects among Protestant women are relatively small (within ±.15 of their average). Among Catholic women, the cohort effects are strong but virtually uninterpretable. A strong negative correlation between these cohort coefficients and the estimates of the effects of age make us wary of any substantive interpretation that might be advanced.

Catholics attend church more often than Protestants, even in this postdecline period. The smallest Catholic/Protestant differences are found

---

[10] An exception to this generalization is the sharp rise in attendance among 40-year-old Protestant men; there is a drop to a lower level among Protestant men ages 45–49 years. We cannot account for this spurt of church going among Protestant 40-year-olds.

Table 4. Change in L^2 Due to the Addition or Deletion of Age and Cohort Effects on Church Attendance by Religion and Sex: 1975–1984

| | Catholics | | | | Protestants | | | |
| | Women | | Men | | Women | | Men | |
	L^2	d.f.	L^2	d.f.	L^2	d.f.	L^2	d.f.
0. Independent	285.90	90	163.10	90	243.90	90	100.10	90
1. Preferred model	68.92	60	83.14	70	74.48	60	59.94	80
2. Add age effects (change in L^2)								
$A4$	—	—	—	—	7.59	10	—	—
$A3$	15.38	10	—	—	—	—	3.73	10
$A2$	—	—	10.97	10	—	—	15.94	10
3. Delete age effects (change in L^2)								
$A4$	160.98	10	41.56	10	—	—	40.16	10
$A3$	—	—	20.16	10	22.56	10	—	—
$A2$	33.68	10	—	—	25.69	10	—	—
4. Add cohort effects (change in L^2)								
$A4$	9.37	10	11.47	10	—	—	8.69	10
$A3$	10.81	10	11.39	10	10.55	10	15.64	10
$A2$	—	—	15.64	10	11.35	10	12.59	10
5. Delete cohort effects (change in L^2)								
$A4$	—	—	—	—	96.02	10	—	—
$A3$	—	—	—	—	—	—	—	—
$A2$	86.78	10	—	—	—	—	—	—

Table 5. Estimates of the Effects of Age and Cohort on Church Attendance by Sex and Religion: 1975–1984

Independent Variable	Weekly : Monthly		Weekly : Yearly		Weekly : Never	
	Women	Men	Women	Men	Women	Men
Catholics						
Age:						
18–20	.53	.25	−.11	.42	—	2.06
21–25	.33	.28	−.31	−.95	.56	.69
26–30	.67	.32	.03	−.43	1.44	1.21
31–35	.97	.58	.33	−.36	3.42	1.28
36–40	1.32	1.39	.68	−.05	3.64	1.59
41–45	1.27	1.50	.63	.18	4.53	1.82
46–50	1.42	1.08	.78	.15	3.84	1.79
51–55	1.90	1.71	1.26	.33	2.78	1.97
56–60	2.21	1.45	1.57	.42	2.73	2.06
61–65	2.14	1.26	1.50	.40	3.62	2.04
66+	2.14	1.63	1.50	.32	2.80	1.96
Cohort:						
Before 1915	—	—	—	—	−1.05	—
1915–19	—	—	—	—	−.33	—
1920–24	—	—	—	—	.31	—
1925–29	—	—	—	—	−.80	—
1930–34	—	—	—	—	−1.26	—
1935–39	—	—	—	—	−2.34	—
1940–44	—	—	—	—	−1.44	—
1945–49	—	—	—	—	−1.11	—
1950–54	—	—	—	—	.37	—
1955–59	—	—	—	—	1.15	—
1960–66	—	—	—	—	2.01	—
Protestants						
Age:						
18–20	—	.17	—	.72	—	.53
21–25	−.19	.16	.12	−.73	.03	.52
26–30	−.07	.31	.20	−.58	.00	.68
31–35	.06	.43	.62	−.45	.29	.80
36–40	.14	.42	.67	−.47	.49	.78
41–45	.04	.76	.33	−.13	.32	1.12
46–50	.22	.53	.66	−.36	.56	.89
51–55	.55	.59	.86	−.30	.45	.95
56–60	.45	.54	1.03	−.34	.64	.91
61–65	.64	.66	.67	−.23	.96	1.02
66+	.79	.93	1.00	.04	.25	1.30
Cohort:						
Before 1915	.69	—	−.15	—	1.39	—
1915–19	.54	—	−.31	—	1.23	—
1920–24	.15	—	−.69	—	.85	—
1925–29	.65	—	−.20	—	1.34	—
1930–34	.38	—	−.47	—	1.07	—
1935–39	.57	—	−.28	—	1.26	—
1940–44	.66	—	−.19	—	1.35	—
1945–49	.35	—	−.49	—	1.05	—
1950–54	.36	—	−.49	—	1.05	—
1955–59	.48	—	−.37	—	1.17	—
1960–66	.62	—	−.23	—	1.31	—

among men between the ages of 20 and 35. Catholic and Protestant men of these ages have nearly the same odds on weekly attendance relative to monthly or yearly, but Catholic men are clearly higher on the odds on weekly versus never attendance, giving them the edge in overall attendance. Although it is not obvious from the parameter estimates (because the cohort effects compound the interpretation), Catholic women are substantially more likely to attend church than are Protestant women of the same age.

Conclusions about Demographic Effects. The Gallup and GenSoc data replicate and extend Greeley's (1980) findings regarding a religious life cycle. Many young people strive to put some social distance between themselves and their religious roots during their years of family formation and career beginnings. Once established, they return to the churches—typically to

332   AMERICAN SOCIOLOGICAL REVIEW

the faith of their parents, although unpublished tables from GenSoc indicate that about 15 percent migrate to the faith of their spouse (also see McCready 1972; Johnson 1980). This life-cycle effect is somewhat stronger for women than for men and substantially stronger for Catholics than for Protestants, but it is significant in all four combinations of sex and religion.

The intersection of life-cycle and the changing age composition of the Catholic population during the late 1960s and early 1970s (as a consequence of the baby boom) is not sufficient to account for the drop in Catholic attendance after the publication of *Humanae Vitae*. Every age group within the Catholic population registered some drop in weekly attendance. The remainder of this paper addresses the sources of declining attendance among Catholics between 1968 and 1975 and the establishment of a new equilibrium in Catholic attendance since 1975.

PAPAL AUTHORITY AND SEXUAL ORTHODOXY: ACCOUNTING FOR THE DECLINE IN CATHOLIC ATTENDANCE

The key event in charting the drop in Catholic church attendance in the United States is the publication of *Humanae Vitae*, Pope Paul VI's encyclical on "artificial birth control." The encyclical was issued in 1968, when weekly attendance among Catholics was 65 percent. As shown in Table 6, weekly attendance then dropped 10 points in the next five years. The American response to the encyclical was as negative as it was because many American Catholic couples had already accepted birth control in practice by 1968 (Westoff and Bumpass 1973). In the climate of change surrounding the Second Vatican Council (1962–65), it was popularly assumed that a change in Church teaching on contraception was also in the offing. When Pope Paul reiterated the traditional ban on birth control methods other than rhythm, even within marriage, the response from American Catholics (along with sisters and brothers elsewhere) was threefold. Some Catholics discredited the Pope's authority to teach on matters of sexuality. Some stopped listening to Church teaching on a wide range of sexual issues, becoming even more liberal on matters of sexual conduct than they were before the encyclical. Some quit going to Church except, in most cases, on major holidays. These responses are correlated. In this section of the paper we explore the correlations.

Some Catholic writers (e.g., Novak 1964; Hitchcock 1971) ascribe blame for falling attendance to the Second Vatican Council. The survey data contradict this surmise. People did

Table 6. Church Attendance in the Last Seven Days: Catholics, 1958–1984

Year	Attendance Rate	Absolute Change per Year
1939	64	—
1950	63	−0.1
1958	74	1.4
1959	72	−2.0
1960	70	−2.0
1965	67	−0.6
1966	68	0.5
1967	66	−2.0
1968	65	−1.0
1969	63	−2.0
1970	60	−3.0
1971	57	−3.0
1972	56	−1.0
1973	55	−1.0
1974	55	0.0
1978	52	−0.8
1979	52	0.0
1980	53	1.0
1981	53	0.0
1982	51	−3.8
1983	52	2.0
1984	51	−1.9

Sources: Gallup (1985, p. 42); Greeley et al. (1976, p. 150); Table 1.
Note: The figures since 1958 combine several surveys taken throughout the year in question.

not leave the Church because they disapproved of the English Mass, the wider role of the laity, modern habits for nuns, folk Masses, or any of the other changes that blew into the Church when Pope John XXIII opened the window to let in some fresh air (Greeley et al. 1976, pp. 125–37; Greeley 1977, pp. 126–51). If the Vatican Council changes had any effect on church attendance at all, it was to stave off a potentially greater defection (note the evidence in Table 6 of declining attendance just prior to the Second Vatican Council).

To assess the effects of declining papal legitimacy and sexual orthodoxy on church attendance, we reanalyze some data from a pair of replicate national surveys of Catholic adults conducted by NORC in 1963 and 1974. The survey populations include individuals who were raised Catholic but who identified with some other religion (or no religion) at the time of the survey; our tabulations include only those currently identifying themselves as Catholic. We analyze items pertaining to *papal authority*, *sexual orthodoxy*, and *church attendance*.[11] The percentages reporting "weekly" or "daily" church attendance by papal authority, sexual orthodoxy, and year are shown in Table 7. Both observed percentages and percentages expected

---

[11] Questionnaire items are available from the *ASR* editorial office.

under a log-linear model described below are presented.

These data span the period of dramatic decline in Catholic church attendance. Weekly (or more frequent) attendance dropped from 71 percent in 1963 to 50 percent in 1974. Papal authority and sexual orthodoxy also decreased over the period. The "certainly true" response to the papal authority item dropped from 70 percent of Catholics to 42 percent. Sexual orthodoxy fell from 75 percent to 35 percent "strongly disagree"). The observed percentages make clear that these three variables are strongly correlated; weekly (or more frequent) church attendance is lower among the sexual unorthodox and among those who question the pope's authority. The observed percentages cannot make clear the extent to which shifts in papal authority and sexual orthodoxy account for the drop in attendance. For some cells of Table 7, there are increases in church attendance between 1963 and 1974. Without statistical analysis we cannot tell if the increases are substantive changes that require discussion or random fluctuations that can be ignored.

Log-linear models are well suited to the separation of substantive change from sampling error. We fit standard hierarchical models (e.g., Goodman 1970, 1972; Fienberg 1980) to test the null hypothesis that year per se has no effect net of the changes in papal authority and sexual orthodoxy. Our search is guided by the bic

statistic introduced by Raftery (1986a, 1986b).[12] Extensive model search through large numbers of cases frequently leads to overfitting, that is, the inclusion of terms in the model for which we have little or no substantive interpretation (except a post hoc invention). In applying bic one chooses the model with the largest negative bic. The search for a preferred model of the complete 5 × 5 × 5 × 2 (attendance by sexual orthodoxy by papal authority by year) table is summarized in Table 8.

The preferred model (7) for these data (by the bic criterion) includes terms for all two-way interactions except [YA]—the effect of year on attendance.[13] Selecting Model 7 implies that the

---

[12] The formula is:

$$bic = L_m^2 - df_m \ln(N)$$

where L_m^2 is the likelihood ratio chi-square statistic for some model m, df_m is the degree of freedom for that model, and N is sample size.

[13] By the more conventional rules of inference we would arrive at Model 13, a complicated model that includes all possible terms except the four-way interaction among all variables. Interpreting Model 13 is very difficult, especially since the effects that it adds to Model 7 are quite small. The version of this paper that we read at the ASA meetings did not make use of the bic criterion. It contains a discussion of the higher-order interactions, noting that most interactions are not individually significant. Among the ten significant effects

Table 7. Weekly or Daily Church Attendance (%) by Sexual Orthodoxy, Papal Authority, and Year: Catholic, 1963–1974

| | Sexual Orthodoxy[a] | | | | | | | | | |
| | Disagree Strongly | | Disagree | | Don't Know | | Agree | | Agree Strongly | |
Papal Authority	63	74	63	74	63	74	63	74	63	74
Observed weekly or										
daily attendance (%)										
Certainly true	84	79	68	78	67	52	57	45	44	25
Probably true	65	57	47	61	—[b]	59	29	42	50	25
Uncertain	51	66	25	30	—	18	14	22	—	17
Probably false	69	38	50	58	—	—	25	26	—	11
Certainly false	60	70	—	—	—	—	—	24	—	5
Expected weekly or										
daily attendance (%)										
Certainly true	82	81	73	71	60	57	55	51	40	36
Probably true	69	67	58	55	43	40	38	35	25	22
Uncertain	55	52	43	39	30	26	26	22	15	13
Probably false	63	61	50	47	34	32	30	27	18	16
Certainly false	61	60	48	46	32	30	27	25	16	15
Number of cases										
Certainly true	1,120	412	143	148	30	21	84	166	41	103
Probably true	208	161	62	121	9	17	45	221	20	83
Uncertain	78	90	12	73	8	22	14	116	4	88
Probably false	45	26	12	38	2	0	12	31	6	28
Certainly false	65	30	5	5	1	0	2	17	5	22

[a] Question wording available from the *ASR* editorial office.
[b] Less than 10 cases.

Table 8. Goodness-of-Fit and Likelihood Ratio Tests for $5 \times 5 \times 5 \times 2$ Cross-Classification of Church Attendance by Sexual Orthodoxy by Papal Authority by Year: Catholics, 1963–1974 ($N = 4,072$)

Model	d.f.	L^2	X^2	bic
1. [YP][YS][PS][A]	212	1,280.65	1,320.24	− 598
2. [YP][YS][PS][YA]	208	1,094.78	1,176.16	− 634
3. [YP][YS][PS][PA]	196	816.82	830.17	− 812
4. [YP][YS][PS][SA]	196	629.18	661.46	− 1000
5. [YP][YS][PS][YA][PA]	192	742.16	756.55	− 854
6. [YP][YS][PS][YA][SA]	192	599.14	627.07	− 997
7. [YP][YS][PS][PA][SA]	180	365.68	362.44	− 1130
8. [YP][YS][PS][YA][PA][SA]	176	348.69	345.90	− 1114
9. [YS][PS][SA][YPA]	160	294.27	289.88	− 1036
10. [YP][PS][PA][YSA]	160	306.06	297.53	− 1024
11. [PS][YPA][YSA]	144	251.33	247.31	− 946
12. [YP][YS][PSA]	99	231.58	211.51	− 591
13. [YPS][YPA][YSA][PSA]	64	79.81	77.17	− 452

Note: Only Model [13] fits at conventional .05 level; bic selects [7].
A: church attendance; P: papal authority; S: sexual orthodoxy; Y: year.
L^2 is likelihood ratio χ^2. X^2 is Pearson χ^2.

changes in papal authority and sexual orthodoxy suffice to account for the changes in church attendance among Catholics between 1963 and 1974.

A critic could make a case for including the [YA] term in the preferred model, that is, for preferring Model 8 over Model 7. The change in L^2 of 16.99 with 4 degrees of freedom is significant at the .05 level.[14] After claiming the significance of the residual changes in church attendance left over after the changes in papal authority and sexual orthodoxy have spent their impact, such a critic would have to note their modest size. The second panel of Table 7 displays the expected percentages attending weekly or daily under Model 8. Most of the changes are of 2 to 4 percentage points. The expected percentages under Model 7 (not shown) do not vary by year; the Model 7 estimate for both years lies between the expected percentages in each year under Model 8. Note how closely the expected percentages in Table 7 reproduce the observed percentages despite the fact that the model does not fit by the L^2 criterion.

A method for assessing change developed by Clogg (1978) underscores the extent to which declining papal authority and sexual orthodoxy account for the fall in church attendance among Catholics. Clogg's technique applies the log-linear results to the demographic standardization techniques of Kitagawa (1966, 1970). The output from the technique is a pair of hypothet-

ical distributions of church attendance that differ from the observed distributions for 1963 and 1974 in specified ways. The first output distribution, labeled "composition" in Table 9, presents our best estimate of what church attendance would have looked like if the declines in papal authority and sexual orthodoxy were the only influences on attendance.[15] The other distribution, labeled "effects," allows the effects of papal authority and sexual orthodoxy to change over time.[16]

The most dramatic aspect of the observed change in church attendance among Catholics is the drop in weekly attendance from 62.2 percent in 1963 to 43.9 percent in 1974. Most of that drop is attributable to changes in papal authority and sexual orthodoxy, as evidenced by the composition column of Table 9. This hypothetical distribution indicates that if the declines in papal authority and sexual orthodoxy produced all of the change in attendance, weekly attendance would have fallen to 48.0 percent (only 4.1 percent less than the observed decline). The whole composition distribution is much closer to the observed 1974 distribution than it is to the observed 1963 distribution. The index of dissimilarity between the observed distributions and the composition distribution is

_____

involving year and attendance, four are positive while six are negative.

[14] The bic criterion leaves the [YA] term out because in a situation such as the present one in which many tests of specific alternative hypotheses against a vague null hypothesis are run, the probability of picking a model that fits as well as Model 8 by chance is much greater than .05.

_____

[15] This distribution is created by estimating the parameters of the saturated log-linear model, then setting the terms pertaining to [YA], [YPA], [YSA], [PSA], and [YPSA] to their 1963 values and calculating hypothetical frequencies in the way expected frequencies are usually calculated. Note that Clogg recommends setting these terms to zero, but that would produce a hypothetical distribution that is for effects with magnitudes that average the years 1963 and 1974. We wanted the effect of 1963 not the average year, so we modify Clogg's procedures accordingly.

[16] We obtained this distribution by using the year-specific values of the [YPA] and [YSA] terms instead of using the 1963 values in both years.

Table 9. Observed and Hypothetical Distributions of Church Attendance: Catholics, 1963–1974

Attendance	Observed	Composition	Effects	Observed
Never	5.7	12.4	8.8	12.5
Yearly	11.6	18.5	26.3	19.9
Monthly	11.9	15.9	13.3	16.8
Weekly	62.2	48.0	44.8	43.9
Daily	8.5	5.2	6.8	6.9
Total	100.0	100.0	100.0	100.0
Dissimilarity				
1963	—	17.5	19.0	19.8
1974	19.8	4.0	7.3	—

4.0 for 1973 and 17.5 for 1963 (the index of dissimilarity between observed distributions is 19.8).

The "effects" distribution includes terms that we excluded from our preferred model. It produces an estimate of the distribution of church attendance if the effects of papal authority and sexual orthodoxy had changed (we concluded above that they did not). Including these interaction effects reduces the hypothetical percentage attending weekly to 44.8 percent, but it produces an estimate of 26.3 percent attending yearly (much too high). This departure from the observed rate of yearly attendance distinguishes the effects distribution from both of the observed distributions; the index of dissimilarity is 19.0 for 1963 and 7.3 for 1974.

This analysis supports conclusions about declining attendance discussed in Greeley (1977, p. 143) and Greeley et al. (1976). Through a very different lens, we see here what was then called "partial alienation of Catholics from the institutional church." We underscore the fact that alienation is no more than partial. Seven out of eight Catholics still were going to church in 1974 (and in 1984)—just not every week. As we

show below, 85 percent of the people who were raised Catholic were still Catholic in 1974, and there has been no erosion of that figure well into the 1980s.[17] The partial alienation of American Catholics was brought on by a crisis of papal authority, largely over the issue of sexual orthodoxy.

Since 1974 the Church's position on matters of sexual conduct has continued to erode, and confidence in "people running organized religion" has fluctuated (see Table 10). Nonetheless the slide in church attendance has come to a halt. The next section addresses this anomaly.

THE NEW EQUILIBRIUM: 1975–1984

In this section we look at three items from GenSoc: *church attendance*, attitudes toward *premarital sex*, and *confidence* in "people running organized religion." The first two items

[17] At one time 91 percent of the people raised Catholic were Catholic as adults, but nearly all of the change is due to increased intermarriage followed by conversion to the spouse's faith (Johnson 1980). We do not see intermarriage as a form of disaffection.

Table 10. Trends in Confidence in the Clergy, Attitudes Toward Premarital Sex, and Weekly Church Attendance: Catholics, 1972–1984

Year	Confid. in the Clergy[a]	Premar. Sex Is Wrong[b]	Weekly Church Attend.[c]	Weekly Church Attend. by Confidence[d]			Weekly Church Attend. by Premarital Sex[e]				Weekly Church Attend. by Confid. & Premar.[f]			
				0	1	2	0	1	2	3	− −	− +	+ −	+ +
1972	—	51.0	61.0	—	—	—	29.1	56.1	68.1	81.2	—	—	—	—
1973	39.9	—	47.9	15.6	45.4	58.7	—	—	—	—	—	—	—	—
1974	52.5	41.2	50.3	27.3	40.6	60.7	27.6	46.7	76.1	69.9	23.3	50.0	34.0	70.8
1975	30.1	39.4	45.6	18.6	45.5	61.3	29.0	45.9	55.0	62.5	23.7	47.6	45.2	67.6
1976	39.4	—	43.3	26.4	43.0	51.4	—	—	—	—	—	—	—	—
1977	43.6	40.6	50.1	27.6	48.0	57.6	29.9	48.4	59.0	72.7	25.9	57.3	36.6	65.8
1978	33.9	37.6	48.2	20.8	45.1	63.8	29.7	39.5	67.3	75.6	22.9	52.8	50.0	71.8
1980	45.6	—	48.1	27.5	43.4	58.4	—	—	—	—	—	—	—	—
1982	37.2	30.7	40.9	23.8	35.3	54.2	22.8	39.6	51.4	75.3	25.7	47.9	30.4	65.6
1983	33.1	28.4	45.4	22.6	42.5	61.2	29.1	43.9	62.2	75.0	26.5	46.8	37.0	76.1
1984	39.8	—	46.0	20.0	46.2	58.8	—	—	—	—	—	—	—	—

[a] Respondents who report "a great deal" of confidence in the clergy.
[b] Respondents who report that premarital sex is "always wrong" or "almost always wrong."
[c] Respondents who report that they attend church "almost every week" or more often than that.
[d] Response categories are (0) "hardly any" [−], (1) "only some" [−], and (2) "a great deal" [+].
[e] Response categories are (0) "not wrong" [−], (1) "sometimes wrong" [−], (2) "almost always wrong" [+], and (3) "always wrong" [+].
[f] The first sign refers to response to the confidence item, the second sign refers to response to the premarital sex item. Each category was given the sign shown in notes (d) and (e).

have obvious substantive overlap with the church attendance and sexual orthodoxy items from our analysis of the 1963 and 1974 surveys of American Catholics. Confidence is a crude substitute for a more direct measure of papal authority.[18] Trends in these items are summarized in Table 10.

The decline in Catholic church attendance continued through early 1975. The fluctuations after 1975 can be attributed to sampling variability ($L^2 = 26.79$; d.f. $= 18$; $p = .08$, for a 7 × 4 table of year by attendance after 1975). The erosion of sexual orthodoxy continues unabated, with those saying that premarital sex is "always wrong" or "almost always wrong" dropping from 51.0 percent in 1972 to 28.4 percent in 1983.[19] The GenSoc data show no evidence of further decreases in papal authority, although the annual fluctuations in confidence are significant.[20]

Why did the continuing changes in the variables responsible for the earlier decline in church attendance not result in further declines? Although the effect of attitudes toward sex and Church leaders might have lost their influence over attendance, the data in Table 11 show a continued association. The odds on weekly attendance were higher for Catholics with "a great deal" of confidence in the people running organized religion than for those with "only some," who, in turn, were more likely to turn up on a weekly basis than those with "hardly any" confidence. Similarly, people with orthodox attitudes toward premarital sex were more likely than others to go to church often. The data indicate that the correlations between attitudes toward sexuality and Church leadership did not disappear during the 1970s, but we need more powerful statistical techniques to determine whether their effects became muted once church attendance leveled off.

Log-linear models of constant association fit the church attendance data, whether we consider attitudes toward premarital sex and confidence in Church leadership separately or together.[21] In

these models the year effects are *positive* to counterbalance the negative effects on church attendance produced by marginal shifts in the predictor variables in a direction that favors lower attendance.

At this point we wish to emphasize that disagreement with the Pope depresses attendance but does not drive the disaffected out of the Church. Only 10 percent of Catholics with double negative attitudes—those who have "hardly any" confidence in the people running organized religion and who say that premarital sex is "not wrong at all"—say they "never" go to church. But what if the most extremely disaffected not only left the churches but left the Church altogether, that is, not only never attend religious services but also say "none" when asked about their religious preference? If so, then the foregoing analysis would underestimate trends in church nonattendance by excluding some nonattenders from the Catholic population. To address this issue we use responses to the GenSoc question (asked since 1973): "In what religion were you raised?" By comparing current and former Catholics, we can assess how much lower church attendance would appear to be if we counted people who quit the Church among the nonattenders.

The key datum is the rate of change in the distribution of current religious preferences among people who were raised Catholic. If the proportion leaving religion is increasing, then our conclusion that church attendance has stopped declining would be wrong. The data in Table 11 show that defection from the Church has not risen. The thesis that church attendance among Catholics stopped falling because the disaffected quit calling themselves Catholic is wrong. Catholic church attendance really has stopped falling.

The distribution of current religions among those who were raised Catholic has not changed significantly ($L^2 = 21.50$; d.f. $= 18$; $p = .10$). Furthermore, a majority of former Catholics have not left religion; three-fifths profess some other faith (mostly Protestant—details not shown). Significantly, current Protestants who were raised Catholic are slightly more likely to report weekly attendance (presumably at Protestant services) than are Protestants who were raised Protestant, although the difference is within the margin of sampling error ($L^2 = 6.51$; d.f. $= 3$; $p = .09$).

The lapsed Catholics are the most disaffected; the odds of being outside the Catholic Church are greatest for those who put hardly any confidence in the people running organized

---

[18] This item (and the related confidence items in GenSoc) has been interpreted in a variety of ways (e.g., Bergesen and Warr 1979; Lipset and Schneider 1983).

[19] The yearly differences are highly significant: $L^2 = 86.52$; d.f. $= 18$; $p < .01$ for the 7 × 4 year by premarital sex table.

[20] For a 9 × 3 table of year by confidence: $L^2 = 81.67$; d.f. $= 18$; $p < .01$.

[21] The log-linear model [YC][YA][CA] fits the three-way cross-classification of year (Y) by confidence (C) by attendance (A): $L^2 = 42.79$ with 42 degrees of freedom ($p = .44$). The log-linear model [YS][YA][SA] fits the three-way cross-classification of year by premarital sex (S) by attendance: $L^2 = 34.66$ with 36 degrees of freedom (p) > .50). The log-linear model

[YCS][YA][CA][SA] fits the four-way cross-classification: $L^2 = 28.50$ with 39 degrees of freedom (p > .50).

Table 11. Distribution of Current Religious Preference by Year, Confidence in the Clergy, and Attitude Toward Premarital Sex: People Raised Catholic

| | Current Religion of People Raised Catholic | | | % Not Catholic | | | |
| | | | | Not Confident | | Confident | |
Year	Catholic	Other Relig.	No Relig.	Not Wrong	Wrong	Not Wrong	Wrong
1973	84.7	9.1	6.2	—	—	—	—
1974	84.8	9.5	5.7	28.6	10.6	13.7	10.0
1975	82.3	9.2	8.5	26.5	19.3	6.9	6.6
1976	82.2	9.4	8.4	—	—	—	—
1977	84.6	10.8	4.6	23.3	13.8	21.3	6.8
1978	84.0	7.9	8.1	24.8	14.6	12.2	7.2
1980	81.5	10.8	7.7	—	—	—	—
1982	80.4	10.3	9.3	26.7	20.1	9.3	10.1
1983	84.2	10.6	5.2	18.5	15.5	12.2	14.9
1984	82.2	10.3	7.5	—	—	—	—

religion and who condone premarital sexual relations. But there is no upward trend in defection, even in this highly disaffected group. Furthermore, there is no way to determine the direction of causality between disaffection and defection. At least some of the former Catholics probably formed their attitudes about Church leaders and unmarried couples after they left the Catholic Church.

If Catholics continued to move away from the Pope on the issues of leadership and sex, what arrested the decline in church attendance? Apparently all of those who were disposed to reduce their participation in the services of the Catholic Church over these issues had done so by 1975. But not all American Catholics who disagree with the Pope stay home from Mass on Sunday. The data collected by Gallup and NORC do not provide us with a direct measure that distinguishes disaffected Catholics who attend Mass weekly from disaffected Catholics who attend Mass yearly. Nonetheless, we have a hunch that the disaffected weekly attenders are a latent class of loyalists committed to participation in Catholic culture at the parish level. In their parishes the Pope's loyal opposition can find many like-minded fellows, including some among the clergy. In the next section we derive some testable hypotheses from this "loyal opposition" thesis.

LOYALTY AND BIRTHRIGHTS: SOME QUANTITATIVE SPECULATION

Among the notions that intrigued us as we began this project was the prospect of integrating research on a number of embattled institutions. In particular, we saw a parallel between the crisis in the Catholic Church and the decline in Americans' identification with political parties. Defections to political independence rocked the major parties during the 1960s (Knoke and Hout

1974; Knoke 1976), just when Catholic church attendance was dropping.

The parties and the Catholic Church share more than just the timing of their troubles; there are similarities in the causes of individual attachments, too. The intergenerational components of religion and party are both strong (McCready 1972; Knoke 1976; McRae 1980; Morgan 1981). The demographic influences are similar (Knoke and Hout 1974), an the unexplained trends toward widespread detachment from party are just as clearly *not* attributable to age or cohort effects as we have shown the trends toward detachment from Church to be (compare our results with Knoke and Hout 1974; Hout and Knoke 1975; Converse 1976). Political behavior research has shown the ways in which the independents are distinct from the party faithful, but just as with the Catholic religious faithful, the party faithful share with the independents many of the attitudes associated with detachment (Sniderman 1981). Those who leave do so because they are alienated, but not everyone who is alienated leaves the institution.

The popular media have drawn attention to the disgruntled Catholic Democrat who votes Republican. But we are less concerned here with *shifting* loyalties than we are with *diminished* loyalty. We ask: Are the Catholics who withdrew from the major political parties in America the same Catholics who quit going to church? Are the disaffected but loyal Catholics also disaffected but loyal Democrats (or Republicans)? More technically, is there a latent hierarchy of "stayers" who have a strong attachment to their party and their church in spite of their disagreements with the leaders of those institutions?

Attendance and partisanship are correlated among Catholics (Table 12). Independents are less likely to attend Mass weekly than are strong partisans (Democrat or Republican). The rela-

Table 12. Percentages Attending Church Weekly by Political Party Preference, Confidence in the Clergy, and Attitudes Toward Premarital Sex: Current Catholics and People Who Were Raised Catholic, 1975–1984 (Pooled)

	Currently Catholic				Raised Catholic			
	Not Confident		Confident		Not Confident		Confident	
Party Preference	Not Wrong	Wrong	Not Wrong	Wrong	Not Wrong	Wrong	Not Wrong	Wrong
Strong								
Democrat	25.6	57.3	51.2	70.4	23.8	55.7	47.5	69.0
Republican	40.0	58.8	54.5	84.6	25.0	50.1	41.7	78.8
Weak								
Democrat	24.7	50.7	33.3	71.8	22.4	46.1	31.0	73.0
Republican	25.0	55.0	30.4	61.7	15.5	50.5	30.0	56.8
Leaning								
Democrat	24.7	46.5	38.9	63.0	17.9	45.5	37.6	64.4
Republican	20.7	50.0	38.5	71.1	11.8	47.2	43.9	67.6
Independent	14.1	35.3	33.3	60.8	12.9	33.3	43.8	60.0

tionship between attendance and partisanship holds up even when we control for our two measures of religious disaffection. Data in Table 13 show that weekly attendance fell much more among independents than among partisans. At the other extreme of partisanship, the decline in church attendance is least and the rate of weekly attendance is greatest among strong partisans.

We do not infer a causal connection from this association between partisanship and attendance. Going to church does not make one more of a partisan,[22] nor do we think that being a partisan, in and of itself, makes people go to church. If the correlation between partisanship and attendance does not stem from a causal

---

[22] In parishes with strong political cultures, partisan discussions after Masses or at church social functions might convert a few uncommitted parishoners to a partisan view. The politically uncommitted parishoner who attends Mass weekly would be more exposed to this influence. If a causal effect of attendance on partisanship exists at all it exists for those who develop a political outlook in this way. However, most parishes are large and heterogeneous enough that all political persuasions, including the apolitical and the non-aligned, can find reinforcement within the congregation.

Table 13. Percentage Attending Church Weekly by Strength of Partisanship and Year: Current Catholics, 1972–1984

Year	Indep.	Leaning	Weak	Strong	$(S-I)^a$
1972	63.0	56.7	58.4	66.7	(3.7)
1973	44.0	56.8	46.7	47.1	(3.1)
1974	48.6	45.3	49.0	60.0	(11.4)
1975	32.7	37.5	49.6	56.1	(23.4)
1976	40.4	37.4	43.8	51.2	(10.8)
1977	43.5	45.7	48.7	58.2	(14.7)
1978	35.7	56.4	42.3	59.0	(23.3)
1980	37.9	43.0	48.3	63.6	(25.7)
1982	24.1	31.2	43.5	52.6	(28.5)
1983	37.2	46.1	43.6	50.0	(12.8)
1984	28.6	49.0	40.9	57.3	(28.7)

[a] Strong minus independent.

relationship, then an exogenous common cause must influence both. We posit that a latent commitment variable *(loyalty)* produces the manifest association. We pursue this line of reasoning using the Rasch models advocated by Duncan (1985a, 1985b; see also Hout, Duncan, and Sobel 1987). The basic premise in our application of the Rasch model is that heterogeneity along the unobserved loyalty dimension is responsible for the manifest association between political commitment and church attendance. The model is derived in the appendix.

The problem with a latent variable approach to an unanticipated association like this one comes when we attempt to say anything authoritative about the substance of the latent variable. We have not observed the exogenous influence that, in the calculations that follow, turns out to be important for understanding the plateau in Catholic church attendance in the mid-1970s. We have inferred the existence of an exogenous influence that we refer to as "loyalty" from the appearance of an unlikely correlation between attachment of two troubled institutions. At the high end of the continuum, loyalty is a disposition to stay with an institution even in the face of opposition from leaders of that institution. At the low end, it is a disposition to disassociate oneself from institutions that endorse moral and political stands contrary to one's own convictions. For most people these choices are situational; they depend on a particular combination of issues and institutions. But to find, as we have, that the same people are detached from two institutions—party and church—because of disputes over different issues, suggests that people differ in their tendencies to make a choice to stay with an institution or leave it when they disagree with the official position of that institution. Our hunch is that, if subjective and objective aspects of loyalty were measured, these subjective choices to stay or leave would be guided by attachments to the rituals, symbols, and community of the local Catholic parish. In the absense of data on loyalty per se, we have to rely on an indirect approach by deriving the consequences of unmeasured loyalty for observable correlations like that between attendance and partisanship.

We can test our hypothesis that the association between church attendance and partisanship is due to the effect of a latent loyalty variable on both items by fitting a log-linear model that will generate the expected frequencies in the second panel of appendix Table A1 to the observed cross-classification of attendance by partisanship among Catholics in the 1972–84 GenSoc surveys (Smith and Davis 1985).

The model can fail to fit the data in two ways. First, the model predicts a particular form for the marginal distributions of church attendance and partisanship. Unlike the standard log-linear or multiplicative model that fits exactly the marginal distributions of the variables in the table, the Rasch model that we have specified allows the sum of expected frequencies for each category of church attendance and for each category of political partisanship to differ from the observed sum. Second, the model predicts a special form for the association between attendance and partisanship, as noted above in the discussion of the relationship between association (as measured by the θ_{ij}) and the score group parameters (S_t). If either aspect of the model is wrong, that is, if the observed marginal distribution of one variable or the other departs from that expected under the model by more than could arise by chance, or if the observed pattern of association (as constrained by the S_t parameters) differs from that expected under the model by more than could arise by chance, then the likelihood ratio chi-square test (L^2) will point to rejection of the model.

We fit our model to the $4 \times 4 \times 11$ cross-classification of church attendance by political partisanship by year (each single year between 1972 and 1984 for which GenSoc data are available) using the GLIM program (Baker and Nelder 1978). We allow the S_t parameters to change between 1972 and 1975, but we constrain them to take fixed values after 1975 (i.e., after the start of the period we have identified as a period of new equilibrium). We do not permit y or the μ parameters to vary over time at all. These are critical restrictions because although S_t may change as the distribution of loyalty shifts downward over time, according to our model the relationship between loyalty and the observed variables—attendance and partisanship—must remain constant. A change in y or the μ parameters would indicate that the meaning of attendance or partisanship for loyalty changed over time, making it much more difficult to sustain our latent variable

interpretation of the relationship (see Duncan 1985a, 1985b).

Our loyalty model fits the data at the .05 level ($L^2 = 153.4$; d.f. $= 130$; $p = .08$), but the probability is close enough to .05 to raise a question as to the homogeneity of loyalty during the period we call the new equilibrium. To investigate the possibility that our equilibrium period masks some significant year effects on the score group parameters (S_t), we add interaction effects between score group and year for each year from our 1976–84 equilibrium (taking one year at a time). The largest reduction in L^2 occurs when we introduce the interaction between the S_t parameters and a dummy variable for 1984. On the basis of this exploration we modify our original loyalty model to allow unique values for the S_t parameters in 1984 as well as for 1972, 1973, 1974, and 1975. We retain 1976–83 as a period of unchanging S_t. The revised model fits well ($L^2 = 132.2$; d.f. $= 124$; $p = .29$), and the improvement over our original model is significant ($L^2 = 21.2$; d.f. $= 6$; $p < .01$). The addition of other year by S_t interactions failed to produce significant improvements in fit.

Our estimates of y and the μ parameters derived from the revised model are (standard errors are given in parentheses):[23]

$$\hat{y} = .3832 \ (.0359)$$
$$\hat{\mu}_2^A = .0904 \ (.0089)$$
$$\hat{\mu}_3^A = .6673 \ (.0612)$$
$$\hat{\mu}_2^P = .9823 \ (.0983)$$
$$\hat{\mu}_3^P = .2706 \ (.0231)$$

Note that the ratio of a given coefficient to its standard error is not a test of its significance because the relevant null hypothesis is centered around one, that is, "no effect" means that the parameter equals 1.0. The two-tailed, 95 percent confidence interval for $\hat{\mu}_2^P$ contains 1.0, so that coefficient is not significant. All of the other parameter estimates are significantly different from one at the .05 level.

These results strongly support our interpretation of the association between church attendance and political partisanship as a function of a latent loyalty variable that declined between

---

[23] The absolute sizes of the S_t parameters are not of interest to us here because they are specific to the sample values of x_i which cannot be observed. It is essential for the Rasch model that they follow a convex pattern (Hout et al. 1987). The S_t for the attendance by partisanship analysis exhibit this pattern clearly. To save space, only the log (S_t) for 1975 are shown. The log (S_t) for other years differ from these by additive constants. The log (S_t) for 1975 are (approximate standard errors in parentheses):

t:	1	2	3	4	5	6	7
	.69	2.07	3.85	5.76	7.29	9.27	11.30
	(.71)	(.31)	(.21)	(.19)	(.26)	(.32)	(.40)

1968 and 1975. Ours is a very strong model that not only implies a specific structure for the association between attendance and partisanship, but also predicts a structure for the observed marginal distributions of those indicators. Despite these specific predictions that make it an easy model to reject, we cannot do so on the basis of the 1972–84 GenSoc data.

Interpretation of the estimated values of the model's parameters yields some additional insight into the process of changing loyalties. First recall that we are trying to explain a drop in the percentage of Catholics attending Mass weekly or more often from 70.8 percent to 50.8 percent (Table 9). In order to use the model to predict the percentage of Catholics attending Mass weekly, we need more knowledge about the distribution of loyalty. Nonetheless, we can get a feel for the kind of drop in loyalty that took place between 1963 and 1974 by calculating the amount of loyalty an individual would need in order to have an expected probability of attending Mass weekly of 70.8 percent and how much loyalty that subject would need in order to have an expected probability of attending weekly of 50.8 percent. Given our estimates of the μ parameters, the values of X that achieve an expected probability of weekly attendance of p^* are the roots of the cubic equation:

$$1 - X + \hat{\mu}_2^{.4} X^2 - [p^*/(p^* - 1)]$$

$$\hat{\mu}_2^{.4} \hat{\mu}_3^{.4} X^2 = 0. \qquad (8)$$

For $p^* = .71$, the only positive root of equation (8) is $X = 8.74$; for $p^* = .51$, the only positive root of (8) is $X = 5.34$. Thus, for an individual's probability of attending weekly to drop as much as the population proportion attending weekly dropped, that individual's loyalty would have to fall 3.40 points.

Turning to partisanship, we note that the model implies the following probability distributions for $X = 8.74$ and $X = 5.34$:

Partisanship	$X = 8.74$	$X = 5.34$
Independent	.039	.106
Leaning	.132	.217
Weak	.435	.436
Strong	.394	.241

These changes tip on the fulcrum of "weak" partisanship. The drop of 15 percentage points in "strong" partisanship is counterbalanced by gains in the expected probability of not affiliating with the major parties either by "leaning" or by declaring oneself "independent." The change in the expected probability distribution for partisanship is not quite as large as the change in the expected probability for church attendance. That is the aspect of changing loyalties tapped by our estimate of $y < 1$.

The estimate of $\hat{\mu}_2^P \approx 1$ means that the

probabilities of "independent," "leaning," and "weak" are all at just about the same level when $X = 1/y = 2.61$. The probability of "strong" partisanship at that point is substantially less than the probability of the other three, as indicated by $\hat{\mu}_3^P < 1$. Indeed, the probability of strong partisanship is generally less than the probability of weak partisanship; strong partisanship is the most probable outcome only when $X > 1/y\hat{\mu}_3^P = 9.64$, a very high level of loyalty.

At the other end of the loyalty scale, we might ask: What value of X is needed to drop the probability of never attending Mass or of identifying oneself as "independent" below some inconsequentially low level, say, .15? To find the answer we plug .15 into the left-hand side of equations (5a) and (6a) in the appendix and solve for the positive roots of X that satisfy those equations. For "never" we obtain $X = 3.07$ from (5a); for "independent" we obtain $X = 4.37$ from (6a). The other roots of both equations are imaginary. Thus, while "yearly" is more probable than "never" for $X > 1$, there is a substantial probability of never attending Mass up to $X = 3.07$. The probability of being independent remains substantial up to $X = 4.37$.

The point of this quantitative conjecture has been to speculate on how the declines in church attendance among American Catholics came to a halt in the mid-1970s. In the joint distribution of political and religious attachment/detachment among American Catholics we have found evidence of a latent loyalty that appears to have been an anchor for many disaffected Catholics. An important facet of that loyalty is its ability to counteract the disorganizing pressure of dissension within the American Catholic Church. Disagreements with Church leaders led to shrinking attendance between 1968 and 1975. The gulf between the hierarchy and the laity has continued to grow, but since the mid-1970s disaffected Catholics have not been reducing their attendance. The active Catholics of the 1980s are less influenced (in their attendance habits) by disagreements with the hierarchy than were the formerly active Catholics who have curtailed their participation. If we are reading this evidence correctly, then further declines in church attendance among Catholics based on matters of "personal morality" must be regarded as unlikely. The negative impact of unpopular teachings about human sexuality has probably spent itself. We expect that a new epoch of declining attendance—should one arise—will come from a new source. Should church attendance among Catholics decline noticeably in the next 15 years or so, it will be because some new shock has eroded the wellspring of communal loyalty in the American Catholic population.

SUMMARY AND DISCUSSION

Contrary to received wisdom in the social sciences and the mass media, we could find no evidence for religious secularization as measured by attendance at religious services in the United States over the past half century. The downward trend in church attendance in the United States during the late 1960s and early 1970s was strictly a Catholic phenomenon. American Catholics reduced their participation in religious services by one-third between 1968 and 1975, while Protestants and Jews did not change. The reduction was evenly distributed throughout the Catholic population—young and old cut back on their frequency of attending Mass. The decline stopped around 1975, as abruptly as it started.

Catholic church attendance began to fall the same year that Pope Paul VI issued *Humanae Vitae*, the encyclical which reiterated the Church's ban on "artificial birth control." We tested the proposition that this coincidence of timing is due to an individual level correlation between attitudes toward papal authority and sexual teaching, on the one hand, and church attendance on the other hand. We found strong support for the position that disagreement with the Pope's sexual teaching, not modernization of church services, sparked the disaffection that reduced attendance. While this perspective on declining attendance has been argued before, it has not been subjected to the rigorous tests applied here.

The decline in church attendance among Catholics was not matched by a departure from Catholicism. The number of lapsed Catholics—people who were raised Catholic but now profess no religion—has not risen, and very few of those Catholics who have reduced their attendance have quit going altogether.

What halted the slide in Catholic attendance? Certainly not a resolution to the crisis of papal authority to teach about sexuality; willingness to accept Catholic ecclesiastical authority on sexual matters has continued to erode since 1975. So why has Catholic attendance remained steady? In particular, what distinguishes those who reject the Church's birth control teaching and continue to be regular churchgoers (the majority) from those who not only reject the birth control teaching but translate thought into inaction by staying home from Mass?

Our answer hinges on the heterogeneity of the Catholic population with respect to the potential influence of attitudes toward Church policy issues on their attendance. Some people go to Mass regularly in spite of their differences with the Pope while others stay home because of those same differences. Attendance varies along a continuum of attachment to the ritual symbols of Catholicism. We call that attachment "loy-

alty." We envisage this loyalty as a tie that goes beyond doctrine. One is tempted to call it an "ethnic" attachment, save that ethnicity is frequently assumed to be susceptible to decline over time. Loyalty divides those who are similar on the predictors of attendance into frequent and infrequent attenders on the basis of susceptibility to the influence of the predictors. Because loyalty goes beyond issues into the realm of birthrights, it is a buffer against the effects of issues that might otherwise reduce attendance. It is loyalty that separates those who stay and fight within the organization from those who get disgusted and leave.

The loyalty thesis assesses the decline and subsequent leveling of Catholic church attendance as the consequence of a one-time shock. *Humanae Vitae* discouraged some American Catholics who expected a revision of Church teaching on married sexuality. Over the course of six or seven years, this discouragement motivated some Catholics to curtail their participation at church services. Others chose to defy the Pope's reaffirmation of traditional teaching by maintaining a high level of participation. For example, among those who continued to attend services, participation became more active. Reception of holy communion increased, even among those using banned methods of contraception (Greeley 1977, p. 142). Lay people took liturgical roles singing, reading scripture, and distributing communion. On the other hand, financial contributions dropped (Greeley and McManus 1986). Using the loyalty thesis, we infer from these trends that church attendance stopped declining around 1975 because the decline was rooted in a single event that had dramatic consequences for church attendance but which ceased to matter once all of those people who were likely to respond had reduced their participation to its lowest limit. Those Catholics of the loyal opposition who continued to be highly active after 1975 despite their disagreements with the Pope on matters of sex are unlikely to reverse themselves at this point and reduce their attendance over the issue of contraception nearly twenty years after *Humanae Vitae*.

Two more questions arise: (1) Where does "loyalty" come from? and (2) What is its content? We have inferred its existence by observing the traces it has left in cross-tabulations; we need to know its origins and substance.

Speculation is easier on the origins than on the substance. It seems reasonable to assume that Herberg (1955) was correct thirty years ago when he suggested that religion is an important part of self-definition in any pluralistic society, especially one as minority-conscious as the United States. On the other hand, religious identification is probably a much weaker ground for self-identification in a homogeneous society. There has to be some variation in religious affiliation before membership in one group can be used to set the self apart from the other.

A crude hypothesis for testing this supposition is that religious observance will be stable in relatively plural societies like the United States and Canada (outside Quebec) where diversity makes religion a potentially powerful means of social location or in countries like Poland and Northern Ireland where religion is a symbol around which cultural nationalism can rally. Homogeneous societies like the Irish Republic and Norway, on the other hand, can be hypothesized to undergo periodic crises of waning attendance because religious affiliation fails to mark the individual. An influx of new religious groups into a formerly homogeneous society, for example, Muslims in France, might even induce increased attendance among the majority. Doubtless the hypotheses would be refined after cross-cultural research, but it would make a good beginning if social scientists could abandon their prejudgment that religion and religious observance must be in decline and adopt an interest in specifying the conditions of decline, increase, and remarkable stability.

We also suspect that if the available data sets were large enough to attempt an analysis of other minority American religions such as Judaism or Orthodoxy (in its various national manifestations) a parallel, perhaps stronger, loyalty factor might be found to be at work.

Since this dimension of religion seems, prima facie, to be an important part of the social cement that holds American social structure in place, it perhaps deserves somewhat more careful consideration than further mindless repetition of hypotheses derived from secularization would make possible.

More difficult than origins is the question of the components of the loyalty factor. To what are Catholics, in the present instance, loyal? Not to the Pope, not to the official teaching, not to their bishop or his support of the Pope. Perhaps the key is contained in the commensurate image of political loyalty uncovered by Sniderman (1981). He found that alienated Americans—no matter how far they cast themselves from the center of the American political scene—have trouble conceiving of themselves as anything other than "Americans." We think that the disgruntled Catholics who score high on the loyalty dimension are like Sniderman's alienated Americans. They stay with their Church because it is their birthright. In their hearts, they are as Catholic as the Pope, whether he thinks so or not.

APPENDIX

Derivation of the Loyalty Model

To derive the Rasch model for loyalty, consider the latent loyalty variable X (defined on the interval $[0, \infty]$ so that it is nonnegative) with unobserved values x_i for $i = 1, \ldots, N$ subjects. Let A_i ($i = 1, \ldots, N$) be a subject's response to the question "How often do you attend religious services?" recoded: (0) never, (1) yearly, (2) monthly, and (3) weekly, as in preceding sections of this paper. Consider the log-odds on being in one category of church attendance, say k, relative to being in the next lower category, $k - 1$:

$$\Phi_{ki}{}^A = \log\left(\frac{\text{prob } (A_i = k|x_i)}{\text{prob } (A_i = k-1|x_i)}\right). \quad (1)$$

Suppose that $\Phi_{ki}{}^A$ is a log-linear function of X and of the "difficulty" of attending church relative to the difficulty of other items used to measure loyalty (label this variable Y^A with value $y_i{}^A$ for subject $i = 1, \ldots, N$):

$$\Phi_{ki}{}^A = \alpha_k{}^A + \beta_{1k}{}^A \log(x_i)$$
$$+ \beta_{2k}{}^A \log(y_i{}^A) \quad (2)$$

for $k \geq 1$, where the α parameters are regression constants and the β parameters are the regression coefficients for the unobserved logit regression of X and Y on $\Phi_{ki}{}^A$. We would expect the odds on a positive response (i.e., k instead of $k-1$) to increase with increases in loyalty (X) and to decrease with increases in difficulty (Y^A), so we expect $\beta_{1k}{}^A > 0$ and $\beta_{2k}{}^A < 0$.

Although unobservable regressions are by now standard elements of measurement models (e.g., Joreskog and Sorbom 1979), Rasch (1966) argues that most "measurement models" of the form of equation (2) do not measure anything because the difference between individuals depends on the item employed and the difference between items depends on which individual is chosen. According to Rasch, a claim that two items "measure" the same thing can be sustained only if difficulty is the same for all subjects ($y_i{}^A = y^A$ for all i), the effect of a change in difficulty is the same for all items (i.e., if $\beta_{1k}{}^A = \beta_1$ for all k and for all items indexed by superscripts) *and* if the effect of a change in the variable being measured (X) is the same for all items (i.e., if $\beta_{2k}{}^A = \beta_2$ for all k and for all items indexed by superscripts).

He then notes that the scale of Y is usually undefined, so it can be normed to be identical to the scale of X by setting $-\beta_2 = \beta_1 = \beta$. In the case of loyalty, we do not know the scale of X, either, so we place the further constraint that $\beta = 1$. If the categories of A form an interval scale with respect to X, then $\alpha_k{}^A$ for all k, justifying a constraint that $\alpha^A = 0$. In our case of church attendance as a measure of loyalty, however, we have no reason to believe that A is an interval scale, so we retain the α parameters. The net result of all of these constraints and definitions is the model:

$$\Phi_{ki}{}^A = \alpha_k{}^A + \log(x_i) - \log(y^A). \quad (3)$$

We can propose similar quantities for the relationship between political partisanship and loyalty. Let P_i ($i = 1, \ldots, N$) be a subject's response to the combined party identification items recoded as in Converse (1976) to reflect partisanship: (0) independent, (1) leaning toward one party or the other, (2) weak Democrat or Republican, or (3) strong Democrat or Republican. The logit regression of loyalty and item difficulty (Y^P) on the log-odds on being in category k of variable P, relative to being in category $k-1$ is given by:

$$\Phi_{ki}{}^P = \alpha_k{}^P + \log(x_i) - \log(y^P). \qquad (4)$$

Equations (3) and (4) are unobservable, but they have implications for the observed distributions of A and P. The first step in deriving those implications is to take the antilogs of both sides of both equations:

$$\exp(\Phi_{ki}{}^A) = \Omega_{ki}{}^A = \mu_k{}^A x_i/y^A \qquad (3')$$

$$\exp(\Phi_{ki}{}^P) = \Omega_{ki}{}^P = \mu_k{}^P x_i/y^P, \qquad (4')$$

where $\mu_k{}^A) = \exp(\alpha_k{}^A$ and $\mu_k{}^P = \exp(\alpha_k{}^P)$. Since we do not know the scale of X, we identify the parameters of (3') and (4') and simultaneously set the scale of X by setting $\mu_1{}^A = \mu_1{}^P = 1$. The sense in which setting the μ_1 parameters equal to one sets the scale of X is explained below.

Following Duncan (1985a, 1985b) we can express the conditional probability of subject i falling into category k of variable A or P as a function of X and the parameters of equations (3') and (4'):

$$\text{prob}(A_i = 0|x_i) = 1/C_i \qquad (5a)$$

$$\text{prob}(A_i = 1|x_i) = x_i/C_i \qquad (5b)$$

$$\text{prob}(A_i = 2|x_i) = \mu_2{}^A x_i{}^2/C_i \qquad (5c)$$

$$\text{prob}(A_i = 3|x_i) = \mu_2{}^A \mu_3{}^A x_i{}^3/C_i \qquad (5d)$$

$$\text{prob}(P_i = 0|x_i) = 1/D_i \qquad (6a)$$

$$\text{prob}(P_i = 1|x_i) = yx_i/D_i \qquad (6b)$$

$$\text{prob}(P_i = 2|x_i) = y^2\mu_2{}^P x_i{}^2/D_i \qquad (6c)$$

$$\text{prob}(P_i = 0|x_i) = y^2\mu_3{}^P x_i{}^3/D_i, \qquad (6d)$$

where $y = (y^A/y^P)$ and where $C_i = (1 + x_i + \mu_2{}^A x_i{}^2 + \mu_2{}^A\mu_3{}^A x_i{}^3)$ and $D_i = (1 + yx_i + y^2\mu_2{}^P x_i{}^2 + y^2\mu_2{}^P\mu_3{}^P x_i{}^3)$ are adjustments that fix the sums of the conditional probabilities at one. These probabilities are undefined if $x_i = 0$. However they approach the limits:

$$\text{prob}(A_i = 0|x_i = 0) = 1$$

$$\text{prob}(A_i = 1|x_i = 0) = 0$$

$$\text{prob}(A_i = 2|x_i = 0) = 0$$

$$\text{prob}(A_i = 3|x_i = 0) = 0$$

$$\text{prob}(P_i = 0|x_i = 0) = 1$$

$$\text{prob}(P_i = 1|x_i = 0) = 0$$

$$\text{prob}(P_i = 2|x_i = 0) = 0$$

$$\text{prob}(P_i = 3|x_i = 0) = 0.$$

We are interested in the values of five parameters: y and the four μ parameters. As noted above, y measures the relative difficulties of A and P. An estimate of $y > 1$ indicates that A is more difficult than P; $y < 1$ indicates the converse. The interpretation of the μ parameters hinges on our earlier claim that setting $\mu_1{}^A = \mu_1{}^P = 1$ fixes the scale of X. To understand this claim, note that by substituting (5a) and (5b) into (1), we obtain: $\Omega_{1i}{}^P = \log(x_i)$. If subject i is indifferent between never attending church and attending yearly, that is, if the probability in (5a) equals the probability in (5b), then $\Phi_{1i}{}^P = 0$, implying that $\log(x_i) = 0$, so $x_i = 1$ when the probability of "never" equals the probability of "yearly." Since the probability of "never" is one and the probability of "yearly" is zero when $x_i = 0$, one unit on the X-scale is the amount of increase in loyalty required to raise the probability of yearly attendance and lower the probability of no attendance to the point of equality.

At that point where $X_i = 1$, the full set of odds for A is

$$\Omega_{1i}{}^A = 1$$

$$\Omega_{2i}{}^A = \mu_2{}^A$$

$$\Omega_{3i}{}^A = \mu_3{}^A.$$

so the $\mu_k{}^A$ parameters give the value of their respective odds at the point where $x_i = 1$. If $\mu_k{}^A > 1$, then the probability of attendance level k is greater than the probability of "never" and "yearly"; if $\mu_k{}^A < 1$, then converse is true. For P,

$$\Omega_{1i}{}^P = y$$

$$\Omega_{2i}{}^P = y\mu_2{}^P$$

$$\Omega_{3i}{}^P = y\mu_3{}^P,$$

so y is the ratio of the probability of "leaning" to the probability of being "independent" when x_i is one. A little algebra reveals that $\Omega_{1i}{}^P = 1$ when $x_i = 1/y$. The interpretation of the $\mu_k{}^P$ is similar to the interpretation of the $\mu_k{}^A$.

The key assumption in deriving the implications of a Rasch model for an observable cross-tabulation is "local independence," that is, the assumption that the joint conditional probability that $A_i = k$ and $P_i = k'$ for a constant value x_i (denoted $p_{kk'i}$) is the product of the two constituent conditional probabilities:

$$p_{kk'i} = \text{prob}(A_i = k|x_i)$$
$$\times \text{prob}(P_i = k'|x_i)$$

$$= (\pi_k\mu_k{}^A)(\pi_{k'}\mu_{k'})$$
$$y^{k'}x_{ikk'}/(C_iD_i). \qquad (7)$$

The top panel of Table A1 contains expressions of this type for the 4 × 4 table at hand. To estimate the identified y and μ parameters, we need an expression of expected frequencies under the model in terms of the y and μ parameters. Expected frequencies are obtained by

344   AMERICAN SOCIOLOGICAL REVIEW

summing joint conditional probabilities over subjects, that is, $F_{kk'} = \Sigma_i p_{kk'i}$, as shown in the second panel of Table A1. The $S_t (t = 0, \ldots, 6)$ parameters are called "score group" parameters. They contain all of the information about heterogeneity on the underlying loyalty dimension, that is, they are the only parameters that are a function of the individual scores (x_i). Note that all of the association between attendance and partisanship is due to heterogeneity on the underlying loyalty dimension, that is, all of the odds ratios for 2×2 subtables of expected frequencies are functions of the score group parameters. For example,

$$\theta_{23} = \log(F_{23}F_{34}/F_{24}F_{33})$$

$$= \log(S_3 S_5 / S_4{}^2).$$

If loyalty is constant, that is, if $x_i = x$ for $i = 1, \ldots, N$, then S_t is a constant for each t ($= 0, \ldots, 6$), and the nine odds ratios for 2×2 subtables formed from adjacent rows and columns are all one, that is, $\theta_{ij} = 1$ ($i = 0,1,2$; $j = 0,1,2$). On the other hand, all else being equal, an increase in the variance of X will increase the strength of the association between A and P. In that sense, then, the association between attendance and political partisanship is spurious when loyalty is controlled.

Table A1. Conditional Joint Probabilities and Expected Frequencies for a Latent Variable Model of the Effect of Loyalty on Church Attendance and Political Commitment for Catholics

Church Attendance	Political Commitment			
	0	1	2	3
Conditional Joint Probabilities				
0	$1/Z_i$	yx_i/Z_i	$\mu_2{}^P y^2 x_i{}^2/Z_i$	$\mu_2{}^P \mu_3{}^P y^3 x_i{}^3/Z_i$
1	x_i/Z_i	$yx_i{}^2/Z_i$	$\mu_2{}^P y^2 x_i{}^3/Z_i$	$\mu_2{}^P \mu_3{}^P y^3 x_i{}^4/Z_i$
2	$\mu_2{}^A x_i{}^2/Z_i$	$\mu_2{}^A y x_i{}^3/Z_i$	$\mu_2{}^P \mu_2{}^A y^2 x_i{}^4/Z_i$	$\mu_2{}^P \mu_3{}^P \mu_2{}^A y^3 x_i{}^5/Z_i$
3	$\mu_2{}^A \mu_3{}^A x_i{}^3/Z_i$	$\mu_2{}^A \mu_3{}^A y x_i{}^4/Z_i$	$\mu_2{}^P \mu_2{}^A \mu_3{}^A y^2 x_i{}^5/Z_i$	$\mu_2{}^P \mu_3{}^P \mu_2{}^A \mu_3{}^A y^3 x_i{}^6/Z_i$
Expected Frequencies				
0	S_0	yS_1	$\mu_2{}^P y^2 S_2$	$\mu_2{}^P \mu_3{}^P y^3 S_3$
1	S_1	yS_2	$\mu_2{}^P y^2 S_3$	$\mu_2{}^P \mu_3{}^P y^3 S_4$
2	$\mu_2{}^A S_2$	$\mu_2{}^A y S_3$	$\mu_2{}^P \mu_2{}^A y^2 S_4$	$\mu_2{}^P \mu_3{}^P \mu_2{}^A y^3 S_5$
3	$\mu_2{}^A \mu_3{}^A S_3$	$\mu_2{}^A \mu_3{}^A y S_4$	$\mu_2{}^P \mu_2{}^A \mu_3{}^A y^2 S_5$	$\mu_2{}^P \mu_3{}^P \mu_2{}^A \mu_3{}^A y^3 S_6$

REFERENCES

Altheizer, Thomas and William Hamilton. 1966. *Radical Theology and the Death of God*. Indianapolis: Bobbs-Merrill.

Alwin, Duane F. 1984. "Trends in Parental Socialization Values: Detroit, 1958–83." *American Journal of Sociology* 90:359–82.

_____. 1986. "Religion and Parental Child-Rearing Orientations: Evidence of a Catholic-Protestant Convergence." *American Journal of Sociology* 92:412–40.

Baker, R.J. And J.A. Nelder. 1978. *The GLIM System: Release 3*. Oxford: Numerical Algorithms Group.

Berger, Peter. 1969. *A Rumor of Angels*. New York: Doubleday.

Bergesen, Albert and Mark Warr. 1979. "A Crisis in the Moral Order: The Effects of Watergate upon Confidence in Social Institutions." Pp. 277–95 in *The Religious Dimension: New Directions in Quantitative Research*, edited by Robert Wuthnow. New York: Academic Press.

Caplow, Theodore, Howard M. Bahr, and Bruce A. Chadwick. 1983. *All Faithful People: Change and Continuity in Middletown's Religion*. Minneapolis: University of Minnesota Press.

Clogg, Clifford, C. 1978. "Adjustment of Rates Using Multiplicative Models." *Demography* 15:523–40.

Converse, Philip E. 1976. *The Dynamics of Party Support: Cohort Analyzing Party Identification*. Beverly Hills, CA: Sage.

Cox, Harvey. 1965. *The Secular City*. New York: Macmillan.

Davis, James A. and Tom Smith. 1984. *General Social Survey Cumulative Codebook: 1972–84*. Storrs, CT: Roper Center.

Duncan, Otis Dudley. 1985a. "Measurement and Structure: Strategies for Design and Analysis of Subjective Survey Data." Pp. 179–230 in *Surveying Subjective Phenomena*, vol. 1, edited by Charles F. Turner and Elizabeth Martin. New York: Russell Sage Foundation.

_____. 1985b. "Rasch Measurement: Further Examples and Discussion." Pp. 367–403 in *Surveying Subjective Phenomena*, vol. 2, edited by Charles F. Turner and Elizabeth Martin. New York: Russell Sage Foundation.

Fienberg, Stephen E. 1980. *The Analysis of Cross-Classified Categorical Data*. 2nd ed. Cambridge, MA: MIT Pess.

Fienberg, Stephen E. and William M. Mason. 1978. "Identification and Estimation of Age-Period-Cohort Effects in the Analysis of Disrete Archival Data." Pp. 1–63 in *Sociological Methodology 1979*, edited by Karl F. Schuessler. San Francisco: Jossey-Bass.

Gallup, George H. 1972. *The Gallup Poll: Public Opinion 1935–71*. New York: Random House.

Gallup, George, Jr. 1985. *Religion in America: Fifty Years, 1935–1985*. Princeton: American Institute of Public Opinion (Gallup Report #236).

Gilkey, Langdon. 1969. *Naming the Whirlwind*. Indianapolis: Bobbs-Merrill.

Glock, Charles Y. and Rodney Stark. 1965. *Religion and Society in Tension*. Chicago: Rand-McNally.

Goodman, Leo A. 1970. "The Multivariate Analysis of Qualitative Data: Interactions Among Multiple Classifications." *Journal of the American Statistical Association* 65:226–56.

_____. 1972. "A General Model for the Analysis of Surveys." *American Journal of Sociology* 77:1035–86.

_____. 1981. "Three Elementary Views of Log-Linear

CHURCH ATTENDANCE IN THE UNITED STATES   345

Models for the Analysis of Cross-Classified Data Having Ordered Categories." Pp. 193–239 in *Sociological Methodology* 1981, edited by Samuel Leinhardt. San Francisco: Jossey-Bass.

Greeley, Andrew M. 1972. *Unsecular Man: The Persistence of Religion*. New York: Shocken Books.

———. 1977. *The American Catholic: A Social Portrait*. New York: Basic Books.

———. 1980. *The Young Catholic Family: Religious Images and Marital Fulfillment*. Chicago: Thomas More Press.

———. 1982. *Religion: A Secular Theory*. New York: Free Press.

———. Forthcoming. *Social Indicators of American Religion*. Cambridge, MA: Harvard University Press.

Greeley, Andrew M. and Mary Greeley Durkin. 1984. *How to Save the Catholic Church*. New York: Viking.

Greeley, Andrew M., William C. McCready, and Kathleen McCourt. 1976. *Catholic Schools in a Declining Church*. Kansas City: Sheed and Ward.

Greeley, Andrew M. and William E. McManus. Forthcoming. *Trends in Catholic Giving*. Chicago: Thomas More Press.

Hanushek, Eric A. and John E. Jackson. 1977. *Statistical Methods for Social Scientists*. New York: Academic Press.

Herberg, Will. 1955. *Protestant Catholic Jew*. New York: Doubleday.

Hitchcock, James. 1971. *The Decline and Fall of Radical Catholicism*. New York: Herder and Herder.

Hout, Michael and David Knoke 1975. "Change in Voter Turnout, 1952–72." *Public Opinion Quarterly* 39:52–62.

Hout, Michael, Otis Dudley Duncan, and Michael E. Sobel. 1987. "Association and Heterogeneity: Structural Models of Similarities and Differences." Pp. 145–84 in *Sociological Methodology* 1987, edited by Clifford C. Clogg. Washington, D.C.: American Sociological Association.

Johnson, Robert A. 1980. *Religious Assortative Marriage in the United States*. New York: Academic Press.

Joreskog, Karl G. and Dag Sorbom. 1979. *Advances in Factor Analysis and Structural Equation Models*. Cambridge, MA: Abt Books.

Knoke, David. 1976. *Change and Continuity in American Politics: The Social Bases of Political Parties*. Baltimore: Johns Hopkins University Press.

Knoke, David and Michael Hout. 1974. "Social and Demographic Factors in American Political Party Preferences, 1952–1972." *American Sociological Review* 39:700–713.

Lenski, Gerhard. 1966. *The Religious Factor*. New York: Doubleday.

Lipset, Seymour Martin and William Schneider. 1983. *The Confidence Gap: Business, Labor, and Government in the Public Mind*. New York: Free Press.

Luckmann, Thomas. 1967. *The Invisible Religion*. New York: Macmillan.

Mason, William M., H.H. Winsborough, and W. Kenneth Poole. 1973. "Some Methodological Issues in Cohort Analysis of Archival Data." *American Sociological Review* 38:242–56.

McCrae, James. 1979. "Intergenerational Transmission of Religious Practice." Ph.D. diss., University of Arizona.

McCready, William C. 1972. "Faith of Our Fathers: A Study of the Process of Religious Socialization." Ph.D. diss., University of Illinois, Chicago Circle.

Morgan, S. Philip. 1981. "Religious Socialization and Prayer." Ph.D. diss., University of Arizona.

Novak, Michael. 1964. *The Open Church*. New York: Macmillan.

Raftery, Adrian E. 1986a. "Choosing a Model for Cross-Classifications." *American Sociological Review* 51:139–41.

———. 1986b. "A Note on Bayes Factors in Log-Linear Contingency Table Models with Vague Prior Information." *Journal of the Royal Statistical Society*, Series B, 48:249–50.

Rasch, Georg. 1960. *Probabilistic Models for Some Intelligence and Attainment Tests*. Copenhagen: Danish Institute for Educational Research. Expanded Edition, Chicago: University of Chicago Press, 1980.

———. 1966. "An Individualistic Approach to Item Analysis." Pp. 89–107 in *Readings in Mathematical Social Science*, edited by Paul F. Lazarsfeld and Neil W. Henry. Chicago: Science Research Associates.

Sasaki, Masamichi and Tatsuzo Suzuki. 1987. "Changes in Religious Commitment in the U.S., Holland, and Japan." *American Journal of Sociology* 92:1055–76.

Sniderman, Paul. 1981. *A Question of Loyalty*. Berkeley: University of California Press.

Westoff, Charles F. and Larry Bumpass. 1973. "Revolution in the Birth Control Practices of U.S. Roman Catholics." *Science* 179:41–44.

Wilson, Bryan. 1976. *Contemporary Transformations of Religion*. New York: Oxford University Press.

———. 1982. *Religion in Sociological Perspective*. New York: Oxford University Press.

258

HALLUCINATIONS AMONG THE WIDOWED

Andrew M. Greeley

University of Arizona

SSR, Volume 71, No. 4, July, 1987

A replication with national probability data is presented of the recent nursing home research by Olson et al., on "Hallucinations of Widowhood." In both data sets almost two-thirds of widows have had some experience of "contact with the dead." In the national sample some two-fifths of all respondents report a "contact with the dead." A simple log linear model, designed to explain the higher incidence of such contact among widows and widowers by a combination of age and intense religious imagination, seemed to fit the data adequately. A second replication, based on the experience of those who had lost siblings in the last five years, raised the question of whether religious imagery disposes a person to a "contact" experience or whether the experience leads to more intense religious imagery. It is suggested that the incidence and prevalence of such experiences requires more careful attention.

Olson and his colleagues (1985) have recently reported a strikingly high incidence of "hallucinations" in which widows experience contact with their dead spouse. The interviews on which the report is based were conducted in nursing homes and do not represent a probability sample of the American population. However, it is possible, using data collected in 1984 as part of NORC's annual General Social Survey, to attempt replication of the work of Olson, et al., and to develop an explanatory model which will account for the higher incidence of such "contacts with the dead" (a term the present author prefers to "hallucination") among those who have lost husbands or wives.

The 1984 General Social Survey questionnaire asked: "How often have you had any of the follow experiences?

Thought you were somewhere you had been before but knew it was impossible.

Felt as though you were in touch with someone when they were far away from you.

Seen events that happen at a great distance as they were happening.

Felt as though you were really in touch with someone who had died.

Felt as though you were close to a powerful, spiritual force that seemed to lift you out of yourself."

The fourth item is the one on which this analysis is based. Note that it does not ask the person reporting such "contact" who the "contacted" dead person was. It was, therefore, entirely possible that those widows and widowers in the NORC sample who reported an experience of contact with the dead were not necessarily "in touch" with their spouse. However, it does not seem unreasonable to assume that a disproportionate incidence of such "contact" among the "widowed" (a term to be used in this analysis to include both men and women) is attributable to a contact with a departed spouse.

Forty-two percent of the respondents (N = 1445) reported "contact" with the dead; forty-one percent of those who were not widowed, and fifty-three percent of the widowed (a statistically significant difference.) Of the 149 widowed, 129 were women and 20 were men. The proportion of widows reporting contact with the dead "at least once or twice" was sixty-four percent, virtually the same proportion as that recorded in the article by Olson, et al. Thus, it would appear that the incidence of contact with the dead reported in the nursing home survey is not substantially different from the incidence in the general population.

That almost two-thirds of the widows in the American population have had some "contact" with a dead person (presumably their spouse) is perhaps less surprising than the fact that two-fifths of the population who are not widowed also report such contact. Olson and his colleagues note "the existence of hallucinatory experiences in a population documented at risk of increased morbidity and mortality." Indeed, yes. But also in the general population (the forty-two percent reporting contact with the dead in the 1984 General Social Survey represents an increase from twenty-five percent in a previous NORC study in 1972 in which exactly the same questions were asked. Perhaps the respondents feel more at ease in reporting such experiences now than they did thirteen years ago).

Haraldsson (1985) reports that the average proportion of the population of fifteen western European countries reporting such experiences was twenty three percent, ranging from forty-one percent in Iceland to nine percent in Norway. In Iceland thirty-one percent of the population reported the visual apparition of a dead person.

The purpose of the present analysis, however, is not to address the rather staggering question of why and how two-fifths of the American population have experienced contact with the dead but why this contact experience is more likely to occur among the widowed (Table 1.)

A contact with the dead experience is somewhat more likely to occur among the older respondents than among younger respondents and the correlation with age (Table 2) is statistically significant. Nonetheless, thirty-eight percent of those in their teens and forty percent of those in their twenties have had such experiences.

Catholics and Baptists are the most likely to have such experiences and those Protestants with no denominational affiliation and Episcopalians are the least likely to report them. Blacks are more likely to record such experiences than whites, women more likely than men, and those who have attended graduate school less likely than the rest of the population.

The model developed for the present analysis assumes that religion might be involved in accounting for the disproportionate experience of "contact" with the dead among those who are widowed. Religion, after all, purports to explain the ultimate purposes and the final tragedies of life. It is to religion that many men and women turn in times of grief. Might it not be that in attempting to resolve the grief of a tragic loss many people develop a religious intensity that disposes them to such encounters--real or imaginary, the social scientist cannot say--with the deceased spouse?

Moreover, since it is known that religious devotion correlates with age (Hout and Greeley, 1985) and since the widowed are older than the rest of the population, might it not be that the positive correlation between being widowed and "contact" with the dead can be accounted for by age and by higher levels of religious intensity or devotion?

Figure 1 presents such a model graphically. It proposes five significant relationships among the four variables: "widowed," "age," "religion," and "contact." If the model can be fit into the data as it stands, without a relationship between widowed and "contact," then one can assert--in the language of log linear model fitting--that it is possible to reject a model which accounts for the disproportionate experience of contact with the dead among the widowed by a combination of age and religion.

Contact with the dead, perhaps not surprisingly, does correlate, and significantly, with a number of different measures of religious behavior (Table 3.) It is more likely to occur among those who believe in life after death--though thirty percent of those who do not believe in life after death still report that they "felt as though they were really in touch with someone who had died"--a finding which surely should be a challenge to any social scientist exploring the incidence and prevalence of paranormal experiences in the American population.

Those who pray frequently are more likely to have such experiences than those who do not as are those who are more likely to imagine God as a lover than as a judge (on a seven-point scale between "Lover" and "Judge," part of a battery of items that NORC uses to measure the religious imagination of its respondents.) The intensity of religious commitment and the frequency of church attendance, however, do not seem to correlate with contact with the dead (though they might for widows and widowers.) Finally, those who have had more than one experience of the other three kinds of psychic phenomena--deja vu, extrasensory perception, and clairvoyance--are almost twice as likely to report contact with the dead as those who have had only one such experience or less. (A psychic experience may not be, strictly speaking, "religious" but the psychic measure is included in Table 3 because the paranormal might be appropriately considered as not unrelated to the supernormal.)

Six log linear models, based on Figure 1, were fitted to the data. Estimates were made of the distribution of respondents for each of these models. The actual distributions of the data were compared to the estimated (or "hypothesized") distribution. In the logic of log linear research, a model can be rejected if the actual distribution differs significantly from the hypothesized distribution. A high chi-square measure relative to the degrees of freedom indicates a statistically significant difference. The model then can be rejected. On the other hand, a low chi-square relative to the degrees of freedom indicates the absence of a statistically significant difference between the hypothesized distribution of respondents and the one actually observed. In the latter case it is said that the model cannot be rejected.

The statistics in Table 5 indicate that when church attendance or prayer or psychic experience or belief in life after death are inserted in the "religion" slot in the model in Figure 1, the observed distribution does differ significantly from the hypothesized distribution and therefore explanatory models containing each one of these variables can safely be rejected. Neither

260

the religious commitment nor the religious imagination items, however, when placed in the "religion" slot, can be rejected. Since the chi-square is lower for the religious imagination item, a model which seeks to explain the higher incidence of contact with the dead among the widowed in terms of a combination of age and religious imagination becomes the preferred model.

The relationship between the image of God as a lover and contact with the dead for those who are widowed is nicely illustrated in the cross-tabulation in Table 5. The image of God as lover does not increase the probability of an experience of contact with the dead for those who are not widowed but for those who are. The ones who imagine God as a Lover are thirty-three percentage points (73% versus 40%) more likely to report a contact experience.

Why then are the widowed more likely to experience contact with someone who has died? They are more likely to do so because they are older and because their religious imaginations are more likely than the imagination of others to think of God as a lover rather than a judge. The larger problem of why so many Americans report contact with the dead has not been solved but the smaller question of why the widowed are more likely even than others to report it seems, tentatively at least, to be solved: the higher incidence among the widowed can be explained by their age and by a religious response to death which falls back on images of God as a lover instead of a judge.

Or so it seems.

One assumes in Figure 1 that the flow of causality moves from left to right, from "widowed" to "religion" (image of God as a lover instead of a judge) to contact with the dead or, as Olson and his colleagues refer to it, a "hallucination" of the lost spouse.

But there is no absolute necessity of this upper path in the model in Figure 1. Might not the final step in the path--a relationship between the image of God as a lover and the experience of contact with the dead--flow in the opposite direction? Might not a bereaved person first have the experience of contact with the dead and then, because of such an experience, shift upward on the judge/lover scale? Logically, at any rate, if not metaphysically or theologically, such a possibility cannot be rejected.

One can imagine in principle a way of deciding the issue. If a religious imagination scale could be administered to a sample of widowed persons shortly after the death of the spouse and then subsequently at periodic intervals administered again with other questions about how the respondent was coping with loss and about possible contact with the dead, one might be able to speak with greater confidence about the causal flow in the upper path of the chart in Figure 1.

But even to fantasize about such research is to understand how extraordinarily complex the issues involved in such matters really are.

In the absence of such an elaborate, not to say virtually impossible experiment, one might at least ask whether the findings reported in this analysis can be replicated in another bereaved population where the grief, however intense it might be, might not normally be so powerful as the grief over the loss of a spouse.

The 1984 General Social Survey also asked whether a respondent had lost a mother, a father, a child, or a sibling at various times in their life. For the purposes of this analysis, the population was divided into two groups on each of these questions--those who had experienced such a loss within the last five years and those who either had never lost the designated relation or whose loss had been prior to the last five years. As Table 6 indicates in each of the cases, those who have suffered the loss are more likely to report a contact experience than those who have not but the only statistically significant difference--and one of about the same order of magnitude as presented in Table 1--is for those who have lost a sibling in recent years. The analytic question then becomes whether the same model that accounted for the higher incidence of contact with the dead among widows and widowers also will explain the higher incidence among those who have lost siblings (only 15% of the widowed reported a death of a sibling in the last five years.) If one distributes a hypothesized population in such a fashion that age and image of God as Lover account for the relationship between the loss of a sibling and contact with the dead, how will such a hypothesized distribution relate to the actual distribution of respondents?

As Table 7 shows, the proposition that the same model explains "sibling contact" and "spouse contact" cannot be rejected. Chi-square is 27.21 with 23 degrees of freedom and a probability of .25. In both cases then, of a higher incident of Olson et al.'s "hallucinations," age and religious imagery account for the differences. That the loss of a sibling normally would not cause as much grief as the loss of the spouse does not seem to matter.

Why sibling and spouse and not parent or child? Perhaps because both sibling and spouse are part of one's own generation and have, in the ordinary course of events, shared life with the self longer than either a parent or a child.

Where does this finding leave us on the intricate question of the direction of the causal flow on the final step of the upper path in our analytic model? While the death of a sibling is surely a tragic experience, it does not seem likely to force a person to fall back on religious beliefs and to revise these beliefs more or less permanently in the direction of a more intense relationship with a God who is a Lover. Or if sibling death does lead to such image modification, it would, one might presume, not exercise quite the same power as the loss of a spouse.

Obviously, one must be very hesitant and cautious in suggesting even a tentative answer to the question but it would seem that the replication of the "spouse loss" phenomenon in the "sibling loss" situation might inch us a little in the direction of a contact > religion causal flow while still leaning preponderantly in the direction of a religion > contact flow. One still would be inclined to believe that it is the changing religious imagery which produces a propensity to experience contact with the dead. Yet the replication in the sibling loss phenomenon of the replication (a duplication of Olson's spouse finding) must cause us to consider more seriously that it is the actual "contact" which affects the religious imagination and not vice versa--or at least that there is an intricate reciprocal flow between the two phenomena.

To consider seriously the possibility that an experience of being in touch with a person who is dead might actually affect the imagination of the bereaved person in the direction of a more benign view of God--and presumably of the purposes of human life--is to make no suggestions at all about the "reality" of such experiences. As one of the founding fathers of modern sociology, W.I. Thomas remarked, if something is defined as real, that definition itself becomes a reality to be studied. Beyond that, empirical social science as we know it must necessarily be agnostic.

The efforts of the Society for Psychic Research, alluded to briefly by Olson and his colleagues, both in its English and American manifestation, despite almost a century of effort, have not been able to settle the issue of whether "the dead return." While a reading of the long history of that debate might lead one to conclude that those who answer "yes" have ever so slightly more evidence on their side than those who would answer "no," the issue has not been settled and is not likely ever to be settled by the techniques of empirical science.

Empirical scientists may then want to say, "Since we can't measure it, it doesn't happen." But such an attitude finally is as dogmatic as the opposite one, "We have measured it and it does happen." A much more modest approach would be to say, "The issue is beyond the skills of our discipline; it might happen, and then again, it might not. But, if a substantial proportion of the population thinks it **has** happened, then the incidence and the prevalence, the antecedents and the consequences of this conviction are well worth studying if only so that those of us who minister in one way or another to human health might not be utterly ignorant of a widespread and quite possibly powerful phenomenon."

Dismissing an experience which seems to affect two-fifths of adult Americans as too absurd to notice would be scientific dogmatism of the most intolerable sort.

REFERENCES

Erlendur Haraldsson "Representative National Surveys of Psychic Phenomena." Journal of the Society for Psychical Research. 53:145, 1985.

Michael Hout and Andrew Greeley, "The Center Does Not Hold." American Sociological Review. In Press. .

P. Richard Olson, Joe A. Suddeth, Patricia J. Peterson, and Claudia Egelhoff, "Hallucinations of Widowhood," J.M. Geriatr Soc 33:543, 1985.

*Manuscript was received February 11, 1987
and reviewed February 14, 1987.*

*Tables start on the following pages. Figure 1
appears on p. 265.*

262

Table 1. "Contact with the dead" for Widows and Widowers

	Men		Women	
	Widowed	Not Widowed	Widowed	Not Widowed
Never	55%	65%	46%	55%
Once or twice	15	23	19	25
Several Times	25	09	28	14
Often	05	03	07	05
Total	100	100	100	100
N =	20	568	129	728

Table 2. Correlates of "Contact with the Dead" experience

Age	Percent reporting "Contact with the Dead"
Teens	38%
Twemties	40
Thirties	44
Forties	39
Fifties	42
Sixties	50
Seventy and other	46

Denomination	
Baptist	47%
Methodist	40
Lutheran	45
Presbyterians	42
Episcopalian	29
Other	44
No Denomination	32
Catholic	46

Race	
White	41%
Black	55

Education	
Grammar School	50%
High School	42
Attended College	42
College Graduate	45
Graduate School	32

Sex	
Men	53%
Women	64

Table 3. Religion and "Contact with the Dead"

Belief in Life after death	
Yes	47%
No	30

Religious Commitment	
Very Strong	43%
Somewhat Strong	43
Not Too Strong	43

Image of God	
Judge	41%
Lover	50

Prayer	
Daily	48%
Weekly	35
Less than Weekly	21
Attendance Monthly or less	42
More than once a month	43
One experience or Less	24
More than one experience	59

Table 4. Explanatory models for "Contact" experiences among Widowed

Variable	Chi square	D.F.	P.=
Church Attendance	41.05	26	.03
Prayer	39.34	26	.04
Psychic Experiences	31.72	26	.06
Belief in life After Death	31.02	26	.07
Religious Commitment	30.85	26	.16
God as lover/Judge	28.62	26	.33

Table 5. "Contact with the Dead" for Widowed by image of God

(Percent Reporting Experience)

	Imagine God as	
	Lover	Judge
Widowed	73%	40%
Not Widowed	46	49

264

Table 6. "Contact with the Dead" by other loss in family*

(Percent reporting contact experience)

	Yes	No
Father	48%	41%
Mother	50	42
Child	45	42
Sibling	57	41

*Difference statistically significant.

Table 7. Model to explain sibling-Loss-Related contact

Variable	Chi square	D.F.	P=
Judge/lover	27.21	23	.25

Table 8. "Contact with the Dead" by loss of sibling and image of God

	(Percent Report Experience) Image of God	
	Lover	Judge
Sibling died in last five years		
Yes	100%	54%
No	44	40

*N = 5

Figure 1. Model to explain disproportionate contact with dead among widowed

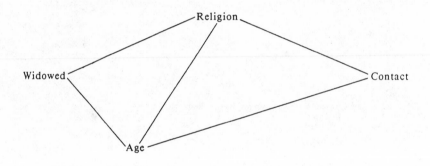

Model to be fitted:

Widow*Age

Widow*Religion

Religion*Contact

Age*Religion

Age*Contact

THE SUCCESS AND ASSIMILATION OF IRISH PROTESTANTS AND IRISH CATHOLICS IN THE UNITED STATES

Andrew M. Greeley
*National Opinion Research Center and
University of Arizona*

SSR, Volume 72, No. 4, July, 1988

This paper compares the success in the United States of persons of two origins, Irish Catholic and Irish Protestant.

Immigrants, on the average, succeed in America. But in their success to they become just like everyone else or do ethnic traits survive, even perhaps to the fourth generation? Does achievement lead to assimilation? What are the circumstances which create a likelihood of successful assimilation?

The present paper, using data from NORC's General Social Survey, asks first about the relative success or failure of Irish Catholic immigrants to the United States. It then inquires whether there are discernible Irish traits which still remain among this population group.

(There are 15,238 respondents in the General Social Survey of whom the ethnic question was asked; 771 are Irish Catholics, who are 16 percent of the Catholic population. The surveys have been taken every year since 1972 with the exception of 1979 and 1981).

To analyze the Irish Catholic story, however, one must also address the puzzling and fascinating question of Irish Protestants. One of the great mysteries of American immigration history is the issue of who they are.

Answers to that question, as we shall see, can only be often with caution.

Irish Catholics are 4.5% of the American population. Irish Protestants are 7.7% of the GSS respondents. The two groups differ greatly in era of immigration, region and place of residence and must be considered to distinct cultural groups. 46% of the Irish Catholics live in the North East of the country but only 7% of the Irish Protestants live in the same region. On the other hand 54% of the Irish Protestants live in the South as opposed to 14% of the Irish Catholics. 11% of the Irish Protestants live in the twelve largest SMSAs (Standard Metropolitan Statistical Areas) but 29% of the Irish Catholics live in these large metropolitan areas. 58% of the latter live in the hundred largest SMSAs but only 34% of the Irish Protestants live in the same areas.

Some 41% of Irish Catholics are fourth generation, while 83% of the Irish Protestants are at least the great grandchildren of immigrants. Almost half the Irish Catholics have attended college, only a little more than a quarter of the Irish Protestants have attended college.

(In the "generation" categories normally used, the "first generation" are the immigrants, the "second generation" are the children of immigrants, the "third generation" are the "grandchildren" of immigrants and the "fourth generation" are at least the great grandchildren of immigrants, all their grandparents having been born in the United States.)

It has been generally assumed that the Irish Protestants are the descendants of the Scotch Irish immigrants who game in massive numbers before the year 1800 and the Irish Catholics are for the most part the descendants of Celtic immigrants who came after the Famines of the eighteen forties or later.

It is also assumed that the Scotch Irish were the descendants of the lowland Scotch who were "planted" in Ulster by Elizabeth and Cromwell and their successors.

A number of scholars have contested this theory in recent years. Professor Grady McWhiney (1987) of Texas Christian University has argued with considerable force that there were not enough lowland Scots in Ulster to account for the size of the eighteenth century Irish migration to America and that therefore the Irish in the southern part of the United States are mostly Celtic.

He suggests, following Professor Emmett Larkin (1972) of the University of Chicago, that these immigrants were Catholics but that the close identification between the Catholic Church and Irish identity, took place only after the Famine and long after these migrants left. Therefore their conversion to Protestantism (thirty percent are Baptists and another thirty-five percent some other kind of fundamentalist Protestant) was a relatively easy matter.

The South, he says, is Celtic -- Irish, Welsh, and Highland Scotch.

Other authors (O'Brien 1979, McDonald 1980, Eid 1986) point out that records of the names of late eighteenth and early nineteenth century immigrants suggest that most of them were Celts. Accounts of their behavior in this country hardly suggest that they were stern, somber, industrious Presbyterians. Rather they earned themselves a reputation for drinking and fighting which would shame John Knox but which was not at all untypical of Celts. Moreover, if they were indeed Ulster Protestants, they did not remain loyal for long to their Presbyterian

230

heritage but were swept by the various revivals into Methodism and then Baptist and other fundamentalist congregations. Only 7% today are Presbyterian. Finally, they hated the name Scotch Irish which was affixed to them by their neighbors. They were Irish and that was that.

(Eventually they accepted the name to distinguish themselves from a later and more devoutly Catholic immigration which was the target of Nativist prejudice.)

Some at any rate of them were Celtic Catholics. How many we may never know.

The weakness of the "Celtic explanation" is that it assumes as given Professor Larkin's theory that the Irish Catholic devotional revival after the Famine shaped the intense loyalty of the survivors to their church, a loyalty which was characteristic of Irish immigrants to the United States after 1870. The early immigrants from Ireland, it is contended, were neither stern Presbyterians nor devout Catholics, but marginal Catholics with little of the loyalty to their Church that marked later Irish immigration.

Larkin's explanation is powerful and persuasive. Yet it seems to allow rather little time for an almost complete transformation of a culture. Granting the blow to the old Irish-language heritage from the Famine, the new post-emancipation strength of the Church, and the astuteness of Paul Cardinal Cullen of Dublin, there still does not seem to be enough time between the Famine and the post Civil War Irish migration to the United States to account for such a complete religious turn around. Is less than a single generation (indeed less than twenty years) enough to accomplish such a thorough going religious revolution?

Connolly (1982) has offered a chilling theory to account for the change, a theory which also helps to account for the differences we shall shortly describe between Irish Protestants and Irish Catholics in this country.

In pre-Famine Ireland there were two major social classes among Irish Catholics, the landless farm laborers and the tenant farmers. The latter were much less devout than the former. They were the ones who were most likely to migrate, and the first to die in the Famine. The devotional revolution of Cardinal Cullen was successful, because most of the less devout were gone, either emigrants or dead.

Post-Famine migration was most likely to be from the families of the more devout tenant farmers. Pre-Famine migration was in substantial part from the less devout "agricultural proletariat" with little strong loyalty to the Catholic Church.

(Connolly should be read in conjunction with McWhiney: the Whiteboys who opposed the clergy in pre-Famine Ireland sound very much like McWhiney's "crackers.")

Larkin (1984), responding to Connolly, clarified and refined his own position and wrote what must for the present be considered the definitive model for the two Irelands and the two Irish migrations:

> I do not think it would be outrageous to maintain, in spite of considerable overlapping, that in pre-Famine Ireland, formal and canonical Roman Catholicism was the religious resort of the argicultural bourgeoisie, while the popular religion was largely the possession of the "agricultural proletariat" . . . I would now be prepared to argue that this elite, which I have defined as the more than thirty-acre, tenant-farmer class, had been in existence from at least the middle of the eighteneth century and that it was this rural bouregeoisie that was the backbone of what constituted formal and practicing Catholicism before the rapid increase in the population between 1800 and 1845 masked their importance as the devotional nucleus and crucial nation forming class. (page 9)

Thus the immigration model: the earlier immigration, mostly to the South, was an immigration (mostly) of the "proletariat." The later immigration, mostly to the North was (mostly) an immigration of tenant farmers (themselves poor but not as poor as their predecessors). Irish Protestants are mostly descendants of the former, Irish Catholics mostly the descendants of the latter. The former probably bore more of the archaic Irish tradition (they were the real "bog Irish") than the latter. The latter class not only were the nation builders of modern Ireland (in the movements from O'Connell to Parnell) as Larkin asserts, they were also the ethnic group builders of contemporary Irish American Catholicism.

Catholicism lost the former both because they were not all that devout to begin with and because there were no priests to accompany their migration. The first Catholic relief act was passed only in 1793 when the migration to the South had already been in full force for at least thirty years. But even if there were priests available they would have found their task much more difficult than the latter clerical immigrants to the big cities of the North who were working with a much more devout population.

In this model (which fits much of the data), the Famine immigration itself represented a transition. Illiterate, Irish-speaking, landless, the Famine Irish quickly earned themselves in New York and Boston a reputation for drinking and fighting not unlike that of their Revolutionary War predecessors. But in the northern Urban Centers, the Catholic Church (now stronger because of Emancipation) had access to them and the big city political machines, together with the Church, provided an urban social structure to sustain them.

The death rates among the Famine immigrants were high in this country (to say nothing on the ships coming to America). Many of the Famine immigrants did not survive to raise children. Despite the importance of the historical myth of Famine immigration, they may not have contributed large numbers of offspring to the Irish Catholic population. It's an open question what proportion of Irish Catholics today are the descendants of pre-Famine, Famine, or post-Famine immigration. It would seem that most of them are from the third category.

Tentatively, then, the Irish Catholics in this analysis are descendants of a very different wave of immigration than the Irish Protestants, some of whom (perhaps even many of whom, even, arguably, most of whom) are also Catholic in remote origins.

Let us turn then to the approximately eleven million Irish Americans whose religious affiliation is Catholic.

The first observation to be made about them is that the majority are substantially removed from the immigrant experience. Only four percent are first generation (immigrants) and nine percent more are second generation (the children of immigrants). (Eighteen percent of Americans are either immigrants or the children of immigrants.) Forty-six percent of Irish Catholics are the grand children of immigrants and forty one percent are fourth generation (as opposed to sixty percent of the total population).

Thus the majority of Irish Catholics are members of families which have been in the United States long enough to be assimilated into main stream American culture, if such assimilation is to occur.

The major immigration of Irish Catholics to this country was completed therefore before nineteen hundred; much of it came before the fall of Parnell and nearly all of it before the Rising and the Troubles and the Civil War. Contemporary Irish Catholic Americans are a century away from Ireland, a point which the recent immigrants and the Irish government seem to forget when they complain about the lack of interest among Irish Americans in Irish political and economic issues.

The immigration has been a fantastic economic and social success. As Table 1 demonstrates the Irish Catholics in the United States are substantially more likely than the average white American to have attended college, to have graduated from college, and to have chosen professional and white collar careers. They are also more likely to be Democrats and to describe themselves as politically "liberal."

Finally their income is almost four thousand dollars a year above the national average. They are in fact the most affluent gentile ethnic group in America.

Nor is this advantage merely the result of the fact that the Irish have been here longer than some other immigrant groups. A comparison between the fourth generation Irish Catholic Americans and other fourth generation Americans (Table 2) indicates that the Irish Catholic lead over these other groups continues even among those who are at least three generations away from the immigrant experience.

In both these tables the Irish Protestants lag not only behind the Irish Catholics but also behind the national average.

Irish Catholics have been far more successful than anyone, including the Irish themselves, would have expected a century ago and far more successful than anyone, Irish included,

seems willing to admit today.

Moreover the stereotype, so beloved by the national media, of the "conservative" Irish Catholic is also unsupported by the data. They are also more likely to describe themselves as both "liberal" and "Democrat."

How long ago was this success achieved? If eighty five percent of Irish Catholics are third or fourth generation, it follows that the immigrant experience for their families must have occurred before nineteen hundred. How soon after that did the immigrants and their children struggle up the ladder to rough social and economic parity with the rest of the country? When did they forge ahead of the national average?

The oft-quoted works of Shannon and Moynihan (1970) argued in the late nineteen fifties and the early nineteen sixties the Irish were still lagging behind the rest of the country, perhaps because of the constraints of their religion and perhaps because of their fondness for the "Creature."

Might the reason for the skepticism about Irish success in this country be the recent nature of that success?

It is possible to use survey data to reconstruct a past era in the history of an ethnic group. Most young people make choices about education, career, and political affiliation in their late teens and early twenties. If one is able to interview people who were born, let us say, in the first decade of this century and learn from them their education, their career, and their political affiliation, then one obtains a brief snap shot of the decisions which were being made by members of that group in the nineteen twenties.

The four figures accompanying this paper are in effect an outline history of the Irish Catholic ethnic group in this country since the First World War and a comparison of their history with that of Irish Protestants during the same era.

(Those who reached their twenties since 1970 are omitted from the graph because many of them were too young to have made these choices at the time NORC interviewed them -- the GSS began in 1972>)

The figures show that by the time our "snapshot" camera was able to operate -- the coming of age during the second decade of this century (1910 to 1920, the era of the First World War) of those born at the turn of the century -- the Irish Catholics had already exceeded the national average in college attendance and graduation and professional and white collar careers. The young men and women who were born at the turn of the century, most of them doubtless the children of immigrants, were already more likely to attend college and choose professional careers than the typical native born American.

At the same time Irish Protestants were close to the national average on these measures and indeed above the national average in white collar careers.

The Irish Catholics continued to move into

232

modest affluence in the nineteen twenties, a memory of which exists in many families today as part of a story of tragic disappointment and disillusion caused by the great depression. (The story was told in classic form in James T. Farrell's Studs Lonigan trilogy).

There was indeed a dip in Irish success during the Great Depression and then a rebound after the War (nineteen forties) which put the Irish Catholics solidly above the national average (and comparable with Jews and Episcopalians for educational and occupational success).

In the meantime the scores of the Irish Protestants on these measures slipped beneath the national average. Their college attendance and choice of professional careers did indeed increase but not at the same rate as the rest of the country. Their relative position vis a vis the rest of the society and especially vis a vis Irish Catholics eroded.

The children of the Irish Catholic immigrants "made it," in the early decades of this century. Despite the setback of the Depression, they continued to expand their success ever since. Moreover this success has not diminished their affiliation with the Democratic party, despites the stereotypes to the contrary. Finally, the cohorts maturing during the last two decades are also notably more likely to describe themselves as politically "liberal" in comparison both with other Americans and with their own predecessor cohorts.

At the same time their Irish Protestant counterparts lost the rough parity they had with the rest of the country in education and won the unenviable position of being the least successful major white ethnic group in the country.

How can one explain this difference in outcome between two groups who at least to some extent share a common ancestry?

The success of immigrants may depend to a considerable extent on the time of immigration, the nature of the immigrants themselves, the occupations at which they worked when they arrived, and the region of the country into which they moved. One must ask what was the "push" in the native land which caused the immigrants to leave, the "pull" in the host country which attracted them, and what was the social class of those who chose to migrate.

The Irish immigrants into the South during the late 18th and early 19th century to some extent were members of a "rural proletariat," landless workers without literacy or extended social structure and perhaps even without a mastery of English. The dangers of ocean travel cut them off from the community they had left behind, a community of which they had been at best marginal members. They became corn and hog farmers in the rural south, and drifted away from the mainstream of American life, especially after the Civil War in which they fought on the losing side.

The immigrants of the years after the Famine were more likely to be the younger children of tenant farmers; they were able to read and write and speak English (in some cases as a second language). They settled in the expanding industrial cities of the North and became an important part of the economic and political life of the cities. The Catholic Church in Ireland (rejuvenated after emancipation and the founding of the seminary in Maynooth) was able to provide a clergy and social structure for them. They quickly became members in and then leaders of the urban political machines. With the advent of safer sailing ships and then steamers, they were able to maintain closer connection with the community they left behind, a community of which to some extent they were still a part. From a different social class, they migrated with different skills to a different place and at a different time than the cousins of their ancestors who had migrated to the rural south a half century and more before them.

Not only were the immigrants of the two movements different, they also were drawn by different opportunity structures. The earlier group were landless farmers searching for land of their own. They found it in the rural south and were able to develop their farms in an environment of personal liberty free from exploitation by government and landlord. They were content, one suspects, with their corn and their hogs, and their music, and their homemade whiskey, all enjoyed with greater freedom and greater abundance that was possible in the old country. Small wonder that they were willing to fight for it during the Civil War, although few of them owned slaves. The industrial (and English) North was perceived as a threat to their life style (they would not have used the words) which they had migrated to protect from English oppression.

The opportunity road down which they walked eventually became a dead end; but it was a road which provided them with the life they wanted. It would not have occurred to them that their opportunity structure would prove a limitation for their descendants. Even if they had thought of such a possibility, there was no alternative for them.

Thus it seems reasonable to believe that the culture we call today Appalachian ("Mountain") is in fact the culture of the agricultural working class of eighteenth century Ireland (and Wales and the Scotch Highlands too). This culture -- described by Fetterman (1967) in Stinking Creek -- certainly seems similar to the life of the Irish countryside as described by visitors for centuries. One might add that it looks much more "Celtic" than the culture of urban Irish American Catholics who came in the years after the Famine.

The opportunity road available for this latter group was provided by the nation's need for unskilled or semi-skilled labor in the factories and mines of the industrial North. They came not seeking land but jobs. Perhaps their predecessors

233

in the South had an easier time of it at first. Life was probably healthier and more pleasant on farms in Mississippi or Alabama than it was in the coal fields of Pennsylvania and the factories of New England.

Nonetheless the post-Famine immigrants became part of the enormous economic expansion of industrial America and were able to profit from it, turn it to their own purposes, and become enormously successful. On the other hand this expansion and the resultant prosperity passed by the rural south and the earlier immigrants.

There is a nice irony: the first immigration was from peasant field to peasant field, in the latter case your own field, and was -- once the Atlantic had been crossed -- probably an easier migration; but the descendants of the immigrants ended up in a backwater of the changing nation. The second immigration was from field to factory; but the descendants of this immigration were to ride the main stream of American expansion to great success.

To confirm the importance of region, we note that there is no statistical difference in education and occupation between the Irish Protestants and Irish Catholics who live in the North East region of the country (New England and Middle Atlantic states). However, it is possible that the Irish Protestants in that region are not part of the same migration as are those in the south. The former may in fact be the descendants of Ulster Protestants or even of Catholics who left their church at an earlier stage in history (only 5% of Irish Protestants were raised Catholic -- the same proportion of Irish Catholics who were raised Protestant.

The Irish Catholics, in other words, lucked out in both time and place of emigration and immigration (though many of the first generation would hardly have thought so). Good fortune was a major cause of their success.

The luck of the Irish! But they're not Irish any more, are they?

That question raises the fascinating issue of the survival of cultural traits after immigration and the equally fascinating question of what it means to be Irish.

I do not attempt to wrestle with the latter issue in detail. Rather I consider four characteristics from the General Social Survey whose Irishness I think that not even the most stuffy Dublin (or Cork) academic will deny: gregariousness, gathering in a public house, religious intensity, and activity in religious organizations.

GSS asks the following four questions:

How often do you spend a social evening with friends?

How often do you spend a social evening in a bar or tavern?

Would you call yourself a "strong" (religious preference)?

Are you a member of a church related organization?

Thirty-eight per cent of all Americans socialize with friends at least several times a month, as 49% of Irish Catholics. 16% of Irish Catholics socialize in a bar several times a week (twice the national average) and 28% socialize in a bar at least several times a month (again twice the national average).

Incidentally 88% of Irish Catholics drink, twenty one percentage points about the national average (and four percentage points above other Catholics -- a statistically significant difference.

Thirty-five per cent of Irish Catholics as opposed to 30% of other Catholics belong to a church related organizations. 51% say that they are "strong Catholics" as opposed to 41% of other Catholic ethnics.

Thus on four characteristics which might well distinguish the real Irish from their counterparts in the Common Market, Irish American Catholics are also distinguished from their fellow Americans.

One hears it heard frequently when Irish and Irish American sociologists gather together (perhaps in public houses) that something has been lost in the transition to American success. In the old country, it is argued, our ancestors were poor but happy. In this country they are affluent but not so happy.

It is impossible to compare the happiness of those alive today with that of their ancestors. But one can at least compare the happiness of Irish Americans with that of other Americans.

Thirty-six per cent of Irish Catholics say they're "very happy," as opposed to 31% of other Catholics; 37% of the Irish Protestants make the same claim compared with 33% of their fellow Protestants. The Irish, whatever their religion, are more likely to claim happiness than other Americans (and at levels of statistical significance). They are also significantly more likely than their coreligionists to claim satisfaction with job and family and happiness in marriage. And to say that their health is excellent and that life is exciting.

Perhaps these similarities in life satisfaction between Irish Catholics and Protestants, despite considerable economic differences, offer some confirmation for Professor McWhiney's suggestion that the his "crackers" are Irish celts.

In any case, immigration does not seem to have depressed the good spirits of either group.

After at least three generations immigration and success have not eliminated Irish cultural traits from the Irish American Catholics. Nor made them unhappy. Their distant cousins in the South, Protestant now, Americans much longer, and not nearly so affluent, are not unhappy either.

There are then still a few Irish around.

REFERENCES

Connolly, S.J. 1982. Priest and People in Pre-Famine Ireland. Dublin: Gill and Macmillan.
Eid, Leroy V. 1986a. "The Colonial Scotch-Irish: A View Accepted

234

Too Readily." Eire-Ireland: A Journal of Irish Studies. 21: 81-105.

--1986b. "Irish,Scotch, and Scotch-Irish, A Reconsideration." American Presbyterians: Journal of Presbyterian History. 67: 4

Fetterman, John (1967). Stinking Creek. New York: E.P. Dutton.

Larkin, Emmet. 1972. "The Devotional Revolution in Ireland, 1850-1875." American Historical Review. 77: 623-652.

--1984. The Historical Dimensions of Irish Catholicism. Washington D.C. The Catholic Univeristy of America Press.

McWhiney, Grady. 1987. Crackers. Sherveport: Louisiana State University Press.

Moynihan, Daniel Patrick. 1970. "The Irish." In Glazer Nathan and Daniel Patrick Moynihan. Beyond the Melting Pot (Second Edition). Boston: MIT Press.

O'Brien, Michael. 1979 Irish Settlers in America. Baltimore: Shannon, William.

McDonald, Forest and Ellen Shapiro McDonald. 1980 "The Ethnic Origins of the American People." William and Mary Quarterly. 37: 179-199.

Manuscript was received May 12, 1988 and reviewed May 15, 1988.

Figure 1. Odds of College Graduation by Cohort, United States, Persons of Irish Catholic and Irish Protestant Origin, 1910-1960.

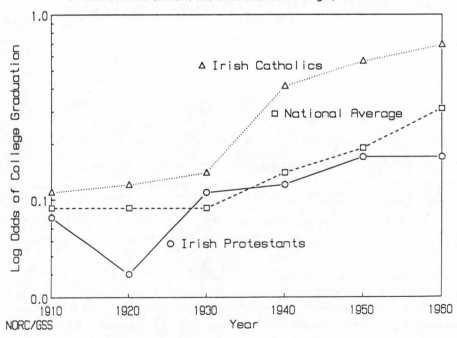

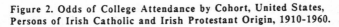

Figure 2. Odds of College Attendance by Cohort, United States,
Persons of Irish Catholic and Irish Protestant Origin, 1910-1960.

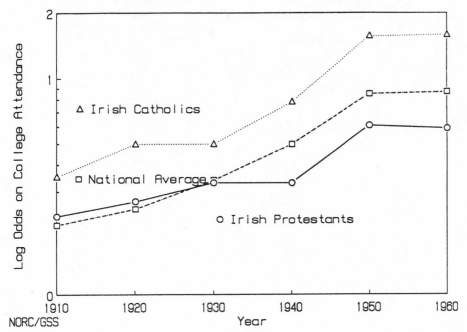

NORC/GSS

Figure 3. Odds of Professional Career by Cohort, United States,
Persons of Irish Catholic and Irish Protestant Origin, 1910-1960.

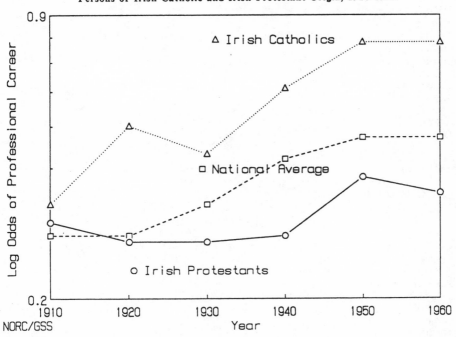

NORC/GSS

236

Figure 4. Odds of While Collar Career by Cohort, United States,
Persons of Irish Catholic and Irish Protestant Origin, 1910-1960.

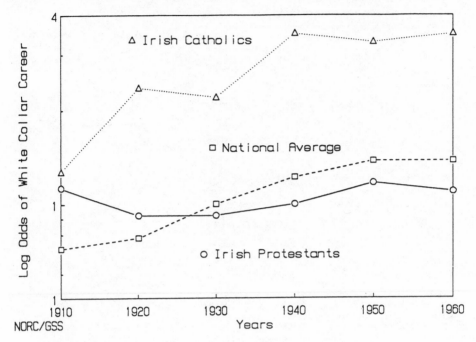

Table 1. Social Indicators for Irish Protestants and Irish Catholics in the United
States, General Social Survey, Data Combined for 1972-1978, 1980, 1982-1987.

	Irish Catholics	Protestants	National Ave. (White)
Attended College	45%	29%	28%
College Graduate	22%	11%	16%
Professional	34%	14%	24%
White Collar	68%	50%	51%
Democrat	61%	54%	50%
"Liberal"	28%	22%	25%
Income (thousands)	$32.4	$26.8	$28.7

Table 2. Social Indicators for Fourth-Generation Irish Protestants and
Irish Catholics in the United States, General Social Survey, Data Combined
for 1972-1978, 1980, 1982-1987.

	Irish Catholics	Protestants	National Ave. (White)
Attended College	53%	31%	38%
College Graduate	24%	13%	16%
Professional	38%	20%	27%
White Collar	71%	51%	51%
Democrat	65%	51%	47%
"Liberal"	32%	23%	24%
Income (thousands)	$40.1	$31.3	$31.5

3

CORRELATES OF BELIEF IN LIFE AFTER DEATH

Andrew M. Greeley
National Opinion Research Center

SSR, Volume 73, No. 1, October, 1988

This paper states and tests three null hypotheses regarding the correlates of belief in life after death. The first, drawn from such writers as Freud, Marx, Nietzche, and Dewey, was that there is no statistically significant relationship between belief in life after death and this-worldly social concerns. The second, based upon the thought of William James, was that belief in life after death makes no "difference" in human behavior. The third, relying on the seventeenth century French philosopher Blaise Pascal, was that belief in life after death is not a wise wager. All three null hypotheses are rejected.

Most of the great philosophers who have shaped modern thought--Marx, Freud, Nietzche for example--have rejected belief in life after death because, they argue, such belief is an "other worldly" escape from responsibility for life in this world. Thus Nietzche (1956) says, "When one places life's center of gravity not in life but in the "beyond"--in nothingness--one deprives life of its center of gravity altogether." And Dewey observes (1956), "The ideal of using the present to get ready for the future contradicts itself."

Life after death, like religion, is an illusion which can have no future (Freud) and an opiate which the people can no longer tolerate (Marx). In Marx's words (1978) "To abolish religion as the illusory happiness of the people is to demand their real happiness." And Freud (1978): asserts that we believe in life after death because we wish there would be life after death. "We shall tell ourselves that it would be very nice if there were a moral order in the universe and an an after-life, but it is a very striking fact that all this is exactly as we are bound to wish it to be."

Many contemporary Christian theologians and philosophers--Ogden (1966, 229-30) for example--accept this argumentation. Professing belief in God, they reject doctrines of personal immortality on the grounds that they are "selfish." "Life is interesting," says Hartshorne, "because of birth and death and not in spite of them." The purpose of our life is to provide happy cells to contribute to God's joy! Schleiermacher (1958) long before espoused a similar theory: "The goal and character of the religious life . . . is the immortality which we can now have in this temporal life. (p.101)

The argument of both pagan philosophers and Christian theologians seems logical enough. If religion promises "pie in the sky when you die," it should surely distract humans from this worldly concerns. Why bother with the problems

and challenges of this life when another and better life awaits you?

A question about belief in life after death has been asked in most years of the General Social Survey (Do you belief in life after death?). Some 71% of Americans reply that they do; 20% respond that they do not and the rest are undecided. The proportions have not changed since the late nineteen thirties. (Greeley 1989) It therefore is possible to test the proposition that belief in a hereafter diminishes concerns with the problems of the here and now.

It is reasonable to assume that those who believe in a world to come would, for example, be less concerned in this world about the rights of blacks and homosexuals, about violence in the nation and in the world, and about the protection of the environment. The General Social Survey provides nine items which enable one to directly test the null hypothesis:

Blacks shouldn't push themselves where they're not wanted. (Agree)

I strongly agree that the government shouldn't give special treatment to blacks.

I'd like you to tell me whether you think we're spending too much money on welfare (the environment, the military, armaments, and defense) too little money or about the right amount (too much on welfare, too much or about right on the environment, too little on arms).

And what about a man who admits that he is a homosexual?

Suppose that this admitted homosexual wanted to make a speech in your community, should he be allowed to speak or not? (not allowed)

Should such a person be allowed to teach in a college or university or not? (not allowed)

If some people in your community suggest that a book he wrote in favor of homosexuality should be taken out of your public library would you favor removing this book or not? (favor).

Would you favor or oppose a law which would require a person to obtain a police permit before he or she could buy a gun?

It can be observed in Table 1 that attitude towards life after death does not correlate significantly with attitudes towards race or welfare but that it does correlate significantly with attitudes towards the rights of homosexuals, the environment, gun control, and investment in

4

arms: there is evidence that belief in life after death lessens concerns for justice and peace in this world. Those who predicted such incompatibility seem to be justified in their expectations.

However, it might also be the case that a conviction of personal immortality might not be the cause of such lower levels of this worldly concern. Rather both variables might relate to an antecedent religious conservatism or fundamentalism which produces both belief in life after death and unconcern about justice and violence. Perhaps those who believe in life after death but are free of such conservatism will not differ in their concerns from those who do not believe in life after death.

In three recent years the General Social Survey asked about belief in the literal interpretation of the bible:

Which of these statements comes closest to describing your feelings about the bible?

The bible is the actual word of God and is to be taken literally, word for word.

The bible is the inspired word of God but not everything in it should be taken literally, word for word.

The bible is an ancient book of fables, legends, history and moral precepts recorded by men.

Thirty eight percent of Americans committed themselves to the first statement, 48% to the second, and 14% to the third. If the respondents are divided into two groups--those who accept the strict literal interpretation of the bible and those who do not--might the negative correlation between belief in life after death and social concerns prove to be spurious?

Table 2 suggests strongly that such is the case. While the number of respondents on which the table is much less (because of the fact that the bible question was asked only three years) and therefore significant differences are harder to come by, there are virtually no differences at all between those who believe in life after death and those who do not among respondents who reject the strict, literal "word for word" interpretation of the bible and only one significant difference (rights of the homosexual to speak) and two "suggestive" (homosexual teacher and concern for the environment) between those who accept immortality and those who reject it among those who believe in the "word for word" interpretation for the bible. The relationship then seems to be spurious or at least "specified" as existing only among those who are biblical literalists.

Thus the enemy against whom the philosophical giants raged seems to be fundamentalism and not belief in immortality.

Why is there conflict between the overwhelming conviction of the philosophical architects of our era and the data? A number of possibilities appear:

First, there may simply have been change. In the nineteenth and early twentieth centuries there may have been an incompatibility between a belief in personal immortality and social and human concerns, but for any number of reasons (most notably perhaps the improvement in standard of living) in contemporary America this incompatibility no longer exists.

Second, there never was an incompatibility. The philosophers were arguing logically and not attending to the possibility that humans can believe in the hereafter and still be strongly committed to the here and now, either because *they* don't see any incompatibility or because they are hedging their bets or because they fall back on "pie in the sky when they die," only when human effort seems no longer to avail or because in some forms of Christianity the rewards of life after death will exist in some rough proportion to concers for the problems of this life, ("Whatever you do to the least of my brothers, you do to me.").

Third, survey questions are not appropriate for measuring the validity of philosophical propositions.

The last proposition assumes that a sweeping generalization about human behavior made by a philosopher is superior to the rigidly precise and empiricist propositions which are the *materia prima* of the survey researcher. However, it should be noted that if philosophers are commenting on human behavior they can safely be presumed to be speaking about observations they have made of a sample of the human race to test implicit propositions. That their sample is not random, their propositions not explicitly operationalized, their observations not carefully controlled and their tests not rigidly examined and subject to replication does not make their propositions about human behavior superior or more wise or more profound than that of the empirical social scientist. It only makes them more vague.

How many philosophers, one may be permitted to wonder, would have objected to the survey items in Table 1 if the apparent negative relationship between belief in personal immortality and social concern had not turned out to be spurious?

The items used, it might also be said, are not appropriate for detecting the impact of other worldly belief on this wordly concerns. Fine, but then let appropriate items be specified. But, it might be replied, in fact the matter is so complicated that no survey instrument can possibly measure the harm done by belief in life after death. That might well be the case, but it would be strange that such a powerful deleterious impact can occur and not affect attitudes towards race, homosexuality, guns, military armaments and the environment. A negative effect which had no influence on such matters would ultimately be trivial.

Finally, in the logic of social research, the only claim made here is that the null hypothesis--no relationship at all between belief in life after death and this worldly commitment --cannot be rejected. It does not follow that it is proven. It only follows that the opposite--incompatibility of belief in immortality and this worldly concern-- remains to be proven.

William James was a dissenting voice from the philosophical tradition which rejected personal immortality. In his Pragmatic perspective, he wondered whether such a belief "made a difference" (James 1902, 466)--the first and most critical question a Pragmatist asks about any proposition. He came to believe that belief in life after death did "make a difference."

This is not the place to present a detailed explanation of the Pragmatic epistemology of William James. It suffices to say that James' position was not as simple as it is often made to sound. He did not contend that if a proposition "worked" it was true, much less that if it felt good, it was true. Rather, much like contemporary empirical social scientists, he believed that the search for truth was a continuous process of "model fitting" (he did not use those words) in which provisionally held truths are tested new insights to see if the new provides congruence (fit with what we already know to be true), luminosity (greater understanding of life) and fruitfulness (make a difference in our behavior and our life). In the Jamesian paradigm this is less a norm for how truth should be sought than a description of how in fact humans search for it. (James 1902, p. 24-25).

James' position on immortality developed during his lifetime. At first he was convinced only that there were other consciousness that existed and overlapped with our own consciousness (1902 p. 463) and that "Where God is, tragedy is only provision and partial and shipwreck and dissolution are not the absolutely final things. Then he began to believe that immortality was likely. As Ralph Barton Perry observes "He had come more and more to feel that death was a wanton and unintelligible negation of goodness." (See Fontinell 1986, p. 214)

In other words, for James' belief in immortality seemed to offer congruence, luminosity and fruitfulness; it seemed to make a difference. Such a belief was not a certainty, only a provisional model to be tested against the data of further experience.

But does belief in immortality make a difference? Is there evidence that it enriches the quality of human life?

One possible test of such a proposition is the quality of relationships one has with other humans. Does belief in life after death facilitate or impede intimacy with others? Or is it simply orthogonal to such relationships?

The General Social Survey provides three items which measure a person's perception of his relationships with others (and, *pace* W.I. Thomas, that perception itself is a reality):

Would you say that most of the time people try to be helpful or that they are mostly just looking out for themselves?

Do you think that most people would try to take advantage of you if they go a chance or would they try to be fair?

Generally speaking, would you say that most people can be trusted or that you can't be too careful in dealing with people?

One can observe in Table 3 that there are statistically significant differences on the three items between those who believe in life after death and those who do not with the former having the more benign view of their fellow human beings. The null hypothesis cannot be rejected. It does not follow in the Jamesian perspective, of course, that immortality is proven but only that belief it "makes a difference" and therefore it is legitimate to pursue it further as a provisional model to be tested (not, be it noted, that one must so pursue it).

Might not this relationship also be spurious, the result of a fundamentalist naivete about other human beings? If the same control applied in Table 2 is used again, might it not eliminate the apparent correlation between belief in immortality and more benign attitudes towards others?

In fact, just the opposite is what occurs. The differences persist among both the literalists and the non literalists (except for trust among the non-literalists) and the highest proportions are to be found among the non-literalists who believe in life after death: those who are most likely to have faith in other humans are precisely those who believe in life after death *and* who reject the literalist interpretation of Scripture. (Table 4)

Perhaps some more benign reading of reality--both of other humans and of the chances for survival--underpins both variables. However, this fact would not undermine James' position. What "makes a difference" is this underlying view of the meaning of life.

Is there not, however, a risk in pursuing James' model- fitting. Granted that a belief in life after death does not seem to diminish social concern and granted too that it seems to improve the quality of human relationships is it still not the case that a conviction of personal immortality is nothing more than wish fulfillment and it therefore interferes with a happy and fully human life?

Such an issue is complicated by the question of whether wishes are predictive. Sometimes they may not be. Other times they may be. If I love Jane and I wish that she would love me, I might be deceiving myself or I might be reading the signs properly. Only time will tell. Either way there is a risk.

Should one run the risk of accepting the notion of life after death? Such a question leads to a the famous gamble offered by the French philosopher Pascal who contended

6

"Pesons le gain et la perte . . . estimons ces deu cas: si vous gagnez,vous gagnez tout; si vous perdez, vous ne perdez, rien."(Pascal 1670, pp. 60-61)

Is this true? Is there nothing to lose as Rohmer(1967) contended in his cinematic version of Pascal's argument? Or does the risk of committing oneself to belief in immortality undermine the possibility of a happy and exciting life because it is a form of self deception incompatible with honesty and maturity?

Three General Social Survey items might test the possibility that the self deception (or wish fulfillment) involved in belief in life after death might be incompatible with an exciting and fulfilling life:

Taken all together, how would you say things are these days--would you say that you are very happy, pretty happy, or not too happy?

Taking all things together, how would you describe you marriage? Would you say that your marriage is very happy, pretty happy or not too happy?

In general, do you find life exciting, pretty routine or dull?

A rejection of the null hypothesis would not prove that there is no self deception or wish fulfillment in a belief in immortality, but only that the belief does not impose a risk in Pascal's gamble that the philosopher did not foresee. Perhaps the gambler who followed his advice would lose happiness and excitement in this world because he gambles on happiness in the next.

However, quite the contrary, those who believe in life after death are significantly more likely to report that they are very happy, that their marriage is very happy, and that their lives are exciting. Moreover in Table 6, while the relationship between a happy marriage and belief in life after death disappears when atti-

tudes towards the bible is taken into account, in general the most excited of all are those who believe in life after death and reject a literal interpretation of the scripture. They might well be deceiving themselves, but there are not obvious negative effects (as measured by these items) in such self deception.

If Pascal had these data available he might have argued that there is a payoff from his gamble in this life too. He may have been the first Jamesian.

Self deception and wish fulfillment, it might be replied, are sufficiently deep seated that men and women may think they are happy and excited when it fact they are unwittingly using denial mechanisms. Perhaps they are, but such deep mechanisms will require other data to establish.

REFERENCES

Dewey, John. 1956. Experience and Education. New York:Macmillan.

Fontinell, Eugene. 1986. Self, God, and Immortality. Philadelphia: Temple University Press.

Greeley, Andrew. 1989. Religious Indicators. Cambridge: Harvard University Press.

Freud, Sigmund 1978 Cited in Kung, Hans. Does God Exist. p.284 New York: Doubleday.

Hartshorne, Charles. 1986. "A Philosophy of Death." Cited in Fontinell (1986 p. 185).

James, William, 1902. (1988) Varieties of Religious Experience. New York: The Library of America

Marx, Karl 1978. Cited in Kung, Hans. Does God Exist. p.230. New York:Doubleday

Nietzsche, Friedrich. 1954 The Antichrist. In The Portable Nietzsche, trans. and ed. Walter Kaufmann. New York: Viking Press.

Ogden, Schubert. 1966. The Reality of God. New York: Harper and Row.

Pascal, Blaise. 1670. Penses et Opuscules. Paris: Librairie Larousse.

Rohmer, Eric. "Ma Nuit Chez Maud. 1967.

Schleiermacher, Friedrich. 1958. On Religion. Translated by John Oman. New York: Harper Torchbooks.

Manuscript was received August 23, 1988 and reviewed August 29, 1988.

7

Table 1. Various Social Attitudes by Belief in Life after Death, General Social Survey, 1972-1987.

N = 21,872

	Belief in Life After Death	
	Yes	No
Blacks Should Not Push (strongly agree)	31%	32%
Government Should Help Blacks (Disagree)	50%	50%
Too Much Spent on Welfare	54%	52%
Homosexual Teacher	46%	40%*
Homosexual Book	44%	37%*
Homosexual Speaker	37%	31%*
Too Much or About Right Spent on Environment	43%	38%*
Oppose Gun Control	29%	22%*
Not Enough Spent on Arms	27%	22%*

*Difference from first column statistically significant.

Conclusion: *On some but not all matters belief in life after death seems to diminish concerns for this life.*

Table 2. Attitudes by Belief in Life after Death by Belief about Literal Interpretation of the Bible, 1972-1987.

N = 21,872

	Interpretation of Bible			
	Literal		Not Literal	
Belief in Life After Death	Yes	No	Yes	No
Homosexual Teacher	61%	56%	27%	28%
Homosexual Book	61%	52%*	18%%	18%
Homosexual Speaker	45%	45%	28%	25%
Too Much or About Right Spent on Environment	40%	34%	31%	32%
Oppose Gun Control	24%	20%	27%	26%
Not Enough Spent on Arms	22%	19%	21%	19%

Conclusion: *Among those who reject literal interpretation of the bible there is no relationship -- positive or negative -- between belief in life after death and social concerns.*

8

Table 3. Attitudes Towards Others By Belief in Life after Death, 1984, 1985, 1987.

N = 2,862

Belief in Life After Death	Yes	No
Trust	62%	56%*
Fair	53%	46%*
Helpful	43%	38%*

*Differences from first column statistically significant.

Conclusion: *Those who believe in life after death are significantly more likely to have positive attitudes towards other human beings.*

Table 4. Attitudes Towards Others by Belief in Life after Death and by Belief in Literal Interpretation of Scripture, 1984, 1985, 1987.

N = 2,862

Belief in life aft. death	Interpretation of Bible			
	Literal		Not Literal	
	Yes	No	Yes	No
Trust	34%	28%*	50%*	47%
Fair	53	47*	62*	57**
Helpful	43	39*	52*	42**

*Statistically sig. difference from first column, p<.05.
**Statistically sig. difference from third column, p<.05.

Conclusion: *attitudes towards literal interpretation of the bible do not explain positive relationship between belief in life after death and favorable attitudes towards other human beings.*

Table 5. Life Satisfactions By Belief in Life After Death, 1984, 1985, 1987.

N = 2,862

Belief in Life After Death	Yes	No
Very Happy	35%	29%*
Marriage Very Happy	67%	63%*
Life Exciting	47%	40%*

*Statistically significant difference from first column

Conclusion: *Those who believe in life after death are more likely to be happy, or at least to express that feeling.*

Table 6. Life Satisfactions by Belief in Life after Death by Belief in Literal Interpretation of Scripture, 1984, 1985, 1987.

N = 2,862

Life After Death	Interpretation of Bible			
	Literal		Not Literal	
	Yes	No	Yes	No
Very Happy	34%	27%*	35%	26%**
Marriage Very Happy	64%	63%	68%	64%
Life Exciting	43%	39%*	51%*	40%**

*Statistically significant difference from first column

**Statistically significant difference from third column.

Conclusion: *relationship between belief in life after death and happiness is not the result of fundamentalist attitudes towards the bible.*

Sociological Analysis 1989, 50:4 393-397

Sociology and the Catholic Church: Four Decades of Bitter Memories

Andrew Greeley
University of Arizona and National Opinion Research Center

The basic premise with which the Catholic Church has related to empirical social research in the last four decades can be stated quite simply: Who needs it?

The Church (by which I mean here bishops and priests) assumes that it has a monopoly on truth. Not only does it not make mistakes; it also knows everything that it needs to know about every possible subject. It understands whatever needs to be understood about human social behavior because of the revelations of God through Jesus to the Church and especially to the Pope. Thus the Church can really learn nothing important from empirical research. At best, such research is a minor help; at worst, it is an obstacle to the Church's work.

No one could possibly adopt such an approach to reality, you say? Read, for example, the writings of the current Archbishop of Cincinnati, the vice president of the American bishops, and see if I'm making it up.

This basic premise underlies the four major assumptions about sociology that I have encountered in the last forty years:

(1) There is no possible distinction between fact and value. Thus, it is the obligation of the scholar to report the way reality should be (which is the way the Pope and the bishops say it should be) and not the way it is.

(2) Empirical research cannot measure the spiritual. It cannot account for the operation of Grace. Therefore it is useless to religion.

(3) Probability samples are a needless luxury.

(4) Anyone can be a sociologist.

An outsider, one not familiar with the relationship between the Church and social sciences, will say that these four assumptions reveal an astonishing amount of ignorance. Indeed they do. But ignorance has never prevented clerics and hierarchs from sounding off before in human history, and they are not likely to stop now.

Let us consider each of the four premises:

There is no possible distinction between fact and value. Thus, it is the obligation of the scholar to report the way reality should be (which is the way the Pope and the bishops say it should be) and not the way it is.

393

When I first became interested in sociology in seminary forty years ago, the only book on the subject in the seminary library was *Catholic Sociology* by a Holy Cross priest from Notre Dame. It argued that a Catholic could not engage in the sociology practiced at the secular universities because that sociology was "value free." Catholics, he argued, could not be neutral about society; therefore they ought to describe society the way it should be. The "value free" sociologists, he contended, believed that what is, is right. They confused description with ethics, actual norms with real norms. The man could simply not comprehend that most sociologists, even in those days, took "value free" to mean only that they tried to prevent their own biases from interfering with an objective report of their findings. Nor did he comprehend that virtually no one thought that moral values should be derived from empirical descriptions. In his world sociology was merely a division of ethics. Its purpose was to teach people how they should behave and to report how they actually did behave. The latter was excluded from Catholic Sociology by definition. The Church had no interest at all in what was actually happening. (For samples of this approach see Furfey, 1936; Struzo, 1943; Ruland, 1942; Lugan, 1928.)

This position ignored St. Thomas on the distinction between disciplines and also ignored traditional Catholic teaching that God speaks through the people to the Church leadership as well as vice versa. But this is still the de facto position of most priests and bishops, who to this day cannot understand that a scholar who reports on reality is neither endorsing that reality as ethically normative nor fitting his description to his own biases and opinions. Does a researcher report that Catholics do not honor the papal birth control teaching? Then he is (a) using data to back his own opinions, (b) suggesting that moral values are determined by taking surveys, and (c) responsible for the fact that Catholics are disobeying the Pope. The logic of the last charge is that if the sociologist did not tell them that they were practicing birth control, the laity would not be doing it. The herald of the bad news is responsible for it.

For a time bishops flirted with social research — mostly as a way of postponing decisions. Then they discovered that the research almost always found bad news and that Rome would promptly demand to know why they were funding research that revealed the Pope's teaching was being ignored. So they backed away from social research. Better not to lift your head out of the sand if the Vatican would object to what you saw when you did look around. For a time they flirted with the notion that research was all right as long as it was confidential. Reality was not a threat, in other words, as long as only the bishops knew about it — neither the people nor the Vatican were to be trusted with accurate social description.

The left is as obdurate as the right on this point. When I was directing a study of the priesthood for the Bishops (as disastrous an effort as any in which I have ever engaged), the president of the National Federation of Priests Councils demanded that I turn the data over to him so that he could hire a sociologist who would analyze the data from the priests' perspective. If I were working for bishops, he seemed to think, I would necessarily report their opinion. Truth would emerge from the conflict of the two biases, a nice Hegelian notion. When I would not accept his charge of bias and refused to turn my data over to him, he commissioned a separate study. I do not know whether he has ever figured out the implication of the fact that the findings of the two studies were virtually identical — despite the intense efforts of his man to refute our work and impugn our objectivity.

I detect no change in this attitude. When I recently reported on the decline of financial contributions in the Church from 2.2 percent per annum to 1.1 percent, the finding was almost universally dismissed as one more example of my "opinions."

Empirical research cannot measure the spiritual. It cannot account for the operation of Grace. Therefore it is useless to religion.

This position is supernaturalism with a vengeance. It assumes, contrary to the Catholic tradition, that grace is totally distinct from nature, that the effects of grace do not exist in the natural world, that grace does not ordinarily work through nature, and that nature does not predispose or impede grace.

Just as no responsible sociologist has ever suggested that values are derived by counting noses, so no responsible sociologist has ever suggested that the supernatural as such can be directly measured. But Church People consistently attribute such attitudes to us and reject our denials (or ignore them).

But since the Catholic tradition has always contended that grace and nature are intimately linked, there is no reason to deny that the natural comcomitants of grace can be studied. If, for example, there is a correlation between age and religious devotion (an ebb from fifteen to twenty-five and a gradual increase till fifty), one is not measuring grace, one is merely observing that grace seems to have an easier time of it after the 25th birthday than it did between the 15th and 25th birthdays.

Probability samples are a needless luxury.

Almost as a matter of principle, research done by the Church or by Church-related organizations avoids probability sampling. The much publicized Notre Dame study of parishes, for example, is not based on a national probability sample of American Catholic parishioners. Most of the "studies" emanating from the Washington offices of the Church (on social action and religious education, for example) are based on self-selected samples. The attitude behind such efforts seems to be that between probability samples and personal opinion there is an acceptable middle ground: very large self-selected samples (of the sort which led the *Literary Digest* to give the 1936 election to Alfred Landon over FDR). At one meeting, a Catholic researcher announced, "we took a random sample, we gave questionnaires to people coming out of Mass on Sunday." Indeed, those who conduct such "surveys" are offended if they are told that their work has no scientific value. One of the reasons for the rejection of probability sampling is that the clergy find it difficult to understand why a thousand respondents chosen according to the rules of random sampling can possibly reflect accurately a large population — while a hundred thousand self-selected respondents reflect nothing but themselves.

One can observe that most American business enterprises expect probability sampling and that explanations for it are to be found in any introductory methods course. Catholic researchers have little time for such courses. Most Church sponsored research would be given a failing grade in such an introductory course, but in the world of the Catholic clergy such a course does represent an important reference point. From the point of view of bishops, however, this research does not get them in trouble with Rome.

396   SOCIOLOGICAL ANALYSIS

Anyone can be a sociologist.

In the late sixties and the seventies, many Catholic institutions turned to "studies" to find the way out of the problems of identity and purpose that affected them in the wake of the Vatican Council. These projects were intended not to provide information for decision making but actually to make the decisions. In effect, the institutions were transferring the goal setting function from themselves and their leadership to researchers.

Most scholars did not succumb to the temptation to engage in such dishonest research. Therefore, the institutions turned to others to do the work for them. Often one would be requested by the "committee" responsible for these projects to spend a day with them developing a questionnaire — usually without any theoretical or substantive issues clearly delineated. The consultant was expected to define the purposes of the research, draw up a research design, and construct a questionnaire — all within eight hours, usually for free.

When one would tell such committees that these functions normally require weeks or months, one would be greeted with disbelief. Why should it take so long? Could not anyone make up a questionnaire over night?

So someone else would make up a questionnaire over night. The project would be executed. The institution would announce a new set of goals and purposes on the basis of "scientific research," in the confident tone of men or women who had solved their problems. And nothing would change.

So maybe they would do another "study." Or, more likely, they would decide that they had already done a "study" and it hadn't worked. Bad research once again had driven good research out of the market. In fact, to paraphrase G. K. Chesterton, social research had not been tried and found wanting, but found hard (and expensive) and not tried.

One might wish to observe that the attitude of the Church towards social research during the present era has been a mixture of ignorance and arrogance, of prejudice and presumption. The Church didn't want its research good; it wanted it quick and cheap. Unfortunately for the Church, the state of clerical education has almost guaranteed such an orientation towards any discipline beyond the clerical trade. There is no reason to believe that this situation has changed or is changing. The absence of any serious dialogue between the Church and social research seems likely to continue indefinitely.

This Society was originally founded with a number of different goals, not necessarily exclusive of one another. It was to be an association of those who were interested in the study of religion or of Catholicism. It was to be a refuge for Catholic scholars when the ASA was (or was presumed to be) hostile. Finally, some hoped that it would be one of a number of Catholic professional organizations that would dialogue with the Church and offer professional skills in service to the Church.

The first two goals are still valid if transformed. Sociology of religion is still a sub-discipline that earns rather little respect in the profession. None of the major universities have hired a scholar whose only specialty is the study of Catholicism. Catholics are not unwelcome in the ASA, but there is no particular place in the organization for their special interests.

By now, however, there is no reason to think that we Catholic sociologists (or sociologists interested in the study of Catholicism) have anything to offer that the Church thinks it needs.

When I was president of the ACSS, I still thought I would be a sociologist in service to my Archdiocese. I still thought that our organization would be of use to the Church. I have never been asked to use my skills in service to the Archdiocese. The Association has never been asked to help the Church. Indeed, it is safe to assume that the Church does not know of its existence.

Once can still earn a living by studying Catholicism, and perhaps even promotion and tenure. One can find the study fascinating and rewarding — and of interest to colleagues, family, and friends. But as far as the Church is concerned we don't even begin to exist.

At least it has not given us the Hans Küng treatment: it hasn't tried to deprive us of the title of "Catholic" sociologists.

REFERENCES

Furfey, P. 1936. *Fire on the Earth.* New York: Macmillan.
Lugan, A. 1928. *Social Principles of the Gospel.* New York: Macmillan.
Ruland, L. 1942. *Morality and the Social Order.* St. Louis: Herder.
Sturzo, L. 1943. *The True Life: Sociology of the Supernatural.* Paterson, NJ: Saint Anthony Guild Press.

Andrew Greeley

My Research on Catholic Schools

Catholic schools are more effective than teachers and administrators might have imagined in their wildest dreams.

Summer 1966: my first summer at Grand Beach (where I had escaped from my alcove in a rectory basement). Monsignor George A. Kelly, a fellow sociologist, was on the phone. (George was then a "liberal" and a close friend, indeed he invited me once to talk to the clergy of New York. Since then, he has turned sharply to the right and blames me and Hans Küng for all the bad things which have happened to the Church. While it is always an honor to be linked with such a scholar as Father Küng, I fear Monsignor Kelly gives me too much credit. Catholic married people did not and do not make their decisions about birth control because of what sociologists write, probably not even because of what theologians, even those as distinguished as Father Küng, write.)

"You're in terrible trouble!"

My stomach turned uneasily. Being in terrible trouble was a new experience for me.

"Did you see the piece about your report in the Times?"

"There was nothing in the Sun-Times about it."

I was still so naive as not to know, except when you are in London or Dublin, that the Times is what Jimmy Breslin calls The New York Times newspaper.

"The New York Times! Spelly has read it and he's furious. You're attacking Catholic schools!"

"You read the manuscript, George. I don't attack the schools."

"It looks that way in the Times and Spelly is fit to be tied."

My stomach had stopped turning. I was a lot less worried about Cardinal Spellman than I was about the new Archbishop of Chicago, John Cody. I had brought him the galleys of *The Education of Catholic Americans* and was greeted with questions about who gave me permission to work at the University of Chicago (his predecessor Cardinal Albert Meyer) and how much money I made and what I did with it. He was uninterested in the report. I departed, as I came, the galleys under my arm.

I did not realize that if something appeared in The Times it was officially true. If The New York Times newspaper reported that our research showed that Catholic schools had failed, then they had officially failed. George Kelly said he would mail me the front page of the second section, special delivery, and suggested I write a refutation and send it to the Cardinal with a nice letter of explanation and a copy of the report.

I was astonished when the Times article arrived at Grand Beach. It was a thoroughly dishonest exercise in selective journalism, the worst I would ever see in all the years of daily reading of the Times since then. The writer had gone through the book and taken out of context everything that might sound unfavorable about Catholic schools and ignored everything favorable, sometimes even cutting out part of a sentence to reverse my meaning.

I wrote a letter of protest to the Times, which was never published. I sent a copy with a letter and the book to Cardinal Spellman who replied very graciously. Much later John Cogley, then the religion writer of the Times, phoned to apologize for the incident, noting that both he and Clifton Daniel, the editor of the Times, were on vacation when it happened. They never did print my reply, however.

The following week, the National Catholic Reporter weighed in with an attack on the *Education of Catholic Americans* (Andrew Greeley and Peter Rossi, Aldine Press, 1966), which had little to do with what the book actually said. I wrote a letter to the editor asking him to document some of the assertions he had made. He replied that he had only glanced at the volume, but was responding to what he knew to be my "general" opinions on the subject of Catholic

RESEARCH   247

schools. He did not apologize, however.

What sociologists find in their research, you see, is dictated by their "general opinion" and not by their data!

The Commonweal had already ridiculed a preliminary report as a "whitewash of Catholic schools."

A few years later, at a wild meeting in the Marriot Hotel near Washington National Airport, a nun/sociologist attacked Catholic high schools on the grounds that students at such schools were racist bigots. It was an era in the late sixties when there was an open season on all things that the Church had ever done before the appearance of Dan and Phil Berrigan. The Greeley/Rossi report, sister continued, proved that Catholic schools did not have any effect on the lives of the people who attended them.

I rose to a point of personal privilege: sister was misquoting the findings of the report. Catholic schools did indeed have a positive impact on the attitudes and behavior of those who attended them, even on their racial attitudes. Afterwards a bevy of angry nuns swarmed around me to castigate me. I knew what sister meant, they insisted; why had I disagreed with her? I replied with more mildness than I felt or they deserved that all I knew was what sister said and what she said was not true.

                                                                     C.C.D

Years later, I was eating breakfast in the historic Roosevelt Hotel in New Orleans before presenting findings from the Knights of Columbus study about the effect of Catholic education on young people growing up in a time of turbulence in both Church and nation. (The presentation would take place in the same Superdome where the Bears would triumph over the Foxboro Patriots). Two of the other priests at the table were diocesan directors of the Confraternity of Christian Doctrine which is responsible for the "religious education" of Catholics who do not attend Catholic schools. What was I going to say, they demanded nervously.

I should have known better by that stage in my life, but I told them the truth. I could find no correlation between attendance at C.C.D programs and adult attitudes and behavior. On the other hand the measures of relationship between Catholic education and adult behavior, which had increased between 1963 and 1974, had increased again and were now quite strong indeed. Moreover, attending Catholic schools had an especially powerful effect on the return to the Church of young people who had drifted away during the bottom of the religious life cycle in their early and middle twenties.

My two companions pleaded with me to suppress the findings. C.C.D was a new movement, it lacked money and resources, it required time to "catch up" with the Catholic schools. My report would discourage bishops from increasing C.C.D funding.

I was unable to see then, and I still cannot see, how they expected to accomplish more in one hour a week (at the most) than the Catholic schools accomplished in twenty-five hours a week, especially since the secret of the religious success of the Catholic schools was their ability to integrate young people into the parish community.

And I do not suppress truth, not then, not ever. Nonetheless they and their colleagues conspired to persuade the Knights of Columbus to delete from our report the observation that the C.C.D had no observable effect.

Our research had started out shrouded with fears that we would destroy Catholic schools, it ended up in fears that we would sustain them. In the interim, it made a rapid journey from inkblot to myth. In the process, the reports went largely unread and the facts largely ignored. Serves me and my colleagues right for becoming involved in such an emotionally charged subject!

Most of our findings, in six projects and as many books were, in fact, more favorable to Catholic schools than not. Nonetheless, in the years between the publication of *The Education of Catholic Americans and Minority Students in Catholic Schools* (1982, Brunswick N.J.: Transaction Books) the construction of new Catholic schools ground to a halt. In Chicago, not a single new one has been opened since 1966. Shows what research findings are really worth.

Even though the books have gone unread, it is now pretty clear to almost everyone that they report findings which indicate that Catholic schools are quite successful. So I find myself both praised and damned as a great "friend" of Catholic education. That is not, however, true. I am rather a friend of empirical evidence. I began my research a dispassionate sceptic, rather impressed by my own Catholic education and by my experience in teaching at Christ the King school as a newly ordained priest, but I was not at all convinced that the schools were worth the cost.

RESEARCH   249

If I now think they are worth the cost (that indeed they pay for themselves), the reason is not that I have a bias in favor of them, but rather that I have been convinced by the evidence.

A TOUCHSTONE

I call the Catholic schools the "touchstone" because opposition to them is so irrational and in such defiance of overwhelming evidence, that I take it to be *prima facie* proof of self-hatred and self-rejection, a turning against the community ethos of the sacramental imagination in favor of the individualist ethos of the dialectical imagination, (dialectical in the strict sense of the word, because opposition to Catholic schools rejects the network of relationships between past and present; between what we did then and what we do now. The sacramental imagination seeks to preserve every last bit of wisdom and sensitivity that the past has to offer, it rejects efforts to link the past with the present only, when the evidence is incontrovertible that a given artifact or custom of the past can no longer be harmonized with the present. The dialectical imagination, for its part, rejects the past as sinful and corrupt in all its particularities and strives to build a new order *de novo,* that is, free from links with the past.) an elitist perfectionism, and an over-reaction to the assimilationist pressures of Americanization.

There is no phenomenon more paradoxical in Catholicism since the Council than the Catholic schools. On the one hand, the evidence is overwhelming that the schools are remarkably successful, both religiously and academically. On the other hand, enrollment in the schools is diminishing and Catholic leadership does not appear to be as committed to Catholic schools as it was before the Vatican Council.

At the time of the 1979 study of young adults, eighty-eight percent of the respondents between eighteen and thirty had some kind of Catholic education: sixty-four percent of these had attended Catholic grade schools for a time; thirty-six percent had attended Catholic grade schools for all of their elementary education; more than a third of those who did not spend all their years in Catholic schools had at least four years of religious instruction. On the other hand, fifty percent of the young adults surveyed received no religious instruction in high school. Of the other fifty percent, twenty-five percent attended C.C.D religious instruction classes. Seventeen percent of the Catholics during their high school years had four years of Catholic high schools, only eight percent had four years of C.C.D. Seventy-three percent of those who attended public schools at least some of the time said there were years when they did not receive religious instruction. The reasons given add up to more than a hundred, because the respondent was permitted many different reasons: twenty-six percent said poor teaching; forty-five percent no interest in religion, eleven percent friends were not going; thirteen percent said there were no classes offered; fourteen percent said parents did not care, and eleven percent said they already knew enough religion.

So one can conclude that the Church gets some instruction to most of its young members, a lot to elementary school children and much less to high school youth. However, poor teaching and the unavailability of religious education classes accounts for about only one-third of the non-attendance at high school religious education classes. Thus, despite the pleas of C.C.D's supporters that, with more classes and better teaching they would attract more "uneducated" young Catholics, the major reasons young people who do not attend Catholic schools also do not seek religious education are a lack of interest in religion and a lack of support from their parents or friends for religious education classes.

The study demonstrated that Catholic school attendance had a statistically significant impact on the religious behavior of young people. Forty-three percent of those who had more than eight years of Catholic school attended Mass every week, as opposed to thirty-two percent who had less; thirty-two percent received communion every week, as opposed to seventeen percent; seventy-two percent believed in life after death, as opposed to sixty percent; thirteen percent belonged to parish organizations, as opposed to five percent; twelve percent had thought seriously of a religious vocation, as opposed to six percent; thirty-seven percent had read a Catholic periodical, as opposed to twenty-five percent; sixty-four percent were opposed to abortion if no more children were wanted by the mother, as opposed to fifty-four percent.

Moreover, these effects of Catholic school education were not merely surrogates for the influence of a religious family or a religious spouse. Rather, they were additional effects when family and spouse influence was held constant. The influence of Catholic school on the religious behavior of young Catholics is stronger than

RESEARCH   251

that of the family of origin. It is only slightly less strong than the
family of procreation, even when the influence of the other is taken
into account. The old explanation of the success of Catholic
schools, that they were merely duplicating the work of the Catholic
family, is simply not valid.

Catholic schools seem to have their effect on those who attend
them, not so much through formal religious instruction class, but
rather through the closeness to the Catholic community which the
experience of attending Catholic schools generates.

Attendance at C.C.D classes does not have anywhere near the
same effect. Indeed, there are virtually no statistically significant
correlations between attendance at C.C.D and later religious beliefs
or behaviors, and there are strong and statistically significant correlations between attendance at Catholic schools and adult religious
behavior.

Attendance at Catholic schools continued in the late 1970s to
have the same moderate and statistically significant impact on the
behavior of young Catholic adults, as had been found in our earlier
studies. More than eight years of Catholic schooling does not produce a statistically significant impact on attitudes towards birth
control, living together, and frequency of prayer. Neither did Catholic education produce such an impact on the analysis reported on
the education of Catholic Americans based on 1974 data. Nor is
there a significant difference between those who had more than
eight years of Catholic schooling. However, on all the other tested
variables—Mass attendance, Communion reception, belief in life
after death, activity in parish organizations, thought of religious vocation, activity in parish organizations, Catholic periodical reading
and TV watching, participation in home liturgy and study groups,
and opposition to abortion—Catholic schools do have a statistically
significant effect.

How impressive is the magnitude of that effect? The question is
not more easy to answer now than it was in either our 1966 or our
1975 report. Those who attended Catholic schools are twice as likely to receive communion almost every week, to belong to parish organizations, to think of religious vocations, and to attend home lit-
urgies. Indeed, only twelve percent of them have considered a
vocation, but that is twice as many as the six percent who have not
had more than eight years of Catholic schooling. Only ten percent
have attended a home liturgy, but that is still twice as high as the

five percent of those who have not had more than eight years of Catholic schooling. Are these differences large or small? A little more than a quarter of those who have attended Catholic schools are uncertain about life after death (less than ten percent say they do not believe in life after death; the others report they do not know for certain). If the goal is 100 percent commitment to belief in human survival, then Catholic schools have failed. If the goal is notably and significantly to improve the likelihood of believing in life after death, then Catholic schools have succeeded.

The Effectiveness of Catholic Schools

In the propaganda for Catholic schools many years ago, it often seemed to be said that Catholic schools would turn out, almost without exception, exemplary Catholics. The critics of Catholic schools, taking that "argument" as a norm, have never ceased to point out enthusiastically the schools simply do not achieve such a goal. The defenders of Catholic schools who accept such a statement of the question have been embarrassed and defensive.

Any serious reading of the educational impact literature would reveal that schools should not reasonably be expected to undo the work of home, family, peer group, neighborhood, social class, and ethnic culture. Though schools can make a difference under some circumstances, the boundless American faith in the power of formal education has never been sustained, either by empirical evidence or by everyday impression.

Where does this leave us on the subject of the effectiveness of Catholic schools? They do not produce graduates who are universally exemplary Catholics. They do have some effect. How much effect? Far more effect, in terms of statistical size, than is used to justify racial integration. Is the effect worth the cost? One would think, given the difficulty of affecting human religious behavior at all, that the effect is worth the cost until an alternate system, technique, or method can be devised that does as well.

This interpretation is basically the same one that was originally presented in the *Education of Catholic Americans* and appeared in *Catholic Schools in a Declining Church*. Catholic schools do have a limited effect, a not unimpressive effect, as educational impact effects go. It does not seem reasonable to give up on them unless one has an alternative system which will produce the same effect at less

RESEARCH   253

cost.

In the three NORC Catholic school studies, 1963, 1974 and 1979 (of young adults), perhaps the most interesting phenomenon was that in each year the importance of Catholic schools to the religious behavior of Catholic adults increased. The correlation between attendance at Catholic schools and a wide range of measures of adults religious attitudes and behaviors—church attendance, reception of communion, attitudes towards vocation, belief in life after death, activity in parish organizations, closeness to the Church—increased as the stability of the Church decreased. The question asked in the second Catholic school study, *Catholic Schools in a Declining Church*, whether Catholic schools were more important in a time of crisis in the Church than a time of stability has been clearly answered and now, twice: "Catholic schools are much more important—as measured by the strength of correlation between Catholic school attendance and adult behavior—in a time of crisis in the Church than in a time of stability. Nevertheless, Catholic school enrollment declines and confidence in the worth of Catholic schools also seems to erode."

In the 1974 study it appeared that the decline in Catholic school attendance was the result of smaller-sized cohorts coming of school age and the failure to build new schools in the areas into which Catholics were moving. The decline in support for Catholic schools thus at that time seemed to be the result of decisions on the part of school administrators not to build new schools, and not the result of decisions by parents not to use the schools that were available. It also appeared on the basis of the 1974 study that, while Catholic schools were a substantial extra cost to a parish, most if not all of this extra cost was absorbed by the larger contributions of parents with children in the Catholic schools, and by the more substantial contributions to the Sunday collection of parishioners who had themselves attended Catholic schools. In fact, this sort of analysis indicated that Catholic schools, actually, not only paid for themselves, but may even have been a money-maker for the parish, in that contributions from present and past users of the Catholic schools more than made up for the costs the schools incurred.

I have reported elsewhere that a life-cycle phase in which young people drift away from religious practice begins after high school graduation and seems to come to an end when the young person approaches his or her thirtieth birthday. The correlation between

Catholic school attendance and return to the Church in one's late twenties is .35, a very powerful correlation. There is no correlation at all between attendance at C.C.D classes and return to frequent religious practice in one's late twenties. Indeed, in some cases the correlation is negative: the more one has attended C.C.D classes, the less likely one is to return to active religious practice in the late twenties. In all the research we have done on the effects of Catholic schools, we have not been able to find persuasive evidence of ANY effect of participation in C.C.D courses on adult religious behavior. For all the enthusiasm, for all the energy, for all the financial commitment, it simply has to be said that, as of 1979, the Confraternity of Christian Doctrine as a substitute for Catholic schools is simply a waste of time. C.C.D does not attract a substantial proportion of Catholics—at least half the Catholics of high school age receive no religious instruction at all, most of them because they do not want to receive religious instruction—and is not in any meaningful sense an adequate replacement for Catholic schools.

The Catholic schools are the most effective contribution the Church is making to the service of the poor. While Catholic school attendance has been declining, the enrollment of Blacks and Hispanics (at least half of the former not Catholic) in Catholic schools has been increasing dramatically. Research done by James Coleman and myself on secondary school students indicates that the Catholic schools have an enormous impact on the sons and daughters of the disadvantaged. Holding constant twelve different parental background variables and academic scores in the sophomore year, the seniors in Catholic schools perform substantially higher on standardized achievement tests than do the seniors in public schools. Moreover, this finding applies not only to Hispanic and to black young men and women but also to white students. The Catholic schools are more effective as secondary educators than public schools for all three racial groups.

It is especially among the disadvantaged and even more among the multiply disadvantaged, that the impact of Catholic secondary schools is likely to be greatest. Those young men and women who are disadvantaged by poverty, by low levels of parental education, by low personal self-esteem, by disciplinary problems when they were sophomores, by being on the fringes of the school community, or by low academic scores in their sophomore year are the ones most likely to benefit from the two years in between sophomore

RESEARCH   255

and senior year in Catholic schools. Most of the effectiveness of Catholic schools in dealing with disadvantaged young men and women can be attributed to the fact that the schools demand more home work from the students and more advanced course work, especially in mathematics and English.

THE DISADVANTAGED

Those public schools which demand several hours of home work a night and more advanced course work have the same effect as do the Catholic schools on disadvantaged young men and women. But many, indeed most, public schools are not either able or willing to demand more home work and more advanced course work. The Catholic schools, perhaps because they have fallen behind the educational fashion, are able to make such demands and thus able to have remarkable academic effect on their students, particularly on those students who come from one or another disadvantaged backgrounds.

On my desk are two newspaper clippings, one a bitter attack by a priest in the *National Catholic Reporter* on Catholic schools, the other a celebration of them by James S. Coleman in the *Wall Street Journal*. The former denounces them as a reactionary fraud on the Catholic people and a misuse of parish funds, the latter praises them as the most effective educational institutions in America.

As Pete Rossi would say, there are a lot of ironies in the fire.

Among the many curious paradoxes that affect the present condition of Catholic schools is that in the years since the Second Vatican Council, and especially in light of the conciliar document *Gaudium et Spes,* the Church has insisted vigorously on its obligations to the poor and on the necessity to exercise the "preferential option for the poor." At the same time, it has phased out as quickly as it could much of the most effective service it has ever done for the inner-city poor in the Catholic schools.

It is difficult to think of any other efforts of the Catholic Church in the larger urban centers of America which reach so many of the poor or reach them with such notable effectiveness. Nonetheless, Catholic schools in the inner city are slowly being closed and there seems to be little protest from those Catholics who are enthusiastically committed to the cause of "justice and peace" and to the "preferential option for the poor".

The evidence is now completely persuasive that Catholic schools do, indeed, render an important service to the poor. It is odd, to say the least, to see these schools being closed precisely at a time when the Church takes frequent public stands in favor of the "preferential option for the poor." Obviously, there was nothing in the documents of the Second Vatican Council which suggested that the Catholic schools should be "phased out" and replaced by some form of "religious education," like the Confraternity of Christian Doctrine program. Nevertheless, in the intellectual and religious climate that developed in the American Church after the Second Vatican Council, the decision to proceed away from Catholic schools and in the direction of C.C.D was made without the benefit of consultation with the Catholic laity, serious consideration of the available empirical research, and public discussion of the reasons behind the decision. Suddenly, the decision had been made: Catholic schools were out and C.C.D was in.

The Catholic schools have not been completely closed down, but new ones are rarely built and enrollment in the old ones is declining as the Catholic population shifts into the new areas of the suburban fringes of the large cities of the country. The religious and community building function of the Catholic school has been sustained by empirical research beyond any reasonable doubt. The service to the poor function of the school is both self-evident and has also been sustained by empirical evidence.

Nonetheless, Catholic schools simply are no longer as important to the ecclesiastical institution as they were at the time of the Vatican Council. Just as there has been a loss of nerve and confidence in the priesthood, despite the fact that priests are more important rather than less important than they used to be, so there is a loss of nerve and of confidence in Catholic schools, even though they are now more important both to Catholics and to disadvantaged non-Catholics than they used to be.

There is no research evidence to explain the reason for either of these losses of nerve. Still, the conclusion is inescapable: Catholic schools are a casualty of the era following the Second Vatican Council. They have not disappeared completely, but they are in trouble—and they are in trouble despite the fact that the consumers of Catholic education are, for the most part, very happy with the product they purchase when they send their young people to parochial schools.

RESEARCH   257

THE SECRET

What is the secret of the "modest" or "moderate" or "important" effect of Catholic education on the behavior of young Catholic adults? (Readers may choose their own word depending on their criteria for educational success—though we would remind them that, in most educational research, relationships of the size reported in our research would be taken very seriously indeed.) How can the effectiveness of Catholic schools be explained? Is it the result of specific religious instruction, of different techniques used, or of the various courses taught? Is it the integration of religion with other parts of the curriculum, or, perhaps, the integration of the educational experience with the liturgical life of the parish or school?

I had begun to assume, in the late nineteen-seventies, that the primary effectiveness of Catholic schooling was based on cultural and social structural factors. Now I would add that these forces are supported by an imagination of God-as-present in the world and in the community. Those who attended Catholic schools, I suspected, would have a closer sense of affiliation to the Church, simply because they had spent more time on Church property and would more likely have more experience with religious personnel, over and above the influences of their families, either of origin or procreation. I argued that it is precisely this sense of "closeness" to the Church which would be the primary intervening variable between Catholic schooling and religious behavior in adult life.

About a third of the difference between those who have had more Catholic education and those who have had less can be accounted for by familial factors, but all of the rest of the difference is accounted for by the fact that those who have gone to Catholic schools feel that they are closer to the Church. It must be remembered that this feeling of "closeness" is over and above whatever closeness to the Church might be accounted for by either spouse or family of origin. It is "pure" Catholic school effect.

The secret of the schools, if it may be called that, is that they integrate young people more closely into the Catholic institutional community. However, not all those who go to Catholic schools are close to the Church. But, it is the greater "closeness" of some of those who go to Catholic schools which "explains" virtually all of the religious effectiveness of Catholic education. The point for Catholic policy makers is clear: if you can find another institution that can have the same effectiveness in integrating young people into the Catholic community and Catholic institutions, you do not need Catholic schools. Unless and until we find such a technique, then the continuing decline of the proportion of Catholic population in Catholic schools will inevitably lead to a diminished level of Catholic commitment in the years ahead.

Finally, does Catholic school attendance incline a young person to choose not merely a spouse who is a Catholic, but also one who is more likely to be a devout Catholic and, therefore, more likely to activate and reactivate a respondent to religious devotion? The question is hard to answer, because it is difficult to separate spouses' influence on respondents from respondents' influence on spouses. Yet, if one considers a three-variable model one can see that it is possible to make a tentative test. We know that Catholic education affects the communion reception of our respondents. We also know there is a relationship among Catholic education, the respondents' own communion reception, and the spouse's communion reception. Logically, there ought not to be a direct correlation between the number of years a respondent went to Catholic schools and the communion of her or his spouse. How, after all, could a husband's Catholic education affect a wife's communion reception, except, say, through the example of the husband's communion reception? Nonetheless, the direct relationship between one's own Catholic school attendance and that of the spouse is also statistically significant. One must assume that the closeness to the Church community—resulting perhaps from joint sacramental imaginations—inclines the family community as such to link itself more intensely with the Church.

MARY PERKINS RYAN

Twenty-five years ago, Mary Perkins Ryan published her controversial book, *Are Catholic Schools the Answer?* It was the beginning of a powerful ideological assault on Catholic education. Mrs. Ryan's answer was a powerful "no." Religious instruction classes of the sort provided by the Confraternity of Christian Doctrine were the answer. From that time on C.C.D, claimed the image of a "movement" in the "new" Church while Catholic schools were relegated to the status of an institution of the "old" Church.

Bishops denounced Mrs. Ryan's solution, but before the decade

RESEARCH   259

was out, all the while protesting their dedication to Catholic schools, the hierarchy was in fact adopting her "answer." Somehow, by a process not yet clear to me, the decision was made by bishops and priests that no more new Catholic schools were to be built and that C.C.D was to become the *de facto* substitute for the schools. Apparently, fears of financial pressures brought on by "inflation" were crucial in this decision (or decisions, since they may have been made independently in many places).

The decision to give up on them—I can think of no other description for what happened—was made in the teeth of research findings: Catholic schools had a religious impact over and above that of the Catholic family. C.C.D had no measurable religious impact. The schools were more important in the transition after the Council than they were before the Council. They paid for themselves, because of the extra Sunday contributions made by those with children in Catholic schools. Perhaps one of the reasons for the continuing decline in Catholic contributions is that parents no longer view their offerings as part of support for the parish school, because there no longer is a parish school. They provided better education than most public schools and as good as the best public schools. They integrated young men and women into parish communities of which they would be part for the rest of their lives. Their students were less prejudiced and more enlightened than Catholics who went to public schools. They were especially successful in educating the disadvantaged—the educationally, emotionally, economically, racially, academically impoverished. Much of their accomplishment, as James S. Coleman has demonstrated, came from their "social capital," the overlapping networks of school, Church, and neighborhood.

The system that Church leadership sent quietly into that good night was abandoned at the height of its success.

Brand new data show how golden the twilight is. In a sense, this conclusion represents the fifth NORC report on Catholic education. Previous reports were *The Education of Catholic Americans, Catholic Schools in a Declining Church, Young Catholics in the United States and Canada*, and *Minority Students in Catholic High Schools*. In their twilight, the Catholic schools have produced substantial impact on the educational, political, moral, religious, sexual and financial behavior of those adults who attended them during their school years, the kind of impact that no other institution can

260   CHICAGO STUDIES

claim. Moreover these effects are not of the sort which could be attributed to the family background of those who attended Catholic schools.

RECENT DATA

In the 1988 General Social Survey, NORC added a special "module" of questions about religion which it will repeat intermittently in years to come. One question asked about the number of years the respondent attended church-related schools. The Catholic population was dichotomized into two segments, the 265 who had less than eight years of Catholic schools (which included all those who had no Catholic schools) and the 109 respondents who attended Catholic schools for more than eight years. With such small numbers only high correlations become statistically significant.

NORC routinely administers to its respondents a ten-word vocabulary test which is a rough measure of intellectual achievement and intelligence. The Catholic school group scored 6.6 on the scale, the other group scored 5.5. The difference, as all that will be reported in this article, was statistically significant.

Those who went to Catholic schools scored systematically higher on measures of support for the equality of women: 90% of them rejected the notion that women should limit themselves to taking care of the home (as opposed to 80% of the other group); 84% approved of women working (as opposed to 76%); 35% strongly rejected the notion that wives should support their husbands careers (as opposed to 21% of the other group); 73% thought that working mothers did not harm their children (as opposed to 63%); 70% disagreed that it was better for the man to work and the woman to take care of the home (as opposed to 58%).

24% of the Catholic school group described themselves as "conservative" (the rest were "moderate" or "liberal"), as did 36% of those who did not have at least eight years of Catholic schools.

The Catholic school group also consistently scored higher on measures of morale: 36% said they were "very happy" (as opposed to 28%); 69% said their marriage was "very happy" (as opposed to 56%); 44% said their health was "excellent" (as opposed to 27%); 47% said they received a "very great deal" of satisfaction from their family life (as opposed to 40%).

Furthermore, they are more likely to take a benign view of their

RESEARCH   261

fellow humans: 47% say that other people can generally be "trusted" (versus 38%); 35% say that most people tend to be "fair" (versus 29%); 63% say that others are "helpful" (versus 45%).

They are also more likely to have benign views of God: 35% say that they imagine God either as a "mother" or equally as a "mother" and "father" (versus 26%); 37% picture God as a "spouse" instead of as a "master" (versus 27%).

They are much more generous to the Church. Those who have had eight or more years of Catholic education give $347 a year to the Church, as opposed to $222. The additional contribution of those who went to Catholic schools, above the average, amounts to 750 million dollars a year, not a bad return on investment.

They are more likely to stress the importance of their own conscience, even above the orders of Church authorities by a rate of 53% to 38%, and they reject the notion that right and wrong are usually a simple matter of black and white, without shades of gray. They are only half as likely to have drifted away from the Church (10% versus 20%). Finally, they are twice as likely (19% versus 9%) to say that intense sexual pleasure has strengthened their religious faith.

Virtually all the criticisms aimed at the Catholic schools are refuted by these data: they are not rigid or repressive or dull or restrictive. On the contrary, they seem to facilitate greater happiness, more support for the equality of women, more confidence in other people, more willingness to see sex as a sacrament, greater generosity to the church, more benign images of God, greater awareness of the complexity of moral decision making, and higher intellectual achievement.

Not bad.

Are these really Catholic school effects or are they the result of the fact that those who go to Catholic school are likely to achieve higher educational levels? Is the effect really a Catholic school function or merely an educational function?

When educational attainment is taken into account, the Catholic school effect diminishes somewhat, but remains statistically significant. Moreover, the correlations do not diminish for Catholics under thirty, those whose Catholic education began after 1964 as the Vatican Council was drawing to an end. Quite the contrary: for some variables, the strength of the relationship increases for those under thirty. On political and feminist attitudes and for happiness, the gap between those who attended Catholic schools and those who did not has grown larger among the post-conciliar generation.

I confess that I found these relationships exciting. I would not have expected most of them beforehand and I certainly would not have expected them to be so strong (as correlations go in social research). I doubt that even the small remnant of enthusiastic supporters of Catholic schools would have anticipated that those adults who attended Catholic schools for eight years or more would be happier, more feminist, smarter, more tolerant of other people, more benign in their images of God, more accepting of moral complexity, and more likely to see sex as sacramental. Catholic schools seem to have been more successful than the teachers and administrators might have imagined in their wildest dreams. The news is almost too good to be true—and some, I think, will say that the findings simply cannot be accurate.

Let the latter do their own research. None of the standard demographic or social explanations account for the findings reported in this article. They appear to be the result of either classroom instruction or the ambience and atmosphere of the schools themselves.

I have no illusion that these data will reverse the decline of Catholic schools. Bishops will continue to think that they cannot afford to build new ones. Suburban pastors will continue to believe that life is a lot more simple without a school to worry about. Those laity who imagine themselves to be independent-minded and sophisticated, because they do not send their children to Catholic schools will continue to congratulate themselves on their own wisdom. The C.C.D "movement" will continue to claim superior virtue for itself, although none of the effects discussed in this chapter can be found for their programs. Catholic educators will continue to feel apologetic and, perhaps, even sorry for themselves. The implacable critics of Catholic education will ignore these findings as they have ignored all previous findings.

James S. Coleman has shown how the effect of Catholic secondary schools can be attributed to the "social capital" created by the overlapping networks of school, parish, and family which enable the Catholic schools to demand more from their students—and get what they demand. My own research demonstrates that it is precisely the "community forming" component of Catholic education which makes them effective—another manifestation of the work of

RESEARCH					263

"social capital."

It does not seem unreasonable to suggest that the Catholic schools were, and still are, an example par excellence of the Catholic communal ethos and the sacramental imagination at work. Not only are Catholics more likely to value community, they are also more predisposed to use it effectively and to be influenced by it. The past impulse to build schools, the dedication to them, and their effectiveness are all proof that Catholics imagine social reality differently and are more like to be affected by it.

The neighborhood parish, I have argued, is a survival of the archaic in the modern world, a residue of the curious notion that God is especially present in the local community where people live. Similarly, the parish school is also an archaic survival, a residue of the curious notion that young people can best be educated, not by outsize educational bureaucracies which care nothing for local communities, but by an interaction network of Church, neighborhood, and school.

However well they might work, the fact that they do work is offensive to those who reject the archaic and the local—and, apparently, to the educators themselves who have lost their nerve and their faith in what they have been doing.

Thus, historians of the future can marvel at how foolish we were to give up, because of loss of nerve and loss of faith, what might have been our best resource.

Catholic schools, after all, were the answer.

"DEVELOPMENT" AND TOLERANCE: THE CASE OF IRELAND

CONOR WARD AND ANDREW GREELEY

SINCE the time of Max Weber,[1] Ferdinand Tonnies[2] and the other founders of modern sociology, it has been assumed that under the impact of industrialization, urbanization, and "rationalization" human societies have been evolving from a condition in which most relationships are "primordially" structured to a condition in which most human relationships are "socially constructed"[3] — that is, from relationships which are a given (marriage, family, local community) to those which are entered into by contractual agreement (trade union, corporation, fraternal association). Consequently, "modernized" society will be more "rational" and less "archaic," more "scientific" and less "superstitious," more "bureaucratic," and less "familial," and more tolerant of diversities based on old and such outmoded social divisions as ethnicity, religion, race, geography, and culture. However, many studies of lesser developed nations have demonstrated that this evolution is anything but one-directional and one-dimensional.[4] Moreover, daily newspaper headlines demonstrate that modernization can coexist with fundamentalist religion and, as Salman Rushdie would agree, powerful intolerance.

Yet, the evolutionary modernization model persists as a presupposition

1 Max Weber, *The Protestant Ethic and the Spirit of Capitalism*, trans. T. Parsons (New York: Scribners, 1958).

2 Ferdinand Tonnies, *Community and Society (Gemeinscahft and Gesellschaft)*, trans. and ed. Charles P. Loomis, (East Lansing: Michigan State University Press, 1957).

3 See James S. Coleman, *Foundations of Social Theory* (Cambridge: Harvard University Press, 1990).

4 See Alex Inkeles and David H. Smith, *Becoming Modern: Individual Change in Six Developing Countries* (Cambridge): Harvard University Press, 1970); Lloyd I. Rudolph and Suzanne Hoeber Rudolph, *The Modernity of Tradition: Political Development in India* (Chicago: The University of Chicago Press, 1967).

of many social scientists: the more sophisticated and better educated a society is — the more "modern" it is — the less likely it is to be troubled by outmoded intolerances, all other things being equal. The United States, for example, is one of the most "modernized" countries in the world. Therefore, its score on measures of tolerance ought to be high, and there should be lower levels of prejudice based on social and demographic differences. On the other hand, Ireland, being a much less "modernized" country, should have higher scores on measures of intolerance. It does not follow that an increase in tolerance at the present time would be more rapid in the United States than in Ireland. The United States may have reached a "ceiling" where modernization has already occurred and had its effect on tolerance, while Ireland, "catching up" in modernization, may also be catching up in tolerance. The present question concerns the present condition of tolerance rather than change from the past.

The two countries chosen for hypothetical comparison in the paragraph above both share some things in common: the United States and Ireland are largely white and mostly English-speaking and heavily, if not entirely, Christian. The reason for this choice, in addition to the fact that data on such countries are available, is that the histories and cultures of various nations are so complex that many comparisons across national lines prove difficult, if not irrelevant. The analyst wants to hold as many demographic variables as constant as possible to determine whether, in fact, a higher position on measures of economic development does indeed produce higher scores on measures of tolerance and to determine that the seeming correlation is not the result of some such extraneous fact as religion, race, or culture.

From the point of view of testing this hypothesis, it is desirable to look at a group of countries which share in some degree a common culture and learn whether there exists a relationship between development and tolerance among those countries. In the English-speaking world, for example, are the more advanced countries also the more tolerant of diversity and deviance?[5] To put the matter more concretely, one might expect

5   This technique of comparing countries in different positions on a variable is often used by scientists as a substitute for measuring one country on its variation over time when time series data are not available. Thus, in the absence of measures on the eyesight of forty-year-olds twenty years ago, we compare the vision of contemporary forty-year-olds with contemporary twenty-year-olds to determine whether aging leads to a decline in the powers of eyesight.

"DEVELOPMENT" AND TOLERANCE: THE CASE OF IRELAND

that Ireland, one of the less developed of the English-speaking coun-tries,[6] would score lower on measures of tolerance than Great Britain and the United States, which are among the most developed countries in the world. That expectation raises a number of similar questions. Is Ireland — the most "backward" in level, if not pace, of economic develop-ment and modernization of the white, English-speaking countries[7] — also a country where high levels of intolerance exist — higher indeed than in any of the other white, English-speaking countries? Compared to the British, Canadians, Americans and Australians, are the Irish a nation of bigots?

The existing research literature on Ireland would suggest that they are.[8] Ireland is an archaic, familial society, conservative, rigid, domi-nated by a reactionary Roman Catholic Church. It is the most agricultural and most rural of the English-speaking nations, its gross national product and levels of educational attainment are the lowest of any of these nations.[9] Many of the events which shaped the modern world — the Renaissance, the Industrial Revolution, the French Revolution — had only marginal impact on Irish life. Ireland is the poorest and the most back-ward of the white, English-speaking nations and, hence, the most likely to be reactionary and intolerant. Who would expect anything differ-ent? Indeed, in *Prejudice and Intolerance in Ireland*, Míceál MacGréil reported high levels of intolerance among Irish respondents, but he was unable, owing to lack of data, to attempt comparisons with other countries.[10]

It is, however, possible to examine these expectations in the data gathered

6 The countries that are available for analysis in the data we use are all "white" English-speaking countries.

7 And also the Western European countries, save for Portugal.

8 For example, Conrad Arensberg and Solon Kimball, *Family and Community in Ireland* (New York: Harcourt, Brace and World, 1965); Rosemary Harris, *Prejudices and Tolerance in Ulster: A Study of Neighbors and "Strangers" in a Border Community* (Manchester: Man-chester University Press 1966); John Messenger, *Inis Beag, Isle of Ireland* (New York: Holt, Rinehart and Winston, 1969); Ann C. Breslin, *Some Correlations of Tolerance Among Adolescents in Ireland* (Ph.D. Dissertation: The University of Chicago, 1979); and Roy F. Foster, *Modern Ireland* (New York: Basic Books, 1989).

9 However, among the current college-age cohort, there is a notable change: 25 percent of the young people attend university and 22 percent graduate.

10 Míceál MacGréil, S. J., *Prejudice and Tolerance in Ireland* (New York: Harper and Row, 1977). MacGréil is currently replicating his earlier work.

"DEVELOPMENT" AND TOLERANCE: THE CASE OF IRELAND

in the International Study of Values.[11] Data on a question about whom one would reject as neighbors were collected in representative samples of five English-speaking countries — Ireland, Britain, the United States, Canada, Australia.[12] Requiring a "yes" or "no" response, the question was worded:

> On this list are various groups of people. Could you please sort out any that you would *not* like to have as neighbors: People with a criminal record, People of a different race, Students, Left-wing extremists, Unmarried mothers, Heavy drinkers, Right-wing extremists, People with large families, Emotionally unstable people, Members of minority religious sects or cults, Immigrant / foreign workers.

One would expect that the Irish respondents would score higher — more "no" responses — than respondents in other white, English-speaking nations on these items, save perhaps with regard to those groups such as people of other races or immigrant workers, both rarely found in Ireland. On all other measures, the theory of development as well as the existing literature on Ireland would lead one to expect that the Irish are

11 The International Study of Values (ISV) project was inaugurated in 1981 by a consortium of research organizations under the loose direction of British Gallup. The purpose of the research was to assemble a massive data file on values in the contemporary world. Its main focus, would seem, is on the relationship between values and religion. Insofar as any theoretical presuppositions guided the project, it would appear that a basic assumption of the research design was that traditional values, especially traditional religious values, are in decline. While some of the reports written about this research suggests that the assumption is correct, our reading of the data suggests just the opposite.

There are a number of serious weaknesses and limitations in the ISV data set: there were no questions on the role of women, the political affiliation question was badly mangled, an inadequate ethnic question was asked in the United States. Nonetheless, the data set is a powerful analytical tool because it provides information on many different nations. The method that is used in the present article is called "secondary" analysis. This means that the researchers came to the data with a question for which the survey was not explicitly designed to elicit a response. Nonetheless, the nature of the data is such that the question may be asked. Increasingly social scientists use this approach which, in effect, considers massive surveys like the ISV as data banks of which many different questions may be asked. The data on which this analysis is based, a subset of more than thirty countries, are available from the archivist at NORC, 1155 East 60th, Chicago, Illinois 60637.

12 Two the countries are technically bilingual — Canada and Ireland. However, they are both inside the cultural, legal, linguistic, and historical boundaries of the English-speaking world. The Irish sample is a combination of a survey done in the Republic of Ireland and another done in the six countries of Northern Ireland.

"DEVELOPMENT" AND TOLERANCE: THE CASE OF IRELAND

less tolerant of deviance and diversity than inhabitants of other English-speaking countries.

In fact, the data presented in Table 1 suggest just the opposite. The Irish, astonishingly, appear to be the most tolerant people in the English-speaking world.[13]

TABLE 1:
Attitudes Towards Potential Neighbors
English Speaking Nations
(% would not want to have as neighbors)

	U.S.	BRIT.	IRE.*	CAN.	AUS.
SOCIAL					
Different Race	07%	09%	07%	04%	07%
Immigrant or Foreign	08%	11%	07%	06%	06%
Students	03%	04%	04%	03%	02%
Unmarried Mothers	04%	03%	03%	02%	03%
Large Families	07%	10%	05%	05%	06%
POLITICAL					
Left-Wing Extremists	29%	25%	22%	27%	30%
Right-Wing Extremists	23%	21%	18%	21%	26%
Minority Sects or Cults	22%	20%	13%	23%	31%
PERSONAL					
Heavy Drinkers	56%	47%	35%	58%	56%
Criminals	47%	36%	42%	37%	42%
Emotionally Unstable	44%	29%	24%	28%	39%
n =	2325	1231	1529	1254	1228

*32 Counties

The data are arranged according to three scales produced by factor analysis, a method of clustering responses into patterns measuring respectively *social* tolerance, *political* tolerance, and *personal* tolerance.

In respect to social intolerance, the proportions of those who rejected the indicated groups as neighbors are all quite small. Insofar as there is any pattern in the responses, the British seem least inclined to accept as neighbors those with the given forms of deviances and the Canadians the

13 In a separate analysis we also discovered that the Irish are the *most* tolerant people in Western Europe, tied with the Dutch.

most inclined to accept them. The Irish in these items are neither the most tolerant nor the least tolerant and, in fact, differ very little from the Americans. However, in respect to political intolerance, the Irish are consistently the *least* likely to reject extremists or cult members as neighbors. Moreover, while the Irish may lack left-wing extremists in their island, there is surely no lack of minority religious groups or right-wing extremists. In respect to personal intolerance, the Irish are more likely than the British and the Canadians, but less likely than the Americans, to reject criminals as neighbors. However, they are substantially less likely to reject either the emotionally disturbed or heavy drinkers as neighbors — and there is no lack of the latter in Ireland. Compared to other English-speaking peoples, the Irish are, therefore, surely not more intolerant and, quite the contrary, seem in fact to be less intolerant than anyone else.

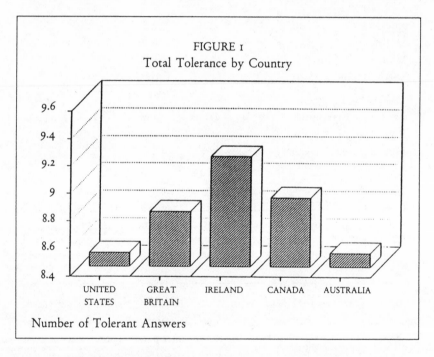

FIGURE 1
Total Tolerance by Country

Number of Tolerant Answers

Figure 1 illustrates reason for not rejecting the null hypothesis. The Irish are the most tolerant group on a summary measure compiled by adding all nine items. The Australians and the Americans rank substantially below them, while the Canadians and the British fall in between. How can one account for such a dramatic refutation of conventional expectation? How can one account for the striking finding that the Irish appear to

"DEVELOPMENT" AND TOLERANCE: THE CASE OF IRELAND

be more tolerant than the rest of the English-speaking world?

What might have survived from archaic society which would sustain such tolerance — and even if, as is possible, the present level might, in theory, represent a decline from previous levels of intolerance? The most obvious difference about Ireland is that, even when one includes the Six Counties, it is an overwhelmingly Roman Catholic country. For all its rigidities and flaws, Catholicism has attempted to be a universal religion — a religion which means, according to Ireland's most famous writer James Joyce, "Here Comes Everyone." The Catholicism of Ireland may account for the greater tolerance to be found in that country, as astonishing as such a suggestion may seem. Might the more communal or analogical religious imagination of Catholics in which God reveals Herself in society, instead of being absent from it as sinful and God-forsaken, encourage a greater toleration for diversity?[14]

TABLE 2:

Correlations between Ireland and Tolerance Scales

A) *Total* Tolerance Scale
(r)

	ALL COUNTRIES	BRITAIN	USA
Simple r	.12	.10	.18
Partial net of Catholic	.08	.00*	.13

B) *Political* Tolerance Scale
(r)

	ALL COUNTRIES	BRITAIN	USA
Simple r	.07	.05	.07
Partial net of Catholic	.03*	.00*	.03*

C) *Personal* Tolerance Scale
(r)

	ALL COUNTRIES	BRITAIN	USA
Simple r	.13	.05	.22
Partial net of Catholic	.07	.00*	.18

*Statistically not significant.

14 The notion of the analogical imagination of Catholics as opposed to the dialectical imagination of Protestants was developed by David Tracy, *The Analogical Imagination* (New York: Seabury 1982). Tracy's analysis was based on the classic theological works of the two

Table 2 suggests that such may be the case. The correlation between Ireland and the three tolerance scales is examined first with all other English-speaking countries, then with Britain, and then the United States. The first coefficient is the simple "r."[15] The second is the standardized "beta" control for the proportion of Catholics in the various countries. In all comparisons, the simple correlation diminishes when the Catholic proportion is taken into account. In the comparison with Britain, the correlation falls to zero. It also falls to statistical insignificance when the dependent variable is political tolerance. This finding means that the Irish are more tolerant in part because they are Catholic. All the variances on all three scales between the Irish and the English are accounted for by the higher proportion of Catholics in Ireland.

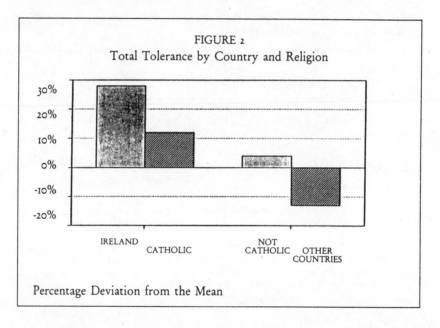

FIGURE 2
Total Tolerance by Country and Religion

Percentage Deviation from the Mean

traditions. The present writer has tested this theory with contemporary empirical data from national samples of lay members. See Andrew Greeley, "Protestant and Catholic — Is the Analogical Imagination Extinct?" *American Sociological Review*, (1989): 485–502.

15 An "r" is a measure of how much variation on the one scale (weight, for example) can be accounted for by a parallel variation on another scale (height, for example). In this instance it shows much of the variation on the summary tolerance measure can be accounted for by being Irish. The "beta" presents the same relationship net of an outside variable. How much of the variance on tolerance can be accounted for by the fact that the Irish are mostly Catholic? The substantial decline of the beta from the r indicates in considerable part the Catholicism of the Irish accounts for their greater tolerance. In this analysis, the important

"DEVELOPMENT" AND TOLERANCE: THE CASE OF IRELAND

Likewise, Figure 2 nicely illustrates the finding using a measure of the percentage of a standard deviation above and below the mean score. Catholics in general are more tolerant than non-Catholics. Moreover, whether Protestant or Catholic, the Irish are more tolerant than other English-speaking peoples, and Irish Catholics are notably more tolerant than their fellow Catholics and their fellow Irish.

Perhaps the most interesting item of the eleven measured is the attitude towards minority religious groups, of which there are plenty on both side of the Six-County border and about which diversity terrorist violence continues in the Six Counties and, occasionally, in the Republic. In this apparent tolerance an Irish or a Catholic phenomenon, or perhaps both?

TABLE 3:

Attitude Towards Members of Minority Religious Groups
as Neighbors in British Isles by Religion

	(% "Would not Want")	
	CATHOLIC	NOT CATHOLIC
Britain	13%	22%*
	(143)	(889)
Ireland	13%	15%
	(1231)	(244)

Significantly different from Catholics in Britain, Catholics in Ireland and Not Catholics in Ireland.

The percentages in Table 3 suggest that it may well be both. The Irish, regardless of their religion, and British Catholics all differ significantly from English non-Catholics in this expression of religious toleration. As measured by this variable, there is more religious toleration in violence-torn Northern Ireland than in peaceful Britain. Since most British Catholics are of Irish origin, there is a suggestion in these data that it is

fact is not the absolute size of the r but its decline when religion is taken into account. It should be noted that, in most social research, a statistically significant r of .12 is not considered trivial. The complexity of human behavior is such that rarely do single demographic variables account for more variation.

not merely Catholicism which makes for tolerance among the Irish but, especially, the specific form of Catholicism which exists in the Irish tradition.

A second measure of advanced attitudes in the International Study of Values data is provided by responses to a question on the purposes of prisons: "To re-educate the prisoner," "To make those who have done wrong pay for it," "To protect other citizens," "To act as a deterrent to others." Those who think of prison as a place for reeducation might reasonably be described as tolerant in comparison to those who choose another of the three responses. The Irish are the most likely, by 42 percent, versus 34 percent for the other countries combined, of the five peoples to assert that the purpose of prison is the rehabilitation of the criminal.

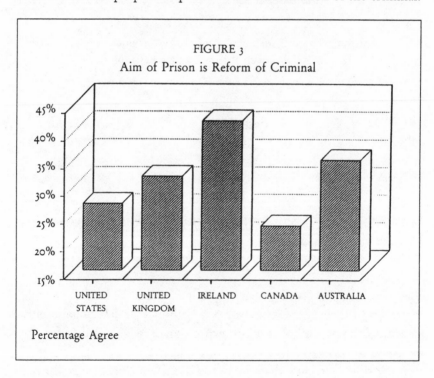

FIGURE 3
Aim of Prison is Reform of Criminal

Percentage Agree

However, the religious explanation does not apply to the Irish advantage on this measure. While the Irish are more "enlightened" about the purpose of prisons than are the citizens of other English-speaking countries, and while Irish Catholics are more "enlightened" by five percentage points than other Catholics, Irish Protestants are the most "enlightened"

"DEVELOPMENT" AND TOLERANCE: THE CASE OF IRELAND

of all: 55 percent of them see the purpose of prison as rehabilitation, twenty percentage points higher than their fellow Protestants.[16]

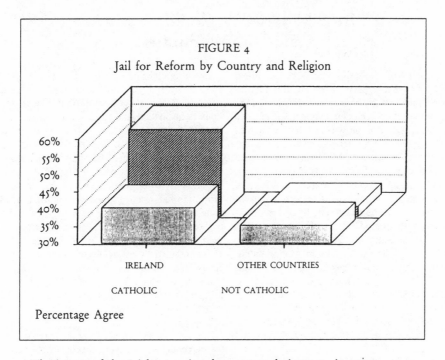

FIGURE 4
Jail for Reform by Country and Religion

Percentage Agree

The image of the Irish as an intolerant people is pervasive, even among the Irish themselves. It is part of a more generalized stereotype, which is not by any means absent among sophisticated elites. In light of suggestions posed by the research reported here, social scientists and other scholars — particularly, if one is permitted to say so, in Ireland — may wish to examine again their images of "development," of religion, of tolerance, and of Ireland.

— *University College, Dublin and
NORC, the University of Chicago*

16   In another analysis currently in process using a different data set, we asked whether the tolerance of Irish Catholics in America is a result of both their Irish and Catholic backgrounds. The answer is that such is, indeed, the case. To those who say that Irish Catholics in America are not tolerant, we reply that numerous studies over the last quarter century demonstrate that they are the most tolerant gentile ethnic group in America.

Americans and Their Sexual Partners

Andrew M. Greeley, Robert T. Michael and Tom W. Smith

In the absence of responsible social research about human behavior, poor research and media-generated folk lore become conventional wisdom. The assumptions of such conventional wisdom are seldom questioned and rarely tested. In few areas of human behavior is the power of conventional wisdom so pervasive as it is when the subject is sex. In matters of research on sexual behavior, as in other arenas, Gresham's Law applies – bad research seems to drive out good research. And there is good research on sexual behavior, as the recent lengthy and informative review by the National Research Council details. It is just less sensational than much of the poorer research, and thus less successful in shaping public perceptions about the facts pertaining to our sexual behavior. Perhaps Gresham's Law should be paraphrased in this context as: sensational findings (often the result of poor or superficial research) drive out carefully balanced and less sensational findings, at least from headlines and thus from public perception.

Bad research, like the self-selected reader surveys in popular magazines and non-random samples such as those gathered for the Hite Report, and the popular metaphor of a "sexual revolution" have created a conventional wisdom that "everyone knows" to be true: marital infidelity and sexual experimentation are widespread among Americans.

But if "monogamy" is defined as having no more than one sexual partner during the past year, research based on a scientifically sound national sample indicates that Americans are a most monogamous people. Only 14 percent of all adult Americans interviewed in a 1988 nationwide survey were not monogamous in this sense; and excluding those who were not sexually active, 18 percent were not monogamous. In only one major population group – young men – were a majority not monogamous.

Our study is based on a supplement to NORC's (the National Opinion Research Center) GSS (General Social Survey) given during the winter of 1988 to about 1500 adults who were scientifically selected from a national probability frame of households in the United States. The questions about sexual behavior were included as a self-administered form during the face-to-face interview conducted in the respondent's home. The self-administered form was sealed by the respondent and returned, unopened, by the interviewer, with the rest of the survey. This procedure reassured respondents that their answers were confidential and to be used only for statistical purposes such as this article. The response rate on the 1988 GSS was 77.3 percent, and 93.9 percent of those who responded did answer the questions about sexual behavior, well within the range of "item nonresponse" that is typical for a lengthy interview. There is no evidence in this survey that respondents felt the questions about sexual partners were particularly intrusive or inappropriate.

We use two definitions of monogamy. We report the percentage of sexually active people with one sexual partner (M1) and the percentage of all people with zero or one sexual partner (M2). In both definitions we exclude those few (6.1 percent) who did not answer the question. Each of the two definitions has some appeal as a measure of the tendency for adults to be monogamous, for the sexually inactive – those who report having no sexual partner within the past twelve months – can be considered in or out of the definition depending on its purpose. They are not monogamous in the social sense of being committed to a sexual relationship with a sole partner, but from the epidemiological standpoint of risks of contracting sexually transmitted diseases such as AIDS, they belong to the category of the monogamous. We caution that as our questionnaire asked the number of partners in the preceding twelve months, we cannot distinguish serial monogamy within the year from having two or more partners in the same interval of time. Our definitions of monogamy exclude persons with more than one partner in a twelve-month period, serially or otherwise. Thus our definition of monogamy represents a lower bound estimate of its prevalence in this respect.

Table 1 shows the basic facts. These facts indicate that a vast majority of adults report monogamous behavior. Among all adults 86 percent were monogamous (M2), while among the sexually active 82 percent were monogamous (M2). More women (90 percent) report being monogamous than men (81 percent). More older respondents report being monogamous than do younger ones with the monogamy rate rising from 61 percent among those under 25 to 96 percent and higher among those over

Table 1

Monogamy in the United States
(Percent of Sexually Active Persons with One Partner During Previous Twelve Months)

	M1 *	M2 *		M1 *	M2 *
All	82%	86%	Divorced	62%	73%
	(1072)	(1390)		(125)	(178)
			Separated	78%	81%
Gender **				(36)	(43)
Women	86%	90%	Never	52%	64%
	(568)	(793)		(205)	(278)
Men	78%	81%			
	(504)	(597)	Race **		
			Black	69%	74%
Age **				(144)	(170)
18-24	56%	61%	White	84%	88%
	(144)	(163)		(889)	(1161)
25-29	77%	79%			
	(157)	(168)	Religion		
30-39	85%	86%	Protestant	83%	87%
	(283)	(308)		(648)	(852)
40-49	86%	88%	Catholic	85%	89%
	(213)	(243)		(281)	(364)
50-59	91%	93%			
	(96)	(132)	Region		
60-69	93%	96%	North East	82%	86%
	(119)	(194)		(216)	(274)
70+	95%	98%	North Central	82%	87%
	(59)	(180)		(288)	(382)
			South	82%	86%
Education				(372)	(482)
Grammar	81%	91%	West	83%	87%
	(70)	(146)		(196)	(252)
High	83%	87%			
	(504)	(644)	Size **		
College	81%	84%	12 SMSA	73%	79%
	(398)	(480)		(202)	(265)
Graduate	84%	86%	Other SMSA	87%	90%
	(99)	(116)		(353)	(440)
			Other Urb	82%	86%
Marital Status **				(400)	(530)
Married	96%	97%	Rural	86%	90%
	(672)	(740)		(117)	(155)
Widowed	71%	93%			
	(34)	(151)			

M1: Monogamy defined as having one partner, people with zero partners, and people who refused to answer are excluded from the sample.
M2: Monogamy defined as having zero or one partner, refusals are excluded.
** Signifies that the percentage differences within this category are significant at the .01 level for M1 and M2. Numbers in parentheses indicate the size of the cell on which the percentage is based.

38 / SOCIETY · JULY / AUGUST 1990

60. Whites (88 percent) have higher monogamy rates than blacks (74 percent), as do residents of smaller sized communities (90 percent) compared to those in large metropolitan areas (75 percent). There appears to be no appreciable difference between Protestants and Catholics or by region of residence in the United States. Marital status has a major influence, as would be expected, with a remarkably high percentage of married persons (97 percent) reporting monogamous behavior. Among sexually active formerly married people, monogamous behavior appears to be the norm as well. Rates of monogamy appear to vary little with educational level (the anomalous high monogamy rate for M2 in Table 1 reflects the large number of elderly people with low levels of education, many of whom are widowed and have no sexual partner). It appears that sexual experimentation exists predominantly among the young and the nonmarried.

Age, gender, and marital status are powerful predictors of monogamy, as Table 2 suggests. The rates for monogamy are strikingly high for both married men and married women in all three age groups – over 90 percent of each group reported themselves monogamous.

For those who have a "regular" sexual partner, the rates of monogamy are decidedly lower, typically falling 25 percentage points for women under 50 and about 40 percentage points for men under 50. Other

Table 2

Rates of Monogamy Among the Sexually Active, by Gender, Age, and Type of Relationship

Women

Age	Married*	Regular Partner	No Regular Partner
< 30*	94% (80)	64% (70)	40% (15)
30-49*	100% (159)	74% (93)	50% (16)
50+*	97% (109)	91% (23)	67% (3)
Total	98% (348)	73% (186)	47% (34)

Men

Age	Married	Regular Partner	No Regular Partner
< 30*	91% (44)	47% (62)	23% (30)
30-49*	95% (163)	55% (53)	42% (12)
50+*	96% (117)	75% (12)	45% (11)
Total	95% (324)	53% (127)	32% (53)

* NB: Row percentages (by partnership for each age group) are statistically significant at the .01 level for all six groups; the column percentages (by age for a given partnership) are significant at the .01 level for only one group, married women.

research suggests that the half-life of a cohabitational union in the United States is only about one year, so if many of those reporting a regular partner are cohabiting, it is likely that they have been in that relationship for less than a full year. Their having more than one sexual partner within a year may cover a period different from that of the regular partnership they report. Many unmarried persons with a "regular" sexual partner may have no expectation about sexual exclusivity, so the lower rates of monogamy for these men and women may not indicate any infidelity.

For those who reported having no regular sexual partner, the rates of monogamy – are much lower, about 50 percentage points for women and 60 percentage points for men. They range from 23 percent of the young men to 67 percent of the older women. The rates rise with age and are higher for women. Of the sexually active respondents in the survey who were not married and had no regular sex partner, about one-third of the men and half of the women nonetheless reported only one partner within the year.

Even among the *nonmonogamous* sexual license is limited. Fifty-seven percent of these women and 32 percent of these men report only two sexual partners. Men, more than women, are likely to report having a large number of partners – and hence to be the primary targets for sexually transmitted diseases. (A quarter of the men who have more than one sexual partner report in fact that they have had at least five such partners and only 8 percent of women had five or more partners.) If we project to life cycle patterns from our cross sectional data, when young people marry or reach the age of thirty or so, a large majority adopt monogamy as their lifestyle.

To see which of these demographic variables had independent effects on monogamy we carried out multiple regression analysis on the M1 definition of

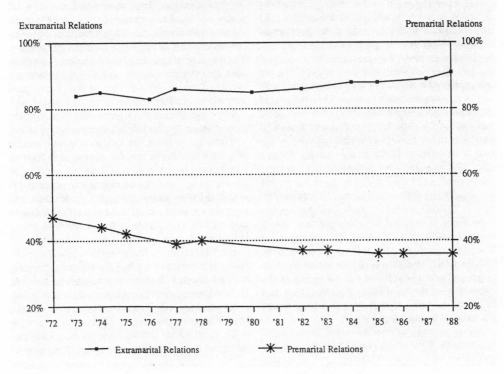

Figure 1
Attitude Toward Nonmarital Sexual Relations
GSS Annual Survey 1972-1988
(Percent Saying Always or Almost Always Wrong)

monogamy. The regressions were run separately for men and for women. They indicate that older people are more likely to be monogamous, that black men (but not black women) are less likely to be monogamous, that those in large cities are less likely to be monogamous, and that compared to the married men and women, those with and those without a regular sex partner are far less likely to be monogamous. The regressions also included information on education level, religion, household age structure, and ethnicity (Hispanics), but none of these variables had any statistically discernible effect on the rate of monogamy.

It is interesting to note, too, that when we reran these regressions on only the persons who were married, there were no significant variables for the women, and only the race variable was significant for the men. That is, marriage is the dominant determinant of the monogamy rate, and within the married population, none of the other factors we looked at – education, city size, household composition, religion, age, (except for race for men) – had an influence that was statistically notable. Again, marital status is clearly the dominant determinant of the monogamy propensity in these data.

One issue that deserves attention, but which we doubtless cannot fully address, is whether the GSS respondents are telling the truth about their sexual behavior. Might they be lying about the number of their sexual partners? Two points can be made. Survey data from the United Kingdom in 1986 reported comparable proportions of the adult population with zero, one and two or more partners. The similarity of these two quite independent surveys provides some face validity for each. The experience of those who have undertaken surveys of sexual behavior is that respondents tend to be remarkably candid. Phrases like "the new permissiveness," "the playboy philosophy," and "open marriage" have become so fashionable and discussions of marital infidelity in popular journals are so commonplace that respondents might be inclined to exaggerate their sexual accomplishments to keep up with the "trends" rather than understate them. Also, if the respondents to the GSS are falsifying accounts of their sexual behavior because of mores which demand monogamy (a circumstance we do not think is the case), then at a minimum they are demonstrating that those mores still strongly support monogamy.

Are the monogamy rates described above "high" by standards of the recent past? Might the situation of widespread monogamy described by our data reflect a response to the fears created by the AIDS epidemic? Does the high rate of monogamy represent a "retreat" from a previous state of "permissiveness" or "liberation"? Have fear and caution made sexual restraint popular?

As our data is only a snapshot about behavior in the past twelve months, it cannot help us determine directly if the fear of AIDS has affected sexual behavior. Finding that monogamy is relatively rare among young men who have never been married and who do not have a regular sexual partner does not inform us, for they might have had even more partners before they became aware of the AIDS danger.

One way our data might indirectly address this question is if we assume that knowing an AIDS victim inhibits sexual permissiveness. We can compare the sexual behavior of those who do know an AIDS victim with the behavior of those who do not know anyone with AIDS, and that can indicate the magnitude of the behavioral response. But those who do know a victim are significantly less likely to be monogamous. Among all adults 76 percent of those knowing an AIDS victim were monogamous, while 87 percent of those not knowing anyone with AIDS were monogamous. Even those who know an AIDS victim who has died are somewhat less likely to report themselves monogamous (70 percent) than those personally unaware of any AIDS fatalities (80 percent). The direction of causation here is probably that those who are not monogamous, and have a lifestyle that exposes them to greater risks of AIDS and other sexually transmitted diseases, are acquainted with more people who are also at greater risk of contracting those diseases. So this line of inquiry is not revealing.

There is, however, no evidence in our data to support a hypothesis that the current high level of monogamy is the result of fear of AIDS. The demographic correlates of monogamy suggest that sexual behavior varies greatly by gender, age, and especially marital status; these powerful predictors may explain much more of the variation in sexual behavior than does fear of AIDS.

But what might the fear of AIDS have added to the levels of monogamy that had already existed among married people? If there were a more permissive attitude among married people towards infidelity five or ten years ago, how great was this permissiveness? Data from prior years of the General Social Survey (with independent national samples of adults) can inform us about how that attitude has changed over the past 15 years. It suggests that norms against extramarital sex were strong even 15 years ago. Studying the trend in attitude toward marital infidelity in the annual GSS questionnaire since 1972, there has been a statistically significant increase in opposition to infidelity. There was an increase from 84 percent to 91 percent of the adult population saying that extramarital sex was always or almost always wrong, as Figure 1 indicates. This hardly indicates a dramatic increase in sexual restraint, especially since disapproval of extramarital sex was quite high in the early 1970s when the GSS was first conducted.

It is worth noting that this increase in opposition to extramarital sex has occurred at the same time as there has been a statistically significant increase in tolerance for premarital sex (an increase in tolerance from 53 percent to 64 percent). The notion that social change is always unidimensional and unidirectional rarely is sustained by empirical data. "Revolutions" in which there is uniformity unmarred by complexity usually exist only in newspaper articles and not in the real world.

Three independent national surveys provide data that enables us to gauge the impact of fear of AIDS on American monogamy. A CBS study in 1986 based on 823 cases reported that 11 percent of Americans said that they had changed their behavior because of AIDS. NBC studies conducted in 1986 and 1987 indicated that 7.3 and 7.4 percent, respectively, said they had modified their behavior.

These levels, when reported, were commonly seen as indicating that people were not reacting responsibly to the risks of AIDS, but our findings suggest another interpretation. If many fewer people were engaged in sexual behavior that was risky, it may be quite sensible that few altered their behavior. This is further supported by a 1987 Gallup survey in which 68 percent indicated that no change in their sexual behavior had been made because they did not need to change their behavior. We cannot be sure, and do not intend to be Pollyannas, but our findings that relatively few adults report having sex with many partners may be one reason only about 10 percent of adults report changing their behavior. Another cautionary note – we focus on only the number of partners, and there are several other dimensions of sexual behavior that one might change in response to the risks of AIDS (*e.g.*, care in the selection of partners, avoidance of high-risk sexual practices, use of condoms, *etc.*), and these are beyond the scope of our survey.

The details of the reported change in behavior motivated by fear of AIDS conform quite well to the details in the GSS tables reported above about which groups are most at risk: in the Gallup survey 7 percent of the married people and 22 percent of the never married reported a change of behavior; 10 percent of the whites and 22 percent of the blacks reported a change in behavior, as did 13 percent of the men and 9 percent of the women, 19 percent of those under 25 and 10 percent of those between 35 and 50. The changes for married people are compatible with the change in attitudes towards extramarital sex during the years Americans have been conscious of AIDS. So one can tentatively estimate that, even in the absence of AIDS, the monogamy rate for married men and women would not be less than 90 percent. For the whole population the rate, without the AIDS scare, might be between 75 percent and 80 percent. We note again the face validity here: those groups who report the lower monogamy rates in the GSS – men compared to women, nonmarried compared to married – are those who report in the Gallup survey the biggest change in behavior for fear of contracting AIDS.

The fear of AIDS may have increased monogamy especially among unmarried people and most especially if they are young, but the rates appear to us to have been quite high in any case. Despite the fear of AIDS the promiscuity rate among the young is still high, especially among young, unmarried men, with resultant dangers to themselves and their future partners.

A Sexual Revolution?

Like all metaphors the phrase "sexual revolution" is apt for some dimensions of social behavior over the past couple decades, but by no means all of it. It might be useful to review a few changes in recent years in demographic features such as marriage and divorce as well as to speculate on how they might have affected the rate of monogamy in the United States as measured by our variables M1 and M2.

Consider the changes in marital status. The divorce rate in the United States (per 1000 married women) rose from 9.2 in 1960 to 14.9 in 1970, 22.6 in 1980, and then declined slightly to 21.5 in recent years. As a result, despite a rise in remarriage rates, the proportion of the adult population currently divorced also rose dramatically from 3.2 percent in 1970 to 7.8 percent in 1986. Divorced adults are much less likely to be monogamous than are married adults, so this trend probably has decreased the number of adults

42 / SOCIETY · JULY / AUGUST 1990

with one sex partner and increased the number with more than one partner and the number with no partner, thus lowering M1 but not necessarily M2.

The median age at first marriage for women in the United States has risen over the past two decades from 20.6 in 1970 to 22.8 in 1984. As a result, the proportion of 20-24 (25-29) year-old men who have never been married rose from 54.7 percent (19.1 percent) in 1970 to 75.5 percent (41.4 percent) in 1986, and for women that proportion for the same age groups rose from 35.8 percent (10.5 percent) in 1970 to 58.5 percent (26.4 percent) in 1986. These are traditionally sexually active ages and the dramatic increases in the proportions still single probably accompany an increase in the average number of sex partners among the sexually active subsets for these growing segments of the population, thus lowering M1.

There has been a relatively large increase in the rate of cohabitation in the United States, from 0.8 percent in 1970 to 2.8 percent in 1988. This rise among young single couples and among the divorced may offset the tendency toward lower rates of monogamy somewhat, if, as the regressions above imply, the rate of monogamy among those with a "regular" sex partner is higher than among those without such a "regular" partner even though it is lower than among those who are formally married. This would tend to lower M1.

Another dimension of the issue is addressed by the earlier onset of sexual activity by teenagers in the United States. For 17-year-old urban women, the proportion who had premarital intercourse rose from 28 percent in 1971 to 41 percent by 1982. The early onset of sexual activity presumably is associated with a decrease in the monogamy rate for the population as a whole. The trends toward earlier age of beginning sexual activity and toward later age of first marriage lengthen the interval of the life cycle in which sexual activity is most associated with multiple sex partners. The resulting increase in premarital sexual activity mirrors the increased acceptance of that behavior, as reflected in the trends in attitude noted above. It probably lowers M1 and also reduces the discrepancy between M1 and M2.

The changes in fertility control through medical technology (such as the oral contraceptive) and legally accepted practices (such as abortion) have dramatically altered the risks of an unwanted birth associated with sexual behavior. That lower risk surely has had some influence, at the margin at least, on the inclination to engage in nonmarital sexual activity. This, too,

may lower M1 and reduce the discrepancy between M1 and M2.

The baby boom of the fifties and early sixties resulted in a disproportionate number of young adults in their twenties over the past decade. As men and women in this age tend to exhibit less monogamy than those in older ages, that demographic bulge itself has tended to lower the overall incidence of monogamy. (This is a trend that can be anticipated with some clarity and as the size of the new cohorts of young adults for the next decade or so will be disproportionately small, this should tend to raise the incidence of monogamy over the next several years, and thus raise M1.)

As this sketchy review of demographic events indicates, there have been several social phenomena that have probably lowered the incidence of monogamy in the past decade or so. Whether these forces have helped create a "sexual revolution" or not, we cannot say. One fact is clear: the high rates of monogamous behavior in the United States exhibited in the GSS data for 1988 do not support the notion that the "revolution," if it occurred, has resulted in a society that does not value or adhere to monogamy.

READINGS SUGGESTED BY THE AUTHORS

Hofferth, S.L., F.R. Kahn, and W. Baldwin. "Premarital Sexual Activity Among U.S. Teenage Women Over the Past Three Decades," *Family Planning Perspectives* 19, (1987).

Michael, R.T., E.O. Laumann, J.H. Gagnon, and T.W. Smith. "Number of Sex Partners and Potential Risk of Sexual Exposure to HIV," *Morbidity and Mortality Weekly Report* 37, (1988).

Turner, C.F., H.G. Miller, and F.E. Moses (eds.). *AIDS: Sexual Behavior and Intravenous Drug Use.* Washington, DC: National Academy Press, 1989.

Andrew M. Greeley is a priest, sociologist, novelist, and journalist. He is a Research Associate at the National Opinion Research Center, University of Chicago, and Professor of Sociology at the University of Arizona. His scholarly writings concentrate on religion and ethnicity. His other writings range from critiques of the Catholic church to best-selling novels.

Robert T. Michael is an economist. He is Dean of the Graduate School of Public Policy Studies, University of Chicago, and former Director of the National Opinion Research Center. His research interests center on the economics of the family.

Tom W. Smith is a survey researcher and historian. He is Director of the General Social Survey at the National Opinion Research Center. His research interests are survey methods and social change.

THE DEMOGRAPHY OF AMERICAN CATHOLICS:

1965-1990

Andrew M. Greeley

This paper is divided into three sections, the first dealing with how many Catholics there are in America, the second with the changing demographic composition of American Catholics, and the third with the continuing of Catholic immigration.

HOW MANY CATHOLICS?

What proportion of Americans are Catholics?

Depending on your sources, the estimates range from 21 percent to 28 percent. The differences are not unimportant: each percentage point represents almost two and a half million people. There may be more than 16 million Catholics for which the low estimate does not account.

Table 1 presents six different estimates. The first is drawn from the largest single study of American religious affiliation ever attempted—the Current Population Survey of the Census Bureau (as it was then called) in 1957. If the proportion Catholic is the same today as it was then, then there are approximately 59 million Catholics in the United States, seven million more than reported in the *Official Catholic Directory* (1986).

Religion and the Social Order, Volume 2, pages 37-56.
Copyright © 1991 by JAI Press Inc.
All rights of reproduction in any form reserved.
ISBN: 1-55938-388-7

Table 1. Various Estimates of Present U.S. Catholic Population

	Proportion	*Population in Millions*
U.S. Census (1957)	25	59
Gallup	28	65
NORC	25	59
Official Directory	22	52
Births*	25	59
Deaths**	21	49

Notes: *Ratio of baptisms to live births.
          **Ratio of funerals to deaths.

Recent surveys of the Gallup organization estimate that 28 percent of Americans are Catholic which would mean a Catholic population of 65 million. The surveys done of religion at the National Opinion Research Center (NORC) since the early 1960s consistently report 25 percent of the population Catholic. The Gallup data, on the other hand, indicate an increase from 23 percent to 28 percent between the early 1960s and the present, a 20 percent increase in the proportion of Americans who are Catholic.

In Which Estimate Should the Most Confidence Be Placed?

The *Official Catholic Directory* figures are helpful but not conclusive because the quality of information available to a pastor when he fills out his annual form varies, as does the care with which the form is filled out. Note in Table 2 that while Gallup portrays an increase in the last quarter century and NORC no change, the *Directory* estimates indicate a decline (from 24% to 22%) in the proportion Catholic—which is compatible with an increase in numbers because the American population is growing at a faster rate than is the proportion affiliated with the church, if the Directory is to be believed.[1]

Baptism and burial records are likely to be more reliable than pastoral estimates of parish size, if only because of canonical regulations about keeping records and because the books are ready at hand when a pastor is required to tally the numbers (which does not necessarily mean that he looks at the books). Thus, at the present time, if the reports are accurate, a quarter of American births are Catholic and 21 percent of deaths are Catholic. These figures suggest that the Gallup numbers are too high—such a gross under-reporting by the country's pastors seems most improbable.

Moreover, the proportion of burials (Catholic burials as a fraction of death statistics) that are Catholic has been consistently at 21 percent since the early 1960s while the proportion of births (baptisms divided by birth statistics) has fallen from 31 percent in 1962 to 25 percent at the present (see Table 2)—a

Table 2. Catholic Population Statistics from the
Official Catholic Directory by Year
(Percentage of Total U.S. Population)

Year	Total	Births*	Deaths**
1960	24	31	21
1965	24	31	21
1970	24	28	22
1975	23	27	22
1980	22	26	21
1985	22	25	21

Notes: *Ratio of baptisms to live births.
**Ratio of funerals to deaths.

finding that is supported by the various fertility studies done at the University of Michigan and Princeton University which show that from the middle 1960s on the Catholic birth rate rapidly declined until it matched the national rate (despite the birth control encyclical).

Why the difference in birth rates and death rates? The higher birth rate causes the lower death rate because it produces a younger population. In NORC's *General Social Surveys* (Davis and Smith 1989) adult Catholics (over age 18) are three years younger on the average than adult Protestants (43 versus 46). The younger population is the result of higher birth rates in the past. It will take many years for the present lower birth rates to begin to age the Catholic population so that it becomes as old (on the average) as the Protestant population.

If Gallup's figures are too high and pastoral estimates too low, why then are the middle range figures (about a quarter of the country is Catholic) so stable in the last 25 years despite the demographic changes which are going on? The answer is that the figures mask a process by which Catholics leave the church and are replaced. In the General Social Survey 28 percent of the respondents said they were raised Catholic. The 25 percent currently Catholic is the result of an equation in which the number of converts and the natural increase from higher birth rates and immigration has been subtracted from the number of defectors. As a result of the decline in the Catholic birth rate and the decline in the number of converts there will be a slow erosion in years to come from the 25 percent figure, though not in actual numbers of Catholics as long as the American population continues to grow. (As we shall see subsequently, immigration may diminish or even cancel out this expected erosion in proportion Catholic.)

In 1960, some 15 percent of those who were raised Catholics are no longer Catholic. Taking into account the shifting age of the American population (and

40   ANDREW M. GREELEY

the propensity of some to return to their denominations as they grow older) that figure has not changed in the last quarter century (Hout and Greeley 1987). Thus, if the proportion Catholic erodes in decades to come it will be the result of changing birth and convert rates (and perhaps changing immigration rates) and not of changing defection rates. As I will note later in this paper, defection is particularly high among Hispanic Catholics and in this population the rate may actually be increasing.

About half of the defectors have left to join another religion, usually in conjunction with a marriage to someone of that religion (Greeley 1979). The other half leave to no religious affiliation. The Catholic defection rate is (and has been) more than half again as high as the Protestant defection rate.

Perhaps the most useful statistic for estimating how many Catholics there are in a given area is a fraction in which the numerator is the number of baptisms the previous year and the denominator is the number of live births in the same area. Thus, by way of example, (using the *Official Directory* for 1986 and the current *Statistical Abstract,* both of which present data for 1985) I calculate that in 1985 37 percent of the live births in the State of Illinois were baptized Catholic or that the population Catholic of the Prairie State is approximately 4.3 million. Diocesan statistics could be calculated using the same formula.

To save overworked Chicago chancery officials the trouble of calculating an estimate, I have done so for them: I estimate 2.57 million Catholics, a little less than 10 percent more than the report in the *Directory* (approximately the same as the national rate of underestimates). This technique must be used with special caution in any area in which there is reason to suppose that the age and ethnic group distribution of Catholics is radically different from the rest of the country as in the States of Florida, Texas, New Mexico, and California with their large Hispanic populations which are younger and more fertile than the national average. (The Hispanic birth rate is 20 per 1,000 as opposed to the 15.5 per 1,000 national rate.)

In many, if not most, cases, however, an estimate using this technique is likely to provide the best possible numbers until the church attempts a census as careful and as comprehensive as the government's. Table 3 presents the proportion Catholic estimated by this technique for each of the nine census regions of the country.

Table 4 presents the proportion Catholic and the estimated Catholic population for each of the states. In any state in which there have been many baptisms of the children of migratory workers from Mexico one should discount somewhat the estimates in this table, and especially as noted previously in such states as Florida, New Mexico, Texas, and California where there are large Mexican American populations.

The shape of the age pyramid of the Catholic population is rather different from that of the rest of the country—smaller at the top, larger in the middle,

Table 3. Proportion* Catholic by Census Region
(In Percent)

New England	58
Middle Atlantic	40
East North Central	37
West North Central	26
South Atlantic	11
East South Central	7
West South Central	23
Mountain	20
Pacific	17

Note: *Ratio of baptisms to live births.

Table 4. Catholic Population by State
(Estimated by the number of baptisms
as percent of live births in the state.)

	Percent Catholic	Total Catholic Population *(in thousands)*
New England		
Maine	27	314
New Hampshire	34	339
Vermont	31	166
Massachusetts	57	3,319
Rhode Island	53	523
Connecticut	55	1,746
Mid Atlantic		
New York	42	7,469
New Jersey	46	3,417
Pennsylvania	34	4,030
South Atlantic		
Delaware	27	167
Maryland and DC	19	953
Virginia	9	523
West Virginia	6	116
North Carolina	3	187
South Carolina	3	100
Georgia	4	239
Florida*	18	2,045

42   ANDREW M. GREELEY

East North Central
Ohio	22	2,364
Indiana	16	879
Illinois	33	3,806
Michigan	24	2,818
Wisconsin	37	1,776

East South Central
Kentucky	13	484
Tennessee	4	190
Alabama	3	120
Mississippi	5	130

West North Central
Minnesota	34	1,426
Iowa	26	750
Missouri	19	956
North Dakota	31	212
South Dakota	31	219
Nebraska	26	449
Kansas	21	514

West South Central
Arkansas	4	94
Louisiana	33	1,478
Oklahoma	6	198
Texas*	24	3,929

Mountain
Montana	13	119
Idaho	23	121
Wyoming	15	76
Colorado	22	719
New Mexico*	42	690
Arizona	22	701
Utah	5	77
Nevada	17	150

Pacific
Washington	12	529
Oregon	11	296
California*	32	8,437
Alaska	10	52
Hawaii	22	231

Note: *Estimates in Florida, Texas, New Mexico, and California are problematic because of their large Hispanic population, with a younger than national average and a higher birth rate.

and then tapering down towards similarity at the bottom. It would be possible to estimate this pyramid from the age of a person at burial. One would calculate the number of deaths by gender in five-year age categories (one year for those under five) and multiply that number by the inverse of the age/sex-specific death rate. However national data for age-specific deaths of Catholics are not available.

An attempt was made to collect this information by the publisher of the *Official Catholic Directory*. It would have been a rather easy task for a pastor to go through his funeral record and tabulate such data. Unfortunately, only about a quarter of the pastors cooperated, making any such estimates virtually impossible.

It is reasonable to conclude that Catholics are about a quarter of the American people, a little less than 60 million in number. Until the American population reaches stability (births replacing deaths but not adding to the population) the Catholic numbers will continue to increase, although the proportion Catholic may decline slightly because of the decline in Catholic birth rate (if that decline is not cancelled by immigration).

There are four possible ways to prevent this slow erosion—more births, more converts, more immigrants, fewer defections. The last might seem the most promising, but it must be noted that, whatever the cause of defections, the present rate is not a result of the Vatican Council, post-conciliar changes in the church, nor changes in American society, because the rate has not changed since 1960. Whatever the nature of the defection problem, its causes are deeper than the current controversies in the church.

One might observe in passing that attempts at "evangelization," which do not ask questions about the high Catholic defection rate, seem to be misplaced—if not foolish. My research suggests that the most serious cause of defection—over and above the "average"—is the way authority is exercised, especially at the parish level (Greeley 1979).

The Mobility of Catholics

In 1961, half the Catholics in the country were immigrants or the children of immigrants. Yet a quarter of the college graduates in the country were Catholic (Greeley 1964). American Catholics had one foot in the immigrant era and one foot in the upper-middle-class professional suburb. Thirty years later, many observers both in and outside the Catholic church are not sure that the descendents of Catholic immigrants have succeeded in American society. In fact, there is no reasonable doubt about that success. In 1987 and 1988, the average white Protestant income was $24,899 (according to NORC's *General Social Surveys*). The average Catholic income was $28,367. Catholic income was fourteen percent higher than Protestant income.

In the middle 1980s,[2] 61 percent of the Catholics in the country were white-collar workers, as opposed to 55 percent of the white Protestants. Twenty-one percent of Catholics were professionals, as opposed to 19 percent of white Protestants. Thirty-nine percent of Catholics had attended college, as had 37 percent of white Protestants.[3]

In the beginning of the 1970s, 27 percent of the Catholic population had attended college and 29 percent of Protestants. Thus the Catholic increase in little more than a decade was 12 percentage points, a 44 percent increase in the number of college educated people within the Catholic population. Those clergy and hierarchy who think that somehow the Big change in the social status of their people is over could not be more wrong. If anything, the pace of change will increase because the proportion of Catholics attending college is still accelerating.

One way of mapping the social change of a population is to consider the educational and occupational decisions made by those who are young adults at different points in the population's history. The 20 thousand cases in NORC's *General Social Surveys* provide enough data for us to be able to "walk back" the Catholic population to the decisions of those who were born before 1900 and who made their career decisions during the First World War. Even at that time, when immigrants were still pouring into the country, 13 percent of young American Catholics were deciding to attend college. During the 1920s, the proportion remained steady at 13 percent. Despite the Great Depression, it rose to 18 percent in the 1930s. In the two decades after the war it increased again, first to 25 percent and then to 31 percent. The biggest increase in the century was during the 1960s when 47 percent of the Catholics coming of age elected to attend college (precisely at the time my own research was documenting the Catholic economic and educational revolution). In the 1970s the proportion increased to 52 percent and in the 1980s to 55 percent.

Catholic college attendance has doubled twice during the century. The proportion of young Catholics choosing professional careers has increased from 8 percent in the World War I era to 25 percent among young people reaching maturity today and the proportion of white-collar workers has risen from 44 percent to almost 70 percent.

These changes are impressive. They are also, given the history of American immigration, ordinary. The research of Barry Chiswick (1978) has shown that it takes the immigrant, on the average, 12 years to catch up in income with the native born of the same educational achievement. The sons of immigrants earn more income (by about 5%) than the sons of native born. America is indeed the land of opportunity, unless you happen to be Hispanic or native born black.

The mistake all along has been to assume that the children, grandchildren, and great grandchildren of Catholic (non-Hispanic) immigrants would somehow be excluded from this process of economic achievement because of handicaps imposed on them by their religion. It is safe to say that the assumption, however strongly some may still hold it (if only preconsciously), has been proven wrong. The Catholic story is merely the immigrant story, writ for a different religious group than the Protestant groups.

There are two different dynamics of upward mobility at work—that which affects the whole of society and that which affects those who at one time were disadvantaged in the society. The first is the enormous increase in higher education of the whole population in this century and the second is the even more rapid increase of certain groups which were catching up. We can picture both of these processes operating at the same time by imagining an ascending curved line (see Figure 1).[4] This represents the log of the odds of college attendance to non-attendance (the best way to measure proportions over time) from 1910 to the present for all white Americans. It is a slowly ascending curve.

Figure 2 smooths the curves in Figure 1 into trend lines. The top line is Irish Catholic, the middle two, (so close as to be almost the same line) are German Catholic and non-Catholic Americans. The bottom two lines, almost on top of one another, are the Polish and Italian Catholics. The ascent of that line to parity with the rest of the country is in a very simple sketch the story of the demography of American Catholics in this century.

One could draw similar upward swinging curves on other sheets of paper to represent proportion choosing white-collar and professional careers. The former is similar to the college attendance curve, the latter also climbs but the slope is more shallow.

Then we plot, on the same page, lines for four major Catholic European ethnic groups—Irish,, German, Italian, and Polish. The German line is more or less the same as the national average. The Irish line begins in 1910 at a level already above the national average and continues to climb so that at the end of the series it is even more distant from the average. There is a sharp drop in the 1930s (during the Great Depression), but the Irish line is still above the national average even then. After the Depression, it soars again.

The Polish and Italian lines are below the national line and move up at about the same rate as the national line (the slopes are a little less steep) until the 1940s; then they suddenly turn sharply upward, cross the national line in the 1960s and at the present stand above the national average, though not yet as high as the Irish.

In a brief scheme, this is the story of Catholic ethnic groups in the twentieth century, one of them on the average, another above the average even at the beginning of the century, the final two "catching up" at the time of the G. I. Bill after the war and moving ahead in the last couple of decades. It is, I emphasize, not an unusual story in itself. What is unusual is that this path up the American ladder of dreams happened to groups who were not supposed to prosper and whose prosperity is still an affront to many, including some of their own (who perhaps like to think that they are ahead of their fellow ethnics).

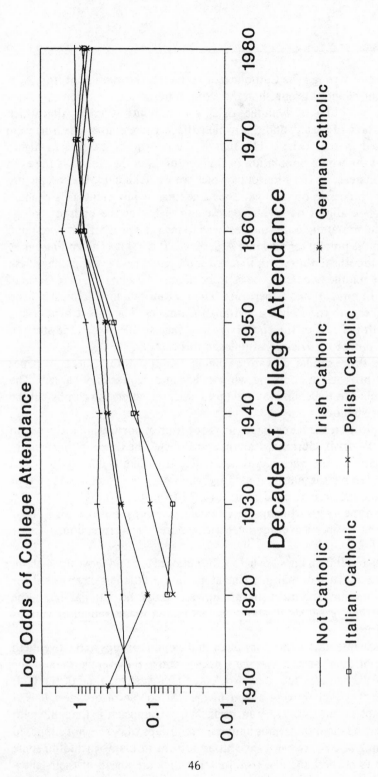

Figure 1. Odds of College Attendance by Religion and Ethnicity

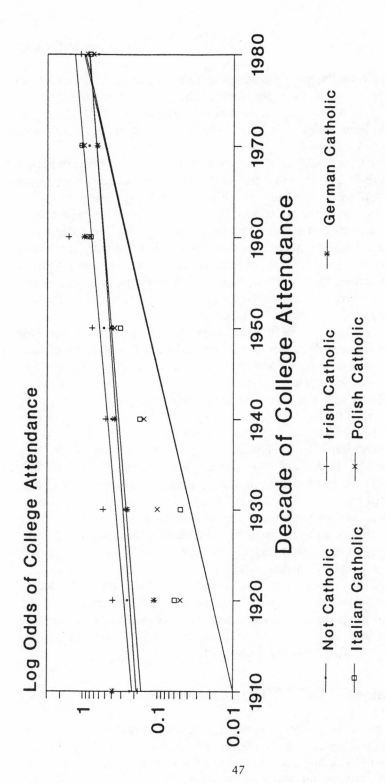

Figure 2. Trends in College Attendance by Religion and Ethnicity

47

Demographically the quarter century since the end of the Vatican Council was an era during which the more recent Catholic immigrant groups caught up with the rest of America in educational attainment. As a result, the proportion college educated in the Catholic population has accelerated dramatically and will continue to do so.

Oddly enough, the image of Catholics on the fringes of American society is shared by some Catholic leaders and theologians. Cardinal Joseph Bernardin writes, "The Church of the future in this country will not be able to rely on general social support, the structures of popular culture or the kind of civic leverage formerly wielded by priests in Bing Crosby movies." And theologian Avery Dulles writes, "We have as yet very few eminent Catholic intellectuals on the national scene. Catholics, whether clerical or lay, are not prominent in science, literature, the fine arts or even, I think, in the performing arts and communications. We have all too few Catholic political leaders and statesmen with a clear apostolic vision and commitment."

One can address the hypotheses in these two statements with data that show whether Catholics are adequately represented in the scholary and artistic elites. In the NORC's *General Social Surveys* (almost 23,000 cases) a little less than 2 percent of Americans fall in the category of scholars, writers, performers, and artists. Catholics are no less likely than anyone else (save for Jews) to be in that 2 percent. Moreover they are as likely to have Ph.D.s as anyone else. In addition, they seem to be successful in these areas because they earn five thousand dollars more than the national average for this category. Finally, they may not have what Father Dulles defines as "clear apostolic vision," but they go to church far more often than do their colleagues who are not Catholic, and more often than typical Catholics. About half of American Catholics go to Mass at least two or three times a month. Among those who fall in the artist-scholar-writer-performer category, 56 percent attend church regularly, a statistically significant difference (only 5% never attend Mass). Is this merely "nominal or perfunctory" membership?

Not only are the Catholic cultural elites still Catholic, they tend to be devout Catholics. If there are 40 million Catholic adults, there are almost a million Catholics who can make some claim to be part of the intellectual and cultural creative elites. More than half of them (approximately a half million) regularly show up at Sunday (or Saturday evening) Mass.

IMMIGRANT CATHOLICISM—STILL ALIVE?

Freedom of inquiry in the United States is limited by an extra-legal restriction on the right of the census to ask a religious affiliation question. Thus the issue of religion and immigration can be addressed statistically only by analyzing survey data. In this section, I propose to rely on data from NORC's *General*

Social Surveys (Davis and Smith 1989). I am at least as well aware as any critic of the limitations of this approach. For example, it is likely to underestimate Hispanics and hence Catholics among immigrants. It is impossible to specify the recency of the immigration event. The wording of NORC's question will include within the "immigrants" respondents who were born of American citizens residing out of the country. Moreover, 7 percent of the "immigrants" list their country of origin in another item as Puerto Rico, which is hardly a foreign country.[5]

As can be observed in Table 5, 42 percent of first generation Americans and 46 percent of second generation Americans are Catholic as opposed to 20 percent of the third generation. Eleven percent of Catholics are immigrants and 22 percent are the children of immigrants. Thus a third of American Catholics are immigrants or children of immigrants[6] Jews, "others," and those with no religion are also over-represented among immigrants. Protestants, in contrast, are drastically under-represented among immigrants—approximately only a third of immigrants. There does not seem to be a shift in these proportions in the last decade (see Table 6). The distribution is basically the same at both time periods.

Table 5. Religion by Generation
(In Percent)

	First[1]	*Second*[2]	*Third*[3]
Protestant	34	37	71
Catholic	42	46	20
Jewish	5	7	1
None	10	7	7
Other	9	3	1
Total	100	100	100
(Total Respondents)	($N = 1003$)	($N = 1855$)	($N = 12,818$)

Notes: [1]"Were you born in this country?" No.

[2]"Were both your parents born in this country?" No.

[3]"Were both your parents born in this country?" Yes.

Source: NORC's *General Social Surveys* for 1977-1988 (Davis and Smith 1989).

Table 6.   Religion of Immigrants by Time of Survey
(In Percent)

	1977-1983	1984-1988
Protestant	35	32
Catholic	42	43
Jewish	5	5
None	9	10
Other	7	10
Total	100	100
(Total Respondents)	(N =514)	(N =489)

Source: NORC's *General Social Surveys* for 1977-1988 (Davis and Smith 1989).

The immigrants (though not their children) are a little less likely to attend church at least two or three times a month than third generation Americans and notably less likely to believe in life after death[7] although this is the result of a larger proportion saying that they are undecided on the subject (see Table 7). Immigrants and their children are as likely as third generation Americans to say that they are "strong" in their denominational affiliation. They are, however, much less likely to belong to "fundamentalist" denominations (Smith 1986).

The difference between the first and second generation and the third generation in belief in life after death cannot be accounted for by different proportions Hispanic, non-European, Catholic, or non-fundamentalist, nor by differences in age or education. Interestingly enough, the differences between generational groups (see Table 8) in belief in life after death is greater among older respondents than among younger respondents—there being no relationship between age and belief among the third generation and a negative relationship among the first and second generation. (Older immigrants and the older children of immigrants are less likely to believe in life after death than younger immigrants and their children.) Thus, the three items that measure religious attitudes and behavior in the *General Social Surveys* do not indicate that immigration will produce a less "religious" population or a more "religious" population. Forty-five percent of the Catholic immigration is "non-European" as opposed to 32 percent of the non-Catholic population; a third of the Catholic immigration is "Spanish Origin" (see Table 9).

The proportion of Protestants, and especially fundamentalist Protestants, in American society will diminish (if only marginally) as immigration accounts for a portion of the "natural" increase in the population. The country seems to be in the process of becoming more Catholic (and more Jewish, "other" and "none"). However, a closer look at the demography of American

Table 7. Religious Behavior and Attitudes by Generation
(In Percent)

	Generation		
	First	*Second*	*Third*
Church at least two or three times a month	42	46	45
Belief in life after death	67	67	81
"Strong" religious affiliation	44	45	44
"Fundamentalist" affiliation	14	12	38

Source: NORC's *General Social Surveys* for 1977-1988 (Davis and Smith 1989).

Table 8. Belief in Life after Death by Generation and Age

	Generation	
Age	*First and Second*	*Third*
20s	70%	78%
	(271)*	(2223)
30s	70%	81%
	(315)	(1954)
40s	68%	81%
	(229)	(1301)
50s	65%	83%
	(241)	(1020)
60s	67%	82%
	(334)	(915)
70s	64%	83%
	(336)	(782)

Note: *Number of respondents in parentheses.
Source: NORC's *General Social Surveys* for 1977-1988 (Davis and Smith 1989).

Table 9.   Origins by Generation and Religion
(Percent Not European)

| | Generation | | |
	First	Second	Third
Catholic	45%	14%	9%
	(414)*	(800)	(2209)
Not Catholic	32%	8%	15%
	(542)	(887)	(7363)

Note: *Number of respondents in parentheses.
Source: NORC's *General Social Surveys* for 1977-1988 (Davis and Smith 1989).

Catholicism suggests that the increase in Catholic affiliation may be less than meets the eye because of the defection rate of American Catholics and especially the defection rate of Catholics of "Spanish Origin" who constitute a third of the Catholic immigrants. As I reported in the first section of this paper, Catholics have constituted about a quarter of Americans for the last 30 years, but this constant proportion masks a shift in distribution within the Catholic population. The Catholic defection rate during the last third of a century has been routinely 15 percent—about one out of every six of those who are raised Catholic are no longer Catholic.[8] Indeed if one looks at the religion in which a respondent was raised, then half of the immigrants and their children were Catholic at one time.

That there are no traces of this decline in the proportion reporting themselves Catholic in national surveys is the result of the high proportion of Catholics among immigrants and their children. The tables in this section of the paper demonstrate that if it were not for the immigrants and their children Catholics would constitute only a fifth and not a fourth of the American population. Given the rate of decline of Catholics among "Spanish Origin" immigrants and their children, it may well be that the increase in Catholicism through immigration will do little more than replace those who have left the Catholic church.

Catholics of Spanish Origin are defecting to Protestant denominations at the rate of approximately 60 thousand people a year. Over the past 15 years this departure from Catholicism has amounted to almost a million men and women, almost one of ten (8%) of the Spanish Catholic population. This conclusion is based on an analysis of respondents of "Spanish Origin" in NORC's annual *General Social Surveys*. There are, according to the census, some 17 million Americans of Spanish Origin. It is routinely assumed that most, if not all, of these are Catholics. In fact, according to the *General Social*

Surveys only 70 percent of those of Spanish origins (Mexican, Puerto Rican, and "Other Spanish") are Catholic and 22 percent are Protestants. Thus, at the most, only 12 million of the population reported by the census are Catholic.

If one pools all the annual *General Social Surveys* since 1972, one has a Spanish Origin sample of 790, a sufficient number for analysis of the change in the last decade and the difference between Protestant and Catholic Hispanics. There are weaknesses in the *General Social Survey* sample: it has been assembled over 16 years, it is not based on a Hispanic sampling frame (which does not exist), it represents interviews only with those who speak English, it probably misses the poorest of Hispanic respondents (as do all surveys). However, it is, as far as I know, the only data set, based on a national probability sample, that provides detailed information on the religion in which a respondent was raised and the religion with which the respondent currently identifies.

In the first four years of the *General Social Surveys* (1972-1975), 16 percent of Spanish Origin respondents were Protestant (and 7% some other religion or no religion). In the four most recent years (1985-1988), 23 percent were Protestant (and 7% other or no religion). Thus, in the early 1970s, 77 percent of the Hispanics were Catholic. In the middle 1980s that had declined to 71 percent. The difference between the two time periods is statistically significant (at the .02 level). The Protestant segment of Americans of Hispanic origin is not only large, it is growing rapidly.

The defection rates are higher among Puerto Ricans (24%) and "others" (26%) than among Mexican Americans (15%). They are lower in the West (17%) than in the East (23%). Thirty-six percent of those who are currently Protestant were raised Protestant, making them at least second generation converts. A little more than three-fifths of both Catholic and Protestant Hispanics are native born. About a third of each group are the children of native born parents (so immigration does not seem to correlate with religious affiliation).

More than three-fourths of the Spanish Origin Protestants are either Baptists or Fundamentalists. Moreover, they are more likely to believe in life after death than their Catholic counterparts (80% as opposed to 64%), more likely to reject abortion on demand (79% as opposed to 69%), more likely to think that premarital sex is always wrong (37% versus 26%), and much more likely to attend church regularly: 23 percent of the Catholics go to church every week as opposed to 49 percent of the Protestants (29% more than once a week). Thus it would seem that the Protestant Hispanics have joined fervent Protestant groups in which their religion provides them with intense activity and community support. By some norms of religious behavior they are better Catholics than those who have stayed.

There are two explanations for the defection of Catholics to Protestant denominations, especially to the sects to which most of them seem to be going:

1.   Because the Catholic Church fails to reach the poorest of its Spanish members a vacuum has been created into which the sects can rush with their enthusiasm, their grass roots ministry, their concern about the religious problems of ordinary people, and their "native" (and married) clergy.

2.   The sects have a special appeal to the new middle class because they provide a means of breaking with the old traditions and becoming responsible and respectable members of the American middle class (much as Catholicism provides a middle-class niche for some upwardly mobile Blacks). The Catholic church's failure in this perspective is to provide community and respectability for the upwardly mobile Hispanic American. This explanation is supported by analysis done (most notably by the late Anne Parsons [1969] of Italian-American Pentecostals during the 1930s and 1940s, an analysis that saw the Protestant sects as a means of "Americanization" for some Italians.

This second model seems to fit the data in Table 10 better than the first. Protestant Hispanics are better educated, make more money, are more likely to be married, and are more likely to be managers and white-collar workers than Hispanic Catholics. Moreover, they come from backgrounds in which there was more paternal education.

Becoming Protestant has apparently an economic and social payoff for Hispanics. The second generation Protestants (those who say they were raised Protestant) have on the average 11.3 years of education and earned on the average $27,000 a year. Fifty-two percent of them are white-collar workers and 28 percent are managers. They remain fervent Protestants—26 percent of them attend church more than once a week.[9]

Table 10.   Differences Between Hispanic Catholics and Protestants

	Protestants (N = 197)	*Catholics* (N = 593)
Income	$25,000	$19,000
Education	10.8 years	10.4 years
Percent Managers	21%	13%
Percent White Collar	45%	38%
Married	70%	63%
Father's Education	7.1 years	6.3 years

Note: All differences are statistically significant at the .01 level.
Source: NORC's *General Social Surveys* for 1972-1988 (Davis and Smith 1989).

Protestant Hispanics do indeed look like an upwardly mobile middle class for whom the Protestant denomination provides both a way of becoming acceptably American and a support community in which they are comfortable as they break with their old religious heritage. It is not only their old religion which is left behind. Fifty-nine percent of Hispanic Catholics are Democrats, while only 44 percent of Spanish Protestants are Democrats.

The success of the sects, then, seems to be the result of the failure of the Catholic church to be responsive to the emotional, communal, and religious needs of some of the new Hispanic middle class. The loss of almost one out of ten members of its largest ethnic group is an ecclesiastical failure of unprecedented proportions, one that is matched only by the failure of the Catholic church in the first half of the nineteenth century to retain the affiliation of Irish rural proletarians (farm laborers) who migrated to the American South before the Great Famine (Greeley 1988; Shaughnessy 1925). Like many of the Hispanic migrants, the Irish speaking prefamine Irish laborers (the so-called bog Irish) were only loosely affiliated with organized Catholicism. However, unlike the present American Catholic church, that of the early nineteenth century lacked the resources of money and personnel to respond to the prefamine immigration.

CONCLUSION

The form of this paper is also a sketch of the demographic history of American Catholicism during the quarter century after the Second Vatican Council—rapid social and economic change between two massive immigrations. Since 1965, the children and the grandchildren of the pre-1920 immigration caught up with and indeed surpassed the rest of the country on the ordinary measures of achievement and at the same time remained Catholic. In the same time period, a new wave of immigration, almost half of which was Catholic in its origins, has arrived on America's shores. Some of that group seems to be leaving the church, threatening a possible long-term decline in the proportion Catholic.

The church which dealt successfully with the beginning of the century crisis seems incapable of responding to the end of the century crisis—even though it has far more resources available now than it did then.

It is hard to see how the Second Vatican Council can be blamed for this latter crisis. However, the independence of the American bishops at the Council may well have so frightened the Roman Curia that it decided to appoint only "safe" bishops—which meant bishops who could not respond to any serious problem, whether it be the disenchantmant of the old wave of immigrants with incompetence and insensitivity or the departure of the new wave.

A three-word summary of the last quarter century: success, then failure.

56   ANDREW M. GREELEY

NOTES

1.   Why would pastoral estimates decline? In part perhaps because of the impression that the number of their parishioners is declining and perhaps in part because they know they will be taxed on the numbers reported.

2.   These statistics represent *General Social Surveys* data pooled in 4-year groupings.

3.   Catholics include Hispanics; and Protestants do not include blacks.

4.   The apparent down sweep of the line in the last two decades is caused by the fact that observations in the *General Social Surveys* began in 1972 and continue to the present. Many young men and women in the last two cohorts were still coming of age during the last two decades and were not yet embarking on their college education.

5.   In this paper, those whose parents are born abroad are called "first" generation, those who are native born with at least one parent born abroad are called "second" generation, and those whose parents were born in the United States are called "third" generation—meaning third and subsequent generations.

6.   In 1960, half of the Catholic population was either first or second generation American.

7.   Question wording: "Do you believe in life after death?"

8.   Some three-fifths of the "defectors" have joined another Christian denomination in conjunction with marriage, the other two-fifths have rejected all denominational affiliation. About half of this latter group eventually return to Catholicism during the life-cycle, a return taken into account in the over all 15 percent defection rate.

9.   The *General Social Survey* is available at most university computer centers. The income variable, based on corrections for inflation developed by Michael Hout, may not be on all data sets yet.

REFERENCES

Chiswick, B.R. 1978. "The Effects of Americanization on the Earnings of Foreign-Born Men." *Journal of Political Economy* 86(5): 897-921.

Davis, J. A., and T.W. Smith. 1989. *General Social Surveys, 1972-1989. Cumulative Codebook.* Chicago: National Opinion Research Center.

Greeley, A. 1964. *Religion and Career.* New York: Sheed and Ward.

————. 1979. *Crisis in the Church.* Chicago: Thomas More Press.

————. 1988. "The Success and Assimilating of Irish Protestants and Irish Catholics in the United States." *Sociology and Social Research* 72:229-236.

Hout, M., and A. Greeley. 1987. "The Center Does Not Hold: Church Attendance in the United States, 1940-1984." *American Sociological Review* 52:325-345.

Official Catholic Directory. 1986. Wilmette, IL: P. J. Kennedy.

Parsons, A. 1969. *Belief, Magic, and Anomie.* New York: Free Press.

Shaughnessy, G. 1925. *Has the Immigrant Kept the Faith? A Study of Immigration and Catholic Growth in the United States.* New York: Longmans, Green.

Smith, T.W. 1986. *Classifying Protestant Denominations.* General Social Survey Technical Report No. 66. Chicago: National Opinion Research Center.

Statistical Abstract. 1985. Washington, DC: Bureau of the Census.

4

American Exceptionalism:
The Religious Phenomenon

Andrew Greeley

I propose in this chapter to present a sketch of religion in the United States based on my professional tools, survey research data, to ask whether this portrait does indeed make American religion 'exceptional', and to suggest some reasons why religion in the United States might differ from religion in Great Britain and on the continent. This is not an essay about the nature of religion. It is rather a much more modest effort to determine whether the tools of survey research are able to confirm the hypothesis that self-reported religious behaviour in America has diminished in the last four decades. To use the language of the logic of social research: can one safely reject the null hypothesis that the survey indicators show no major change in American self-reported religious behaviour?

To anticipate my conclusions:

1. There have been only marginal changes in American religious attitudes and behaviours since the first years when survey material was available to us. Projections based on age and cohort analysis suggest that there will be no major changes in the years immediately ahead.

2. There is some question as to whether the high levels of religious devotion in the United States are 'exceptional' in the English-speaking world of the North Atlantic. More probably, if there is an exception, it is Great Britain not the United States—and only in one component of the British population.

3. Religion in the United States seems to differ from religion in Great Britain in that it has more capability to confer identity in the former than in the latter. In those British groups where one may assume that religion does have some identity-conferring potential, the levels of religious devotion do not differ from those in the United States.

Because my argument may seem strange even to some of my American colleagues—counter-intuitive, opposed to what everyone knows to

The Religious Phenomenon 95

be true—I must set the argument in the context of my own approach to research, a context which at the very beginning must express systematic scepticism about what everyone knows to be true. Whatever I may be when I wear other hats, I am an empiricist when I am doing social research; that is to say, I begin by seeking evidence to disconfirm the null hypothesis at the start of my investigations. In this case the null hypothesis is that there is no social change. Only when I can reject that hypothesis do I endeavour to explain the social change I have tentatively established.

Another way of describing this approach is to say that if a proposition cannot be falsified it cannot be verified. If research is not structured in such a way that the thesis of the researcher is not subject to falsification, then it cannot be established as even provisionally true. Thus when Professor Bellah and his colleagues tell me that civil responsibility in America has declined and individualism has increased during the last hundred years, I beg to be excused from accepting such an assertion in the absence of any serious attempt to falsify it, to confirm the null hypothesis that there is no such change.[1] The intensity with which Professor Bellah and his colleagues feel the truth of their argument is not a substitute for the search for evidence to disconfirm it. The evidence does not have to be survey evidence of the sort I use in my own work. Obviously surveys were not taken during the last century. But I want some evidence which, if the indicators go the 'wrong' way, would disprove their thesis. Until I observe the search for such evidence, I simply will not accept an argument as anything more than a deeply felt opinion.

Secondly, I am interested in the behaviour of people and not of church leaders, theologians, or church organizations. When someone purports to describe the changes in American religion by detailing the changing stands of theologians, the changing editorials of church publications, or the changing resolutions of clergy in solemn assembly, I take these data as proving only that there have been changes in institutional leadership. That some priests march on picket lines indicates only an upswing in clerical involvement in politics and *not* a change in political attitudes of the men and women who belong to the institution.

Thirdly, while I am aware of the weaknesses of my own data and willingly accept other data sources, I will not apologize for survey data.

[1] Robert N. Bellah *et al.*, *Habits of the Heart: Individualism and Commitment in American Life* (Berkeley: University of California Press, 1985). See also Bellah, *The Broken Covenant: American Civil Religion in Time of Trial* (New York: Seabury Press, 1975).

96   *Andrew M. Greeley*

Everyone uses samples of some sort and everyone asks questions. The issue is how the samples are chosen, how the questions are worded, how the data are collected, and how the data are analysed. What a professor hears at a cocktail party, what a pastor thinks about his parish, and what everyone knows to be true are also findings that represent results of informal surveys. I am not prepared to admit that my data are inferior.

Minimally, I expect scholars using other data sources to take survey findings seriously, especially when such findings challenge their own conclusion. Survey results may not capture the whole of reality; neither do any other kinds of data. But they do measure at least one aspect of reality and hence cannot be lightly dismissed, especially when they run against what everyone knows to be true. I confess to a certain impatience with some historians and humanists who dismiss survey scholarship from the lordly position of their own wisdom, or assert that respondents are not telling the truth, or try to refute survey findings with anecdotes.

In each case, their own methods are not more solid but only less explicit. The historian tries to recreate the past from documents which are a sample of possible descriptions of the past, usually a sample with a powerful élite bias. Moreover, the historian picks and chooses from the testimony of his or her documents, usually without any explicit description or explanation for the decisions made about judging testimony. Finally, the anecdote-teller's stories may be more interesting than survey results and more entertaining than survey tables. None the less, he or she is reporting from a sample of data and, like the historian, is also sampling within the data sets available in his or her memory. The only real difference between these two kinds of wise and witty critics and the survey scholar is that the latter has eliminated personal bias from the process of sample selection and has been forthright about the limitations of his data.

'But there has been change', some critics say of my failure to find much change in American religion in the last half century. Surely some things have changed, but some things have remained remarkably consistent too. The consistencies must not be dismissed merely because everyone knows that they cannot be true—not when a legitimate mode of analysis demonstrates that what everyone knows to be true is not *in fact* true. For a number of years I worked on a board of an international Catholic magazine which wanted (or thought it wanted) an American empiricist among its members. Whenever I would present an article about the work of my colleagues and myself, continental theologians would first of all label it as 'positivism', as though such a label dismissed it out of hand. Then they would ask why I had not taken into account the theories of the Marxists or of the Frankfurt school. To which I would reply that I did not give a damn about either unless they had evidence that called into question my own evidence. I cite this not to establish the correctness of my position but rather to illustrate what my position is.

The conventional wisdom among those Americans who write about religion—clergymen, journalists, academics, even sociologists not specializing in empirical sociology of religion—is that American religion is 'declining'. When I was asked by the Social Science Research Council to write a monograph on American religion for the Harvard University Press social indicators series on America, I was told that my principle task would be to document the ever-increasing power of secularization in American society. I replied that I would be happy to write the book, but no one should count on that being the finding. It took a year-and-a-half struggle with referees who 'knew' that I had to be wrong before the book was finally forced towards publication. Something had to have changed, had it not?

The problem is that those who write on religion and most academics are not religious themselves. Neither are their families or friends. Since many of them came from religious backgrounds, they naturally assume that their own biographies are typical. Scholarly restraint ought to incline them to scepticism about their own typicality. But, on the subject of religion, scholarly restraint is a notoriously weak quality.

A typical élite position on American religion was expressed one night on the NBC evening news when Tom Brokaw reported that the latest edition of the Statistical Abstract contained one more piece of evidence for the declining importance of American religion: there had been no increase in the previous year in church membership. When the absence of an increase is taken to be proof of a decline we have left behind all the rules of logic and entered the area of religious faith! *Credo ut intelligam.* (I believe so that I may understand.) Incidentally, while one can hardly expect TV news writers to be aware of it, any decline or indeed any levelling off of increase in a society with a disproportionately youthful population (as the United States still is, under the impact of the 'baby boom') must be examined to determine whether the change is the result of age composition and not of cultural or structural change.

Alongside the conventional wisdom that American religion is in decline is the opposite conventional wisdom of a 'surge' of religious fundamentalism, of the 'emergence' of the 'religious right' or the 'moral

98   *Andrew M. Greeley*

majority'. On the one hand, the forces of secularization are eroding religion; on the other, the radical fundamentalists are increasing in numbers, importance, and influence: this, I submit, is the conventional wisdom not only of the national press but also of the faculty dining rooms.

How can such positions be held with any consistency? Since both of them are in fact pre-conscious imagery and not explicitly articulated propositions, there is no necessity for consistency. One can feel, on the one hand, quite confident that science and education are diminishing the importance of religion and, on the other hand, frightened about the effect of massive waves of fundamentalists on society. If one strives for some sort of consistency, one can always use the strategy of Peter Berger and talk about 're-sacralization', a countervailing force to 'secularization'.

One can use such an approach if one has no concern about empirical evidence. Yet it is very difficult indeed to find any—I repeat, *any*— evidence of either phenomenon in the survey data. When George Gallup, sen., asked the first question about whether you 'happened' to attend church or synagogue last week in the early 1940s, the proportion that had 'happened' to attend church was 40 per cent. It's still 40 per cent almost a half-century later.

In the first Roper question about belief in life after death, also in the 1940s, a little more than 70 per cent of Americans said that they were 'certain' about such continuance of life. In the 1987 NORC General Social Survey the proportion was exactly the same. Nor does such a conviction correlate with age or education at either point in time; both the young and the old, the college-educated and those who did not even attend secondary school, believe in survival in almost exactly the same proportions.

As to the 'rise' of the fundamentalists, twenty years ago some 22 per cent of Americans believed in the literal interpretation of the Bible, described themselves as 'born again', and said that they had tried to convert someone else to Jesus. This proportion has not changed. Indeed, acceptance of the literal interpretation has not declined, as we shall see shortly. The 'fundamentalist' right is now, as it was two decades ago, about a fifth of the American population. It has always been an important part of the American religious scene. The First Great Awakening, after all, occurred in 1744. The change in the last decade is that the élite media in New York, under the impact of the Reagan election, have rediscovered the fundamentalist fifth of Americans. As a rule of thumb, most 'trends' reported in *Time* and *Newsweek* and similar media outlets

The Religious Phenomenon 99

are a rediscovery of something that has always existed outside of New York, Washington, and Boston.[2]

But surely the 'moral majority' has more political clout than it used to have? When I'm asked that, I reply by asking if the questioner has ever heard of Prohibition? A surprising number either have not heard of it or do not see the point. So I have to explain that the religious right wing of our nation deprived the rest of the country of the right to consume alcoholic beverages for a decade and a half in the early part of this century. The rise of the moral majority is a falsehood on all three counts—it has not risen, it is not especially moral, and it certainly is not a majority.

To summarize what has happened to American religion during the era of social surveys (twenty-five years for most items, almost fifty for some): with the exception of some shuffling of denominational affiliation, Protestantism has not changed. Catholicism has changed, but not much, and the change is over.[3]

Most of the lines one would draw on a graph of American religious behaviour through the years are straight lines: more than 95 per cent believe in God; 77 per cent believe in the divinity of Jesus; 72 per cent believe in life after death with certainty, while another 20 per cent are unsure; 70 per cent believe in hell, 67 per cent in angels, 50 per cent in the devil; 34 per cent belong to a church-related organization; a third have had some kind of intense religious experience; half pray at least once a day and a quarter pray more than once a day; a third have a great deal of confidence in religious leadership; more than half think of themselves as very religious. Defection rates have not increased since 1960 and intermarriage rates have not changed significantly across Protestant and Catholic lines in the same time period.

Only three indicators show a decline—church attendance, financial contributions, and belief in the literal interpretation of the scripture. All three declines are limited to Catholics. The decline among Catholics in the acceptance of the literal interpretation of the Bible is limited to the young and the college-educated, and especially the young who are college-educated. Moreover, it is a decline accounted for by a change

[2] Tom Smith of the staff of NORC's General Social Survey has studied in detail the membership patterns of 'fine-tuned' denominational affiliation—the sort which distinguish, for example, among the various Baptist sub-denominations—and reports that there has been no statistically significant increase in the proportion (about 35%) of Americans in fundamentalist denominations since 1967.

[3] Andrew M. Greeley, *Religious Change in America* (Cambridge, Mass.: Harvard University Press, 1989).

100   *Andrew M. Greeley*

to a position which is quite properly orthodox for Catholics—acceptance of the general message of the scripture as inspired without believing the literal interpretation of each word.

In 1968, 65 per cent of American Catholics attended Mass every week. Seven years later, 1975, that proportion had fallen to 50 per cent. In the ensuing thirteen years there has been no further decline. In 1960, 12 per cent of those born Catholic no longer described themselves as Catholic. By 1987 that proportion had increased, age composition taken into account, to 13 per cent. The traumatic change of the quarter-century had led to an increase of 1 per cent in the Catholic 'defection' rate—leading one to observe that there is probably nothing more that the clergy, the hierarchy, and the Vatican could do that would drive American Catholics out of the church.

In 1960 Protestants contributed 2.2 per cent of their income to their churches. In 1985 they continued to contribute the same 2.2 per cent. In 1960 Catholics also gave 2.2 per cent. In 1985 this proportion had declined to 1.1 per cent, costing the Catholic Church six billion dollars in lost income. Both the decline in Mass attendance and in financial contribution can be accounted for (statistically) by lay anger over the encyclical on birth control. Moreover, this anger affected different segments of the Catholic population differently. Church attendance declined only six percentage points among Catholics who described themselves as 'strong' Democrats or Republicans and thirty percentage points among those who described themselves as 'pure' political independents. Loyalty to the party and loyalty to the church, in other words, correlated with one another.

Michael Hout of the University of California and I subjected the correlation to a stringent statistical analysis developed by the Swiss psychometrician George Rasch to determine whether there was a latent variable linking the two, one that responded to certain precise constraints.[4] There did indeed seem to be such a relationship which we dubbed 'loyalty', a variable which resisted the negative impact of the birth control encyclical. This finding is, I believe, central to the American religious phenomenon: denominational heritages have a strong grip on Americans. They are given up only reluctantly because they are so integral to the specific forms of American pluralism. One is constrained to be loyal to that which defines what one is.

In addition to measuring simple change from survey to survey, it is

[4] Michael Hout and Andrew M. Greeley, 'The Center Doesn't Hold: Church Attendance in the United States, 1940–1984', *American Sociological Review*, 52 (June 1987), 325–45.

possible, if one has enough measures at different points in time, to analyse the relationship between age and cohort to determine if more recent age cohorts are less religious than their predecessors when the latter were the same age. Many European sociologists use an age relationship (religious variables correlating negatively with age) to prove a decline of religion. They forget that young people are less likely than older people to have made definite choices about career, job, party affiliation, place of residence, and permanent sexual partner. There is no reason to assume on a priori grounds that religion would be an exception to this pattern. That the more recent cohorts are less religious than their predecessors cannot be assumed, but remains to be proven.

In the cohort analysis in which Hout and I have engaged, the four following findings have emerged:

1. There is relationship between age and religion which affects most religious measures. Religious behaviour declines sharply between 18 and 25, begins to climb again in the late 20s and increases sharply in the 30s and 40s, then tapers off in the 50s. In general, this curve fits the most recent cohorts as well as the cohorts born in the 1920s.

2. Moreover, since the intercepts of the various cohorts (the rate of religious behaviour at which they enter the 'system' in their late teens) do not differ significantly, it is possible to simulate models which project church attendance rates till the year 2000. The most recent cohorts (born in the 1960s) will be as likely as their parents to attend church weekly: when the former reach their 40s, some three-fifths will be weekly church-goers.

3. There is, as noted briefly above, a shift of denominational affiliation occurring among Protestants, away from the 'main line' churches and towards the more conservative churches. Especially hard hit are the Methodists who were 22 per cent of Protestants born in the 1920s and only 11 per cent of those born in the 1960s. However, this 'realignment' has not involved any change in doctrinal position (including views on the literal interpretation of the Bible), church attendance, or political and social and moral positions.

4. When age is taken into account, there is a marginally significant relationship (.03) between cohort and denominational affiliation ('Protestant', 'Catholic', 'Jew', or 'other'). At present, some 3 per cent of Americans over 50 have no denominational affiliation. That will increase in years to come, we project, to 6 per cent. This increase is entirely explained by the later age at marriage and the proportion of the population never marrying. Both the change in marriage patterns and in

102   *Andrew M. Greeley*

denominational affiliation were phenomena of the 1970s. Since 1980, neither have changed.

The power of cohort analysis as a tool is enormous because it can demonstrate whether there are signs of deviation from the life-cycle path of religious behaviour in cohorts that were born forty years apart. Almost no such deviations are to be found among Americans. Indeed, among Catholics the decline in Mass attendance in response to the birth control encyclical was evenly distributed in all age cohorts and not limited merely to the younger generations. Thus my two sentences stand. With the exception of denominational rearrangements, American Protestantism has not changed. Catholicism has changed, but the change seems to have stopped.

Yet those two sentences of summary seem absurd. Protestantism has experienced the rise and fall of Neo-orthodoxy, the death and rebirth of the Social Gospel, migration from farm and small town to the city, the appearance of the electronic evangelist, the 'surge' (or rediscovery) of fundamentalism and evangelicalism, the musical chairs of various denominational mergers, social and political conflict between activist clergy and conservative laity, the clerically launched and led Civil Rights Movement, renewed controversy between literalist and non-literalist interpretation of scripture, and the endless battle between science and religion.

Catholicism has experienced the twin transformation of the embourgeoisement of the children of the immigrant and the *aggiornomento* of the Second Vatican Council. Its people have moved from the immigrant city to the professional suburbs, from unquestioning loyalty to frequently contentious independence, from Latin to English, from the Counter-reformation to the ecumenical age, from pious and docile nuns to strident supporters of the ordination of women, from the Baltimore Catechism to the Charismatic Renewal. Priests and nuns have left the active ministry by the thousands, others have become involved in radical political and social movements, sometimes with Marxist tones, still others have doffed distinctive garb, insist on being called by first names, and instead of pretending that they have no personal problems, insist that their problems become the topic of constant conversation. Non-Catholic students flock to parochial grammar schools, Liberation Theology is taught in Catholic high schools, professed atheists hold chairs of theology in Catholic universities.

How can I possibly argue that there has been no change in Protestantism and only minor change in Catholicism? There are two answers to the question. The first is to question whether there is as much change as meets the eye in the descriptions of the previous paragraphs and to wonder how much the actual changes affect the daily religious life and faith of ordinary Catholic and Protestant laity. Is not the 'changing church' a concern of the clergy, the lay élites, and the denominational journals of opinion rather than of the typical congregants? Is not the 'changing church' model an example of the 'Future Shock' fallacy, the utterly gratuitous assumption that changes in technology and environment must, without any need for proof, cause a change in fundamental dimensions of human life? Have not church members through the years shown remarkable skill in drawing from their faith what they want and need regardless of what the current organizational and theological fashions might be among their élites?

Priests on picket lines are news. But as dramatic as TV clips of such activity may be, is there any reason to think that such clips have any but peripheral effects on the religious life of Catholics? The protests of Catholic activists during the Vietnam War are frequently alleged to have turned the Catholic laity from hawks to doves. But survey data show that Catholics were always more dovish than typical white Americans, that their turn against the war antedated the Catholic Peace Movement, and that after each major public anti-war demonstration, there was an increase in support for the Nixon administration's conduct of the war.

Are Catholics more likely than Protestants to oppose nuclear arms because of a pastoral letter by the American hierarchy? Or is the letter itself a result of lay concern? The survey data show that Catholics were more likely to think that too much money was being spent on weapons ten years ago, long before the pastoral letter. In other words, the ecclesiastical changes which the mass media note may have little effect on the religious life of individuals, families, and local communities. Such effect needs to be proven, not assumed.

A second response is to concede the fact and the importance of the changes in American Christianity, and then add that social indicator research cannot hope to describe all the aspects of a phenomenon but only those for which there exist time-series data. Social indicators are at best a skeleton of a body politic or a body religious, an incomplete trajectory, an outline, a sketch. They represent truth as far as they go, but not surely the whole truth. The ingenious reader will perceive that the second argument is merely a less contentious version of the first. A little less explicitly than the first it hints, 'alright, give us an operational measure of religious change and we'll try to find data to test it. Till then

104   *Andrew M. Greeley*

we stand by the data we have: The null hypothesis cannot be rejected!'

Catholic church attendance rates fell sharply from 1969 to 1975 but the decline stopped in 1975 and a new level of stability has been in effect since then. The decline was caused by the birth control encyclical, the stability by an underlying loyalty to the church. Bible reading has increased over the last century; prayer may have increased in the last fifteen years; certainly the willingness to admit to ecstatic and paranormal experiences has gone up.

There has been no discernible change in belief in God, the divinity of Jesus, life after death, the existence of heaven, and divine influence on the Bible. The pattern of denominational affiliations has not changed (save for a decline in Methodism) nor has propensity to become a church 'member' and to belong to a church-affiliated voluntary organization (which organizations still have the largest claim on American organizational membership). The self-professed 'strength' of religious affiliation has not changed and this 'strength' is proven by the fact that even among the most unreligious age group—those in their early 20s—half the Christians in the United States are inside a church at least once a month.

Basic doctrines, church attendance, prayer, organizational affiliation and activity, religious experience, location on the political spectrum—are not these indicators, as superficial and as naïve as they might seem, at least a rough measure of the basic condition of religion in America? If they have not changed, is there not reason to assert that there is a certain long-term stability in American religious behaviour, whatever important changes might also be occurring? If the null hypothesis—no change in American religious behaviour— is to be rejected, must not support for such rejection be found in data other than survey data? And where is such data to be found?

Theodore Caplow and his colleagues in their study of the religion of 'Middletown' (Muncie, Indiana, first studied by Robert and Helen Lynd in 1924) note that in the late 1970s and early 1980s Middletown's religion had not changed on eleven major indicators for which there were measures at the beginning and the end of the sixty-year period:

If secularization is a shrinkage of the religious sector in relation to other sectors of society . . . then it ought to produce some or all of the following indications: (1) a decline in the number of churches per capita of the population, (2) a decline in proportion of the population attending church services, (3) a decline in the proportion of rites of passage held under religious auspices (for example, declining ratios of religious to civil marriages and of religious to secular funerals), (4) a decline in religious endogamy, (5) a decline in the proportion of the labor force engaged in religious activity, (6) a decline in the proportion of income devoted to the support of religion, (7) a decline in the ratio of religious to non-religious literature, (8) a decline in the attention given to religion in the mass media, (9) a drift toward less emotional forms of participation in religious services, (10) a dwindling of new sects and of new movements in existing churches, and (11) an increase in attention paid to secular topics in sermons and liturgy.[5]

While admitting that religion has changed greatly in Middletown since the 1920s, Caplow found no support for any of the eleven hypotheses. Muncie, Indiana, is the nation described in the present essay writ small, a place of remarkable continuity in religious behaviour.

In certain academic, journalistic, and religious circles, the response to the obvious fact of the sustained religiousness of the American people in comparison with the behaviour of Western Europeans is to dismiss the American religious 'phenomenon' as 'not authentic'. American devotion, we are told, is to 'the American way of life' and not to God. It is a 'civil religion', a 'culture religion', a reinforcement of patriotism and political conservatism, a 'religion in general' without specific doctrinal challenge or content, a materialistic creed supporting American 'consumerism' (a favourite phrase of Pope John Paul II).

Why, it is often asked by those who are prepared to accept the data that researchers like Caplow have gathered, is the United States so different from Europe, where 'secularization' is so much further advanced? The tone of voice in which the question is asked seems to imply that it is a mark of inferiority to lag behind Europe in a matter so important as religion. I shall leave to others the question of how secularized Europe actually is and merely suggest that, if it is indeed secularized, then a consideration of the rest of the world suggests not that North America is unique, but that Europe is. Religion has lost none of its power in the Third World, despite the energies which we group under the label 'modernization'. Is Iran secularized? Brazil with its powerful syncretistic cults? Is Poland? Or Croatia? Indeed the non-Western religions all seem to be undergoing dramatic revivals—not that Judaism and Christianity can properly be called 'Western'. The apparent failure of Christianity in some countries in Europe is the deviant case if one takes a world perspective, not the norm, a fact which orthodox sociology—based as it is on the work of three great theorists of 'secularization', Marx, Durkheim, and Weber—is most reluctant to admit.

[5] Theodore Caplow *et al., All Faithful People: Change and Continuity in Middletown's Religion* (Minneapolis: University of Minnesota Press, 1983), 34–45.

106   *Andrew M. Greeley*

Our European counterparts, those who advance the civil religion argument seem to imply, may not be devout but at least they are hard-headed and not hypocritical. The proponents of a 'civil religion' interpretation in effect argue that there has been a notable change in American religion but that survey indicators cannot measure the phenomenon because the change—in the direction of secularization—is masked by the 'civil religion', the religion of 'the American Way of Life', of American patriotism.

The most sophisticated supporters of the theory of 'civil religion'—a term introduced into the discussion by the sociologist, Robert Bellah, in an article analysing not the religious behaviour of Americans but presidential inauguration addresses—cite the French sociologist, Emile Durkheim (along with the German, Max Weber, one of the two founding fathers of modern sociology) as the theorist behind their position. Durkheim argued that religion originates in the feelings of 'effervescence' by which society becomes conscious of itself in moments of enthusiasm during collective ritual. The American 'civil religion' is a religion of enthusiasm for the American political and social culture.

The trouble with applying Durkheim's model to contemporary Western society is that one is still faced with the question of why collective effervescence produces religious devotion in the most advanced industrialized nation in the world and not in Europe. *Qui nimis probat, nihil probat*: if you prove too much, you prove nothing. In fact, if one tries to test the 'civil religion' theory, one is hard put to find any support. Thus if one tries to find correlations between regular church attendance and militaristic attitudes (a demand for more money spent on the military and weapons), no such relationship emerges. Civil religion has flourished as a theory for more than twenty years without any substantial statistical support. Such findings are dismissed by the 'civil religion' theorists as being naïve and unsophisticated.

If a social change, a major trend in religious attitudes and behaviours, is too subtle to measure save by the wise men and women who do not need empirical data to establish trends, then it might well be true, but it is not a scientific proposition. Rather, it is an exercise in prophecy. Thus the available survey evidence cannot refute the null hypothesis that American religion continues substantially unchanged over the last three to five decades and seems likely to continue at the same levels into the third millennium of Christian history.

European scholars frequently argue that 'secularization' is the result of 'urbanization and industrialization'. That this is the case in some

The Religious Phenomenon 107

countries seems to be unarguable. Yet it did not happen in the United States, so the explanation is obviously inadequate. Scholars would be much better advised to put aside arguments based on such sweeping and irresistible historical trends and engage in cross-national research that asks why the migration to the cities in England (for the sake of an example) led to a decline in religious practice when the same migration in the United States and Canada did not produce similar results. Indeed, Finke and Stark have demonstrated that, in the United States at the turn of the present century, urbanization actually led to an increase in religious mobilization.[6]

There are a number of areas of explanation for the failure to replicate European trends in America. America lacks a history of feudalism, monarchy, and an established church. Thus religion in America has never been identified with any particular side in class struggles in the way it has been in Europe. 'Clericalism', in so far as it exists at all, is not perceived of as 'the enemy', as it was and is in France and has therefore not generated a virulent 'anticlericalism' (save in certain minute portions of the population) which views religion as the enemy of freedom and progress. It is not necessary today, not even in most liberal academic circles, to break with religion in order to establish one's credentials as an opponent of obscurantism, privilege, and reaction.

Moreover, on the positive side, the deliberately self-conscious pluralism which is both the official and unofficial policy of American society, has created a situation in which one's self-definition and social location have become an important part of one's personal identity. If religion is about believing and belonging, if it provides a community to which one can belong and find explanation and reinforcement for the ultimate values (symbols) one shares with other members of that community, then there is little in American experience to persuade most Americans that they should avoid such community and much to persuade them that they should join and be active in religious communities—to ask not why be religious, but rather to ask why not be religious.

Unintentionally, perhaps, American life seems to reinforce the loyalty factor which Hout and I found latent in both political affiliation and church attendance. The factor is both discrete and continuous. There is a threshold of loyalty that a person apparently elects to cross or not to cross in the late teens or early 20s. Once one chooses to be a religious

[6] Roger Finke and Rodney Stark, 'Religious Economies and Sacred Canopies: Religious Mobilization in American Cities, 1906', *American Sociological Review* 53 (Feb. 1988), 41–9.

108   *Andrew M. Greeley*

and/or political alienate at that threshold, one is likely to remain in that social location for the rest of one's life. On the other hand, if one crosses the threshold, even to the extent of identifying with a party by reporting that one is an independent 'leaning' towards one party or the other or by attending church at least once a year, then one has embarked on a path which is likely to 'slide' upward politically and/or religiously as life continues.

Why this slide upward in political and religious affiliation, once one has elected to find some of one's social location in party and church? Perhaps age makes one more conservative and more in need of firm guidelines. Or perhaps with the passage of time one becomes more aware of the complexity of human existence, and hence more tolerant of the imperfections of one's church and one's party and more in need of clearly marked guideposts along the path. Or perhaps one wants to be able to pass on such useful guideposts to one's children, so that they can chart a safe and happy path through life's confusions. Or perhaps all of these three explanations come to the same thing: some guideposts, and some community to set up the posts and maintain the signs on them, are better than none; one's party and one's church may not be much, but, it turns out, they are all one has.

These possible explanations can be converted into operational measures; but social scientists will only begin to work on such measures when they are convinced that religion is not losing its importance in American life and hence is still worth studying as a major component of social structure and of the glue which holds the society, however precariously at times, together.

I am not equating religion with the social and structural characteristics which seem to facilitate it in some societies and impede it in others. I do not want to slip into a crude form of societal reductionism. I am merely suggesting that in some societies it is easy to be religious and in other societies it is easy to be non-religious. If a propensity to seek transcendental meanings for life is part of the human condition because humans are both conscious of their own mortality and apparently incurably hopeful that death is not the end, then the form and style in which individuals respond to such a propensity is likely to be shaped by the structure and culture of the given society in which individuals live.

It is possible, under these conditions, to develop a 'rational choice' theory which explains the persistence of religion in America. In American society a further 30 per cent of the population does consciously decide between their twenty-fifth birthday and their fortieth birthday to

The Religious Phenomenon 109

become regular church-goers (this increase from 30 to 60 per cent being an estimate based on age/cohort analysis). An additional 10 per cent of the population also decide to move (back in most cases) from religious non-identification to religious identification. Perhaps many more make decisions, in their early and middle 20s, about *continuing* their original religious identification and the devotional levels of their middle teens.

In the United States, more than 80 per cent of those who are born Catholic and more than 90 per cent of those who are born Protestant or Jewish eventually opt for their own religious heritage. Why? I would suggest that the reason for this is that, in the calculus of benefits, the choice of one's own religion seems to most Americans, finally, to confer the most benefits. You have to be something. For example, you don't want to be Jewish or Protestant because such a choice seems strange to you. So, perhaps reluctantly and perhaps with a sigh of resignation, you end up (on the average) being Catholic just as your parents were.

The choice of the religion of one's parents may suggest a certain 'addiction', a propensity to choose the familiar because so much has been invested in the familiar, perhaps a phenomenon not unlike the decision to remain with one's original word-processing programme even if other programmes promise more benefits, because (quite rationally) it is calculated that the advantages of Word Perfect over Microsoft Word are not worth the investment of start-up time required to obtain skill in the programme.

Stigler and Becker propose a theory of 'addiction' or 'consumption capital' that may be pertinent here.[7] To paraphrase the authors (on the subject of 'addiction' to classical music), an alternative way to state the same analysis is that the marginal utility of time allocated to a given denomination is increased by an increase in the stock of religious capital. Thus the consumption of a given religious heritage could be said to rise with exposure to the heritage because the marginal utility of time spent on the heritage rose with exposure. Could one be said to be 'addicted' to one's religious (or word-processing) heritage because one has acquired consumption capital in that heritage?

It's hard enough to learn one religion—its rituals, its protocols, its doctrines. Why bother learning another when the extra benefit does not seem all that great? Most Americans (we need not debate about how many exceptions there might be) are born into a religious heritage. Quite

[7] George J. Stigler and Gary S. Becker, 'De Gustibus Non Est Disputandum', *American Economic Review*, 67 (Mar. 1977), 76–90.

110   *Andrew M. Greeley*

likely one could extend the assertion to say that most people in the world are born into some religious or quasi-religious heritage. There are five components of that heritage which may be conveniently considered:

(i) A set of symbols which, *pace* Clifford Geertz, purport to explain uniquely the real, to provide answers to problems of injustice, suffering, and death.

(ii) A set of rituals which activate these symbols at crucial life-cycle turning-points and inculcate the paradigms which the symbols can contain.

(iii) A community which is constituted by and transmits these symbols and rituals.

(iv) A heritage to pass on, should one wish, to one's children.

(v) A differentiation, thick or thin, from those who are not born inside the heritage.

Let us consider the schedule of benefits a person faces (for the sake of this presentation in her/his middle 20s) when considering a religious decision. First of all, the community provides a pool of preferred role opposites, friends, marital partners, perhaps business or professional colleagues. Secondly, it offers familiar rituals for crucial turning-points in one's life. Thirdly, it offers symbols, usually absorbed very early in childhood, which express meaning when one is in a situation which requires meaning. Fourthly, it offers social and organizational activities which confer advantages of various sorts on its members.[8]

In each of the cases, there will be considerable cost in giving up these utilities. Other role opposites may not respond to the most familiar interactive cues. One may lose valuable relationship networks. One may have to learn new symbols and integrate them into one's personality orientations, not an easy task in adulthood, perhaps for many not even a possible task. One may have to engage in ritual behaviours with which one is not familiar and which one might even find distasteful. One may have to find new organizational activities with relative strangers. Or one may have to live without symbols, rituals, and community. Or to try to do so.

What are the alternative benefits on the schedule of options which would attract a person to choose a heritage other than one's own or, if it be possible, no heritage at all?

---

[8] I note here that the more actively one engages in religious activities—up to a certain point, perhaps—the more available these resources may become. There may also be a law of diminishing returns: Sunday Mass attendance may find you a spouse; daily Mass may not notably enhance the chances of finding one.

The Religious Phenomenon   111

1. One attractive possibility is that such a choice would punish parents and church leaders with whom one is angry.

2. Another attraction is upward social mobility. If one is not a Catholic or a Jew one might have access to élite social positions or more esteem in élite circles. It was only in the last two decades, for example, that Catholics and Jews earned access to college presidencies.

3. One might also win freedom for oneself from what one takes to be the restraints, the superstitions, the repressions, and the tyrannies that are inherent in one's heritage and community. One can, for example, eat bacon for breakfast or, in the old days, meat on Friday. One can use the birth-control pill with a clear conscience. One need not take seriously what the local pastor or priest has to say. One can ignore the Pope and refuse to be worried about Israel.

4. One is free to engage with a clear conscience in pleasurable practices on which one's religious heritage seems to frown or to embrace social and ethical concerns which do not preoccupy one's religious leaders—when was the last time the Catholic Church launched a campaign for good government?

5. By rejecting one's religious heritage one may obtain access to particularly desired role opposites—a potential spouse in most cases—who would otherwise not be available.

How does one deal with the loss of such benefits if one chooses to stay within the heritage in which one is raised (since in the concrete, this option—leave or remain—is the usual contact for religious choice)? One may choose to ignore the restraints and the liabilities that the tradition seems to impose. One can remain Catholic, devoutly Catholic in one's own estimate, and still practice birth control because one is able to appeal from a church leadership, which does not understand, to a God that does. (I presume that such behaviour would be called 'free-riding' by economists—a phenomenon which marks all religions, even Catholicism in the days since the decline of the Inquisition.)

This is the ordinary strategy in religious choice, I submit, since most Americans do indeed elect to remain in their own heritage. The choice becomes more desirable and hence more rational to the extent to which one is able, one way or another, to diminish the costs of the choice. In sum, the 'familiarity' factor (or religious consumption capital)—broadly understood—explains why it seems rational, finally, for most people in the United States to opt for their own heritage.

It is worth nothing here that there are differences in both the way the religious choice is made and the degree of religious intensity that is

112   *Andrew M. Greeley*

chosen. For some, the choice is merely a drift in the direction of least resistance—towards a renewal, not necessarily enthusiastic, of the religious identification of their childhood (or of their spouse's childhood identification, as in the case of most religious changers in America). For others, the decision is more conscious and perhaps leads to greater religious intensity. In most of the various solutions that are reached, however, the decisions are sociological in the strict sense of that word. They are the result, I suggest, of patterns of interaction with parents, spouse, friends, neighbourhood, and perhaps children, and not the result of pressures of the so-called 'mass society'.

Religious choice is more likely to be 'intimate' (that is to say, to result from interaction with close role opposites) than political choice and less likely to be intimate than marital choice. This 'intimate' nature of religious choice may be hard for scholars from other countries to comprehend because they are more familiar with religious indifference, that is to say, situations in which religion does not play an important role in identity formation.

One is forced to say to such scholars that religion is more important in this respect in America than it is in other countries and ask that they not dismiss this fact by begging the question with an assertion that such importance merely proves that Americans are not very enlightened. Such a position betrays the powerful theological assumption that religion *ought* to be unimportant, an assumption which has no place in social science discourse.

Why, then, is it rational for Americans to be more devout than the English or the French? Why is it rational for the Irish to be even more devout than Americans? (They are, be it noted, less likely to describe themselves as 'very religious', an option which, in my convert's zeal for rational choice, I think can be said to be quite rational too.) There are two possible paths to follow: one may note, with Avis, that a 'minority' religion, that is to say, one that is not established or quasi-established, is likely to try harder. It may offer more services (one thinks of parochial schools in the United Kingdom) to attract and hold its members. It thus becomes increasingly rational to stay in your tradition and reap the extra benefits that the tradition confers because of its 'minority' status—in America all religions are 'minority' as the word is being used here. Moreover, there may well be a relationship between the degree of religious devotion and activity in which you engage and the services which the institution (in the interests of its own self-preservation) will make available to you: if you are not a devout Catholic, you may not

The Religious Phenomenon   113

be able to take advantage of the parochial schools. In the 'minority' or pluralistic situation, the church may go out of its way to help find you a presentable marriage partner, more out of its way than it would in a situation where it has a near-monopoly on available spouses. It is rational to take advantage of such a situation. But the variety and quality of the pool may depend to some extent on your willingness to engage in high levels of religious behaviour.

This essay is not the place to discuss at length the question of why large numbers of 'minority' group members (in the usual sense of that word) do not desert their group when there seem to be ample benefits in doing so. I merely want to note that it seems to be true that for many within the minority group, the fact of being in a disadvantaged group merely intensifies the identification. Why such an 'identity' is a benefit is an interesting question but beyond my concerns at the present. That it is a benefit in a pluralistic society seems obvious enough. ('Yes, I'm Jewish and proud of it.') That which strengthens identity is often estimated to be worth the cost.

So I propose that the combination of symbol, ritual, and community provides a partial 'identity', a useful response to the question 'what are you?', an answer often stated with pride and even defiance. Such an answer signals to others (and to oneself) one's symbolic and ritual orientation and one's potential pool of preferred role opposites.

I finally propose by way of summary that a religion attracts loyalty and devotion from its members in proportion to the thickness of the differentiation and that for two reasons: (a) Ordinarily the religion will offer more services when its membership is sharply distinguished over and against the rest of society, and hence perhaps in jeopardy of defection. (b) Paradoxically, and despite the fears of religious leaders of the risk of defection, the distinction is a benefit itself; hence the more loyal one is to one's heritage, the stronger the distinction and the more proudly it is professed.

If your church does not perceive itself as threatened and your membership in it adds little to the identity into which you are born as a member of a society, if it does not differentiate you sharply from the rest of society, then there are lower costs and lower benefits in making your choice, and hence less pay-off for you in engaging in actions or professing beliefs which would link you more closely to your church. Concretely, in one-religion societies (either *de facto* or in the case of established churches *de jure*) the differentiation is thin indeed and the efforts the church perceives as necessary to attract and hold members

114   *Andrew M. Greeley*

are minimal. Hence it is less rational to commit oneself to higher levels of religious behaviour.

As a rule of thumb, I hypothesize, if you are born into a religion almost by the fact of birth in a society, then religion adds rather little to your identity and makes little demands on your behaviour to sustain that identity. On the other hand, if you are born into a pluralistic society where there is no official or quasi-offical religion, then your religious choice (even if it is to remain in the denomination of your parents) helps notably to define who you are. In such circumstances, higher levels of devotional and organizational behaviour are important to maintain your self-definition (on the average, of course).

In Great Britain, I would suggest as a hypothesis to be considered, being an Anglican adds little to the identity of being British (or English, if that word is more appropriate) and hence the affiliation can be maintained without substantial devotional activity. On the other hand, if you choose to belong to one of the 'non-established' churches, for one reason or another (including birth), then such a choice becomes an important norm in defining yourself over against the rest of British (or English) society and imposes on you constraints for devotional and organizational behaviour not unlike those experienced by your counter-parts in other (English-speaking) societies.

This would lead one to hypothesize that those identifying in England with non-Anglican denominations, whether Catholic or Protestant, would be as likely as Americans to believe, for example, in the existence of God and life after death and to attend church regularly. To put it a little differently, the difference between the United States and England, the fact of British exceptionalism, would be essentially an Anglican difference, an Anglican exceptionalism.

In point of fact, this is precisely the case: 81 per cent of the population of Great Britain believes in God as opposed to 96 per cent in the United States; 14 per cent of the people of Great Britain attend church every week (23 per cent at least once a month) as opposed to 44 per cent in the United States; 57 per cent of Britons believe in life after death as opposed to 70 per cent of Americans. But there is no difference between Roman Catholics in the United States and Roman Catholics in Great Britain and between Protestants in the United States and (non-Anglican) Protestants in Great Britain in belief in God and life after death and in church attendance. Forty-two per cent of the Protestants in both countries go to church every week, as do 50 per cent of the Catholics. Approxi-mately 70 per cent of both religious groups in both countries believe in

The Religious Phenomenon   115

life after death. Ninety-eight per cent of the Catholics in both countries believe in God, 94 per cent of the Protestants. The percentages in English-speaking Canada are virtually the same as in the United States: 94 per cent believe in God, 70 per cent in life after death, 44 per cent attend church regularly. (The numbers for francophones are virtually the same.)

The lower levels of religiousness in England are purely an Anglican phenomenon. Among the four English-speaking nations of the North Atlantic, then, the exception in levels of religious practice is to be found only among British Anglicans.

It is interesting to note in passing that in Australia and New Zealand, the percentages on these three items are even lower among Protestants and Catholics then they are in the English-speaking countries of the North Atlantic. The exceptions, then, in the six English-speaking countries are the inhabitants of the countries in the South Pacific and the British Anglicans. Why those from the South Pacific are exceptions is a fascinating question, indeed, but obviously beyond the scope of this exercise.

By way of conclusion, there are many differences in religion between the United States and the United Kingdom. But the point here is that, in basic essentials, the difference seems to be the result of the different identity-conferring role of religion in a society with an established (or quasi-established religion) and in a society without such an established church.

Who's exceptional, then? Australia, not America. Why did immigration and pluralism produce higher levels of religious behaviour in the latter than in the former? This is the pertinent question. It will be asked seriously, I suspect, only when scholars who study or pontificate about religion are willing to put aside their myths about broad, uni-dimensional, and uni-directional social changes (as have demographic historians) and focus on comparisons which ask why religious practice has declined in some countries and not in other very similar countries. Monopoly, official or unofficial, does not seem to help religion. Poland, however, is a clear exception. Pluralism does seem to help religion. Australia is a clear exception. Scholarship requires more than an expression of personal opinion about the reasons why.

126

RELIGION AND ATTITUDES TOWARDS AIDS POLICY

Andrew M. Greeley
The University of Arizona
The National Opinion Research Center

SSR, Volume 75, No. 3, April, 1991

In the modern world there is relatively little connection in ordinary circumstances between religion and public policy with regard to contagious diseases. The quarantine rules about leprosy (a much wider collection of diseases than what is now called Hansen's Disease) in the Mosaic law -- rough and ready public health measures in retrospect -- are now enforced by governmental agencies and not by religion.

Acquired Immune Deficiency Syndrome, however, is a special case both because of the inevitably fatal outcome of the disease and because it is normally transmitted through sexual contact, is especially likely to spread under conditions of sexual promiscuity, and in the United States has in fact spread in great part through homosexual contact. Since the traditional religions have disapproved of promiscuity and homosexuality, AIDS has become or seem to have become an issue of morality as well as of public health. Indeed some religious leaders have pronounced it a punishment of God on immorality and especially homosexual immorality.[1]

Thus the question arises as to whether religious affiliation and devotion might have an impact on AIDS policy issues and decisions. Will the more devout have more repressive attitudes towards those who are victims of AIDS?

The 1988 General Social Survey (Davis and Smith 1988) contained two additional modules beyond the usual sets of GSS questions, the fortuitous combination of which makes it possible to address this question.[2] The first module was a battery of questions about AIDS funded by NORC;[3] the second was an extensive series of items about religion.

The eight AIDS policy items[4] were as follows (the percentage in parenthesis indicates the proportion of respondents who took a position that indicated hostility towards AIDS victims):

Do you support or oppose the following measures to deal with AIDS:

A) Prohibit students with AIDS virus from attending public schools. (26%)

B) Develop a government information program to promote safe sex practices, such as the use of condoms. (14%)

C) Permit Insurance companies to test applicants for the AIDS virus. (62%)

D) Have the government pay all of the health care costs of AIDS patients. (67%)

E) Conduct mandatory testing for the AIDS virus before marriage. (89%)

F) Require the teaching of safe sex practices. such as the use of condoms in sex education courses in public schools. (88%)

G) Require people with the AIDS virus to wear identification tags that look like those carried by people with allergies or diabetes. (63%)

H) Make victims with AIDS eligible for disability benefits. (40%)

The impact of denominational affiliation, frequent church attendance and religious imagery on responses to these items will be explored in the remainder of this note.

Denominational Affiliation. Statistically significant correlations were found between Protestant[5] affiliation and negative AIDS attitudes on three items -- sex information (.10), sex education (.11), and identification tags(.16).

Seventy percent of the Protestants in the sample supported the imposition of indentification tags on AIDS victims as opposed to 54% of the Catholics. Some of this difference was concentrated among members of Fundamentalist denominations (Smith 1986), of whose members 73% supported the identification tags and Conservative denominations, of whose members 72% approved of the identity tags. However, 61% of Protestants in liberal denominations also supported identification tags for AIDS victims; the difference between them and Catholics is not statistically significant.

In an endeavor to explain the differences between Catholics and Protestants, this ,writer tried to reduce the .16 correlation (sixteen percentage points difference) to statistical insignificance through the use of multiple regression equations into which religious variables would be entered successively. My assumption was that variables associated with fundamentalist religious orientations would account for much of the differences between Protestants and Catholics.

When three items were inserted which measured attitudes towards the Bible[6], the correlation (as measured by the beta in the regression equation) diminished to .11. Catholics, in other words are less likely to support identification tags for AIDS victims than are conservative and fundamentalist Protestants because they are less likely to emphasize the Bible, as literally interpreted, than are Protestants.

The correlation was diminished to .09 when an attitude about formal church membership when growing up[7] is inserted in the equation and to .07 and statistical insignificance when the South as a region of the country is added.

Catholics are baptized into the Church and usually do not consciously reaffiliate in their adolescent years. However, members of the more conservative Protestant denominations are more likely to go through such a process of formal reaffiliation. It would appear that those who do are somewhat more likely to have a repressive attitude towards AIDS. Finally, Protestants, being disproportionately Southern in comparison with Catholics, may share a cultural attitude towards morality which has an impact above and beyond biblical fundamentalism.

Thus one can account for differences between Fundamentalist and Conservative Protestants and Catholics in their attitudes towards identification tags for AIDS victims by a model which takes into account explicit beliefs about the Bible, early formal relationship to a church, and region of origin.

It should be noted that 38% of all Americans believe in the strict literal interpretation of the Bible and 26% both believe in this interpretation and support prayer and bible reading in the public schools. 47% of Protestants believe in literal interpretation and 36% of Protestants believe in this interpretation and support prayer and bible reading in public schools. The "fundamentalist" strain in American religion is thus large. Moreover, it is not a new phenomenon. According to a Gallup index composed of the experience of being born again,

belief in a literal interpretation of scripture, and an attempt to persuade others to "decide" for Christ, a fifth of the American population has been "fundamentalist" for the last several decades with neither increase nor decrease during that period of time. (Greeley 1989) Fundamentalism is a major component of American religion which did not "emerge" during the nineteen eighties; rather the national elites and the national media discovered (again) what has existed in the United States since the First Great Awakening -- in 1744. In attempting to understand the relationship between Fundamentalism and AIDS attitudes it is helpful to realize that half of the population of the south believe in the literal interpretation of the Bible as opposed to a quarter of the rest of the country.

There are also somewhat smaller relationships between Protestant affiliation and attitudes on AIDS education. 8% of Catholics oppose sex education about AIDS in public schools as opposed to 16% of Protestants. 10% of Catholics as opposed to 17% of Protestants oppose government information campaigns about "safe sex." Again there are no statistically significant differences between Catholics and liberal Protestants. Opposition among fundamentalist Protestants is higher - - 20% against sex education in the public schools and 25% oppose government information campaigns about "safe sex."

While there is, then, a correlation between Protestantism and especially fundamentalist Protestant and opposition to information campaigns about AIDS, it is nonetheless true that at least three quarters of the fundamentalists do NOT oppose such campaigns.

Regression models based on the three biblical items used to account for differences between Protestants and Catholics on the issue of identification tags for AIDS victims reduce to statistical insignificance the differences between the two denominations in attitudes on information campaigns, both in the schools and outside the schools. It is precisely rigid biblical literalism which accounts for greater Protestant opposition to such campaigns.

Church Attendance. Church attendance does not correlate with attitudes towards identification tags for AIDS victims, but it does correlate negatively and powerfully with attitudes on sex education in the public schools and government information campaigns -- -.32 and -.24. 38% of those who attend church weekly or more often oppose sex

128

education about AIDS in public schools (as opposed to 6%) and 29% opposed government campaigns about "safe sex."

Again the differences between frequent attenders and others can be diminished substantially by use in multiple regression equations of models based on biblical and moral rigidity. The -.24 relationship with opposition to sex education in public schools is reduced to .13 by taking into account belief in biblical literalism and frequent reading of the Bible. It diminishes to -.08 (and statistical insignificance) when three attitudes on moral decision making are entered into the equation.[8] The difference in attitudes towards government informational campaigns is reduced by half by the same model: the correlation decreases from -.32 to -.16, though the difference remains statistically significant.

Those who attend church frequently are more likely to be opposed to AIDS education programs in substantial part because they accept a more literal interpretation of the Bible and because they see moral decisions in a more simplistic fashion than to those who do not attend church so frequently. Among those regular church-goers who do not have such rigid religious orientations there is less difference (or no statistically significant difference) from those who do not attend church weekly.

In one sense it is not such a striking series of findings that are reported here: The religious correlation with negative attitudes towards AIDS victims or AIDS education is the result of moral and religious narrowness among certain members of the more devout population. It is what one might have expected. Nonetheless this finding establishes that it is not religion as such but a certain highly specific type of religious orientation which tends to induce hostility on the subject of AIDS. While this religious orientation represents a strong component of American culture and society, it is not a majority orientation; and even among fundamentalists the majority support AIDS education programs.

The question remains, however, whether other kinds of religious orientation correlate positively with compassion on AIDS issues. Obviously more flexible attitudes on biblical inspiration and moral decision making produce greater tolerance and sympathy. But are there other indices of religious devotion

which are likely to induce such positive attitudes?

Religious Images. Religion according to a theory developed elsewhere (Greeley 1982, 1988, 1990) finds its origins and its raw power in the imaginative dimension of the self. It begins with 1) *experiences* which renew hope, which experiences are encoded in 2)*images* (or symbols) stored in the imaginative memory, and shared in 3) *stories* with members of a 4) *community* with a common narrative and symbolic tradition, and often acted out in community 5) *rituals*. This paradigm is pictured not as a line but as a circle so that symbols, stories, community, and rituals in their turn shape the hope-renewing experiences of those who are part of a tradition. The symbols, stories, and rituals constitute a (pre-rational) system which purports to explain what creation and human life mean.

It is suggested that a quick and crude measure of the religious imagination can be obtained by measuring a person's image of God, since it is this image which summarizes in an abbreviated fashion the stories and symbols in a person's imagination. For several years NORC has been administering a battery of four items which attempt to measure a person's image and story of God and their relationship with Her/Him.[9]

A scale was constructed from these items in which one point was given for each response that picture God as mother, spouse, lover, and friend[10.] The scale is referred to in the literature dealing with this theory as the GRACE scale because it purports to measure a more gracious story of what life means and to predict a more graceful response to problems and concerns of life. A person with a higher score on the GRACE scale, it is theorized, will have experienced a more benign relationship with the powers (or Powers) which govern the cosmos and hence will be more benign in his attitudes towards and relationships with other human beings.

There are modest but statistically significant positive relationships between the grace and tolerance on the AIDS questions -- those who are more likely to have a gracious image of God are less likely to approve of identification tags for AIDS victims (-.13), of the exclusion of AIDS victims from public schools (-.14) and of premarital AIDS tests (-.09). They are also more likely to support education about "safe sex" in public schools

129

(.11).

Thus religion measured not by affiliation nor by church attendance but by images of God correlates with tolerance and flexibility towards AIDS policy issues.

The four graphs illustrate the nature of this relationship for Catholics and Protestants. For both groups tolerance increases with GRACE on all measures -- save for attitudes towards premarital tests among Catholics. On two of the four measures -- identification tags and attendance at public schools (Figures 1 and 3) -- the correlation is essentially the same for Protestants and Catholics, though on both Catholics are more tolerant than Protestants (only slightly more tolerant on the subject of public school attendance).

On the other two measures -- premarital tests and AIDS education in the schools (Figures 2 and 4) -- there is essentially no difference between Catholics and Protestants at the higher end of the GRACE scale because the scale leads to an increase in tolerance for Protestants and no significant changes for Catholics.

Thus images of God's -- codes which tell stories of a person's relationship with God and provide templates for relationships with other human beings -- do correlate with AIDS policy attitudes. To understand the relationship between religion and AIDS policy attitudes, one needs to know not only about attitudes towards the Bible and moral decision making but also about the religious imagination which, according to the theory, underlies the formation and expression of such cognitive attitudes.[11]

Conclusion. Since 1988 Americans may have become more tolerant on such matters as identity tags for AIDS victims and premarital testing. Moreover, some religious denominations, especially liberal Protestant and Catholic, have insisted vigorously on the need for compassion for victims -- though Catholic leaders have campaigned (with their usual success in such matters) against "safe sex" education campaigns. It would be useful to know whether these changes, should they have taken place, might also relate to religious convictions, practices, and images. One would predict that the greatest resistance to attitudinal change would come from those with rigid religious orientations and the highest likelihood of attitudinal change from those with the most gracious images of God.

It is to be hoped that a future research project would include both the religious measures and the policy attitudes discussed in this note.

NOTES

1. It is perhaps appropriate that, as a cleric, at the beginning that I note that the God I know doesn't work that way. Are children born with AIDS guilty of anything? However, it is also true that in a non-promiscuous population, the disease would spread much less rapidly. This is a fact of epidemiology and not of divine justice.

2. The General Social Survey is funded by the National Science Foundation, which of course is not responsible for this analysis.

3. Unfortunately there was no funding available for subsequent replications of the questions so there are no data on changes in these policy attitudes since 1988. The first four items were asked of one half of the sample and the other four of the second half.

4. The size of the sample permitted only comparisons between Protestants and Catholics. For the total sample N=1381. Since the items on AIDS policy were administered to only half the sample, the number of cases on each of these questions does not exceed 700.

5. The size of the sample permitted only comparisons between Protestants and Catholics. For the total sample N=1381. Since the items on AIDS policy were administered to only half the sample, the number of cases on each of these questions does not exceed 700.

6. The wording of the three items:
-- Which of these statements comes closest to describing your feelings about the Bible: a)The Bible is the actual word of God and is to be taken literally word for word; b)The Bible is the inspired word of God but not everything in it should be taken literally, word for word; c) the Bible is an ancient book of fables, legends, history and moral principles recorded by men.
-- The United States Supreme Court has ruled that no state or local government may require the reading of the Lord's Prayer or Bible verses in public schools. What are your views on this -- do you approve or disapprove of the court ruling.
-- How important is each of the following in helping you to make decisions about life -- the Bible.

7. Did you ever join a church when you were growing up, that is become a member by confirmation or such?

8. The items:
-- Morality is a personal matter and society should not force anyone to follow one standard.
-- Immoral actions by one person can corrupt society in general.
-- Right and wrong are not usually a simple matter of black and white; there are many shades of gray.

9. The question: There are many different ways of picturing God. We'd like to know the kinds of images you are most likely to associated with God. Here is a card with sets of contrasting images. On a scale of 1-7 where would you place your image of God between the two contrasting images: Mother, Father; Master, Spouse; Judge, Lover; Friend; King.

10. Or equally Mother and Father etc.

11. The scale correlates negatively with ALL the variables in the models discussed in previous sections of this paper Literalism -.22; Bible reading -.10; Bible in public schools -.11; Morality is personal not social .08; Morality is a matter of black and white not gray -.15; Immoral actions can corrupt society -.12.

REFERENCES

Davis, James A. and Tom Smith. 1988. General Social Surveys 1972 - 1988: Cumulative Codebook. Chicago: The National Opinion Research Center.

130

Greeley, Andrew. 1982. Religion: A Secular Theory. New York: The Free Press.

-- 1988. "Evidence That A Maternal Image of God Correlates with Liberal Politics." Sociology and Social Research. 73:3-8.

-- 1989. Religious Change in America. Cambridge Mass: Harvard University Press.

-- 1990. The Catholic Myth. New York: Charles Scribner.

Smith, Tom. 1986. "Classifying Protestant Denominations," GSS Technical Report No. 67, Chicago: NORC.

Manuscript was received March 25, 1991
and reviewed March 27, 1991.

131

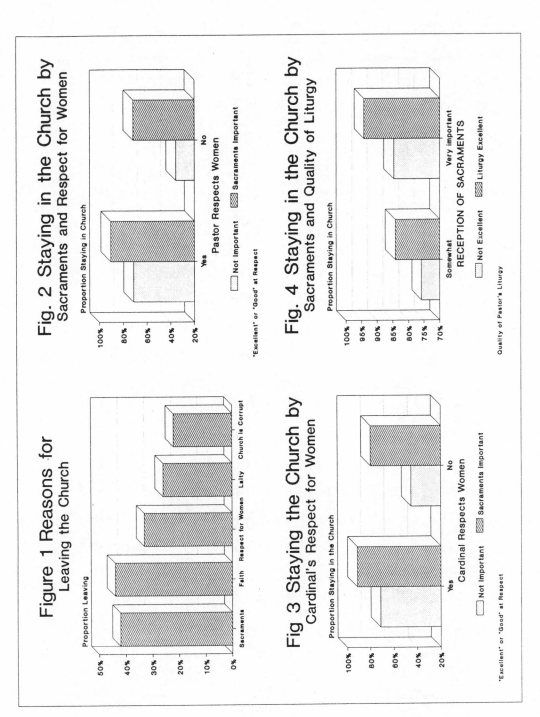

Figure 1 Reasons for Leaving the Church

Fig. 2 Staying in the Church by Sacraments and Respect for Women

Fig 3 Staying the Church by Cardinal's Respect for Women

Fig. 4 Staying in the Church by Sacraments and Quality of Liturgy

132

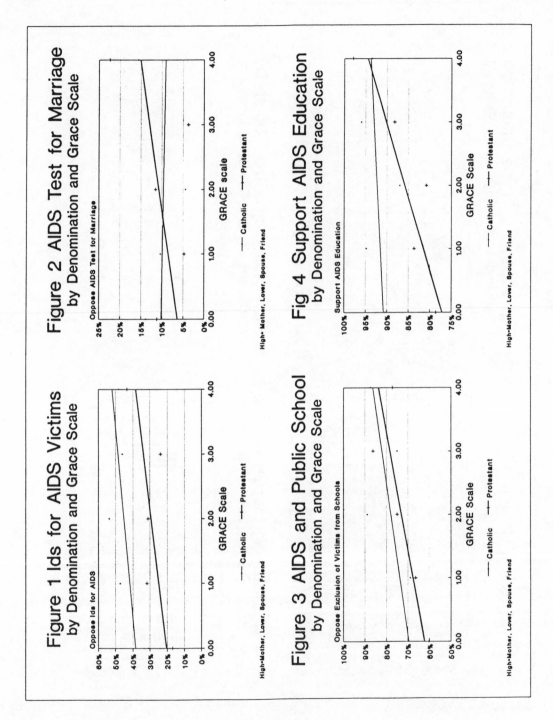

Figure 1 Ids for AIDS Victims
by Denomination and Grace Scale

Figure 2 AIDS Test for Marriage
by Denomination and Grace Scale

Figure 3 AIDS and Public School
by Denomination and Grace Scale

Fig 4 Support AIDS Education
by Denomination and Grace Scale

The Paranormal is Normal: A Sociologist Looks at Parapsychology

ANDREW GREELEY

ABSTRACT: From a sociological viewpoint, based on survey research, the paranormal or psi phenomena are normal. The advantages of the sociological approach to research on such phenomena are pointed out. The author also presents his personal views, briefly describes the results of various surveys of attitudes toward the paranormal, and criticizes the scientistic approach to psi experiences.

A sociologist who considers research on the paranormal can make two important observations:

1. The paranormal is normal (Greeley, 1975).

2. The inability of a sociologist, using the tools of his or her trade, to comment on the "reality" of paranormal experiences is not the disadvantage it may seem.

There has been a substantial amount of research done in many different countries on the prevalence and incidence of paranormal experiences, much of it summarized by Erlendur Haraldsson of the University of Iceland (Haraldsson, 1985; Haraldsson & Houtkooper, 1991). In a survey of Europe and the U.S. in the early 1980s, Haraldsson & Houtkooper (1991) report striking national differences in belief in the paranormal and frequency of experiences. For example, for those reporting *any* type of psi experience, 60% of those polled in Italy and the United States responded positively, as opposed to 24% in Norway. Nonetheless, these surveys indicate that for a significant number of people in the Americas, Europe, and Asia the extraordinary is ordinary, the astonishing is commonplace, the wonderful is mundane. This finding is so unexpected and so powerful that both sides in the debate about the paranormal should stop their arguments and listen to it. Whether parapsychological phenomena are real or not is notably less important than the sheer fact that experiences of such phenomena, whatever their physical or metaphysical nature, are commonplace.

In the United States, for example, in 1986 67% of the population reported having had an ESP experience, 31% a clairvoyant experience, and 42% contact with the dead (Greeley, 1987). Haraldsson and Houtkooper (1991) report that in the early 1980s, 54% of Americans reported telepathy experiences, 25% clairvoyance, and 30% contact with the dead. In a 1990 Gallup poll of belief in the paranormal, 49% of Americans believed in

ESP, 26% in clairvoyance, and 25% in "ghosts" (Gallup & Newport, 1991).[1]

Whenever I mention these findings (based on national probability samples), I am almost instantly challenged: Are they telling the truth? Do the phenomena really happen? Are they not deceiving themselves?

I always reply that to answer those questions is not my job. I lack the tools to say as a sociologist whether there is a world of spirit or whether the human self survives after death. As a sociologist I don't give a hoot about the answers to such metaphysical questions. It's my task to report the prevalence and incidence of such phenomena and to leave to others the (perhaps pointless) debate about what, if anything, the existence of such phenomena proves about the nature of the universe.

If a phenomenon is widespread in the human condition, then it is worth studying. Even if there is no "reality" of mental communication with those who are at a distance, the very phenomenon that most Americans think they have experienced such communication is a fact not to be dismissed. The survey sociologist wants to know who those people are, what was the nature of the experience, what effect did it have on their lives, and how do they explain what happened.

Thus, in my own research on contact with the dead (Greeley, 1985), I discovered that three fifths of the widows and widowers in America reported such contact, that the experience was benign, that it was as likely to occur among men as among women and among the well educated as among the less educated, and that it correlated with the image of God as a lover. Presumably, I said, those with that image would be more open to experiencing contact with the dead, though it was remotely possible that the experience may have changed the image of God. I then discovered that reported contact with the dead correlated not with the loss of a parent or a child but with the loss of a sibling, and that among those with sibling loss and contact with the dead, the image of God as lover was also more likely. Since sibling loss, as traumatic as it might be, does not usually produce the same grief as spouse loss and hence does not seem likely to force a person to fall back on religious beliefs and to revise those beliefs more or less permanently in the direction of a more intense image of God, I speculated that perhaps the experience *does* influence the image of God, instead of vice versa. In any event, I concluded in the paper I wrote on the subject (Greeley, 1985) that the phenomenon was sufficiently widespread that

---

[1] The questions used in the NORC studies (Greeley, 1975, 1987) and later in the International Study of Values, which provided the data for Haraldsson's (1985) and Haraldsson & Houtkooper's (1991) analysis, were as follows: How often have you had any of the following experiences:

—Thought you were somewhere you have been before but knew it was impossible.

—Felt as though you were in touch with someone when they were far away from you.

—Seen events that happen at a great distance as they were happening.

—Felt as though you were really in touch with someone who had died.

those elderly folk who reported it should not be ridiculed or dismissed as victims of wish fulfillment.

The fact that we would very much like to have contact with the dead does not mean in itself and in the absence of other proof that the contact experience is a form of self-deception. It might only mean that a response to our wish is possible (Greeley, 1988).

My investigation was instigated by a research article in a gerontology journal by a family practice team that had found such "hallucinations" (their quotation marks) among widows and widowers (Olson, Suddeth, Peterson, & Egelhoff, 1985). I tried to replicate their findings with my national sample data and found virtually identical percentages. I submitted my article to the same journal as a follow-up to theirs. The journal had acquired a new editor in the interim, however. He rejected my article with a contemptuous and insulting letter.

Note that neither the family practice group nor I had made any claims that widows and widowers "really" were in touch with their spouses. We had only reported that the phenomenon is widespread and benign and that those who work in the gerontological fields should be aware of this. But even to report that undeniable fact was sufficient to incite dogmatic academic nastiness.

Call out the thought police!

Erlendur Haraldsson has an excellent Icelandic data set on contact with the dead experiences. Yet every major publishing house in New York has rejected an outline of a book on his data, and despite the enormous success of Raymond Moody's (1975, 1977) work on near-death experiences (NDEs). Dogma clearly cancelled out marketing potabilities.

Never having been a dogmatic materialist (and being a theist who is convinced that the best argument is Pascal's wager[2]), I find such rigid obscurantism both unbelievable and dreadful. Of what, I wonder, are they so afraid? Could it be, as the late Morris Janowitz once remarked to me, that an agnostic is someone who is afraid that there might be a God after all?

There is a vast amount of research that can be done on paranormal phenomena through the techniques of survey research. Indeed, I once prepared a questionnaire for a national survey on contact with the dead and a proposal for a study of the phenomenon. I was not trying to "prove" that there was life after death or that contact with the dead was possible. I was merely attempting to obtain a profile of the men and women who have such experiences, their descriptions of the experiences, and the impact of the experiences on their lives.

---

[2] Pascal reasoned that on the assumption that either God does or does not exist and we are unable to discern which alternative is correct, it is better to choose that God does exist, because if He does, we stand only to gain, whereas if God does not exist, we would not lose anything. On the other hand, if God does exist and we choose not to believe it, we may lose thereby.

370   *Journal of the American Society for Psychical Research*

If such experiences improve the quality of life and the emotional well being of the bereaved, if they correlate with positive mental health (and they do), then are they not worth studying?

"They're deceiving themselves," I was told. "We can't encourage self-deception no matter how benign its effect."

To which I would routinely reply, "how do you know that they're deceiving themselves?"

"They *have* to be deceiving themselves."

I know dogma when I hear it.

The dogma not only rejects the laboratory experiments about the paranormal, it also rejects findings that most people experience the paranormal (thus making it normal) on the grounds that people *shouldn't* have such experiences.

It can't be happening, you see; and, since it can't be happening, those who experience it as happening should not be experiencing it, and therefore there is no reason to study them. Hence it would be wrong to study them.

Moreover, those of you who want to study them are dangerous because in your hearts you believe the paranormal is possible and you're trying to prove it by collecting data on the poor idiots who think it is possible. Don't deny what you're up to. We see through your pose of academic agnosticism.

Got it?

There are only so many projects one can attempt in a life, and this project seemed doomed to both funding rejection and ridicule. There were, I decided, other things to do.

As a transition from my first point to my second point, I will state what I believe about such matters. I believe first of all in spirit, even in Spirit, but I don't think She is demonstrable by social science research—or refutable by such research either.

Secondly, I believe with G. K. Chesterton that life, is too important to ever be anything but life. However, I do not believe that human survival can be proven by parapsychological research. The NDE does no more than prove that at the outside there is a period of survival after death. It tells us nothing about the long term, should there be a long term. Contact with a dead person, however persuasive and reassuring it may be to the one who has such a contact, proves nothing at all to those who reject the possibility of life after death. Religion will make few converts on the basis of parapsychological research because faith knowledge operates with a different set of criteria and a different way of knowing than does scientific knowledge—it asks different questions and must select from different possible answers.

So my Catholic faith is not validated by paranormal research—it would be a weak faith indeed if it were. If Saints Patrick, Bridget, and Columba should wander into my apartment tonight, along with a couple of my friends who have recently died, that might notably strengthen my religious commitment. But I don't need and ought not to need such phenomena for basic faith.

It might be fun to meet them, however, especially Bridget. I would ask her if she really ordained priests!

Hence I would not try to impose on others my belief in spirit or in survival on the basis of parapsychological research or even on the basis of my imagined meeting with the Holy Saints of Ireland. Those who are familiar with the end of *The Varieties* will recognize that here, as in so many other ways, I am a disciple of William James (1902). I add that I believe we live in an open universe, filled with wonder and surprise, and that the wise person does not deny on a priori grounds any possibility for surprise.

Is there a Bigfoot? I rather think not, but I would be delighted if there were, and I'm open to looking at the evidence. Is there cold fusion? I guess not, but I would be overjoyed if there would be because I'd like to see someone make fools out of all the arrogant scholars who ridiculed the possibility. You can't really be a scholar unless you have an open mind and are willing to listen. Paradigms are to be defended vigorously but not by obscurantist dogmatists.

Because of my religious position on the paranormal (religiously who needs it?), I am at ease with my sociological agnosticism on the *reality* of the widespread paranormal experiences of the general population. No better statement of that agnosticism can be found than the remark made long ago by one of the fathers of American sociology, W. I. Thomas (Thomas with Thomas, 1928, p. 572): If people judge something to be real then that judgment itself is a reality to be studied. Would Thomas have approved of my research on the prevalence of the paranormal? I have no idea, but logically he should have.

There is in the American academy precious little room for maneuver on the subject of the paranormal, precious few people with an open mind on the subject. Most academics reject in principle and on a priori philosophical grounds the possibility of such phenomena. A small minority are committed to studying the phenomena and proving that they can and do occur. In between there are very few who will say "show me" or tell me about it. Empiricist principles yield to materialist dogma.

Survey sociologists are freed from such debates because their discipline is not equipped to do any empirical testing of psychic phenomena. They can happily say "agnosco" when asked if they *really* believe in them. The activist protectors of materialist dogma may demand an act of faith (or even an *auto da fe*) against the paranormal; but sociologists, if they are real scholars, must reply, "darned if I know." They may not get their grants, but at least they are protected from the necessity of useless arguments.

Indeed, since the founding in 1882 of the Society for Psychical Research in Britain, the argument has raged on and on, and, as far as I am aware, it is no closer to resolution now than it was then. I therefore ask myself whether the argument is useless and rejoice in the fact that my sociological limitations bar me from participating in it.

Carol Zaleski (1987), in her wonderful book *Otherworld Journeys,* rehearses at considerable length the arguments about the validity of NDEs (which she shows ingeniously were reported in the literature of the Middle Ages). At the end of her review, Zaleski concludes, wisely I think, that the argument is both endless and useless and may be about the wrong question. Neither side will ever convince the other, because one side enters the discussion convinced that the experience is impossible and the other convinced that the experiences do in fact occur. She even cites the case of a skeptic who had an NDE and afterwards rejected it completely, though he admitted that it did make him less afraid of death.

Also a disciple of William James, Zaleski asks whether it might not be better to consider such phenomena as signs or hints which, when taken together and integrated with other experiences and insights, suggest the probability of grace or even Grace. She thereby shifts the epistemology of the discussion from the rhetoric of science, in which the discussion can never be resolved, to the rhetoric of religion, where it can be resolved—though not with the same kind of certainty that science produces or seems to produce.

Religious knowledge is based on what John Henry Newman called converging probabilities (an alternative version, I think, of Pascal's wager). The various signs and wonders we encounter in our lives contribute or can contribute to that convergence. For some people, the paranormal signs enter into the calculus of probabilities. That seems, in Zaleski's perspective, all that one can say and enough for one to say.

Having said that, one can return to the study of the paranormal with a sigh of relief. The metaphysical has been dismissed, or at least relegated to its proper sphere, and the empirical investigation can continue.

Yet, since I am both a practicing Catholic priest and an empirical researcher, I must pause to answer some questions: Do I accept the findings of paranormal research, the dogmatist may demand of me. To which I reply that as an empirical scholar I find them very interesting indeed and that I want to know more about them (which means I want to see the research continue); and I add, stubbornly perhaps, that I am also fascinated by the prevalence of paranormal experiences in our society and want to learn more about that too—though I doubt the dogmatists will permit me to do so.

Have I ever had any paranormal or mystical experiences? No.

Would such experiences enhance my faith? Perhaps. I don't seek them however, any more than I seek the miraculous at shrines—which I consistently avoid (despite my devotion to the Mother of Jesus).

Do the findings of paranormal research fit into the converging probabilities of my religious faith? At most marginally—in that they add a little bit to my conviction that the cosmos we live in is both mysterious and wonderful. My interest is empirical rather than religious.

One of the advantages of having established empirical norms for the prevalence of paranormal phenomena is that one can, by simply quoting the statistics, establish an environment in which it becomes possible for people to talk securely and openly about experiences they have mentioned to no one.

Thus, in a seminar I taught at the University of Arizona a number of years ago, most of the students were working in hospices or in cancer wards at hospitals. As soon as I had established the "normalness" of such experiences, their stories of strange and wonderful deathbed experiences flooded out. Since then I periodically accuse doctors of treating these phenomena as ugly little secrets. No doctor has ever denied the truth of my charge. The standard reply is, "we don't like to think about them, much less talk about them."

Surely, there ought to be research on such matters. But just as surely, in the present state of academic dogmatism, one would be naive to expect it. So the anecdotes pile up, particularly of NDEs and contact with the dead. They are always great stories, filled with wonder and surprise. Each time I hear one I feel sad that academic social science forbids the study of such phenomena. However, they do provide wonderful material for novels— such as the incident narrated in my novel *Saint Valentine's Night* (Greeley, 1989).

If only I could tell you some of the stories. For example this woman. . . .

REFERENCES

GALLUP, G. H., JR., & NEWPORT, F. (1991). Belief in paranormal phenomena among adult Americans. *Skeptical Inquirer, 15,* 137–146.

GREELEY, A. (1975). *The Sociology of the Paranormal: A Reconnaissance.* Beverly Hills, CA: Sage Publications.

GREELEY, A. (1985). Hallucinations among the widowed. *Sociology and Social Research, 77,* 258–265.

GREELEY, A. (1987, January/February). Mysticism goes mainstream. *American Health, 6*(1), 47–49.

GREELEY, A. (1988). Correlates of belief in life after death. *Sociology and Social Research, 73,* 3–8.

GREELEY, A. (1989). *Saint Valentine's Night.* New York: Warner.

HARALDSSON, E. (1985). Representative national surveys of psychic phenomena: Iceland, Great Britain, Sweden, USA and Gallup's multinational survey. *Journal of the Society for Psychical Research, 53,* 145–158.

HARALDSSON, E., & HOUTKOOPER, J. M. (1991). Psychic experience in

374   *Journal of the American Society for Psychical Research*

the multinational Human Values Survey: Who reports them? *Journal of the American Society for Psychical Research, 85,* 145–165.

JAMES W. (1902). *The Varieties of Religious Experience.* New York: Longmans, Green.

MOODY, R. (1975). *Life After Life: The Investigation of a Phenomenon— Survival of Bodily Death.* St. Simon's Island, GA: Mockingbird Books.

MOODY, R. (1977). *Reflections on Life After Life.* Harrisburg, PA: Stackpole Books.

OLSON, P. R., SUDDETH, J. A., PETERSON, P. J., & EGELHOFF, C. (1985). Hallucinations of widowhood. *Journal of the American Geriatric Society, 33,* 543–547.

THOMAS, W. I., WITH THOMAS, D. S. (1928). *The Child in America: Behavior Problems and Programs.* New York: Knopf.

ZALESKI, C. (1987). *Otherworld Journeys: Accounts of Near-Death Experience in Medieval and Modern Times.* New York: Oxford University Press.

Department of Sociology
University of Arizona
Tucson, Arizona 85721

This article analyzes a general model of religious choice under uncertainty by interpreting Pascal's wager as an expected utility problem and faith as insurance. The authors assert that the basic religious choice is one of faith and that religious practice is essentially the allocation of time required to maintain a level of faith in an uncertain environment. The optimal amount of faith and hence the optimal amount of religious practice are determined in part by the costs of maintaining faith, which depend on, among other things, the level of religious capital. The solution to the expected utility problem yields several interesting predictions regarding both the high percentage of individuals choosing at least some positive level of faith and the variation in faith levels across individuals. A series of regressions provide evidence indicating general support for the main predictions of the model.

A Model of Religious Choice Under Uncertainty

ON RESPONDING RATIONALLY TO THE NONRATIONAL

JOHN T. DURKIN, Jr.
University of Chicago

ANDREW M. GREELEY
University of Arizona

Most rational choice models of human behavior operate under the assumption of perfect information. In other words, individuals face no uncertainty or risk in making their decisions. Although the perfect information assumption is sufficient at least as a first approximation, for most choices, the uncertainty inherent in many decisions implies that a rational choice model that does not account for this uncertainty is incomplete. No individual

Authors' Note: *We would like to thank Gary Becker, James Coleman, and Michael Hechter for their valuable comments and suggestions on earlier versions of this article. We also received helpful comments from two referees and from participants at the Rational Models Seminar at the University of Chicago.*

RATIONALITY AND SOCIETY, Vol. 3 No. 2, April 1991 178-196
© 1991 Sage Publications, Inc.

decision involves more uncertainty than religious choice. Information regarding the existence of God or the afterlife is notoriously imperfect and does not appreciably improve with time. However, uncertainty and risk are important components of religious choice. Indeed, part of the incentive for religious choice is that it provides meaning and purpose in the face of uncertainty. Does this imply that a religious choice is irrational or that a rational choice perspective cannot be applied to religious behavior?

Several centuries ago, Blaise Pascal (1670) proposed a gamble: If one chooses for religion and in the event is proven correct (necessarily posthumously it would seem), then one has been very wise indeed. The utility from the choice is reported to be considerable in that posthumous situation and is also present in greater peace and contentment short of that ultimate condition. If one is proven wrong in the event, than one will never know that one was wrong. If, on the other hand, one chooses against religion and is wrong, one might find oneself in a very awkward position. If one is right in the choice, one will never be able to enjoy vindication and will miss out on the consolations of being religious in the present condition. "Pesons le gain et la perte . . . estimons ces deu cas: si vous gagnez, vous gagnez tout; si vous perdez, vous ne perdez, rien" (Pascal 1670, 60-61).

In this article, we develop a rational model of religious choice under uncertainty which restates Pascal's wager in terms of expected utility. In so doing, we feel that we have created the first rational choice model of religious behavior which illustrates that the special nature of the uncertainty inherent in religious choice helps explain some of the patterns of religious behavior we observe.

In the first section, we describe a rational choice problem in which an individual chooses an optimal level of faith based on the maximization of expected utility. Faith influences expected utility in two ways. First, like insurance, faith allows one to insure against the uncertainty regarding the existence of life after death. Short of the afterlife, faith also provides meaning and purpose to one's life and raises utility independent of whether the afterlife exists. Because of the uncertainty, faith is costly to maintain, and the optimal faith choice depends heavily on those costs. The main determinant of the cost of maintaining faith is the level of "religious human capital." The level of religious capital reflects the degree of knowledge about the rites, traditions, and dogma of a particular religion. Religious capital is accumulated over the life cycle through religious participation and is positively related to the optimal level of faith.

The next section provides some empirical evidence that the choice under uncertainty framework helps explain patterns of religious behavior. The main results are summarized as follows. Using data from the National Opinion Research Center's (NORC) 1988 General Social Survey (GSS), regression results reveal two independent components that help explain variation in faith and religious practice: considerations of the afterlife and costs of maintaining faith in this life. Moreover, the evidence indicates that it is necessary to account for both effects to explain variation in faith and practice. In addition, by considering the effect of duration of marriage on faith and practice for endogamous versus exogamous marriages, we find evidence that there is indeed some kind of religious capital accumulation effect taking place. Finally, there is evidence that faith is an increasing function of observing others' faith, as determined by looking at the effect of denominational population shares on faith and practice.

A MODEL OF RELIGION AS INSURANCE

This section describes a model constructed from our reflections on Pascal's wager that attempts to derive an optimal level of faith. This represents a substantial departure from earlier rational choice models of religious behavior in which the relevant choice variable was religious participation. Azzi and Ehrenberg (1975) examined a model in which individuals choose a level of participation in order to improve the quality of the afterlife. Iannoccone (1989a) analyzed a household production theory model in which religious participation is an input into the production of religious satisfaction during this lifetime. Our model takes the analysis one step backward to investigate the faith decisions that provide a motivation for religious participation. The benefits from faith will be increases in utility both in the afterlife and during this life. Although this section is entirely heuristic, a mathematical appendix analytically solves the expected utility problem described here for the optimal level of faith.

Exactly what we mean by an optimal level of faith requires some explanation. Terms like faith and belief are frequently associated with expectations. When someone remarks that "I have faith in the Cubs this year," we normally interpret this as implying that he or she has a high (probably irrational) expectation that the Cubs will win the pennant. In this case, faith is more a reflection of subjective probability than a choice variable. With regard to religion, the term faith is often used as a dichotomous indicator of whether or not one believes in God and not as a continuous choice variable. In this article, faith represents the priority that an individual attaches to religion or God, given, among other things, his or her expectation that God exists. In other words, faith is a measure of how close one chooses to be to God or the importance an individual attaches to God in making other nonreligious choices. In this sense, it is not something that one has or does not have but, rather, is a continuous variable. God has varying degrees of importance in people's lives. Some dedicate their careers to religious work, while many express only weak faith and infrequent practice.

The individual maximization problem is to choose a level of belief or faith given expectations of the probability of life after death, the effect of faith on the quality of the afterlife should it occur, and the effect of the level of faith on lifetime utility. The analysis is similar to the standard insurance problem in that faith can be viewed as having many of the same characteristics as insurance. Using expected utility theory language, in the standard insurance problem there are two "states of the world": one in which a fire occurs and burns down your house and one in which a fire does not occur. The fire reduces total wealth. The rational agent does not know which state will occur, so instead he or she maximizes expected utility, which is the wealth in State 1 times the probability of State 1 occurring plus the wealth in State 2 times the probability of State 2 occurring:

Expected utility = (State 1 probability) (wealth − premium) + (State 2 probability) (wealth − fire loss + insurance),

with the premium and insurance terms equal to zero if no insurance is purchased. By paying the insurance premium, the maximizing agent is willing to give up wealth in the state in which no fire occurs in order to receive insurance and reduce the potential loss in the state in which the fire does occur.[1] In so doing, the agent reduces the differential between the two states and maximizes total expected utility.[2]

In the model considered here, faith is the means by which an individual can reduce the difference in wealth or utility between two states: one in which the afterlife exists and one in which it does not. In State 1, the existence of God becomes known in some form of an afterlife; in State 2, there is no afterlife. The individual is assumed to have a given subjective expectation, ranging from 0 to 1, of the probability that each state will occur.

The utility in each state is the result of the level of income in that state. Endowed income is simply the income in each state if zero faith is chosen. Endowed income in State 2 is equal to lifetime pecuniary wealth, while endowed income in State 1 is also a function of the quality of the afterlife if the individual chooses zero faith. We assume that if the individual does indeed choose zero faith and State 1 occurs, then that person experiences a loss in income; if, however, the individual chooses a positive level of faith and State 1 occurs, that person experiences an improvement in income. Thus we can alternatively view faith as producing some net improvement in income or utility if State 1 occurs.

Income in each state also has a nonpecuniary component. Nonpecuniary wealth is simply the meaning and purpose that an individual is able to derive from his or her life in the face of uncertainty regarding the existence of God or an afterlife. Indeed, people have a need for meaning and purpose in their lives due to the uncertainty regarding the existence of God and an afterlife. Nonpecuniary wealth is a positive function of faith because faith increases our religious satisfaction, which gives our lives meaning and purpose.

The level of faith carries with it certain costs. If an individual chooses a high level of faith, he or she must adhere strictly to the moral structure associated with the existence of some supernatural force: Those who tend to view morality more subjectively will incur higher costs for a given level of faith. In addition, faith carries with it certain pecuniary costs in terms of time and money, such as time spent at church services or in prayer and contributions to the church. Given that information regarding the existence of God is not based on any direct prior experience and cannot improve over time, faith is something that needs to be maintained by religious practice. The assumption we adopt is that higher levels of faith require more practice to maintain and hence proportionately higher costs. When an individual chooses a level of faith, he or she is aware that maintaining that level will require a certain amount of practice and therefore a known cost. For example, if one chooses God to be very important in one's life, then given the nature of the information regarding the existence of God, he or she must have a high level of participation in order to maintain that faith.

The cost of maintaining a given level of faith is a function of many factors, the first of which we refer to as the market price of faith. If we think of faith as insurance and assume that the insurance is provided by churches or religious organizations, we can view the price of faith as simply the insurance premium. In the insurance problem, the cost of the premium is a function of the degree of competition in the insurance industry. Maintenance of a level of faith requires a given amount of religious participation. To achieve this level of participation, most churches require some form of membership. This membership is attained at a given price in terms of contributions or time spent at church functions. As is true in the insurance industry, the price which the churches are able to charge depends on the degree of monopoly power. The more competition among churches, the lower the price and the higher the level of faith. Iannoccone (1989b) developed a model of competition among churches and showed, using cross-country data, that respondents in countries in which one church dominates or countries where one church has a monopoly are less likely to say that God is very important in their life.

Second, the cost of faith is determined by the amount of faith exhibited by *all* participants in a particular religious community. Religion is almost universally practiced in groups, as individuals get more out of the practice when others are involved. Because of the uncertainty inherent in faith, observing others' faith should reduce the costs. Therefore, the cost of maintaining faith is determined by the number of members of a religious community and their faith levels.

Third, the costs of faith depend on what we refer to as the level of religious human capital or technical ability to maintain faith. This is similar to the approach adopted in Iannoccone (1989a). Religious capital is knowledge about the traditions, rites, and dogma of a particular religion. The more religious capital, the lower the cost of maintaining a given level of faith. The level of religious capital is a function of the sum of past levels of faith because the capital is accumulated primarily by religious participation through a "learning by doing" effect. For example, if two individuals are at a particular religious service and both are identical in every respect except that one has attended the service before and the other has not, then the former's faith will be strengthened more by the service — a direct result of having more religious capital.

The ability to accumulate religious capital is not identical for all individuals. We assume that this ability is higher for married people and still higher in endogamous than exagamous marriages, and it should also be a function of total number of family members who participate together. This is again due to the uncertainty inherent in religious choice. If religious participation is a shared and reinforcing experience, then for a given level of participation, more capital should be accumulated from joint participation of married couples and their children and even more from couples who share the same religion.

The individual choice problem can be stated as follows. Assume that when an individual enters adult life, he or she is forced to make a religious choice. That choice available is a lottery not unlike Pascal's wager. The individual chooses an optimal level of faith to maximize his or her total expected utility. Leaving the explicit solution of the analytic model for the appendix, we can state that the optimal level of faith is a positive function of the probability of life after death and the meaning that one can produce in a lifetime for a given level of faith. The optimal faith choice is a negative function of the cost of maintaining faith, which depends positively on the price of faith and negatively on the level of religious capital and the size of one's congregation.

To clarify the issues surrounding the optimal faith choice, it is helpful to first consider the limiting case in which the individual is not able to produce any lifetime meaning or nonpecuniary wealth from his or her faith. As such, the optimal faith choice depends solely on the ability to influence income in the afterlife. In this case, expected utility can be written as follows:

Expected utility = (State 1 probability) (wealth − costs + afterlife) + (State 2 probability) (wealth − costs).

It is easy to see that in these circumstances the faith choice is very similar to the insurance choice. In the insurance problem, the rational agent is willing to reduce income in the state in which no fire occurs in order to increase income in the state in which it does. In this model, even if the agent is not able to produce any lifetime benefit from faith, it may still be rational to reduce income in the state without the afterlife in order to increase income in the state in which there is life after death. A necessary condition for a positive faith choice is that the quality of the afterlife is an increasing function of the level of faith. Within the Christian tradition, the promise of eternal life for believers implies that this derivative is certainly positive, potentially quite large, and possibly even infinite. Another necessary condition for a positive faith choice is that the subjective expectations that the afterlife exists must be greater than zero. If both of these conditions are met, the individual will choose at least some positive level of faith.

The data on levels of faith and practice in the United States reveal that 95% of all Americans choose at least some positive level of faith and an equally large percentage conduct some kind of religious practice.[3] Given that there is no direct evidence regarding the existence of God, these percentages are quite high. Previous sociological attempts to explain such a high proportion focused on the "social return" to religion, that is, yielding to community pressures to become involved in religious activities. From the perspective of Pascal's wager, however, since both of the conditions necessary for a positive level of faith are likely to be met, the high percentages can be explained by the fact that if small levels of faith can result in near infinite returns in the afterlife, a rational agent will always choose a positive level of faith even if the probability of life after death is very small.

Next, what if an individual is able to increase nonpecuniary wealth in this lifetime by deriving meaning and purpose from faith choice or what if

Pascal's "no lose" situation is possible? Recall Pascal's suggestion that even if you are wrong, you will still be able to achieve the greater peace and contentment associated with a positive faith choice. In this case, the individual can increase utility in both states independent of which state occurs, as shown by the statement:

Expected utility = (State 1 probability) (wealth + purpose + afterlife − costs) + (State 2 probability) (wealth + purpose − costs).

This provides an extra incentive to choose positive faith and implies a higher optimal level of faith. Moreover, a positive faith choice is possible now even if the quality of the afterlife is independent of faith. If so, a positive faith choice would occur if the benefits of meaning and purpose from faith are greater than the cost of maintaining that faith.

The most important determinant of the cost of maintaining faith and the lifetime benefits from faith is religious capital. However, since the level of religious capital is partly a function of past religious participation, to fully contemplate the intertemporal aspects of the faith choice, we need to consider in more detail the influence of religious capital on faith. We can think of faith choices over the life cycle as taking place as follows. An individual enters his or her adult life with a given level of religious capital. We assume that the individual is aware of the influence of his or her current faith choice on future religious capital levels. In this case, the individual chooses an entire path of optimal faith choices until death, updating those choices only when shocks occurred that altered any of the other parameters.

One implication of the intertemporal approach is that for an initial positive faith choice, the optimal level of faith rises through time, ceteris paribus. This is due to the fact that as one participates in religious activities, one's religious capital increases. This lowers the cost of maintaining a given level of faith, which implies a higher optimal level of faith. In addition, those who were brought up in more religious households should begin their adults lives with more religious capital and therefore have higher levels of faith throughout the life cycle. Since switching religions would imply lowering one's religious capital and raising the costs of maintaining a given level of faith, the model predicts that individuals who retain the religion in which they were raised have more religious capital, which would lead to a higher level of faith. Moreover, at any point in time, the cost of switching religions is positively related to the level of religious capital because those with high levels of religious capital give up more when they switch.

In addition, as explained earlier, a household with an endogamous marriage accumulates more religious capital per level of participation. Thus the cost of maintaining a given level of faith declines more rapidly in endogamous marriages. We should expect to see both higher faith and participation levels in endogamous marriages at any point in time and a faster rate of increase over the life cycle than in exagamous marriages. Moreover, within those endogamous marriages, we should observe religious capital being accumulated at a faster rate for those who participate jointly on a more frequent basis.

We previously defined the price of maintaining faith as a price for participation imposed by churches. Since maintaining faith is a time-intense activity, we can instead adopt the assumption used by Azzi and Ehrenberg (1975) that the price of faith is actually the relative price of time spent participating compared to time spent on other activities. If so, it is likely that the relative price will change during the life cycle. Since the value of time in the labor market changes, we should expect that the optimal level of faith will be negatively related to the value of time or the wage rate.

Finally, it is possible that expectations about the existence of the afterlife will change through time. We stated earlier that individuals have no direct evidence about the existence of God or the afterlife and that this information could not improve over time. They do, however, base their subjective expectations on indirect information through experiences. It is likely that one's expectations are based on personal experiences. Bad experiences of catastrophes, such as the unexpected death of loved ones or some perceived injustice inflicted on a person, could reduce an individual's expectation that God exists and, therefore, lower the optimal level of faith. Good experiences could have the opposite effect. Moreover, the kind of paranormal experiences reported in Greeley (1975), which bring someone closer to God or in which they experience a dead loved one, should increase the expectation of the good state occurring and increase the optimal level of faith. Indeed, the simple correlation coefficient between belief in life after death and having had such an experience is statistically significant at .17.[4]

EMPIRICAL RESULTS

The model described in the previous section yields several interesting predictions regarding the nature of religious choice and patterns of religious behavior:

1. The assumption that participation is proportional to faith implies that the variables which influence the faith choice should influence participation to roughly the same degree.
2. The optimal faith choice is an increasing function of expectations regarding the existence of God and the afterlife and the ability to influence the quality of the afterlife through faith.
3. The lifetime benefits from faith depend negatively on the cost of maintaining faith. The costs are primarily a function of the several factors, including the level of religious capital.
4. The level of religious capital is determined by the amount of religious capital accumulated in one's formative years or prior to the faith decisions, whether one is married to someone of the same religion, the number of family members who participate jointly, and one's age.

Thus, to understand the patterns of faith and participation that we observe, we need to take into consideration both the impact of faith on the afterlife and the impact of faith on lifetime utility, ignoring either of these considerations severely limits the ability to predict variation in faith and participation.

The primary difficulty in testing these predictions lies in finding data which accurately reflect variation in either expectations, faith levels, participation, or religious capital. We feel that the data from the NORC's 1988 GSS give us the best opportunity to do so. The 1988 GSS contained a special religion module from which 1,481 individuals from a random probability national sample were asked a series of questions regarding their religious beliefs and behavior.

As interpreted in this model, faith represents the importance of God in one's life. The GSS provided us with two variables that we feel reflect variation in faith. First, the survey asked respondents to state how important the teachings of their church or religion were in helping them make decisions regarding their life (DECCHURH).[5] Second, respondents were asked to state how close they felt to God (NEARGOD).[6] We used both as dependent variables to test the robustness of our results. Since practice is simply proportional to faith, we used yearly church attendance as a measure of practice (YRMASS).

The expected utility problem is set up such that the existence of God becomes known in some form of the afterlife, so there is no important distinction between expectations regarding the existence of God or the afterlife. The survey also asked respondents two questions which should reveal variation in expectations: whether they believe in life after death (POSTEXP)[7] and their degree of doubt regarding the existence of God (NODOUBT).[8] Again, we used both as proxy variables for expectations as a test of the sensitivity of the results.

TABLE 1:   Simple Correlation Coefficients

	DECCHURH	NEARGOD	YRMASS
POSTEXP	.21	.31	.19
NODOUBT	.41	.45	.35
STAY	.08	.03*	−.01*
AGE	.18	.15	.15
MAYRMASS	.18	.15	.26
HOMPOP	.07	.01*	.09
ENDOG	.15	.10	.20
MORALSUB	−.11	−.03*	−.12
WAGE	−.05*	−.07*	−.05*

* = not statistically significant.

We used a number of variables to reflect variation in costs. As discussed, religious capital should be an increasing function of age (AGE), retaining one's original religion (STAY), whether someone is in an endogamous marriage (ENDOG), and the number of family members (HOMPOP). In addition, we used the frequency of the respondent's parent's church attendance to reflect variation in the starting level of religious capital (MAYRMASS). The remaining nonreligious capital variables, which we used to depict variation in costs of maintaining faith, were the relative price of faith (WAGE) and the tendency of respondents to view morality subjectively (MORALSUB).

Table 1 shows the simple correlation coefficients between all the relevant variables considered in the first set of tests. For the most part, all of the appropriate dependent variables (DECCHURH, NEARGOD, and YRMASS) were, as predicted, positively correlated with expectations (POSTEXP and NODOUBT), retaining one's religion (STAY), being in an endogamous marriage (ENDOG), one's age (AGE), parental church attendance (MAYRMASS), and family size (HOMPOP) and negatively correlated with wages (WAGE) and the tendency to view morality subjectively (MORALSUB). Two outcomes were not predicted: NEARGOD was negatively correlated with HOMPOP, and YRMASS was negatively correlated with STAY. However, in both cases, the relationship was not statistically significant. In nearly all other instances, however, the relationships were significant. The primary exception is that wages are not significant related to any of the dependent variables.

In Tables 2 through 4, the first group of tests attempt to show that it is necessary to consider both the expectations of the afterlife and the effect of

TABLE 2:   Regressions of Expectations and Costs on DECCHURH

Independent Variable	Dependent Variable				
	DECCHURH	DECCHURH	DECCHURH	DECCHURH	DECCHURH
POSTEXP	.23		.21		
	(9.1)		(8.4)		
DOUBT		.41		.36	
		(17.5)		(14.1)	
STAY			.08	.07	.08
			(3.3)	(3.2)	(3.0)
AGE			.21	.16	.20
			(7.6)	(5.8)	(7.0)
MAYRMASS			.13	.09	.16
			(5.3)	(3.8)	(6.4)
HOMPOP			.14	.12	.13
			(4.9)	(4.2)	(4.4)
ENDOG			.19	.14	.21
			(4.1)	(3.2)	(4.5)
MORALSUB			−.09	−.07	−.09
			(3.5)	(3.3)	(3.5)
WAGE			−.04	−.04	−.04
			(1.7)	(1.4)	(1.6)
MARRIED			−.13	−.26	−.12
			(2.6)	(2.0)	(2.6)
R^2	.05	.17	.16	.23	.11

NOTE: Standardized regression coefficients, with absolute value of t statistics shown in parentheses.

faith on lifetime utility to explain variation in faith and practice. Tables 2 through 4 each show the results from regressions run on DECCHURH, NEARGOD, and YRMASS, respectively. For each dependent variable, we ran three separate sets of regressions. The first set used both expectations terms as independent variables and only those variables. The second added a series of variables reflecting costs, and the third used only the cost variables.

The main results from the tables are summarized as follows. For each dependent variable, the regressions which controlled for both costs and expectations had the highest R^2, while the same held true for the adjusted R^2 Moreover, the fact that few of the coefficients changed across regressions in any statistically significant sense as variables were added or subtracted indicates that the costs and expectations exerted independent effects. Taken together, these results provide general support for main predictions of the model, namely, that a combination of costs and expectations determine faith.

190 RATIONALITY AND SOCIETY

TABLE 3: Regressions of Expectations and Costs on NEARGOD

Independent Variable	Dependent Variable				
	NEARGOD	NEARGOD	NEARGOD	NEARGOD	NEARGOD
POSTEXP	.34		.32		
	(13.7)		(8.4)		
DOUBT		.45		.42	
		(19.5)		(17.3)	
STAY			.03	.02	.03
			(1.3)	(1.0)	(1.0)
AGE			.15	.09	.14
			(5.5)	(3.1)	(4.6)
MAYRMASS			.10	.07	.15
			(4.1)	(2.7)	(5.6)
HOMPOP			.07	.03	.05
			(2.4)	(.88)	(1.6)
ENDOG			.13	.09	.17
			(2.9)	(2.1)	(3.5)
MORALSUB			−.02	.01	−.03
			(.63)	(.25)	(.61)
WAGE			−.05	−.04	−.05
			(2.1)	(1.8)	(1.9)
MARRIED			−.11	−.07	−.10
			(2.3)	(1.6)	(2.1)
R^2	.11	.21	.16	.23	.06

NOTE: Standardized regression coefficients, with absolute value of t statistics are shown in parentheses.

More specific, for the equations with DECCHURH and YRMASS as dependent variables, those equations containing only cost variables explained more variation than the regressions, with only expectations if POSTEXP was used as an explanatory variable but less if NODOUBT was used. NODOUBT always had a larger and more significant coefficient than POSTEXP, and equations using NODOUBT always had a higher R^2. One interpretation of this difference is that because of the manner in which the POSTEXP and NODOUBT questions were asked and coded, the NODOUBT variable better reflects the true variation in expectations.

Also, for the regressions on NEARGOD, expectations explained more of the variation than costs. Indeed, NODOUBT dominated the regression containing all the variables to such an extent that the only cost variables which were significant were AGE and MAYRMASS. These difference are

TABLE 4:   Regressions of Expectations and Costs on YRMASS

Independent Variable	Dependent Variable				
	YRMASS	YRMASS	YRMASS	YRMASS	YRMASS
POSTEXP	.19			.15	
	(7.8)			(8.4)	
DOUBT		.33			.28
		(14.5)			(11.4)
STAY			−.04	−.04	−.04
			(1.6)	(1.9)	(1.7)
AGE			.14	.10	.14
			(5.3)	(3.9)	(4.9)
MAYRMASS			.24	.21	.26
			(9.6)	(8.6)	(10.5)
HOMPOP			.10	.09	.09
			(3.5)	(3.1)	(3.1)
ENDOG			.15	.13	.17
			(6.0)	(5.3)	(3.8)
MORALSUB			−.09	−.08	−.09
			(3.9)	(3.5)	(3.8)
WAGE			−.03	−.02	−.03
			(1.3)	(1.0)	(1.2)
MARRIED			−.10	−.07	−.11
			(2.1)	(1.4)	(2.0)
R^2	.04	.12	.17	.22	.14

NOTE: Standardized regression coefficients, with absolute value of t statistics shown in parentheses.

likely due to the ability of the DECCHURH and NEARGOD variables to reflect the true variation in faith. Neither completely captured faith as interpreted in this article, but each captured some of the characteristics of faith. We can interpret the fact that the expectations dominated the regressions on NEARGOD as a function of the fact that expectations, especially NODOUBT, had a larger impact on the characteristics captured by NEARGOD.

Of the nonreligious capital variables reflecting cost differences, MORAL-SUB had the strongest effect. It was negative, as predicted, in all regressions and significant in the regressions on DECCHURH and YRMASS. WAGE was also negative, but the t statistics were between 1 and 2 in all but one regression. In general, the variables used to indicate variation in religious capital were significant and had the predicted sign. AGE and MAYRMASS were positive and significant in all regressions, while HOMPOP and ENDOG were positive in all regressions but insignificant in some of the regressions on NEARGOD. The notable exception regarding the religious capital variables was STAY, which was positive and significant in the regressions on DECCHURH, positive and insignificant in those on NEARGOD, and negative and significant in the regressions on YRMASS.

MARRIED, a dummy variable indicating whether one is married, was included in the regressions with ENDOG to determine if the effect of ENDOG was due simply to marriage and independent of the fact that the marriage was endogamous. That the ENDOG coefficients were positive and significant with MARRIED included demonstrates that the effect is due strictly to the endogamous nature of the marriage. This result lends support to the model's suggestion that entering an endogamous marriage increases one's stock of religious capital and therefore increases the optimal level of faith.

In addition, the model assumes that an endogamous marriage also increases one's ability to accumulate additional human capital. If this is true, ceteris parabus we should see religious capital being accumulated at a higher rate in endogamous than exogamous marriages. In other words, the effect of an endogamous marriage on faith should be an increasing function of the duration of the marriage (DURMAR). In Table 5, the next set of regressions attempted to test this relationship by adding an interactive term between ENDOG and DURMAR. The GSS data allowed us to determine the duration of marriage only for those in their first marriage, so the n in Table 5 reduces to 572. As predicted, the interactive term was positive and significant in all regressions. We interpret this result as evidence that there is, indeed, an accumulation effect taking place and that, as predicted, it is stronger in endogamous marriages.

The final set of tests attempted to determine the effect of the faith of fellow worshipers on the optimal level of faith. Since costs depend negatively on the faith of fellow worshipers, larger congregations should imply higher levels of faith. Because the data on individual congregation sizes were not directly comparable to the GSS, we calculated a variable representing the percentage of the sample in each of the main Christian denominations (RELPER), which should, at least in part, capture this effect. The regressions in Table 6 added, RELPER to the earlier regressions but used only cases for Christians, which reduced the n to 962. The RELPER coefficient was positive and significant in all three regressions, which suggest that there is an positive effect on the optimal level of faith associated with observing other's faith.

TABLE 5:   Regressions Testing Accumulation Effect

Independent Variable	Dependent Variable		
	DECCHURH	NEARGOD	YRMASS
POSTEXP	.19	.28	.19
	(4.8)	(7.3)	(5.0)
STAY	.07	−.01	−.09
	(8.4)	(.23)	(2.5)
MAYRMASS	.07	.12	.27
	(1.8)	(3.1)	(6.9)
HOMPOP	.12	.03	.09
	(2.9)	(.63)	(2.2)
MORALSUB	−.11	−.03	−.09
	(2.6)	(.68)	(2.3)
WAGE	−.08	−.11	−.03
	(1.7)	(2.8)	(.85)
ENDOG	.06	.06	.11
	(1.3)	(1.4)	(2.4)
DURMAR × ENDOG	.20	.11	.16
	(4.1)	(2.2)	(3.2)
R^2	.13	.15	.19

NOTE: Standardized regression coefficients, with absolute value of t statistics shown in parentheses.

CONCLUSION

This article made four main contributions. First, as opposed to previous models of religious choice which modeled religious behavior, we asserted that the primary religious choice is one of faith and that the faith choice is made in an environment of uncertainty regarding the existence of God and the afterlife. Second, we developed a formal model in which a rational individual chooses an optimal level of faith to both improve the quality of the afterlife and increase lifetime utility and found that, interpreted in this light, faith has many of the characteristics of insurance. Third, we argued that religious practice is essentially time costs allocated to maintain faith in the uncertain environment and interpreted the costs to be a function of the level of religious capital. Finally, the model predicted that variation in faith should depend on variation in expectations regarding the afterlife and the costs of maintaining faith, and through a series of regressions, we found support for these predictions.

TABLE 6: Regressions Testing Congregation Size Effect

Independent Variable	Dependent Variable		
	DECCHURH	NEARGOD	YRMASS
POSTEXP	.16	.24	.13
	(5.0)	(7.5)	(4.3)
STAY	.04	−.04	−.05
	(1.4)	(1.3)	(2.6)
MAYRMASS	.12	.08	.24
	(3.7)	(2.5)	(8.1)
HOMPOP	.08	.06	.05
	(2.3)	(1.6)	(1.5)
MORALSUB	−.09	−.02	−.08
	(3.1)	(.57)	(2.7)
WAGE	−.04	−.04	−.02
	(1.3)	(1.3)	(.45)
ENDOG	.06	.00	.14
	(1.9)	(.00)	(4.5)
RELPER	.07	.11	.13
	(2.3)	(3.4)	(4.1)
R^2	.12	.10	.17

NOTE: Standardized regression coefficients, with absolute value of t statistics shown in parentheses.

MATHEMATICAL APPENDIX

Let p be the probability of State 1 occurring, $(1 - p)$ be the probability of State 2 occurring, and f be the level of faith. Let W be lifetime pecuniary wealth. Let A(f) be the quality of the afterlife if State 1 occurs. Assume $f \geq 0$ and $A(f) < 0$ for $f = 0$, $A(f) > 0$ for $f > 0$. Let M(f) be lifetime nonpecuniary wealth: meaning and purpose.

Define a cost function $C(p_f, R, F, f)$ as the cost of maintaining faith. Let p_f be the fixed market price of faith or the "insurance premium." Let $F = \Sigma^N_{i=1} f_i$ be the total amount of faith of all participants in a religious community and $R_t = (\Sigma_{t=0} \alpha f_{t-1})$ be the religious capital at time t, with α as ability to accumulate religious capital for a given level of participation.

Endowed income is the income if no faith is chosen. Let I_1^e and I_2^e be the endowed incomes in States 1 and 2 and I_1 and I_2 be the incomes for a positive level of faith. Thus

$$I_1^e = W + A(f), \quad I_2^e = W,$$

$$I^1 = W + A(f) + M(f) - C(f), \quad I^2 = W + M(f_i) - C(f_i).$$

The expected utility function is

$$EU(f) = pU_1(I_1) + (1 - p)U_2(I_2) \tag{1}$$

Defining π as the price of faith measured in terms of income in State 1, the budget constraint or the amount of income that can be transferred between states is represented by

$$I_2^e - I_2 = \pi(I_1 - I_1^e). \tag{2}$$

The individual choice problem can be stated as follows. Assume that when an individual enters adult life, he or she is forced to make a religious choice. The individual chooses an optimal level of faith f^* to maximize his or her expected utility function (Equation 1) subject to the constraint (Equation 2). The first-order condition from the maximization problem is

$$\pi = pU_1' / (1 - p)U_2', \tag{3}$$

with $U_1' = (\partial U_1/\partial I_1) (\partial I_1/\partial f)$ and $U_2' = (\partial U_2/\partial_i 2) (\partial I_2/\partial f)$. By employing specific function forms for U, C, and A, we can solve for $f^* = f(p, p_f, R, F, \partial A/\partial f, A(0))$. The signs of the derivatives are

$$f_1^* > 0, f_2^* <, f_3^* > 0, f_4^* > 0, f_5^* < 0.$$

The optimal level of faith is a positive function of the probability of life after death, the level of religious capital, and the faith of one's fellow worshipers and a negative function of the size of the income loss in the afterlife, if zero faith is chosen, and the relative price of faith.[9]

NOTES

1. The way in which the problem is stated here, the insurance is net of premium.

2. For a good general description of the choice under uncertainty framework, an explicit description of the insurance problem, and a list of further references, see Deaton and Muellbauer's (1980) chapter 14.

3. Data are taken from the NORC's 1988 General Social Survey (GSS).

4. Ibid.

5. The variables are coded between 1 and 5, with 1 as very important and 5 as not important. We switched the coding around so that higher numbers reflected more importance.

6. The responses are coded from 1 to 5, with 1 as extremely close and 5 as does not believe. Again, we recoded so that higher numbers reflected more closeness.

7. The possible responses are yes, no, and undecided. We coded yes as 1, undecided as .5, and no as 0.

8. The responses are coded from 1 to 7, with 1 as no doubt and 7 as mixed with doubt. We recoded so that higher numbers reflected higher expectations.

9. For a more detailed treatment of the technical issues and the signs of the derivatives in an insurance problem, see Becker and Erlich (1972).

REFERENCES

Azzi, C., and R. Ehrenberg. 1975. Household allocation of time and church attendance. *Journal of Political Economy* 83:27-55.

Becker, G., and I. Erlich. 1972. Market insurance, self-insurance and self protection. *Journal of Political Economy* 80:623-47.

Deaton, A., and J. Muellbauer. 1980. *Economics and consumer behavior.* Cambridge: Cambridge University Press.

Greeley, A. 1975. *Sociology of the paranormal.* Beverly Hills, CA: Sage.

Iannaccone, L. 1989a. Three examples of the rational choice approach to religion. Manuscript, University of Santa Clara.

———. 1989b. Religious practice: A human capital approach. Manuscript, University of Santa Clara.

Pascal, B. 1670. *Penses.* Paris: Editions.